Vera Simone was born in Germany, but has lived most of her life in New York City. She received her B.A. from Queens College and did graduate work in Chinese studies at the University of Michigan. Her Master's dissertation was a comparative study of Lenin and Mao Tse-tung, and she is in the process of completing her doctoral dissertation in Political Theory. She has taught in the Department of Political Science at Queens College for the past four years.

The Political Perspectives Series

Two generations ago historians in the United States were calling for a "New History" that would put the study of the past at the service of the present and future. The demand is now even more urgent.

This series of books is intended to fill this need. Under the overall title "Political Perspectives," a wide variety of books will be issued in inexpensive format. The series will include original works and anthologies, as well as reprints of important older books and monographs. The common theme will be the placing of contemporary political problems in their historical perspective.

MARVIN E. GETTLEMAN

China in
Revolution

History, Documents, and Analyses

Edited with an Introduction and
Commentary by
VERA SIMONE
Queens College

A Fawcett Premier Book
Fawcett Publications, Inc., Greenwich, Conn.
Member of American Book Publishers Council, Inc.

CONTENTS

15447

THREE Nationalism and the Transition
to a Modern Society

INTRODUCTION   115

To someone very special
whose critical judgment was surpassed
only by his loving support

PREFACE

CHINA AND THE U. S. appear headed on a collision course. The U. S. escalates the war in Vietnam on grounds of a Chinese threat and China prepares herself for American aggression. The easing of tensions between the Soviet Union and the United States has led to a redefinition of the Cold War as a battle of wits and ultimately strength between the two major powers, the United States and China. But neither power really understands the other and the guessing games that result from this impasse play havoc with human civilization itself.

There is, in addition to an alarming lack of reliable information available to the American public, a total absence of any political and historical context within which to grasp the meaning of events. Despite the vast amounts of knowledge accumulated by experts, little has been communicated to those beyond the pale of specialization. How are we to understand and evaluate the policy of our Government concerning China if we are ignorant of the nature of Chinese society?

There is an historical parallel that underlines the justification for this book. It is the parallel between 19th century European attitudes towards "democratic America" and contemporary American contempt for "communist China." Threatened by the revolutionary claims of a youthful China embarked on a bold course of independent action, the U. S. refuses to entertain even the remotest possibility of a Chinese "manifest destiny" to rival her own. China is at the beginning of her industrial development and reminds us vaguely of an America of the past—a society fired with energy, enthusiasm, bravado, optimism and an irrepressible impatience with European decadence. But this America is a part of our past, now enveloped by the nostalgia of old age and disillusionment, while China is in the present and our enemy so the reminiscence is rejected. Instead there is a steadfast blankness, a refusal to see that which we have denied in ourselves.

China is more than Red Guards, teeming millions and a cultural revolution. It is a history 4,000 years old and a future that will break present-day boundaries of man's imagination

13

and experience. But to learn about China is not the same as to understand China. This book is an attempt to stimulate the understanding of an historical process. It is an attempt to present a documentary and analytical selection of China's past and present with a view to capturing her history and development. Out of this, hopefully, will come some sense of her possible future. The reader is asked to step into another culture, experience its existence and the unfolding drama of a continuing transformation.

Any selection of information involves interpretation which is all the more significant when crossing cultural boundaries. The interpretive motif of this book is the breakdown of a highly advanced but traditional agricultural society, and the problems of a people agonizingly impelled towards modernization. If Americans are to grasp the full implications of this process, however, they must confront a special problem. This problem derives from the fact that their conception of a revolution and their interpretation of historical change sets them apart from the rest of the world today.

Because they left feudalism behind when they settled in the New World, Americans developed a singular idea of revolution based on a unique historical experience. Revolution was construed as a purely constructive act of liberation from external bonds of oppression. Today this historical experience, through its legacy of ideas, prevents Americans from fully appreciating the stranglehold that a deeply entrenched social order can exercise on man's development. When they observe the social revolutions in today's world, Americans judge events in terms of their own past, blithely ignoring, or worse, denying the role that destruction plays in the revolutionary process.

For many of us, our own fortunate circumstances, past and present, afford us highly delicate sensibilities which are continually being violated by the price revolution exacts in the twentieth century world. Attributing the hardships of revolutionary change to the "totalitarian" techniques of communist leadership, we assume a self-righteous position that an alternative—ours—is possible and indispensable. The element of self-delusion in this is costly for if reality *is* harsh and *other* people's conditions and aspirations legislate actions that offend our judgment, there is an additional price to be paid for the luxury of denying it.

There is a lesson to be learned from the evolution of modern China: that destruction, whether we like it or not, is inherent in the modernization of a society that is radically transforming itself under contemporary conditions. The old order, the traditional patterns of behavior and thinking must be forced to give way to the imperatives of a modern, industrial society. In another way, then, this book is motivated by a concern with new patterns of revolution and what Americans can learn about themselves by studying them.

The book is divided roughly into three distinct periods: traditional China, the failures of the Republican era, and Communist China, the thread of external involvement running throughout. There are general introductions preceding each chapter in which I have singled out the major problems, characters and situations, pointing out recurrent themes, future possibilities or simply gaps in our knowledge. Many of the selections, especially the primary documents, are necessarily abridged but there is an attempt to retain the spirit of the original. And in the case of Chinese materials, with the kind permission of the translator in some cases and the absence of legal arrangements in others, I have relied exclusively on existing translations.

In the selection of articles for a Reader there is inevitably a projection of personal values. Although all of the differing views on China are not included, I have nonetheless made use of articles whose explicit value judgments are opposed to my own. What is more important than the vast number of contradictory opinions is the data itself, the knowledge of what China is, does and hopes to do in the future.

In the final analysis there are two basic orientations: whether we are interested in China because of her effect on *us* and *our* position in the world, or whether we are interested in China because of what is in the best interests of the Chinese themselves and all of mankind, ultimately. My inclination is the latter, but in either case it is necessary to have as accurate and as full a picture as possible of life in China—her past, present and future aspirations.

1

TRADITIONAL CHINA:
CONTINUITIES AND DISCONTINUITIES
IN IMPERIAL CHINA

ALTHOUGH CHINA has only recently impinged on the consciousness of most Americans she boasts an ancient civilization. Over a thousand years before Christ a civilization emerged which endured relatively intact into the twentieth century. There were changes, territorial as well as social, the civilization expanding at times and contracting at other times. But the remarkable characteristic of its history is continuity. Given the size and level of achievements of Chinese civilization, what continues to amaze the historian of western civilization is the longevity of its economic and political institutions. Throughout the rise and fall of successive dynasties, which to the Chinese took on the appearance of a never-ending cycle of nature, there was a persistent pattern of social arrangements. We refer to this pattern as "traditional China."

Among the recurring facets of traditional China were problems of organization. When 17th century Europeans "discovered" China, they were enormously impressed by the sophistication of the Chinese and their civilization. What they neglected to note was that these were products of a highly centralized society which had, in the manner of countless predecessors, a seamier side of social costs and pressures towards disintegration. This aspect of Chinese civilization, less visible to the 17th century European, was a constant source of disruption in the lives of the majority of Chinese throughout their history.

There were perennial inter-related problems of size, population, food and the impossibility of securing any *lasting* unity. Every strong dynasty eventually weakened. When it did, a period of chaos, decentralization, starvation and rebellion followed. Periodically a new dynasty, under the leadership of a powerful and capable leader, pulled the parts of the sprawling society together by a thorough housecleaning of the state bureaucracy only to have his work undone—unobtrusively

as it were, within a period of decades, sometimes centuries—
by the ever-present centrifugal forces of family interests and
regional particularisms.

The state bureaucracy, as Etienne Balazs documents in his
selection on "tradition and revolution," was the pivotal institution. When it functioned well, i.e. as a civil service based
on merit, it secured a sufficient degree of centralization to
ensure economic and political stability. But by the very nature
of the society in which it functioned, the bureaucracy was
intrinsically subject to those forces of "decay" that it was
supposed to counteract. The educated elite, the scholar-gentry,
who occupied bureaucratic posts invariably used their position
to protect particular interests of family, clan and region, thereby contributing to the periodic breakdown of the entire system. This internal contradiction was insoluble under the conditions of pre-industrial society.

Traditional China was an agricultural society with a very
high ratio of population to arable land. As a result, production
was labor-intensive and depended heavily on a state-con-
structed and maintained system of irrigation works. Society
was stratified so that outside of a small number of merchants
and soldiers there were two major classes: the large peasant
class whose cultivation of the land supported the costs of
civilization, and the elite gentry class whose position was based
on a combination of land ownership and government connections. The state bureaucracy, theoretically open to all Chinese
who successfully passed through an extensive education and
civil service examinations, was usually filled by members of
the gentry class. Its function was to administer the complex
irrigation system and provide some centralized control and
coordination over the vastly dispersed resources necessary for
the task. Stability, under these circumstances, depended on
the ability of the bureaucracy to integrate an immense empire
so that it functioned as a whole. Throughout Chinese history,
this was possible only for limited spans of time in which the
combination of scarcity of resources and their unequal distribution prevented the majority of people from enjoying
anything but bare subsistence, even in those periods marked
by relative prosperity.

Despite a relatively sophisticated technology, traditional
China did not generate industrialization. This has intrigued
the student of western civilization perhaps more than any
other fact. The reasons offered in explanation leave a great
deal to be desired and are too complex to encompass here,
but two factors seem to be significant: the fact that the role

of the merchant was sharply circumscribed by the dominance of the scholar-bureaucrats, and the fact that the scholar-bureaucrats' preeminent position was sanctioned by the generally accepted ideology of Confucianism. Merchants, according to the Confucian scale of values, had the lowest status in society. When they acquired great wealth, therefore, they aspired to higher rungs on the social ladder. This could be achieved by investing in land, assuming gentry graces and educating their sons to enter the state bureaucracy—the pinnacle of the Chinese social order. There was little added incentive or reward for the discovery of new commercial avenues.

"The Sacred Edict" of Emperor K'ang Hsi (selection four) illustrates the use made of Confucian ideas to bolster the traditional structure of Chinese society. The emphasis on harmony, learning as the basis of good government, and the importance of weeding out unorthodox ideas lest they subvert law and order promoted a general acceptance of the hardships of the traditional order, especially for those on the bottom of it. And whenever conditions deteriorated in the Empire, it was attributed to a declining faith in Confucian principles. People starved, presumably, because of the moral laxity of their officials which caused the disintegration of the body politic. The remedy, therefore, was to recruit men of talent and virtue. The idea, expressed in the Doctrine of the Mean, one of the Confucian classics is

When the right men are available, government flourishes.
When the right men are not available, government declines.

As a result, reform in traditional China, recurrent as it was, was never oriented towards structural change but always to a return of the old principles. When the state was ineffectual against foreign enemies, racked by internal unrest and the depletion of resources, the fault, and therefore the solution, centered on the scholar-official's lack of moral fibre. From a historical perspective, however, this was an underlying dilemma, a set of problems endemic to the institutional structure of traditional China.

The legacy of this past is not yet dead but continues to shape and mold present-day events in China. Beneath the recent clamor of the "cultural revolution," the purges, and what appear to be chaotic activities of the Red Guards, are age-old problems of organization. The centralized bureaucracy, as pivotal as it was in imperial China, is just as prone to corrosive elements; the difference lies in the communist approach to these problems. In the past, reforms, eroded by concessions to the traditional order, invariably gave way to the overwhelming force of the affliction even as they do today in the midst of the first successful attempt to eradicate the very conditions that breed the trouble. The Communist leadership seems to be acutely aware of the hold past has on present. It is extraordinarily attentive to the fact that, more often than not, splendid ideas and the best of intentions are eviscerated by the invisible and often dormant weight of tradition and habit.

One solution has been to anticipate repetitions of the past and take concrete and radical measures to check them. Criticism, self-criticism, public humiliation, the mass line can be seen as techniques designed to combat any restoration of traditional disorders. This concern is probably not unrelated to the ousting of men like P'eng Chen and Teng Hsiao-p'ing and major structural shake-ups of the kind recently being witnessed. Individuals, entrenched in bureaucratic or regional positions of power, invite official opposition because they present a historically recognizable threat which cannot be countenanced by a centralized government bent on creating an egalitarian society. Given the twin objectives of unification and egalitarianism the present leadership, symbolized by Mao Tse-tung, leaves no room for pockets of vested interest, whether regional or structural; and it is probable that the recent upheaval testifies more than anything to the attention that Communists pay to historical precedent.

This is so despite the fact that the continuity of problems, past and present, is not publicly proclaimed in the official rhetoric. It is nonetheless important. Although the Communists eschew all reminders and attachments to Confucian society, their imperative is different from ours: they are changing society, we are only trying to understand this change. For this reason, in trying to explain their behavior we cannot take at face value the Communist denial of the deterministic aspects of China's history. When they insist that the past is dead, conquered and buried, we should, as observers, reserve the possibility that this is still part of what they are trying to accomplish. The Chinese have their mountains to move in bringing about large-scale change under severe conditions, as we shall see in later chapters. But in order for us to accurately perceive and comprehend why and how these changes occur, Americans must begin to understand China's past.

Tradition and Revolution in China*

ETIENNE BALAZS

To ATTEMPT, in a few pages, to assess the forces of tradition and revolution in China is a presumptuous task. Indeed, the very idea is quite absurd, for if the task were to be carried out at all adequately, familiarity with various specialized branches of knowledge, a mastery of world history, and a global point of view would be required, since the problems involved have eventuated in the complete recasting of one of the greatest and most ancient of civilizations and in the violent upheaval of a quarter of mankind—an event that will have incalculable consequences and will alter the balance of forces in the world as we know it. I am fully aware how complex the problems are and how ill-equipped I am to deal with them, and all I can hope to do is draw attention to one or two aspects of the present extremely serious situation.

I shall begin by telling a story. One evening in A.D. 731 a poor peasant and an old Taoist called Liu met together in an inn on the road to Han-tan. In order to forget how hungry they were, they started to chat while the innkeeper prepared a bowl of gruel for their supper. The peasant spoke of the cares and anxieties of his poverty-stricken life, but when the strange old man offered him a curious porcelain pillow, scarcely had he laid his weary head upon it than he was transported to a wonderful land of dreams, where he possessed a house of his own, was married to a daughter of one of the best families, was rich, looked up to, and respected, and had passed the civil service examinations with distinction. After filling a number of important posts, he was appointed governor of the capital, and in this capacity, conquered an army of barbarians. As a reward, the Emperor made him a minister; but a rival faction was successful in its plot to bring about his downfall, and his headlong plunge from the heights of power to the depths of a dungeon nearly ended in his being decapitated. Only at the last minute did he escape execution, and he was then restored to office, and given a title to make up for the injustice he had suffered. His five sons, all high officials, provided him with numerous descendants, and he had come to

* From CHINESE CIVILIZATION AND BUREAUCRACY by Etienne Balazs, translated by H. M. Wright, edited by Arthur F. Wright, New Haven and London: Yale University Press, 1964, pp. 150–170. Copyright © 1964 by Yale University.

the point of contemplating retirement, happy to end his days in peace, and looking forward to a final resting place with his ancestors, when he suddenly wakened to find himself once again in the vile inn, where the pot of gruel was still heating on the stove, and the old Taoist was smiling at him and saying, with a wink: "That's the way life passes, quick as a flash."

This little tale, known in Chinese as "The Yellow Millet Dream," dates from the end of the eighth century,[1] and later supplied the theme for a number of stories and plays. The story is remarkable, because it contains the dream of happiness shared by all Chinese, and expresses it with the utmost conciseness yet without leaving out a single salient feature. It is as if the writer had striven to put all his experience into a nutshell, and in doing so he has summarized two thousand years of history, during which the ideal of every Chinese had always been to become an official, this being regarded as the height of power and the sum of happiness. It was, however, an ideal that could be realized only by a tiny minority of the elect, and the fate of the vast majority was to remain a peasant, an artisan, or a merchant—in short, one of the *misera plebs,* the humble subject of those remote, haughty, flesh-and-blood divinities of the terrestrial universe, the officials.

Is it possible that a thousand-year-old tale should contain a valid image of the past and present of a society so vast in extent both in space and in time? Is it no more than a fantasy to imagine that a constant feature can be detected throughout such a broad and lengthy development? The answer to these pertinent questions brings us to the fundamental problems of China's history.

Nothing is further from the truth than the picture of China as a calm, unchanging, smiling land suddenly transformed into a blazing inferno by the flaming torch of twentieth-century social and nationalist revolutions; of China as an amiable giant, torn from three thousand years of somnolence amidst gracious works of art, sophisticated customs, and mystical wisdom, by the shrill call to arms of foreign emissaries and agitators. For just as false as that other legend of her immobility and impassivity is the extremely tenacious legend of the social harmony that prevailed in the old China. If even a minimum of objectivity is to be attained when speaking of tradition and revolution in China, it will be necessary first to rid ourselves of the tissue of falsehoods arising from gross ignorance and deep-seated prejudice.

[1] Cf. E. D. Edwards, *Chinese Prose Literature of the T'ang Period* (London, 1938), 2, 212–15.

Our own eventful eighteenth century formed an idealized picture of the distant Celestial Empire as an idyllic, stable society, well balanced and well content, automatically following a rhythm similar to that of the recurring seasonal cycle. This was a Utopian vision that had more relevance to those who invented it than to the unknown country that served them as model; for, however dear it may be to harassed Westerners in search of ideals, it will not stand up for an instant under serious examination. The smiling landscape is found to be a veil which, when torn asunder, reveals a craggy vista of precipices and extinct volcanoes, reminiscent of the visions with which most Chinese landscape painters were obsessed.

It is, however, by no means true that the idealized picture of the Chinese landscape was pure invention. It had some element of historical truth. The force of inertia in a social mechanism whose driving power is generated by conflicting pulls easily gives the impression of a pre-established harmony. Tensions are kept under control by force, and thus tend to cancel each other out, so that the internal dynamic force appears to be in a state of constant equilibrium.

What were the factors that were responsible for the continuity of one of the most stable social structures ever known? This question must be asked, in view of the fact that the old order lasted for over two thousand years—if the abolition of the ancient form of feudalism by Ch'in Shih-huang in the third century B.C. is taken as the beginning of the period occupied by the Chinese Empire, and the irruption of Western civilization in the nineteenth century as the end. Convenient though it is to make vague generalizations, it would nevertheless be simplifying in the extreme if, by omitting every detail that might detract from such a generalization, one were to say that Chinese society never changed and always followed the same pattern. The only excuse for doing so would be to facilitate comprehension of the essential otherness of the old China, in order to distinguish it both from the West and from the new China. It would be a device for taking a mental stance that might provide a point of departure. Let us, then, adopt such a stance for a moment and attempt to compress China's history in order to bring the main trends into relief.

Traditional China was a well articulated agrarian society divided into four sharply demarcated classes, each following a hereditary occupation. The largest of these classes was the peasantry, forming the wide base of the social pyramid. The peasant's life was hard but honorable, for the well-being of the entire community depended upon his labors. Hence his was regarded as a fundamental occupation, honored in the national pantheon in the form of the Divine Farmer. Once a year, the Emperor dutifully rendered homage to him by personally plowing a symbolic furrow. The peasant family was self-sufficient, for apart from its agricultural tasks, each peasant household did its own spinning, weaving, and all the work required for making its tools and utensils. This self-sufficiency explains why the other two occupations—craftsmanship and commerce —were regarded as much less important. Merchants and craftsmen not only lagged far behind numerically, but their social position was also less respectable. Although they had a far better life than the peasant from every point of view, having less hard work, more wealth, and more chance of rising in the social scale, their prestige was incomparably lower—was, in fact, almost non-existent, because they were looked upon as people who practiced an intermediary occupation. The profession of craftsman, and even more that of merchant, since both were dependent on the fundamental classes, traditionally bore the stigma of being superfluous and parasitical.

When we come to the apex of the pyramid, we find a small social group such as has never been known in the West. We must examine this group more closely, for it is this social stratum—tiny, but of considerable specific gravity—that determines the total structure. By exploring the nature and role of this peculiar class we may find the key that will explain the structure of every regime, past and present, of eternal China.

It was a class that was unproductive, or rather not directly productive, but which possessed aristocratic privileges and, as a rule, landed property. Nevertheless, it was not landownership, nor even heredity, that conferred upon it its special position and its extraordinary power; it was its indispensable social function. The Chinese official—the dominant, central figure of the old regime—may have found a certain amount of material security in having a country estate and useful kinship relations, for this enabled him to be educated, and facilitated his passing the examinations and attaining a career in the service of the state. But it was only by being in office that he was able to make full use of his privileges, for then he no longer had to pay taxes and was exempted from corvée and, usually, from military service. The mere fact of being in office guaranteed to officials and their descendants the monopoly of education that provided such an inestimable source of prestige amidst a sea of illiterates. It also conferred special rights which in practice amounted to complete immunity before the law, in a country where the ordinary subject was deprived of all legal rights and at any moment was in danger of being sentenced to deportation, banishment, or decapitation by judges who could only be described as guardians of the law in the interests of, and by virtue of being, officials—"official" and "magistrate" being synonymous terms. Moreover, official status allowed those who enjoyed it to enrich themselves by every means, legal or illegal, and to acquire new lands, or enlarge the family estate. The combination of these factors enabled the scholar-official gentry to continue in office and perpetuate themselves as the mandarinate that remained the ruling class until recent times.

Thus we find that, at bottom, Chinese society consisted of a vast majority of illiterate workers without legal rights, and a tiny minority of cultivated literati who planned, directed, supervised, and officered the work of others—in short, who assumed all the tasks of organization, coordination, and administration, and without whom the social organism could not have functioned at all. A passage from Mencius, who gave popular form to Confucian thought, will give a much better idea of the general picture than any amount of sociological discussion: "Great men have their proper business, and little men have their proper business . . . . Some labor with their minds, and some labor with their strength. Those who labor with their minds govern others; those who labor with their strength are governed by others. Those who are governed by others support them; those who govern others are supported by them." [2]

The necessity for government if the cohesion of a vast agrarian empire was to be maintained explains why the ruling class was able to cling so tenaciously to their prerogatives and last for such an astonishing length of time. Without strict fulfillment of its coordinating function by the mandarinate, China with its mixture of races and tribes would quickly have disintegrated and fallen prey to the dissensions of particularism. It was only constant supervision and harmonization of individual efforts that prevented the system of communications from becoming disorganized, the vital tasks of water conservation and utilization from being neglected, and roads, canals, dikes, and dams from falling into a state of disrepair. The calendar, too, depended upon the mandarinate, and without it all the agricultural tasks of the peasantry would have fallen into indescribable chaos. But the Chinese people had to pay an exorbitant price for all this. The bureaucracy was a hard taskmaster, and its tentacles reached everywhere. It marked

[2] *Mencius* III A, 4.

every member of society and every sphere of life with its stamp. Nothing escaped it; for the least deviation from prescribed paths had to be kept in check lest it should lead to rebellion, and any dislocation, however slight, was a threat to the system as a whole.

After much hesitation, the officials adopted the Confucianist doctrine as being the ideology that best expressed their way of life, since, in spite of preaching respect for others, justice, and reciprocity, these virtues were reserved for relations between educated people, whereas for the ordinary subject, the cardinal virtue was absolute obedience. Its unalterable aim was to maintain the status quo of the social hierarchy. Ancestor worship, divested of its earlier religious character, geared the social mechanism, regulating every detail of social relations. Respectfulness, humility, deference, docility, complete submission and subordination to elders and betters— these were the dominant features of the Confucian ethic that helped to cement the hierarchy, creating a patriarchal, paternalistic world in which gradations of rank, from the sovereign downward, were marked by the reciprocal relations of favor and obligation, and individual rights, initiative, and liberty were entirely lacking. In the Confucian view, the family was the main pillar of society. Not only was it the smallest social unit in which relations of dominance—subservience obtained (although here somewhat tempered by kinship solidarity), and hence regarded as the very embodiment of the moral code, but it was also, on the administrative level, the vector of the system of collective responsibility, for the whole family had to expiate for a crime committed by one of its members.

The picture I have drawn of Chinese society as it used to be is, of course, incomplete and one-sided—if you like, tendentious. I have deliberately omitted the brighter side, left out all the nuances, passed over the humor, the easy-goingness, and all the other pleasant characteristics that graced Chinese life. For it is my firm conviction that they flourished not because conditions were favorable, but as by-products of a harsh reality that would have justified a more tragic outlook on life.

It is inconceivable that a society as regimented as this one was, with every member obliged to conform from the cradle to the grave, should have remained permanently content to follow the prescribed patterns of behavior. Indeed even its privileged members sometimes suffered under the pressures brought to bear by its institutions, for although as a class they were both masters and the main prop and stay of the state, as individuals they were its humble servants and often its victims.

State ceremony and the rules of propriety were as far as Confucianism went in the direction of religious feeling (it is indeed doubtful if anything so sober and so lacking in feeling as Confucianism can be described as a religion at all), which was scarcely enough to satisfy the human desire to transcend circumstances and move toward a worthier destiny. This must be borne in mind when we try to understand why Taoism (the other basic attitude open to the Chinese that ran parallel with Confucianism) maintained a permanent appeal. It was the philosophy adopted both by peasant revolts and by frustrated individuals. Its basic ideas were in direct contrast to those of Confucianism: spontaneity, nonintervention, nonaction (*wu-wei*), and a return to nature, as against duty to the state, regulations, propriety, and moral obligations; nature as the absolute, spontaneous and untrammeled, the primal autonomous and self-sufficient community, characterized by metaphysics, mysticism, and meditation, as against the works of man, represented by civilization, order, the state, rationalism.

It was, however, not only on the plane of ideas that the subjects of the state withheld their obedience. They rebelled in practice whenever the officials exerted too much pressure on them, and the moment when this would inevitably occur was determined by time and patience, or, to apply the measurement used by Cocteau in his definition of courage, by knowing when one has reached the end of one's tether. China's history is one long chain of peasant revolts, and it is not surprising to find that their ideology always had pronounced Taoist features. Every time the amount of land under cultivation was reduced through floods, drought, or overpopulation, and the fiscal screw was tightened; every time the usurers began foreclosing on mortgaged plots of land, and exploitation and exactions reached the point where they could no longer be endured—a leader arose and gathered round him bands of peasants in revolt. The smouldering resentment of the ragged, ill-organized masses then burst forth, and, like some elemental force, they hurled themselves upon the country, charging blindly against each and every representative of authority. The devastation and depopulation brought about by civil war then frightened the forces of law and order into declaring a remission of taxes and a redistribution of land, which restored some measure of equilibrium, even if it was only a compromise that would last until the next revolt broke out.

After the Northern Sung dynasty had fallen, waves of fugitives poured southward with the cavalry of the Ju-chen barbarians at their heels, and the country was once again sufficiently out of control to provide opportunity for a peasant rising. The central government was powerless to prevent bands of peasants from roaming the country, and local authorities did not know whose orders to obey—the usual state of affairs during times of disorder. A peasant leader then arose in Honan and proclaimed himself king. A contemporary account tells us:

For twenty years he has been leading the masses astray with his heresies. He calls himself the "Great Celestial Saint," and claims that his spiritual powers enable him to get into communication with Heaven and to heal the sick. But in secret he says to his followers: "The law that divides commoners from nobles, that separates the poor man from the rich, is not a good law. The law which I shall introduce will confer equality of rank on commoners and nobles, and level degrees of poverty and wealth." It is with words such as these that he rouses the common people. So that within an area of several hundred leagues, the common people in their ignorance follow him, keep him supplied, and call him Revered Father.[8]

The account then describes how the partisans of the thaumaturge, originally recruited from the regular peasant militia, turned their arms against the authorities and set fire to government offices, monasteries, towns, and landowners' houses, and massacred everyone who might—however vaguely—be regarded as an official.

There are a number of other examples I could have chosen instead, but this one gives a good enough idea of the usual stages peasant revolts went through and of how their social demands were expressed in religious terms. Nor was the name this rebel gave to his ephemeral kingdom a fortuitous one. He called himself the King of Ch'u, because the area over which he reigned had once formed part of the powerful ancient kingdom of Ch'u. Ancient names, hallowed by history, were often revived in China. It is a familiar feature of Western history as well to disguise something new in historical costume, but in China the habit went much further, and might almost be described as something organic—a visceral reflex, as it were. Utopias were always placed in the distant past, in the earliest times of the Sage Kings. This golden age provided a meeting place for the Confucianist reformer, who had to clothe his proposals in historical precedents in order to get them ac-

[8] *Chien-yen i-lai hsi-nien yao-lu* (Chronicle of the Period 1127–1162) 31.613 (*Ts'ung-shu chi-ch'eng* edition).

cepted, and the Taoist dreamer, who longed for the lost paradise—the primitive stateless community, where there were neither lord nor servants, and everyone lived in peace and contentment. This archaistic tendency set severe limitations on peasant movements. The eyes of the rebels were always firmly fixed on the past, and no new horizons opened up for them. No one could escape these limitations. The unprecedented filled the guardians of tradition with terror, but even those who wanted to make changes were unable to go beyond the sacred ideas of the past. "He who succeeds becomes Emperor, he who fails is a bandit" is a Chinese proverb that expresses this attitude with all the ripe wisdom of practical experience.

In point of fact, few of the innumerable bandits in Chinese history succeeded in founding a dynasty, although most dynasties fell as a result of agrarian crises. For instance—to name the most important—the Former Han dynasty perished in the anarchy created by the rebels who called themselves the "Red Eyebrows," and the Later Han went down in one of the bloodiest of all peasant wars, the revolt of the "Yellow Turbans" under its banner of the "Great Peace" (*T'ai-p'ing*). The T'ang fell under the blows of a rebel who combined in his own person all varieties of the humiliated and dispossessed: he was the son of a peasant, a candidate who had failed the examinations, and a smuggler. The Mongol conquerors were expelled by a movement that had at first a social and later a national character; its leader founded the Ming dynasty, which, in turn, was removed by a peasant rising, whereupon the vacant throne was occupied by the Manchu conquerors. This last dynasty never recovered from the blow dealt it by the T'ai-p'ing, those peasants who rose, inspired by a chiliastic faith half Taoist and half Christian, who ruled over the greater part of China for about a decade, and whose exploits have now became a favorite subject for study in present-day China.

Thus we find that, until recent times, there has always been a combination of traditional and revolutionary elements at those turning points in Chinese history when a latent agrarian crisis accelerated events and all problems had to be solved at once within a few feverish years or decades. Nevertheless, it was seldom the same person who stayed the course from the fall of the old regime to the establishment of a new one. Rarely were the grave diggers of a decadent dynasty able to fulfill their promise of founding the next. Leaders falling by the wayside and upstarts who know how to profit from the occasion are phenomena typical of times of upheaval found in our own history as well as in China's, with this difference only: in China, whether a new dynasty was founded by an adventurer or carried to victory by the peasants, sooner or later it was taken over by the literati, the traditional intelligentsia, who, being both staunchly conservative and experienced as administrators, always brought the revolutionary forces under control, canalized them, tamed them, and rendered them harmless. Whence the awkward paradox that while revolutionary features marked the founding of every new dynasty (and heaven knows the Confucian high priests of history had plenty of difficulty in justifying the unforeseen leaps taken by their god, and in endeavoring to interpret disobedience—*post festum* and because of exceptional circumstances—as the most sacred of duties), yet the founding of a new dynasty after the fall of an old one, its rise to prosperity and subsequent gradual deterioration, was a pattern that repeated itself so monotonously that it became like a series of ritual gestures where no deviation is permissible, or the movements of a ballet in which the choreography is always the same. I would even go so far as to say (with certain reservations to which I shall return presently), that in the last of the great and victorious peasant wars —the one that led to the founding of the empire of Mao Tse-tung—historical parallels have, either consciously or unconsciously, played as important a part as the new foreign doctrines, although in very different circumstances. The peasant's son, poor and unknown, who finally succeeds after many misfortunes in overcoming his rivals and, despite the wiles of his enemies, mounts the imperial throne in the role of magnanimous conqueror, and reigns as the wise Son of Heaven, surrounded by a circle of counselor-companions—this is an epic conception of the founders of dynasties that has entered so deeply into Chinese consciousness, thanks to popular historical novels, that striking parallels must constantly emerge. Even the most Westernized of intellectuals must find it difficult to resist the temptation of drawing them.

So far I have spoken only of the traditional forms of revolution, or rather simply of tradition, emphasizing the features common to the past and the present. Now it is time to turn our attention to the uprooting of traditions that has taken place— the revolutionary transformation of all accepted values that has been mainly brought about by a truly revolutionary revolution. I assume there is no need for me to repeat facts that are known to everybody, nor any need to rehash events which, in many different ways, all illustrate the same basic theme:

the irruption of the West in China. (And an irruption it certainly was: the abrupt entry of Western technology, economic institutions, habits of thought, and ways of feeling, into a pre-industrial subcontinent.) For, although it is not yet ended, the world conflict that arose from the dynamic expansion of Western capitalism confronted with primitive communities or with societies that were perhaps dormant or at all events static, is now a matter for school textbooks. The steam engine and Gauguin, impersonal technology as against the Russian or the Chinese or the Negro soul (one or another to be chosen at random), material well-being as against spiritual joys, unrelenting progress coupled with hygiene on the one hand and passive contemplation accompanied by vermin on the other —such were the facile terms in which awareness of the immense and potentially tragic conflict was expressed.

The stages in the Chinese version of the conflict can be labeled as follows: the Opium War, the imposed treaties, the extortion of foreign concessions, consular jurisdiction, the Sino-Japanese War, the Boxer Rising, the Republic, Sun Yat-sen, Chiang Kai-shek, the Manchurian incident and the Japanese invasion, the Soviets and Mao Tse-tung. What lies concealed beneath these headlines of recent history? What is the underlying trend of events that began with the violent opening of China's ports, and has finally made this most civilized of great nations close her frontiers against the West and remain entrenched behind them? To answer these questions briefly, it is necessary to oversimplify and do violence to historical facts.

The inborn xenophobia of the Chinese marked their first reaction to the interminable series of humiliations inflicted upon them. But since they were the inheritors of a civilization that had either repulsed or else swallowed and digested so many different barbarians, they felt they could afford to greet such happenings with a smile that was haughty rather than indignant. But these new barbarians from the West were made of different stuff from the others. Not only did they refuse to become assimilated, but they continued to carve out for themselves larger and larger slices of Chinese territory. What was worse, the competition among them, which prevented any one of the great powers from swallowing the whole indigestible morsel, did not stop them from combining to nibble away the very substance of China, changing the lives and innermost being of the Chinese people with their corrosive, disintegrating influence.

I should like to mention here, parenthetically, that the powers of resistance of one of the higher civilizations, when confronted with an industrialized civilization, are quite different from those of a primitive people. The higher civilization is at once more resistant and more easily contaminated: more resistant, because it has something solid for the corrosive forces to work upon; more easily contaminated, because it has more sensitive organs whose receptivity favors the possibility of contamination. The relations between China and the West might be compared with those of Russia and the West, if only one century instead of two lay between Peter the Great and Stalin. In any case, it was the Russians themselves who asked the foreigners for help, and they always remained their own masters, whereas China became a mere chattel in the hands of foreigners who came uninvited and arrogated to themselves extraterritorial rights within the country. While we are on the subject of the instructive comparison between Russia and China, it should also be mentioned that, apart from the forced industrialization of the last twenty years, the Europeanization of Russia has been a slow process similar to the blending of liquids, whereas the bombardment of China's atoms by Western influences is like nothing so much as the nuclear disintegration that takes place in a giant cyclotron.

The second phase of China's conflict with the West was resignation in the face of an unavoidable evil, and might be given the descriptive label "learning from the barbarians." After the bitter experience of the 1895 war with Japan, the Chinese were anxious to imitate the barbarians, to see through their tricks and adopt their techniques and their technology without however in any way damaging their own institutions. This was a period of investigation and of travels abroad for study purposes, of tentative reforms and of struggles against the ultraconservatives; it gave rise to some remarkable men who, with touching naiveté, attempted to grapple with the insoluble problem of trying to borrow from the West what was technologically useful, and combine it with all that was of permanent value in the East. The problem was insoluble because it very soon appeared that what was thought to be of value was perhaps not so sound as it seemed, and that it was clearly impossible to attach new hands and feet to the old torso without also renewing the head. Every attempt at adaptation failed. On the one hand, the dynasty, with senile obstinacy, refused to countenance even the most inoffensive of reforms. On the other, technology proved to have a voracious appetite, and engulfed a far wider sphere than had been expected. It was simply not possible to go on studying the classics, observing the rules of propriety, respecting one's ancestors, and condemning all specialists, and at the same time be busily occupied in constructing railways. The old civilization was totally unable to withstand the shock of the introduction of a textile industry, of artillery, and of blast furnaces, once the decision had been taken no longer merely to endure them as evils introduced by hostile foreigners, but to make active use of them and integrate them into the life of the country.

From this time on, traditional ways were perceptibly in retreat. Within the space of two generations, from the middle of the nineteenth century to the beginning of the twentieth, the West, on its irresistible march, captured one stronghold after the other of China's three-thousand-year-old culture. Once the field of technology had been conquered, those of economics, science, the arts, and even the old conception of the universe all had to capitulate. As retreat followed upon retreat, all hope of holding the lines of defense had to be abandoned. The two generations concerned were mercilessly pulverized in the process. Only future historians will be able to do justice to the tragic greatness of the men of these condemned generations. Their tragedy consisted in the rapidity with which the efforts of Chinese progressives became outdated. It took more courage to declare oneself a constitutional monarchist in 1890 than to become a republican in 1910, or confess to being a Communist in 1930.

The hard apprenticeship, which had been nearly completed toward the end of World War I and the beginning of the Russian Revolution, can thus be seen to have brought about profound changes. The degree of change varied considerably according to whether the situation was viewed from Shanghai or from a village in the depths of the country. But since the history of the countryside has so far been little studied, while that of the treaty ports will continue to occupy historians for some time to come, it is from this angle that I shall attempt to show how values were transformed and how tradition and revolution exercised an alternating influence on events.

The greatest upheaval of all must undoubtedly have been the painful collapse of the old world view, the conception of the Chinese Empire as the universe, the *t'ien-hsia,* with China at its center, and all other peoples grouped around it ranked according to their degree of participation in the one civilization worthy of the name—the Chinese civilization. Now, China had become merely one among many other countries, and could not even claim a place in the concert of nations, having been reduced to helplessness—a mere bone of contention between the great powers. The shift in the center of gravity and the changed view of the world (the Chinese world having shrunk, while the world of the West had been enlarged) had one inevitable consequence: the birth of nationalism. The Chinese had formerly had a certain pride in their civilization, a firm awareness of its exclusive value, and a feeling of vocation for governing the world, which after all was simply the *t'ien-hsia*. But a prickly, touchy, demanding kind of nationalism, all the more virulent because of the mortal wound to their former feeling of superiority, was something entirely new to them.

After many avenues had been explored, nationalism finally found expression in the noisy demonstrations of the student movement. The universities and colleges became the hotbed of feverish agitation, reminiscent of the patriotic student movement of the "people's springtime" in 1848. The younger generation was strongly opposed to all that was reactionary, and wanted to emancipate everything—in the first place, themselves, from the tutelage of their fathers, and secondly, the Chinese language, from the shackles of the literary style (which played a role similar to that of our dead languages), so that they could express their ideas in journals and reviews in a way that everyone could understand, thus enabling them to speak to the people. But there could be no real freedom from the yoke of tradition until family ties were loosened and the emancipation of women was achieved, just as the national shame of the iniquitous unequal treaties could not be wiped out until riddance was made of the puppets of the foreign powers, those shady war lords, governors, and generals whose names are now forgotten but who, in the years around 1920, exercised a wide influence and were responsible for much bloodshed. Thus it was through the linguistic reform of 1917 and the famous May Fourth movement of 1919—a protest from the universities against the megalomaniac demands of Japan—that nationalism was brought to birth. Soon a wave of nationalism was to flood the whole of China.

Before long, however, it was realized that national resurgence could not take place without the accompaniment of a social revolution—another feature reminiscent of Europe in 1848. Hence the fanatical champions of independence for China became eager apostles of social emancipation. At the beginning of the eventful twenties, scholars were turning from translating *Werther,* Dickens, and John Stuart Mill to translating Maupassant, Chekhov, and Karl Marx, and education by missionaries was being replaced by university lectures given by men of the caliber of Bertrand Russell. Anticolonialist America, the champion of the "open-door" policy, was still regarded as the disinterested friend of China, although the recent October Revolution in the great neighboring country was already arousing eager echoes. This was the time when the Chinese Communist Party came into being. It was founded by a professor, and its first members were students.

That a revolution that would be both nationalist and social was next on the program was a belief shared by all progressives, whether they belonged to the Nationalist People's Party (the Kuomintang) or were members of the tiny Communist Party. They were also unanimous in proclaiming the slogan that united everyone without exception: the struggle against imperialism! The only thing the intellectuals disagreed about was who was to carry out and direct the revolution. At first the question was a purely academic one, for on both sides power was still in the hands of the intelligentsia, and relations between the Kuomintang and the Communists were still those of friendly collaboration. But the revolution of 1926-27 was a prompt catalyst of events. A military march was planned, such as had never before been seen, and was expected to conquer the whole country. But General Chiang Kai-shek, who led the northern military expedition, turned against his Communist companions-in-arms, whom he succeeded in duping, and hoped to exterminate. The massacre of the Communists fixed the fronts for the next twenty years. The dividing line ran through the little word "and," the copulative conjunction linking the nationalist *and* social revolution. The Kuomintang more and more confined itself to being the mouthpiece of the nationalist cause, and proved to be not only set upon maintaining the established order, but because of its niggardliness, certain to preserve all the traditional ills of poverty. The nationalist bourgeoise of the Kuomintang equaled the officials of the Celestial Empire in corruption, nepotism, bureaucracy, and inefficiency, and it was only to be expected that this national-socialist police state should finally restore Confucianism and inscribe the ancient Confucian virtues upon its flag. Those who resent this realistic assessment as being too harsh, or who do not find it convenient to subscribe to it, place themselves in a position from which it is impossible to form a cool, dispassionate judgment about either the present or the future.

On the other side of the dividing line, the Communist Party—decimated, proscribed, and forced to go underground—grew rapidly. Although, in spite of many internal crises, it continued to preach the social and nationalist revolution, it adapted its doctrines to the necessities of the situation and changed from being a party representing the interests of a minute urban proletariat (without, however, renouncing any of its Marxist jargon) into a body of political and military cadres for organizing a mass movement of peasants. The striking thing about the civil war that shook China during the years between 1930 and 1950 was that it invariably recalls the peasant rising of former days, in spite of modern techniques used. The red partisans were described as bandits, whose extermination was triumphantly announced by the government month after month for years on end. These same bandits, while ceaselessly harassing their enemies (whom of course they also described as bandits) with guerrilla warfare, also found time to set up a countergovernment in the territories they had gradually succeeded in occupying, known as Soviet districts, and to organize an army and stubbornly prepare themselves for the final struggle. But of course when drawing these historical parallels, we must not forget the modern context, which was something quite new. The pious legend —half believed in, half invented according to the ends in view—which represents Mao Tse-tung in the reassuring guise of an ordinary agrarian reformer, does not become true by constant repetition on the part of people anxious to be persuaded of its truth.

Indeed, all the analogies I have suggested are no more than approximations, and can be justified only as part of an attempt to understand the new complex situation by bringing out certain constant factors. For example, if one were to compare the Chinese revolution with the French revolution, the comparison—which is quite a valid one—is permissible only if one bears in mind the fact that making a revolution in a Europe of absolutism and stagecoaches is one thing and making the same sort of revolution in mid-twentieth century, in a highly industrialized world of interdependence and atomic bombs, is quite another. Those who wish to see Mao as nothing more than an agrarian reformer must ask themselves whether it is still possible to carry through a simple agrarian reform nowadays without setting off a whole chain of reactions. Not a single one of the measures introduced by the present rulers of China can be regarded in the abstract, leaving other things out of consideration. The same reservations must be made when comparing the aims, methods, stages and tempo of the Russian revolution with those of the Chinese revolution. Any sociologically minded observer would at once be struck by certain obvious features they have in common. Both revolutions took place in a pre-industrial, underdeveloped country, where existing conditions were the outcome of a long period of autocracy and absolutism. In both countries the overwhelming majority of the inhabitants were peasants. Consequently, the bourgeoisie was relatively unimportant. All the more important, therefore, was the role of the intelligentsia, consisting of the sons of officials, peasants, and petty bourgeois. In addition, both revolutions were made by peasants and soldiers, but directed, in the name of the working class, by the intelligentsia, and it is they who were the first to derive palpable benefits.

These analogies must be borne in mind when we come to consider the sequence of events, the results achieved, and the future prospects of the immense experiment taking place in China today. That this again has salient features in common with the Russian experiment is natural only if account is taken of the direct influence Russia had on the Chinese revolution. On the other hand, many elements in the Russian situation are understandable only if we remember the Asiatic factors common to the developments of both countries.

It is unnecessary to linger over the seizure of power by the Chinese Communists, for it is still fresh in everyone's memory, and all witnesses of the great event are in agreement as to its explanation. Their unanimous verdict is simply that Mao owed his triumph to the shortcomings of Chiang Kai-shek. The regime of the Kuomintang, which collapsed like a house of cards, was marked by its inefficiency and muddle, by nepotism and greed, corruption and disorganization; the trumps held by the army known as the "liberation" army were its efficient organization, its discipline, the incorruptibility of its soldiers and staff, and their devotion to the tenets of the movement. How long these virtues will last remains to be seen, but no one can deny that they existed, nor that they were of decisive importance at the crucial moment; and that is what counted. No doubts can any longer be held that the government of the Generalissimo, who was at one time acclaimed as the nation's savior, gradually and irretrievably alienated nearly the whole of the Chinese people. Everything it did seemed designed to lose the support of liberal intellectuals, which would have been such an asset, and to push them into the arms of the Communists. Students deprived of bread, liberty, and hope, professors who had been hauled over the coals for their opinions, starving writers, artists, and teachers, salaried workers without salaries, employees without employment, peasants who bore the brunt of the accumulation of follies and muddles prepetrated by the regime—all nursed a unanimous hatred for the chicaneries of the speculators and the activities of the police, and fell an easy prey to the cunningly modulated song of the Communist sirens. The dust of which Secretary of State Acheson spoke is still far from being laid.

A vast country, backward and poverty-stricken, and in addition ravaged and disorganized by a long civil war; a population of nearly 500 million, 90 per cent of whom are peasants; a working class that is half peasant, scarcely literate, and numerically insignificant; an infinitesimal number of skilled workers, engineers, and technicians; finally a complete lack of capital and little hope of getting any from abroad—these are the main factors in the present situation. To state them is alone enough to reduce any talk of socialism to its proper value as mere verbiage. But socialism is referred to only in the future tense or the conditional mood; even more than in Russia, is it a far-off paradise. Present reality, since it must be given a name, is called state capitalism. With more of state than of capitalism, the system is marked by the pronounced disadvantages of all state capitalisms: shortages, restraints, and bureaucracy. There is a shortage of everything, of the means of production as much as of articles of consumption. When things are in short supply, regulated distribution becomes a necessity, as even the wealthiest nations discovered during the last war. And when food rationing is unavoidable and a system of priorities has to be operated, in which appropriate shares must be distributed as equitably as possible according to need, bureaucracy is inescapable. The more poverty there is, the more regulations, restraints, and bureaucracy there are. Is this not reminiscent of the former institutions of imperial China?

The economic activities of the present regime consist mainly in grandiose public works on the one hand, and on the other, in state monopolies of all kinds—neither of which, it must be admitted, are exactly a novelty for China. One of the first state farms, now known as "sovkhoz" was established by soldiers on uncultivated land in Turkestan; does this not recall the agricultural military colonies of long-forgotten dynasties? Public works on a gigantic scale, carried out by a servile labor force, have existed in China from time immemorial; nor are state monopolies something new, any more than are their consequences—measures carried through by force, direction of the economy, compulsory saving, red tape, falsified reports, misappropriation of funds, maladministration, top-heavy over-organization, and the inevitable piling up of incidental expenses.

The complete regimentation of public and private life has a long tradition behind it. State officials and party cadres are as privileged today as the mandarins used to be, and prescribe in as much detail the duties of the ordinary mortal, who has not become any more precious in their eyes. The fountain pen is used instead of the writing brush and the Communists have replaced the Confucianists as the official party, but at bottom it is the same intelligentsia that assumes the indispensable function of direction, command, and administration. Even their mentality often recalls that of the autocratic and authoritarian tyrants of former days.

The stifling of all criticism, the muzzling of opinion, the punishment of the slightest sign of opposition as if it were a crime; threatening the faintest suspicion of heresy with serious penalties, deporting political adversaries to deserted regions, terrorizing kin through the system of collective responsibility, extorting confessions by refined forms of torture and elevating suicide to the level of an act of mercy—all such features of totalitarian power do not need to be borrowed from their neighbor by the Chinese Communists, for all are to be found in abundance in the storehouse of their own national traditions.

On the other hand, what does appear as a surprising novelty are the methods of agitation and propaganda used by the official party for taming the masses. Bringing politics into the daily life of the whole population has radically altered their former habits. Innumerable demonstrations, reunions, marches, committees, meetings, and public trials; theatrical performances, dances, public rejoicings; notices, pamphlets, journals— by every possible means official slogans are constantly drilled into every brain. In this way, what was formerly a sluggish, lethargic, undifferentiated mass of people has been shaken up, wakened up, enlivened, turned topsy-turvy, thus releasing an elemental force that will have incalculable consequences. Equally new, and with potential consequences whose importance it is impossible to exaggerate, is the enforced breakup of the traditional form of the family. It has been slowly disintegrating for the past century, but the Communists want to push the process to its logical conclusion. If they succeed in transforming family loyalties into submission to the state, and persuade the individual to transfer his allegiance from the family to the state, they will have accomplished one of those memorable feats that change the course of history, for suppression of the clan spirit at the same time removes the main causes of nepotism and corruption. It is, however, too soon to judge whether the official ideology of collectivism and what can only be described as state slavery will be capable of dislodging deeply ingrained attitudes toward the family. Only one thing can be predicted with any certainty, and that is that in China individual liberty is not yet on the program; for the present it remains the cherished inheritance of the West and the secret dream of the Taoist sages.

I should like to conclude with a declaration of faith that our present Russian-American century will be succeeded by a Chinese twenty-first century. All the potential is there. Is this tantamount to saying that the "yellow peril"—that specter invented by a Victorian generation of Malthusians with a bad conscience—will actually eventualize? No. If peril there be, it is not a yellow one. I hope I have succeeded in giving some slight indication of the very different and far more serious nature of the danger that does actually confront us, and that it is not simply a question of what will happen in China, but of what will happen in the world as a whole.

The Course of Pre-Revolutionary Chinese History*

KENNETH SCOTT LATOURETTE

OUR KNOWLEDGE of man in China takes us back into a remote antiquity. In the twentieth century there came to light in a cave in the north bones of what because of their location is known as Peking man, or, more technically, as Sinanthropus. Here was a primitive man who lived scores of thousands of years ago. A feature of his skull may indicate that the modern Chinese have him among their ancestors. Later, but still very remote, is evidence of Old Stone Age man underneath the mantle of loess and thus ante-dating its deposit. Still later are remains, more abundant and varied, of New Stone Age man. Much of these is in the form of pottery. Some is in stone implements and some in the traces of dwellings, partly below the level of the surrounding earth. They show that there was not one civilization, but several cultures, possible indications of diverse races and origins. Where these peoples came from and who they were we do not know. We wait for archaeology to tell us more. It seems significant that much of the evidence is in the north. It may point to migrations of people or cultural forms from Central and Western Asia along the corridor which leads into the

* From A HISTORY OF MODERN CHINA by Kenneth Scott Latourette, (Penguin Books, 1954), pp. 24–46. Reprinted by permission of Penguin Books, Ltd.

north-west of China proper. Yet some and perhaps much may have come from the south. Between these New Stone Age cultures and the China of subsequent centuries no sharp break occurred. There was a continuous development.

Chinese legends and myths which became part of the familiar folk-lore profess to tell of beginnings and give accounts of ancient rulers. Among the latter were the 'model emperors' Yao, Shun, and Yü, who were held to be paragons of virtue, giving themselves wholly to the welfare of their subjects. The third of them, Yü, is said to have drained the land of a great flood and to have founded the first of the dynasties, Hsia. However, we cannot be certain that a reigning line of that name existed. If it did, its domains must have been small and were in the north, somewhere in the valley of the Yellow River.

Here is seen, presumably although not certainly read back by later generations, what became a pattern of Chinese history. That history moved by dynasties. Each of the major dynasties coincided with a distinct epoch in the life of China.

We are first on fairly firm ground in the first half of the second millennium before Christ. There was then in existence a state which we know as Shang. Chinese historians have called it the Shang (or Yin) Dynasty, the successor of the Hsia. Its centre was in the lower part of the valley of the Yellow River and it comprised much of the north-east of what we have described as China proper. In the present century the remains of its capital have been uncovered and we have learned much about it, supplementing what has been handed down in ancient Chinese writings. The Shang had a high and distinctive culture. So far as we know, it was purely a creation of the Chinese, with no influence from the outside. It had writing, through characters to which can be traced many of those now in use in China. It displayed great skill in the casting of bronze, beautiful examples of which have survived to this day. There were numerous domestic animals, among them the dog, the pig, fowls, and the elephant. Society was based upon agriculture. There seems to have been a marked class structure with a sharp division between the aristocracy and the common people. There were armies, and we hear of one which numbered at least 5,000. The chariot was in use. At the head of the state was a ruler with the title of Wang, and the position was kept in the same family. The Shang had a long duration, of about six centuries. The traditional dates are 1766–1122 B.C. While they are probably incorrect, the Shang period covered about the same number of years as that between Edward III of England and the middle of the twentieth century, and fully a third more than have elapsed since the discovery of America by Columbus.

The Shang were displaced and succeeded by the Chou. By their success the Chou inaugurated an era which bears their name and which continued for almost a millennium, until the middle of the third century before Christ. Here was a span of time much greater than that of the Shang, more than twice that of any later dynasty, and longer than that between the Norman conquest of England and our own day. It was marked by the gradual extension of what may be called Chinese culture over most of China proper north of and including the Yangtze Valley. The rule of the Chou was not effective over all this area. Indeed, the authority of the Wang, as the monarch was still called, declined and eventually was little more than ceremonial. The realm was more and more divided into a number of states, some large and some small. The period is often called feudal, but in the technical use of that term, as it was employed to describe what arose in Western Europe in the eighth, ninth, and tenth centuries and prevailed there in the Middle Ages and what was seen in Japan for several centuries, that designation is inaccurate. With local variations, the Chinese of the Chou were conscious of possessing a common culture and the conviction was cherished that all mankind should be one in civilization and under a unified administration headed by one ruler.

From these long centuries and this culture there came many contributions to the later China, some of which were still potent in the nineteenth century and early in the twentieth century. What became the classics, standard for literature, were chiefly from these times. They included what were later esteemed as the *Five Classics,* i.e. *The Classic of History* (*Shu Ching*), a collection of ancient documents, *The Classic of Poetry* (*Shih Ching*), an anthology of poems of many dates and authors, *The Spring and Autumn* (*Ch'un Ch'iu*), the annals of the state of Lu, long said to have been written or at least edited by Confucius, *The Record of Rites* (*Li Chi*), dealing with ritual and much of it from a later era, and *The Classic of Change* (*I Ching*), arising from practices of divination some of which went back to the Shang and possibly earlier. There were also many other books. Writing was largely on bamboo slips incised or written with a brush pen, and in characters which were a modified continuation of those of the Shang. The sharp distinction between social strata persisted from the Shang. The upper classes made much of the ceremonies in honour of their ancestors.

The Chou was especially marked by the development of schools of thought which were to contend for the mastery. All were to be remembered and to leave their impress on the later China. One of them, what is usually known in the West as Confucianism, although the term more often employed by the Chinese is *Fu Chiao,* or "the Teaching of the Learned," was eventually to become dominant as the major body of ideas which shaped Chinese culture, but that was not until after the passing of the Chou.

The Chou, and especially the latter half of the Chou, was a time of intense intellectual ferment and vigorous debate. The focus of attention was largely on what constitutes ideal human conduct, and on the closely related subjects, the function and structure of society, including especially the family and the state. To anyone who thought more than superficially on these issues, it must have been clear that they could not be long discussed without entering into such questions as the nature of man and of the world in which man finds himself, and the relations of the two to each other. These, then, also became controversial topics. The approach, however, was primarily practical and utilitarian. Interest centred on the queries: What is the ideal society and how can that society be achieved? What in the broadest sense of that term is religion was inevitably involved and religious beliefs and ceremonies came in for discussion. Most of the scholars who engaged in the debates were socially and politically minded. Numbers of them either held political office or aspired so to do. Many of the discussions were at the courts of the princes of the states into which the realm was divided.

As its name indicates, Confucianism had as its most revered figure Confucius. Confucius, whose generally accepted dates are 551–479 B.C., did more to shape his people than any other individual in history. He early showed a deep interest in ceremonies and in the ways and records of the past and become their lifelong student. For a time he held office in his native state, but much of his later years he spent traveling from court to court, hoping vainly that he could find a ruler who would employ him on the high conditions which he laid down. A man of force of character and integrity, he was a teacher who attracted loyal disciples who recorded for posterity his words and his actions. A lover of music, conscientious, courteous, placing a high value upon the proprieties, dignified, but with a sense of humour, affable, serene, quietly assured that Providence had committed to him a mission, he carried through that assignment as a statesman and a teacher of ethics.

Deeply concerned for the disorder which he saw about him, Confucius held that it could be met by a return to what he believed to have been the policies of the model rulers of China's past. As a way of education and social control, he would have the ceremonies of antiquity revived and maintained, including those of religion. He held that if the upper classes, especially the monarchs, were upright and had the welfare of those below them at heart, the masses of men would be happy, contented, and peaceful. Government was to be more by moral influence than by force. He sought through his teaching and through companionship with his students to produce cultivated men of superior character. The example of men of this stamp, would, he believed, lead others to imitate them, and thus the ideal society would be achieved.

Holding to much the same principles as Confucius, but more than a century after him, was Mencius, whose traditional dates are 373–288 B.C. Next to Confucius he was the teacher most honoured by the orthodox schools of later generations. He, too, was interested in government and spent much of his life journeying from one capital to another of the states of his day, seeking to induce princes to accept his programme. Even more than Confucius, he insisted that if the rulers set worthy examples their subjects would conform to them. Consistently with this conviction, he held that men are by nature good and will respond if those who are over them are devoted to the welfare of those whom they govern.

In sharp contrast with Confucianism was a school which is generally called Taoism and which, next to Confucianism, was to be the most persistent. Its most highly esteemed expression is in the little book or tract, the *Tao Tê Ching*. Ascribed to Lao Tzŭ, whom the Taoists represented as being an older contemporary of Confucius, it is of much later date than the latter and of uncertain authorship. Of Lao Tzŭ almost nothing that is dependable is known, and it is sometimes said that he never existed. The *Tao Tê Ching* advocated, as the correct way for men and society, conformity to the *Tao,* a term long in use in Chinese thought, by which the Taoists meant the great reality which creates and controls the universe. Conformity with the *Tao* entailed what is sometimes called 'inaction', but which is probably better described as 'doing everything by doing nothing'. The *Tao Tê Ching* was critical of what was most prized by the Confucianists—the regard for elaborate ceremonies, the zealous cultivation of morals, and a highly organized government and economic structure. It advocated the simplest society possible. It decried the prizing of wealth, for were it not for that, so it said, there would be no coveting and no stealing. The *Tao Tê Ching* held up as the ideal a society in which village dwellers would be aware that there were other villages because they could hear their roosters crowing in the mornings, but would have no desire to know who dwelt in them. This meant no communication between villages, no commerce, and no elaborately ordered state.

In later centuries, as we are to see, Taoism was to undergo many changes. It was to take many forms. It was to become a religious cult, eventually borrowing from the imported Buddhism and having in it much of magic. It was to stress the achievement of personal immortality, a goal to be attained partly through diet and a physical and mental regimen, and entailing the search for the elixir of life. Yet through it many sensitive and thoughtful souls were seeking for a quietistic way of life, emancipated from the demands of a complex society.

Born in the small state of Lu in the present Shantung, as were Confucius and Mencius, younger than the former but older than the latter, was Mo Ti, also called Mo Tzŭ. For centuries his influence rivaled that of these two fellow products of that principality, but eventually it waned and he was remembered only by scholars and as one who had deviated from what later was regarded as orthodoxy. Deeply religious, he regarded the dominant power in the universe not as unvarying law, as was the tendency about him, but as a personal Supreme Being who, with the spirits, punishes those who do evil. He argued against the current scepticism regarding the existence of spirits. He stood for what he believed would make for the welfare of men. He taught, as a basic ethical principle, 'universal love'. He would have all men love one another as much as they loved themselves or their nearest of kin. He believed that if practised this would end war. He was immensely critical of war, but held that when waged in defence it was justifiable. He opposed as harmful the lavish burial ceremonies and extended mourning which were regarded as obligatory, and the elaborate ceremonial dances and the music which accompanied them. In contrast with the Confucianists, who argued that men's course is determined by fate, he stoutly maintained that men have free will. His followers separated into at least two schools, one stressing his religious beliefs and ethical precepts, working hard and living simply, and the other developing the logic which they found in his teachings.

Still another school which was developed in the long Chou era was that of the Legalists. It arose rather late, when China was being torn by wars among the states. It despaired of achieving stability and order by the Confucian way of a good moral example which postulated the basic goodness of human nature. It was also critical of the 'universal love' of Mo Ti. It insisted that what was needed for a body of laws, regulatory of imperfect human nature and impartially administered.

It was the Legalists, or School of Law, which at first seemed to succeed. As the central authority of the Chou Wang declined and as the culture associated with the Chou expanded over more and more of what we have called China proper, the wars between the states which made up the China of that time were intensified. Indeed, this stage of China's history is known as that of the Contending States (*Chan Kuo*). In the course of the struggle one state, Ch'in, with its centre in the north-west, emerged triumphant. It subdued its rivals and erased the last feeble remnants of Chou power. This last was in either 256 B.C. or 249 B.C. Ch'in had been organized according to the principles of the Legalists and seems to have owed its victory partly to this fact.

The undisputed dominance of Ch'in was short, from the defeat of its last rival in 221 to 206 or 202 B.C. Yet it was decisive. These brief years saw the culmination of a revolution from which emerged what in several ways was a new China. Some have maintained that it was through the Ch'in that the Chinese Empire really arose. It is significant and fitting that our word China, by which the land is now known, is from Ch'in. Certainly the Ch'in ruler believed that he was making a new beginning. In contrast with the title Wang, which the Shang and Chou monarchs had borne, he adopted a title, Huang Ti, and called himself the first (Shih) to bear it. He is thus known to history as Shih Huang Ti, or, to prefix it by the name of the state, the designation also given to the dynasty which he inaugurated, Ch'in Shih Huang Ti.

How much of Shih Huang Ti's achievements were due to him and how much to his chief minister, Li Ssŭ, has been debated. Certainly they would have been impossible without the foundations laid by earlier rulers and ministers of Ch'in. Shih Huang Ti mastered not only his rivals in what then might be called China, but also extended his domains along the south coast into what was later called Indochina, a region which until then had been outside the circle of Chinese culture. He applied to all China the Legalist system which had been adopted in Ch'in. As had been true in Ch'in, the land was distributed among those who cultivated it, a process which was to be repeated more than once in later centuries, notably by the Communists in the mid twentieth century. He sought to eliminate the last traces of the states which had long been a divisive element and to end the debates between the several philosophic schools, for these might weaken the Legalism on which his rule was built. He had the arms of his former rivals melted down, reserving weapons to his own armies. He stopped the discussions of non-Legalist scholars with their criticisms of his regime and ordered the books on which they relied to be burned, exempting only a few categories and copies which were to be preserved in the imperial library. Through a system of roads he attempted to tie his realms to his capital, near the present Hsian, in the original territories of the Ch'in. A new style of script was promoted to make the writing of the Empire uniform and thus foster unity. To defend the Empire on its most vulnerable frontier, the north, Shih Huang Ti had the Great Wall constructed. It was not entirely a fresh creation, but took advantage of earlier barriers built by the individual states.

When, in 210 B.C., death removed the strong hand of Shih Huang Ti, the dynasty which he had so hopefully formed did not long survive. Revolts broke out, in part reactions against his radical, autocratic measures and protests against the distress brought by the vast expenditures and the conscription of labour entailed in his gigantic building enterprises. The regime collapsed in a welter of murders and civil strife.

The Ch'in Dynasty was succeeded by the Han Dynasty, inaugurated by a general of lowly birth who emerged as master in the contest for power. With an interruption about the time of Christ brought by an ambitious magnate who attempted to supplant it with one founded by himself, the Han Dynasty ruled the Empire for a little over four centuries, from shortly before 200 B.C. to A.D. 220. It marks a distinct period in China's history. Contemporary with the founding and the heyday of the Roman Empire, its territories were probably fully as extensive as the land area of that realm. It was not as populous, and it may not have been as wealthy as the Roman domains, but it had a high and creative civilization. With the one exception of the Roman Empire, no other state of its day equalled it in power, prosperity, and geographic extent. The Han Empire embraced all of China proper except the south-west, and at one time or another it also included what were later South Manchuria, North Korea, much of Sinkiang, and part of Indochina.

The outstanding monarch of the Han was Wu Ti, who was on the throne from 140 B.C. to 87 B.C., or a little over fifty years. Under him military operations greatly expanded the territories of the Empire—to the north-west into the later

Sinkiang, to the north-east into Korea, along the south coast into what is now Indochina, and to a certain extent in the south-western mountains and plateau, the later Yünnan and Kweichow. He undertook vast public works, exalted the power of the throne over local magnates, and had a state monopoly of iron and salt. Yet his ambitious programme brought financial difficulties and entailed heavy taxation and the debasing of the currency.

He whom Chinese historians have regarded as a usurper, Wang Mang, in the first century after Christ put himself on the throne and attempted to found a new dynasty. He entered upon a comprehensive economic reorganization of the realm. He abolished the huge landed estates, nationalized the land and divided it among the cultivators, altered the currency, endeavoured to fix prices, and instituted state loans at moderate rates of interest to those requiring them for productive enterprises and for funeral and sacrificial purposes.

Under the renewal of the Han after Wang Mang's downfall, Chinese territory was extended afresh into what was later Sinkiang and beyond it into Central Asia. Caravan routes to the west were thus controlled and trade along them flourished. The Pan family from which came the generals chiefly responsible for these conquests also provided China with some of its notable historians.

In political structure and in culture the China of the Han was both a continuation of the past and made significant modifications and contributions. With some delay it checked the threatened renewal of the partition of the Empire into states with hereditary rulers. To prevent this it began the recruiting of a bureaucracy through civil service examinations, a principal which, much elaborated by later strong dynasties, persisted into the twentieth century. In place of Legalism the Han made Confucianism orthodox and for part of its course the realm was dominated by great families who were committed to that school and whose wealth was based upon the land. The Legalists did not give way without a struggle, and records survive of lively debates between them and the Confucianists over political and economic theory and specific measures. It was a modified Confucianism which triumphed, a Confucianism more theistic than the Confucianism of the Chou. It made much of impersonal forces, such as the elements *yin* and *yang,* the former roughly equated with the female and negative and the latter with the male and positive elements in the universe. It viewed the universe as operating through their interaction.

The Han scholars endeavoured to recover and edit the literature of the Chou which had been scattered or destroyed in the wars in which that period had come to an end, by the measures of Shih Huang Ti, and in the disorder that had accompanied and followed the collapse of the Ch'in. Sharp differences of major proportions arose between those who held to what were called the Old Texts, written in archaic characters but forgeries of the Han, and those who clung to the New Texts, genuine survivals from the past but recorded in a simplified form of the characters which, prevailing under the Han, become standard for succeeding ages. Fresh literature was composed in large quantities, some of it in philosophy and much of it historical. The latter included a voluminous and comprehensive account of China's past by Ssŭ-ma Ch'ien, who is regarded as China's greatest historiographer. It was to be continued from time to time down into the twentieth century as the Dynastic Histories, the standard but not the only mine of information for the course of the Chinese people, their state, their achievements, and their culture. Members of the Pan family were responsible for the first notable continuation of Ssŭ-ma Ch'ien's history. Literature was furthered by the invention of paper, which provided a less bulky and a cheaper form of its dissemination and which, incidentally, eventually spread to Europe, becoming the source of the manufacture of paper in the Occident.

A distinctive and notable art developed, some of it showing the influence of the Chou and the Shang, some of it inspired by contacts with peoples to the west, and some of it original.

By the end of the Han, of the schools of thought which had flourished in the Chou, only Confucianism and Taoism survived. The latter was modified, prospered, and became the system around which centred a movement which for a time created a regime that made a bid for the Empire.

Contacts were had with foreign peoples. Trade was carried on indirectly with the Roman Empire, and Chinese silk, conveyed by way of the caravan routes that led from the northwest of China proper, became common among the wealthy of that realm. Contributions came to China from the outside. In its effects the chief of these was Buddhism. It made its way to China and gained adherents, but it did not at once attain the popularity which it was eventually to enjoy.

When, in the first half of the third century of the Christian era, the Han Dynasty went the way of its predecessor, there ensued more than three and a half centuries of disunion. Much of it was marked by internal wars, and the earlier portion, that of the Three Kingdoms, in the half century which followed the Han, became famous in Chinese romance. In it flourished a trio of China's most notable military heroes. For a brief time later in the third and early in the fourth century most of what we have called China proper was nominally under one ruling house, but even in that brief interval of unity non-Chinese peoples, 'barbarians' from the north, were making themselves masters of much of the land. In the fourth, fifth, and sixth centuries the Yangtze Valley and the south were under a kaleidoscopic series of Chinese ruling houses and the north was divided among a succession of states in which the monarchs were non-Chinese invaders. The period paralleled the decline of the Roman Empire and the invasion of the Mediterranean Basin by the barbarians from the north.

Under these circumstances Chinese culture offered less resistance to foreign influences than at any time until late in the nineteenth century. It persisted, but Confucianism lost the dominance which it had enjoyed under the Han. Buddhism grew in popularity and became firmly established. It was furthered by missionaries from abroad and by Chinese pilgrims who, having journeyed to the centres of their faith in India, returned, their enthusiasm heightened by what they had seen and heard. Buddhism brought much of the voluminous literature, including works of high philosophic and religious quality, which it had produced in the course of its pilgrimage, now of nearly a millennium, and great quantities of it were translated into Chinese. With it also came rich and varied art forms, some of them developed in Central Asia and North-West India under Hellenistic influences. It spawned sects, several imported and others primarily Chinese creations. Now, too, Taoism reached the apex of its popularity. It influenced Buddhism and was even more profoundly shaped by the foreign faith. It possessed a highly organized religious community made up of a majority who might be called the laity and of experts who constituted a minority. Its attraction was its promise of personal immortality, to be achieved by a varied regimen by which the physical body was transformed into one which was imperishable.

Other cultural developments there were—in literature, and in forms of writing. The drinking of tea, of southern origin, spread through the south and centre of China. Not until the eighth and ninth centuries did it become popular in the north. Eventually it played a large part in the life of China and was one of China's main contributions to the rest of the world. The invention of the wheelbarrow, a vehicle widely used on the narrow roads and streets which characterized the south and the Yangtze Valley, is also ascribed to the early part of this period.

The reunion of China was achieved by a dynasty, the Sui,

in A.D. 589, but which, like the Ch'in eight centuries earlier, did not long survive its success. It was followed, in A.D. 618, by a dynasty, the T'ang, which ruled the Empire for nearly 300 years, until A.D. 907, one of the most glorious periods in the history of the Empire. In the early and more prosperous years of the T'ang, China embraced more territory and was probably more populous, wealthier, and more highly cultured than any other realm on the planet. In the seventh century its capital, Ch'ang-an, of which the present Hsian is a shrunken survival, was then almost certainly the largest city on the globe. From it the T'ang ruled an even larger area than had the Han. Its realms included not only all of China proper except the mountainous south-west, South Manchuria, and the later Sinkiang with its westward-stretching caravan routes, but also an alliance with a Korean kingdom which brought all that peninsula under its jurisdiction, and protectorates which included Afghanistan and the caravan cities in Central Asia and the valley of the Oxus.

Probably the ablest monarch of the T'ang was the second of the line to bear the imperial title. He is generally known as T'ai Tsung. He contributed markedly to his father's winning of the throne and to the firm establishment of the dynasty. On his father's abdication (627) he reigned in his own right until his death over two decades later (649). Under him Chinese rule was again extended into the Tarim basin and was pushed even farther westward, until the caravan cities Samarkand and Bokhara and much of the later Afghanistan and Russian Turkestan acknowledged his suzerainty. He strengthened the examination system for the recruitment of members of the bureaucracy. He emphasized Confucianism and ordered temples in honour of Confucius to be erected in every administrative subdivision of the realm. He fostered agriculture and commanded the reestablishment of public granaries in which stores could be accumulated in seasons of plenty for distribution in years when the crops were poor.

During the T'ang there lived and wrote the two men who are usually considered the outstanding poets of China, the bibulous, bohemian, and stylistically daring and original Li Po and, even greater as an artist and a genius, the conscientious Tu Fu, intimately acquainted with both beauty and tragedy and, like so many of the literary men of China, with ambition and experience in the service of the state. Prominent also was Po Chü-i, who, living in the later turbulent years of the dynasty as a poet of the common people, was to be emphasized by the Communists in the twentieth century. Partly under the inspiration of Buddhism, painting flourished. It was then that one of the most famous of the many Chinese experts with the brush, Wu Tao-hsüan (or Wu Tao-tzŭ) lived and worked. Buddhism reached its apex and began the slow decline that marked its later course in China. Taoism was also popular. Significantly Confucianism revived and resumed the dominance which it had held under the Han and which it was to retain until the twentieth century. This was partly because it was deemed necessary to the state and partly because of the further development of the civil service examinations. These were largely based on the literature honoured by Confucian scholars, and this entailed its study in the schools through which preparation was made for them. Fiction, much of it tales long told by professional entertainers, was given written form in the vernacular. Printing made its appearance, apparently for the first time in the history of mankind, and later, combined with the use of paper which had come down from the Han, enabled the Chinese to multiply books beyond anything known elsewhere in the world until the nineteenth century. Partly through the elaboration of the civil service, the central government acted more directly on the masses of the people than formerly—a feature which was continued under subsequent dynasties.

The China of the T'ang had extensive contacts with other peoples and through them it both received and gave. Merchants came, some overland by the historic caravan routes and others by the sea. Foreigners of many peoples and cultures were to be seen on the streets of Ch'ang-an and in the ports on the south coast. Through them entered both Christianity and Islam, the latter faith then in the first stages of its amazing spread. However, both were represented only by small minorities and by the end of the T'ang Christianity had disappeared. Chinese Buddhist pilgrims continued to make their way to the central shrines of their faith in India and to return with sacred books and enhanced zeal. Several food plants were introduced and enriched the Chinese diet. It was possibly then that the use of optical lenses was acquired from India. Chinese influences flowed outward, notably into Japan. The adoption and adaptation of Chinese culture by the Japanese, begun earlier, was now accelerated.

As had its great predecessors, the T'ang passed off the scene in a welter of rebellions and civil strife. These first assumed large proportions during the reign of him who is usually known as Ming Huang. Ming Huang was on the throne from 712 to 756, longer than any other monarch of the dynasty. Under him the T'ang reached its climax. In the West a military expedition carried Chinese arms into the upper reaches of the Oxus and the Indus. It was under him that Li Po, Tu Fu, and Wu Tao-hsüan (Wu Tao-tzŭ) flourished. But it was in his later years, when he became infatuated with one of the most infamous of China's beauties, that a rebellion broke out which caused him to flee from his capital and abdicate in favour of one of his sons. The revolt dealt the T'ang a blow from which it never fully recovered.

The disorder which followed the T'ang lasted for a little over half a century and was marked by five short dynasties. In 960 a new dynasty, the Sung, was founded by a successful warrior. It remained in power until 1279, or slightly longer than had the T'ang, but not as long as had the Shang, the Chou, and the Han. However, at no time did it control as much territory as had the Han or the T'ang. Its rule extended very little beyond China proper. Moreover, during the latter part of the Sung much of the north of China proper was in the hands of various alien conquerors. Yet the Sung was a period of striking cultural achievement. Porcelain and painting were notable. Printing was further developed and extant specimens witness to a superb technique. The printers aided the circulation of a voluminous literature, some of it old but much of it a fresh creation. Because of printing the reading public increased. Huge histories were written. Confucianism was re-formulated under Buddhist and Taoist influence with Chu Hsi as its outstanding synthesizer. That which emerged eventually became standard, and was accepted as orthodox until the twentieth century. Much attention was given to the civil service. The examinations which led to it were further developed. The state instituted and supported more schools which prepared for them. The professional civil servants took the lead in scholarship. Striking social experiments were undertaken which were associated with the programme of Wang An-shih and which included the monopoly of commerce by the Government and loans to farmers by the state at rates of interest which were much lower than could be had from private sources. Foreign commerce was attracted and much of it was by sea through the ports on the south coast.

In the thirteenth century the Sung succumbed to the Mongols, the first time that all of China had been mastered by foreigners. China was the richest and most populous part of an empire which stretched from the China Sea across the heart-land of Eurasia into what we think of as Russia, in area and probably in population the largest realm which until then had been brought under one rule. For a time the capital was at Cambaluc, approximately the later Peking. Foreigners from many nations and races entered the country, some of them as merchants and some employed by the Mongols. It was during Mongol times that the first Western Europeans reached China, some of them merchants, some missionaries, and at least one engineer, the vanguard of the invasion which in the nineteenth and twentieth centuries was to work the most basic revolution that China had known. All of China proper was brought under Mongol rule, including the south-west, now for the first time fully incorporated in the realm. Through immigration and attendant conversions Islam gained the extensive foothold as an important minority which it has since retained.

In the fourteenth century the Mongol Empire broke into fragments. In China a rebellion which was partly nationalistic and anti-foreign swept out the Mongols. A new dynasty, the Ming, was founded by a successful general of humble origin who had once been a member of a Buddhist community. The Ming ruled China from 1368 to 1644. It was a period of prosperity, but it was shorter than that of the Han, the T'ang, and the Sung, and did not display as much cultural creativity and originality as had any of these three great predecessors. Its territorial extent was approximately that of the Sung, although it now included the south-west as the latter had not, but with one exception it did not reach out as successfully beyond the borders of China proper as had the Han and the T'ang. That one exception was fairly early in the dynasty, when formidable naval expeditions, under official auspices, semi-commercial and semi-political, went to South-East Asia, including Java, Sumatra, and Ceylon. They were not followed by the extension of China's rule, but they were significant as part of the movement of Chinese into that general area which attained increasing importance in the twentieth century. Ming painting and porcelain brought Chinese art to a new level of skill in technique. At first Nanking was the capital, but soon Peking was substituted for it, and it was at this time that Peking was given the great walls, temples, and palaces which in their main outlines persisted into the twentieth century and made it architecturally one of the most impressive cities of the world. Literature was produced and circulated in great quantities. Here and there fresh adventures were undertaken in philosophy and scholarship, among them one movement to get behind the Sung Neo-Confucianism to primitive Confucianism as seen in the Han editions of the works of the Chou period. However, in neither art nor scholarship were the Chinese doing or saying anything essentially new. In government they were perfecting the civil service examinations based on Confucianism, but this and the education which prepared for them tended to imprison the Chinese mind and outlook in patterns framed centuries earlier. Before the end of the dynasty, Europeans, led by the Portuguese and followed by the British and others, were again making their way to China by the sea routes, but they had little immediate effect on the Empire. The re-introduction of Christianity by Roman Catholic missionaries affected only infinitesimal minorities.

In the middle of the seventeenth century the Ming regime was terminated by foreign conquerors, the Manchus. Like the other invaders who had established themselves in China, they were from the north, the direction of chronic danger. As had the Mongols, after prolonged fighting they made themselves masters of all China, the second occasion in history that this had been accomplished by aliens. They remained in power until 1912. Thus for more than half the time after the Sung the Chinese were governed by foreigners. Here was a thought-provoking fact, fraught with implications for the future. Had the Chinese lost the ability to maintain their independence? As a qualifying consideration it must immediately be said that both Mongols and Manchus did not attempt to displace Chinese culture or Chinese institutions. They governed as native Chinese rulers had done and were regarded by the Chinese historians as in the legitimate succession to the dynasties. The Mongol Emperors had the dynastic title of Yüan and the Manchus that of Ch'ing.

The Manchus brought what we usually know as the Chinese Empire to its widest extent. Under them it included all of China proper and what we have called the outlying dependencies—Manchuria, Mongolia, Sinkiang, and Tibet. In addition several states were in a subordinate position which was without exact parallel in western international law. Of these the chief were Korea, Annam, Burma, and Nepal. Although this vast realm was gathered by the great Manchu Emperors, the Chinese regarded it as theirs and the regimes which succeeded the Manchus sought to extend their control over it—with the exception of Outer Mongolia, the recognition of whose independence was brought by Russian pressure, and of Burma and Nepal, which were never brought within the Manchu administrative system.

The first century and a half of Ch'ing rule was vigorous and under it the population of China rose to unprecedented proportions. Two reigns, known by the name of K'ang Hsi (1661–1723) and Ch'ien Lung (1736–96), covered most of that period and the Emperors who are usually remembered by those names were able and masterful. It was under them that the Manchu rule reached its greatest territorial dimensions. Population statistics for China are very uncertain, but the totals seem to have fluctuated greatly. During the prolonged internal strife which marked the end of the great dynasties they declined sharply, sometimes by as much as two-thirds. Yet until the Ch'ing they seem never to have been much above 100 millions. At the outset of the Ch'ing the total may have been 75 or 100 millions. By the end of the eighteenth century it had reached about 300 millions, and perhaps more. This means that it had multiplied between three- and four-fold in a century and a half. Why this was so we do not know. Although it appears to have begun in the later decades of the Ming, the increase may have been in part because of the strong government in the K'ang Hsi and Ch'ien Lung periods. Some have ascribed it to mounting food supply due to the introduction of maize, peanuts, and the sweet potato in the latter part of the Ming era and their rapid spread in the seventeenth century. The growth of population, continuing as it did in the nineteenth and twentieth centuries, although at not so rapid a rate, became one of the major problems of China.

In culture the China of the Ch'ing saw few innovations, but was largely a prolongation of that of the Ming. The Manchus continued to recruit the civil bureaucracy through the competitive examinations which were begun at least as early as the Han and were elaborated by the later major dynasties. Based as they were mainly on the classics esteemed by that school, they reinforced the hold of Confucianism on the Chinese. The Neo-Confucianism of the Sung remained orthodox. Literature was produced in vast quantities. With modifications, porcelain and painting were largely in the Ming tradition.

A feature of the great years of the Ch'ing was the continuation of the contacts with the Occident which had been renewed under the Ming. They were chiefly by sea and were deliberately restricted by the state. In the sixteenth century Portugal had acquired a foothold at Macao, a shallow harbour on a rocky island not far from Canton, and this she maintained. The Ch'ing attempted, and on the whole with success, to limit the sea-borne commerce to Canton and there to confine the foreign traders to a narrow strip along the river front outside the city wall, where were the 'factories', or places of business and residence of the merchants. True to the historic Chinese tradition, the Ch'ing refused to recognize any government as of equal rank with its own or to enter into the kind of diplomatic relations to which European governments had become accustomed in the family of nations which constituted the Western world. Before the Ch'ing had been in power many years the eastward expansion of Russia across Asia began to impinge upon the northern frontiers. Armed conflict followed, with a check to Russian southward advance into Manchuria. The resulting treaties (1689 and 1727) defined the boundary between the two empires, especially in the north-east, and provided for a limited overland trade and a semi-diplomatic Russian mission in Peking. Roman Catholic missions which had been renewed under the Ming were augmented under the first part of the Ch'ing regime. Jesuit representation at Peking was increased and the missionaries had charge of the mathematical and astronomical computations which regulated the official calendar. At imperial request they made maps of the realm, did paintings in European style, and supervised the erection of buildings in Western architecture at the summer palace. By the beginning of the eighteenth century there were between 200,000 and 300,000 Christians scattered through all but one of the provinces of China proper.

However, except for the possible contribution of the new food plants from the Americas to the startling increase in population, the effect of the Occident upon China as a whole was very slight. A combination of factors prevented an increase in the number of Christians in the eighteenth century, and at the dawn of the nineteenth century Christianity seemed again to be dying out. Foreign merchants and trade were still closely restricted, and efforts from the West, notably from Great Britain, to establish continuing diplomatic relations after the European manner were rebuffed. China was the most populous empire on the face of the globe. Serene in their conviction of self-sufficiency and cultural superiority, the ruling classes wished to hold at arm's length the troublesome 'barbarians' who came by way of the sea.

The reverse effect, that of China upon Europe, was more marked. Many in Europe, especially among the intellectuals, warmly admired China. Gardens, pagodas, and pavilions were built after the Chinese style; lacquer, incense, and the Chinese manner of painting were popular; sedan chairs came into use, wall-papers were imitations and adaptations of Chinese models; numbers of Chinese plants and flowers were introduced; the drinking of tea became general, and the fashionable deism was reinforced by what was known of Confucianism, esteemed as that was by an example of the 'natural religion' which the deists prized in opposition to 'revealed religion'.

By the end of the eighteenth century the Ch'ing rule was beginning to give evidence of the decline which had characterized the later stages of earlier Chinese dynasties. In the nineteenth century, with occasional partial recovery, this became progressively more marked. Monarchs of mediocre or inferior ability followed the Ch'ien Lung Emperor and in general the Manchus deteriorated. As we are to see, a reprieve, temporary as it proved, was won through the energy and initiative of outstanding Chinese. Yet, when pressure from the Occident began to mount steeply, as it did in the nineteenth century, China had the misfortune to be handicapped by the decadence of the Manchus, aliens who clung to the power won for them by their vigorous ancestors.

THE FOUNDATIONS OF TRADITION

In 221 B.C. the Ch'in state, subduing all rival Chinese states, unified the territory we refer to as China, our name deriving from this venture. The ruler, Shih Huang Ti, and his chief minister, Li Ssŭ, embarked on an ambitious course. They eliminated the vestiges of separate states which had long been a divisive element, and within a short time succeeded in extending the domain of China into what was later called Indochina.

To secure this strongly centralized empire, all opposition was quelled and the land was divided among the cultivators. It was at this time also that a uniform script was adopted and an extensive system of public works constructed among which was the Great Wall. The cement of this first great Empire, put together through a combination of force and wile, was an administrative system based on legalism. Opposed to the older school of Confucianism, the legalists despaired of relying on moral example to achieve order and stability and substituted the unifying principle of a body of impartially administered laws to regulate the imperfections of human nature.

The opposition to Shih Huang Ti's innovations was spearheaded by the scholars. Li Ssŭ, recognizing the dangers of philosophical criticism of the new regime, drafted a decree ordering the burning of books of old knowledge, exempting only a few categories and copies to be preserved in the Imperial library. In this way he hoped to deprive the critics of their historical ammunition, the precedents that were used to interfere with the Imperial aim of centralization. The following selection of Li Ssŭ's comments and the decree banning the books presents a picture of the underlying conflict from the perspective of the unifiers, the advocates of change.

To a westerner, Li Ssŭ comes closest to Machiavelli in his concern for power and his reasoning that unification demands the obliteration of all potential sources of opposition. In the first instance this means the feudal baronies and secondly, the ideological weaponry of the scholars. In his decree banning the books Li Ssŭ argues, much as the present Communist leadership does, that the scholars are narrow in their outlooks and opposed to change. Despite the improvements engineered by the new regime they "do not conduct themselves in the new way, but study the past in order to defame the present." Ironically, Confucianism in the 3rd century B.C. was a major threat to the foundation of an Imperial system it was later to justify. But there is a certain parallel in the objectives of the present Chinese leadership with those of Li Ssŭ: the aim is to change an entire social order. The recent Maoist campaign to bring intellectuals into line is reminiscent of Li Ssŭ's comparable task and suggests an additional dimension to the present ideological disputes—the problem of unification. Therefore, although the Ch'in dynasty's undisputed dominance of China was short-lived, it highlights a pervasive problem in Chinese history, one that continues to face China's present-day unifiers.

The Biography of Li Ssŭ in the Shih Chi*

DERK BODDE

LI SSŬ was a native of Shang-ts'ai in Ch'u. When a young man, he became a petty clark of his district. In the toilet room belonging to his official quarters, he noticed that there were rats that ate the filth, and that the approach of man or dog would repeatedly frighten them. But upon entering the granary, he observed that the rats there were eating the stored up grain. They lived beneath the great side-galleries, and did not evidence any uneasiness from man or dog. Thereupon Li Ssŭ sighed and said: "A man's ability or non-ability is similar to [the condition of] these rats. It merely depends upon where he places himself." He thereupon became a follower of Hsün Ch'ing in studying the methods of emperors and kings.

In advising the King of Ch'in he said: "The small man is one who throws away his opportunities, whereas great deeds are accomplished through utilizing the mistakes (of others),

* From Derk Bodde, CHINA'S FIRST UNIFIER, A STUDY OF THE CH'IN DYNASTY, AS SEEN IN THE LIFE OF LI SSŬ, 1938, pp. 12–14. By permission of E. J. Brill Ltd., Publishers, London.

and inflexibly following them up. Why is it that in ancient times Duke Mu of Ch'in (659–621), as Lord Protector, did not in the end annex the Six States in the east? It was because the feudal lords were still numerous, and the power of Chou had not yet decayed. Hence the Five Princes who arose one after the other, still continued to honor the House of Chou. But from the time of Duke Hsiao of Ch'in (361–338) onward, the House of Chou has declined, and the feudal lords have been annexing one another's [states]. East of the pass lie the Six States and Ch'in, availing itself of its victories, has now indeed for six generations brought the feudal lords into servitude.

"The feudal lords at the present time are paying allegiance to Ch'in, as if they were its commanderies and prefectures. With Ch'in's might and its great King's ability, [the conquest of the other states would be] like sweeping [the dust] from the top of a kitchen stove. [Ch'in's power] is sufficient to obliterate the feudal lords, bring to reality the imperial heritage, and make of the world a single unity. This is the one time of ten thousand generations. If now you are negligent and do not press to a finish, the feudal lords will return to strength, and will combine to form north-to-south alliances against you, so that although you had the ability of the Yellow Emperor, you would be unable to bring them into unity. . . ."

Li Ssŭ's Decree Banning the Books*

"THE FIVE Emperors[1] did not copy each other, the three dynasties [Hsia, Shang and Chou] did not imitate their predecessors. Each had its particular form of government. It was not that they were opposed to the methods of their forerunners, but that times had changed. Now Your Majesty has accomplished for the first time a great achievement. He has founded a glory which will endure for ten thousand ages. This is what narrow scholars cannot understand. Moreover, the matters about which Shun-yu has spoken[2] concern the three dynasties.

* From C. P. Fitzgerald, CHINA: A SHORT CULTURAL HISTORY (London: The Cresset Press, 1935), pp. 142–143. By permission. (Latest revised edition, 1962.)

[1] The five legendary emperors who preceded the Hsia dynasty, Huang Ti, Chuan Hsiu, K'u, Yao and Shun.

[2] Shun-yu Yüeh, a conservative minister had just proposed the re-establishment of feudal fiefs, basing his argument on the fact that such fiefs had always existed under the preceding dynasties.

Why should we take them as a model? Formerly the princes were continually at war. They esteemed the wandering scholars and sought their advice. Now the empire has been pacified. Laws and commands emanate from a single authority. The common people are engaged in industry and agriculture, the superior classes study law and the methods of administration. Nevertheless the scholar nobles [*chün tzŭ*] do not conduct themselves in the new way, but study the past in order to defame the present. They cause doubt and trouble among the black haired people [the Chinese]. The Counsellor, your subject, Li Ssŭ, not disguising from himself that he merits death[3] advises: in the past the empire was troubled and divided. No one could succeed in uniting it. Thus the princes reigned simultaneously. In their discussions the scholars speak of ancient times in order to decry the present. They use false examples to stir up confusion in the actual state of affairs, they proclaim the excellence of the doctrines they have studied to abuse what Your Majesty has established. Now that the Emperor possesses the whole land and has imposed unity, they honour the past and hold private consultations. These men who oppose the new laws and commands, as soon as they hear of a new edict, discuss it in accordance with their doctrines. When they are at Court they conceal their resentment, but when they are elsewhere they debate these matters in the public streets and encourage the common people to believe calumnies. This being the case, unless we take action the authority of the sovereign will be abased, the associations of the malcontents will grow powerful. It is necessary to prevent this. Your subject proposes that the histories [of the feudal states], with the exception of that of Ch'in, shall all be burnt. With the exception of those holding the rank of 'Scholars of Great Learning, all men in the entire empire who possess copies of the *Shu Ching*, the *Shih Ching*, and the works of the Hundred Schools, must all take these books to the magistrates to be burnt. Those who dare to discuss and comment the *Shu Ching* and *Shih Ching* shall be put to death and their bodies exposed in the market place. Those who praise ancient institutions to decry the present régime shall be exterminated with all the members of their families. Officials who condone breaches of this law shall themselves be implicated in the crime. Thirty days after the publication of this decree, all who have not burnt their books will be branded and sent to forced labour on the Great Wall. Those

[3] A formula of respect used when offering advice, which, in theory, might be displeasing to the sovereign and so justify the death of him who offered it.

books which shall be permitted are only those which treat of medicine, divination, agriculture and arboriculture. As for those who wish to study law and administration, let them take the governing officials as their masters."

The decree, as drafted by Li Ssŭ, was "approved."

The downfall of the Ch'in dynasty was followed by a period of disorder after which a new dynasty was established, the Han. China under the Han rulers (200 B.C.–220 A.D.) expanded roughly to the size of its contemporary in the West, the Roman Empire. By continuing the process of centralization, recruiting a civil service, and replacing the legalists' orthodoxy with a modified form of Confucianism, the Han dynasty crystallized the social pattern that we refer to as "traditional China." It was this same social pattern that continued to shape Imperial China through its last great dynasty (and beyond), the Ch'ing, which fell in 1912.

In many ways the Ch'ing dynasty, although it was established by conquering aliens, exemplifies for us the principles of organization so thoroughly tested in preceding dynasties. In the middle of the 17th century the Manchus, coming from what is today an integral part of China, the northeastern provinces, conquered all of China. They governed as native Chinese rulers had done and were regarded as legitimate heirs of the dynastic 'Mandate of Heaven' bearing the title of Ch'ing. Under the able leadership of Emperors K'ang Hsi (1661–1723) and Ch'ien Lung (1736–96), the Chinese Empire expanded both territorially and numerically. The Manchus adopted what were from the days of the Han dynasty the methods used by the ruling elite to reinforce its position and consolidate the Empire.

At the core of this system, as always, was Confucianism. Based on the assumption that man was by nature good, Confucianism appealed to reason and worthy example to sustain harmonious relations between men whether in state or personal affairs. The state was, after all, only an extension of the family, the same principles applying to everyone. So long as men adhered to the dictates of this "secular religion" the realm was secure. With its emphasis on reason, the "suitable words" and filial piety, Confucian ethics sanctified the acceptance of a social hierarchy at the top of which were the privileged scholar-bureaucrats who by their position preserved the status quo inherent in Chinese civilization, from the 3rd century B.C. to the middle of the twentieth century.

The following selection, from an Edict of Emperor K'ang Hsi, is included as a testament to the enduring contours of Chinese civilization. It vividly hints at how Confucianism, one pillar of this ancient system, fostered the kind of behavior that complied with the needs of Imperial China. What is especially interesting for us in light of today's events in China is the sharp contrast in values between Confucian society and those of New China. The exhortation to "kindly excuse people's errors; and though wrongfully offended, settle the matter according to reason" has today been replaced by the positive worth of conflict and struggle as a means of achieving progress. To build a new society, the Chinese are urged actively to resist the yoke of the past so strikingly represented in the Emperor's Edict. Behavior such as the humiliation of elderly people by youthful Red Guards and the public parading of respectable officials in dunce caps fly directly in the face of century-old and ingrained social norms; they can only be fully understood in this context.

The Sacred Edict of Emperor K'ang Hsi (1663–1722)*

LET CONCORD ABOUND AMONG THOSE WHO DWELL IN THE SAME NEIGHBOURHOOD, IN ORDER TO PREVENT LITIGATIONS.

Amplification

IN ANCIENT times, five *Tsoh* formed a *Tang,* and five *Chows,* a *Heang.* In them the doctrines of peacefulness, harmony, friendship, and compassion, were ever held in honour. But as the population of the *Heang* and *Tang*[1] daily increases, so habitations approximate, little inadvertencies occur, closer intimacies are formed, and trifling debates take place; from these, in an unguarded hour, strife arises which terminates in subjecting the person to public disgrace, and in delivering over the body to the police to be punished. The loser feels himself without character; and at the gainer every one looks askance. When those living closely together in the villages, become suspicious

* THE SACRED EDICT CONTAINING SIXTEEN MAXIMS OF THE EMPEROR K'ANG HSI (Shanghai: American Presbyterian Mission Press, 1870) pp. 26–29, 60–63, 70–73.

[1] *Heang* and *Tang* are nearly synonymous with the English word "*neighbourhood*," and are here sometimes rendered by it.

of each other, and seek mutual revenge, what plan can then be devised to establish their employment, and prolong their posterity?

Our sacred father, the benevolent Emperor, grieved at men's love of strife, and thinking to promote the renovating doctrine of good agreement, purposely extended his admonitions to the *Heang* and *Tang;* and said, "Harmony is that by which litigations may be rooted out before they bud." We, desiring the concord of the myriads of the people, also repeatedly enjoin it upon you to magnify the doctrine of harmony. The *She* says—

> "From sauceless food
> Folks' quarrels oft arise";

The meaning of which is, that strife, often by slow degrees, rises out of small beginnings. The *Yeh-tsung* says, "The man of superior virtue, in all affairs, commences by deliberately forming his plan." This expresses that, in preventing litigations the chief stress should be laid on suppressing their first beginnings.

It is therefore evident that a man should receive all, both relatives and indifferent persons, with mildness; and manage all, whether great or small affairs, with humility. Let him not presume on his riches, and despise the poor; not pride himself of his illustrious birth, and condemn the ignoble; not arrogate wisdom to himself, and impose on the simple; not rely on his own courage and shame the weak; but let him, by suitable words, compose differences; kindly excuse people's errors; and, though wrongfully offended, settle the matter according to reason. The one party displaying this largeness of mind, the other must feel remorse and shame. He who can bear for a morning, the village will bestow on him the epithet of "virtuous." He who will not wrangle about a trifling offence, the neighbours will proclaim his magnanimity. Great are the advantages of harmony among neighbours! The ancients said, "divination is not used for the sake of selecting an habitation, but neighbours." In favourable and unfavourable circumstances, there are none on whom we can so well depend as on our neighbours.

Let the aged and the young in the village, be united as one body; and, their joys and sorrows viewed as those of one family. When the husbandman and the merchant mutually lend, and when the mechanic and the shopman mutually yield; then the people will harmonize with the people. When the military mutually learn to exercise, and the guards to aid each other; then the soldiers will harmonize with the soldiers. When the soldiers exert their strength to protect the people, let the people nourish that strength. When the people spend their money to support the soldiers, let the soldiers be sparing of that money; thus both soldiers and people will harmonize together. From hence no more strifes will arise about a plate of food or a cup of sauce. . . .

The opulent and the aged who are looked up to in the villages; the learned and the able who are the glory of the neighbourhood, ought to go before, in the spirit of harmony, as an example to the place. . . .

The whole empire is formed by a collection of villages; hence you ought truly to conform yourselves to the sublime instructions of our sacred father, and honour the excellent spirit of harmony: then, indeed, filial and fraternal duties would be more attended to; kindred, more respected; the virtue of villages become more illustrious; approximating habitations prosper; litigations cease; and man enjoy repose through the age and ages! The union of peace will extend to myriads of countries; and superabounding harmony diffuse itself through the universe!

We, with our soldiers and people, must for ever make this dependence. . . .

MAGNIFY ACADEMICAL LEARNING, IN ORDER TO DIRECT THE SCHOLAR'S PROGRESS.

Amplification

OF OLD, families had their schools; villages, their academies; districts, their colleges; and the nation, her university. Of consequence, no one was left uninstructed. Places were appointed to which the scholars repaired, and a literary Mandarin set over them as a general superintendent. By these means, human talent was perfected, and manners improved. The intelligent, the simple, the bold, and the timid, were reduced to one rule. Our sacred father, the benevolent Emperor, attained to venerable old age; elevated the people, purposely magnified the schools; and left nothing that regarded the scholar's encouragement and the mode of instruction, unprepared.

The scholar is the head of the four classes of the people. The respect that others show to him, should teach him to respect himself, and not degrade his character. When the scholar's practice is correct, the neighbourhood will consider him as a model of manners. Let him, therefore, make filial and fraternal duties the beginning, and talent the end; place enlarged knowledge first, and literary ornaments last. Let the books he reads be all orthodox; and the companions he chooses, all men of approved character. Let him adhere rigorously to propriety, and watchfully preserve a sense of shame, lest he ruin himself and disgrace the walls of his college, and lest that, after having become famous, the shadows of conscious guilt and shame should haunt him under the bed cover. He who can act thus is a scholar.

But there are some who keenly contend for fame and gain; act contrary to their instructions; learn strange doctrines and crooked sciences; not knowing the exalted doctrine. Giving wild liberty to their words, they talk bigly, but effect nothing. Ask for the name, and they have it; search for the reality, and they are void of it.

The honour of the schools, it is true, depends, in a good degree, on the authorized teacher's maintaining uniformity and discipline; but it does still more depend on the scholar's regard to his own person and name. When the scholar's character is correct, then her literary compositions will not be mere bombast, or his actions a mere ostentatious show. He who can, while at home, support the dignity of the learned, will, when called to office, be a meritorious minister. How important are such consequences!

With respect to you, soldiers and people, it is to be feared that you are not aware of the importance of education; and suppose that it is of no consequence to you. But though not trained up in the schools, your nature is adapted to the common relations. *Mung-tsze* said, "Carefully attend to the instructions of the schools—repeatedly inculcate filial and fraternal duties." He also said, "When the common relations are fully understood by superiors, affection and kindness will be displayed among inferiors." Then it is evident that the schools were not intended for the learned only, but for the instruction of the people also.

In the seminaries there are both civil and military candidates. Though government and tactics, which form the objects of their pursuit, be different, yet, to act filially at home and affectionately abroad, are things in which they ought all to unite. The exertions of the scholar and the husbandman are not very different. If the husbandman can exert his strength in the field and duly attend to his duty, then he is a scholar.

Nor is it otherwise with the soldiers than with the people. When the soldiers all know to venerate their superiors and love their relatives, then they also are scholars. Do you not see, then, soldiers and people, that you ought to view the schools as important? That you ought to imitate learned persons of approved character? Who among you has not the common relations of prince and subject, parent and child? What one is without the radical dispositions of benevolence, justice, propriety, and wisdom?—say not then that education was intended only for the class of the learned. Mutually counsel to that which is good; and mutually caution against that which is evil. Keep your eye on the cultivation of proper manners; exert yourselves in the practice of that which is meritorious. Then the most stupid of the people will consider propriety and righteousness as their implements of husbandry; and the blustering soldier, view the *She* and *Shoo* as his coat of mail! The lovely uniformity of ancient principles and customs will re-appear! . . .

DEGRADE STRANGE RELIGIONS, IN ORDER TO EXALT THE OR-
THODOX DOCTRINE.

Amplification

WE, IN ORDER to improve manners, must first rectify the human heart—desiring to rectify the human heart, we must first have sound principles.

When man, obtaining the medium of nature, is brought into being, he has only the common relations, the radical virtues, and his daily bread, to mind. To these, both the wise and simple, should alike attend. To seek for that which is hidden, and practice that which is marvellous, are things not admitted of by the sages. . . .

With respect to books which are not written by the sages, and unsanctioned records, which alarm the age, and astonish the vulgar; which promote irregularities, and eat the people as a canker,—these all contain strange dogmas which should be rooted out.

Among you, soldiers and people, are many good and well-meaning persons; but there are some also who are blindly led into these devious paths, and exposed to punishment. We greatly pity such.

From of old three sects have been delivered down. . . . Afterwards, however, there arose a class of wanderers, who, void of any source of dependence, stole the names of these sects, but corrupted their principles. The sum of what they do is to feign calamity and felicity, misery, and happiness, in order to make merchandize of their ghostly and unexamined tales. At first they swindle people out of their money, in order to feed themselves. By degrees they proceed to collect assemblies to burn incense, in which males and females promiscuously mingle. The labours of the husbandman are inspected and all talk of wonders.

And what is still worse, lascivious and villainous persons creep in secretly among them; form brotherhoods; bind themselves to each other by oath; meet in the night, and disperse at the dawn; violate the laws, corrupt the age, and impose on the people;—and behold! one morning the whole business comes to light. They are seized according to law—their innocent neighbours injured—their own families involved—and the chief of their cabal punished with extreme rigour. What they vainly thought would prove the source of their felicity becomes the spring of their misery. . . .

The sect of the Western Ocean which honours *Teen-choo*, ranks also among those that are corrupt; but because these men [*i. e.* the Romish missionaries] understand the mathematics, therefore government employs them: of this you ought to be aware. To walk in these by-roads and deceive the people is what the law will not excuse. The intention of government in enacting these laws was none other than to prohibit the people from doing evil, and encourage them to do good; to induce them to degrade the corrupt, and honour the pure; to retire from danger, and advance to repose.

Should you, soldiers and people, intrusted with bodies descended from your parents, living in days of undisturbed prosperity, having food and raiment, and without cause of sorrow either above or below you;—should you still blind your nature, follow those lawless banditti, and have to suffer punishment for transgressing the law, would it not be indicative of the very extreme of stupidity?

By his benevolence, our sacred father, the benevolent Emperor, refined the people; by his rectitude, he polished them; by his most exalted talents, he set forth in order the common relations and radical virtues. His sublime and luminous instructions form the plan by which to rectify the hearts of the men of the age. A plan the most profound and excellent!

Soldiers and people! act conformably to his sacred injunctions; and stop the progress of these strange sects as you would that of torrents, flames, robbers, and thieves. Indeed the injury of torrents, flames, robbers, and thieves, terminates on the body; but that of false religions extend to the human heart. Man's heart is originally upright and without corruption; and, were there firm resolution, men would not be seduced. A character, square and upright, would appear. All that is corrupt would not be able to overcome that which is pure. In the family there would be concord; and on meeting with difficulties, they would be converted into felicities.

He who dutifully serves his father, and faithfully performs the commands of his prince, completes the whole duty of man; and collects celestial favour. He who seeks not a happiness beyond his own sphere, and rises not up to do evil, but attends diligently to the duties proper for him, will receive prosperity from the gods.

Attend to your agriculture, and to your tactics. Be satisfied in the pursuit of the cloth and the grain, which are the common necessaries. Obey this true, equitable, and undeviating doctrine. Then false religions will not wait to be driven away: they will retire of their own accord. . . .

EARLY CHINESE RELATIONS WITH THE WEST

As far back as Han times the Chinese had contact with such remote civilizations as the Roman Empire. But in the long course of her history, China for the most part confronted peoples of more primitive accomplishments than her own convincing the Chinese of their superiority. As a result they evolved a pattern of treating foreign emissaries as tribute-bearers. Since China was the 'Middle Kingdom,' the center of the world map, it was assumed that foreigners came to seek peaceful relations with a powerful neighbor or simply to ask favors. They were treated kindly but always in a condescending manner symbolized by their being called "barbarians."

This was true for the Europeans who came in the 13th and again in the 16th century as it was for others. The commercial activities of Europeans that began to flourish after the 16th century were firmly restricted by the Imperial Government. Even the most persistent merchants, the British, were confined to foreign 'factories' (residences) on the river bank in Canton and allowed dealings only with government-appointed Chinese merchants. The same was true of the missionaries; their activities and residences were just as sharply curtailed. After 1807, when the first Protestant missionary from Britain established a foothold in Canton, the Chinese were so effective in preventing missionary work that most of the missionaries established themselves among Chinese colonies where they were more hospitably received.

By the end of the 18th century Great Britain found the Chinese restrictions on their trade intolerable. Canton, the exclusive port for international trade conducted on the Chinese side by a number of chartered firms known as Cohongs, no longer offered Great Britain sufficient trade opportunities. In order to persuade the Chinese government to change this policy, missions were sent in 1787, 1793 and 1816. The following reply of Emperor Ch'ien Lung to the demands made by the British missions in 1787 is characteristic of the nonchalance of the Middle Kingdom in face of western aggressiveness.

The Emperor Ch'ien Lung's 'Mandates' to King George III*

"You, O KING, live beyond the confines of many seas, nevertheless, impelled by your humble desire to partake of the benefits of our civilisation, you have dispatched a mission respectfully bearing your memorial. Your Envoy has crossed the seas and paid his respects at my Court on the anniversary of my birthday. To show your devotion, you have also sent offerings of your country's produce.

"I have perused your memorial: the earnest terms in which it is couched reveal a respectful humility on your part, which is highly praiseworthy. In consideration of the fact that your Ambassador and his deputy have come a long way with your memorial and tribute, I have shown them high favour and have allowed them to be introduced into my presence. To manifest my indulgence, I have entertained them at a banquet and made them numerous gifts. I have also caused presents to be forwarded to the Naval Commander and six hundred of his officers and men, although they did not come to Peking so that they too may share in my all-embracing kindness.

"As to your entreaty to send one of your nationals to be accredited to my Celestial Court and to be in control of your country's trade with China, this request is contrary to all usage of my dynasty and cannot possibly be entertained.

*From Harley Farnsworth MacNair, MODERN CHINESE HISTORY, SELECTED READINGS (Shanghai: The Commercial Press, Ltd. 1933), pp. 2–9.

It is true that Europeans, in the service of the dynasty, have been permitted to live at Peking, but they are compelled to adopt Chinese dress, they are strictly confined to their own precincts and are never permitted to return home. You are presumably familiar with our dynastic regulations. Your proposed Envoy to my Court could not be placed in a position similar to that of European officials in Peking who are forbidden to leave China, nor could he, on the other hand, be allowed liberty of movement and the privilege of corresponding with his own country; so that you would gain nothing by his residence in our midst.

"Moreover, Our Celestial dynasty possesses vast territories, and tribute missions from the dependencies are provided for by the Department for Tributary States, which ministers to their wants and exercises strict control over their movements. It would be quite impossible to leave them to their own devices. Supposing that your Envoy should come to our Court, his language and national dress differ from that of our people, and there would be no place in which to bestow him. It may be suggested that he might imitate the Europeans permanently resident in Peking and adopt the dress and customs of China, but, it has never been our dynasty's wish to force people to do things unseemly and inconvenient. Besides, supposing I sent an Ambassador to reside in your country, how could you possibly make for him the requisite arrangements? Europe consists of many other nations besides your own: if each and all demanded to be represented at our Court, how could we possibly consent? The thing is utterly impracticable. How can our dynasty alter its whole procedure and system of etiquette, established for more than a century, in order to meet your individual views? If it be said that your object is to exercise control over your country's trade, your nationals have had full liberty to trade at Canton for many a year, and have received the greatest consideration at our hands. Missions have been sent by Portugal and Italy, proferring similar requests. The Throne appreciated their sincerity and loaded them with favours, besides authorizing measures to facilitate their trade with China. You are no doubt aware that, when my Canton merchant, Wu Chao-ping, was in debt to the foreign ships, I made the Viceroy advance the monies due, out of the provincial treasury, and ordered him to punish the culprit severely. Why then should foreign nations advance this utterly unreasonable request to be represented at my Court? Peking is nearly two thousand miles from Canton, and at such a distance what possible control could any British representative exercise?

"If you assert that your reverence for Our Celestial dynasty fills you with a desire to acquire our civilisation, our ceremonies and code of laws differ so completely from your own that, even if your Envoy were able to acquire the rudiments of our civilisation, you could not possibly transplant our manners and customs to your alien soil. Therefore, however adept the Envoy might become, nothing would be gained thereby.

"Swaying the wide world, I have but one aim in view, namely, to maintain a perfect governance and to fulfil the duties of the State: strange and costly objects do not interest me. If I have commanded that the tribute offerings sent by you, O King, are to be accepted, this was solely in consideration for the spirit which prompted you to dispatch them from afar. Our dynasty's majestic virtue has penetrated unto every country under Heaven, and Kings of all nations have offered their costly tribute by land and sea. As your Ambassador can see for himself, we possess all things. I set no value on objects strange or ingenious, and have no use for your country's manufactures. This then is my answer to your request to appoint a representative at my Court, a request contrary to our dynastic usage, which would only result in inconvenience to yourself. I have expounded my wishes in detail and have commanded your tribute Envoys to leave in peace on their homeward journey. It behoves you, O King, to respect my sentiments and to display even greater devotion and loyalty in future, so that, by perpetual submission to our Throne, you may secure peace and prosperity for your country hereafter. Besides making gifts (of which I enclose an inventory) to each member of your Mission, I confer upon you, O King, valuable presents in excess of the number usually bestowed on such occasions, including silks and curios—a list of which is likewise enclosed. Do you reverently receive them and take note of my tender goodwill towards you! A special mandate."

(A further mandate to King George III dealt in detail with the British Ambassador's proposals and the Emperor's reasons for declining them) "You, O King, from afar have yearned after the blessings of our civilisation, and in your eagerness to come into touch with our converting influence have sent an Embassy across the sea bearing a memorial. I have already taken note of your respectful spirit of submission, have treated your mission with extreme favour and loaded it with gifts, besides issuing a mandate to you, O King, and honouring you with the bestowal of valuable presents. Thus has my indulgence been manifested.

"Yesterday your Ambassador petitioned my Ministers to memorialise me regarding your trade with China, but his proposal is not consistent with our dynastic usage and cannot be entertained. Hitherto, all European nations, including your own country's barbarian merchants, have carried on their trade with Our Celestial Empire at Canton. Such has been the procedure for many years, although Our Celestial Empire possesses all things in prolific abundance and lacks no product within its own borders. There was therefore no need to import the manufactures of outside barbarians in exchange for our own produce. But as the tea, silk and porcelain which the Celestial Empire produces, are absolute necessities to European nations and to yourselves, we have permitted, as a signal mark of favour, that foreign *hongs* (Chinese business associations) should be established at Canton, so that your wants might be supplied and your country thus participate in our beneficence. But your Ambassador has now put forward new requests which completely fail to recognise the Throne's principle to 'treat strangers from afar with indulgence,' and to exercise a pacifying control over barbarian tribes, the world over. Moreover, our dynasty, swaying the myriad races of the globe, extends the same benevolence towards all. Your England is not the only nation trading at Canton. If other nations, following your bad example, wrongfully importune my ear with further impossible requests, how will it be possible for me to treat them with easy indulgence? Nevertheless, I do not forget the lonely remoteness of your island, cut off from the world by intervening wastes of sea, nor do I overlook your excusable ignorance of the usages of Our Celestial Empire. I have consequently commanded my Ministers to enlighten your Ambassador on the subject, and have ordered the departure of the mission. But I have doubts that, after your Envoy's return he may fail to acquaint you with my view in detail or that he may be lacking in lucidity, so that I shall now proceed to take your requests *seriatim* and to issue my mandate on each question separately. In this way you will, I trust, comprehend my meaning.

"(1) Your Ambassador requests facilities for ships of your nation to call at Ningpo, Chusan, Tientsin and other places for purposes of trade. Until now trade with European nations has always been conducted at Aomen,[1] where the foreign *hongs* are established to store and sell foreign merchandise. Your nation has obediently complied with this regulation for years past without raising any objection. In none of the other ports named have *hongs* been established, so that even if your vessels were to proceed thither, they would have no means of disposing of their cargoes. Furthermore, no interpreters are available, so you would have no means of explaining your wants, and nothing but general inconvenience would result. For the future, as in the past, I decree that your request is refused and that the trade shall be limited to Aomen.

"(2) The request that your merchants may establish a repository in the capital of my Empire for the storing and sale of your produce, in accordance with the precedent granted to Russia, is even more impracticable than the last. My capital is the hub and centre about which all quarters of the globe revolve. Its ordinances are most august and its laws are strict in the extreme. The subjects of our dependencies have never been allowed to open places of business in Peking. Foreign trade has hitherto been conducted at Aomen, because it is conveniently near to the sea, and therefore an important gathering place for the ships of all nations sailing to and fro. If warehouses were established in Peking, the remoteness of your country lying far to the north-west of my capital, would render transport extremely difficult. Before Kiakhta was opened, the Russians were permitted to trade at Peking, but the accommodation furnished to them was only temporary. As soon as Kiakhta was available, they were compelled to withdraw from Peking, which has been closed to their trade these many years. Their frontier trade at Kiakhta is on all fours with your trade at Aomen. Possessing facilities at the latter place, you now ask for further privileges at Peking, although our dynasty observes the severest restrictions respecting the admission of foreigners within its boundaries, and has never permitted the subjects of dependencies to cross the Empire's barriers and settle at will amongst the Chinese people. This request is also refused.

"(3) Your request for a small island near Chusan, where your merchants may reside and goods be warehoused, arises from your desire to develop trade. As there are neither foreign *hongs* nor interpreters in or near Chusan, where none of your ships have ever called, such an island would be utterly useless for your purposes. Every inch of the territory of our Empire is marked on the map and the strictest vigilance is exercised over

[1] Macao [Ed. note].

it all: even tiny islets and far-lying sandbanks are clearly defined as part of the provinces to which they belong. Consider, moreover, that England is not the only barbarian land which wishes to establish relations with our civilisation and trade with our Empire: supposing that other nations were all to imitate your evil example and beseech me to present them each and all with a site for trading purposes, how could I possibly comply? This also is a flagrant infringement of the usage of my Empire and cannot possibly be entertained.

"(4) The next request, for a small site in the vicinity of Canton city, where your barbarian merchants may lodge or, alternatively, that there be no longer any restrictions over their movements at Aomen, has arisen from the following causes. Hitherto, the barbarian merchants of Europe have had a definite locality assigned to them at Aomen for residence and trade, and have been forbidden to encroach an inch beyond the limits assigned to that locality. Barbarian merchants having business with the *hongs* have never been allowed to enter the city of Canton; by these measures, disputes between Chinese and barbarians are prevented, and a firm barrier is raised between my subjects and those of other nations. The present request is quite contrary to precedent; furthermore, European nations have been trading with Canton for a number of years and, as they make large profits, the number of traders is constantly increasing. How would it be possible to grant such a site to each country? The merchants of the foreign *hongs* are responsible to the local officials for the proceedings of barbarian merchants and they carry out periodical inspections. If these restrictions were withdrawn, friction would inevitably occur between the Chinese and your barbarian subjects, and the results would militate against the benevolent regard that I feel towards you. From every point of view, therefore, it is best that the regulations now in force should continue unchanged.

"(5) Regarding your request for remission or reduction of duties on merchandise discharged by your British barbarian merchants at Aomen and distributed throughout the interior, there is a regular tariff in force for barbarian merchants' goods, which applies equally to all European nations. It would be as wrong to increase the duty imposed on your nation's merchandise on the ground that the bulk of foreign trade is in your hands, as to make an exception in your case in the shape of specially reduced duties. In future, duties shall be levied equitably without discrimination between your nation and any other, and, in order to manifest my regard, your barbarian merchants shall continue to be shown every consideration at Aomen.

"(6) As to your request that your ships shall pay the duties leviable by tariff, there are regular rules in force at the Canton Custom house respecting the amounts payable, and since I have refused your request to be allowed to trade at other ports, this duty will naturally continue to be paid at Canton as heretofore.

"(7) Regarding your nation's worship of the Lord of Heaven, it is the same religion as that of other European nations. Ever since the beginning of history, sage Emperors and wise rulers have bestowed on China a moral system and inculcated a code, which from time immemorial has been religiously observed by the myriads of my subjects. There has been no hankering after heterodox doctrines. Even the European (missionary) officials in my capital are forbidden to hold intercourse with Chinese subjects; they are restricted within the limits of their appointed residences, and may not go about propagating their religion. The distinction between Chinese and barbarian is most strict, and your Ambassador's request that barbarians shall be given full liberty to disseminate their religion is utterly unreasonable.

"It may be, O King, that the above proposals have been wantonly made by your Ambassador on his own responsibility, or peradventure you yourself are ignorant of our dynastic regulations and had no intention of transgressing them when you expressed these wild ideas and hopes. I have ever shown the greatest condescension to the tribute missions of all States which sincerely yearn after the blessings of civilization, so as to manifest my kindly indulgence. I have even gone out of my way to grant any requests which were in any way consistent with Chinese usage. Above all, upon you, who live in a remote and inaccessible region, far across the spaces of ocean, but who have shown your submissive loyalty by sending this tribute mission, I have heaped benefits far in excess of those accorded to other nations. But the demands presented by your Embassy are not only a contravention of dynastic tradition, but would be utterly unproductive of good result to yourself, besides being quite impracticable. I have accordingly stated the facts to you in detail, and it is your bounden duty reverently to appreciate my feelings and to obey these instructions henceforward for all time, so that you may enjoy the blessings of perpetual peace. If, after the receipt of this explicit decree, you lightly give ear to the representations of your subordinates and allow your barbarian merchants to proceed to Chêkiang and Tientsin, with the object of landing and trading there, the ordinances of my Celestial Empire are strict in the extreme, and the local officials, both civil and military, are bound reverently to obey the law of the land. Should your vessels touch the shore, your merchants will assuredly never be permitted to land or to reside there, but will be subject to instant expulsion. In that event your barbarian merchants will have had a long journey for nothing. Do not say that you were not warned in due time! Tremblingly obey and show no negligence! A special mandate!"

In studying China's history, westerners invariably face an emotional difficulty. They not only confront a strange culture but one that insists on its superiority. Beginning with the 18th century, culture contacts between Chinese and westerners were based on mutual hostility which, while it has abated in some cases, continues to plague the relations between China and both the United States and the Soviet Union. The opening of China, the opium trade, the demise of traditional Confucian society, and the misery and deterioration in the first half of the twentieth century are identified in the minds of the Chinese with western imperialism, including U. S. imperialism. To the extent to which the Soviet Union has in the past accelerated its pace in the industrial race at the expense of China and other underdeveloped areas, and in the present seeks to identify its interests with the U. S., it too fits in that category. The following selection provides background to this long-standing contention.

The initial response of the Chinese towards the westerners was to treat them as another variety of barbarian tribute-bearers who, so long as they respected the customs and laws of the Middle Kingdom, could not only be tolerated but warmly and generously received. This attitude of noblesse oblige, portrayed in Emperor Ch'ien Lung's Mandates to George III, appears from a westerner's hindsight as charmingly ingenuous. He politely refuses English demands for increased trade rights on grounds that China has no need of them. The westerners, of course, are persistent. They become increasingly infuriated by China's blithe assumption of superiority and intransigence, a situation in which patience soon gives way to righteous indignation and aggression.

The following selection of the first American missionary to China's observations, Elijah Coleman Bridgman, reflects the westerner's reaction to Chinese stubbornness and sets the stage

> for the ultimate showdown between the Manchu dynasty and the western imperialists. The outcome was disastrous for traditional Chinese society which did not long survive the death of its last dynasty, the Manchu dynasty.

First American Missionary's Remarks on Chinese Government's Attitude Toward Foreign Powers*

ELIJAH COLEMAN BRIDGMAN

DURING THE long period which has elapsed since an intercourse was commenced between Portugal, Spain, Sweden, Denmark, Holland, France, England, and other nations of the west on one side, and the Chinese on the other, negotiations, becoming the character of great and independent nations, seem never to have been undertaken. Numerous envoys, legates, embassadors, &c., have been sent from Europe to the court of China. They have been fitted out at great expense, and have usually been men of great abilities: but they have always been considered by the Chinese as *kung sze,* 'tribute bearers;' have frequently been treated with neglect and indignity; and after all have effected little or nothing for the benefit of those who sent them, or for the world. Two or three of these missions will afford us a tolerably correct idea of the whole. . . .

Thus it appears, from a long series of historical facts, that the Chinese practically deny the existence of relative rights among nations. The government proceeds on the supposition that its subjects have no rights; this position once established, all rights and immunities are and must be denied to outside barbarians. 'As there is but one sun in the heavens, so there can be but one great supreme power on earth:' that power is the emperor. He is the viceregent of heaven; and to his sway all both within and without the four seas must submit and whoever and whatever does not, ought to be annihilated. In this assumption of all right and dominion, foreigners have acquiesced. This acquiescence has grown out of the doctrine (very prevalent in the west), that nations have a right to manage their own affairs in their own way, and have no responsibilities in reference to other portions of the human family; and that so long as one permits intercourse in a way it chooses, and refuses it in any other way, or interdicts it altogether, other

* "Mr. Elijah Coleman Bridgman on China's Attitude Toward Foreign Powers," THE CHINESE REPOSITORY (Canton, 1831–1847) Vol. III, pp. 417–420.

nations have no right to interfere or complain. . . . The doctrine is equally opposed to the laws of God, to reason, and to common sense. Ignorance, superstition, pride, and ambition, have acted jointly to strengthen, establish, and perpetuate it. . . .

A just view of this doctrine will be obtained, if we suppose it to be carried into effect in a small community. Imagine then an extensive estate equally divided among twelve sons. Together with a large landed property, and flocks and herds, it embraces a variety of manufactories; rivers, canals, and highways intersect the whole, and in such a manner as to make each one of the parts, in a measure dependent on and serviceable to all the other parts. This mutual relation was designed; and eleven of the sons perceive this, and act accordingly, keeping up the relation and the intercourse which their father had established for their mutual benefit. But to their surprise, one of the twelve takes a very different course; he draws around his portion a line of separation, and declares death to any one of his domestics who shall pass that line; and enacts the same penalty against his brothers and any members of their households, who shall presume to enter the forbidden territory. And he stops not here. He denies the existence of any relationship or obligation to his brothers; denounces them as barbarians; and treats them accordingly. But some of them venture to enter a remote corner of his part of the estate, and after many disputes, are at length 'graciously permitted' to lodge there, and buy and sell: but all intercourse beyond this is interdicted.

It is unnecessary to pursue this illustration farther; it shows at once, in a clear light, the very unnatural attitude which China has assumed. And what, in the case supposed, ought to be the course of conduct pursued with regard to the individual who has adopted this exclusive system? He has evidently frustrated the intentions of his father, much to the injury of the whole family. His brothers have perceived this, have felt the injury, and have tried various expedients to remove the evil. They have sent messengers to him, repeatedly and at great expense; but he has treated them with neglect, contempt, and insult, requiring them to do him homage in the name of their masters. With regard to an individual of this description, there would be evidently but one course that could be pursued with strict justice. It would be necessary, as a matter of expediency and of duty, to restrict and restrain him, and with a hand so strong as to prevent the possibility of his doing injury to his neighbors. With special care being taken not to do him any harm, this rigid course should be followed up till he acknowledges and respects his kindred, reciprocates their offices of kindness, and gives bonds for good behavior in future. So it should be with China.

2

THE IMPACT OF MODERNIZATION AND THE DISINTEGRATION OF TRADITIONAL SOCIETY

THROUGHOUT CHINESE history there were periods of decay in which the regime was collapsing, chaos reigned and the people waited for the Mandate of Heaven to pass on to a new ruler. It was not unusual for a dynasty, when it was declining, to withdraw its garrisons from the northern outposts with the result that nomadic invaders—"barbarians"—came in, conquered crucial areas and ultimately installed themselves as rulers of China. The Manchu dynasty had been established in this way. But the Chinese were self-assured. They believed that all barbarians, whatever their intentions, inevitably assimilated the civilization and became more Chinese than the Chinese. And this in fact was the case with the Manchus as it had been earlier in Chinese history.

In the nineteenth century all this was changed. The Europeans, "barbarians" from the west, unlike earlier assailants, were not impressed with the splendor and achievements of Imperial China. They did not come as conquerors nor did they perceive themselves as "barbarians." They had little desire to learn about China and insisted on the equality of their status as members of their own civilization. It was impossible for the Chinese to fit these new invaders, their ideas or behavior, into any of the traditional categories of experience. True, there had been Europeans in China earlier, in the sixteenth century, but the Jesuits, proficient in western science and the Chinese language, had not prepared Chinese for the westerners who came to China in the nineteenth century. They had been scholarly, respectful and desirous of mutual cultural exchange as the means of converting China from the top down.

The Europeans had indeed changed since the sixteenth century. They had developed an industrial technology and along with it a set of nationalistic attitudes that placed Europeans not only apart from but on top of other peoples in the world. The expanded trade operations growing out of the industrial revolution brought a new class of Europeans into contact with Chinese civilization. Unlike the Jesuits, these Europeans came to China in search of trade not missionary work and were surprised to find China uninterested. This imposed sharp limits on the commercial intercourse between Europe and China. But for the most part, despite the westerners' frustrations, these early trade relations were peaceful. The cultural aspects of this contact, however, were far less sanguine.

English merchants, lacking the education and sophistication of China's earlier visitors from Europe, derided Chinese customs without attempting to understand them. And the Chinese for their part, though more circumspect in manner, reciprocated the feelings. All foreigners were known as "foreign devils" with their peculiar attributes used to refer to them: the English became known as "red-headed devils," the Americans as the "flowery-flag devils." Western dress and manners were a source of amusement to the Chinese and even the westerners' physical features evoked laughter. (Today they are still referred to as "long noses" as Jean-Louis Vincent writes from China, see pp. 494-504.) The following example of a Chinese reaction to westerners' appearance is not without wit:

Their thick coats fit tightly around their arms and body, narrow trousers restrict the movements of their knees, tough leather pinches their feet, and hats unyielding in shape grip their heads. Their movements, nevertheless, are quick and abrupt; what they would do without the restraint of their garments, I do not fancy; perhaps, these cramping clothes are a necessary check to their fury, instituted by their sages.

Despite the underlying rancor, however, as long as there was simply a relationship between private western merchants (the British East India Company had a monopoly) and the Chinese (who also worked through a monopoly) for the most part things were judiciously expedited. This was not the case in official relations between agents of foreign countries and the ruling house of China which were far less cordial from the start. The Middle Kingdom, still firm in its belief of celestial superiority and economic self-sufficiency dealt with the foreign envoys summarily. Treating them as "barbarians," the Chinese Emperor granted the westerners certain rights to trade but only out of a sense of *noblesse oblige*. What mystified Chinese officialdom was the westerners' dissatisfaction with this arrangement, a situation the Chinese attributed to his greed.

The Englishman, for his part, was frustrated by the absurd and willful obstructionism of the Chinese officials and irked at the self-centered complacency which led China to refuse further trade privileges in the interior of China. Englishmen came half way around the world to do business. For the Chinese state to interfere in this endeavor was hardly tolerable. The situation rapidly assumed explosive proportions and opium was the point of contention.

The immediate impetus for the Opium Wars came from the success of the industrial revolution in England. Being the major power in Far Eastern waters, England took the initiative and opium was used to entice the Chinese away from the steadfast proscription of their rulers. The end of the British East India Company's monopoly (1833) led to more belligerent pressure by the British for the elimination of these restrictions on their trade. In 1834, Lord Napier arrived at Canton to seek negotiations with the Chinese government for new trade concessions but to no avail and the smuggling of opium continued to be the major source of profit. And it was a profitable enterprise for all concerned. To simply identify the British as villain and China as victim hardly does justice to the complexity of the situation. While the British brought the opium to China (prohibited by law), the Chinese merchants capitalized on the opportunity to make enormous profits.

The assignment of an Imperial envoy, Lin Tse-hsu, to handle the increasing irritations between westerners and Chinese engaged in this singular "trade" in Canton did little but raise tensions. The Chinese officials, in anticipation of his arrival, refused the bribes of the foreign smugglers who in turn became increasingly impatient with what appeared to them as the capriciousness of the Chinese in enforcing the restrictions. The sum total of factors in this first round of opium smuggling posed not only a moral headache to Chinese officialdom but a threat to the stability of the Manchu dynasty. The edicts prohibiting the use and importation of opium, far from being a solution, served to whet the British appetite for a showdown victory and a final end to the trade restrictions. As a result, the Manchus, and all Chinese, deluded by their own experiences, were unwittingly forced to taste the bitter truth of their own weakness in a modern world that transcended their wildest dreams.

"It is a regrettable fact," as C. P. Fitzgerald says, "that the value of a nation's contribution to civilization, her place in the world, tends to be judged, from age to age, by the strength or weakness of her military power." By the middle of the nineteenth century Europeans had completely reversed their earlier high estimation of the celestial Empire. China was now seen as weak, corrupt, poorly governed, pagan, ignorant in the ways of science and stupidly opposed to change. Chinese officials could no longer be allowed to stand in the way of progress. If the end result was the destruction of the entire fabric of the Confucian world order this was not what the British intended. They went to war against the Chinese to secure the inviolability of the opium trade. If this undermined Chinese society it was no fault of the British; changing backward and corrupt ways was progress: a phenomenon no nation questions so long as it is identified with its own national interest.

Once England was embarked on this course, there was nothing China could do to save her ancient system from crumbling under the onslaught of western demands. The Manchu dynasty had already fallen prey to the traditional disease: the erosion of centralized power. Military complacency, corruption and inefficiency in the state bureaucracy, peasant rebellions, China had all the earmarks of dynastic decline. But there was a difference this time. The Manchus were not simply giving way to a new dynasty; they were ushering in the end of the entire dynastic system. The "foreign devils," by exacerbating the ills of traditional mismanagement, were throwing the Chinese into a bottomless abyss. The changes that would make their way into the traditional Chinese way of life were not even guessed at, let alone understood, until it was too late for the Chinese, or anyone, to preside over an orderly transformation. Modernization assumed its own course in China, haphazardly destroying the age-old structure of Chinese society, making promises to those who would be robbed of their fulfillment and yielding immediate gains only to the assailants and opportunists.

By 1858, the western powers had succeeded in "opening" China. They gained access to Peking and five treaty ports from where they could pursue their trading activities. The decisive factor—military superiority—was sufficient to convince the Chinese of the threat of the foreigners but insufficient to propel them in the direction of change. The extraordinary weakness of the Middle Kingdom in the face of western industrial might was too rude and traumatic an awakening. The reaction was like that of a dazed victim, uncoordinated and ineffective. The external threat was compounded by increasing internal unrest, creating confusion in the minds of even the ablest scholars. Baffled, they tried to learn from the westerners but failed to perceive the source of their strength. Under the leadership of prominent men, modern arsenals were built and institutes for western learning were founded. But modernization was not clearly understood.

There was an inclination to adapt only the techniques of westerners and then only in those areas visibly suffering from the comparison with western might. It was assumed, even by the most liberal proponents of reform, that the practical knowledge of the Occident could be separated from western culture and grafted onto the moral and political foundations of Chinese society. When Chang Chih-tung advocates "self-strengthening" for China in 1898, he stresses a return to Confucian virtues and support of the dynastic order as necessary prerequisites for the effective acquistion of western technical skills.

But if the reformers did not accurately gauge the extent to which modernization subverted the foundations of Confucian society, the opponents of reform, the conservatives, did. They were acutely sensitive to the threat westernization posed for China and rejected all attempts at learning from or compromising with the foreigners. In order to turn the clock back, however, and rid China of these alien and dangerous possibilities, the foreigners had to be forcibly removed from Chinese territory. The movement that came closest to accomplishing this was the Boxer Rebellion.

The Boxers, for the most part village peasants, untutored and destitute, were opposed to the Manchus because of their weakness and inability to defend China against foreign interests. As the movement grew the primary focus of attack became Christianity, the most widespread symbol of the westerner's subversion of Chinese civilization. They vented their hatred and anger first on Chinese converts to Christianity, then on missionaries and eventually on all foreigners, hoping thereby to cleanse China of its alien disease. Their behavior, in fact, exhibited the characteristics of a holy war: they combined an impressive aggressiveness and bravery with a superstitious belief in their own powers (they believed themselves immune to bullets). In July 1900, the Boxers, encouraged by the Empress Dowager, made their way to Peking and lay siege to the foreign legations until the western nations sent an expedition to rescue their citizens.

Unlike the earlier Taiping Rebellion (1850-1864) which was a revolutionary attack on the Manchu dynasty based on an alternative ideology and organization of society, the Boxer Rebellion was a more spontaneous and desperate expression of frustration aimed at the foreigner. And it had the implicit support of the government. Although in 1842 the Manchu dynasty had hastily met the terms of the British (Treaty of Nanking) because they feared open rebellion by the Taipings, by 1900 it was easier for the dynasty to deflect internal discontent from itself onto the foreigners thereby, perhaps, killing off two birds with one stone.

What an official had prophesied at the time of the first British victory over the Chinese in 1841, had come to pass: "On account of these disgraceful events (the fall of Canton) I am quite overwhelmed and ready to destroy myself; yet it would avail very little. Henceforth we shall be an object of contempt to other nations, and the native villains will gain strength and oppose the government."[1] In 1911, after a long series of accumulating crises, the Manchu dynasty was overthrown. The proclamation of a Republic, however, did not put an end to dynastic ambitions. In 1915 Yüan Shih-k'ai, having prevented the Republicans from effectively establishing a national government, attempted unsuccessfully to found a new dynasty. It was too late to restore the Empire; it was too late for reform within the old order. Revolution became the order of the day and if there was uncertainty about the direction of change there was at least no doubt that Imperial China was a thing of the past.

The Western Impact*

HAROLD C. HINTON

THE WESTERN impact on China has been one of the most important facets of what is perhaps the salient feature of the whole of modern history, the expansion of Europe. Unlike many other areas so affected, China was not transformed into a European political dependency. It was, however, confronted with a challenge too severe for its traditional ideas and institutions to cope with.

Until the end of the nineteenth century, Western influences came to China mainly in the baggage of the Western merchant and the Western missionary. Broadly speaking, the

* From "China" by Harold C. Hinton, in MAJOR GOVERNMENTS OF ASIA, edited by George McTurnan Kahin, 2nd edition, 1963. © 1958 and 1963 by Cornell University. Used by permission of Cornell University Press. Pp. 15–20.

[1] Quoted in Sir John Francis Davis, *China During The War And Since The Peace,* London, 1852, vol. 1, p. 127.

former brought with him Western commodities and technology, and the latter Christianity and European culture.

Portuguese merchants began to come to China in limited numbers in the sixteenth century, and they were followed in the subsequent century by Dutch, French, British, and Russian rivals. China at that time was in advance of Europe in most material respects; Chinese goods, especially tea, silk, and porcelain, were in great demand in Europe, but there was no corresponding demand in China for European goods. The foreigners were therefore faced with a serious payments problem, which they solved by importing silver bullion and coins. The situation was greatly eased by the British discovery in the late eighteenth century that opium grown in the newly acquired British territories in India could be sold at handsome prices in China.

The Chinese government during this early period generally considered foreign trade a minor nuisance that should be tolerated but not encouraged. By about 1760, however, the Ch'ien Lung Emperor had banned trade with the Western nations except at the port of Canton, and even there it was subjected to very strict regulation.

By the beginning of the seventeenth century a group of Jesuit missionaries had begun to gain acceptance at the Chinese court as a first step toward Christianizing China. They hoped, very unrealistically, to convert the Emperor himself and thus create a Chinese Constantine. Unfortunately for them and their cause, the Jesuits aroused the jealousy of other Catholic missionary orders by their successes in China and by certain concessions they made to Chinese culture, such as allowing their converts to perform the rites of "ancestor worship." When it became clear that the Holy See was inclining against the Jesuit position in the so-called Rites Controversy, the K'ang-hsi Emperor in 1706 decreed that only those missionaries would be allowed to preach in China who adhered to the Jesuit view on the questions in dispute. After 1742, when the Jesuit position was officially condemned at Rome, this edict had the effect of putting a virtual end to Catholic missions in China for the time being.

China's contacts with both the foreign merchant and the foreign missionary entered a new phase in the early nineteenth century. China's foreign trade was transformed during that period by two new features. The first was the growing trade in opium, which was smuggled into China and adversely affected not only the health but the finances of the coastal population of South China. The second was the industralization of Britain, which rendered British manufacturers and exporters anxious to sell their goods, especially textiles, on the supposedly limitless Chinese market. In 1833 Parliament abolished the British East India Company's monopoly on British trade with China. The company had not taken part in the opium trade directly and had tended to act as a check valve on Sino-British trade in general. With its removal, China began to feel the full impact of British pressure for expanded trade.

The so-called Opium War (1839–1842) between Britain and China resulted from China's refusal to permit normal diplomatic relations and free trade between the European nations and itself, from the Chinese insistence on subjecting foreign nationals accused of crimes to the brutalities of Chinese criminal procedure, and from a determined Chinese effort to put an end to the opium trade. The decayed might of the Manchu empire proved no match for the small British expeditionary force sent against it. The Treaty of Nanking, imposed by the British in 1842, set the pattern for a long series of what the Chinese came to call "unequal treaties."

Under these treaties, which China was compelled to sign with all principal foreign powers including the United States and Japan, China lost much of its sovereignty. It could no longer try foreigners on its soil, but had to allow them to be tried by their own courts and under their own law. It could no longer fix its own tariffs on foreign goods entering its ports; these were set by treaty at a very low rate. It was compelled to establish conventional diplomatic relations with the treaty powers. It was forced to open numerous "treaty ports" to foreign trade and allow the establishment in them of foreign concessions, in which foreigners could lease land and carry on business and which were not subject to Chinese administration. It was made to legalize the importation of opium, to allow the establishment of foreign-owned factories in the treaty ports, and to open its inland waterways to foreign shipping.

The advantages which these treaties gave to foreign manufacturers and merchants were considerable. Foreign goods, especially opium and cotton textiles, entered in increasing quantities and tended to disrupt the Chinese economy by creating an unfavorable trade balance and wiping out local handicrafts. China's two major traditional exports, tea and silk, were almost driven off the world market about the end of the nineteenth century by British and Japanese competition respectively.

The nineteenth-century Western impact began to undermine not only China's economic self-sufficiency but also its cultural self-confidence. About the middle of the century, under the protection of the "unequal treaties," Christian missionaries both Catholic and Protestant came to China in sizable numbers and made steady but not spectacular progress in the field of conversions. They also set up schools, hospitals, and orphanages, which helped to acquaint the Chinese with Western ethics and culture. They waged war on Chinese superstitions and on cruel customs such as the binding of the feet of upper-class girls. Less tolerant than the earlier Jesuits, they denounced the Confucian basis of Chinese culture and thus sowed doubt in the minds of some and resentment in the minds of others.

In 1898 some of the powers began to establish "spheres of influence" for themselves in China: a Russian sphere in Manchuria (the southern third of which was taken over by the Japanese after the Russo-Japanese War of 1904–1905), a German sphere in Shantung, a British sphere in the Yangtze Valley, a Japanese sphere in Fukien, and a French sphere in Southwest China. Within each sphere the power in question held a near monopoly on investment and the development of communications. The fact that this trend did not lead to an outright partition of China into a number of foreign possessions was due to two main causes: the first and more important was the rivalry among the powers themselves, which culminated in the First World War and which preserved a precarious balance among their interests in China; the second was the policy of the United States.

The United States was reluctant to see China partitioned into Western spheres of influence or outright colonies. This reluctance found expression in Secretary of State John Hay's two famous Open Door notes, the first (1899) of which attempted to secure equality of opportunity for American trade within the newly created foreign spheres of influence and the second (1900) of which requested the other powers to respect the "territorial and administrative entity" of China. The Open Door Policy had a slight, but only a slight, effect in checking foreign pressures on China; it would have had more effect if there had been any reason to think that the United States would fight to enforce it.

The Chinese response to the challenge posed by the Western impact in the nineteenth century was slow, uncertain, and much less effective than Japan's contemporary response to the same challenge. The Chinese were handicapped from the outset by their complacency and cultural superiority complex, as well as by their ignorance of the West and of its true strength. Few Chinese could deny after 1842, however, that Western armies and navies were stronger than those of China. During the terrible Taiping Rebellion (1850–1864), which if it had not been suppressed would have resulted in the overthrow of the Ch'ing dynasty by a pseudo-Christian successor dynasty, both sides made some use of Western weapons and military techniques. The years after the rebellion, known to the Chinese as the T'ung-chih Restoration (1861–1874), saw the building of a limited number of modern arsenals and dockyards with the help of foreign technicians, the translation of some Western technical treatises into Chinese, the training of a few young Chinese in Western languages and studies, and the beginning of Chinese diplomatic representation abroad. These essentially technical innovations continued, at a moderate pace that was far from adequate to the need, during the remainder of the nineteenth century.

The early Chinese modernizers responsible for these innovations were mainly officials committed to the traditional values of Chinese culture, though they made use of foreign advisers and Chinese compradors (agents for foreign firms doing business in the treaty ports). The aim of these officials was not to abandon or even modify the essentials of Chinese culture, but rather to preserve them by arming them with efficient modern military and economic techniques.

Toward the end of the nineteenth century it became clear to a growing number of Chinese, though not yet to the dynasty itself, that this formula was not good enough. Western technology would not flower in China unless some of the institutional soil in which it thrived at home were transplanted as well. The earliest convincing demonstration of this truth was the Sino-Japanese War (1894–1895), in which China was roundly defeated by another Asian power that had modernized far more effectively than China and had adopted not only Western techniques but also some Western institutions, such as a constitution and a parliament. The next demonstration was the "Scramble for Concessions" of 1898, which showed the Chinese how weak they still were and how close China had come to being partitioned by the powers.

The seriousness of the situation lent force to the arguments of a rising group of Chinese who favored the institutional as well as technical modernization of China under a constitutional monarchy of either the authoritarian Japanese or the liberal British type. The leaders of this group were two prominent intellectuals named K'ang Yu-wei and Liang Ch'i-ch'ao. In the spring of 1898 they gained the confidence of the young and well-meaning Kuang-hsü Emperor (1875–1908) and persuaded him to implement their program. There ensued the so-called Hundred Days Reform (June–September 1898), during which the Emperor promulgated a series of decrees aimed at modernizing the armed forces, the bureaucracy, the legal and educational system, and the economy. The people remained apathetic, however, and the bureaucracy was strongly hostile to the reforms. These reforms were nearly all canceled when the Empress Dowager Tz'u-hsi, the Emperor's aunt, who had dominated the court in her capacity of regent during most of the period from 1861 to 1889, resumed power and overthrew the reformers.

Even the Empress Dowager, however, became convinced of the urgent necessity for reform as a result of the Boxer Rebellion (1899–1900). This was an antiforeign, and especially anti-Christian, rising of lower-class Chinese in the northern provinces. The Empress Dowager lent the movement encouragement and support and even went so far as to declare war on the foreign powers (June 1900) and besiege the Legation Quarter in Peking. In mid-August, however, an international relief expedition moved up from Tientsin, took Peking, and drove the Empress Dowager and court into exile. The dynasty then had to put its seal on a humiliating peace treaty which included a large indemnity.

Convinced too late of the need for modernization, the Empress Dowager proceeded to put into effect a reform program basically similar to the abortive one attempted by the Emperor in 1898. Usually known as the Manchu Reform Movement, this program showed some genuine if inadequate progress until the Empress Dowager's death in 1908, but thereafter tended to flounder for lack of strong leadership. The most concrete success was the almost complete eradication of opium production in China and a simultaneous agreement by the powers to eliminate gradually the importation of opium into China from abroad. Others were the creation of a modernized model army of six divisions under the able but unscrupulous official Yuan Shih Kai, a partial modernization of the bureaucracy, the promulgation of a monarchical but parliamentary constitution modeled largely on the Japanese, the construction of a sizable mileage of railways by foreign firms and groups of provincial gentry, and the drawing up of modernized legal codes.

But this official program of reform, like the private one

led by K'ang Yu-wei, and Liang Ch'i-ch'ao, was too little and too late. China was growing ripe for revolution.

In the following Edict sent by the Emperor to enforce the decree prohibiting the illicit opium trade, the Imperial High Commissioner Lin Tse-hsü ordered the foreigners to surrender their stocks of opium to be confiscated. In addition, they had to sign oaths to discontinue the trade "under penalty of death." The next day, March 19, 1839, foreigners were forbidden to leave the city of Canton. With this decisive act on the Chinese government's part and the virtual incarceration of foreigners in Canton, the Chinese became embroiled in a sequence of events that led to the Opium War with Great Britain.

The treaties that were the aftermath of China's defeat in the Opium War presented new problems for the Ch'ing regime. The Manchus in government, more conciliatory to the westerners than the Chinese, seem to have been primarily concerned with the survival of the dynasty rather than the welfare of all of China. In following a policy of appeasement towards the "barbarians," the Manchus hoped to buy them off with concessions which would save the dynasty even if it was at the expense of Chinese pride and economic interest. In this respect Lin Tse-hsu, a high Chinese official, was associated both before (as in the selection) and after the Opium War with a policy of non-appeasement towards the western powers.

Before the war he favored harsh measures against the western transgressors of Chinese law, threatening military resistance and the permanent expulsion of all foreigners from China. As a result when the Chinese suffered the first reverses of the war, Imperial Commissioner Lin was dismissed and recalled to Peking. After the Opium War Lin Tse-hsü remained a firm advocate of "controlling the barbarians" but by learning their skills, especially their military skills, from them rather than bowing to them as the Manchus were inclined to do.

Edict from the Imperial Commissioner Lin to Foreigners of All Nations*

LIN, HIGH Imperial commissioner of the Celestial Court, a director of the Board of War, and governor of Hookwang, issues his commands to the foreigners, requiring of all full acquaintance with the tenor thereof.

* Edict in CHINESE REPOSITORY, Vol. VII, op. cit., pp. 610-615.

It is known that the foreign vessels, which come for a reciprocal trade to Kwangtung, have derived from that trade very large profits. . . . It is because our great emperors, in their universal benevolence, have granted you commercial privileges, that you have been favored with these advantages. Let our ports once be closed against you, and for what profits can your several nations any longer look? Yet more,—our tea and our rhubarb,—seeing that, should you foreigners be deprived of them, you therein lose the means of preserving life— are without stint or grudge granted to you for exportation year by year beyond the seas. Favors never have been greater! . . .

I, the high commissioner, having my home in the maritime province of Fuhkeen, and consequently having early had intimate acquaintance with all the arts and shifts of the outer foreigners, have for this reason been honored by the great emperor with the full powers and privileges of 'a high imperial commissioner, who, having repeatedly performed meritorious services, is sent to settle the affairs of the outer frontier.' . . .

I find that on board the warehousing vessels which you now have lying at anchor in the Lintin and other offings, there are stored up several times ten thousand chests of opium, which it is your purpose and desire illicitly to dispose of by sale. . . .

I proceed to issue my commands. When these commands reach the said foreign merchants, let them with all haste pay obedience thereto. Let them deliver up to government every particle of the opium on board their store-ships. Let it be ascertained by the hong merchants, who are the parties so delivering it up, and what number of chests is delivered up under each name, and what is the total quantity in catties and taels. Let these particulars be brought together in a clear tabular form, and be presented to government, in order that the opium may all be received in plain conformity thereto, that it may be burnt and destroyed, and that thus the evil may be entirely extirpated. There must not be the smallest atom concealed or withheld.

At the same time let these foreigners give a bond, written jointly in the foreign and Chinese languages, making a declaration of this effect: 'That their vessels, which shall hereafter resort hither, will never again dare to bring opium with them: and that should any be brought, as soon as discovery shall be made of it, the goods shall be forfeited to government, and the parties shall suffer the extreme penalties of the law: and that such punishment will be willingly submitted to.' . . .

After this, you will continue to enjoy the advantages of commercial intercourse; and, as you will not lose the character of being 'good foreigners', and will be enabled to acquire profits and get wealth by an honest trade, will you not indeed stand in a most honorable position?

If, however, you obstinately adhere to your folly and refuse to awake,—if you think to make up a tale covering over your illicit dealings,—or to set up as a pretext that the opium is brought by foreign seamen, and the foreign merchants have nothing to do with it . . . it will be evident that you retain a spirit of contumacy and disobedience, that you uphold vice and will not reform. Then . . . it will become requisite to comprehend you also in the severe course of punishment prescribed by the new law. . . . I swear that I will progress with this matter from its beginning to its ending, and that not a thought of stopping halfway shall for a moment be indulged.

Furthermore, observing the present condition of the popular mind, I find so universal a spirit of indignation aroused, that, should you foreigners remain dead to a sense of contrition and amendment, and continue to make gain your sole object, there will not only be arrayed against you the martial terrors and powerful energies of our naval and military forces;—it will be but necessary to call on the able bodied of the people, and these alone will be more than adequate to the placing all your lives within my power. Besides, either by the temporary stoppage of your trade, or by the permanent closing of the ports against you, what difficulty can there be in effectually cutting off your intercourse? Our central empire . . . has no benefit to derive from the purchase of your foreign commodities, and you may therefore well fear, that from the moment such measures are taken, the livelihood of your several nations must come to an end. . . . It rests with yourselves alone to choose whether you will have weal or woe, honor or disgrace. . . . Do not indulge in idle expectations, or seek to postpone matters, deferring to repent until its lateness render it ineffectual. A special edict.

Taoukwang, 19th year, 2nd month, 4th day (March 18th, 1839).

> Although the treaties that ended the Opium War extended the rights of westerners in China to five "treaty ports" where they were allowed to reside and trade, there were continuing disputes between the Chinese and foreigners over the interpretation of these rights. In Canton the dispute raged over the question of foreign residence within the walled city of Canton. The English insisted on their right to reside inside the city while the Chinese, fearful of the foreigners' conquest of the

city, interpreted their right of residence as ending at the city walls. That this was a matter of principle for the British was clear from the fact that in the port of Shanghai, where the British were allowed to reside inside the city, they soon chose to live outside, giving rise to the International Settlement.

By this time the British, busily "proving" their superiority, were in no mood to tolerate Chinese resistance. The emotions of the Cantonese, on the other hand, rose to fever pitch during the years of conflict and were accompanied by the posting of placards on the streets and walls of the city.

The following excerpt from a Cantonese denunciation of the British in 1841 is eloquent testimony to the acrimonious feelings of the Chinese. There is an interesting parallel here with the bitter, strong language of the big-lettered wall posters that are a part of the Chinese landscape today. In both cases, the violence of the language expressing Chinese emotions contrasts paradoxically with the correct behavior of most Chinese in their relations with their "enemies." There is a story presently circulating in knowledgeable circles about the Chinese staff in the British Embassy who, en masse, formally requested permission from their English employers during one of the recent stormy demonstrations outside the legation, to join the demonstrators. Obtaining permission, they joined the protest returning afterwards to their regular duties without further incident. Regardless of its origin the story contains a certain "truth." It is important, I think, to evaluate Chinese behavior, both past and present, in the context of the distinctive cultural patterns of the Chinese.

Cantonese Denunciation of the British, 1841*

THE THOROUGHLY LOYAL and patriotic people of the whole province of Kwantung instruct the rebellious barbarian dogs and sheep for their information. We note that you English barbarians have formed the habits and developed the nature of wolves, plundering and seizing things by force. . . . in trade relations, you come to our country merely to covet profit. What knowledge do you have? Your seeking profit re-

* Document 4, p. 36, reprinted by permission of the publishers from Ssu-yu Teng and John K. Fairbank, CHINA'S RESPONSE TO THE WEST, Cambridge, Mass.: Harvard University Press, Copyright, 1954, by the President and Fellows of Harvard College.

sembles the animal's greed for food. You are ignorant of our laws and institutions, ignorant of right principles. . . . You have no gratitude for the great favor of our Celestial Court; on the contrary you treat us like enemies and do us harm. You use opium to injure our common people, cheating us of our silver and cash. . . . Although you have penetrated our inland rivers and enticed fellows who renounce their fathers and their rulers to become Chinese traitors and stir up trouble among us, you are only using money to buy up their services— what good points have you? . . . Except for your ships being solid, your gunfire fierce, and your rockets powerful, what other abilities have you? . . .

We patriots have received the favor of the Celestial Dynasty in nourishing us for two centuries. Today, if we do not exterminate you English barbarians, we will not be human beings. You have killed and injured our common people in many villages, and seriously hurt the universal harmony. You also completely destroyed the coffins in several places, and you disastrously damaged the Buddhist statues in several monasteries. This is properly a time when Heaven is angered and mankind is resentful; even the ghosts and spirits will not tolerate you beasts. . . .

Our hatred is already at white heat. If we do not completely exterminate you pigs and dogs, we will not be manly Chinese able to support the sky on our heads and stand firmly on the earth. Once we have said this, we will never go back on it, even if frustrated ten thousand times. We are definitely going to kill you, cut your heads off and burn you to death! Even though you ask people to admonish us, we will not obey. We must strip off your skins and eat your flesh, and then you will know how tough (*li-hai*) we are. . . . We ought really to use refined expressions. But since you beasts do not understand written characters, therefore we use rough, vulgar words to instruct you in simple terms. . . .

THE LEGAL ASPECTS OF WESTERN SUPERIORITY

A complicating factor in the early relations between Chinese and westerners was the issue of extraterritoriality, the legal right the westerners reserved for themselves not to submit to Chinese law. The operation of this principle meant that westerners committing any crime (according to Chinese law) on Chinese soil would not be subject to the Chinese authorities. This had been one of the issues sparking the Opium War. In 1844 Caleb Cushing at the head of an American delegation signed the Treaty of Wanghsia, whereby China was forced to recognize the principle of extraterritoriality with respect to Americans. Eventually this was applied to all foreigners.

The following selection from a letter of Caleb Cushing explains the westerner's point of view according to which the principle of extraterritoriality was not only necessary but just, regardless of the difficulties this imposed on the Chinese. For the Chinese, this principle came to symbolize western imperialism and the national weakness and humiliation of China.

Statement of Principle of Extraterritoriality by Caleb Cushing, American Commissioner to China, 1844*

"The nations of Europe and America form a family of States, associated together by community of civilisation and religion, by treaties, and by the law of nations.

"By the law of nations, as practised in Europe and America, every foreigner, who may happen to reside or sojourn in any country of Christendom, is subject to the municipal law of that country, and is amenable to the jurisdiction of its magistrates on any accusation of crime alleged to be committed by him within the limits of such country. Here the minister or consul cannot protect his countrymen. The laws of the place take their course.

"In the intercourse between Christian States on the one hand, and Mohammedan on the other, a different principle is assumed, namely, the exemption of the Christian foreigner from the jurisdiction of the local authorities, and his subjection (as the necessary consequence) to the jurisdiction of the minister, or other authorities of his own government.

"One or other of these two principles is to be applied to the citizens of the United States in China. There is no third alternative. Either they are to be surrendered up to the Chinese authorities, when accused of any breach of law, for trial and punishment by the magistrates of China, or (if they are to have protection from their country) they come under the jurisdiction of the appointed American officer in China.

"In my opinion, the rule which obtained in favour of Europeans and Americans in the Mohammedan countries of Asia is to be applied to China. Americans are entitled to the protec-

---

* Letter to the American Consul at Canton, in H. B. Morse, International Relations of the Chinese Empire (Shanghai: The Commercial Press, Ltd., 1910), p. 329.

tion and subject to the jurisdiction of the officers of their government. The right to be protected by the officers of their country over them, are inseparable facts.

"Accordingly, I shall refuse at once all applications for the surrender of the party who killed Hsü A-man; which refusal involves the duty of instituting an examination of the facts by the agency of officers of the United States. . . ."

> The following selection is from a publication written by a British consulate interpreter, Thomas Taylor Meadow, Desultory Notes on the Government and People of China. The book is based on personal observations of the difficulties involved in communication and understanding between Chinese and foreigners.
>
> The westerner, it is important to note, assumes that the physical superiority of the West is proof of a moral superiority which the Chinese are too proud to admit or even understand.

A Nineteenth-Century Westerner's Analysis of Chinese-European Relations*

THOMAS TAYLOR MEADOW

THERE SEEMS to be an idea now somewhat prevalent in England, that the Chinese generally have, in consequence of the late war, attained a much more correct knowledge of foreigners and the power and state of their countries than formerly. This is, however, very far from being the case. Those who saw and felt us, though sufficient in number to populate a first-rate European kingdom, form but a very small portion of the Chinese people; and the great body of the nation, inhabiting districts and provinces that we have never yet reached, can only look on the late war as a rebellious irruption of a tribe of barbarians; who, secure in their strong ships, attacked and took some places along the coast; and even managed to get into their possession an important point of the grand canal, whereby they forced the Emperor to make them certain concessions.

So much for the nation generally; as to those who have come, and continue to come into contact with us, let the reader remember how very few foreigners speak Chinese; that only the Canton and Macao Chinese speak a little English,

* Thomas Taylor Meadow, DESULTORY NOTES ON THE GOVERNMENT AND PEOPLE OF CHINA (London: Witt. Allen & Co., 1847), pp. 228–235.

and that so badly as to be barely intelligible even when speaking of matters relating to their own occupations of tradesmen, mechanics, or menials;—let the reader recall this to his mind, and he will perceive that, even if the Chinese were eager inquirers into foreign matters, and knew how to put their questions, they must from the want of opportunity alone, be woefully ignorant of us. But the apathy with respect to foreign things generally, even of the higher and, in the Chinese sense of the word, educated classes, and that when they meet a foreigner who understands their own language, is to an European quite astonishing. . . . Their exclusion of foreigners and confinement to their own country has, by depriving them of all opportunities of making comparisons, sadly circumscribed their ideas; they are thus totally unable to free themselves from the dominion of association, and judge every thing by rules of purely Chinese convention.

"It is in the great size and wealth and the numerous population of our country; still more in its excellent institutions, which may contain some imperfections, but which after all are immeasurably superior to the odd confused rules by which these barbarians are governed; but, above all, in its glorious literature which contains every noble, elegant, and in particular, every profound idea; every thing, in short, from which true civilization can spring, that we found our claim to national superiority." So thinks even the educated Chinese; and so the whole nation will continue to think until we have proved to them—no easy nor short task—our mental as well as our physical superiority. When some good works shall have been compiled in Chinese on natural law, on the principles of political economy, and on European national and international policy, then (after such works have obtained a wide circulation) when they perceive how much more deeply metaphysics have been explored by us than by them, and how studiously the best established principles of the sciences included under that term have been brought into practical operation by us, then, but not till then, will the Chinese bow before the *moral* power of the civilized west.

At present they take the tone of superiors quite unaffectedly, simply because they really believe themselves to be superior. I do not remember meeting among educated Chinese with a single instance of any want of candour in regard to this subject; whenever their minds once acknowledge anything foreign as superior to the Chinese article of the like sort, they at once admit it to be so. For instance, when a mandarin who has never spoken to a barbarian, and never seen one of their books, who, perhaps, has hitherto always doubted that they had anything deserving of the name, is first shown one, he admires the decided superiority of the paper at once. . . .

All Chinese who have seen them, are perfectly ready to allow, that our ships, our guns, watches, cloths, &c., are much superior to their own articles of the like sort; and most of them would frankly admit us to be superior to them in all respects, if they thought so. But as above said, they do not. They are quite unable to draw conclusions as to the state of foreign countries, from an inspection of the articles produced or manufactured in them. They cannot see that a country where such an enormous, yet beautiful fabric as a large English ship is constructed—an operation requiring at once the united efforts of numbers, and a high degree of skill—*must* be inhabited by a people, not only energetic, but rich and free to enjoy the fruits of its own labour; that such a country *must*, in short, have a powerful government, good laws, and be altogether in a high state of civilization. All this the Chinaman, having never compared the various states of different nations, is not only quite unable to perceive of himself, but often not even when it is pointed out to him at great length. We have, it is true, the power to do some great and extraordinary things, but so have the elephants and other wild animals, he occasionally sees and hears of; in his eyes, therefore, we are all barbarians, possessing perhaps some good qualities, congregated perhaps together in some sort of societies, but without regular government, untutored, coarse, and wild.

THE TAIPING REBELLION

The Taiping Rebellion was the first major rebellion facing the Manchu Dynasty, (1850–1864). Its near-success frightened not only the ruling elite but the foreigners as well who finally helped the Manchus quell the revolution.

In addition to its effective organization and military victories the significance of the Taiping Rebellion was its modernity. The movement incorporated Christian ideology as a revolutionary ethic and displayed an amazing sensitivity to the ideas of modernization. The rebels adopted an economic and industrial program for China's future development and recognized the need to abolish such practices as long fingernails, foot-binding, sale of slaves and infanticide. They seemed, at least in the abstract, to appreciate the technology of the West and China's need to introduce it.

The following selections give a sketch of the origins of the

Taipings written by one of the revolutionaries himself, and a translation of the Taiping notification to the citizens of Nanking that they were to be safe under the rule of their new dynasty.

An Autobiographical Account of the Taipings
By One of the Leaders*

THE TIEN-WANG [the leader of the Taiping Rebellion] was a native of Hua-sien in the Canton province, and from that place through Kuangsi, and other places extending several thousand li, his followers were sprinkled like stars. The Tien-Wang was constantly concealed amongst the hills, carrying on his work of reformation, and out of ten families he either made converts of three or five or even eight of them. Students and those of good sense would not follow him, but only the agricultural labourers and those in distress were willing to join him, and of these latter there was an immense number. The preconceived design of ultimately establishing a government was known only to the Tung-Wang (Eastern King), Yang-siu-ch'ing, the Hsi-Wang (Western King), Hsiao-ch'aoKuei, the Nan-Wang (Southern King), Fung-yun-shan, the Pei-Dang, (Northern King), Wei-Ch'ang-hui, the Yi-Wang Shih-ta-k'ai, and the spiritual Minister of State, Ch'in-yih-c'hang. None but the above six were aware of it. The only object the remainder of the people had in following the Tien-Wang was for the sake of obtaining a subsistence. The Eastern King . . . lived . . . in the neighbourhood of Kuei-p'ing (hsien), and depended for his existence on the sale of firewood and charcoal. He had no knowledge of military tactics until after he had worshiped Shangti, when unexpectedly heaven wrought a great change in him. He enjoyed above all others the confidence of the Tien-Wang, and had the general management of affairs entrusted to him. His orders were strict and proper, and his rewards and punishments administered impartially. . . .

The great distress of our home was the sole cause of my leaving it. Our family lead a very precarious existence, having to subsist in the best way we could. From the age of 8 to 10 I was engaged in study, but at that period I was obliged to

* "The Origin of the Taiping Leaders," Document 218, pp. 335–336, from Harley Farnsworth MacNair, MODERN CHINESE HISTORY, SELECTED READINGS (Shanghai: The Commercial Press, Ltd., 1933).

assist my father and mother in working for our daily sustenance. It was not until I had attained the age of 26 that I heard of Hung-siu-tseuen projecting a new doctrine.

Taiping Proclamation to the People of Nanking*

Ye people, this announcement is to set your minds at rest,
And hinder you from fleeing to the East and to the West.
The hearths and altars of the Mings—that dynasty sublime—
Have been usurped by Mantchou hordes until the present time.
But now we hurl the Tartars down, and raise the Chinese throne,
The greedy crew of magistrates shall perish every one.
Our deeds are surely virtuous, when Heaven we obey,
So do not, O ye people, to vain alarms give way.
Since first our mighty force began to penetrate the land,
Upon the honest citizen we ne'er have laid a hand.
The ashes of our ancestors are in your neighbourhood,
And urged by their example we protect the just and good.
Against the robbers of the place all due precautions take,
And do not waste your courage for the vile oppressor's sake.
At Houang-Tcheou and at Han-Yang many valiant warriors fell,
Because the hardy peasants for their tyrants fought too well.
But though a hundred millions should oppose us in our course,
As dust by wind is scattered, we shall dissipate their force.
When the Kiang-Nan and the Chang-Toung shall at last submissive be,
You shall all enjoy the blessings of a long tranquillity.
To these few words of warning you will now attention pay
Nor be by disobedience nor by terror led astray.

Although the failure of the Taiping Rebellion removed the immediate internal threat to the Manchus, the Ch'ing dynasty was more than ever fettered by the escalating demands of the external aggressors. The western powers had, after all, come to the rescue of the dynasty in its rather enfeebled struggle against the rebels. But while the Manchus, for the sake of expediency, allied themselves with the western powers (Eng-

* "The Proclamation to the people of Nanking," in Callery and Yvan, HISTORY OF THE INSURRECTION IN CHINA (New York: Harper & Brothers, 1853), pp. 257–258.

land and France) they were themselves the losers in a three-way struggle. The Chinese population, oppressed on the one hand by the mismanagement of the Manchus and on the other by the economic dislocations set into motion by the "foreign devils," had little recourse for its grievances. Most of its anger was vented on the outsider. And usually in retaliation for either a real or imaginary Chinese attack on foreigners, the western powers sent expeditionary forces to extend their control in the interior of China, making life for the Manchu government that much harder. In this way, the Manchu dynasty was unable to prevent western expansion within China and therefore unable in the long run to safeguard its position vis-à-vis the Chinese population.

In December 1856 the European 'factories' at Canton were set on fire which provoked a series of Anglo-French expeditions, in each instance western military superiority spelling swift and easy victories for the invaders. The Treaties of Tientsin (June 1858), concluded separately between China and each of the foreign powers (England, France, the United States and Russia) provided for the residence of western diplomats at Peking, the opening of five more treaty ports, Chinese toleration of Christian missions and permission for foreigners to travel in the interior of China. The Manchu dynasty, caught in a vicious circle, tried to extricate itself through self-defeating measures; Imperial Edicts called on the population to resist foreign invaders even while the Court promised to come to terms with western demands, thus leading to further European expeditions and so on.

It was clear to some, however, that in the attempts to remove the foreign "curse" from China's border, cunning and deceit were insufficient. There were scholars, faithful servants of the Emperor, who studied western learning and concluded that China's salvation lay in her learning from the western powers the skills necessary for "self-strengthening." Thus Feng Keui-fen, in a series of essays written in 1860, argued for the adoption of western knowledge and the manufacture of foreign weapons in order to oppose rebellion from within and aggression from abroad.

In the following selection from one of those essays, Feng tries to pinpoint the errors of the past and outline suggestions for the future. The basic idea was characteristic both in its boldness of sentiment and its limited understanding: learn from the westerners the source of their strength so as to use it against them. Unfortunately, this contained the basic flaw that continued to plague Chinese reformers until the middle

of the twentieth century; namely, that westernization, even in
the limited form imposed on China, entailed the complete
overhaul of its institutions—moral, social, economic and
political.

On the Manufacture of Foreign Weapons*

THE MOST unparalleled anger which has ever existed since the
creation of heaven and earth is exciting all who are conscious
in their minds and have spirit in their blood; their hats are
raised by their hair standing on end. This is because the largest
country on the globe today, with a vast area of 10,000 *li*, is
yet controlled by small barbarians. . . . According to a
general geography by an Englishman, the territory of our
China is eight times larger than that of Russia, ten times that
of America, one hundred times that of France, and two hundred times that of England. . . . Yet now we are shame-
fully humiliated by those four nations in the recent treaties—
not because our climate, soil, or resources are inferior to
theirs, but because our people are really inferior. . . . Why
are they small and yet strong? Why are we large and yet
weak? We must try to discover some means to become their
equal, and that also depends upon human effort. Regarding
the present situation there are several major points: in making
use of the ability of our manpower, with no one neglected,
we are inferior to the barbarians; in securing the benefit of the
soil, with nothing wasted, we are inferior to the barbarians;
in maintaining a close relationship between the ruler and the
people, with no barrier between them, we are inferior to the
barbarians; and in the necessary accord of word with deed,
we are also inferior to the barbarians. The way to correct these
four points lies with ourselves, for they can be changed at
once if only our Emperor would set the general policy right.
There is no need for outside help in these matters. [Here Feng
goes on to point out that the only help China needs from the
West is in modern arms, and claims that in recent contests with
Western troops the Chinese army has not been inferior in
physical qualities, nor even sometimes in morale, but always
in arms.]

* Document 9, pp. 52–54, reprinted by permission of the publishers from Ssu-yu Teng and John K. Fairbank, CHINA'S RESPONSE
TO THE WEST, Cambridge, Mass.: Harvard University Press, Copyright, 1954, by the President and Fellows of Harvard College.

What we then have to learn from the barbarians is only the one thing, solid ships and effective guns. When Wei Yuan discussed the control of the barbarians, he said that we should use barbarians to attack barbarians, and use barbarians to negotiate with barbarians. Even regardless of the difficulties of languages and our ignorance of diplomatic usages it is utterly impossible for us outsiders to sow dissension among the closely related barbarians. Moreover, he considered the various barbarian nations as comparable to the Warring States [403–221 B.C.], but he did not realize that the circumstances are different. Wei saw quite a number of barbarian books and newspapers and should not have made any such statement It is probably because in his life and academic ideas he was fond of regarding himself as a political strategist. In my opinion, if we cannot make ourselves strong [*tzu-ch'iang*] but merely presume on cunning and deceit, it will be just enough to incur failure. Only one sentence of Wei Yuan is correct: "Learn the strong techniques of the barbarians in order to control them. . . ."

Funds should be assigned to establish a shipyard and arsenal in each trading port. Several barbarians should be invited and Chinese who are good in using their minds should be summoned to receive their instructions so that they may in turn teach many artisans. When a piece of work is finished and is indistinguishable from that made by the barbarians, the makers should be given a *chü-jen* degree as a reward, and be permitted to participate in the metropolitan examination on an equal footing with other scholars. Those whose products are superior to the barbarian manufacture should be granted a *chin-shih* degree as a reward, and be permitted to participate in the palace examinations on the same basis as others. The workers should be double-paid so as to prevent them from quitting.

Our nation has emphasized the civil service examinations, which have preoccupied people's minds for a long time. Wise and intelligent scholars have exhausted their time and energy in such useless things as the eight-legged essays [highly stylized essays for the civil service examination, divided into eight paragraphs], examination papers, and formal calligraphy. . . . Now let us order one-half of them to apply themselves to the pursuit of manufacturing weapons and instruments and imitating foreign crafts. . . . The intelligence and wisdom of the Chinese are necessarily superior to those of the various barbarians, only formerly we have not made use of them. When the Emperor above likes something, those below him will pursue it even further, like the moving of grass in the wind or the response of an echo. There ought to be some people of extraordinary intelligence who can have new ideas and improve on Western methods. At first they may learn and pattern after the foreigners; then they may compare and try to be their equal; and finally they may go ahead and surpass them—the way to make ourselves strong actually lies in this. . . .

Two years ago the Western barbarians suddenly entered the Japanese capital to seek trade relations, which were permitted. Before long the Japanese were able to send some ten steamships of their own over the western ocean to pay return visits to the various countries. They made many requests for treaties which were also granted by these countries, who understood Japan's intentions. Japan is a tiny country and still knows how to exert her energy to become strong. Should we, as a large country, alone accept defilement and insult throughout all time? . . . We are just now in an interval of peaceful and harmonious relations. This is probably an opportunity given by heaven for us to strengthen ourselves. If we do not at this point quickly rise to this opportunity but passively receive the destiny of heaven, our subsequent regret will come too late. . . . If we live in the present day and speak of rejecting the barbarians, we should raise the question as to what instruments we can reject them with. . . .

Some suggest purchasing ships and hiring foreign people, but the answer is that this is quite impossible. If we can manufacture, can repair, and can use them, then they are our weapons. If we cannot manufacture, nor repair, nor use them, then they are still the weapons of others. When these weapons are in the hands of others and are used for grain transportation, then one day they can make us starve; and if they are used for salt transportation, one day they can deprive us of salt. . . . Eventually we must consider manufacturing, repairing, and using weapons by ourselves. . . . Only thus will we be able to pacify the empire; only thus can we play a leading role on the globe; and only thus shall we restore our original strength, and redeem ourselves from former humiliations.

Despite considerable discussion and examination of the source of China's weakness in the 1860's (as typified in the last selection) little was accomplished in the way of actual change. Internal rebellion, incurable disorganization, corruption and the irresistible external encroachments had taken a heavy toll. And in addition to the western powers, Japan was emerging as a powerful expansionist nation. She was surpassing China in learning from the West and appeared on the Chinese horizon to further emphasize China's abject state of affairs.

The following warning in 1874 precedes by twenty years the first major defeat of China by Japan. Wen-Hsiang reiterates the need for Imperial expenditures on defense rather than on needless public works (or luxuries) like the elaborate Summer Palace the Empress Dowager was having constructed.

Wen-Hsiang's Warnings of Disaster, 1874

WHEN THE peace negotiations were completed [in 1860] everybody spoke of the necessity for self-strengthening, yet during the last ten years or more there has been little achievement The reason is that those who look down upon and disregard foreign affairs merely have empty discussions without actual accomplishment, whereas those who are accustomed to the peaceful situation are content when nothing happens for fear that if anything is done it may arouse the suspicion of the foreigners. Even those who carefully discuss defense measures are hindered by the insufficiency of funds, and nothing can be done or developed. Now the (Formosa) incident has already taken shape, a war crisis is imminent. If we still do not pay attention to it and suddenly the great enemy (Japan) confronts us, what can we rely upon? It is humbly hoped that imperial orders will be sent to the Ministry of Revenue and the Imperial Household Department to raise plenty of the necessary supplies, to cut off lavish expenditures, to stop public works which are not urgent [i.e., the construction of the Summer Palace], and to plan for the most needed coastal defense; so that the ministers at the capital and in the provinces can all devote their energy to the scheme.

As for the way to make ourselves strong, it lies first in our readiness to accept advice in a humble manner in order to seek out the good and bad points of our administration. One should not take agreeable and soothing words as a source of pleasure and take straightforward and frank advice as distasteful. When Your Majesty is concerned to work diligently

* Document 22, p. 90, reprinted by permission of the publishers from Ssu-yuteng and John K. Fairbank, CHINA'S RESPONSE TO THE WEST, Cambridge, Mass.: Harvard University Press, Copyright, 1954, by the President and Fellows of Harvard College.

and alertly, then your ministers within and without the capital will be stimulated in spirit and not dare to follow their traditional dawdling habits. Otherwise they will remain accustomed to taking things complacently and will never think of reforms, in which case, I fear that internally and externally the country will fall apart, the people's confidence will be shaken, and the disaster will be unspeakable.

China during the 1880's and 90's continued her steady decline. The Empress Dowager Tzu Hsi, who combined an impressive shrewdness with a colossal ignorance, had the Summer Palace built with the funds originally allocated for the reconstruction of the Chinese fleet (destroyed by the French). The western powers, meanwhile, rapaciously carved out their spheres of influence, the rivalries amongst them getting keener as the task became easier. In 1894 Japan found her opportunity for a swift victory, precipitated by intrigues in Korea which had long been subject to the suzerainty of China. The outcome was another humiliating treaty, the Treaty of Shimonoseki (April 1895), which further underscored China's helplessness even against the "dwarf bandits." China was forced to recognize Korea's independence, ceded Formosa to Japan in addition to paying a huge indemnity and opened four more ports to foreign commerce.

The proponents of reform had not vanished, however. K'ang Yu-wei, greatly influenced by Japan's rapid transformation into a powerful modern nation, had launched a Reform Society in the 1880's. By 1889, when the young Emperor Kuang-Hsü came of age, the writings of K'ang Yu-wei had attracted considerable attention. Anxious to overcome the Empress Dowager's overbearing control, the Emperor in 1898 embarked on what has come to be known as the "Hundred Days of Reform." Between June 11 and September 16, 1898 a series of reform decrees were issued under the inspiration of K'ang Yu-wei ordering sweeping changes in age-old customs and institutions. But opposition to these reforms was both widespread and organized. It centered around the Empress Dowager, who though semi-retired was far from inactive. With the help of her trusted friend and military commander, Jung Lu, and the complicity of Yüan Shih-k'ai, who was later to become President of the Chinese Republic, she carried out a coup d'état in September 1898, making short shrift of the reformers and imprisoning the Emperor. The reformers, hampered from the start by a lack of experience and popular support, were succeeded by the conservatives.

A wave of xenophobia swept through China, spearheaded by the Boxer Movement. Christian converts, missionaries and eventually all foreigners came under open attack as the Boxer Rebellion gained momentum. Chinese officialdom more or less openly tolerated and protected the Boxers with the expected result that the rebels became bolder in their anti-foreign activities. The Empress Dowager, firmly in control since her coup, maneuvered between two rival factions in the Court: an extremist party hoping to use the Boxers to expel all foreigners from China and a moderate group led by her friend, Jung Lu, opposing the Boxers. In the following selection from a letter of Jung Lu to the southern viceroys pleading for their help, the effects of the Empress Dowager's last-minute support of the extremists is delineated. The Boxers, rampaging the countryside with the Court's official blessing, had little chance of success. Jung Lu, sensing the disaster, urged the southern viceroys to protect their provinces.

An Imperial Minister's Account of the Boxer Rebellion*

JUNG LU

THE SAME DAY [June 22, 1900] at the Hour of the Dog (7–9 P.M.).—I learn that Jung Lu has just sent off a courier with a telegram, which Yüan Shih-K'ai is to send on to the Viceroys of Canton, Nanking and Wuch'ang. Prince Li has sent me a copy, which I am to keep secret; it reads as follows:—

"With all respect I have received your telegrams. Where one weak people dares to oppose ten or more powerful nations, the inevitable result can only be complete ruin. It has always been maintained as a fixed principle with civilized nations, that, in the event of war between any two Powers, their respective Envoys should be treated with respect. Can it now be that this our great inheritance, founded by our remote ancestors at so great a cost of toil and danger, is to be endangered, and suddenly brought to ruin, by these false workers of magic? Shall the fate of the Dynasty be staked on a single throw? It requires no peculiar sagacity to see that these Boxers' hopes of success are nothing but the shadow of a dream. It is true and undeniable, that, from Their Majesties on the Throne down to the very lowest of our people, all have suffered from

* "Jung Lu's Telegram to the Southern Viceroys," pp. 591–592 from Harley Farnsworth MacNair, MODERN CHINESE HISTORY, SELECTED READINGS (Shanghai: The Commercial Press, Ltd., 1933).

the constant aggression of foreigners and their unceasing insults. For this reason these patriotic train-bands have been organised, claiming a divine mission of retaliation; but the present crisis is all-serious, and although I have used every effort to explain its dangers, I have laboured in vain. I am sick and suffering from lameness, but since I obtained leave of absence I have already submitted seven separate memorials denouncing these Boxers. Seeing that they produced no result, I have now left my sick bed, in order, if possible, to explain the situation clearly to Their Majesties; and this also has been in vain.

"All the Princes and Ministers of State who surround the Throne now cry out against me with one voice, as your Excellencies can readily believe. I dare not quote in this place the words of Her Majesty, but I may say that the whole of the Imperial family have joined the Boxers, and at least two-thirds of our troops, both Manchu and Chinese, are with them. They swarm in the streets of our capital like a plague of locusts, and it will be extremely difficult to disperse them.

"Even the divine wisdom of Her Majesty is not sufficient to stand against the will of the majority. If Heaven is not on our side, how can I oppose its will? For several days past I have been pondering night and day on some way out of our difficulties, some forlorn hope of escape. Therefore yesterday morning (June 20th) I arranged for a meeting with the foreign Ministers at the Tsung-li Yamen, with a view to providing a safe-conduct for the entire foreign community, with my own troops, to Tientsin. This course appeared to me to hold out some reasonable chances of success, but Prince Tuan's soldiery slew the German Minister, and since then the situation continues to develop from hour to hour with such extraordinary rapidity that words fail me to describe it. On my side, in the discussion of the Grand Council and the Chamberlains of the Presence, are Prince Ch'ing and Wang Wen-shao, but the former, following his usual practice, has applied for leave, and Her Majesty will have nothing to do with him; so that these two are of no real assistance to me. I have no fear of death, but I grieve at the thought of the guilt which will be recorded against me in history; Heaven knows that I am overwhelmed with grief and shame. I have received great favors at the hands of the Throne, and can only now pray to the spirits of the Dynastic ancestors to protect our Empire. The situation here is well-nigh lost, but it remains for your Excellencies to take all possible steps for the protection of your

respective provinces. Let each do his utmost, and let proper
secrecy be maintained." Signed "Jung Lu, with tears in his
eyes."

Through her support of the Boxers, the Empress Dowager
had gambled on a desperate attempt to divert mounting opposition towards the corruption and inefficiency of the Manchu
dynasty against the foreigners. The Boxer Rebellion was
quelled by the western powers, and the Ch'ing dynasty was
made to pay heavily for its mistake. Unable to restore China's
strength through traditional devices, the government turned
again towards reform. Tzu Hsi, returning to Peking in 1902
after her ignominious flight at the height of the Boxer ram-
page, made an about-face and passed a number of decrees instituting basic reforms. They were too late and when she died
in 1908, the dynasty was for all intents and purposes dead.
The Mandate of Heaven had long before fallen on the young
revolutionaries in China and abroad who realized the necessity
for a Republican China that could guide the Chinese into the
ways and means of the modern world.

The aspirations as well as the limitations of the revolutionaries as late as 1911, when the abdication of the Manchus was
imminent, is evident in the following Manifesto. In addition
to the obvious desire to placate foreign anxieties, there is a
naiveté with respect to the depth of the changes necessary to
resurrect China which characterized even those people who
like Sun Yat-sen lived and studied in the West. China was left
on the doorstep of chaos.

The Revolutionists' Manifesto to the Foreign World
on the Aims of the Revolution and the
Provisional Government,* November 17, 1911

TO OUR FOREIGN FRIENDS

PROMPTED by many inquiries by leading articles in the Press
and by the letters which have appeared in the *North China
Daily News* and other papers, we feel it incumbent upon us
to express the deep sense of our appreciation of the evident

* "The Revolutionists' Manifesto to the Foreign World," from
P. H. Kent, THE PASSING OF THE MANCHUS (London: 1912), pp.
210–212.

world-wide interest and sympathy taken in the revolutionary movement and briefly to set forth the position of the Revolution party to-day.

It is unnecessary to indulge in lengthy explanations of the reasons leading to the present Revolution. They are notorious. The Manchu Government has in the course of its dominance of China demonstrated its incapacity to rule its people or conduct the affairs of the nation in a manner compatible with the forward movement signalising the modern history and development of the civilized world. The Manchu Dynasty has, by its benighted conceptions and barbaric leaning, brought China to a position of degradation. The nation is scorned, and its institutions and general retrogressive policy are the objects of contempt.

For decades the enlightened among the Chinese endeavored by peaceful means to promote and establish ambition among the people for an elevated line of progressive conduct. They have failed. .

The foreign powers individually and collectively have stood hammering at the door of China for centuries pleading for the diffusion of knowledge, a reformation of national services, the adoption of Western sciences and industrial processes, a jettisoning of the crude, out-of-date and ignoble concepts which have multiplied to keep the nation without the pale of the great family constituting the civilized world. They have failed.

The Manchu Dynasty has triumphantly carried on its reactionary policy despite the strongest pressure exerted from within and without until the oppressed people could endure the disgrace and the contumely of it no longer. They rose, and with what result the history of the past few weeks has shown.

The Manchu Dynasty has been tried by a patient and peaceful people for centuries, and has been found more than wanting. It has sacrificed the reverence, forfeited the regard, and lost the confidence freely reposed in it by all Chinese.

Its promises in the past have proved delusions and snares. Its promises for the future can carry no weight, deserve no consideration, and permit no trust.

The popular wish is that the dynasty must go.

The leaders of thought in the revolutionary movement abhor bloodshed.

We have, it is safe to say, evidenced a toleration unexpected by our foreign friends.

We have controlled the forces for evil in a manner which should characterize this revolution as the least sanguinary in the history of the world, when the sins of the country and nature of the masses are taken into consideration.

We have memorialised the Prince Regent to secure the abdication of the Manchus upon the guarantee of full protection for the life and property not only of the Imperial family, but of all Manchus.

We have issued a manifesto to every province urging upon a common ground.

We have exhorted the whole of the people to sink racial prejudices, to combine for the betterment and advancement of the nation, and to respect and protect, not only their own, but foreign interests to the utmost extent in our power.

We have striven for order and have created no chaos in those provinces, cities, and towns that have of their own volition come under our banners.

We have retained officers of the old régime where such have desired to remain, and have subscribed to the new regulations for conduct of provincial affairs. The Viceroy of Yunnan, the Governor of Soochow, the Governor of Anking are instances in point.

We have issued telegraphic appeals to the fourteen provinces that have declared for independence from Manchu dominance to send delegates to Shanghai to form a National Assembly.

We have, in short, taken every possible step to protect vested interests, safeguard international obligations, secure continuance of commerce, and shield education and religious institutions; and what is even more important, striven continually to maintain law and order, sustain peace, and promote a constructive policy upon sound and enduring grounds.

The mind of the people is made up for a change. The shameless destruction of life and property that has signalised the latter days of the Manchus' attempt to resist the termination of their reign is but their characteristic valedictory message to the world.

To the Manchus is the blame for a continuance of hostilities and the perpetration of outrage. They have received from a majority of the provinces an unmistakable pronunciamento of the popular wish; they know that their race is run and that the China of to-morrow can never be as China of Yesterday.

The revolutionary leaders appealed to them to abdicate in order to put a period to the useless fighting in the field, to prevent wanton bloodshed, to restore the peace of mind of the whole of the populace and to tranquillise trade.

The hand of the people is now at the plough, and they must of necessity push on to the uttermost end of the furrow.

We ask our foreign well-wishers to unite with us in our appeal to the Prince Regent to abdicate and so end the strife that is now shaking the land. For our part, our conduct is open to the full view of the world. We are fighting for what Britain fought in the days of old; we are fighting for what America fought; we are fighting for what every nation that is now worthy of the name has fought in its days.

We are fighting to be men in the world; we are fighting to cast off an oppressive, vicious, and tyrannous rule that has beggared and disgraced China, obstructed and defied the foreign nations, and set back the hands of the clock of the world.

We must not be judged by the past; we are trying to bring China into her own; to elevate her to the standard that the people of the Occident have ever been urging her to attain, and the stumbling block of to-day as it has been during the past centuries, is the Manchu Dynasty.

Our foreign friends must from a sheer sense of fairness concede that we have the right to win the laurels of freedom by fair fight in the field, and to avoid the rest we again appeal to them to use their influence to secure in the Manchu mind recognition of the utter hopelessness of the continuance of the dynasty.

That is all that China requires. The Manchus may remain in full enjoyment of citizenship, will be entitled to the fullest equality and freedom, and are urged to rest in possession of their lands and property for the future good of the State.

3

NATIONALISM AND THE TRANSITION
TO A MODERN SOCIETY

WHEN THE Manchu dynasty fell in 1911 there was nothing to take its place. The Republic, for which Sun Yat-sen and others had struggled, was stillborn; democracy was a farce. China could move neither forward nor backward, yet she did not stagnate. While the western powers engaged each other in the First World War and the Chinese warlords fought over the division of territory, the youth of China and the intellectuals grappled with the possibilities of a resurrection. Western ideas were seriously studied, students traveled abroad to learn, alternative solutions for saving China were eagerly debated, and even warlords were experimenting with new equipment and modern techniques if only for their own selfish aims. The entire Chinese situation was in a state of ferment.

For over three decades while the fabric of Confucian life and culture continued to deteriorate, a host of revolutionary movements crystallized. Like a kaleidoscope in the hand of a child, the situation offered up innumerable possibilities and variations: each new arrangement being discarded in turn for a newer one. Nationalism was the only consistently recurrent theme. The idea of restoring China's greatness was in some cases identified with linguistic and cultural reforms and sometimes with ideas of political, economic and military reforms as in Sun Yat-sen's "Three People's Principles" (see pp. 142-146) and Mao Tse-Tung's writing (pp. 169-186). The cataclysm that China endured during this period included so vast a number of rapidly changing attempts at modernization that it escapes any orderly arrangement. But whatever the differences among substantive prescriptions, nationalism provided the revolutionary momentum. It exploded the neat categories of Confucian thinking and opened the Pandora's Box of modernization.

The generational differences in these decades are the key to understanding the radical nature of the transformation taking place. In traditional China ancestors were worshipped and the closer one came to becoming an ancestor the greater one's prestige and authority. Older people's authority stemmed from their accumulated experience. Since they knew a thing or two more about life and living than the young they were accepted authorities, listened to and emulated. But the process of modernization inevitably changes all this. Industrialization puts youth in the limelight. It replaces the sanctity of tradition with the ethic of perpetual motion. Technology, skills and values change so rapidly that every successive generation knows more from its latest experience than any of its predecessors.

Youngsters growing up in China in the opening decades of the twentieth century felt this for the first time. There was such a gap separating them from their parents, who bemoaned the loss of traditional virtues, that communication across the generations was barely possible. The young people felt the full brunt of oppression and confusion that resulted from the imposition of imperialism on a weak, disoriented civilization. They were, through their exposure to western education, acutely sensitive to the glaring gap between the thread-bare traditions of an emasculated China and the promise of new ideas, the inherent potentialities of modernization. Unlike the older generations, they had no sense of resignation to a past they scarcely remembered except in terms of personal frustration and national humilation. The breeding ground for such youthful sentiments was the university and the city where the sons of gentry were more in evidence than sons of peasants.

Time is relative, and nowhere is this so evident as in China in the first two decades of the twentieth century. Centuries of experimentation and innovation were contracted and concentrated into a short span of time, in which young Chinese intellectuals experienced a multitude of ideas stemming not only from different parts of the world but from different historical eras. The intellectual horizon shifted so swiftly that Darwin, Nietzsche and Comte were literally pushed aside by the onrushing ideas of Lenin and Trotsky. In the whirlwind of diverse ideas to which Chinese students exposed themselves there was one fixed point: the desire to change their progressively deteriorating civilization into a powerful, modern nation-state. They were especially attracted, therefore, to those theories and prescriptions that were appropriate and fertile within the context of Chinese conditions.

In 1915, Ch'en Tu-hsiu took up the "Call to Youth" (see pp. 128-133) and urged young Chinese to assume their responsibilities and opportunities. Youth was to lead the way in changing the antiquated culture of China and its lost illusions into a modern reality. European progress was held up as the standard of evaluation, science and liberalism as the source of inspiration. It was not long, however, before Ch'en Tu-hsiu, with lightning speed, relinquished the liberal-democratic ideas of Bentham and Mill for the revolutionary and communist ideas of Marx and Lenin.

By the close of World War I the students had moved from theory to action, from the realm of ideas to the arena of demonstrations. The May Fourth Movement (see pp. 140-141), stimulated by the events of World War I and Japanese expansion into China, was a response to the international situation and the threat it posed to China's *national* interests. It was a protest against imperialism and a demand for a new national integrity. As C. P. Fitzgerald points out, the students "shook the corrupt government of the day and forced it to refrain from some of the more inept and even treasonable activities which its self-seeking members favored.* In these lofty national sentiments the students were joined by other segments of the population, most importantly the laborers in coastal cities. In these expanding centers of trade and industry, modernization had gone furthest; cities like Shanghai had come to symbolize the twin evils of foreign exploitation and native capitalist enterprise. It was the working class in these urban centers, therefore, who responded to the force and significance of the student-inspired May Fourth Movement. This was the first instance of an alliance between idealistic and militant youths and the small but "modern" working class, an alliance that seemed to fit the model of a Marxist revolution. And those who used a Marxist blueprint for social change after 1919 found the explosive nationalist atmosphere in the cities ripe for building a revolutionary base with which to forge a new China.

But the nature of the revolution, how it would occur and who would play what role, was still a problem. The warlords controlled most of the interior of China. In the coastal cities the segment of Chinese population that did come into contact with modern ways was either, as with the working-class, in the pay of the foreigner or seeking to exploit their connections to advance their individual fortunes. All of China was split between the masses of peasantry and rural gentry on the one hand and the minute working class and Chinese bourgeoisie on

* C. P. Fitzgerald, *The Chinese View of Their Place in the World* (Oxford University Press, 1964), p. 43.

the other. Where to begin making a revolution: in the interior (the countryside) of China against the power of the independent warlords, or in the coastal cities against the foreign imperialists? Who could be mobilized to carry out the revolution: the workers in the cities or the "backward" Chinese peasants who had rarely if ever confronted westerners? What would the role of the native (and wealthy) bourgeoisie be? Could they be counted on to support a Chinese revolution against the foreign investor or would they, when the time came for a choice, be too frightened of Chinese radicalism to risk a break with the militarily superior protection of the foreigner? These were imponderables.

The young revolutionaries, all of them fervent nationalists, agreed on the general objectives—a two-pronged revolution: the ousting of foreign interests in China, and the transformation of a "backward," disintegrated social order into a powerful modern nation. But they differed on how to achieve these objectives. The situation was not an easy one to pin down, even analytically. The strange alliance of foreign imperialism (the bearer of modernization) and home-grown warlordism, which very often stood for traditions and backwardness (certainly in fact if not in intention) was an intricate and elusive network to combat. The accomplices of the voracious foreigners—Japan adding insult to injury—were Chinese, themselves dissipating national resources through their corruption and internecine warfare.

The central problem was unification. By the 1920's it seemed clear that in order to unify and modernize China, revolution and war were necessary. The country had to be integrated by force as well as persuasion and the first requisite was a unified revolutionary force. This entailed burying doctrinal differences, forging an effective party organization, training a modern military force and mobilizing the support of the Chinese people behind the common effort. In 1924 the two major revolutionary groups, the Kuomintang and the Communist Party, joined ranks to effect such a union. The Kuomintang, under Sun Yat-sen's leadership had formally incorporated principles of radical social change within a nationalist framework (see pp. 142-146) and agreed to cooperate with the Communists who, as individuals, became members of one national revolutionary party—the Kuomintang.

Despite Kuomintang and Communist cooperation after 1924 the First United Front failed. In 1927 Chiang Kai-shek, at the head of the army engaged in the Northern Expedition, betrayed the Communists in the first major incident (see pp.

165-167), and from then on there was continued hostility of the Kuomintang (under the leadership of Chiang) towards the Communists, ending in full-scale civil war. For the Communists this turn of events led to a major transformation in the Party itself. Contrary to the advice of the Russians, some of the Communists withdrew from the cities and began to think in terms of organizing the vast peasantry that constituted the majority of Chinese (see pp. 169-179).

The following selections cover the beginning of the story of China's full-scale modernization. It spreads over social and intellectual lightyears, and, yet, actually takes place in a short span of physical time. It starts with a momentum of great optimism and ends with the sober reconsideration of the immense difficulties that have to be encountered if China is to be brought into the twentieth century as a powerful independent nation.

The theme of this period is revolution as it is affected by continuing external stimuli. The early attempts at keeping the western "barbarians" out of China had been futile; the hurried second thoughts of reformers that urged China to adopt, selectively, certain technical aspects of western knowledge had been inundated and swept over by the rush of events. And now that the Manchu dynasty, like Humpty-Dumpty, had fallen, the serious business of how to put the pieces of society back together again in some new form was confronted by Chinese still reacting to external stimuli. The first United Front was built on the advice of Russians. It was only when it failed that some Chinese began to pursue policies that were based on the independent application of theories, such as Marxism, to Chinese conditions as understood by themselves not outsiders.

The Revolutionary Movement*

HAROLD C. HINTON

THE CAUSE of revolution in China, like that of reform, received its first major stimulus from the Japanese defeat of China in

* From "China" by Harold C. Hinton, in MAJOR GOVERNMENTS OF ASIA, edited by George McTurnan Kahin, 2nd edition, 1963. © 1958 and 1963 by Cornell University. Used by permission of Cornell University Press. Pp. 20–28.

1894–1895. The Japanese defeat of Russia in 1904–1905 gave further impetus to the revolutionary movement, especially in view of the contrast between Japan's strength and the miserable weakness that China had displayed at the time of the "Scramble for Concessions" and the Boxer Rebellion. Japan appeared to Chinese, Indians and other Asians, suffering in varying degrees from the effects of the Western impact, as the light of Asia. Attracted also by the comparative nearness and cheapness of the Japanese schools and universities, Chinese and other Asian students flocked there in the early years of the twentieth century. Some were sent on scholarships provided by the Ch'ing dynasty, but regardless of the source of their support most of these students were extremely nationalistic, anti-Manchu, and susceptible to the propaganda of revolutionaries.

There is space here only for an account of the most important of these revolutionaries, Sun Yat-sen. Born near Canton in 1866, into a poor family, Sun received a secondary and advanced education of the Western type in Hawaii and Hong Kong. In 1895 he founded the first of a series of secret organizations dedicated to the overthrow of the Manchus. Between then and the Revolution of 1911 he launched ten risings, some comic, some tragic, and all unsuccessful. In the intervals he spent most of his time traveling in America, Europe, and the Far East, soliciting funds and support for his movement from overseas Chinese. These he received, but the movement was doomed to frustration by its limited membership and conspiratorial methods. This political ineffectiveness acted as a check on the influence of Sun's political ideas, which had begun to take shape by about 1905.

By 1911 both the finances and the prestige of the Ch'ing dynasty had reached an extremely low point. On October 10 of that year a mutiny began in a government garrison at Wuchang, near Hankow, among troops who had been infected by revolutionary propaganda. This mutiny rapidly grew into a revolt which by the end of the year swept most of South China clear of Manchu authority. Representatives of the revolutionary groups met at Nanking in December, proclaimed the Republic of China, and elected Sun Yat-sen, then returning from the United States, its provisional President.

Meanwhile the Ch'ing government, under pressure of the crisis and at the insistence of its own National Assembly, had appointed Yuan Shih-kai Premier with dictatorial powers and the mission of suppressing the revolt. He had other ideas, however, and after inflicting some sharp defeats on the insurgents he opened secret negotiations with them in December 1911. The outcome was a celebrated agreement betwen Yuan and Sun Yat-sen in January 1912, under whose terms Sun resigned the provisional presidency in Yuan's favor and Yuan for his part agreed to compel the Manchu boy Emperor to abdicate and thereby to extend the authority of the revolutionary government to North China. This Yuan did in February, but he violated other commitments to the revolutionaries by removing the capital from Nanking to Peking and negotiating for a foreign loan to render himself financially independent of them. It was clear that Yuan intended to dominate, and perhaps to overthrow, the infant republic.

In preparation for the parliamentary elections scheduled for the winter of 1912–1913, a number of new political parties arose. Among these was the Kuomintang (National People's Party), which though led by Sun Yat-sen and composed of his followers was so reorganized and revitalized at that time by Sun's leading lieutenant, Sung Chiao-jen, that it may be regarded as virtually a new party. The Kuomintang won a plurality in both houses of parliament in the elections, and Sung would probably have become Premier if he had not been assassinated at Yuan Shih-kai's instigation in March 1913. Revolts, in which the Kuomintang was heavily implicated, broke out in some southern provinces during the following summer, but Yuan suppressed them without much difficulty.

He then dissolved the parliament, outlawed the Kuomintang (most of whose leaders fled to Japan), and proceeded to promulgate a constitution under which he, as President, became a virtual dictator. He ruled with an iron hand and gave China the most orderly and oppressive government it had known for more than a century. He was soon ruined, however, by Japanese enmity and his own ambition.

The Japanese government was opposed to the unification of China under a strong leader, which would render China less susceptible to Japanese influence. Yuan seemed to be such a leader, and he had earned additional hatred from the Japanese by opposing their encroachments in Korea during the decade preceding the Sino-Japanese War. In August 1914 the Japanese government entered the First World War on the Allied side, primarily in order to acquire German holdings in the Pacific. Having seized the German sphere of influence in Shantung, the Japanese presented Yuan Shih-kai in the spring of 1915 with the notorious Twenty-one Demands, which if accepted in their entirety would have transformed China into a virtual Japanese protectorate. Backed by world opinion, Yuan was able to secure a considerable modification of these demands, but he had to acquiesce in the Japanese position in Shantung.

The final Japanese blow to Yuan was delivered in connection with his plans to make himself Emperor. Late in 1915 he manipulated a show of popular support for his plans and announced that he would establish a new dynasty. This step aroused widespread opposition and even revolts in China, and the Japanese and other governments added their disapproval of the scheme. Yuan abandoned his imperial ambitions, and in June 1916 he died, while trying vainly to suppress the revolts that his announcement had touched off.

After Yuan's death the constitution and parliament of 1913 were restored. Within about a year, however, the republic was gravely weakened by the defection of the Kuomintang, which proceeded to set up a rival regime at Canton, and by widespread opposition to the government's action in taking China into the First World War on the Allied side. This it did at American insistence and mainly in order to secure a seat at the peace conference, from which it could press for abrogation of Japan's position in Shantung.

In fact, the republic soon degenerated into a dismal farce, which did much to disillusion Chinese intellectuals with Western parliamentary institutions, as embodied in the half-dozen constitutions drawn up in China between 1912 and 1928, and to pave the way for avowedly authoritarian alternatives. [The recognized government at Peking became the plaything of shifting combinations of disreputable generals usually referred to as warlords.] The typical warlord was a man of humble birth who had acquired at least the rudiments of a modern military education either in China or abroad and who after the Revolution of 1911 had become military governor of a province. Controlling the armed forces of the province, he also dominated its political life. He fought frequently with nearby rivals and generally treated the province as his private preserve, taxing the population almost beyond endurance. A few particularly powerful generals, who could be called superwarlords, controlled entire regions such as Manchuria (Chang Tso-lin) and Northwest China (Feng Yü-hsiang). Although often colorful and not always vicious, these warlords had a bad effect on China. Domestic militarism and Western imperialism came to rank in the eyes of Chinese revolutionaries as the two major evils which must be eliminated if China was to progress. Nevertheless, warlordism survived the fall of the republic in 1928 and continued to plague China until at least as late as 1949.

Several important trends operating during the period from 1912 to 1928 need to be mentioned before discussion of the republic and the warlords is concluded and the rise of the Kuomintang is considered. One was the tendency of the outlying parts of the former Manchu empire to separate themselves from China after 1912 and go their separate ways. The peoples of Outer Mongolia, Sinkiang, and Tibet had regarded themselves as subjects of the Manchus, not of the Chinese. Some of them, furthermore, had been antagonized by Chinese immigration into their territories, which the Manchus had encouraged after about 1900 as a precaution against absorption of the regions by Russia or Japan. After the Revolution, Outer Mongolia became independent of China in all but name and came under Soviet domination after 1921; Sinkiang fell under a succession of local Chinese warlords and was subject to powerful Soviet economic and political penetration from 1932 to 1942; and Tibet remained largely free of Chinese influence until the Chinese Communists overran it in 1950–1951.

The tendency toward gradual economic modernization, especially in the coastal regions of China, that had been in effect during the nineteenth century continued to operate during the republican period. Western commodities came increasingly into use, except in the most remote regions, and the growing of cash crops such as cotton or tobacco partially replaced subsistence farming in some coastal areas. On the whole, however, the peasant was more affected during this period by domestic political disorder than by foreign economic influences. No important change occurred in his agricultural techniques or in the trend toward more widespread tenancy. This trend was especially prevalent near the coastal cities and was the result primarily of the growth of population and the traditional preference of Chinese investors for land as the safest and most respectable outlet for their capital. Modern enterprises, both Chinese and foreign in ownership, continued to grow in the cities, but they were still far too few to make much of an impression on China's poverty and backwardness. China remained an overwhelmingly agrarian country, and the living standards of its people tended on the whole to get worse rather than better.

The most important trend of all was the growth of Chinese nationalism, in protest against both foreign imperialism and domestic militarism. One aspect of this trend was cultural and is usually known as the Chinese Renaissance. The two main leaders were Hu Shih, who had studied at Cornell and Columbia universities, and Ch'en Tu-hsiu, a professor who later became a founder of the Communist Party of China. Both men, and especially Ch'en, favored an almost complete scrapping of traditional Chinese culture and the substitution of Western culture in its materialistic and scientific aspects; Hu also led an ultimately successful campaign for the use of *pai-hua* (the vernacular) in literature, instead of classical Chinese.

Still more important were the political manifestations of nationalism, which may be said to have begun to affect the intellectuals about 1895, the merchants a few years later, the small but growing industrial working class about 1918, and the peasants about 1925. The decision of the Versailles Conference in 1919 awarding the former German sphere in Shantung to Japan and the willingness of the pro-Japanese clique then in control of the Peking government to accept that award promptly touched off the first major manifestation of modern Chinese nationalism, the so-called May Fourth Movement. This movement, which began with student demonstrations in Peking and spread from there to other parts of the country, had the effect of preventing Chinese adherence to the Treaty of Versailles and of raising nationalist feeling to new heights. It later rose to fever pitch at the time of the May Thirtieth Movement of 1925, which was precipitated by the shooting of Chinese demonstrators by British-officered police in the International Settlement at Shanghai. For the next two years antiforeignism in China raged unchecked, and many Christian missionaries found it wise to leave their mission stations for safer places.

This upsurge of Chinese nationalism, combined with a rising feeling in foreign countries that China had been unjustly treated and *that Japan must be checked,* led to some improvements in China's international position. At the Washington Conference (1921–1922), Japan agreed to evacuate Shantung, the Open Door Policy was written into treaty form for the first time (in the Nine Power Pact), and it was agreed in principle that the obnoxious features of the "unequal treaties" ought to be abrogated. Lenin's Bolshevik government made a very favorable impression on China by issuing in 1919 a ringing renunciation of former tsarist special privileges in China, though it was careful to regain in 1924 the right to operate the Chinese Eastern Railway through Manchuria to Vladivostok. From 1913 to 1923 Sun Yat-sen's position was pathetic. His party was weak and ineffective, and he was largely dependent for what power he had on temporary alliances with unreliable warlords or other revolutionary factions. His futility was to a great extent the result of his own character, which was unselfish, patriotic, and sincere, but also impulsive, vacillating, and naïve. Even his political philosophy was not especially remarkable, but since it later became the official philosophy of China it deserves some attention.

Sun held that China could and should be transformed through the implementation of what he called the Three Principles of the People (San Min Chu I). Sun had advocated these principles as early as 1905, but they did not take final form until 1924, by which time Sun had become disillusioned with the Western democracies and favorably impressed by some aspects of Bolshevism.

The first was Nationalism, which meant the elimination of foreign imperialism and domestic militarism from China and the creation of a united but nonaggressive national state embracing not only the Chinese but also the Manchus, the Mongols, the Muslims of Northwest China and Sinkiang, and the Tibetans.

The second principle was Democracy, by which Sun meant a form of government in which the people should exercise the rights of election, recall, initiative, and referendum, but in which only educated and qualified persons should be admitted to the civil service and to political office. The government was to be divided into five branches corresponding to what Sun considered the major functions of government: executive, legislative, judicial, examination (roughly equivalent to the imperial civil service examination system), and control (roughly equivalent to the imperial censorate). Democracy as Sun defined it, however, was to be attained only in the last of three constitutional stages. During the first stage, the Kuomintang would unify China by force of arms. In the second, known as the period of Political Tutelage, the Kuomintang would exercise a monopoly of political power but use that power to train the people in the arts of self-government, so as to make possible the establishment of democracy and constitutional government.

The third principle was People's Livelihood, meaning the redistribution of land among the actual cultivators and state control of communications and heavy industry, all for the public benefit. As the comparative mildness of this program shows, Sun was far from being a Marxist.

It hardly seems necessary to comment on the vagueness and

naïveté of these principles, except to emphasize Sun's un-realism in expecting a party once entrenched in dictatorial power to work for the abolition of its own dictatorship.

Sun's political ideas would not warrant even this brief summary if he had not found an ally to help him implement them. At that time Lenin and the Comintern (Third International) were casting about for Asian nationalist movements with which they might ally themselves in a joint struggle against the position of the Western powers in Asia. In 1922 they fixed on the Kuomintang as the most likely prospect in China, and a fateful alliance was accordingly concluded in 1923.

Under the terms of this alliance, the Comintern and the Soviet government provided the Kuomintang with arms, funds, and a staff of military and political advisers. The advisers reorganized the Kuomintang from top to bottom along the "democratic centralist" lines of the Soviet Communist Party and thereby transformed it for the first time into an effective political instrument. The Kuomintang also began to acquire something else it had lacked before—a reliable and effective army, which was built around an officer corps trained at the newly founded Whampoa Military Academy, near Canton.

There was another important aspect to the Kuomintang-Comintern alliance, namely, a coalition between the Kuomintang and the young and far weaker Communist Party. Sun Yat-sen insisted that Communists could enter the Kuomintang only as individuals, not as a bloc, and that they must abide by the usual conditions of membership, including party discipline. The Comintern compelled the Chinese Communists, against the better judgment of their leaders, to comply. They did so with the aim of using the Kuomintang for their own purposes, if possible.

The alliance between the Kuomintang on the one hand and the Comintern and the Chinese Communist Party on the other conferred during its brief existence considerable benefits on both parties, especially on the Kuomintang. It gave the latter not only efficient party and military machinery, but also a revolutionary zeal and a corps of agitators and propagandists, mostly Communists, who were of inestimable value in forming labor and peasant unions and in undermining the will of war-lord armies to resist. The alliance, however, was an unstable one, because the parties to it had incompatible aims and distrusted each other.

The alliance began to show signs of strain not long after the death of Sun Yat-sen in March 1925. A year later General

Chiang Kai-shek, the Kuomintang's leading military figure, brought off a coup which severely limited the power of the Soviet advisers and the Communists over party affairs. Stalin and the Comintern, however, decided to ignore the challenge, on the theory that everything must be subordinated to the success of the Northern Expedition, as the projected military campaign for the unification of China was called. Later, as Stalin put it, Chiang Kai-shek could be cast aside, like a squeezed lemon.

The Northern Expedition accordingly got under way in the summer of 1926 and from the beginning won brilliant successes. The rabble armies of provincial militarists melted away before the advance of the Kuomintang forces and their accompanying agitators. By the end of 1926 most of South China and the Yangtze Valley had been conquered, and the capital of the Kuomintang revolutionary regime and its party headquarters were transferred from Canton to Hankow. There they fell under the virtually complete control of the Soviet advisers, the Communists, and those elements within the Kuomintang which favored a leftist orientation for the party.

Chiang Kai-shek, whose forces were advancing farther to the east, in the lower Yangtze Valley, noted this trend with disapproval. To protect his own position and prevent the Bolshevization of the Kuomintang, he prepared to strike. Against his blow his leftist opponents took no adequate steps to protect themselves, mainly because of Stalin's insistence that everything possible must be done to avoid giving Chiang offense. Having entered Shanghai with the active and effective cooperation of the Communist-led labor unions of that city, Chiang turned on them suddenly on April 12, 1927, and crushed them. He then set up a rival capital at Nanking in opposition to the one at Hankow.

Stalin now had to admit that Chiang Kai-shek had betrayed the common cause, but he still would not allow the Chinese Communists to break off their alliance with the Kuomintang. On the contrary, he sent them directives instructing them to seize control of the Kuomintang's party machinery and embark on a program of revolutionary class warfare. Having learned of this policy, however, the Left Kuomintang at Hankow broke with its dangerous allies on July 15, 1927, and expelled the Communists and the Soviet advisers. Soon afterward most of the Left Kuomintang leaders submitted to Chiang Kai-shek.

By the spring of 1928 Chiang had consolidated his position within the party sufficiently to resume the Northern Expedition. In spite of a Japanese attempt to block the advance of his armies by sending troops back to Shantung, he took Peking in June 1928. The Kuomintang thereupon transferred the capital of China from Peking (which was then renamed Peiping) to Nanking and officially proclaimed the military unification of China to be complete. The second of Sun Yat-sen's three constitutional stages, that of Political Tutelage, had begun.

Ch'en Tu-hsiu, the son of a rich family, studied in France and returned to China to found a magazine in Shanghai in 1915 called The New Youth. In his capacity as a professor at Peking University he exercised enormous influence on the young generation of students pursuing solutions to China's problems. He gave his approval to the founding of the Society for the Study of Marxism at the University. Its members were made up of students many of whom, such as Chang Kuo-t'so and Mao Tse-tung (who was a librarian's helper), were later destined to play leading roles in the Communist movement. At its inception the society was little more than a study group for investigating the doctrine which the Russian revolution had brought into such prominence. Later in their movement into the Marxist-Leninist circles men such as Ch'en and Li Ta-chao carried with them a whole host of students influenced to some extent by the weight of their intellectual authority. In 1921 Ch'en Tu-hsiu became one of the founders of the Chinese Community Party, only to be discredited in the Party shake-up that followed the dissolution of the first United Front.

Ch'en Tu-hsiu's "Call to Youth," 1915*

THE CHINESE compliment others by saying, "He acts like an old man although still young." Englishmen and Americans encourage one another by saying, "Keep young while growing old." Such is one respect in which the different ways of thought of the East and West are manifested. Youth is like early spring, like the rising sun, like trees and grass in bud, like a newly sharpened blade. It is the most valuable period of life. The

* Document 59, pp. 240–245, reprinted by permission of the publishers from Ssu-yu Teng and John K. Fairbank, CHINA'S RESPONSE TO THE WEST, Cambridge, Mass.: Harvard University Press, Copyright, 1954, by the President and Fellows of Harvard College.

function of youth in society is the same as that of a fresh and vital cell in a human body. In the processes of metabolism, the old and the rotten are incessantly eliminated to be replaced by the fresh and living. . . . If metabolism functions properly in a human body, the person will be healthy; if the old and rotten cells accumulate and fill the body, the person will die. If metabolism functions properly in a society, it will flourish; if old and rotten elements fill the society, then it will cease to exist.

According to this standard, then, is the society of our nation flourishing, or is it about to perish? I cannot bear to answer. As for those old and rotten elements, I shall leave them to the process of natural selection. I do not wish to waste my fleeting time in arguing with them on this and that and hoping for them to be reborn and thoroughly remodeled. I only, with tears, place my plea before the young and vital youth, in the hope that they will achieve self-awareness, and begin to struggle. What is this self-awareness? It is to be conscious of the value and responsibility of one's young life and vitality, to maintain one's self-respect, which should not be lowered. What is the struggle? It is to exert one's intellect, discard resolutely the old and the rotten, regard them as enemies and as the flood or savage beasts, keep away from their neighborhood and refuse to be contaminated by their poisonous germs. Alas! Do these words really fit the youth of our country? I have seen that, out of every ten youths who are young in age, five are old in physique; and out of every ten who are young in both age and physique, nine are old in mentality. Those with shining hair, smooth countenance, a straight back and a wide chest are indeed magnificent youths! Yet if you ask what thoughts and aims are entertained in their heads, then they all turn out to be the same as the old and rotten, like moles from the same hill. In the beginning the youth are not without freshness and vitality. Gradually some are assimilated by the old and rotten elements; then there are others who fear the tremendous influence of those elements, who hesitate, stammer and stall, and dare not openly rebel against them. It is the old and rotten air that fills society everywhere. One cannot even find a bit of fresh and vital air to comfort those of us who are suffocating in despair.

Such a phenomenon, if found in a human body, would kill a man; if found in a society, would destroy it. A heavy sigh or two cannot cure this malady. What is needed is for one or two youths, who are quick in self-consciousness and brave in a struggle, to use to the full the natural intellect of man, and judge and choose all the thoughts of mankind, distinguishing which are fresh and vital and suitable for the present struggle for survival, and which are old and rotten and unworthy to be retained in the mind. Treat this problem as a sharp tool cleaves iron, or a sharp knife cuts hemp. Resolutely make no compromises and entertain no hesitations. Consider yourself and consider others; then perhaps society can hope to become clean and peaceful. O youth, is there anyone who takes upon himself such responsibilities? As for understanding what is right and wrong, in order that you may make your choice, I carefully propose the following six principles, and hope you will give them your calm consideration.

1) *Be independent, not servile.*

All men are equal. Each has his right to be independent, but absolutely no right to enslave others nor any obligation to make himself servile. By slavery we mean that in ancient times the ignorant and the weak lost their right of freedom, which was savagely usurped by tyrants. . . .

Emancipation means freeing oneself from the bondage of slavery and achieving a completely independent and free personality. I have hands and feet, and I can earn my own living. I have a mouth and a tongue, and I can voice my own likes and dislikes. I have a mind, and I can determine my own beliefs. I will absolutely not let others do these things in my behalf, nor should I assume an overlordship and enslave others. For once the independent personality is recognized, all matters of conduct, all rights and privileges, and all belief should be left to the natural ability of each person; there is definitely no reason why one should blindly follow others. On the other hand, loyalty, filial piety, chastity and righteousness are a slavish morality. (Note: The great German philosopher Nietzsche divided morality into two categories—that which is independent and courageous is called "morality of the noble," and that which is humble and submissive is called "morality of the slave.") . . . Therefore, before we speak of contributing to mankind in moral example or in deed, we must first make this distinction between the independent and the servile.

2) *Be progressive, not conservative.*

"Without progress, there will be retrogression" is an old Chinese saying. Considering the fundamental laws of the universe, all things or phenomena are daily progressing in evolution, and the maintenance of the *status quo* is definitely out of the question; only the limitation of man's ordinary view has rendered possible the differentiation between the two states of things. . . . Considered in the light of the evolution of human affairs, it is plain that those races that cling to antiquated ways are declining, or disappearing, day by day, and the peoples who seek progress and advancement are just beginning to ascend in power and strength. It is possible to predict which of these will survive and which will not. Now our country still has not awakened from its long dream, and isolates itself by going down the old rut. . . . All our traditional ethics, law, scholarship, rites and customs are survivals of feudalism. When compared with the achievement of the white race, there is a difference of a thousand years in thought, although we live in the same period. Revering only the history of the twenty-four dynasties and making no plans for progress and improvement, our people will be turned out of this twentieth-century world, and be lodged in the dark ditches fit only for slaves, cattle, and horses. What more need be said? . . . The progress of the world is like that of a fleet horse, galloping and galloping onward. Whatever cannot skillfully change itself and progress along with the world will find itself eliminated by natural selection because of failure to adapt to the environment. Then what can be said to defend conservatism!

3) *Be aggressive, not retiring.*

While the tide of evil is now rushing onward, would it not be rare virtue for one or two self-respecting scholars to retire from the world, to keep themselves clean? But if your aim is to influence the people and establish a new tradition, I suggest that you make further progress from your present high position. It is impossible to avoid the struggle for survival, and so long as one draws breath there can be no place where one can retire for a tranquil hermit's life. . . . Stated in hostile terms, it is a phenomenon of the weak who are unable to struggle for survival. . . . Alas! The war steeds of Europe are intruding into your house. Where can you quietly repose under a white cloud? I wish that our youth would become Confucius and Mo-tzu and not [the hermits] Ts'ao-fu and Hsü Yu, and I do not wish so much that our youth be Tolstoi and Tagore (Note: R. Tagore, an escapist poet of India) as that they become Columbus and An Ch'ung-ken [the Korean patriot who assassinated Prince Ito on October 26, 1909].

4) *Be cosmopolitan, not isolationist.*

Any change in the economic or political life of one nation will usually have repercussions over the whole world, just as the whole body is affected when one hair is pulled. The prosperity or decline, rise or fall of a nation of today depends half on domestic administration, and half on influences from outside the country. Take the recent events of our country as evidence: Japan suddenly rose in power, and stimulated our revolutionary and reform movements; the European War broke out, and then Japan presented her demands to us; is this not clear proof? When a nation is thrown into the currents of the world, traditionalists will certainly hasten the day of its fall, but those capable of change will take this opportunity to compete and progress. According to the pessimists, since the opening of the treaty ports our country has been losing territory and paying indemnities to the point of exhaustion. But according to the optimists, we would still be in the age of the eight-legged essay and the queue were it not for the blessings of the Sino-Japanese War of 1895 and the Boxer Uprising of 1900. Not only are we unable to support an isolationist and closed-door policy, but circumstances also are unfavorable to it. . . .

5) *Be utilitarian, not formalistic.*

The social system and the thought of Europe have undergone a change since J. S. Mill's advocacy of utilitarianism in England and Comte's advocacy of positivism in France. More recently their system and thought have undergone another change, with the great advancement of science in Germany, where material civilization has reached its pinnacle of achievement. In all that concerns the administration of government, the aims of education, and the fashions in literature and the crafts, there is nothing that is not focusing on the road of better livelihood and greater usefulness, like ten thousand horses galloping toward the same point. Meanwhile all things that are formalistic, utopian, and useless to practical life are almost completely rejected. . . .

The age-long precepts of ethical convention, the hopes and purposes of the people—there is nothing which does not run counter to the practical life of society today. If we do not restring our bow and renew our effort, there will be no way to revive the strength of our nation, and our society will never see a peaceful day. As for praying to gods to relieve flood and famine, or reciting the *Book of Filial Piety* to ward off the Yellow Turbans [i.e., bandits]—people are not infants or morons, and they see through these absurdities. Though a thing is of gold or of jade, if it is of no practical use, then it is of less value than coarse cloth, grain, manure or dirt. That which brings no benefit to the practical life of an individual or of society is all empty formalism and the stuff of cheats. And even though it were bequeathed to us by our ancestors, taught by the sages, advocated by the government and worshiped by society, the stuff of cheats is still not worth one cent.

6) *Be scientific, not imaginative.*

. . . There was only imagination and no science in the un-enlightened days of old, as well as among the uncivilized peoples of today. Religion, art, and literature were the products of the period of imagination. The contribution of the growth of science to the supremacy of modern Europe over other races is not less than that of the theory of the rights of man. . . . Our scholars do not know science, therefore they borrow the *yin-yang* school's notions of auspicious signs and of the five elements to confuse the world and cheat the people, and the ideas of topography and geomancy to beg for miracles from dry skeletons (spirits). Our farmers do not know science; therefore they have no technique for seed selection and insecticide. Our industrialists do not know science; therefore goods lie wasted on the ground, while we depend on foreign countries for everything that we need in warfare and in production. Our merchants know no science; therefore they are only concerned with obtaining short-term profits, and give not a thought to calculating for the future. Our physicians know no science; not only are they not acquainted with human anatomy, but also they do not analyze the properties of medicines; as for bacteria and contagious diseases, they have never heard of them. They can only parrot the talk about the five elements, their mutual promotions and preventions, cold and heat, *yin* and *yang,* and prescribe medicine according to ancient formu-lae. Their technique is practically the same as that of an archer. . . . All these nonsensical ideas and unreasonable be-liefs can be cured at the root only by science. For to explain truth by science means proving everything with fact. Although the process is slower than that of imagination and arbitrary decision, yet every step taken is on firm ground; it is different from those imaginative flights which eventually cannot advance even one inch. The amount of truth in the universe is bound-less, and the fertile areas in the realm of science awaiting the pioneer are immense! Youth, take up the task!

> For some men greatness is in small enough proportions to measure during their lifetime. For others personal greatness assumes historic proportions immeasurable within the time categories of one life or even one generation. These men be-

come the center of cults, subject to effervescent adulation long before they are dead and long before the record can objectively be evaluated. Whether history makes them or they make history is a meaningless question. They are artists using the materials of their time to carve out new opportunities, a new human landscape for future generations. Their ideas fertilize unknown territories which because they are uncharted defy immediate observation.

In his lifetime Mao Tse-tung is such a man. He arouses our curiosity, as all great men do, without satisfying our need to know the man, the personal life behind the public figure. The facts of his private life are scanty indeed and come to us for the most part from his "official biography" as told to Edgar Snow. They provide a skeleton of dates and places but the man himself, the sense of a private consciousness is absent. It is as if Mao Tse-tung the person was so totally fused with Mao the revolutionary that his private history is indistinguishable from the history of the Communist movement in China.

In the following selection from Edgar Snow's Red Star over China we glimpse, through Mao's recollections, a picture of his youth prior to his association with the circle of intellectuals later to become the nucleus of the Communist Party.

"Genesis of a Communist"—Autobiographical Notes of Mao Tse-tung*

"MY SCHOLASTIC adventure was in the First Provincial Middle School. I registered for a dollar, took the entrance examination, and passed at the head of the list of candidates. It was a big school, with many students, and its graduates were numerous. A Chinese teacher there helped me very much; he was attracted to me because of my literary tendency. This teacher loaned me a book called the *Chronicles with Imperial Commentaries* (*Yü P'i T'ung Chien*), which contained imperial edicts and critiques by Ch'ien Lung.

"About this time a Government magazine exploded in Changsha. There was a huge fire, and we students found it very interesting. Tons of bullets and shells exploded, and gunpowder made an intense blaze. It was better than firecrackers.

* Reprinted from RED STAR OVER CHINA by Edgar Snow, by permission of Grove Press, Inc. Copyright © 1938, 1944 by Random House, Inc. pp. 141–148.

About a month later T'an Yen-k'ai was driven out by Yüan Shih K'ai, who now had control of the political machinery of the Republic. T'ang Hsiang-ming replaced T'an Yen-k'ai and he set about making arrangements for Yuan's enthronement.

"I did not like the First Middle School. Its curriculum was limited and its regulations were objectionable. After reading *Chronicles with Imperial Commentaries,* I had also come to the conclusion that it would be better for me to read and study alone. After six months I left the school, and arranged a schedule of education of my own, which consisted of reading every day in the Hunan Provincial Library. I was very regular and conscientious about it, and the half-year I spent in this way I consider to have been extremely valuable to me. I went to the library in the morning when it opened. At noon I paused only long enough to buy and consume two rice cakes, which were my daily lunch. I stayed in the library every day reading until it closed.

"During this period of self-education I read many books, studied world geography and world history. There for the first time I saw and studied with great interest a map of the world. I read Adam Smith's *The Wealth of Nations,* and Darwin's *Origin of Species,* and a book on ethics by John Stuart Mill. I read the works of Rousseau, Spencer's *Logic,* and a book on law written by Montesquieu. I mixed poetry and romances, and the tales of ancient Greece, with serious study of history and geography of Russia, America, England, France and other countries.

"I was then living in a guild house for natives of Hsiang Hsiang district. Many soldiers were there also—'retired' or disbanded men from the district, who had no work to do and little money. Students and soldiers were always quarrelling in the guild house, and one night this hostility between them broke out in physical violence. The soldiers attacked and tried to kill the students. I escaped by fleeing to the toilet, where I hid until the fight was over.

"I had no money then, my family refusing to support me unless I entered school, and since I could no longer live in the guild house I began looking for a new place to lodge. Meanwhile, I had been thinking seriously of my 'career' and had about decided that I was best suited for teaching. I had begun reading advertisements again. An attractive announcement of the Hunan Normal School now came to my attention, and I read with interest of its advantages: no tuition required, and cheap board and cheap lodging. Two of my friends were also urging me to enter. They wanted my help in preparing entrance essays. I wrote of my intention to my family, and received their consent. I composed essays for my two friends, and wrote one of my own. All were accepted—in reality, therefore, I was accepted three times. I did not then think my act of substituting for my friends an immoral one; it was merely a matter of friendship.

"I was a student in the Normal School for five years, and managed to resist the appeals of all future advertising. Finally I actually got my degree. Incidents in my life here, in the Hunan Provincial First Normal School, were many, and during this period my political ideas began to take shape. Here also I acquired my first experiences in social action.

"There were many regulations in the new school and I agreed with very few of them. For one thing, I was opposed to the required courses in natural science. I wanted to specialize in social sciences. Natural sciences did not especially interest me, and I did not study them, so I got poor marks in most of these courses. Most of all I hated a compulsory course in still-life drawing. I thought it extremely stupid. I used to think of the simplest subjects possible to draw, finish up quickly and leave the class. I remember once drawing a picture of the 'half-sun, half-rock,[1] which I represented by a straight line with a semi-circle over it. Another time during an examination in drawing I contented myself with making an oval. I called it an egg. I got 40 in drawing, and failed. Fortunately my marks in social sciences were all excellent, and they balanced my poor grades in these other classes.

"A Chinese teacher here, whom the students nicknamed 'Yuan the Big Beard,' ridiculed my writing and called it the work of a journalist. He despised Liang Ch'i-ch'ao, who had been my model, and considered him half-literate. I was obliged to alter my style. I studied the writings of Han Yü, and mastered the old Classical phraseology. Thanks to Yuan the Big Beard, therefore, I can today still turn out a passable Classical essay if required.

"The teacher who made the strongest impression on me was Yang Chen-ch'i, a returned student from England, with whose life I was later to become intimately related. He taught ethics, he was an idealist, and a man of high moral character. He believed in his ethics very strongly and tried to imbue his students with the desire to become just, moral, virtuous men, useful in society. Under his influence, I read a book on ethics translated by Ts'ai Yuan-p'ei and was inspired to write an essay which I entitled 'The Energy of the Mind.' I was then an

[1] The reference is to a line in a famous poem by Li T'ai-po.

idealist and my essay was highly praised by Professor Yang Chen-ch'i, from his idealist viewpoint. He gave me a mark of 100 for it.

"A teacher named T'ang used to give me old copies of the *People's Paper* (*Min Pao*), and I read them with keen interest. I learned from them about the activities and programme of the T'ung Meng Hui.[1] One day I read a copy of the *Min Pao* containing a story about two Chinese students who were travelling across China and had reached Tatsienlu, on the edge of Tibet. This inspired me very much. I wanted to follow their example; but I had no money, and thought I should first try out travelling in Hunan.

"The next summer I set out across the province by foot, and journeyed through five counties. I was accompanied by a student named Hsiao Yü. We walked through these five counties without using a single copper. The peasants fed us and gave us a place to sleep; wherever we went we were kindly treated and welcomed. This fellow, Hsiao Yü, with whom I travelled, later became a Kuomintang official in Nanking, under Yi Pei-chi, who was then president of Hunan Normal College. Yi Pei-chi became a high official at Nanking and got Hsiao Yü appointed to the office of custodian of the Peking Palace Museum. Hsiao sold some of the most valuable treasures in the museum and absconded with the funds in 1934.

"Feeling expansive and the need for a few intimate companions, I one day inserted an advertisement in a Changsha paper, inviting young men interested in patriotic work to make a contact with me. I specified youths who were hardened and determined, and ready to make sacrifices for their country. To this advertisement I received three and one-half replies. One was from Liu Chiang-lung, who later was to join the Communist Party and afterwards to betray it. Two others were from young men who later were to become ultra-reactionaries. The 'half' reply came from a noncommittal youth named Li Li-san.[2] Li listened to all I had to say, and then went away without making any definite proposals himself, and our friendship never developed.

"But gradually I did build up a group of students around

[1] The T'ung Meng Hui, a revolutionary secret society, was founded by Dr. Sun Yat-sen, and was forerunner of the Kuomintang, which now has power in Nanking. Most of its members were exiles in Japan, where they carried on a vigorous "brush-war" against Liang Ch'i-ch'ao and K'ang Yu-wei, leaders of the "reformed monarchist" party.

[2] Li Li-san later became responsible for the famous "Li Li-san line," which Mao Tse-tung bitterly opposed. Farther on Mao tells of Li's struggle with the Red Army, and of its results.

myself, and the nucleus was formed of what later was to become a society[3] that was to have a widespread influence on the affairs and destiny of China. It was a serious-minded little group of men and they had no time to discuss trivialities. Everything they did or said must have a purpose. They had no time for love or 'romance' and considered the times too critical and the need for knowledge too urgent to discuss women or personal matters. I was not interested in women. My parents had married me when I was fourteen to a girl of twenty, but I had never lived with her—and never subsequently did. I did not consider her my wife and at this time gave little thought to her. Quite aside from the discussions of feminine charm, which usually play an important rôle in the lives of young men of this age, my companions even rejected talk of ordinary matters of daily life. I remember once being in the house of a youth who began to talk to me about buying some meat, and in my presence called in his servant and discussed the matter with him, then ordering him to buy a piece. I was annoyed and did not see this fellow again. My friends and I preferred to talk only of large matters—the nature of men, of human society, of China, the world, and the universe!

"We also became ardent physical culturists. In the winter holidays we tramped through the fields, up and down mountains, along city walls, and across the streams and rivers. If it rained we took off our shirts and called it a rain bath. When the sun was hot we also doffed shirts and called it a sun bath. In the spring winds we shouted that this was a new sport called 'wind bathing.' We slept in the open when frost was already falling and even in November swam in the cold rivers. All this went on under the title of 'body-training.' Perhaps it helped much to build the physique which I was to need so badly later on in my many marches back and forth across South China, and on the Long March from Kiangsi to the North-west.

"I built up a wide correspondence with many students and friends in other towns and cities. Gradually I began to realize the necessity for a more closely knit organization. In 1917, with some other friends, I helped to found the Hsin Min Hsüeh Hui ('New People's Study Society'). It had from seventy to eighty members, and of these many were later to become famous names in Chinese Communism, and in the history of the Chinese Revolution. Among the better-known Communists who were in the Hsin Min Hsüeh Hui were: Lo Man, now secretary of the Party Organization Committee;

[3] The Hsin Min Hsüeh Hui.

Hsia Hsi, now in the Second Front Red Army; Ho Hsien-hôn, who became high judge of the Supreme Court in the Central Soviet regions and was later killed by Chiang Kai-shek; Kuo Liang, a famous labour-organizer, killed by General Ho Chien in 1930; Hsiao Chu-chang, a writer now in Soviet Russia; Ts'ai Ho-shêng, a member of the Central Committee of the Communist Party, killed by Chiang Kai-shek in 1927; Yeh Li-yün, who became a member of the Central Committee, and later 'betrayed' to the Kuomintang, and became a capitalist trade-union organizer; and Hsiao Chen, a prominent Party leader, one of the six signers of the original agreement for the formation of the Party, but who died not long ago from illness. The majority of the members of the Hsin Hsüeh Hui were killed in the counter-revolution of 1927.

"Another society that was formed about that time, and resembled the Hsin Min Hsüeh Hui, was the 'Social Welfare Society' of Hupeh. Many of its members also later became Communists. Among them was Wen Teh-ying, its leader, who was killed during the counter-revolution by Chiang Kai-shek. Lin Piao, now president of the Red Army Academy, was a member. So was Chang Hao, now in charge of work among White troops. In Peiping there was a society called Fu Hsieh, some of whose members later became Reds. Elsewhere in China, notably in Shanghai, Hangchow, Hankow and Tientsin,[4] radical societies were organized by the militant youth then beginning to assert an influence on Chinese politics.

"Most of these societies were organized more or less under the influence of *New Youth* (*Hsin Ch'ing Nien*), the famous magazine of the Literary Renaissance, edited by Ch'ên Tu-hsiu. I began to read this magazine while I was a student in the normal college and admired the articles of Hu Shih and Ch'ên Tu-hsiu very much. They became for a while my models, replacing Liang Ch'i-ch'ao and Kang Yu-wei, whom I had already discarded.

"At this time my mind was a curious mixture of ideas of liberalism, democratic reformism, and Utopian Socialism. I had somewhat vague passions about 'nineteenth-century democracy,' Utopianism and old-fashioned liberalism, and I was definitely anti-militarist and anti-imperialist.

"I had entered the normal college in 1912. I was graduated in 1918."

[4] In Tientsin it was the Chou-Wu Hsüeh Hui, or "Awakening Society," which led in organization of radical youth. Chou En-lai was one of the founders. Others included: Miss Teng Ying-ch'ao (now Mrs. Chou En-lai), Ma Chun, who was executed in Peking in 1927; and Sun Hsiao-ch'ing, now secretary of the Canton Committee of the Kuomintang.

On May 4, 1919 the students in Peking held a demonstration against their government's humiliating acceptance of Japan's demands on Chinese territory following World War I. They were angered not only at their government for acquiescing to the colonial expansion of Japan but also at the Allies who, after fighting the war for high ideals, supported Japan's claims on Chinese territory formerly belonging to Germany.

The May Fourth Movement was more than an event on that date. It was the beginning of a revolutionary process that had its roots in a cultural transformation and has its continuation in the present-day "cultural revolution." As a result of China's contact with the West the students had become conscious of new literature, science, democracy, modernization and social reforms. They were young, restless and idealistic and rallied behind them workers and even peasants.

The following selection is a manifesto drawn up by the students before the meeting that initiated the demonstration. It is as fervently nationalistic, idealistic and militant in its expression as any contemporary declaration of Chinese students. The aspirations have changed, perhaps, but the style and intensity of commitment remain the same.

Declaration of the Students of Peking, May 4, 1919*

ALAS, CITIZENS! Our dearest, most respected, and most patriotic brethren! The five Great Powers first promised to seek our consent for the solution they will reach regarding the humiliating secret and dangerous treaties forced upon us by Japan and the long-prayed-for return to us of Tsingtao and other German privileges in Shantung. But now they leave these problems to direct negotiation between China and Japan. This ominous news robs the light from our skies. When the Paris Peace Conference was convened, was it not our hope and happy anticipation that right, humanitarianism, and justice would prevail in the world? To return Tsingtao to us and to abolish the Sino-Japanese secret treaties and military conventions and other unequal treaties are right and just; to surrender right to might, to place our territory at the disposal of the five Great

* "The Declaration of Students," pp. 107–108, reprinted by permission of the publishers from Chow Tse-tung, THE MAY FOURTH MOVEMENT, Cambridge, Mass.: Harvard University Press, Copyright, 1960, by the President and Fellows of Harvard College.

Powers, and to treat us like the defeated Germany and Austria are not right and and are unjust. Now right and justice have been further violated; the Great Powers ask China and Japan to negotiate the Shantung question directly. Japan, tiger-like and wolf-like, has been able to wrest privileges from China simply by sending us a sheet of paper, the Twenty-one Demands. Our further negotiation with her will certainly mean the loss of Tsingtao and Shantung. Shantung, strategically controlling Chihli and Shansi to the north and Hupei and Kiangsu to the south, and situated in the middle of the Peking-Hankow and Tientsin-Nanking Railroads, is actually the throat and heart of the South and North. The loss of Shantung means the subjugation of China. How can our brethren, dwelling in this land as owners of these mountains and rivers, while looking on the insult and oppression and the attempt to enslave us, refrain from crying out for last-ditch salvation? The French in their struggle for Alsace-Lorraine cried, "Give us our wish or give us death." The Italians in their struggle for the Adriatic Straits cried, "Give us our wish or give us death." The Koreans in their struggle for independence also cried, "Give us our wish or give us death." We now approach a crisis in which our country is threatened with subjugation and her territory is going to be ceded. If her people still cannot unite in indignation in a twelfth-hour effort to save her, they are indeed the worthless race of the twentieth century. They should not be regarded as human beings. Are there not some of our brethren who cannot bear the torture of being slaves and beasts of burden and steadfastly desire to save their country? Then the urgent things we should do right now are to hold citizens' meetings, to make public speeches, and to send telegrams to the government in support of our stand. As for those who willingly and traitorously sell out our country to the enemy, as a last resort we shall have to rely on pistols and bombs to deal with them. Our country is in imminent peril—its fate hangs on a thread! We appeal to you to join our struggle.

The Kuomintang, or Nationalist Party, of China was organized in 1912 and reorganized in January, 1924. The following declaration was adopted at the National Convention held at the time of reorganization and incorporates Sun Yat-sen's SAN MIN CHU I (Three People's Principles). These principles were supposed to lay the groundwork for China's modernization. Unfortunately, the Kuomintang in later years, despite its avowed allegiance to these founding principles, failed to translate them into reality. The Communists also claiming

these principles as their heritage, while they interpreted their
meaning quite differently from the Kuomintang, certainly did
more in the direction of enacting them in the form of effective
policies.

The Kuomintang Declaration at Its First National Convention,* January 1924

SUN YAT-SEN

THE PRINCIPLES OF THE KUOMINTANG

The principles of the Kuomintang are really the *San Min*
Doctrine or the Three Principles of the People as outlined by
Dr. Sun. As the faithful execution of these principles is the
only way to national salvation, the political platform of the
Party is based upon these principles and the entire program of
the people's revolution has been determined in accordance
with them.

The purpose of the present reorganization of the Party is to
maintain better discipline of Party members, so that the Party
can have an early realization of the *San Min* Doctrine.

THE DOCTRINE OF NATIONALISM

The Kuomintang's Doctrine of Nationalism has two implications: the first is the emancipation of the Chinese people,
and the second is the equality of all the races within China.

First of all, the purpose of the Kuomintang's Doctrine of
Nationalism is to restore liberty and independence to the Chinese people. Before 1911, the Chinese people were governed
by the Manchus who, in turn, were not free, but were under
the dominant influence of the imperialistic Powers. At that
time, the function of the Nationalist movement was, on the
one hand, to free the Chinese people from the Manchu rule,
and on the other hand, to prevent the partition of China by
the Powers. The first object, namely, the overthrowing of the
Manchu rule, was accomplished by the revolution of 1911.
But the imperialistic Powers have still kept a dominant influence in China.

Although the danger of political partition seems to be
averted, the danger of international control is imminent. In

* "The Manifesto of the First National Convention," pp. 120–
140 from SUN YAT-SEN: HIS POLITICAL AND SOCIAL IDEALS, by Leon-
ard Shihlien Hsu, Copyright, 1933, University of Southern California
Press. By permission of the University of Southern California.

other words, the Powers have substituted for their policy of military conquest a policy of economic exploitation; and the result of imperialistic economic exploitation is the same as the result of military conquest, namely, the loss of independence and liberty on the part of the Chinese people. Not only are the militarists in the country allying themselves with the imperialists, but the capitalist class is also trying to get as much as possible from the common people. Thus, the Chinese people are prevented from making progress in economic activities as well as in political activities.

Seeing the present status of affairs, the members of the Kuomintang feel in duty bound to work for the liberation of the Chinese people from economic and political exploitation. In this struggle, we must have the support of the mass of the people including support from the intellectual class, from the farmers, from the workers, as well as from the merchants.

Since Nationalism aims to stop the imperialistic invasion of China, it is a doctrine by which all classes will be equally benefited. Without the realization of the Doctrine of Nationalism, the manufacturers will be forever hindered from achieving economic prosperity and development by the foreign domination of business in China. At the same time, the workers will have to depend for their living upon either foreign capitalists or Chinese militarists, and so will have to keep on living in a status of slavery.

The motto in the present struggle for national liberation is "Anti-imperialism," because the downfall of imperialism in China will enable the mass of people to organize; to consolidate, and to continue the nationalist struggle. We pray, therefore, for close co-operation between the Kuomintang and the mass of the people in order to enable the Chinese people to regain their real liberty and their independence.

The second aspect of the Doctrine of Nationalism is racial equality. . . .

Unfortunately, the present government of China is controlled by the surviving elements of old officialdom who know nothing of racial equality and freedom; and consequently the other races in China are discontented with the present status of affairs.. . . . We hereby repeat solemnly that we recognize the right of self-determination for all peoples in China, and that a free united Republic of China based upon the principles of free alliance of the different peoples will be established after the downfall of imperialism and militarism.

THE DOCTRINE OF DEMOCRACY

The Kuomintang's Doctrine of Democracy includes direct democracy and indirect democracy. This means that the people will not only have the right to suffrage, but also the rights of initiative, referendum, and recall. . . . It has been found that so-called representative governments often have not been truly representative of the people, and that they have been only tools used by capitalists to exploit the common people. According to the Kuomintang's Doctrine of Democracy, the people's rights should be enjoyed by all the people, not by a few privileged individuals only.

It should also be pointed out that the Kuomintang's Doctrine of Democracy is different entirely from the doctrine of natural rights. Our doctrine is based upon the actual needs of the present revolutionary cause in China; for the safety of the nation can be maintained only when all the political power is enjoyed by all the people of the Republic, not by those individuals who are opposed to the Republic and who may use the power to work indirectly against the interest of the nation. In other words, all individuals or organizations sincerely opposed to militarism may enjoy all the direct rights of the people, and all the individuals or organizations who are betraying the nation's interest by working in the interest of the imperialists or militarists will forfeit their rights.

THE DOCTRINE OF LIVELIHOOD

The Kuomintang's Doctrine of Livelihood includes two essential points: first, the equalization of land ownership; and second, the regulation of capital. The greatest cause of economic inequality in society is the private ownership of land. It is necessary, therefore, for the state to enact laws to regulate the ownership of land and the collection of land tax. Land owned by private individuals should be assessed and reported to the government, which will levy the tax according to the value of the land; and, if necessary, buy it from private owners at the assessed rate. This is the essence of the principle of equalization of land ownership.

As to the regulation of capital: big industries such as banks, railways, and steamship lines which can be favorably operated by a monopoly or are of such dimensions as to exceed the power of individual investment, should be managed by the state. In this way, the private capitalists can have no power to interfere with the normal economic life of the people. We believe that if these two principles are successfully carried out, a sound foundation will have been laid for the solution of the problem of the people's livelihood. We should like to say this to the farmers: China has been and still is an agricultural nation, and of all the classes of people, the agricultural class has suffered the most from economic exploitation.

According to our Doctrine of Livelihood, the state will provide land for cultivation to those farmers who have been deprived of their land or to those who have suffered from their landlords. Irrigation systems will be provided, and colonization schemes will be devised to help those farmers who are without land of their own. Farmers' banks will be established to facilitate rural credits. It is the earnest hope of the Party that everything be done to restore normal happiness to the farmers.

To the workers, the Kuomintang has also a special message. For centuries, the Chinese government has not done anything to ensure the livelihood of the working class. According to our principles, the state should help the unemployed and pass laws to improve the conditions of the laborers. Systems for the relief of the aged, for the care of children, for providing pensions for the disabled, and for providing education for the mass of the people will also be attended to by the Party in order to better the conditions of the less fortunate classes.

Throughout the length and breadth of China, there is no place where we cannot find destitute farmers and exploited workers. Because their conditions are so difficult, their desire for emancipation is correspondingly great. So the laborers and farmers may be counted among those who will most strongly oppose imperialism, and who will help in our work toward a national revolution. On the one hand, the people's revolution can achieve victory only when the farmers and laborers of the country give it their wholehearted support. On the other hand, the Kuomintang will do its best to help peasant and labor movements in order to strengthen the people's revolution.

Both the farmers and the workers are asked to join the Kuomintang and to give their continuous devotion and efforts to promoting the People's Revolution. . . .

The above is an exposition of the content of the *San Min* Doctrine. After the reorganization of the Party, strong discipline will be enforced in order to strengthen the Party. Every means will be used to strengthen the members of the Party and to make them capable of propagating the Party principles and of becoming leaders in popular movements. At the same time, the Party will try its best to spread its influence and to get new adherents throughout the country, in the hope that the people of the entire nation will arise to struggle against their enemies and to demand the supreme political power.

In this way we shall be able to prevent further counter-revolutionary activities, to discover any new intrigues of the imperialists against our people, and to remove all hindrance to the realization of our Party principles. At that time, the central executive power of the nation will be in the hands of the Party itself, for, we believe that only with a strong Party organization based upon popular support will the Party be able to serve the country. . . .

METHODS OF CARRYING OUT THE PROGRAM

1. The reconstruction program will be divided into three periods: (1) the period of military dictatorship; (2) the period of political tutelage; and (3) the period of constitutional government.

2. During the period of military dictatorship, all political machinery will be placed under the direct control of the military government. The Government, in order to bring about national unification, will, on the one hand, overcome internal discord by military force, and on the other hand, endeavor to wake up the people through propaganda.

3. When a province has been completely brought within military control, the period of political tutelage begins and the period of military dictatorship ends. During the period of political tutelage, the Government will send to different *hsien* qualified experts who have passed satisfactorily the required civil service examinations to assist the people of the different *hsien* in organizing local self-government. . . .

4. When all the *hsien* in a province have evolved a working self-government, then the provinces are to pass into the period of constitutional government. The Representatives' Assembly will elect a provincial governor to supervise the provincial self-government. In matters within the sphere of the national administration, the governor will receive orders from the Central Government. . . .

> *The following is a selection from John K. Fairbank's classic work,* The United States and China. *One of the eminent scholars of China, John K. Fairbank, in this excerpt traces the rise of the Communist Party from its early gropings through 1945.*

The Rise of the Communist Party*

JOHN K. FAIRBANK

EARLY TWISTS IN THE PARTY LINE

THE CHINESE Communists had begun by dividing Chinese society into the classes of workers (proletariat), peasants, petty bourgeoisie, national bourgeoisie (capitalists) and other, reactionary classes (militarists, "feudal" landlords, *et al.*). Their first manifesto of June 1922 (a year after their formal founding) called for a united front against the militarists in which the CCP would represent the workers (assuming with Marx that a party can really be an organ of only one class) and also poor peasants, while the "democratic party" (the KMT) would represent bourgeois elements. This concept was abruptly overruled when the Comintern shortly declared that the KMT was actually, and quite anomalously, a "bloc of four classes" (bourgeoisie, petty bourgeoisie, workers, and peasants) and that the CCP, instead of seeking a united front with it as a "bloc without" (*i.e.*, from outside) should do as a "bloc within," *i.e.* by having CCP members as individuals become KMT members while still remaining part of the CCP apparatus. The CCP Third Congress in June 1923, in confirming this ingenious idea, echoed the Comintern declaration that the KMT "should be the central force of the national revolution." When dual membership was accepted by the KMT in January 1924, the race began to see which party apparatus could make more use of the other. Communists gained key posts in the KMT organization.

Adhering to this approach (advocated by Stalin, criticized by Trotsky), the Comintern in December 1926 ordered the CCP to join the left wing of the KMT in the National Government at Hankow, which it now defined to be a "bloc of three classes" (workers, peasants, and petty bourgeoisie). The aim was to effect a transition by which the national bourgeoisie would be excluded from the revolutionary movement. As a result the CCP continued to seek power as a "bloc within," even though its subordination to Hankow prevented its exploiting the peasant unrest of the time. The final fiasco of the

* Pp. 229–245, reprinted by permission of the publishers from John King Fairbank, THE UNITED STATES AND CHINA, Cambridge, Mass.; Harvard University Press, Copyright, 1948, 1958, by the President and Fellows of Harvard College.

Comintern's "bloc within" strategy was signalized first by the split between the left KMT at Hankow and the right KMT at Nanking (February-April 1927) and then by Hankow's expulsion of the Communists (July 1927).

Under Comintern orders the CCP now reoriented itself (August 1927). It condemned Ch'en Tu-hsiu (who later was expelled) and "the Party's leading cadres" (who themselves participated in the condemnation) for "opportunism." "Their constant vacillation, their false, unrevolutionary theories . . . in complete contradiction to the resolutions and instructions of the Comintern . . . in reality betrayed the revolution." At the same time the CCP accepted Stalin's view that the revolution was entering a "higher" stage which must be marked by secret conspiracy and armed insurrections in city and country-side. Yet lip service was still paid to the necessity of achieving "hegemony within the KMT," a statement without meaning except as support of Stalin against Trotsky.

Following this new line the CCP staged the Autumn Harvest uprising in Hunan (led by Mao Tse-tung) and seized the South China port of Swatow for a week, in September 1927. In December it contrived a four-day uprising in Canton (the "Canton Commune"). These and similar efforts all failed.

The Sixth Congress of the CCP, meeting in Moscow with 16 or more members present in July-September 1928, again condemned Ch'en Tu-hsiu for his "opportunist" right deviation mentioned above, and now equally condemned his successor for the "putschist" left deviation which had resulted in unsuccessful uprisings. The new line stated that the revolution was now in a "trough between two waves" and the CCP must prepare for armed insurrections in view of the inevitable arrival of a new "revolutionary rising tide." This laid the basis for the disastrous "Li Li-san line" of 1929-30.

The Sixth Congress of 1928 had decreed that the agrarian revolution was the main "content" of the Chinese revolution as a whole, but that the agrarian revolution could be achieved only under "proletarian hegemony." This meant that the CCP must recapture the leadership of the urban proletariat. At the same time it must prepare armed insurrection so as to be ready for the new "rising tide" of revolution. The result was that under Li Li-san, as secretary general appointed by Moscow, the CCP apparatus had to organize city workers for political strikes and armed uprisings, exploiting the labor union members for party ends rather than representing their economic grievances. In the face of the KMT white terror and its competing "yellow" labor union movement, Li Li-san and his close ally in this period, Chou En-lai, got nowhere. No tide rose, least of all in the cities. In 1926 two-thirds of the party had been classed as proletarian and another fifth as intellectuals. In 1930 Chou En-lai reported that out of 120,000 party members, only about 2,000 were industrial workers.

The climax of Li Li-san's insurrectionary effort came in July 1930 when Communist forces made front-page news by seizing Changsha, the capital of Hunan, only to be expelled a few days later. Li Li-san's downfall followed in the usual way. He was condemned for both "opportunism" and "putschism." He had struggled "against the Comintern line, disobeyed Comintern discipline, and adopted the arguments used by the leftist and rightist rebels against the Comintern by saying that the Comintern did not understand the Chinese situation," et cetera. Li Li-san recanted and went to Moscow "for study" (to reappear in Manchuria in 1946). Chou En-lai, after confessing his "cowardly rotten opportunism," remained on the Central Committee. The latter was now dominated by a "returned-student" group of comrades newly trained in Moscow who still assumed that the urban proletariat must lead China's revolution.

The failure of the first decade of Chinese Communism reflected the difficulty of importing and adapting a foreign faith and its institutions. Leninist party discipline included the fiction that Moscow could not err and that the faithful executor of the Comintern line, if he failed, was himself at fault. The irrationality of this latest importation from the West was not attractive to most Chinese intellectuals, even though reminiscent of the Emperor's holding a local mandarin responsible for acts of God within his bailiwick. In Chinese politics the CCP leadership was something new, a band of professional revolutionists, disciplined and trained to concentrate in Leninist ideological terms upon the organization and seizure of power. The decisive feature of their party was that, unlike the Kuomintang which had borrowed a similar Leninist structure, it functioned as an ideological entity. The line set by the leadership on reasoned "dialectical" grounds, was capable of shifts and reversals, resilient in adversity and flexible when opportunity offered, always sacrificing individuals as expendable in the total cause.

Comintern directives, often concocted with one eye on Stalin's enemies in Moscow, had been disastrously doctrinaire. Yet as political platform documents they regularly included contradictory alternatives which could later be cited to prove wrong those who, like Li Li-san, had followed their main tenor. For example, the CCP Sixth Congress of 1928 in Moscow had foreseen "a war in the Pacific for the partition of China . . . the coastal provinces . . . will become the battle-ground." It declared that "the reformist devices of the bour-geoisie cannot solve the agrarian problem." It called for "al-liance with the petty bourgeoisie and the rich peasants" (with-out, however, abandoning "the class struggle against the rich peasants"). It urged support of peasant guerrilla warfare, de-velopment of the Red Army, organization of peasant women and youth, the setting up of Soviet bases. In short, like a cam-paign platform, it covered all eventualities and so in later retro-spect could be cited to prove Moscow's foresight, even though its main directive had led to defeat.

Thus by 1931 the first decade of Communism in China had created a Leninist party, in spite of the failure of Comintern policy. The second decade was to see an indigenous adaptation of Marxism-Leninism to Chinese potentialities. (One cannot help thinking back, in a general way, to the adaptation of Buddhism some 14 centuries before, to find points of compari-son and of contrast.)

THE RISE OF MAO AND THE YENAN PERIOD

The Rise of Mao Tse-tung. The Comintern had reiterated that only the proletariat could lead the peasantry. It regarded peasants, in orthodox Marxist-Leninist fashion, as capable only of auxiliary action. But Mao Tse-tung's famous report on the peasant movement in Hunan foreshadowed what Benjamin Schwartz has called "the Maoist strategy." Written in February 1927, before the debacle of that year, this report asserted heretically that the "revolutionary vanguard" in China was not the proletariat but the "poor peasantry." When Mao's Autumn Harvest uprising of 1927 failed, he was temporarily dismissed from the CCP Politburo but he continued his work in the Hunan countryside. Convinced that mass revolution in China must be based on the peasantry, Mao learned from experience the necessity of combining mass organization with military power. Building up rural guerrilla forces, he began to create "soviets" (as Trotsky had advocated) even before the Comin-tern sanctioned it. With Chu Teh as military commander he took refuge in the winter of 1927-28 in the mountainous Chin-kanshan region on the Hunan-Kiangsi border, collecting some 10,000 men, together with arms for perhaps 2,000.

Here developed a territorial base, to be fused with the other components—a Leninist party, support from the peasant masses, a Red Army—in the "Maoist strategy." The territorial base, Mao declared in 1928, must have a food supply and a strategic location, preferably on the rugged natural border between two provinces. Collecting here the traditional sinews of rebellion, man power and grain, Mao kept his movement ideologically orthodox in form if not in substance. The Chinese Soviet Republic was proclaimed at Juichin, Kiangsi, in November 1931 as a "democratic dictatorship of the proletariat and peasantry," using Lenin's formula of 1905 in utterly different circumstances. The non-existent "proletariat" were favored by excellent labor laws on paper and given greater representation than the peasantry in the system of soviets, the same as in Russia. The Red Army was specially privileged as a political class army. Land was violently redistributed, both in the time-honored fashion of peasant uprisings and also in terms of class warfare and for purposes of establishing political control. Collectivization, then the Russian fashion, was not pushed. In fact the Soviet Republic in Kiangsi was in no position to coerce all the soviets organized in and around its base area. Some rich peasants and landlords organized soviets so as to make peace with it. But Mao's rural strategy was like Lenin's: rely on the poor peasants and destroy the landlords, treating the middle peasants (until later) as allies and the rich peasants usually as class enemies.

Mao Tse-tung's ascendancy came slowly, some time after KMT arrests and executions had forced the Central Committee to abandon Shanghai for Kiangsi in the autumn of 1932. Chiang Kai-shek's extermination campaigns, in late 1931, May-June and July-October 1932 and again in 1933 had been checked by guerrilla tactics which drew KMT columns into the mountains and concentrated superior force against isolated units. In 1934, however, a systematic, German-devised, KMT blockade with networks of blockhouses began to strangle the Soviet base. The Red Army's efforts at positional defense proved disastrous. After receiving permission from Moscow by radio, over 100,-000 CCP personnel in October broke out of their Kiangsi redoubt, moving swiftly by night on the beginning of the Long March. Only now, when Chinese Communism was out of touch with Moscow and irrevocably committed to survive in the countryside or not at all, was the Moscow-trained element in the party leadership obliged to acknowledge Mao's dominance. Mao's rise was not decreed from the Kremlin.

Yenan and Wartime Expansion. After marching and fighting on a circuitous route of 6000 miles or more through half a dozen provinces of Southwest China, surviving perils and hardships now legendary, most of the CCP leaders and probably less than 20,000 troops reached northern Shensi province in the latter part of 1935, transferring their headquarters to Yenan at the end of 1936. Here in the arid, sun-baked Northwest, half-way from Nanking to the border of Soviet Outer Mongolia, a new chapter opened with the second united front, this time against Japan.

Since general Chinese resistance to Japan would serve a dual purpose, diverting Japan from attacking Russia and Nanking from attacking the CCP, it is not surprising that at the beginning of August 1935 both the CCP and the Comintern called for nationwide resistance in a new united front. With some exceptions the CCP statements now offered to join with the archenemy, Chiang Kai-shek; but he remained deaf to this proposal until after his spectacular kidnapping at Sian in December 1936 by Manchurian troops who chafed to fight Japanese invaders, not Chinese rebels. Chou En-lai on Russian orders mediated to secure the release of Generalissimo Chiang, who now reached the zenith of his career as the indomitable symbol of national resistance.

Subsequent pourparlers and the unleashing of Japan's attack near Peiping on July 7, 1937, led to a second KMT-CCP marriage of convenience, an uneasy armed truce which began in an atmosphere of patriotic enthusiasm but soon deteriorated. The Communists now met Nanking's demands and promised to support Sun's *Three Principles,* to give up overthrowing KMT by force and abandon the soviet campaign against landlordism, to democratize their local regime, and to put their troops under Nationalist command. These were of course temporary tactical expedients by which to expand CCP power in the wholly new context of a national war of resistance.

This relatively moderate program, during a period when violent change was being brought about by the Japanese invasion, recognized that China's war of resistance was in itself a revolution. The Communists had only to go along with it and give leadership in the mobilization of a people's army, the organization of local government, and the coordination of autonomous popular movements. By riding with the patriotic tide and on the crest of the popular wave, the Communist organization soon became the over-all government, the only coordinating mechanism, in the densely populated countryside of North China within and without the Japanese strong points and lines of communication.

This process of expansion was first of all military. The name of the Red Army was abolished in 1937 and it was put nominally under the orders of the Central Government, which named it the Eighth Route Army. By degree its forces pushed into the mountain-ringed province of Shansi and thence out onto the North China plain. In the second year of the war the Communists organized the New Fourth Army from remnant forces left in the lower Yangtze region and extended their organization also into the seacoast province of Shantung. The war bases which they organized centered in the less accessible border areas between provinces, beginning with the Shansi-Hopeh-Chahar Border Region set up in 1938, which eventually contained roughly 20 million people. By 1941 the last area of the Nien rebellion of 1853-1868 on the Shansi-Hopeh-Honan-Shantung borders was unified as another such Region with a population of perhaps 30 million. By war's end there were 19 bases, mostly called Liberated Areas, with a total population of 70 to 90 millions, protected by about 2 million militia and by Communist armies said to total 910,000 troops.

The Nationalist Government, never locally dominant in much of North China, could not prevent this expansion. Its modernized forces, absorbed in stemming the main Japanese war effort in such areas as the Hunan rice-bowl, were trained for positional, not guerrilla, warfare. Chiang Kai-shek's troops were also handicapped by the Chinese military tradition which kept the army separate from the people.

Throughout Chinese history an armed populace had invariably endangered the established order, while the soldier had been held in low esteem, kept ignorant, used wastefully, and bought and sold as a mercenary. Armies had lived off the countryside and been the scourge of the people. Politically indoctrinated armies were a new thing in Modern China. In this as in other respects it was typical of the Kuomintang that it had modernized its military machine to the point of giving social prestige to a patriotic new officer corps and giving new arms and training to their peasant soldiers, but it had not reached the point of indoctrinating the ordinary rifleman to fraternize with the farmer and fight in his behalf, because this would have been revolutionary. For that very reason Mao and Chu from the beginning had trained their troops to regard themselves as the defenders of the populace. In practice this meant paying for supplies, helping the households on whom they were quartered, and making the Eighth Route Army the friend of the people. As the Communists put it, "the soldiers are fish and the people water"—the army depended upon popular support. This slogan is an illuminating contrast to the orthodox statement of the philosopher Hsün-tzu (ca. 300–235 B.C.) that "the people are the water and the ruler is the boat; the water can support the boat but it can also sink it." The Communists, so to speak, by being immersible among the people added a dimension to their movement.

This fraternization with the populace meant that the Communist troops could dispense with the modern paraphernalia of a central commissary. By using civilian intelligence networks they could more easily decentralize their military organization. This enabled the Eighth Route Army to operate as a scattered, mobile force, appearing and disappearing in the populated farm land behind the Japanese lines. This was something that the Central Government forces could not do unless they combined their military operations with a more popular political program.

In their political organization the Chinese Communists expanded to fill a vacuum. Local politicians had been the first to go as the Japanese advanced, and in some cases had gone over to puppetry. New leadership had arisen locally, teachers from Peiping in some cases becoming chairmen of guerrilla governments. Into these local situations where new leadership was arising came a great influx of young students from the coastal centers. Intellectuals from Yenching and the big government universities at Peiping, inheritors of the spirit of the May Fourth Movement, packed their belongings in a bundle and joined the guerrillas. Living close to nature and the common people, they emulated the adventurous heroes of Chinese folklore, daring all with loyal comrades in a righteous cause to succor the downtrodden, like the famous characters of the picaresque novel *Shui-hu-chuan* (translated by Pearl Buck as *All Men Are Brothers*).

The migration of patriots was common to both South and North, but with different effect. In the more modern centers of the unoccupied Southwest, the students became symbols of the country's future technological development and remained in the universities-in-exile. In the Border Regions and Liberated Areas of North China, on the other hand, where universities were lacking, they were recruited to be Communist cadres, in teams of political workers. The Communist area during the early united front period attracted venturesome idealists who sought action. By degrees the Communists organized these diverse individuals into a network of decentralized government.

Organization of Popular Support. In their land policy the Communists temporarily abandoned their program of land confiscation and redistribution in favor of rent reduction. This merely carried out the Kuomintang law of 1930 which limited rent to 37½ per cent of the crop. At this time landlords were very generally left in possession, guaranteed a reduced rent and also allowed to vote in local elections, so that there was no great flight of the propertied class from the Communist area. Instead of their former soviet system, the Communists announced direct elections by the so-called three-thirds system in which they would confine their own representation to one-third and seek to retain Kuomintang and independent participation in the other two-thirds of the offices. This was based on the theory that in a community unified against the Japanese the Communists would provide leadership most effectively by refraining from a monopoly of government. The system had the merit of apparent competition. Although the Communists had preponderant force in reserve, their local political representatives had to prove their administrative competence and political wisdom before the bar of public opinion. While this was a passive Chinese type of public opinion, expressed by tacit acquiescence and lack of protest rather than by speeches and editorials, it was still a determining factor in wartime politics. Like traditional contenders for the Mandate of Heaven, the Communists had to steer by the willingness of the populace to put up with their regime rather than turn against it. In practice the Communist movement and the Eighth Route Army in these years could prosper only in proportion as the populace actually supported them, for the war period was one of free political competition, in which the Japanese and their Chinese puppets as well as the Kuomintang offered feasible alternatives to the Communist regime.

The key to popular support lay in the CCP leadership of a patriotic war of resistance and, at the same time, in the Communists' economic program. In the densely populated North China plain where some fifteen hundred people try to live off each square mile of cultivated land, food was more important than civil liberties. The latter had been unknown. Chinese governments had never countenanced the active participation of the farmer in politics. Privately sponsored meetings and speeches had been seditious, elections unheard of, and freedom to publish meaningless among illiterate peasants.

Against this tradition it was comparatively easy to develop an effective economic program. This included production drives both by troops and by farmers which sought to achieve the self-sufficiency of each area in food supply and, with more difficulty, in cotton production. The Communists were not well supplied with improved seeds and farming techniques such as those developed by scientific farming in the West. But they made up for this lack by their emphasis upon cooperation in land reclamation, labor exchange among farmers, transport cooperatives, and small-scale industrial cooperatives. Since the old order had inveterately discouraged the cooperative association of peasant households in any way which might threaten authority, the immense potentialities of peasant cooperation at the village level were ready at hand for Communist exploitation. By bringing the farmers into associations for common ends and controlling these associations through leadership and propaganda, the Communists found a new road to political power.

Compared with the years of decline and disaster in the wilderness after 1927, the Yenan decade of the united front after 1936 was full of vitality, growth and innovation. While not renouncing their orthodox Communist aims, the CCP now stressed "agrarian reform," though far from being "mere agrarian reformers." When an enterprising American journalist, Edgar Snow, interviewed Mao and his colleagues after the Long March, he found a self-confident and even jovial band of veteran revolutionaries, whose homespun earthiness and evident devotion to the peasant's cause, brilliantly portrayed in *Red Star Over China*, captured the imagination of readers around the world. During World War II the electric optimism and sunny atmosphere of Yenan impressed foreign visitors, who invariably came there from the clammy fog and frustration of the capital at Chungking. Communist propaganda in this period sang a liberal tune, for "national independence, democratic liberty and the people's welfare" (paraphrasing Sun's *Three Principles*), with no further stress on soviets, bolshevization, class war, dictatorship or even the absent proletariat. This façade for outside observers, however, did not disclose the Party's inner aims and methods, nor its problem of organizing central power during its wartime growth. . . .

In the early 1920's the Kuomintang was attempting to organize itself into a national party under the leadership of Sun Yat-sen. There was, however, a fragmented situation in which various warlords independently controlled parts of China, even in the South, the stronghold of the Kuomintang. There was the possibility of compromise but no unity.

The Communist Party in its first Manifesto argues against any Kuomintang compromise with the warlords on the grounds that unification has to precede abolition of foreign interests in China. Before throwing the foreigners out, internal conditions have to be radically altered and the Communists want to abolish the military power of the warlords as the first step in this process of unifying China politically, economically and socially.

This document precedes the first United Front by two years and provides us with some idea of the underlying differences between the Communists and the Kuomintang. These differences, submerged during the period of coalition, came to the fore once again after 1927.

First Manifesto of the CCP on the Current Situation*
(June 10, 1922)

FOR THOUSANDS of years China has endured feudal economic conditions. Agriculture has been the basis of China's economy. Hence, China has been socially disunited and has lacked organizational strength and (so has lacked) interest in the country's political life. Not until the second half of the nineteenth century did the development of world capitalist production raise before the capitalist governments the problem how to use the boundless (extent of) China as a market. China, which had previously been inaccessible to alien influence for thousands of years, was now subjected to oppression by other states. During the period when the annexationist aspirations of capitalist states were asserting themselves, China's masses attempted to resist the conqueror by direct action. After the popular revolt was crushed, China began to feel the yoke of foreign enslavement more than ever and to discover at the same time the mercenary and sinful nature of her own government.

In the process of the struggle the Chinese popular masses learned the truth that the country's defence from foreign enslavement was impossible without a decisive change of the entire political system of the country.

The revolution of 1911 had two historical tasks: first, the overthrow of the Manchu dynasty and, second, the liberation of China from foreign oppression and the transformation of China into an independent state. In this second objective the 1911 revolution aimed to create, within a framework of racial and national independence, favourable conditions for the industrial development of China. The 1911 revolution expressed the transition from the political system of feudalism to a democratic régime, from manual labour and an artisan economy to capitalist production.

* Excerpts from Brandt, Schwartz and Fairbank, A DOCUMENTARY HISTORY OF CHINESE COMMUNISM (London: George Allen and Unwin, Ltd., 1952), pp. 54–63. By permission.

The revolution in China—under the definite conditions of its historical environment—did not consummate a victory. The democratic party [presumably, the Kuomintang], which expressed the demands of liberal social strata, resorted to a compromise with the counter-revolutionary class of feudal lords. . . .

The result of the revolution's defeat has been a strengthening of the world imperialist yoke in China and of the reactionary régime of her own militarists. The so-called republican rule is in the hands of militarists who, under conditions of a semi-feudal economy, use it to join their own actions with those of the world imperialists, who are concluding an agreement with the Chinese military clique regarding loans for their military needs and for the state's self-preservation. The foreign states are making use of the opportunity to invest their capital in China, thus acquiring, by means of a system of financial enslavement, "spheres of influence" in China and special rights and privileges.

But the maintenance of civil war in China is of first importance to the world imperialists, for it delays China's progress, prevents China from developing her own industry, saturates the Chinese market with goods of their own foreign manufacture, and also prevents the Chinese bourgeoisie from utilizing the country in the interests of domestic exploitation. Under these historical conditions the development of Chinese industry is hindered by unequal competition on Chinese territory between Chinese and foreign capital, which has insured its own dominance through measures of economic pressure (a tariff system, etc.), by the civil war, by local disturbances, by the looting of the population by the officials, and by every type and form of oppression.

The socio-economic conditions in China affect the middle, intermediary classes with particular force. The owners of small enterprises are being deprived of property; artisans fill the ranks of the army of the unemployed; peasants sell their land to landlords for absurd sums of money because they are unable to conduct their own economy, owing to the continuously rising cost of living.

These conditions will remain unchanged so long as power remains in the hands of the feudal-lord government, in the hands of militarists; so long as power is not seized from their hands; and so long as a democratic government is not established.

Democratic government means a democratic party government. We have in mind the creation of power on the basis of a total reorganization of the entire political system of administration. Basically, this demand entails the overthrow of the authority of the reactionary, counter-revolutionary elements and groups by revolutionary methods, by a democratic party, or by a bloc of democratic groupings which will organize power to conform to the historical requirements of their own country and with consideration for the realities of the new international environment. . . .

The postulate must be clear to everyone that the political struggle is not a struggle between individuals for power, but a manifestation and expression of class struggle—the social struggle of the proletariat against the bourgeoisie in the period of revolution and, in the period of bourgeois revolution, the struggle of the bourgeoisie against the feudal lords and the system of feudal economy. The postulate must also be clear that only such freedom is precious as is achieved in the process of hard struggle and at the price of human blood, in distinction from those methods of struggle which are used by our class enemies.

The struggle for democracy is a struggle of one class, a struggle which aims to overthrow the dominance of another class; it is the replacement of one system by another, and in no event can it be regarded as a struggle of one individual or one group for the overthrow of another individual or group.

A real democratic party must possess two characteristic elements: (1) its principles must be correlated with the concepts of democracy; and (2) its actions must consist in an active struggle against feudalism in the form of the military. Of all the political parties existing in China, only the KMT can be characterized as a revolutionary party, yet it possesses only a relative amount of democratic and revolutionary spirit. The programme of this party has not yet been fully elaborated. But its three principles, "of the people, for the people, and by the people" [evidently an oblique reference to Sun Yat-sen's Three People's Principles], in conjunction with plans for the industrial development of China [cf. Sun's *International Development of China*, 1922 (1919)] reflect the democratic spirit of the KMT. In addition to this party's participation in the revolutionary struggle through its parliamentary members, the KMT has offered a number of other proofs of its democratic spirit, namely: the Canton government [headed by Sun Yat-sen, 1921–2] has not been restricting the labour movement; it has abolished police regulations in regard to "public order and national security"; and it has abolished the law by which workers were deprived of the right to strike. Not infrequently, however, this party's actions have been contradictory in nature. On occasion the KMT manifests a friendly attitude even with respect to . . . [periods as in original] monarchists, and an inclination for a rapprochement "for tactical reasons" with the "Pei-yang" military clique. If the KMT, as a party, wishes to play a definite role in the revolutionary struggle for the consolidation of democracy in China, it must renounce once and for all every policy of vacillation, compromise, and endless zigzags. . . .

Members of the KMT! You were originally revolutionary fighters for the triumph of democracy. You should also conduct a revolutionary struggle now for democracy and prefer to perish in this struggle than to vanish from the socio-political arena in consequence of a policy of compromise. During the first year of the existence of the Chinese Republic [1912] you were deceived by Yüan Shih K'ai, who tried his best to demonstrate his loyalty to the republic. You were cruelly deceived also by Tuan Ch'i-jui, when he proposed the restoration of parliament and of the constitution [1916–17]. Do not let yourselves be deceived now by all this talk about restoring parliament, abolishing the *tu-chün* system, demobilizing provincial troops, for the sake of concluding another compromise with the military of North China. Does the present constitutional parliament differ in any way from the parliament of the fifth and the sixth year of the Republic [1916–17]? Aren't the hopes for abolishing the *tu-chün* system and for demobilization merely hopes that the tiger may shed its own skin? . . .

Is there any hope whatever for a troop demobilization at a time when war between militarists is at its height? Little Hsü (General Hsü Shu-cheng, an active Anfuist) said: "I am an advocate of disarmament, but wait until my soldiers are adequately trained and equipped, so that I may disarm the soldiers of my adversaries." . . .

Workers, peasants, students, soldiers, policemen, and merchants! So long as the authority of the military is not overthrown, there will be no hope of disarming the provincial armies and abolishing the *tu-chün* system. So long as the authority of the military is not overthrown, there will be no hope of reducing the demands for national funds, which are used to cover war expenses and further to disrupt the entire national and local financial system. So long as the authority of the military is not overthrown, all conditions will be present to allow the military to secure new loans from foreigners and thus bring about an intensification of foreign influence in China. So long as the authority of the military is not overthrown, there will be no hope that the military will cease imposing heavy imposts on the citizens of China; there will be no hope that looting may cease, no hope that order may be restored in all regions of China. So long as the authority of the military is not overthrown, there will be no hope of a broad development of education in China and of industrial progress in our country. So long as the authority of the military is not overthrown, there will be no hope that the struggle among militarists for the expansion of their own spheres of influence may cease. Peasants and merchants are always war victims. These wars will be inevitable and endless if they are not stopped by the people themselves.

For all of us, the only way by which we can liberate ourselves from the hard yoke of the military is to join the democratic struggle against the relics of the past—a struggle for freedom and peace. The government opposition game, played by the bourgeoisie, the intelligentsia, and the politicians, cannot be trusted. We all want peace, but real peace rather than false peace. We welcome a war to achieve the triumph of democracy, to overthrow the military and the militarists and to liberate the Chinese people.

The CCP, as the vanguard of the proletariat, struggles for working-class liberation and for the proletarian revolution. Until such time as the Chinese proletariat is able to seize power in its own hands, considering the present political and economic conditions of China's development and all the historical processes now going on in China, the proletariat's urgent task is to act jointly with the democratic party to establish a united front of democratic revolution to struggle for the overthrow of the military and for the organization of a real democratic government.

The concrete aims of the present political struggle cannot be limited to a fight for the publication of data on government finances or for surveillance over the activity of the parliament or of local organs of administration.

Our most immediate aims are as follows:

(1) Revision of the system of tariffs forcibly imposed on China by world capitalism; abolition of consular jurisdiction [extra-territoriality] and of the entire system of privileges for foreigners; the estimation of railway subsidies made to China by foreign capital and the immediate transfer of all railways to the hands of the state.

(2) Abolition of the régime of the military and of the mercenary bureaucrats; confiscation of the property of the mili-

tarists and distribution of their large landholdings among the poorest peasants.

(3) General suffrage.

(4) Freedom of assembly, speech, and press; annulment of laws for the safeguarding of "public order" by police; freedom to strike.

(5) Restricted taxation on land.

(6) Compulsory education.

(7) Prohibition of child and woman labour; laws pertaining to sanitary conditions in factories and shops; laws on workers' insurance.

(8) Abolition of all tariff surtaxes and of the *likin* system [provincial transit taxes on domestic trade].

(9) Revision of the entire Law Code with immediate abolition of the death penalty and physical torture.

Equality of the rights of men and women.

Introduction of a progressive income tax.

Under the rule of feudal militarists, none of this minimum programme can be carried out by the methods of compromise, petition, or requests. The CCP takes the initiative in calling a conference, to be participated in by the revolutionary elements of the KMT and revolutionary socialists, to discuss the question of creating a united front for struggle against warlords of the feudal type and against all relics of feudalism. This struggle along a broad united front is a war to liberate the Chinese people from a dual yoke—the yoke of foreigners and the yoke of powerful militarists in our country—a war which is just as urgently needed as it is inevitable.

The Central Committee of the Chinese Communist Party.

> The relationships among the various participants in the Chinese revolution are so complex and intricately interwoven that it is often necessary to read between the lines of documents to get the full import of slogans and policy decisions. In the following document of the Delegation of the Communist International in Hankow in April 1927, Chiang Kai-shek is attacked for betraying the nationalist revolution. The full implications of the Comintern reaction, however, are only clear if one keeps in mind the realities of the developing situation in which the Russians played a significant role.
>
> Russian influence became prominent in Chinese revolutionary circles after 1921. The success of the Bolshevik Revolution and the friendly overtures of the new Soviet government towards Asian nationalists were sufficient to recommend the services of Russian advisers. This was true of both the

Kuomintang, the Nationalist Party, and the newly-formed Communist Party. Eventually these two, with Russian help, were brought together in a united front.

In 1924 Russian advisers, with Sun Yat-sen's approval, supervised the reorganization of the Kuomintang as an armed party modeled along Soviet lines. They urged members of the Communist Party to join the Kuomintang and work through its structure thus securing a united front of all nationalist Chinese to eliminate imperialism and wrest control of China from the corrupt rule of local warlords. While this objective was shared by Communists and Nationalists alike the means for achieving it proved disastrous for the Communists. Within four years Chiang Kai-shek had killed thousands of Communists and left-wing workers for the Kuomintang, the united front policy was abandoned without the unification of China and Russian influence was on the wane.

Although the Russians had taught the Chinese revolutionaries (including Chiang Kai-shek) a great deal about organization and revolutionary tactics their strategy did not have the desired consequences largely because of their idealized and illusionary picture of the situation in China. Contrary to formal appearances the Kuomintang even under Russian tutelage had not really changed from the early days when it was a loose conglomeration of revolutionaries sympathetic to the ideals of modernization. The Kuomintang remained precariously bound together first by a personal loyalty to Sun Yat-sen, and after his death, by the shifting fortunes of local leaders who needed one another to retain their power. This was not the instrument of revolutionary unity that the Russians had envisioned and on which their policy was based.

After Sun Yat-sen's death in 1925 the rifts among rival factions of the Kuomintang became more pronounced until a new personality emerged to fill Sun's position as center of gravity. A young ambitious general who had risen to preeminence from his position as Commander of the Whampoa Military Academy, Chiang Kai-shek adroitly maneuvered himself among the shifting sands of the Party's coalitions to become the indispensable leader of the Kuomintang. Once on his way to national power Chiang determined to eliminate competing centers of power within the Party. Unlike Sun Yat-sen he was not inclined to accept Soviet assistance, and within two years after Sun's death had already dismissed the advisers and declared open war against both the Communists and left-wing members of the Kuomintang. As Commander-in-Chief of the Kuomintang forces in the Northern Expedition (intended to unify

China under the united front) Chiang was in a position to betray the united front effectively. This was accomplished in the "purge" of Shanghai in April of 1927 and the crushing of a Communist-inspired uprising in Canton some months later.

From Chiang's point of view the united front was over by 1927. The Kuomintang under his leadership was determined to go it alone and in so doing relinquished the idea of a grass-roots revolution in favor of an alliance with the "upper" bourgeoisie. The latter—powerful figures in the large coastal cities —were linked, in turn, to the world of western imperialism thereby closing the vicious circle that once again engulfed China's first attempts at modernization on a nation-wide scale.

From the perspective of the Chinese Communists, in retrospect, 1927 marks the end of the first round of a battle against time and the forces of reaction. It was a resounding victory for Chiang Kai-shek and the Nationalist Party, the two becoming synonymous subsequently. The Communist Party was left a shambles, an easy victim for the Kuomintang "extermination campaigns." If it can be said that there was any responsibility for the loss of lives and time it had to be shared by the members of the Communist International under Stalin's direction. The Comintern directives failed to comprehend the meaning of events in China thus further leading the Chinese Communists astray.

This is the import of the following document of the Delegation of the Communist International in Hankow. In denouncing Chiang for his betrayal of the Communists in Shanghai Comintern officials assume that he alone was villain in defecting from the cause. Firm in their belief that the united front remained intact, Comintern officials continued to advise the Communists to work within the Kuomintang. For most Communists and many revolutionary members of the Kuomintang this policy was disastrous. For some it provided the first lesson in the reliability of non-Chinese sources of advice and support.

Chiang Kai-shek—Traitor to the People and Instrument of Imperialism

Declaration of the Delegation of the Communist International*
(April 22, 1927)

THE FAST tempo of the development of the Chinese revolution has intensified the struggle against imperialism. [The attempt] to arrest the victorious march of the revolution by indirect pressure through native militarism did not succeed, *and international imperialism decided upon open military intervention.* Not only is Shanghai virtually occupied by imperialist powers; other important points inside the country and, especially, Wuhan—the seat of the national government—are under the threat of an imposing line of warships. This is a grand-scale "demonstration."

Arguing with weapons, the imperialist bandits present the Chinese people with a demand for surrender. Identical notes from England, America, France, Italy, and Japan lay down impossible conditions to the national government. If these conditions are fulfilled, the national government would have to declare foreign imperialism, and not the Chinese people, to be the master of China. Nevertheless, the national government gave a very reasonable—perhaps overly conceding—reply to the brazen ultimatum of the powers. But this does not temper the wrath of imperialism which prefers to demonstrate the use of brute force rather than turn to the League of Nations, as the national government suggests. The League of Nations is a smoke screen for the predatory policy of imperialism. But in China the rapacity of imperialism is so frank that there is no need for such a smoke screen.

The Chinese people must meet this imperialist attack with a united revolutionary front. Never in the history of the national movement has it been so essential to have unity of purpose and leadership of revolutionary forces as at the present time. Nevertheless, it was at this very time that the feudal-bourgeois elements in the Kuomintang, headed by Chiang Kai-shek, destroyed the unity of national forces. Thus Chiang Kai-shek and all those whose interests he represents have become a

* Document 8, pp. 183–185 from Robert C. North and Xenia J. Eudin, M. N. ROY'S MISSION TO CHINA (Berkeley and Los Angeles: University of California Press, 1963). Reprinted by permission.

counter-revolutionary instrument of imperialism. It was precisely Chiang Kai-shek's revolt against the central national power and his efforts to split the Kuomintang that allowed imperialism to adopt such an aggressive position.

The counterrevolutionary activities of Chiang Kai-shek culminated in the creation of a parallel "national government" in Nanking. This action of his is even more unpardonable than his numerous acts of violence that preceded it, namely: the *coup* of March 20, the actions against the revolutionary wing of the Kuomintang, the suppression of the workers' and peasants' movement in Kiangsi and Chekiang, the attempt to establish his own dictatorship and, finally, the executions of Shanghai workers. We followed with great anxiety all these violent actions by Chiang Kai-shek and his agents, and we hoped that he would not bring himself to become an open traitor of the national movement. In this critical period of the national revolution, the maintenance of a united front is so essential that the crimes of those who fight against imperialism can be left temporarily unpunished. But the egotistical interests of the feudal-bourgeois class are hostile not only to the interests of workers and peasants, but also to the entire people. The crimes of Chiang Kai-shek, therefore, were not confined to murders of workers in Kiangsi and Shanghai. They culminated in a revolt against the people's party and the people's government. Chiang Kai-shek is trying to deceive the people when he proclaims his loyalty to the Kuomintang and places the responsibility for the split on the Central Committee of the Party. We testify that this is an outrageous lie. When the conflict between him and the Central Committee became acute, Chiang Kai-shek approached the Communist International with the request that it send a delegation to him in China. On the eve of our departure to him we received the news that he had called a meeting in Nanking of several members of the Central Committee and the [Central] Control Commission to accuse the united conference in Wuhan of splitting the Party. We advised him immediately by telegraph to break off the conference and to fulfill the conditions of the agreement he had concluded with Comrade Wang Ching-wei in Shanghai or referring all questions at issue to the plenum of the Central Committee, with his participation. In the same telegram we informed him that if he accepts our advice we will meet with him to discuss ways and means of preserving the unity of revolutionary forces in the face of an attack by the imperialists. He did not respond to our telegram and pursued further his plan for destroying the Party.

In declaring Chiang Kai-shek to be an instrument of imperialism, a murderer of workers and peasants, and a traitor to the people, we assert at the same time, before the broad public, that the defection of Chiang Kai-shek is not merely a revolt of one or more individual persons: an entire class has deserted and has turned against the national revolution. It is necessary to overthrow not only Chiang Kai-shek and the Kwangsi generals—the murderers who surround him and who have usurped the power. *The feudal-bourgeois elements must be annihilated* in the whole country. The roots of Chiang Kai-shekism must be destroyed. One must not only move on Nanking and Shanghai in order to fight Chiang Kai-shek. One can fight his power in any village, in any town, by destroying the power of feudalism and the reactionary bourgeoisie. Destruction of the roots of Chiang Kai-shekism—this is what will be the principal feature of the next stage of the national revolution.

The consolidation of the alliance of the revolutionary-democratic forces in territories under the control of the Kuomintang will compensate for the losses inflicted on the national-revolutionary movement by the betrayal and the revolt of the bourgeois-feudal elements. Encouraged by the betrayal of the feudal-bourgeois class and by the counterrevolutionary activity of the neomilitarism of Chiang Kai-shek, the imperialists are trying to threaten the national government. *But supported by the combined forces of the town and village democracy, that is, the proletariat, the peasantry and the petty bourgeoisie, the national government will be in a position to rebuff the attack by imperialism and to develop the national revolution in a direction which will lead to the consolidation of its base in the popular masses.* Then the national revolution will be rid of the dangers of betrayal by reactionary elements, and its victory will be assured.

> DOWN WITH CHIANG KAI-SHEKISM
> DOWN WITH THE COUNTERREVOLUTIONARY FEUDAL BOURGEOISIE!
> DOWN WITH IMPERIALISM!
> LONG LIVE THE NATIONAL GOVERNMENT!
> LONG LIVE THE KUOMINTANG!

Delegation of the Communist International in China
Hankow, April 22, 1927

At the time Chiang Kai-shek was moving northwards with his army, communists were active in a number of capacities. There were those who organized strikes and insurrections in the cities following an orthodox Marxian guideline. Others conducted campaigns in the rural areas among the peasants of the central provinces. At least one investigation of such peasant revolutionary activities, "Report on an Investigation of the Peasant Movement in Hunan" by Mao Tse-tung came up with astounding conclusions. The peasants in action, according to Mao, were more revolutionary and effective in their activities than other segments of the Chinese population. For Mao the question was whether the Chinese intellectuals who had set themselves up as leaders of a Chinese revolution were willing to recognize the masses of illiterate peasants as true revolutionary forces capable of challenging traditional Chinese institutions. From his observations, the peasants on their own were advancing in a revolutionary direction and the intelligentsia had the choice of acknowledging this and leading them or losing the initiative and ending up behind them.

Peasant uprisings were not new to China. Historians point to the innumerable changes of dynasty that were the result of peasant movements, and Mao, it has been observed, was from early childhood brought up on the legends of peasant rebellions. But there was a new element in Mao's formulation, one that won for him the wrath of two important groups of people: (1) the orthodox members of both the Communist International and the Chinese Communist Party and (2) the broad range of Chinese intellectuals who to this day are wary of the uneducated masses of peasants. The novel element of Mao's proposition was that the intellectual elite (sons of gentry) should not only learn from the peasants the techniques of revolution but that they should join them, work amongst them, in order to become a part of that China from which they had always remained aloof.

It should be stressed that the importance of fostering a "rural revolution" was not original with Mao. (A great deal of debate has centered on this issue.) The Comintern directives emanating from the Soviet Union before 1927 had adopted the official position of recognizing the agricultural problems in "backward" societies and went so far as to explicitly warn the Chinese revolutionaries not to overlook them. But this policy remained on the books, the central focus of activities continued to be the miniscule urban proletariat. While "orthodox" members of the Communist Party paid lip service to the notion of a rural revolution, Mao Tse-tung took it to heart and emphasized the immediacy of acting on it.

On account of Mao's enthusiastic reliance on the peasantry's central role in the Chinese revolution (and, of course, his base of operations in the hinterland throughout most of the revo-

lutionary period) he was thought of at one time as simply an agrarian revolutionary. Mao's writings (Maoism) as Marxist "theory" have been attacked as "heretical" for similar reasons. It is interesting, therefore, to discover that not only in this early article but also in his later writings, Mao Tse-tung never actually substituted the peasantry for the working-class as "vanguard of the proletarian revolution." The Party, he carefully reiterates time and again, must be a working-class party. How, then, reconcile a hypothetical working-class Party with the fact that its membership is constituted of peasants? One answer is that Mao has always exhibited a capacity to play revolution as much by "ear" as by doctrine. Another clue and one which pays greater homage to the man as a Marxist theoretician is that Mao in his later writings evolves a conception, though never explicitly, of "the Party" as an instrument for the socialization of peasants into revolutionary proletarians. In the selection following this, "On Correcting Mistaken Ideas in the Party," written in 1929, there is a first hint of the problems faced by a Communist Party (and army) whose recruits are illiterate peasants bringing with them the attitudes and behavior of life in traditional China. The education they receive through apprenticeship in the "movement," which includes Party and Army, is "political" which in Communist argot means learning new ways of thinking about the whole range of human activities they are engaged in other than fighting, i.e., the militaristic approach.

The following excerpt is from Mao's "Report" which, although it is instructive in its own right, remains the center of a great deal of controversy over the relative "heresy" or "orthodoxy" of Maoism.

Report on an Investigation of the Peasant Movement in Hunan,* March 1927

MAO TSE-TUNG

THE IMPORTANCE OF THE PEASANT PROBLEM

During my recent visit to Hunan I made a first-hand investigation of conditions in the five counties of Hsiangtan, Hsianghsiang, Hengshan, Liling and Changsha. In the thirty-two days from January 4 to February 5, I called together fact-

* Mao Tse-tung excerpts from "Report on an Investigation of the Peasant Movement in Hunan," SELECTED WORKS, vol. I, (Peking: Foreign Languages Press, 1954), pp. 23–34.

finding conferences in villages and county towns, which were attended by experienced peasants and by comrades working in the peasant movement, and I listened attentively to their reports and collected a great deal of material. Many of the hows and whys of the peasant movement were the exact opposite of what the gentry in Hankow and Changsha are saying. I saw and heard of many strange things of which I had hitherto been unaware. I believe the same is true of many other places, too. All talk directed against the peasant movement must be speedily set right. All the wrong measures taken by the revolutionary authorities concerning the peasant movement must be speedily changed. Only thus can the future of the revolution be benefited. For the present upsurge of the peasant movement is a colossal event. In a very short time, in China's central, southern and northern provinces, several hundred million peasants will rise like a mighty storm, like a hurricane, a force so swift and violent that no power, however great, will be able to hold it back. They will smash all the trammels that bind them and rush forward along the road to liberation. They will sweep all the imperialists, warlords, corrupt officials, local tyrants and evil gentry into their graves. Every revolutionary party and every revolutionary comrade will be put to the test, to be accepted or rejected as they decide. There are three alternatives. To march at their head and lead them? To trail behind them, gesticulating and criticizing? Or to stand in their way and oppose them? Every Chinese is free to choose, but events will force you to make the choice quickly.

GET ORGANIZED!

The development of the peasant movement in Hunan may be divided roughly into two periods with respect to the counties in the province's central and southern parts where the movement has already made much headway. The first, from January to September of last year, was one of organization. In this period, January to June was a time of underground activity, and July to September, when the revolutionary army was driving out Chao Heng-ti, one of open activity. During this period, the membership of the peasant associations did not exceed 300,000-400,000, the masses directly under their leadership numbered little more than a million, there was as yet hardly any struggle in the rural areas, and consequently there was very little criticism of the associations in other circles. Since its members served as guides, scouts and carriers of the Northern Expeditionary Army, even some of the officers had a good word to say for the peasant associations. The second period, from last October to January of this year, was one of revolutionary action. The membership of the associations jumped to two million and the masses directly under their leadership increased to ten million. Since the peasants generally enter only one name for the whole family on joining a peasant association, a membership of two million means a mass following of about ten million. Almost half the peasants in Hunan are now organized. In counties like Hsiangtan, Hsianghsiang, Liuyang, Changsha, Liling, Ninghsiang, Pingkiang, Hsiangyin, Hengshan, Hengyang, Leiyang, Chenhsien and Anhua, nearly all the peasants have combined in the peasant associations or have come under their leadership. It was on the strength of their extensive organization that the peasants went into action and within four months brought about a great revolution in the countryside, a revolution without parallel in history.

DOWN WITH THE LOCAL TYRANTS AND EVIL GENTRY! ALL POWER TO THE PEASANT ASSOCIATIONS!

The main targets of attack by the peasants are the local tyrants, the evil gentry and the lawless landlords, but in passing they also hit out against patriarchal ideas and institutions, against the corrupt officials in the cities and against bad practices and customs in the rural areas. In force and momentum the attack is tempestuous; those who bow before it survive and those who resist perish. As a result, the privileges which the feudal landlords enjoyed for thousands of years are being shattered to pieces. Every bit of the dignity and prestige built up by the landlords is being swept into the dust. With the collapse of the power of the landlords, the peasant associations have now become the sole organs of authority and the popular slogan "All power to the peasant associations" has become a reality. Even trifles such as a quarrel between husband and wife are brought to the peasant association. Nothing can be settled unless someone from the peasant association is present. The association actually dictates all rural affairs, and, quite literally, "whatever it says, goes." Those who are outside the associations can only speak well of them and cannot say anything against them. The local tyrants, evil gentry and lawless landlords have been deprived of all right to speak, and none of them dares even mutter dissent. In the face of the peasant associations' power and pressure, the top local tyrants and evil gentry have fled to Shanghai, those of the second rank to Hankow, those of the third to Changsha and those of the fourth to the county towns, while the fifth rank and the still lesser fry surrender to the peasant associations in the villages.

"Here's ten yuan. Please let me join the peasant association," one of the smaller of the evil gentry will say.

"Ugh! Who wants your filthy money?" the peasants reply.

Many middle and small landlords and rich peasants and even some middle peasants, who were all formerly opposed to the peasant associations, are now vainly seeking admission. Visiting various places, I often came across such people who pleaded with me, "Mr. Committeeman from the provincial capital, please be my sponsor!" . . .

In short, what was looked down upon four months ago as a "gang of peasants" has now become a most honourable institution. Those who formerly prostrated themselves before the power of the gentry now bow before the power of the peasants. No matter what their identity, all admit that the world since last October is a different one.

"IT'S TERRIBLE!" OR "IT'S FINE!"

The peasants' revolt disturbed the gentry's sweet dreams. When the news from the countryside reached the cities, it caused immediate uproar among the gentry. Soon after my arrival in Changsha, I met all sorts of people and picked up a good deal of gossip. From the middle social strata upwards to the Kuomintang right-wingers, there was not a single person who did not sum up the whole business in the phrase, "It's terrible!" Under the impact of the views of the "It's terrible!" school then flooding the city, even quite revolutionary-minded people became down-hearted as they pictured the events in the countryside in their mind's eye; and they were unable to deny the word "terrible." Even quite progressive people said, "Though terrible, it is inevitable in a revolution." In short, nobody could altogether deny the word "terrible." But, as already mentioned, the fact is that the great peasant masses have risen to fulfill their historic mission and that the forces of rural democracy have risen to overthrow the forces of rural feudalism. The patriarchal-feudal class of local tyrants, evil gentry and lawless landlords has formed the basis of autocratic government for thousands of years and is the cornerstone of imperialism, warlordism and corrupt officialdom. To overthrow these feudal forces is the real objective of the national revolution. In a few months the peasants have accomplished what Dr. Sun Yat-sen wanted, but failed, to accomplish in the forty years he devoted to the national revolution. This is a marvellous feat never before achieved, not just in forty, but in thousands of years. It's fine. It is not "terrible" at all. It is anything but "terrible." "It's terrible!" is obviously a theory for combating the rise of the peasants in the interests of the landlords; it is obviously a theory of the landlord class for preserving the old order of feudalism and obstructing the establishment of the new order of democracy, it is obviously a counter-revolutionary theory. No revolutionary comrade should echo this nonsense. If your revolutionary viewpoint is firmly established and if you have been to the villages and looked around, you will undoubtedly feel thrilled as never before. Countless thousands of the enslaved—the peasants—are striking down the enemies who battened on their flesh. What the peasants are doing is absolutely right; what they are doing is fine! "It's fine!" is the theory of the peasants and of all other revolutionaries. Every revolutionary comrade should know that the national revolution requires a great change in the countryside. The Revolution of 1911 did not bring about this change, hence its failure. This change is now taking place, and it is an important factor for the completion of the revolution. Every revolutionary comrade must support it, or he will be taking the stand of counter-revolution.

THE QUESTION OF "GOING TOO FAR"

Then there is another section of people who say, "Yes, peasant associations are necessary, but they are going rather too far." This is the opinion of the middle-of-the-roaders. But what is the actual situation? True, the peasants are in a sense "unruly" in the countryside. Supreme in authority, the peasant association allows the landlord no say and sweeps away his prestige. This amounts to striking the landlord down to the dust and keeping him there. They fine the local tyrants and evil gentry, they demand contributions from them, and they smash their sedan-chairs. People swarm into the houses of local tyrants and evil gentry who are against the peasant association, slaughter their pigs and consume their grain. They even loll for a minute or two on the ivory-inlaid beds belonging to the young ladies in the households of the local tyrants and evil gentry. At the slightest provocation they make arrests, crown the arrested with tall paperhats, and parade them through the villages, saying, "You dirty landlords, now you know who we are!" Doing whatever they like and turning everything upside down, they have created a kind of terror in the countryside. This is what some people call "going too far," or "exceeding the proper limits in righting a wrong," or "really too much." Such talk may seem plausible, but in fact it is wrong. First, the local tyrants, evil gentry and lawless landlords have themselves driven the peasants to this. For ages they have used their power to tyrannize over the peasants and trample them underfoot; that is why the peasants have reacted so strongly. The most violent revolts and the most serious disorders have invariably occurred in places where the local tyrants, evil gentry and lawless landlords perpetrated the worst outrages. The peasants are clear-sighted. Who is bad and who is not, who is the worst and who is not quite so vicious, who deserves severe punishment and who deserves to be let off lightly—the peasants keep clear accounts, and very seldom has the punishment exceeded the crime. Secondly, a revolution is not a dinner party, or writing an essay, or painting a picture, or doing embroidery; it cannot be so refined, so leisurely and gentle, so temperate, kind, courteous, restrained and magnanimous. A revolution is an insurrection, an act of violence by which one class overthrows another. A rural revolution is a revolution by which the peasantry overthrows the power of the feudal landlord class. Without using the greatest force, the peasants cannot possibly overthrow the deep-rooted authority of the landlords which has lasted for thousands of years. The rural areas need a mighty revolutionary upsurge, for it alone can rouse the people in their millions to become a powerful force. All the actions mentioned here which have been labelled as "going too far" flow from the power of the peasants, which has been called forth by the mighty revolutionary upsurge in the countryside. It was highly necessary for such things to be done in the second period of the peasant movement, the period of revolutionary action. In this period it was necessary to establish the absolute authority of the peasants. It was necessary to forbid malicious criticism of the peasant associations. It was necessary to overthrow the whole authority of the gentry, to strike them to the ground and keep them there. There is revolutionary significance in all the actions which were labelled as "going too far" in this period. To put it bluntly, it is necessary to create terror for a while in every rural area, or otherwise it would be impossible to suppress the activities of the counter-revolutionaries in the countryside or overthrow the authority of the gentry. Proper limits have to be exceeded in order to right a wrong, or else the wrong cannot be righted. Those who talk about the peasants "going too far" seem at first sight to be different from those who say "It's terrible!" as mentioned earlier, but in essence they proceed from the same standpoint and likewise voice a landlord theory that upholds the interests of the privileged classes. Since this theory impedes the rise of the peasant movement and so disrupts the revolution, we must firmly oppose it.

THE "MOVEMENT OF THE RIFFRAFF"

The right-wing of the Kuomintang says, "The peasant movement is a movement of the riffraff, of the lazy peasants." This view is current in Changsha. When I was in the countryside, I heard the gentry say, "It is all right to set up peasant associations, but the people now running them are no good. They ought to be replaced!" This opinion comes to the same thing as what the right-wingers are saying; according to both it is all right to have a peasant movement (the movement is already in being and no one dare say otherwise), but they say that the people running it are no good and they particularly hate those in charge of the associations at the lower levels, calling them "riffraff." In short, all those whom the gentry had despised, those whom they had trodden into the dirt, people with no place in society, people with no right to speak, have now audaciously lifted up their heads. They have not only lifted up their heads but taken power into their hands. They are now running the township peasant associations (at the lowest level), which they have turned into something fierce and formidable. They have raised their rough, work-soiled hands and laid them on the gentry. They tether the evil gentry with ropes, crown them with tall paper-hats and parade them through the villages. (In Hsiangtan and Hsianghsiang they call this "parading through the township" and in Liling "parading through the fields.") Not a day passes but they drum some harsh, pitiless words of denunciation into these gentry's ears. They are issuing orders and are running everything. Those who used to rank lowest now rank above everybody else; and so this is called "turning things upside down."

VANGUARDS OF THE REVOLUTION

Where there are two opposite approaches to things and people, two opposite views emerge. "It's terrible!" and "It's fine!", "riffraff" and "vanguards of the revolution"—here are apt examples.

We said above that the peasants have accomplished a revolutionary task which had been left unaccomplished for many years and have done an important job for the national revolution. But has this great revolutionary task, this important revolutionary work, been performed by all the peasants? No. There are three kinds of peasants, the rich, the middle and the poor peasants. The three live in different circumstances and so have different views about the revolution. In the first period, what appealed to the rich peasants was the talk about the Northern Expeditionary Army's sustaining a crushing defeat in Kiangsi, about Chiang Kai-shek's being wounded in the leg and flying back to Kwangtung, and about Wu Pei-fu's recapturing Yuehchow. The peasant associations would certainly not last and the Three People's Principles could never prevail, because they had never been heard of before. Thus an official of the township peasant association (generally one of the "riffraff" type) would walk into the house of a rich peasant, register in hand, and say, "Will you please join the peasant association?" How would the rich peasant answer? A tolerably well-behaved one would say, "Peasant association? I have lived here for decades, tilling my land. I never heard of such a thing before, yet I've managed to live all right. I advise you to give it up!" A really vicious rich peasant would say, "Peasant association! Nonsense! Association for getting your head chopped off! Don't get people into trouble!" Yet, surprisingly enough, the peasant associations have now been established several months, and have even dared to stand up to the gentry. The gentry of the neighbourhood who refused to surrender their opium pipes were arrested by the associations and paraded through the villages. In the county towns, moreover, some big landlords were put to death, like Yen Jung-chiu of Hsiangtan and Yang Chih-tse of Ninghsiang. On the anniversary of the October Revolution, at the time of the anti-British rally and of the great celebrations of the victory of the Northern Expedition, tens of thousands of peasants in every township, holding high their banners, big and small, along with their carrying-poles and hoes, demonstrated in massive, streaming columns. It was only then that the rich peasants began to get perplexed and alarmed. During the great victory celebrations of the Northern Expedition, they learned that Kiukiang had been taken, that Chiang Kai-shek had not been wounded in the leg and that Wu Pei-fu had been defeated after all. What is more, they saw such slogans as "Long live the Three People's Principles!" "Long live the peasant associations!" and "Long live the peasants!" clearly written on the "red and green proclamations." "What?" wondered the rich peasants, greatly perplexed and alarmed, " 'Long live the peasants!' Are these people now to be regarded as emperors?" So the peasant associations are putting on grand airs.

People from the associations say to the rich peasants, "In another month, the admission fee will be ten yuan a head!" Only under the impact of all this are the rich peasants tardily joining the associations, some paying fifty cents or a yuan for admission (the regular fee being a mere ten coppers), some securing admission only after asking other people to put in a good word for them. But there are quite a number of diehards who have not joined to this day. When the rich peasants join the associations, they generally enter the name of some sixty or seventy year-old member of the family, for they are in constant dread of "conscription." After joining, the rich peasants are not keen on doing any work for the associations. They remain inactive throughout.

How about the middle peasants? Theirs is a vacillating attitude. They think that the revolution will not bring them much good. They have rice cooking in their pots and no creditors knocking on their doors at midnight. They, too, judging a thing by whether it ever existed before, knit their brows and think to themselves, "Can the peasant association really last?" "Can the Three People's Principles prevail?" Their conclusion is, "Afraid not!" They imagine it all depends on the will of Heaven and think, "A peasant association? Who knows if Heaven wills it or not?" In the first period, people from the association would call on a middle peasant, register in hand, and say, "Will you please join the peasant association?" The middle peasant would reply, "There's no hurry!" It was not until the second period, when the peasant associations were already exercising great power, that the middle peasants came in. They show up better in the associations than the rich peasants but are not as yet very enthusiastic; they still want to wait and see. It is essential for the peasant associations to get the middle peasants to join and to do a good deal more explanatory work among them.

The poor peasants have always been the main force in the bitter fight in the countryside. They have fought militantly through the two periods of underground work and of open activity. They are the most responsive to Communist Party leadership. They are deadly enemies of the camp of the local tyrants and evil gentry and attack it without the slightest hesitation. "We joined the peasant association long ago," they say to the rich peasants, "why are you still hesitating?" The rich peasants answer mockingly, "What is there to keep you from joining? You people have neither a tile over your heads nor a speck of land under your feet!" It is true the poor peasants are not afraid of losing anything. Many of them really have "neither a tile over their heads nor a speck of land under their feet." What, indeed, is there to keep them from joining the associations? According to the survey of Changsha County, the poor peasants comprise 70 per cent, the middle peasants 20 per cent, and the landlords and the rich peasants 10 per cent of the population in the rural areas. The 70 per cent, the poor peasants, may be sub-divided into two categories, the utterly destitute and the less destitute. The utterly destitute, comprising 20 per cent, are the completely dispossessed, that is, people who have neither land nor money, are without any means of livelihood, and are forced to leave home and become mercenaries or hired labourers or wandering beggars. The less destitute, the other 50 per cent, are the partially dispossessed, that is, people with just a little land or a little money who eat up more than they earn and live in toil and distress the year round, such as the handicraftsmen, the tenant-peasants (not including the rich tenant-peasants) and the semi-owner-peasants. This great mass of poor peasants, or altogether 70 per cent of the rural population, are the backbone of the peasant associations, the vanguard in the overthrow of the feudal forces and the heroes who have performed the great revolutionary task which for long years was left undone. Without the poor peasant class (the "riffraff," as the gentry call them), it would have been impossible to bring about the present revolutionary situation in the countryside, or to overthrow the local tyrants and evil gentry and complete the democratic revolution. The poor peasants, being the most revolutionary group, have gained the leadership of the peasant associations. In both the first and second periods almost all the chairmen and committee members in the peasant associations at the lowest level were poor peasants (of the officials in the township associations in Hengshan County the utterly destitute comprise 50 per cent, the less destitute 40 per cent, and poverty-stricken intellectuals 10 per cent). Leadership by the poor peasants is absolutely necessary. Without the poor peasants there would be no revolution. To deny their role is to deny the revolution. To attack them is to attack the revolution. They have never been wrong on the general direction of the revolution. They have discredited the local tyrants and evil gentry. They have beaten down the local tyrants and evil gentry, big and small, and kept them underfoot. Many of their deeds in the period of revolutionary action, which were labelled as "going too far," were in fact the very things the revolution required. Some county governments, county headquarters of the Kuomintang and county peasant associations in Hunan have already made a number of mistakes; some have even sent soldiers to arrest officials of the lower-level associations at the landlords' request. A good many chairmen and committee members of township associations in Hengshan and Hsianghsiang Counties have been thrown in jail. This mistake is very serious and feeds the arrogance of the reactionaries. To judge whether or not it is a mistake, you have only to see how joyful the lawless landlords become and how reactionary sentiments grow, wherever the chairmen or committee members of local peasant associations are arrested. We must combat the counter-revolutionary talk of a "movement of riffraff" and a "movement of lazy peasants" and must be especially careful not to commit the error of helping the local tyrants and evil gentry in their attacks on the poor peasant class. Though a few of the poor peasant leaders undoubtedly did have shortcomings, most of them have changed by now. They themselves are energetically prohibiting gambling and suppressing banditry. Where the peasant association is powerful, gambling has stopped altogether and banditry has vanished. In some places it is literally true that people do not take any articles left by the wayside and that doors are not bolted at night. According to the Hengshan survey, 85 per cent of the poor peasant leaders have made great progress and have proved themselves capable and hardworking. Only 15 per cent retain some bad habits. The most one can call these is "an unhealthy minority," and we must not echo the local tyrants and evil gentry in undiscriminatingly condemning them as "riffraff." This problem of the "unhealthy minority" can be tackled only under the peasant associations' own slogan of "strengthen discipline," by carrying on propaganda among the masses, by educating the "unhealthy minority," and by tightening the associations' discipline; in no circumstances should soldiers be arbitrarily sent to make such arrests as would damage the prestige of the poor peasants and feed the arrogance of the local tyrants and evil gentry. This point requires particular attention. . . .

> In the following selection Mao Tse-tung attacked some of the problems faced by the Party and the Army in the early days when recruits brought with them the attitudes and behavior of life in "traditional China."
>
> The general theme, that politics is more important than simply the militaristic approach, i.e., fighting, is one that is

paramount today in the cultural revolution. This is emphasized by the fact that this article is currently being reprinted and used as basic "reading."

On Correcting Mistaken Ideas in the Party
December 1929*

MAO TSE-TUNG

THERE ARE various non-proletarian ideas in the Communist Party organization in the Fourth Red Army which greatly hinder the application of the Party's correct line. Unless these ideas are thoroughly corrected, the Fourth Army cannot possibly shoulder the tasks assigned to it in China's great revolutionary struggle. The source of such incorrect ideas in this Party organization lies, of course, in the fact that its basic units are composed largely of peasants and other elements of petty-bourgeois origin; yet the failure of the Party's leading bodies to wage a concerted and determined struggle against these incorrect ideas and to educate the members in the Party's correct line is also an important cause of their existence and growth. In accordance with the spirit of the September letter of the Central Committee, this congress hereby points out the manifestations of various non-proletarian ideas in the Party organization in the Fourth Army, their sources, and the methods of correcting them, and calls upon all comrades to eliminate them thoroughly.

ON THE PURELY MILITARY VIEWPOINT

The purely military viewpoint is very highly developed among a number of comrades in the Red Army. It manifests itself as follows:

1. These comrades regard military affairs and politics as opposed to each other and refuse to recognize that military affairs are only one means of accomplishing political tasks. Some even say, "If you are good militarily, naturally you are good politically; if you are not good militarily, you cannot be any good politically"—this is to go a step further and give military affairs a leading position over politics.

2. They think that the task of the Red Army, like that of the White army, is merely to fight. They do not understand that the Chinese Red Army is an armed body for carrying out the political tasks of the revolution. Especially at present, the

* Mao Tse-tung, "On Correcting Mistaken Ideas in the Party," SELECTED WORKS, op. cit., vol. I, pp. 105–115.

Red Army should certainly not confine itself to fighting; besides fighting to destroy the enemy's military strength, it should shoulder such important tasks as doing propaganda among the masses, organizing the masses, arming them, helping them to establish revolutionary political power and setting up Party organizations. The Red Army fights not merely for the sake of fighting but in order to conduct propaganda among the masses, organize them, arm them, and help them to establish revolutionary political power. Without these objectives, fighting loses its meaning and the Red Army loses the reason for its existence.

3. Hence, organizationally, these comrades subordinate the departments of the Red Army doing political work to those doing military work, and put forward the slogan, "Let Army Headquarters handle outside matters." If allowed to develop, this idea would involve the danger of estrangement from the masses, control of the government by the army and departure from proletarian leadership—it would be to take the path of warlordism like the Kuomintang army.

4. At the same time, in propaganda work they overlook the importance of propaganda teams. On the question of mass organization, they neglect the organizing of soldiers' committees in the army and the organizing of the local workers and peasants. As a result, both propaganda and organizational work are abandoned.

5. They become conceited when a battle is won and dispirited when a battle is lost.

6. Selfish departmentalism—they think only of the Fourth Army and do not realize that it is an important task of the Red Army to arm the local masses. This is cliquism in a magnified form.

7. Unable to see beyond their limited environment in the Fourth Army, a few comrades believe that no other revolutionary forces exist. Hence their extreme addiction to the idea of conserving strength and avoiding action. This is a remnant of opportunism.

8. Some comrades, disregarding the subjective and objective conditions, suffer from the malady of revolutionary impetuosity; they will not take pains to do minute and detailed work among the masses, but, riddled with illusions, want only to do big things. . . .

The sources of the purely military viewpoint are:

1. A low political level. From this flows the failure to recognize the role of political leadership in the army and to recognize that the Red Army and the White army are fundamentally different.

2. The mentality of mercenaries. Many prisoners captured in past battles have joined the Red Army, and such elements bring with them a markedly mercenary outlook, thereby providing a basis in the lower ranks for the purely military viewpoint.

3. From the two preceding causes there arises a third, overconfidence in military strength and absence of confidence in the strength of the masses of the people.

4. The Party's failure actively to attend to and discuss military work is also a reason for the emergence of the purely military viewpoint among a number of comrades.

The methods of correction are as follows:

1. Raise the political level in the Party by means of education, destroy the theoretical roots of the purely military viewpoint, and be clear on the fundamental difference between the Red Army and the White army. . . .

2. Intensify the political training of officers and men and especially the education of ex-prisoners. . . .

3. Arouse the local Party organizations to criticize the Party organizations in the Red Army and the organs of mass political power to criticize the Red Army itself, in order to influence the Party organizations and the officers and men of the Red Army.

4. The Party must actively attend to and discuss military work. All the work must be discussed and decided upon by the Party before being carried out by the rank and file.

5. Draw up Red Army rules and regulations which clearly define its tasks, the relationship between its military and its political apparatus, the relationship between the Red Army and the masses of the people, and the powers and functions of the soldiers' committees and their relationship with the military and political organizations.

ON ULTRA-DEMOCRACY

Since the Fourth Army of the Red Army accepted the directives of the Central Committee, there has been a great decrease in the manifestations of ultra-democracy. . . . Actually, however, this decrease is only temporary and superficial and does not mean that ultra-democratic ideas have already been eliminated. . . .

The methods of correction are as follows:

1. In the sphere of theory, destroy the roots of ultra-democracy. First, it should be pointed out that the danger of ultra-democracy lies in the fact that it damages or even completely wrecks the Party organization and weakens or even

completely undermines the Party's fighting capacity, rendering the Party incapable of fulfilling its fighting tasks and thereby causing the defeat of the revolution. . . .

2. In the sphere of organization, ensure democracy under centralized guidance. It should be done on the following lines:

(1) The leading bodies of the Party must give a correct line of guidance and find solutions when problems arise, in order to establish themselves as centres of leadership.

(2) The higher bodies must be familiar with the life of the masses and with the situation in the lower bodies so as to have an objective basis for correct guidance.

(3) No Party organization at any level should make casual decisions in solving problems. Once a decision is reached, it must be firmly carried out.

(4) All decisions of any importance made by the Party's higher bodies must be promptly transmitted to the lower bodies and the Party rank and file. The method is to call meetings of activists or general membership meetings of the Party branches or even of the columns (when circumstances permit) and to assign people to make reports at such meetings.

(5) The lower bodies of the Party and the Party rank and file must discuss the higher bodies' directives in detail in order to understand their meaning thoroughly and decide on the methods of carrying them out.

ON THE DISREGARD OF ORGANIZATIONAL DISCIPLINE

Disregard of organizational discipline in the Party organization in the Fourth Army manifests itself as follows:

A. Failure of the minority to submit to the majority. For example, when a minority finds its motion voted down, it does not sincerely carry out the Party decisions.

The methods of correction are as follows:

1. At meetings, all participants should be encouraged to voice their opinions as fully as possible. The rights and wrongs in any controversy should be clarified without compromise or glossing over. In order to reach a clear-cut conclusion, what cannot be settled at one meeting should be discussed at another, provided there is no interference with the work.

2. One requirement of Party discipline is that the minority should submit to the majority. If the view of the minority has been rejected, it must support the decision passed by the majority. If necessary, it can bring up the matter for reconsideration at the next meeting, but apart from that it must not act against the decision in any way. . . .

ON ABSOLUTE EQUALITARIANISM

Absolute equalitarianism became quite serious in the Red Army at one time. Here are some examples. On the matter of allowances to wounded soldiers, there were objections to differentiating between light and serious cases, and the demand was raised for equal allowances for all. When officers rode on horseback, it was regarded not as something necessary for performing their duties but as a sign of inequality. Absolutely equal distribution of supplies was demanded, and there was objection to somewhat larger allotments in special cases. In the hauling of rice, the demand was made that all should carry the same load on their backs, irrespective of age or physical condition. Equality was demanded in the allotment of billets, and the Headquarters would be abused for occupying larger rooms. Equality was demanded in the assignment of fatigue duties, and there was unwillingness to do a little more than the next man. It even went so far that when there were two wounded men but only one stretcher, neither could be carried away because each refused to yield priority to the other. Absolute equalitarianism, as shown in these examples, is still very serious among officers and soldiers of the Red Army. . . .

The method of correction: We should point out that, before the abolition of capitalism, absolute equalitarianism is a mere illusion of peasants and small proprietors, and that even under socialism there can be no absolute equality, for material things will then be distributed on the principle of "from each according to his ability, to each according to his work" as well as on that of meeting the needs of the work. The distribution of material things in the Red Army must be more or less equal, as in the case of equal pay for officers and men, because this is required by the present circumstances of the struggle. But absolute equalitarianism beyond reason must be opposed because it is not required by the struggle; on the contrary, it hinders the struggle. . . .

ON INDIVIDUALISM

The tendency towards individualism in the Red Army Party organization manifests itself as follows:

1. Retaliation. Some comrades, after being criticized inside the Party by a soldier comrade, look for opportunities to retaliate outside the Party, and one way is to beat or abuse the comrade in question. They also seek to retaliate within the Party. "You have criticized me at this meeting, so I'll find some way to pay you back at the next." Such retaliation arises

from purely personal considerations, to the neglect of the interests of the class and of the Party as a whole. . . .

2. "Small group" mentality. Some comrades consider only the interests of their own small group and ignore the general interest. . . .

3. The "employee" mentality. Some comrades do not understand that the Party and the Red Army, of which they are members, are both instruments for carrying out the tasks of the revolution. They do not realize that they themselves are makers of the revolution, but think that their responsibility is merely to their individual superiors and not to the revolution. This passive mentality of an "employee" of the revolution is also a manifestation of individualism. . . .

4. Pleasure-seeking. In the Red Army there are also quite a few people whose individualism finds expression in pleasure-seeking. They always hope that their unit will march into big cities. They want to go there not to work but to enjoy themselves. The last thing they want is to work in the Red areas where life is hard.

5. Passivity. Some comrades become passive and stop working whenever anything goes against their wishes. This is mainly due to lack of education, though sometimes it is also due to the leadership's improper conduct of affairs, assignments of work or enforcement of discipline.

6. The desire to leave the army. The number of people who ask for transfers from the Red Army to local work is on the increase. The reason for this does not lie entirely with the individuals but also with: (1) the material hardships of life in the Red Army, (2) exhaustion after long struggle, and (3) the leadership's improper conduct of affairs, assignment of work or enforcement of discipline.

The method of correction is primarily to strengthen education so as to rectify individualism ideologically. Next, it is to conduct affairs, make assignments and enforce discipline in a proper way. In addition, ways must be found to improve the material life of the Red Army, and every available opportunity must be utilized for rest and rehabilitation in order to improve material conditions. In our educational work we must explain that in its social origin individualism is a reflection within the Party of petty-bourgeois and bourgeois ideas.

ON THE IDEOLOGY OF ROVING REBEL BANDS

The political ideology of roving rebel bands has emerged in the Red Army because the proportion of vagabond elements is large and because there are great masses of vagabonds in

China, especially in the southern provinces. This ideology manifests itself as follows: (1) Some people want to increase our political influence only by means of roving guerrilla actions, but are unwilling to increase it by undertaking the arduous task of building up base areas and establishing the people's political power. (2) In expanding the Red Army, some people follow the line of "hiring men and buying horses" and "recruiting deserters and accepting mutineers," rather than the line of expanding the local Red Guards and the local troops and thus developing the main forces of the Red Army. (3) Some people lack the patience to carry on arduous struggles together with the masses, and only want to go to the big cities to eat and drink to their hearts' content. All these manifestations of the ideology of roving rebels seriously hamper the Red Army in performing its proper tasks; consequently its eradication is an important objective in the ideological struggle within the Red Army Party organization. It must be understood that the ways of roving rebels of the Huang Chao[1] or Li Chuang[2] type are not permissible under present-day conditions.

The Kuomintang in Power (1928–1937)*

HAROLD C. HINTON

THE UNITY achieved in 1928 was much more nominal than real. The new government at Nanking controlled little more

* From "China" by Harold C. Hinton, in MAJOR GOVERNMENTS OF ASIA, edited by George McTurnan Kahin, 2nd edition, 1963. © 1958 and 1963 by Cornell University. Used by permission of Cornell University Press. Pp. 28–34.

[1] Huang Chao was the leader of the peasant revolts towards the end of the Tang Dynasty. In A.D. 875, starting from his home district Tsaochow (now Hotse County in Shantung), Huang led armed peasants in victorious battles against the imperial forces and styled himself the "Heaven-Storming General." In the course of a decade he swept over most of the provinces in the Yellow, Yangtse, Huai and Pearl river valleys, reaching as far as Kwangsi. He finally broke through the Tungkuan pass, captured the imperial capital of Changan (now Sian in Shensi), and was crowned Emperor of Chi. Internal dissensions and attacks by the non-Han tribal allies of the Tang forces compelled Huang to abandon Changan and retreat to his native district, where he committed suicide. The ten years' war fought by him is one of the most famous peasant wars in Chinese history. Dynastic historians record that "all people suffering from heavy taxes and levies rallied to him." But as he merely carried on roving warfare without ever establishing relatively consolidated base areas, his forces were called "roving rebel bands."

[2] Li Chuang, short for Li Tzu-cheng the King Chuang (the Dare-All King), native of Michih, northern Shensi, was the leader of a peasant revolt which led to the overthrow of the Ming Dynasty.

than the eastern provinces; elsewhere, especially in Southwest and Northwest China, provincial or regional militarists still exercised effective power. The Kuomintang was never able to subdue some of these militarists; instead, it generally followed a policy of giving them high military and political posts in their own provinces or regions, in the hope of securing their loyalty. The support purchased in this way resulted in little of actual value, for some of these generals proved unreliable against the Japanese and still later proved unreliable against the Communists.

After the failure of a disarmament conference in 1929 showed how unwilling the regional militarists were to subordinate themselves in fact to the National Government, there occurred a series of revolts against the power and policies of Chiang Kai-shek. Only the most serious of these need be mentioned. In 1929 there was a revolt by the so-called Kwangsi Clique led by Li Tsung-jen and Pai Chung-hsi; in 1930, one by a formidable combination of Feng Yu-hsiang, Yen Hsi-shan (the warlord of Shansi), and Wang Ching-wei (a prominent Left Kuomintang leader); in 1931, one by a group of Left Kuomintang politicians at Canton; in 1933, one by (non-Communist) Left Kuomintang generals and politicians in Fukien; and in 1936, another by the Kwangsi Clique. Chiang overcame all these revolts by force or diplomacy. His army, trained by German advisers, was easily the strongest in China, although it could not eliminate Chiang's most dangerous and elusive enemies, the Communists.

From having been a decidedly revolutionary party under Sun Yat-sen and during the brief life of its alliance with the Communists, the Kuomintang after 1927 rapidly turned into a conservative and even reactionary party. Under Chiang Kai-shek's stultifying influence it ceased to produce able, prominent, and original political thinkers, and therefore had no choice but to deify Sun Yat-sen and his ideas and parrot them without developing them further. Since Sun's political ideas had serious weaknesses, the uncritical propagation of them, combined with a rejection of the generous spirit which had been behind Sun's ideas, imparted to the Kuomintang a rigid and unattractive quality which tended to minimize popular support for it. Chiang Kai-shek and other prominent Kuomintang figures began to preach a return to the ancient Confucian virtues of loyalty, propriety, and the like, ideas which no longer held compelling appeal for a people becoming increasingly convinced of the possibility of and necessity for progress and modernization. One of the least attractive features of official

Kuomintang thinking was its strong tendency toward xeno-phobia; in Chiang Kai-shek's famous tract, *China's Destiny* (published in 1943), for example, almost all China's ills and problems are attributed to Western influence. This strong anti-Western feeling, although to some extent justified, had the effect of making the Western powers less enthusiastic than they would otherwise have been about supporting the National Government against Japanese encroachments.

Another source of weakness was the fact that, although it retained the "democratic centralist" organization imparted to it during the period of the Communist alliance, the Kuomintang was never truly a "monolithic" party of the Communist type. On the contrary, it was ridden with competing cliques whose selfish interests generally outweighed whatever loyalty to a common ideology, common party organization, and common cause they may have had. Basically, the Kuomintang was an unstable coalition of military leaders, businessmen, and rural landlords. More precisely, it was composed of the following major cliques.

On the extreme right stood the CC (or Organization) Clique, so called because it was controlled by the Ch'en brothers. The elder, Ch'en Kuo-fu, was the leading specialist in party organization and controlled most of the local party branches. He was therefore always in a strong position at the rather infrequent party congresses (there were six between 1924 and 1945), whose membership was elected by the local party organs. His younger brother, Ch'en Li-fu, was a leading party ideologist and specialist in education and public indoctrination. He preached a strange philosophy called Vitalism, which represented a blend of Confucianism with nineteenth-century European idealism and enjoyed a decidedly limited popularity. The CC Clique was strongly anti-Communist, dominant in the secret police, and very conservative in its views on social and economic questions.

Slightly less to the right stood the so-called Whampoa (or Military) Clique. Although also conservative and anti-Communist, this group was more concerned with problems of power than with party organization or ideology. Being specialists in force, the group generally held the balance of power in the party, which it did not, however, entirely dominate.

Another faction was the Political Science Clique. It was composed largely of bureaucrats and intellectuals devoted to the goal of modern and efficient administration, but without any clearly defined political program.

Apart from these cliques, there were two other groups

worth mentioning, though they were not well organized or very influential. The first was a handful of Left Kuomintang politicians, of whom Wang Ching-wei and Sun Yat-sen's son, Sun Fo, were the most prominent. The other group comprised a number of wealthy businessmen, Chiang Kai-shek's able but temperamental brother-in-law T. V. Soong being the best known.

The keystone in the entire arch of Kuomintang power was Chiang Kai-shek himself. He was by no means all-powerful or universally respected within the party, yet he alone commanded both enough power and enough loyalty to lead the party over a long period of time. Of humble origin, having close connections with the Shanghai underworld, militaristic by training and background, conservative by inclination, and intensely patriotic in a way which led him to consider the maintenance of his own power as essential to the good of the country, Chiang personified both the strengths and the weaknesses of the Kuomintang. A strong man himself, he could not tolerate disagreement from other strong men and preferred to surround himself with sycophants. Personally honest, he refused to credit, or at any rate to punish, the widespread and increasing corruption among his associates and subordinates. Even more addicted than other Kuomintang leaders to multiple office holding, he held a list of posts in the party, government, and armed forces so long that it would be tedious to reproduce it. If he lacked both the dictatorial power and the charismatic appeal of a Hitler, he was nevertheless a powerful party boss with a secret police force and an army at his disposal.

During the period under consideration, China's constitutional structure, like its political life, reflected the official view that the Kuomintang enjoyed a monopoly of legal political power. As early as 1928 the Kuomintang set up a central government containing five Yuan (branches) corresponding to the five envisioned by Sun Yat-sen: Executive, Legislative, Judicial, Examination, and Control. This was a departure from Sun Yat-sen's program, for Sun had intended the fivefold governmental structure to be introduced at the end, not at the beginning, of the period of Political Tutelage. In most other respects the regime established in 1928 conformed to Sun's plan. The officials of the five Yuan were appointed Kuomintang members whose work was supervised by the Central Executive Committee of the Kuomintang through one of its agencies, the Political Council. Among the Yuan themselves, the executive was by far the most important, though of course it was still bound by party directives. At the top of the government structure, though also subject to control by the Kuomintang, stood the State Council, whose chairman was the nearest thing China had to a chief of state. Provincial and local offices were appointive and controlled by the central government and the Kuomintang.

In 1931 a semblance of greater constitutionality was conferred on the National Government through the adoption, by a National People's Convention whose membership had been hand-picked by the Kuomintang, of a provisional constitution. The main change that this constitution made in the preexisting situation was that it decreased the powers of the chairman of the State Council, which post Chiang Kai-shek had just given up as a sop to his opponents, who were then very vocal. He continued, however, to be very powerful in the government, in the party, and (through his chairmanship of the Military Affairs Commission) in the armed forces. The provisional constitution contained no procedure for its own amendment and vested the important power of constitutional interpretation in the Central Executive Committee of the Kuomintang. It was, in short, a legalization of Political Tutelage.

With amazing optimism the Kuomintang had promised in 1929 to complete the tasks of Political Tutelage within six years, and accordingly as early as 1933 it began work on a draft constitution for the last stage, that of constitutional government. After numerous revisions the draft was published with the party's blessing in May 1936. Unfortunately, it had several serious defects. The Executive Yuan was to be responsible, not to the Legislative Yuan in the British manner, but to a large and infrequently convened National Assembly. The powers of the President of the Republic, the chief of state, who was to be elected by the National Assembly, were so broad that it seemed likely that he would dominate the five Yuan and their respective presidents. The powers of the provincial and local governments were insufficiently protected from possible encroachments by the central government, and civil liberties were subject to restriction by legislation. It was very probable that under this constitution the Kuomintang would continue to dominate the political life of the country. It did in fact dominate elections held in 1936 for the members of a National Assembly to which the draft constitution was to be submitted for consideration; the convening of the Assembly, however, was prevented by the outbreak of war with Japan in July 1937.

The question of how the National Government of China functioned in practice during the period from 1928 to 1937 is a very important one, for it was then that the Kuomintang had its best chance to show what it could do for China. It is true that Kuomintang was faced with enormous obstacles, such as a backward economy, domestic insurrections, and continuous Japanese pressure after 1931, but even when allowance is made for these difficulties its record remains far from impressive.

By 1937, and for that matter as late as 1949, not a single one of the 2,000-odd *hsien* in China had attained the state of local self-government that Sun Yat-sen had considered a prerequisite to the establishment of self-government on the provincial and national scales. Nor was the mere absence of self-government the worst feature of Political Tutelage. The latter also carried with it a rigorous punitive censorship of the press, a large network of secret police and prisons, and a massive "white terror" flourishing in the cities and towns and directed not only against real or suspected Communists but also against others to whose actions or statements the Kuomintang objected. In some rural areas, especially those reconquered from the Communists, the National Government introduced after the mid-1930s the oppressive *pao-chia* system of collective responsibility for the crimes of individuals. To propagandize its official ideals of obedience and propriety, the Kuomintang inaugurated in 1934 a so-called New Life Movement, which was, however, perhaps more comic than oppressive in its actual working.

Unfortunately, the absence of freedom was not compensated by any significant increase in efficiency or mitigated by any noteworthy progress in the social and economic fields. Much praiseworthy legislation was promulgated, but it remained largely on paper. This was true, for example, of a law of 1930 fixing maximum rents on agricultural land at three-eighths of the annual crop. The unfortunate effects of the Depression, which included an outflow of silver, led to the introduction of a managed currency in 1935, under which the right of note issue was profitably confined to four central banks controlled respectively by T. V. Soong, H. H. Kung, the Ch'en brothers, and Chiang Kai-shek. The Kuomintang's approach to economic questions, at least in practice, was essentially one of dipping its hand as often as possible into a stagnant pool of wealth rather than one of trying to stir up the pool and increase its size.

In the field of foreign affairs the Kuomintang was slightly more successful. By 1931 it had successfully asserted its right to fix its own tariff rates and was on the way to abolishing the extraterritorial rights of citizens of all but the major foreign powers (the United States, Great Britain, and Japan). But these successes were dearly won, for the extreme antiforeignism of the Kuomintang tended to alienate the Western powers and render them less sympathetic to China's case against its major enemy, Japan, than they might otherwise have been.

At the hands of Japan the Kuomintang suffered a long series of injuries and humiliations: the conquest of Manchuria in 1931–1932, an attack by the Japanese navy on the "native" city of Shanghai in 1932, the occupation of Jehol province and the forced demilitarization of the Peiping-Tientsin area in 1933, an unsuccessful attempt in 1935 to make five provinces of North China and Inner Mongolia "autonomous" and thus more susceptible to Japanese penetration, and an extraordinary set of demands in 1936 which if accepted would have transformed Nationalist China into a virtual Japanese protectorate.

Until 1936 the National Government's response to these outrages was one of temporizing, for it feared the power of the Japanese and in any case was more interested in trying to suppress the Communists. This negative policy served only to whet the Japanese appetite and to arouse further the indignation of the articulate Chinese public. In 1935 the chorus of protest, to which the Communists contributed a share but only a share, reached fever heat. Thereafter the Kuomintang was under increasing pressure to stop fighting the Communists and ally with them to resist the Japanese.

4

JAPANESE IMPERIALISM AND THE COMMUNIST ASCENDANCY

By 1936 Japan was embarked on a full-scale conquest of China, taking advantage of China's deteriorating internal situation. China was in the midst of a civil war between the Kuomintang and the Communists, with innumerable fragments of the first united front somewhere between the two. The split between the Communists and the Kuomintang had become more than a simple divergence over means of achieving the same end; it involved a basic conflict between two opposing objectives.

This division and the open struggle between the Nationalists and the Communists were related to internal changes within each of the Parties. The Communist Party under the leadership of nondoctrinaire radicals had taken to the rural areas for their base of operations while the Kuomintang under the firm grip of Chiang Kai-shek remained firmly ensconced in the foreign-dominated coastal cities. Both were nationalists but each had a different conception of what nationalism entailed. Both considered themselves heirs of Sun Yat-sen but each had a different substantive interpretation of Sun's legacy. The Communists were revolutionary foot soldiers who merged their vision of a distant future with the practicable needs of the peasants, while the Nationalists remained doctrinaire in their hostility to rural China and waged war on their opposition, the Communists.

The Chinese Communists, having survived first the annihilation campaigns launched against them by the Kuomintang and then the Long March (on foot) across China, had miraculously re-established themselves in the interior Northwest. There they settled, integrating and developing new communities. In addition to cultivating the land, organizing the population, and educating them the Communists were training an army in guerrilla tactics. They accepted the fact that the Japanese had to be vanquished to prevent the permanent subjugation of China, and by 1935 were extending the first call for united action against the Japanese (see pp. 197-202).

In the meantime, the Kuomintang was moving, roughly, in the opposite direction. The Nationalist Government at Nanking increasingly became the personal tool of Chiang Kai-shek; it alienated itself first from the peasantry, then in successive stages from the intellectuals, the workers and the soldiers until eventually it had isolated itself from all nationalist sentiment. The weaknesses and internal contradictions of the Party infused the rest of the society under its control. In those areas dominated by the National Government, there was economic instability perpetuated by a repressive structure of taxation and widespread corruption. Inflation was endemic, and the economic and political policies pursued in response to it were inadequate.

By 1936 the Kuomintang had lost its vision of social revolution. It sounded the hollow notes of nationalistic rhetoric, further debasing its own ideological currency by drawing attention to the contrast between its own regime and that of the Communists. Instead of land reform, the alleviation of taxation, the reduction of rent and the curtailing of usury and corruption in the countryside, Chiang Kai-shek pursued a rural policy based on a combination of indifference and force. Far from being simply a matter of ignorance this policy was an outgrowth of the way in which the Kuomintang functioned; it reflected a basic mistrust of the masses of illiterate peasants. The overriding concern of Chiang Kai-shek was to secure his pinnacle of power against the encroachments of the Communists. From 1927 through 1936 his primary objective remained their elimination and everything was subordinated to this end. This policy, referred to as 'internal pacification before resistance to external attack,' was the raison d'etre of the Kuomintang.

There was a national crisis in China by 1936 as a result of the endless Japanese aggression. Students were, of course, in the forefront of activities demanding a united front but students and Communists were not alone in their desire to actively oppose the external threat. This feeling spread throughout the population. The December 9th, 1935 movement of students and workers hastened the formation of the people's National Salvation Movement, a patriotic organization that urged the government of Chiang Kai-shek to assume responsibility for the defense of China and restore internal unity towards that end. More and more Chinese (even within the Kuomintang) felt that an enormous expenditure of resources, human and material, was being wasted on a futile struggle against the Communists, who were Chinese, while the Japanese already dominated the vast and rich expanse of Manchuria and were using it as a base to take over the rest of China. What was also clear to some was that the source of Communist strength was not military prowess alone but their mobilization of peasant support.

While Chiang Kai-shek argued and pleaded for "time" to strengthen the body politic (see pp. 202-206)—by which he meant the elimination of the Communists and the mobilization of a strong, modernized military force—, the Communists recognized that "time" was not something that could be shortened or lengthened depending on need or will. Japan was not about to wait for China to strengthen her defenses. The old saying that time and tide wait for no man applies equally well to war and conquest, and the Communists wisely adapted themselves to the requirements at hand. If they had only illiterate and unarmed peasants to fight with, they would have to simultaneously teach and arm them with whatever was available. If the external threat of Japan's invasion overshadowed the civil war between the Kuomintang and the Communists, they would have to make "friends" with their enemies until such time that China was left for the Chinese to dispute over.

In December, 1936, Chiang, planning one more 'extermination drive' against the Communists, went to Sian to encourage reluctant allies into the campaign. He was captured by Allied troops whose opposition to the Japanese took precedence over their dislike of the Communists and who had agreed with the Communists to coax Chiang into relinquishing his battle against them. In return for his agreement to a second united front against the Japanese, the Communists agreed to accept Chiang's authority as head of state. The second united front, even more than the first, was thus externally precipitated and built on only the flimsiest cooperation. It allowed the Kuomintang to plan a strategy of national defense against the invaders and took the pressure off the Communists so that they too could concentrate on fighting the Japanese.

The united front was an uneasy alliance at best. Since the Communists were on the ascendancy while the Kuomintang was in decline, Chiang Kai-shek was continually torn between fighting one or the other of his enemies. If he concentrated on the Japanese he was inevitably strengthening his Chinese adversary. He had felt all along that it was impossible to defeat the Japanese with his own forces, and as the war stretched on he relied more and more exclusively on a big-power victory to save China. This outlook got to the point where it interfered with Allied attempts to defeat the Japanese. Chiang Kaishek repeatedly refrained from using his troops against the Japanese, preferring to save them for a future confrontation with the Communists. But the Kuomintang was receiving extensive aid from the U. S. on the grounds of the war effort, and American military advisers like Stilwell (see pp. 312-315) became increasingly disillusioned with Chiang's regime.

The Communists, on the other hand, benefited from the united front. It was a moral victory for them as well as a respite from continual harassment. Their extraordinary reputation for self-sacrifice, effective guerrilla activities against the Japanese, and skillful organization of peasants gained enormous popularity for them as national heroes. While the Kuomintang alienated nationalistic sentiment and became identified with corruption and inefficiency, the Communists acquired the respect not only of the intellectual community but of all fervent nationalists.

The Yenan period, as it is referred to, greatly strengthened the Communist movement. The contrast between life in the Communist-dominated area and the Kuomintang stronghold in Chungking added to their popular support, internationally as well as nationally. Unaided by Soviet "advice" or aid, the Communists retained their *de facto* independence of the central government throughout the united front period. Although there was military cooperation between Communists and Nationalists, it did not extend to the social and territorial distance between the Kuomintang and the Chinese Communist Party. They fought on different fronts, in different ways, and with different degrees of effectiveness. The CCP did most of the fighting behind Japanese lines while Chiang Kai-shek, relying heavily on the U. S. for aid, made promises and tried to maintain the semblance of a fighting force, but was continually embarrassed by corruption, inflation, inefficiency and, finally, outright defection of his armed forces.

Before the final defeat of Japan, the civil war between the Kuomintang and the Communists emerged into the open again. When the Japanese were finally defeated there was a race between the two groups to reoccupy Chinese territory. The United States having already committed itself in support of Chiang Kai-shek provided air transportation for the Nationalist troops to be flown into the major urban centers of the North. The final outcome was that the Communists, controlling the major rural areas of central and northern China, proceeded to move towards the cities while the Kuomintang, occupying these cities, tried to maintain a deteriorating defense. Chiang Kai-shek would not come to terms with the Communists on a coalition government, but rather held on to the hope of defeating the Communists with the help of the United States. The Communists, however, already had the solid foundations of a new China and with time, captured military equipment and the growing majority of the population on its side; they were assured of the future control of China.

The role of the United States in the final phase of the civil war in China and the resulting victory of the Communists has been the subject of bitter controversy. Given the great distance between the U. S. and China, the lack of reliable, firsthand knowledge of events as they happened and the inevitable bias of the U. S. perspective, it is reasonable to be critical of those who charged the U. S. with having "sold out" Chiang Kai-shek. I have in this section attempted to present the views and analyses of those American foreign service officials *in China* at the time (pp. 315-324) with the hope that in the context of all we know about China up to and including that time, the reader will be able to judge for himself the extent and nature of the U. S. commitment and the limitations imposed on the U. S. by the nature of the regime under Chiang Kai-shek.

Communist Declaration on Unity (1935)*

Issued on August 31, 1935 by the Chinese Soviet Government and the Central Committee of the Chinese Communist Party.

To MEN and women in all walks of life—labor, industry, agriculture, military affairs, politics, commerce and education—in China as well as abroad:

Japanese imperialism is increasing its offensive against our country. Step by step the treacherous Nanking government is continuing its capitulation to Japan. Following the fate of the four north-eastern provinces [the three provinces in Manchuria and that of Jehol—*Editor*], our northern provinces [Chahar, Hopei, Shansi, Suiyuan and Shantung—*Editor*] are virtually lost.

* CHINA TODAY (New York) December 1935, pp. 58–59.

Peiping and Tientsin, cities which have been centers of culture for thousands of years; Hopei, Shansi, Honan, Shantung and other provinces which have unlimited natural resources; Chahar, Suiyuan and other territories which have most decisive strategic significance; the Peiping-Mukden, Peiping-Hankow, Peiping-Pukow, Peiping-Suiyuan and other railroads which hold the threads of the political and economic life of all China—all of these are virtually under the control of the Japanese military forces. The headquarters of the Japanese Kwantung Army is actively carrying out the plan of creating "Mongolkuo" and "Hwapeikuo" [Japanese puppet states in Mongolia and north China—*Editor*]. Since the Japanese invasion of Manchuria in 1931 Japan has advanced from Manchuria to Jehol, from Jehol to the Great Wall, from the Great Wall to the "Luantung Demilitarized Region" and from that region to the virtual occupation of Hopei, Chahar, Suiyuan and other northern provinces.

During this period of less than four years, a large part of the territory of China has been occupied by the Japanese invaders. The vicious plan for the complete annexation of our country sketched out in the Tanaka memorandum, is being systematically carried through. If this aggression continues, our provinces in the Yangtze and Pearl valleys [central and south China—*Editor*] and other remaining territories will also gradually be seized by the Japanese plunderers. And with this, our country, which possesses a history of five thousand years, will be completely transformed into a colony and our 450,-000,000 countrymen will be wholly enslaved.

In the last few years our country and our nation has been placed in a most precarious situation. Resistance to the Japanese invasion means the road to life, while non-resistance means the road to death. To resist the Japanese invasion and save our country has become the "holy duty" of every Chinese citizen.

But the most regrettable fact is that among our great people there exists a handful of corrupt elements who has "human faces, but beastly hearts"—Chiang Kai-shek, Wang Ching-wei, Chang Hsueh-liang and other traitors; Yang Yung-tai, Huang Fu, Wang I-tang, Chang Chung and other old agents of Japanese imperialism. All of them have betrayed our country by their policy of "nonresistance," they have advocated acceptance of the Japanese demands under the slogan of "meet reverses by submission." They carry on civil war and suppress all anti-imperialist movements with demagogic propaganda—"In order to resist external enemies, internal order must be achieved first." They have prevented the people from resisting Japan by deceitful slogans— "Ten years of propagation," "Ten years of education," "Prepare for revenge." They have forced our people to wait for destruction with the treacherous tactics of "Wait for the outbreak of the second World War."

Recently these traitors to their native land, under the slogans of "Sino-Japanese friendship and cooperation" and "Pan-Asianism" have carried out an openly corrupt and disgraceful policy of capitulation, unmatched either in the history of China or of the world. The Japanese imperialists demanded the withdrawal of the troops of Yu Hsueh-chung, Sung Chih-yuan and others from north China, and all of these troops were immediately withdrawn to the south and the west to carry on an internecine war against their own people. The Japanese imperialists demanded the removal of certain political and military officials, and all of these officials were immediately removed from their posts. The Japanese imperialists demanded the removal of the Hopei provincial government from Tientsin, and it was immediately transferred to Paoting. The Japanese plunderers demanded the banning of Chinese newspapers and journals which did not suit them, and all these papers and journals were immediately banned. The Japanese imperialists demanded the punishment of the editor of the *New Life Weekly*, and other editors and correspondents of Chinese newspapers and journals, and immediately all these people were subjected to arrest and imprisonment. The Japanese imperialists demanded the introduction into Chinese schools and universities of the slave system of pro-Japanese education, and all advanced Chinese literature was immediately burned; numerous honest boys and girls, who did not want to become the slaves of an alien state, were either arrested or executed. The Japanese imperialists demanded that the Japanese should be invited as counsellors in all Chinese state institutions, and Chiang Kai-shek immediately opened the doors of all these institutions to Japanese spies. The Japanese imperialists even demanded the disbanding of the Kuomintang organization, and its local organizations in north China and in Amoy were immediately disbanded. The Japanese imperialists demanded the disbanding of the "Blue Shirt" organization, and its leaders in north China, Tsen Kwang-ching and Chiang Hsiao-hsien, immediately resigned their posts.

The Chinese Soviet Government and the Communist Party of China recognize that the acts of the Japanese plunderers and Chinese traitors are an unparalleled disgrace to the Chinese nation. The Soviet Government and the Communist Party emphatically declare, "We not only vigorously oppose the invasion of our territory and interference in our internal political affairs by the Japanese imperialists, but we strongly protest against the Japanese demands for the disbanding of the Kuomintang and 'Blue Shirt' organizations." From the viewpoint of the Communist Party and the Soviet Government, all the affairs of the Chinese people should be handled by the Chinese themselves. No matter how great the crimes committed by the Kuomintang and the "Blue Shirt" organizations, the Japanese should certainly have no voice in the matter.

Province after province is being occupied by foreign invaders. Millions upon millions of citizens are being enslaved. City after city, village after village is being washed with blood. Emigrants abroad are everywhere being persecuted and deported. Internal as well as foreign affairs are being dictated by our enemies. How can this be called a state! How can this be called a nation!

Fellow countrymen! Ethiopia, with a meager population of eight million, is offering armed resistance to Italian imperialism in defence of her territory and people; then can a great country like ours, with a population of four hundred million, fold its hands and wait for death? The Soviet Government and the Communist Party firmly believe that with the exception of a handful of traitors and agents of the Japanese imperialists, who are willing to follow the example of Li Wang-yun, Cheng Hsiao-shu, Chang Ching-hwei and Henry Pu Yi, the absolute majority of our countrymen in all walks of life—labor, industry, agriculture, military affairs, commerce and education—refuse to become the slaves of the Japanese imperialists. . . .

"All countrymen who are not willing to be enslaved!

All sincere military officers and soldiers!

All members of political parties and organizations, and all who are willing to participate in the movement against the Japanese invasion and for the salvation of China!

All the Kuomintang youth and "Blue Shirt" organizations who are nationally-minded!

All Chinese emigrants who are concerned about their fatherland!

All oppressed nationalities in China! (Mongolians, Mohammedans, Koreans, Miaos, Tibetans, Lolos, Yaos, Fans, etc.)

All arise! Smash through the thousand-fold oppressions of

the Japanese imperialists and Chiang Kai-shek, and valiantly fight together with the Chinese Soviet Government and anti-Japanese governments in various places in the northeast for the formation of a united national defense government! Form a united anti-Japanese army with the Red Army and the Northeastern Peoples Army and all anti-Japanese volunteers!"

The main task of the national defense government should be resistance to Japan and the salvation of our country. Its political program should include the following points:—

1. Resistance to Japanese invasion and the recovery of lost territories.

2. Assistance to the famine-stricken; the undertaking of extensive river conservancy work for the purpose of preventing inundations and drought.

3. Confiscation of all the properties of the Japanese imperialists in China to finance the war against the Japanese invasion.

4. Confiscation of all the properties, stored food and land owned by the traitors and the agents of the Japanese imperialists, to be used by the poor countrymen and anti-Japanese fighters.

5. Abolition of onerous taxes and fees, reorganization of finance and currency, and the development of industry, agriculture and commerce.

6. Increase of the salaries, wages, and soldiers' pay and improvement of living conditions of workers, peasants, soldiers, students, teachers, etc.

7. Exercise of democratic rights and liberation of all political prisoners.

8. Free education and provision of jobs for the unemployed youth.

9. Equality for all nationalities residing in the territories of China. Protection of the life, property, and freedom of residence and business of the Chinese emigrants abroad.

10. Union with all anti-imperialist elements—the toiling people of Japan, Korea, Formosa and other oppressed nations—as our allies. Union with all nations which are sympathetic to the liberation movement of the Chinese nation, and the establishment of friendly relations with those nations which maintain good-will and a neutral attitude toward this movement.

The united anti-Japanese army should be composed of all armed forces willing to resist Japan, and a central commanding staff of that army should be organized under the leadership of the national defense government. This staff should be com-

posed of delegates elected by the anti-Japanese commande
and soldiers of all armies, or it should be organized throu
such other forms as may be decided by delegates representi
all shades of public opinion. The Red Army will be the fi
to join unconditionally the united army to fight against t
Japanese invasion and for the liberation of our country.

In order to enable the national defense government to be
the heavy responsibility of national defense, and the unite
army to fight against the Japanese invasion, the Commun
Party and Soviet Government call upon all fellow-countrym
who have money to contribute money, who have weapo
to contribute weapons, who have food stores to contribu
food, who are able to work to contribute work, who are e
perts and professionals to contribute services. The Comm
nist Party and the Soviet Government firmly believe that
we, four hundred million countrymen, have a united natior
defense government to lead us, a united army to act as o
vanguard, millions of armed masses as reserves, and countle
numbers of the proletarians and masses in the Far East a
all over the world as our allies, then we can certainly defe
Japanese aggression which is opposed by its own people
Japan and by the powers abroad!

Fellow countrymen! Arise!
Fight for the life of our Fatherland!
Fight for the existence of our nation!
Fight for the independence of our country!
Fight for our territorial integrity!
Fight for our human rights and liberties!

Long live the unity of the Chinese nation for the strug
against Japanese imperialism and for national existence!

The Chinese Soviet Government
Central Committee, Communist Party of China

Chiang Kai-shek on Resistance to Aggression and Renaissance of the Nation*

JUST BEFORE the Japanese attacks on Shanghai on January
1932, I published an article in which I quoted some words

* Chiang Kai-shek, "Resistance to Aggression and Renaissance
the Nation," Prologue to THE COLLECTED WARTIME MESSAGES
CHIANG KAI-SHEK (The John Day Company, N.Y., 1946),
10–17.

our late Leader addressed to the people of China. "All our fellow countrymen," he said, "should realize that if we were rashly to fight Japan before the opportune moment had arrived, Japan would be able to occupy all the most important points in China within ten days, and then destroy China." These are the words of our great Leader, taken from the Three Principles of the People, in which he earnestly warned our nation of the dangers besetting it. Later some reactionaries asserted these words were my own, and insinuated that I was afraid of the Japanese, and dared not go to war with them. Whether the words are mine or those of our great Leader can be decided at once by reference to his published works.

We can afford to ignore these reactionaries, even though they spend their whole time in helping Japan by attacking their own government. But we ought to consider carefully why our late Leader said, "Japan could destroy China in ten days." It is because China does not possess the necessary equipment for waging modern warfare, and is not in a position to fight the troops of a modern state. If we do not wait for the opportune moment, but start war rashly and prematurely, the result will be only defeat and ruin. Not ten days but three days would suffice for the Japanese to seize all the strategic points on the coast or along the rivers. In fact, they could seize any place they wanted. In the west they could seize not merely Chung-king, but even Chengtu; in the south they could occupy not only Kwangtung, but Wuchow and Yungning (in Kwangsi). Their potential strength has already been mobilized to the full, while their fleet has been stationed at strategic points up and down the coast. But it is not merely places on the coast or along the rivers that they could seize; any place is within their reach.

Not merely have the four Northeastern Provinces been seized, but the whole of North China is already virtually under their control. In North China all the important points on the railways and the convenient lines of communication through difficult but strategic ravines and passes were long ago the scene of Japanese military preparations, and can at any time be taken entirely under their control. Take the case of the Tsing-tao-Tsinan Railway. Although ostensibly they have not sent troops to take control of it, the Japanese workmen and merchants along the line are all ex-soldiers. The Japanese in Tien-tsin, Hankow, and similar important ports; in Chahar, Kalgan, and other places are all officers in plain clothes. With conditions as they are, all the Japanese have to do is to issue an

order, and within three days they would be in possession of all
the strategic points in China, and in a position to destroy
us. . . .

Despite these conditions we ourselves have made no preparations; we have made no arrangements for the defense of the
State. If now we were rashly to enter upon a war with Japan,
would it not simply mean the destruction of our nation, and
that to no purpose? Would this not be the height of folly? When
you have made no preparations, but your enemy has already
laid an ambush all around you, and is only waiting for you to
move in order immediately to rise up and surround you, is it
not suicidal for you to take the initiative, and so play into his
hands? Anyone, therefore, who says that we can go to war with
Japan at the present time is living in a fool's paradise. He
simply does not know his own condition, and he doesn't know
his enemy.

Then how can we resist Japan and restore our nation? Ought
we to put our whole effort into preparations for national defense, and use every ounce of strength in manufacturing planes
and guns? Could we then fight Japan? You officers know perfectly well that even if we began immediately to increase our
total military equipment, and to reorganize our whole national
defense, we could not get ready in time, we could not resist
Japan. Not only so, but if we began now and continued to put
our whole strength and soul into military preparations for the
next thirty years, it would not be enough. At the end of thirty
years, the idea of defeating Japan by means of our material
resources would still be nothing more than an idle dream—
particularly when we realize that Japan would never allow us
to perfect our preparations for national defense, and would
never give us the chance of manufacturing the weapons we
need. But suppose for the sake of argument that Japan should
allow us to continue putting our full strength into preparations
for national defense, do you think for one moment that we have
adequate resources in men and material to carry out such a
program in time? For instance, we want to build fortifications
along the frontiers and forts along the sea-coast, but a single
24-centimeter gun costs $4,000,000, exclusive of shells. Just
this one item is beyond our resources, financial or technical.
And when you remember that Japan would certainly never
allow us to make any preparations of this kind, that wherever
we began to prepare or reorganize, along would come Japanese
warships to bring pressure to bear on us and create disturb-

ances, making it impossible for us to begin, you can see how impossible it all is.

All of you must clearly understand that so long as Japan is undefeated, our preparations for national defense cannot be perfected, the State cannot be made secure, and there cannot be any hope for the preservation of our nation. You should all wake up to the realization of this fact: that so long as Japan has any military might, she will not allow us to reorganize our national defense, or to become united as a nation. This being so, how can we possibly make any adequate preparations to fight Japan? We have neither the opportunity nor the ability. Let us not indulge in wishful thinking.

THE NEED OF PATIENCE AND PERSEVERANCE

The more difficult the circumstances in which we Chinese soldiers find ourselves, and the greater our responsibilities, the more we need the spirit of self-sacrifice, the more we need patient perseverance, steadfast endurance, and strong self-reliance. We must in particular guard all military secrets. Foreign armies are able, in accordance with prearranged plans and protected by arrangements for national defense, to train their troops and to prepare for war without any feeling of insecurity. But we have no means of co-ordinating the whole of our national defense and of making all necessary preparations in accordance with a fixed plan. We are everywhere subject to enemy pressure, and unable to secure any protection through our "national defense." The enemy is watching us every moment and is constantly creating disturbances. In fact he is in a position to annihilate us. If the Japanese want to send troops to any place, they can immediately do so. If they wish to dispatch warships to a certain point, the warships can immediately proceed thither. If their navy and army cannot reach a place, they can always send their planes and destroy it with their bombs. At present the life of our nation and people is entirely in the hands of the Japanese. We have no freedom of action. . . .

SPIRIT WILL OVERCOME MATTER

Since we have no national defense—for the Japanese will not allow us to have any—and our military equipment and our educational system are as they are, while our nation and society are so out of date that we cannot be called a modern state, how are we to meet foreign insult and regenerate the nation? It is true the enemy has guns, but guns are not necessarily the most effective way of meeting him. He has airplanes, but airplanes are not necessarily the best way to resist him. Naturally we cannot do without guns; we cannot do without airplanes; but we do not necessarily have to pit only guns against guns, and planes against planes. We can by our spirit overcome his material advantages; we can by increasing our knowledge resist his material strength. . . .

When, therefore, our Revolutionary Army fights with anti-revolutionary troops, or a country that is invaded resists the invading hordes, we must employ our Revolutionary Army's special strategy and its revolutionary spirit to resist the invader's ruthless force and his superior material equipment. In other words, we must rely simply on the whole nation making a superhuman effort, putting all our heart and strength into the struggle. Each person must do the work of two; five of us must do what it will take ten of the enemy to accomplish. We must use every ounce of our mental and physical powers, we must be willing to pour out our life's blood in resisting the enemy mechanical strength and in overcoming his superior material equipment. If only we will get ready regardless of the cost—even though the cost be death—we shall certainly find ways and means, and above all a suitable opportunity to overcome our difficulties, and to complete our mission of reviving China. . . .

> Mao Tse-tung is both theoretician and revolutionary. He is a revolutionary with a strong pragmatic bent, and his theory ranges broadly over the spectrum of problems facing China in the twentieth century. After 1936 the problem that superseded all others was fighting an effective guerrilla war against the Japanese. Mao therefore directed his attention to the problems of warfare, the principles involved and the tactics to be adopted. His military writings have been translated into innumerable languages and have shown an amazing relevancy for people throughout the world. Some scholars even claim that his genius and originality is most evident in his understanding and application of military strategy.
>
> In the following two selections from "Problems of Strategy in Guerrilla War Against Japan" and "On Protracted War," Mao Tse-tung exhibits a thorough knowledge of the classics. His familiarity with a Chinese classic, Sun Tzu's The Art of War, stands him in good stead. From Sun Tzu, Mao inherited universal principles of warfare embodying a psychology of combat appropriate for varying physical and social conditions. Mao Tse-tung in eclectic fashion incorporates the useful aspects of this ancient scholar's wisdom into the totality of his Marxist approach. Sun Tzu's principles of warfare become part of an

entire approach which can be used in all areas of planning and organization whether it be to build an army or pursue a foreign policy.

The Communists' early period in Kiangsi (1930–1934) and the Long March were "military laboratories" and Yenan was the retreat, a time for taking stock of experiences and evaluating shortcomings. In his writing Mao often goes into lengthy discussion of failures. As Sun Tzu noted long before Mao, it is a major strength to know your weaknesses.

Problems of Strategy in Guerrilla War Against Japan*
May 1938

SIX SPECIFIC PROBLEMS OF STRATEGY IN GUERRILLA WAR AGAINST JAPAN

Now let us see what policies or principles have to be adopted in guerrilla operations against Japan before we can attain the object of preserving ourselves and destroying the enemy. Since the guerrilla units in the War of Resistance (and in all other revolutionary wars) generally grow out of nothing and expand from a small to a large force, they must preserve themselves and, moreover, they must expand.

Generally speaking, the main principles are as follows: (1) the use of initiative, flexibility and planning in conducting offensives within the defensive, battles of quick decision within protracted war, and exterior-line operations within interior-line operations; (2) co-ordination with regular warfare; (3) establishment of base areas; (4) the strategic defensive and the strategic offensive; (5) the development of guerrilla warfare into mobile warfare; and (6) correct relationship of command. These six items constitute the whole of the strategic programme for guerrilla war against Japan and are the means necessary for the preservation and expansion of our forces, for the destruction and expulsion of the enemy, for co-ordination with regular warfare and the winning of final victory.

CO-ORDINATION WITH REGULAR WARFARE

. . . There are three kinds of co-ordination between guerrilla and regular warfare, co-ordination in strategy, in campaigns and in battles.

* Mao Tse-tung, excerpts from "Problems of Strategy in Guerrilla War Against Japan," SELECTED WORKS, op. cit., Vol. II, pp. 81–111.

Taken as a whole, guerrilla warfare behind the enemy lines, which cripples the enemy, pins him down, disrupts his supply lines and inspires the regular forces and the people throughout the country, is co-ordinated with regular warfare in strategy. . . . Not only are the guerrilla units performing the function of co-ordination with the regular forces in our present strategic defensive, when the enemy is on the strategic offensive; not only will they co-ordinate with the regular forces in disrupting the enemy's hold on the occupied territory, after he concludes his strategic offensive and switches to the safeguarding of his gains; they will also co-ordinate with the regular forces in driving out the enemy forces and recovering all the lost territories, when the regular forces launch the strategic counter-offensive.

In addition, guerrilla warfare performs the function of co-ordination with regular warfare in campaigns. In performing a task of this sort, the leaders of each guerrilla base behind the enemy lines, or the commanders of a guerrilla formation temporarily dispatched there, must dispose their forces well and, by adopting different tactics suited to the time and place, move energetically against the enemy's most vital and vulnerable spots in order to cripple him, pin him down, disrupt his supply lines, inspire our armies campaigning on the interior lines, and so fulfil their duty of co-ordinating with the campaign. If each guerrilla zone or unit goes it alone without giving any attention to co-ordinating with the campaigns of the regular forces, its role in strategic co-ordination will lose a great deal of its significance, although it will still play some such role in the general strategy. All guerrilla commanders should give this point serious attention. To achieve co-ordination in campaigns, it is absolutely necessary for all larger guerrilla units and guerrilla formations to have radio equipment.

THE ESTABLISHMENT OF BASE AREAS

The third problem of strategy in anti-Japanese guerrilla warfare is the establishment of base areas, which is important and essential because of the protracted nature and ruthlessness of the war. The recovery of our lost territories will have to await the nation-wide strategic counter-offensive; by then the enemy's front will have extended deep into central China and cut it in two from north to south, and a part or even a greater part of our territory will have fallen into the hands of the enemy and become his rear. We shall have to extend guerrilla warfare all over this vast enemy-occupied area, make a front out of the enemy's rear, and force him to fight ceaselessly throughout the territory he occupies. Until such time as our strategic counter-offensive is launched and so long as our lost territories are not recovered, it will be necessary to persist in guerrilla warfare in the enemy's rear, certainly for a fairly long time, though one cannot say definitely for how long. This is why the war will be a protracted one. And in order to safeguard his gains in the occupied areas, the enemy is bound to step up his anti-guerrilla measures and, especially after the halting of his strategic offensive, to embark on relentless suppression of the guerrillas. With ruthlessness thus added to protractedness, it will be impossible to sustain guerrilla warfare behind the enemy lines without base areas.

What, then, are these base areas? They are the strategic bases on which the guerrilla forces rely in performing their strategic tasks and achieving the object of preserving and expanding themselves and destroying and driving out the enemy. Without such strategic bases, there will be nothing to depend on in carrying out any of our strategic tasks or achieving the aim of the war. It is a characteristic of guerrilla warfare behind the enemy lines that it is fought without a rear, for the guerrilla forces are severed from the country's general rear. But guerrilla warfare could not last long or grow without base areas. The base areas, indeed, are its rear.

History knows many peasant wars of the "roving rebel" type, but none of them ever succeeded. In the present age of advanced communications and technology, it would be all the more groundless to imagine that one can win victory by fighting in the manner of roving rebels. Therefore the struggle against the roving-rebel ideology is an inevitable process. Only when this ideology is thoroughly overcome and the policy of establishing base areas is initiated and applied will there be conditions favourable for the maintenance of guerrilla warfare over a long period. . . .

THE TYPES OF BASE AREAS

Base areas in anti-Japanese guerrilla warfare are mainly of three types, those in the mountains, those on the plains and those in the river-lake-estuary regions.

The advantage of setting up base areas in mountainous regions is obvious. They are all places where anti-Japanese guerrilla warfare can be maintained for the longest time and are important strongholds for the War of Resistance. We must develop guerrilla warfare and set up base areas in all the mountainous regions behind the enemy lines.

Of course, the plains are less suitable than the mountains, but it is by no means impossible to develop guerrilla warfare or establish any base areas there. . . . Broadly speaking, when the strategic offensive of the enemy is brought to a halt and he enters the stage of safeguarding his occupied areas, he will undoubtedly launch savage attacks on all the guerrilla base areas, and those in the plains will naturally be the first to bear the brunt. . . . But in the circumstances of our national war it is not impossible for numerous small guerrilla units to keep going in various counties over the vast plains and adopt a fluid way of fighting, *i.e.*, by shifting their bases from place to place. It is definitely possible to conduct seasonal guerrilla warfare by taking advantage of the "green curtain" of tall crops in summer and of the frozen rivers in winter. As the enemy has no strength to spare now and will never be able to attend to everything even when he has the strength to spare, it is absolutely necessary for us to decide on the policy, for the present, of spreading guerrilla warfare far and wide and setting up temporary base areas in the plains and, for the future, of preparing to keep up guerrilla warfare by small units, if only seasonally, and of creating base areas which are not fixed.

Objectively speaking, the possibilities of developing guerrilla warfare and establishing base areas are greater in the river-lake-estuary regions than in the plains, though less than in the mountains. The dramatic battles fought by "pirates" and "water-bandits," of which our history is full, and the guerrilla warfare round the Hunghu Lake kept up for several years in the Red Army period, both testify to the possibility of developing guerrilla warfare and of establishing base areas in the river-lake-estuary regions. So far, however, the political parties and the masses who are resisting Japan have given this possibility little attention. Though the subjective conditions are as yet lacking, we should undoubtedly turn our attention to this possibility and start working on it. . . . By overlooking this aspect we are virtually providing the enemy with water transport facilities; this is a gap in our strategic plan for the War of Resistance which must be filled in good time.

GUERRILLA ZONES AND BASE AREAS

In guerrilla warfare behind the enemy lines, there is a difference between guerrilla zones and base areas. Areas which are surrounded by the enemy but whose central parts are not occupied or have been recovered, . . . are ready-made bases for the convenient use of guerrilla units in developing guerrilla warfare. But elsewhere in these areas the situation is different. When guerrilla warfare began, the guerrillas could not completely occupy these places but could only make frequent raids; they are areas which are held by the guerrillas when they are there and by the puppet regime when they are gone, and are therefore not yet guerrilla bases but only what may be called guerrilla zones. Such guerrilla zones will be transformed into base areas when they have gone through the necessary processes of guerrilla warfare, that is, when large numbers of enemy troops have been annihilated or defeated there, the puppet regime has been destroyed, the masses have been roused to activity, anti-Japanese mass organizations have been formed, people's local armed forces have been developed, and anti-Japanese political power has been established. By the expansion of our base areas we mean the addition of areas such as these to the bases already established. . . .

Thus the transformation of a guerrilla zone into a base area is an arduous creative process, and its accomplishment depends on the extent to which the enemy is destroyed and the masses are aroused.

Many regions will remain guerrilla zones for a long time. In these regions the enemy will not be able to set up stable puppet regimes, however much he tries to maintain control, while we, on our part, will not be able to achieve the aim of establishing anti-Japanese political power, however much we develop guerrilla warfare. Examples of this kind are to be found in the enemy-occupied regions along the railway lines, in the neighbourhood of big cities and in certain areas in the plains.

As for the big cities, the railway stops and the areas in the plains which are strongly garrisoned by the enemy, guerrilla warfare can only extend to the fringes and not right into these places which have relatively stable puppet regimes. This is another kind of situation.

Mistakes in our leadership or strong enemy pressure may cause a reversal of the state of affairs described above, *i.e.*, a guerrilla base may turn into a guerrilla zone, and guerrilla zone may turn into an area under relatively stable enemy occupation. Such changes are possible, and they deserve special vigilance on the part of guerrilla commanders. . . .

The economic policy of the guerrilla base areas must follow the principles of the Anti-Japanese National United Front by equitably distributing the financial burden and protecting commerce. Neither the local organs of political power nor the guerrilla units must violate these principles, or otherwise the establishment of base areas and the maintenance of guerrilla warfare would be adversely affected. The equitable distribution of the financial burden means that "those with money should contribute money," while the peasants should supply the guerrilla units with grain within certain limits. The protection of commerce means that the guerrilla units should be highly disciplined and that the confiscation of shops, except those owned by proved traitors, should be strictly prohibited. This is no easy matter, but the policy is set and must be put into effect. . . .

THE RELATIONSHIP OF COMMAND

The last problem of strategy in guerrilla war against Japan concerns the relationship of command. A correct solution of this problem is one of the prerequisites for the unhampered development of guerrilla warfare.

Since guerrilla units are a lower level of armed organization characterized by dispersed operations, the methods of command in guerrilla warfare do not allow as high a degree of centralization as in regular warfare. If any attempt is made to apply the methods of command in regular warfare to guerrilla warfare, its great flexibility will inevitably be restricted and its vitality sapped. A highly centralized command is in direct contradiction to the great flexibility of guerrilla warfare and must not and cannot be applied to it.

However, guerrilla warfare cannot be successfully developed without some centralized command. When extensive regular warfare and extensive guerrilla warfare are going on at the same time, their operations must be properly co-ordinated; hence the need for a command co-ordinating the two, *i.e.*, for a unified strategic command by the national general staff and the war-zone commanders. In a guerrilla zone or guerrilla base area with many guerrilla units, there are usually one or more guerrilla formations (sometimes together with regular formations) which constitute the main force, a number of other guerrilla units, big and small, which represent the supplementary force, and many armed units composed of people not withdrawn from production; the enemy forces there usually form a unified complex to concert their operations against the guerrillas. Consequently, the problem arises of setting up a unified or centralized command in such guerrilla zones or base areas.

Hence, as opposed both to absolute centralization and to absolute decentralization, the principle of command in guerrilla war should be centralized strategic command and decentralized command in campaigns and battles.

Centralized strategic command includes the planning and direction of guerrilla warfare as a whole by the state, the co-ordination of guerrilla warfare with regular warfare in each war zone, and the unified direction of all the anti-Japanese armed forces in each guerrilla zone or base area. Here lack of harmony, unity and centralization is harmful, and every effort must be made to ensure all three. In general matters, that is, matters of strategy, the lower levels should report to the higher and follow their instructions so as to ensure concerted action. Centralization, however, stops at this point, and it would likewise be harmful to go beyond it and interfere with the lower levels in matters of detail like the specific dispositions for a campaign or battle. For such details must be settled in the light of specific conditions, which change from time to time and from place to place and are quite beyond the knowledge of the distant higher levels of command. This is what is meant by the principle of decentralized command in campaigns and battles. The same principle generally applies in regular operations, especially when communications are inadequate. In a word, it means guerrilla warfare waged independently and with the initiative in our hands within the framework of a unified strategy.

Where a guerrilla base area constitutes a military area divided into sub-areas, each comprising several counties, each of which is again divided into districts, the relationship between the various levels, from the headquarters of the military area and sub-areas down to the county and district governments, is one of consecutive subordination, and every armed force must, according to its nature, be under the direct command of one of these. On the principle that has been enunciated, in the relationship of command at these levels matters of general policy should be centralized in the higher levels, while actual operations should be carried in the light of the specific circumstances by the lower levels, which should have the right of independent action. If a higher level has something to say about the actual operations undertaken at a lower level, it can and should advance its views as "instructions" but must not issue hard and fast "commands." The more extensive the area, the more complex the situation and the greater the distance between the higher and the lower levels, the more advisable it becomes to allow greater independence to the lower levels in their actual operations and thus give those operations a character conforming more closely to the local requirements, so that the lower levels and the local personnel may develop the ability to work independently, cope with complicated situations, and successfully expand guerrilla warfare. For an armed unit or bigger formation which is engaged in a concentrated operation, the principle to be applied is one of centralization in its internal relationship of command, since the situation is clear to the higher command; but the moment this unit or formation breaks up for dispersed action, the principle of centralization in general matters and of decentralization in details should be applied, for then the specific situation cannot be clear to the higher command.

Absence of centralization where it is needed means negligence by the higher levels or usurpation of authority by the lower levels, neither of which can be tolerated in the relationship between higher and lower levels, especially in the military sphere. If decentralization is not effected where it should be, that means monopolization of power by the higher levels and lack of initiative on the part of the lower levels, neither of which can be tolerated in the relationship between higher and lower levels, especially in the command of guerrilla warfare. The above principles constitute the only correct policy for solving the problem of the relationship of command.

On Protracted War *is especially valuable for its applicability to present-day situations in the world. It provides a clear-cut model for revolutionaries faced with prolonged struggles like that in Vietnam. If one substitutes 'United States' for 'Japan' in the following passages and 'Vietnamese communists' for 'Chinese communists,' one discovers a startling resemblance of the Chinese experience to contemporary revolutions in Asia, Africa and Latin America. The Chinese from their own ordeals have refined the art of patience and methodical planning for the future. They are reconciled to the futility of relying on short-cuts.*

The following analysis of warfare is significant in highlighting the Communist strength in dealing with all problems in terms of their widest ramifications. Military problems require more than a knowledge of fighting. A military problem always encompasses social, political, economic and cultural factors which can be neglected only at the cost of victory. Mao emphasizes that in the midst and as part of the military struggle against Japan, the Communists must engage in cultural work:

"The enemy has transformed our former cultural centres int culturally backward areas, and we on our part must transforn the former culturally backward areas into cultural centres. Lin Piao's prediction of the eventual encirclement of the urba imperialist centers of culture by the rural peoples of the worl in revolution is an extension of this.

On Protracted War*
May 1938

STATEMENT OF THE PROBLEM

It will soon be July 7, the first anniversary of the great Wa of Resistance Against Japan. Rallying in unity, persevering i resistance and persevering in the united front, the forces of th whole nation have been valiantly fighting the enemy for almoʂ a year. The people of the whole world are attentively follow ing this war, which has no precedent in the history of the Eas and which will go down as a great war in world histor too. . . .

The question now is: Will China be subjugated? The answe is, No, she will not be subjugated, but will win final victory Can China win quickly? The answer is, No, she cannot wi quickly, and the War of Resistance will be a protracted war. . .

THE BASIS OF THE PROBLEM

Why is the War of Resistance Against Japan a protracte war? Why will the final victory be China's? What is the bas for these statements?

The war between China and Japan is not just any war, it specifically a war of life and death between semi-colonial an semi-feudal China and imperialist Japan, fought in the Nin teen Thirties. Herein lies the basis of the whole problem. Th two sides in the war have many contrasting features, which w be considered in turn below.

The Japanese side. First, Japan is a powerful imperiali country, which ranks first in the East in military, economic an political-organizational power, and is one of the five or s foremost imperialist countries of the world. These are the bas factors in Japan's war of aggression. The inevitability of th war and the impossibility of quick victory for China are due Japan's imperialist system and her great military, econom

* Mao Tse-tung, "On Protracted War," SELECTED WORKS, c
cit., vol. II, pp. 113–189.

and political-organizational power. Secondly, however, the imperialist character of Japan's social economy determines the imperialist character of her war, a war that is retrogressive and barbarous. In the Nineteen Thirties, the internal and external contradictions of Japanese imperialism have driven her not only to embark on an adventurist war unparalleled in scale but also to approach her final collapse. Thirdly, Japan's war is conducted on the basis of her great military, economic and political-organizational power, but at the same time it rests on an inadequate natural endowment. Japan's military, economic and political-organizational power is great but quantitatively inadequate. Japan is a comparatively small country, deficient in manpower and in military, financial and material resources, and she cannot stand a long war. Japan's rulers are endeavouring to resolve this difficulty through war, but again they will get the very reverse of what they desire; that is to say, the war they have launched to resolve this difficulty will eventually aggravate it and even exhaust Japan's original resources. Fourthly and lastly, while Japan can get international support from the fascist countries, the international opposition she is bound to encounter will be greater than her international support. These are the characteristics on the Japanese side.

The Chinese side. First, we are a semi-colonial and semi-feudal country. The Opium War, the Taiping Revolution, the Reform Movement of 1898, the Revolution of 1911 and the Northern Expedition—the revolutionary or reform movements which aimed at extricating China from her semi-colonial and semi-feudal state—all met with serious setbacks, and China remains a semi-colonial and semi-feudal country. We are still a weak country and manifestly inferior to the enemy in military, economic and political-organizational power. Here again one can find the basis for the inevitability of the war and the impossibility of quick victory for China. Secondly, however, China's liberation movement, with its cumulative development over the last hundred years, is now different from that of any previous period. Although the domestic and foreign forces opposing it have caused it serious setbacks, at the same time they have tempered the Chinese people. Although China today is not so strong as Japan militarily, economically and culturally, yet there are factors in China more progressive than in any other period of her history. The Communist Party of China and the army under its leadership represent these progressive factors. It is on the basis of this progress that China's present war of liberation can be protracted and can achieve final victory. By contrast with Japanese imperialism, which is de-

clining, China is a country rising like the morning sun. China's
is progressive, hence its just character. Because it is a just
it is capable of arousing the nation to unity, of evoking
ympathy of the people in Japan and of winning the support
of most countries in the world. Thirdly, and again by contrast
with Japan, China is a very big country with vast territory, rich
resources, a large population and plenty of soldiers, and is capable of sustaining a long war. Fourthly and lastly, there is
broad international support for China stemming from the
progressive and just character of her war, which is again
exactly the reverse of the meagre support for Japan's unjust
cause. To sum up, China's disadvantage lies in her military
weakness, and her advantages lie in the progressive and just
character of her war, her great size and her abundant international support. These are China's characteristics.

The war is a contest between these characteristics. They will
change in the course of the war, each according to its own
nature; and from this everything else will follow. These characteristics exist objectively and are not invented to deceive
people; they constitute all the basic elements of the war, and
are not incomplete fragments; they permeate all major and
minor problems on both sides and all stages of the war, and
they are not matters of no consequence. If anyone forgets
these characteristics in studying the Sino-Japanese war, he will
surely go wrong; and even though some of his ideas win
credence for a time and may seem right, they will inevitably
be proved wrong by the course of the war. On the basis of
these characteristics we shall now proceed to explain the
problems to be dealt with.

THE THEORY OF NATIONAL SUBJUGATION IS WRONG
AND THE THEORY OF QUICK VICTORY IS LIKEWISE WRONG

The subjugationists stress the contradiction between strength
and weakness and puff it up until it becomes the basis of their
whole argument on the question, neglecting all the other contradictions. Their preoccupation with the contrast in strength
shows their one-sidedness, and their exaggeration of this one
side of the matter into the whole shows their subjectivism.
Thus, if one looks at the matter as a whole, it will be seen
that they have no ground to stand on and are wrong. . . .

The exponents of quick victory are likewise wrong. Either
they completely forget the contradiction between strength and
weakness, remembering only the other contradictions, or they
exaggerate China's advantages beyond all semblance of reality
and beyond recognition, or they presumptuously take the bal-

ance of forces at one time and place for the whole situation
as in the old saying, "A leaf before the eye shuts out Mo
Tai." In a word, they lack the courage to admit that the ene
is strong while we are weak. They often deny this point an
consequently deny one aspect of the truth. Nor do they hav
the courage to admit the limitations of our advantages, an
thus they deny another aspect of the truth. The result is tha
they make mistakes, big and small, and here again it is sub
jectivism and one-sidedness that are doing the mischief. Thes
friends have their hearts in the right place, and they, too, ar
patriots. But while "the gentlemen's aspirations are indee
lofty," their views are wrong, and to act according to ther
would certainly be to run into a brick wall. For if appraisa
does not conform to reality, action cannot attain its objectiv
and to act notwithstanding would mean the army's defeat an
the nation's subjugation, so that the result would be the sam
as with the defeatists. Hence this theory of quick victory wil
not do either. . . .

Taking an objective and all-sided view, we recognize th
two possibilities of national subjugation and liberation, stres
that liberation is the dominant possibility, point out the con
ditions for its achievement, and strive to secure them. . . .

Not that we would not like a quick victory; everybody woul
be in favour of driving the "devils" out overnight. But we poin
out that, in the absence of certain definite conditions, quicl
victory is something that exists only in one's mind and not in
objective reality, and that it is a mere illusion, a false theory
Accordingly, having made an objective and comprehensiv
appraisal of all the circumstances concerning both the enem
and ourselves, we point out that the only way to final victor
is the strategy of protracted war, and we reject the groundles
theory of quick victory. . . .

WHY A PROTRACTED WAR?

Let us now examine the problem of protracted war. A cor
rect answer to the question "Why a protracted war?" can b
arrived at only on the basis of all the fundamental contrast
between China and Japan. For instance, if we say merely tha
the enemy is a strong imperialist power while we are a weal
semi-colonial and semi-feudal country, we are in danger o
falling into the theory of national subjugation. For neither in
theory nor in practice can a struggle become protracted by
simply pitting the weak against the strong. Nor can it becom
protracted by simply pitting the big against the small, the pro
gressive against the reactionary, or abundant support agains

meagre support. The annexation of a small country by a big one or of a big country by a small one is a common occurrence. It often happens that a progressive country which is not strong is destroyed by a big, reactionary country, and the same holds for everything that is progressive but not strong. Abundant or meagre support is an important but a subsidiary factor, and the degree of its effect depends upon the fundamental factors on both sides. Therefore when we say that the War of Resistance Against Japan is a protracted war, our conclusion is derived from the interrelations of all the factors at work on both sides. The enemy is strong and we are weak, and the danger of subjugation is there. But in other respects the enemy has shortcomings and we have advantages. The enemy's advantage can be reduced and his shortcomings aggravated by our efforts. On the other hand, our advantages can be enhanced and our shortcomings remedied by our efforts. Hence, we can win final victory and avert subjugation, while the enemy will ultimately be defeated and will be unable to avert the collapse of his whole imperialist system.

Since the enemy has advantages only in one respect but shortcomings in all others and we have shortcomings in only one respect but advantages in all others, why has this produced not a balance, but, on the contrary, a superior position for him and an inferior position for us at the present time? Quite clearly, we cannot consider the question in such a formal way. The fact is that the disparity between the enemy's strength and our own is now so great that the enemy's shortcomings have not developed, and for the time being cannot develop, to a degree sufficient to offset his strength, while our advantages have not developed, and for the time being cannot develop, to a degree sufficient to compensate for our weakness. Therefore there can as yet be no balance, only imbalance. . . .

But circumstances are continually changing. In the course of the war, provided we employ correct military and political tactics, make no mistake of principle and exert our best efforts, the enemy's disadvantages and China's advantages will both grow as the war is drawn out, with the inevitable result that there will be a continual change in the difference in comparative strength and hence in the relative position of the two sides. When a new stage is reached, a great change will take place in the balance of forces, resulting in the enemy's defeat and our victory.

At present the enemy can still manage to exploit his strength, and our War of Resistance has not yet fundamentally weakened him. The insufficiency in his manpower and material resources is not yet such as to prevent his offensive; on the contrary, they can still sustain his offensive to a certain extent. The reactionary and barbarous nature of this war, a factor which intensifies both class antagonisms within Japan and the resistance of the Chinese nation, has not yet brought about a situation which radically impedes his advance. The enemy's international isolation is increasing but is not yet complete. In many countries which have indicated they will help us, the capitalists dealing in munitions and war materials and bent solely on profit are still furnishing Japan with large quantities of war supplies, and their governments are still reluctant to join the Soviet Union in practical sanctions against Japan. From all this it follows that our War of Resistance cannot be won quickly and can only be protracted war. . . .

THE THREE STAGES OF THE PROTRACTED WAR

Since the Sino-Japanese war is a protracted one and final victory will belong to China, it can reasonably be assumed that this protracted war will pass through three stages. The first stage covers the period of the enemy's strategic offensive and our strategic defensive. The second stage will be the period of the enemy's strategic consolidation and our preparation for the counter-offensive. The third stage will be the period of our strategic counter-offensive and the enemy's strategic retreat. It is impossible to predict the concrete situation in the three stages, but certain main trends in the war may be pointed out in the light of present conditions. The objective course of events will be exceedingly rich and varied, with many twists and turns, and nobody can cast a horoscope for the Sino-Japanese war; nevertheless it is necessary for the strategic direction of the war to make a rough sketch of its trends. Although our sketch may not be in full accord with the subsequent facts and will be amended by them, it is still necessary to make it in order to give firm and purposeful strategic direction to the protracted war.

The first stage has not yet ended. The enemy's design is to occupy Canton, Wuhan and Lanchow and link up these three points. To accomplish this aim the enemy will have to use at least fifty divisions, or about one and a half million men, spend from one and a half to two years, and expend more than ten thousand million yen. In penetrating so deeply, he will encounter immense difficulties, with consequences disastrous beyond imagination. . . . In this stage the form of fighting we should adopt is primarily mobile warfare, supplemented by guerrilla and positional warfare. Through the subjective errors of the Kuomintang military authorities, positional warfare was assigned the primary role in the first phase of this stage, but it is nevertheless supplementary from the point of view of the stage as a whole. . . .

The exponents of quick victory, however, do not realize that war is a contest of strength, and that before a certain change has taken place in the relative strength of the belligerents, there is no basis for trying to fight strategically decisive battles and shorten the road to liberation. Were their ideas to be put into practice, we should inevitably run our heads into a brick wall. Or perhaps they are just talking for their own pleasure without really intending to put their ideas into practice. In the end Mr. Reality will come and pour a bucket of cold water over these chatterers, showing them up as mere windbags who want to get things on the cheap, to have gains without pains. . . .

That the war will be protracted is certain, but nobody can predict exactly how many months or years it will last, as this depends entirely upon the degree of the change in the balance of forces. All those who wish to shorten the war have no alternative but to work hard to increase our own strength and reduce that of the enemy. Specifically, the only way is to strive to win more battles and wear down the enemy's forces, develop guerrilla warfare to reduce enemy-occupied territory to a minimum, consolidate and expand the united front to rally the forces of the whole nation, build up new armies and develop new war industries, promote political, economic and cultural progress, mobilize the workers, peasants, businessmen, intellectuals and other sections of the people, disintegrate the enemy forces and win over their soldiers, carry on international propaganda to secure foreign support, and win the support of the Japanese people and other oppressed peoples. Only by doing all this can we reduce the duration of the war. There is no magic short-cut.

A WAR OF JIG-SAW PATTERN

We can say with certainty that the protracted War of Resistance Against Japan will write a splendid page unique in the war history of mankind. One of the special features of this war is the interlocking "jig-saw" pattern which arises from such contradictory factors as the barbarity of Japan and her shortage of troops on the one hand, and the progressiveness of China and the extensiveness of her territory on the other. . . . Its jig-saw pattern manifests itself as follows:

Interior and exterior lines. The anti-Japanese war as a whole is being fought on interior lines; but as far as the relation between the main forces and the guerrilla units is concerned, the former are on the interior lines while the latter are on the exterior lines, presenting a remarkable spectacle of pincers around the enemy. The same can be said of the relationship between the various guerrilla areas. From its own viewpoint each guerrilla area is on interior lines and the other areas are on exterior lines; together they form many battle fronts, which hold the enemy in pincers. In the first stage of the war, the regular army operating strategically on interior lines is withdrawing, but the guerrilla units operating strategically on exterior lines will advance with great strides over the wide areas to the rear of the enemy—they will advance even more fiercely in the second stage—thereby presenting a remarkable picture of both withdrawal and advance.

Possession and non-possession of a rear area. The main forces, which extend the front lines to the outer-limits of the enemy's occupied areas, are operating from the rear area of the country as a whole. The guerrilla units, which extend the battle lines into the enemy rear, are separated from the rear area of the country as a whole. But each guerrilla area has a small rear of its own, upon which it relies to establish its fluid battle lines. The case is different with the guerrilla detachments which are dispatched by a guerrilla area for short-term operations in the rear of the enemy in the same area; such detachments have no rear, nor do they have a battle line. "Operating without a rear area" is a special feature of revolutionary war in the new era, wherever a vast territory, a progressive people, and an advanced political party and army are to be found; there is nothing to fear but much to gain from it, and far from having doubts about it we should promote it.

Encirclement and counter-encirclement. Taking the war as a whole, there is no doubt that we are strategically encircled by the enemy because he is on the strategic offensive and operating on exterior lines while we are on the strategic defensive and operating on interior lines. This is the first form of enemy encirclement. We on our part can encircle one or more of the enemy columns advancing on us along separate routes, because we apply the policy of fighting campaigns and battles from tactically exterior lines by using numerically preponderant forces against these enemy columns advancing on us from strategically exterior lines. . . . Campaigns and battles fought by the two sides resemble the capturing of each other's pieces, and the establishment of enemy strongholds (such as Taiyuan) and our guerrilla base areas (such as the Wutai Mountains) resembles moves to dominate spaces on the board. If the game of *weichi* is extended to include the world, there is yet a third form of encirclement as between us and the enemy, namely, the interrelation between the front of aggression and the front of peace. The enemy encircles China, the Soviet Union, France and Czechoslovakia with his front of aggression, while we counter-encircle Germany, Japan and Italy with our front of peace. But our encirclement, like the hand of Buddha, will turn into the Mountain of Five Elements lying athwart the Universe, and the modern Sun Wu-kungs—the fascist aggressors—will finally be buried underneath it, never to rise again. Therefore, if on the international plane we can create an anti-Japanese front in the Pacific region, with China as one strategic unit, with the Soviet Union and other countries which may join it as other strategic units, and with the Japanese people's movement as still another strategic unit, and thus form a gigantic net from which the fascist Sun Wu-kungs can find no escape, then that will be our enemy's day of doom. Indeed, the day when this gigantic net is formed will undoubtedly be the day of the complete overthrow of Japanese imperialism. We are not jesting; this is the inevitable trend of the war.

Big areas and little areas. There is a possibility that the enemy will occupy the greater part of Chinese territory south of the Great Wall, and only the smaller part will be kept intact. That is one aspect of the situation. But within this greater part, which does not include the three northeastern provinces, the enemy can actually hold only the big cities, the main lines of communication and some of the plains—which may rank first in importance, but will probably constitute only the smaller part of the occupied territory in size and population, while the greater part will be taken up by the guerrilla areas that will grow up everywhere. That is another aspect of the situation. . . . The enemy has transformed our former cultural centres into culturally backward areas, and we on our part must transform the former culturally backward areas into cultural centres. At the same time, the work of developing extensive guerrilla areas behind the enemy lines is also extremely important, and we should attend to every aspect of this work, including the cultural. All in all, big pieces of China's territory, namely, the rural areas, will be transformed into regions of progress and light, while the small piece, namely, the enemy-occupied areas and especially the big cities, will temporarily become regions of backwardness and darkness. . . .

FIGHTING FOR PERPETUAL PEACE

The protracted nature of China's anti-Japanese war is inseparably connected with the fight for perpetual peace in China and the whole world. Never has there been a historical period such as the present in which war is so close to perpetual peace. For several thousand years since the emergence of classes, the life of mankind has been full of wars; each nation has fought countless wars, either internally or with other nations. In the imperialist epoch of capitalist society, wars are waged on a particularly extensive scale and with a peculiar ruthlessness. . . . Why then do we say the present war is near to perpetual peace? The present war is the result of the development of the general crisis of world capitalism which began with World War I; this general crisis is driving the capitalist countries into a new war and, above all, driving the fascist countries into new war adventures. This war, we can foresee, will not save capitalism, but will hasten its collapse. It will be greater in scale and more ruthless than the war of twenty years ago, all nations will inevitably be drawn in, it will drag on for a very long time, and mankind will suffer greatly. But, owing to the existence of the Soviet Union and the growing political consciousness of the people of the world, great revolutionary wars will undoubtedly emerge from this war to oppose all counter-revolutionary wars, thus giving this war the character of a struggle for perpetual peace. Even if later there should be another period of war, perpetual world peace will not be far off. Once man has eliminated capitalism, he will attain the era of perpetual peace, and there will be no more need for war. Neither armies, nor warships, nor military aircraft, nor poison gas will then be needed. Thereafter and for all time, mankind will never again know war. The revolutionary wars which have already begun are part of the war for perpetual peace. . . .

History shows that wars are divided into two kinds, just and unjust. All wars that are progressive are just, and all wars that impede progress are unjust. We Communists oppose all unjust wars that impede progress, but we do not oppose progressive, just wars. Not only do we Communists not oppose just wars, we actively participate in them. As for unjust wars, World War I is an instance in which both sides fought for imperialist interests; therefore the Communists of the whole world firmly opposed that war. The way to oppose a war of this kind is to do everything possible to prevent it before it breaks out and, once it breaks out, to oppose war with war, to oppose unjust war with just war, whenever possible. Japan's war is an unjust war that impedes progress, and the peoples of the world, including the Japanese people, should oppose it and are opposing it. In our country the people and the government, the Communist Party and the Kuomintang, have all raised the banner of righteousness in the national revolutionary war against aggression. Our war is sacred and just, it is progressive and its aim is peace. The aim is peace not just in one country but throughout the world, not just temporary but perpetual peace. To achieve this aim we must wage a life-and-death struggle, be prepared for any sacrifice, persevere to the end and never stop short of the goal. However great the sacrifice and however long the time needed to attain it, a new world of perpetual peace and brightness already lies clearly before us. . . .

MAN'S DYNAMIC ROLE IN WAR

. . . When we say we are opposed to a subjective approach to problems, we mean that we must oppose ideas which are not based upon or do not correspond to objective facts; because such ideas are fanciful and fallacious and will lead to failure if acted on. But whatever is done has to be done by human beings; protracted war and final victory will not come about without human action. For such action to be effective there must be people who derive ideas, principles or views from the objective facts, and put forward plans, directives, policies, strategies and tactics. Ideas, etc. are subjective, while deeds or actions are the subjective translated into the objective, but both represent the dynamic role peculiar to human beings. We term this kind of dynamic role "man's conscious dynamic role", and it is a characteristic that distinguishes man from all other things. All ideas based upon and corresponding to objective facts are correct ideas, and all deeds or actions based upon correct ideas are correct actions. We must give full scope to these ideas and actions, to this dynamic role. The anti-Japanese war is being waged to drive out imperialism and transform the old China into a new China; this can be achieved only when the whole Chinese people are mobilized and full scope is given to their conscious dynamic role in resisting Japan. If we just sit by and take no action, only subjugation awaits us and there will be neither protracted war nor final victory. . . .

In seeking victory, those who direct a war cannot overstep the limitations imposed by the objective conditions; within these limitations, however, they can and must play a dynamic role in striving for victory. The stage of action for commanders in a war must be built upon objective possibilities, but on that stage they can direct the performance of many a drama, full of sound and colour, power and grandeur. . . . Swimming in the ocean of war, they must not flounder but make sure of reaching the opposite shore with measured strokes. Strategy and tactics, as the laws for directing war, constitute the art of swimming in the ocean of war.

WAR AND POLITICS

"War is the continuation of politics." In this sense war is politics and war itself is a political action; since ancient times there has never been a war that did not have a political character. The anti-Japanese war is a revolutionary war waged by the whole nation, and victory is inseparable from the political aim of the war—to drive out Japanese imperialism and build a new China of freedom and equality. . . .

But war has it own particular characteristics and in this sense it cannot be equated with politics in general. "War is the continuation of politics by other . . . means." When politics develops to a certain stage beyond which it cannot proceed by the usual means, war breaks out to sweep the obstacles from the way. . . . Thus anyone who seeks a compromise before the task of the anti-Japanese war is fulfilled is bound to fail, because even if a compromise were to occur for one reason or another, the war would break out again, since the broad masses of the people would certainly not submit but would continue the war until its political objective was achieved. It can therefore be said that politics is war without bloodshed while war is politics with bloodshed.

From the particular characteristics of war there arise a particular set of organizations, a particular series of methods and a particular kind of process. The organizations are the armed forces and everything that goes with them. The methods are the strategy and tactics for directing war. The process is the particular form of social activity in which the opposing armed forces attack each other or defend themselves against one another, employing strategy and tactics favourable to themselves and unfavourable to the enemy. Hence war experience is a particular kind of experience. All who take part in war must rid themselves of their customary ways and accustom themselves to war before they can win victory.

POLITICAL MOBILIZATION FOR THE WAR OF RESISTANCE

A national revolutionary war as great as ours cannot be won without extensive and thoroughgoing political mobilization. Before the anti-Japanese war there was no political mobilization for resistance to Japan, and this was a great drawback, as a result of which China has already lost a move to the enemy. After the war began, political mobilization was very far from extensive, let alone thoroughgoing. It was the enemy's gunfire and the bombs dropped by enemy aeroplanes that brought news of the war to the great majority of the people. This was also a kind of mobilization, but it was done for us by the enemy, we did not do it ourselves. Even now the people in the remoter regions beyond the noise of the guns are carrying on quietly as usual. This situation must change, or otherwise we cannot win in our life-and-death struggle. . . . The mobilization of the common people throughout the country will create a vast sea in which to drown the enemy, create the conditions that will make up for our inferiority in arms and other things, and create the prerequisites for overcoming every difficulty in the war. . . . To wish for victory and yet neglect political mobilization is like wishing to "go south by driving the chariot north", and the result would inevitably be to forfeit victory.

What does political mobilization mean? First, it means telling the army and the people about the political aim of the war. It is necessary for every soldier and civilian to see why the war must be fought and how it concerns him. . . . Secondly, it is not enough merely to explain the aim to them; the steps and policies for its attainment must also be given, that is, there must be a political programme. . . . Without a clear-cut, concrete political programme it is impossible to mobilize all the armed forces and the whole people to carry the war against Japan through to the end. Thirdly, how should we mobilize them? By word of mouth, by leaflets and bulletins, by newspapers, books and pamphlets, through plays and films, through schools, through the mass organizations and through our cadres. What has been done so far in the Kuomintang areas is only a drop in the ocean, and moreover it has been done in a manner ill-suited to the people's tastes and in a spirit uncongenial to them; this must be drastically changed. Fourthly, to mobilize once is not enough; political mobilization for the War of Resistance must be continuous. Our job is not to recite our political programme to the people, for nobody will listen to such recitations; we must link the political mobilization for the war with developments in the war and with the life of the soldiers and the people, and make it a continuous movement. This is a matter of immense importance on which our victory in the war primarily depends.

THE OBJECT OF WAR

. . . The object of war is specifically "to preserve oneself and destroy the enemy" (to destroy the enemy means to disarm him or "deprive him of the power to resist," and does not mean to destroy every member of his forces physically). In ancient warfare, the spear and the shield were used, the spear to attack and destroy the enemy, and the shield to defend and preserve oneself. To the present day, all weapons are still an extension of the spear and the shield. The bomber, the machinegun, the long-range gun and poison gas are developments of the spear, while the air-raid shelter, the steel helmet, the concrete fortification and the gas mask are developments of the shield. The tank is a new weapon combining the functions of both spear and shield. Attack is the chief means of destroying the enemy, but defence cannot be dispensed with. In attack the immediate object is to destroy the enemy, but at the same time it is self-preservation, because if the enemy is not destroyed, you will be destroyed. In defence the immediate object is to preserve yourself, but at the same time defence is a means of supplementing attack or preparing to go over to the attack. Retreat is in the category of defence and is a continuation of defence, while pursuit is a continuation of attack. It should be pointed out that destruction of the enemy is the primary object of war and self-preservation the secondary, because only by destroying the enemy in large numbers can one effectively preserve oneself. Therefore attack, the chief means of destroying the enemy, is primary, while defence, a supplementary means of destroying the enemy and a means of self-preservation, is secondary. In actual warfare the chief role is played by defence much of the time and by attack for the rest of the time, but if war is taken as a whole, attack remains primary.

How do we justify the encouragement of heroic sacrifice in war? Does it not contradict "self-preservation"? No, it does not; sacrifice and self-preservation are both opposite and complementary to each other. War is politics with bloodshed and exacts a price, sometimes an extremely high price. Partial and temporary sacrifice (non-preservation) is incurred for the sake of general and permanent preservation. This is precisely why we say that attack, which is basically a mean of destroying the enemy, also has the function of self-preservation. It is also the reason why defence must be accompanied by attack and should not be defence pure and simple.

The object of war, namely, the preservation of oneself and the destruction of the enemy, is the essence of war and the basis of all war activities, an essence which pervades all war activities, from the technical to the strategic. . . . What for instance is meant by the principle of "taking cover and making full use of fire-power" in shooting? The purpose of the former is self-preservation, of the latter the destruction of the enemy. The former gives rise to such techniques as making use of the terrain and its features, advancing in spurts, and spreading out in dispersed formation. The latter gives rise to other techniques, such as clearing the field of fire and organizing a fire-net. As for the assault force, the containing force and the reserve force in a tactical operation, the first is for annihilating the enemy, the second for preserving oneself, and the third is for either purpose according to circumstances—either for annihilating the enemy (in which case it reinforces the assault force or serves as a pursuit force), or for self-preservation (in which case it reinforces the containing force or serves as a covering force). . . .

OFFENCE WITHIN DEFENCE, QUICK DECISIONS WITHIN A PROTRACTED WAR, EXTERIOR LINES WITHIN INTERIOR LINES

Now let us examine the specific strategy of the War of Resistance Against Japan. . . . In general, to achieve quick decision, we should attack a moving and not a stationary enemy. We should concentrate a big force under cover beforehand alongside the route which the enemy is sure to take, and while he is on the move, advance suddenly to encircle and attack him before he knows what is happening, and thus quickly conclude the battle. If we fight well, we may destroy the entire enemy force or the greater part or some part of it, and even if we do not fight so well, we may still inflict heavy casualties. This applies to any and every one of our battles. . . .

If we resolutely apply "quick-decision offensive warfare on exterior lines" on a battlefield, we shall not only change the balance of forces on that battlefield, but also gradually change the general situation. . . . After many such battles have been victoriously fought, the general situation between us and the enemy will change. That is to say, through the accumulation of victories on many battlefields by quick-decision offensive warfare on exterior lines, we shall gradually strengthen ourselves and weaken the enemy, which will necessarily affect the general balance of forces and bring about changes in it. When that happens, these changes, together with other factors on our side and together with the changes inside the enemy camp and a favourable international situation, will turn the over-all situation between us and the enemy first into one of parity and then into one of superiority for us. That will be the time for us to launch the counter-offensive and drive the enemy out of the country. . . .

INITIATIVE, FLEXIBILITY AND PLANNING

. . . The initiative here means an army's freedom of action as distinguished from an enforced loss of freedom. Freedom of action is the very life of an army and, once it is lost, the army is close to defeat or destruction. The disarming of a soldier is the result of his losing freedom of action through being forced into a passive position. The same is true of the defeat of an army. For this reason both sides in war do all they can to gain the initiative and avoid passivity. . . .

Initiative is inseparable from superiority in capacity to wage war, while passivity is inseparable from inferiority in capacity to wage war. Such superiority or inferiority is the objective basis of initiative or passivity. It is natural that the strategic initiative can be better maintained and exercised through a strategic offensive, but to maintain the initiative always and everywhere, that is, to have the absolute initiative, is possible only when there is absolute superiority matched against absolute inferiority. When a strong, healthy man wrestles with an invalid, he has the absolute initiative. If Japan were not riddled with insoluble contradictions, if, for instance, she could throw in a huge force of several million or ten million men all at once, if her financial resources were several times what they are, if she had no opposition from her own people or from other countries, and if she did not pursue the barbarous policies which arouse the desperate resistance of the Chinese people, then she would be able to maintain absolute superiority and have the absolute initiative always and everywhere. In history, such absolute superiority rarely appears in the early stages of a war or a campaign but is to be found towards its end. . . . As already explained, it is possible to escape from our position of relative strategic inferiority and passivity, and the method is to create local superiority and initiative in many campaigns, so depriving the enemy of local superiority and initiative and plunging him into inferiority and passivity. These local successes will add up to strategic superiority and initiative for us and strategic inferiority and passivity for the enemy. Such a change depends upon correct subjective direction. Why? Because while we seek superiority and the initiative, so does the enemy; viewed from this angle, war is a contest in subjective ability between the commanders of the opposing armies in their struggle for superiority and for the initiative on the basis of material conditions such as military forces and financial resources. Out of the contest there emerge a victor and a vanquished; leaving aside the contrast in objective material conditions, the victor will necessarily owe his success to correct subjective direction and the vanquished his defeat to wrong subjective direction. We admit that the phenomenon of war is more elusive and is characterized by greater uncertainty than any other social phenomenon, in other words, that it is more a matter of "probability". Yet war is in no way supernatural, but a mundane process governed by necessity. That is why Sun Wu Tzu's axiom, "Know the enemy and know yourself, and you can fight a hundred battles with no danger of defeat," remains a scientific truth. Mistakes arise from ignorance about the enemy and about ourselves, and moreover the peculiar nature of war makes it impossible in many cases to have full knowledge about both sides; hence the uncertainty about military conditions and operations, and hence mistakes and defeats. But whatever the situation and the moves in a war, one can know their general aspects and essential points. It is possible for a commander to reduce errors and give generally correct direction, first through all kinds of reconnaissance and then through intelligent inference and judgement. Armed with the weapon of "generally correct direction," we can win more battles and transform our inferiority into superiority and our passivity into initiative. . . . The fact that every ruling dynasty was defeated by revolutionary armies shows that mere superiority in certain respects does not guarantee the initiative, much less the final victory. The inferior side can wrest the initiative and victory from the superior side by securing certain conditions through active subjective endeavour in accordance with the actual circumstances.

To have misconceptions and to be caught unawares may mean to lose superiority and initiative. Hence, deliberately creating misconceptions for the enemy and then springing surprise attacks upon him are two ways—indeed two important means—of achieving superiority and seizing the initiative. . . .

Let us now discuss flexibility. What is flexibility? It is the concrete realization of the initiative in military operations; it is the flexible employment of armed forces. The flexible employment of armed forces is the central task in directing a war, a task most difficult to perform well . . . unless the time, the place and the troops are well chosen. For example, in attacking an enemy force on the move, if we strike too early, we expose ourselves and give the enemy a chance to prepare, and if we strike too late, the enemy may have encamped and concentrated his forces, presenting us with a hard nut to crack. This is the question of the time. If we select a point of assault on the left flank which actually turns out to be the enemy's weak point, victory will be easy; but if we select the right flank and hit a snag, nothing will be achieved. This is the question of the place. If a particular unit of our forces is employed for a particular task, victory may be easy; but if another unit is employed for the same task, it may be hard to achieve results. This is the question of the troops. We should know not only how to employ tactics but how to vary them. . . .

The ancients said: "Ingenuity in varying tactics depends on mother wit"; this "ingenuity," which is what we mean by flexibility, is the contribution of the intelligent commander. Flexibility does not mean recklessness; recklessness must be rejected. Flexibility consists in the intelligent commander's ability to take timely and appropriate measures on the basis of objective conditions after "judging the hour and sizing up the situation" (the "situation" includes the enemy's situation, our situation and the terrain), and this flexibility is "ingenuity in varying tactics." . . .

Let us now discuss the question of planning. Because of the uncertainty peculiar to war, it is much more difficult to prosecute war according to plan than is the case with other activities. Yet, since "preparedness ensures success and unpreparedness spells failure," there can be no victory in war without advance planning and preparations. . . . We are comparatively certain about our own situation. We are very uncertain about the enemy's, but here too there are signs for us to read, clues to follow and sequences of phenomena to ponder. These form what we call a degree of relative certainty, which provides an objective basis for planning in war. Modern technical developments (telegraphy, radio, aeroplanes, motor vehicles, railways, steamships, etc.) have added to the possibilities of planning in war. However, complete or stable planning is difficult because there is only very limited and transient certainty in war; such planning must change with the movement (flow or change) of the war and vary in degree according to the scale of the war. Tactical plans, such as plans for attack or defence by small formations or units, often have to be changed several times a day. A plan of campaign, that is, of action by large formations, can generally stand till the conclusion of the campaign, in the course of which, however, it is often changed partially or sometimes even wholly. A strategic plan based on the over-all situation of both belligerents is still more stable, but it too is applicable only in a given strategic stage and has to be changed when the war moves towards a new stage. The making and changing of tactical, campaign and strategic plans in accordance with scope and circumstance is a key factor in directing a war; it is the concrete expression of flexibility in war, in other words, it is also ingenuity in varying one's tactics. Commanders at all levels in the anti-Japanese war should take note. . . .

The period of validity of a plan for a campaign is shorter than that of a strategic plan, and for a tactical plan it is shorter still, but each is stable over a given period. Anyone denying this point would have no way of handling warfare and would become a relativist in war with no settled views, for whom one course is just as wrong or just as right as another. No one denies that even a plan valid for a given period is fluid; otherwise, one plan would never be abandoned in favour of another. But it is fluid within limits, fluid within the bounds of the various war operations undertaken for carrying it out, but not fluid as to its essence; in other words, it is quantitatively but not qualitatively fluid. . . .

WAR OF ATTRITION AND WAR OF ANNIHILATION

As we have said before, the essence, or the object, of war is to preserve oneself and destroy the enemy. Since there are three forms of warfare, mobile, positional and guerrilla, for achieving this object, and since they differ in degrees of effectiveness, there arises the broad distinction between war of attrition and war of annihilation.

To begin with, we may say that the anti-Japanese war is at once a war of attrition and a war of annihilation. Why? Because the enemy is still exploiting his strength and retains strategic superiority and strategic initiative, and therefore, unless we fight campaigns and battles of annihilation, we cannot effectively and speedily reduce his strength and break his superiority and initiative. We still have our weakness and have not yet rid ourselves of strategic inferiority and passivity;

therefore, unless we fight campaigns and battles of annihilatior we cannot win time to improve our internal and internation situation and alter our unfavourable position. Hence campaign of annihilation are the means of attaining the objective c strategic attrition. In this sense war of annihilation *is* war c attrition. It is chiefly by using the method of attrition throug annihilation that China can wage protracted war.

But the objective of strategic attrition may also be achieve by campaigns of attrition. Generally speaking, mobile warfar performs the task of annihilation, positional warfare perform the task of attrition, and guerrilla warfare performs both sin ultaneously; the three forms of warfare are thus distinguishe from one another. In this sense war of annihilation is differen from war of attrition. Campaigns of attrition are supplemen tary but necessary in protracted war. . . .

The strength of the Japanese army lies not only in its wea pons but also in the training of its officers and men—its degre of organization, its self-confidence arising from never havin been defeated, its superstitious belief in the Mikado and i supernatural beings, its arrogance, its contempt for the Chines people and other such characteristics, all of which stem fron long years of indoctrination by the Japanese warlords and fron the Japanese national tradition. This is the chief reason wh we have taken very few prisoners, although we have killec and wounded a great many enemy troops. It is a point that ha been underestimated by many people in the past. To destro these enemy characteristics will be a long process. The firs thing to do is to give the matter serious attention, and then pa tiently and systematically to work at it in the political field anc in the fields of international propaganda and the Japanese peo ple's movement; in the military sphere war of annihilatior is of course one of the means. . . . The chief method of de stroying them is to win over the Japanese soldiers politically We should understand, rather than hurt, their pride and chan nel it in the proper direction and, by treating prisoners of wa leniently, lead the Japanese soldiers to see the anti-popular character of the aggression committed by the Japanese rulers. On the other hand, we should demonstrate to the Japanese soldiers the indomitable spirit and the heroic, stubborn fighting capacity of the Chinese army and the Chinese people, that is, we should deal them blows in battles of annihilation. . . . From the viewpoint of destroying the enemy's overweening arrogance through battles of annihilation, such battles are one of the prerequisites for shortening the war and accelerating the emancipation of the Japanese soldiers and the Japanese people. Cats make friends with cats, and nowhere in the world do cats make friends with mice. . . .

THE POSSIBILITIES OF EXPLOITING THE ENEMY'S MISTAKES

The enemy command itself provides a basis for the possibility of defeating Japan. History has never known an infallible general, and the enemy makes mistakes just as we ourselves can hardly avoid making them; hence, the possibility exists of exploiting the enemy's errors. . . . Of course, we should not take it as an important basis for our strategic planning; on the contrary, the only reliable course is to base our planning on the assumption that the enemy will make few mistakes. Besides, the enemy can exploit our mistakes just as we can exploit his. It is the duty of our command to allow him the minimum of opportunities for doing so. . . . However, although much of the enemy's strategic and campaign command is incompetent, there are quite a few excellent points in his battle command, that is, in his unit and small formation tactics, and here we should learn from him.

THE QUESTION OF DECISIVE ENGAGEMENTS IN THE ANTI-JAPANESE WAR

The question of decisive engagements in the anti-Japanese war should be approached from three aspects: we should resolutely fight a decisive engagement in every campaign or battle in which we are sure of victory; we should avoid a decisive engagement in every campaign or battle in which we are not sure of victory; and we should absolutely avoid a strategically decisive engagement on which the fate of the whole nation is staked. . . . Undoubtedly, if we are to avoid decisive engagements, we shall have to abandon territory, and we must have the courage to do so when (and only when) it becomes completely unavoidable. At such times we should not feel the slightest regret, for this policy of trading space for time is correct. History tells us how Russia made a courageous retreat to avoid a decisive engagement and then defeated Napoleon, the terror of his age. Today China should do likewise. . . .

Is it not self-contradictory to fight heroically first and then abandon territory? Will not our heroic fighters have shed their blood in vain? That is not at all the way questions should be posed. To eat and then to empty your bowels—is this not to eat in vain? To sleep and then to get up—is this not to sleep in vain? Can questions be posed in such a way? I would suppose not. To keep on eating, to keep on sleeping, to keep on fighting heroically all the way to the Yalu River without a stop—these are subjective and formalist illusions, not realities of life. As everybody knows, although in fighting and shedding our blood in order to gain time and prepare the counter-offensive we have had to abandon some territory, in fact we have gained time, we have achieved the objective of annihilating and depleting enemy forces, we have acquired experience in fighting, we have aroused hitherto inactive people and improved our international standing. Has our blood been shed in vain? Certainly not. Territory has been given up in order to preserve our military forces and indeed to preserve territory, because if we do not abandon part of our territory when conditions are unfavourable but blindly fight decisive engagements without the least assurance of winning, we shall lose our military forces and then be unable to avoid the loss of all our territory, to say nothing of recovering territory already lost. A capitalist must have capital to run his business, and if he loses it all he is no longer a capitalist. Even a gambler must have money to stake, and if he risks it all on a single throw and his luck fails, he cannot gamble any more. Events have their twists and turns and do not follow a straight line, and war is no exception; only formalists are unable to comprehend this truth. . . .

When we say that Japan will finally be defeated despite her technical superiority, we mean that the blows we deliver through annihilation and attrition, apart from inflicting losses, will eventually shake the morale of the enemy army whose weapons are not in the hands of politically conscious soldiers. With us, on the contrary, officers and men are at one on the political aim of the War of Resistance. This gives us the foundation for political work among all the anti-Japanese forces. A proper measure of democracy should be put into effect in the army, chiefly by abolishing the feudal practice of bullying and beating and by having officers and men share weal and woe. Once this is done, unity will be achieved between officers and men, the combat effectiveness of the army will be greatly increased, and there will be no doubt of our ability to sustain the long, cruel war.

The richest source of power to wage war lies in the masses of the people. It is mainly because of the unorganized state of the Chinese masses that Japan dares to bully us. When this defect is remedied, then the Japanese aggressor, like a mad bull crashing into a ring of flames, will be surrounded by hundreds of millions of our people standing upright, the mere sound of their voices will strike terror into him, and he will be burned to death. China's armies must have an uninterrupted flow of reinforcements, and the abuses of press-ganging and of buying substitutes, which now exist at the lower levels, must immediately be banned and replaced by widespread and enthusiastic political mobilization, which will make it easy to enlist millions of men. We now have great difficulties in raising money for the war, but once the people are mobilized, finances too will cease to be a problem. Why should a country as large and populous as China suffer from lack of funds? The army must become one with the people so that they see it as their own army. Such an army will be invincible, and an imperialist power like Japan will be no match for it.

Many people think that it is wrong methods that make for strained relations between officers and men and between the army and the people, but I always tell them that it is a question of basic attitude (or basic principle), of having respect for the soldiers and the people. It is from this attitude that the various policies, methods and forms ensue. If we depart from this attitude, then the policies, methods and forms will certainly be wrong, and the relations between officers and men and between the army and the people are bound to be unsatisfactory. Our three major principles for the army's political work are, first, unity between officers and men; second, unity between the army and the people; and third, the disintegration of the enemy forces. To apply these principles effectively, we must start with this basic attitude of respect for the soldiers and the people, and of respect for the human dignity of prisoners of war once they have laid down their arms. Those who take all this as a technical matter and not one of basic attitude are indeed wrong, and they should correct their view. . . .

My lectures end here. The great War of Resistance Against Japan is unfolding, and many people are hoping for a summary of experience to facilitate the winning of complete victory. What I have discussed is simply the general experience of the past ten months, and it may perhaps serve as a kind of summary. The problem of protracted war deserves wide attention and discussion; what I have given is only an outline, which I hope you will examine and discuss, amend and amplify.

"On New Democracy" is a theoretical framework for the United Front strategy. It appeared as an article in the first issue of a magazine, in January 1940, at about the time ominous rifts between the Kuomintang and the Chinese Com-

munist Party were breaking through to the surface. It is thus at one and the same time a recognition of the United Front strategy and a forecast of its ultimate dissolution. Mao Tse-tung's prediction, that the Communist Party was to return to its independent objectives and their achievements, was not long in being fulfilled.

Throughout the Yenan period the Communists gathered experience with "self-reliance." There was no outside advice or interference, and the success of their own efforts was astounding. In "On New Democracy," two characteristics illustrate the self-confidence engendered by this. One is Mao's claim that his ideas constitute a new contribution to Marxist-Leninist theory, and the other is the assertion of the autonomous nature and personality of the Chinese Communist movement as such.

On New Democracy*

(January 1940)

WHITHER CHINA?

A LIVELY atmosphere has prevailed throughout the country ever since the War of Resistance began, there is a general feeling that a way out of the impasse has been found, and people no longer knit their brows in despair. Of late, however, the dust and din of compromise and anti-communism have once again filled the air, and once again the people are thrown into bewilderment. Most susceptible, and the first to be affected, are the intellectuals and the young students. The question once again arises: What is to be done? Whither China? On the occasion of the publication of *Chinese Culture* [a magazine founded in Yenan] it may therefore be profitable to clarify the political and cultural trends in the country. I am a layman in matters of culture; I would like to study them, but have only just begun to do so. Fortunately, there are many comrades in Yenan who have written at length in this field, so that my rough and ready words may serve the same purpose as the beating of the gongs before a theatrical performance. Our observations may contain a grain of truth for the nation's advanced cultural workers and may serve as a modest spur to induce them to come forward with valuable contributions of

* Mao Tse-tung, "On New Democracy," SELECTED WORKS, vol. II, pp. 339–382.

their own, and we hope that they will join in the discussion to reach correct conclusions which will meet our national needs. To "seek truth from facts" is the scientific approach, and presumptuously to claim infallibility and lecture people will never settle anything. The troubles that have fallen our nation are extremely serious, and only a scientific approach and a spirit of responsibility can lead it on to the road of liberation. There is but one truth, and the question of whether or not one has arrived at it depends not on subjective boasting but on objective practice. The only yardstick of truth is the revolutionary practice of millions of people. This, I think, can be regarded as the attitude of *Chinese Culture*.

WE WANT TO BUILD A NEW CHINA

For many years we Communists have struggled for a cultural revolution as well as for a political and economic revolution, and our aim is to build a new society and a new state for the Chinese nation. That new society and new state will have not only a new politics and a new economy but a new culture. In other words, not only do we want to change a China that is politically oppressed and economically exploited into a China that is politically free and economically prosperous, we also want to change the China which is being kept ignorant and backward under the sway of the old culture into an enlightened and progressive China unde the sway of a new culture. In short, we want to build a new China. Our aim in the cultural sphere is to build a new Chinese national culture.

CHINA'S HISTORICAL CHARACTERISTICS

We want to build a new national culture, but what kind of culture should it be?

Any given culture (as an ideological form) is a reflection of the politics and economics of a given society, and the former in turn has a tremendous influence and effect upon the latter; economics is the base and politics the concentrated expression of economics. This is our fundamental view of the relation of culture to politics and economics and of the relation of politics to economics. It follows that the form of culture is first determined by the political and economic form, and only then does it operate on and influence the given political and economic form. Marx says, "It is not the consciousness of men that determines their being, but, on the contrary, their social being that determines their consciousness." He also says, "The philosophers have only *interpreted* the world, in various ways; the point, however, is to *change* it." For the first time in human history, these scientific formulations correctly solved the problem of the relationship between consciousness and existence, and they are the basic concepts underlying the dynamic revolutionary theory of knowledge as the reflection of reality which was later elaborated so profoundly by Lenin. These basic concepts must be kept in mind in our discussion of China's cultural problems.

Thus it is quite clear that the reactionary elements of the old national culture we want to eliminate are inseparable from the old national politics and economics, while the new national culture which we want to build up is inseparable from the new national politics and economics. The old politics and economics of the Chinese nation form the basis of its old culture, just as its new politics and economics will form the basis of its new culture.

What are China's old politics and economics? And what is her old culture?

From the Chou and Chin Dynasties onwards, Chinese society was feudal, as were its politics and its economy. And the dominant culture, reflecting the politics and economy, was feudal culture.

Since the invasion of foreign capitalism and the gradual growth of capitalist elements in Chinese society, the country has changed by degrees into a colonial, semi-colonial and semi-feudal society. China today is colonial in the Japanese-occupied areas and basically semi-colonial in the Kuomintang areas, and it is predominantly feudal or semi-feudal in both. Such, then, is the character of present-day Chinese society and the state of affairs in our country. . . .

It is precisely against these predominant political, economic and cultural forms that our revolution is directed. What we want to get rid of is the old colonial, semi-colonial and semi-feudal politics and economy and the old culture in their service. And what we want to build up is their direct opposite, *i.e.,* the new politics, the new economy and the new culture of the Chinese nation.

What, then, are the new politics and the new economy of the Chinese nation, and what is its new culture?

In the course of its history the Chinese revolution must go through two stages, first, the democratic revolution, and second, the socialist revolution, and by their very nature they are two different revolutionary processes. Here democracy does not belong to the old category—it is not the old democracy, but belongs to the new category—it is New Democracy.

It can thus be affirmed that China's new politics are the

politics of New Democracy, that China's new economy is the economy of New Democracy and that China's new culture is the culture of New Democracy. . . .

THE CHINESE REVOLUTION IS PART OF THE WORLD REVOLUTION

The historical characteristic of the Chinese revolution lies in its division into the two stages, democracy and socialism, the first being no longer democracy in general, but democracy of the Chinese type, a new and special type, namely, New Democracy. . . .

Clearly, it follows from the colonial, semi-colonial and semi-feudal character of present-day Chinese society that the Chinese revolution must be divided into two stages. The first step is to change the colonial, semi-colonial and semi-feudal form of society into an independent, democratic society. The second is to carry the revolution forward and build a socialist society. At present the Chinese revolution is taking the first step.

The preparatory period for the first step began with the Opium War in 1840, *i.e.,* when China's feudal society started changing into a semi-colonial and semi-feudal one. . . .

A change, however, occurred in China's bourgeois-democratic revolution after the outbreak of the first imperialist world war in 1914 and the founding of a socialist state on one-sixth of the globe as a result of the Russian October Revolution of 1917.

Before these events, the Chinese bourgeois-democratic revolution came within the old category of the bourgeois-democratic world revolution, of which it was a part.

Since these events, the Chinese bourgeois-democratic revolution has changed, it has come within the new category of bourgeois-democratic revolutions and, as far as the alignment of revolutionary forces is concerned, forms part of the proletarian-socialist world revolution.

Why? Because the first imperialist world war and the first victorious socialist revolution, the October Revolution, have changed the whole course of world history and ushered in a new era. . . .

The "world revolution" no longer refers to the old world revolution, for the old bourgeois world revolution has long been a thing of the past; it refers to the new world revolution, the socialist world revolution. Similarly, to form "part of" means to form part not of the old bourgeois but of the new socialist revolution. This is a tremendous change unparalleled in the history of China and of the world. . . .

This revolution has the proletariat of the capitalist countries as its main force and the oppressed peoples of the colonies and semi-colonies as its allies. No matter what classes, parties or individuals in an oppressed nation join the revolution, and no matter whether they themselves are conscious of the point or understand it,

In China, it is perfectly clear that whoever can lead the people in overthrowing imperialism and the forces of feudalism can win the people's confidence, because these two, and especially imperialism, are the mortal enemies of the people. Today, whoever can lead the people in driving out Japanese imperialism and introducing democratic government will be the saviours of the people. History has proved that the Chinese bourgeoisie cannot fulfil this responsibility, which inevitably falls upon the shoulders of the proletariat.

Therefore, the proletariat, the peasantry, the intelligentsia and the other sections of the petty bourgeoisie undoubtedly constitute the basic forces determining China's fate. These classes, some already awakened and others in the process of awakening, will necessarily become the basic components of the state and governmental structure in the democratic republic of China, with the proletariat as the leading force. The Chinese democratic republic which we desire to establish now must be a democratic republic under the joint dictatorship of all anti-imperialist and anti-feudal people led by the proletariat, that is, a new-democratic republic, a republic of the genuinely revolutionary new Three People's Principles with their Three Great Policies. . . . The numerous types of state system in the world can be reduced to three basic kinds according to the class character of their political power: (1) republics under bourgeois dictatorship; (2) republics under the dictatorship of the proletariat; and (3) republics under the joint dictatorship of several revolutionary classes. . . .

The third kind is the transitional form of state to be adopted in the revolutions of the colonial and semi-colonial countries. Each of these revolutions will necessarily have specific characteristics of its own, but these will be minor variations on a general theme. So long as they are revolutions in colonial or semi-colonial countries, their state and governmental structure will of necessity be basically the same, *i.e.*, a new-democratic state under the joint dictatorship of several anti-imperialist classes. In present-day China, the anti-Japanese united front represents the new-democratic form of state. It is anti-Japanese and anti-imperialist; it is also a united front, an alliance of several revolutionary classes. . . .

The state system, a joint dictatorship of all the revolutionary classes and the system of government, democratic centralism—these constitute the politics of New Democracy, the republic of New Democracy, the republic of the anti-Japanese united front, the republic of the new Three People's Principles with their Three Great Policies, the Republic of China in reality as well as in name. Today we have a Republic of China in name but not in reality, and our present task is to create the reality that will fit the name. . . .

THE ECONOMY OF NEW DEMOCRACY

If such a republic is to be established in China, it must be new-democratic not only in its politics but also in its economy.

It will own the big banks and the big industrial and commercial enterprises.

Enterprises, such as banks, railways and airlines, whether Chinese-owned or foreign-owned, which are either monopolistic in character or too big for private management, shall be operated and administered by the state, so that private capital cannot dominate the livelihood of the people: this is the main principle of the regulation of capital.

This is another solemn declaration in the Manifesto of the Kuomintang's First National Congress held during the period of Kuomintang-Communist co-operation, and it is the correct policy for the economic structure of the new-democratic republic. In the new-democratic republic under the leadership of the proletariat, the state enterprises will be of a socialist character and will constitute the leading force in the whole national economy, but the republic will neither confiscate capitalist private property in general nor forbid the development of such capitalist production as does not "dominate the livelihood of the people," for China's economy is still very backward.

The republic will take certain necessary steps to confiscate the land of the landlords and distribute it to those peasants having little or no land, carry out Dr. Sun Yat-sen's slogan of "land to the tiller," abolish feudal relations in the rural areas, and turn the land over to the private ownership of the peasants. A rich peasant economy will be allowed in the rural areas. Such is the policy of "equalization of landownership." "Land to the tiller" is the correct slogan for this policy. In general, socialist agriculture will not be established at this stage, though various types of co-operative enterprises developed on the basis of "land to the tiller" will contain elements of socialism.

China's economy must develop along the path of the "regulation of capital" and the "equalization of landownership," and must never be "privately owned by the few"; we must never permit the few capitalists and landlords to "dominate the livelihood of the people"; we must never establish a capitalist society of the European-American type or allow the old semi-feudal society to survive. Whoever dares to go counter to this line of advance will certainly not succeed but will run into a brick wall. . . .

REFUTATION OF BOURGEOIS DICTATORSHIP

What about the road to a capitalist society under bourgeois dictatorship? To be sure, that was the old road taken by the European and American bourgeoisie, but whether one likes it or not, neither the international nor the domestic situation allows China to do the same. . . .

In the first place international capitalism, or imperialism, will not permit the establishment in China of a capitalist society under bourgeois dictatorship. Indeed the history of modern China is a history of imperialist aggression, of imperialist opposition to China's independence and to her development of capitalism. Earlier revolutions failed in China because imperialism strangled them, and innumerable revolutionary martyrs died, bitterly lamenting the non-fulfilment of their mission. Today a powerful Japanese imperialism is forcing its way into China and wants to reduce her to a colony; it is not China that is developing Chinese capitalism but Japan that is developing Japanese capitalism in our country; and it is not the Chinese bourgeoisie but the Japanese bourgeoisie that is exercising dictatorship in our country. . . .

In the second place, socialism will not permit it. All the imperialist powers in the world are our enemies, and China cannot possibly gain her independence without the assistance of the land of socialism and the international proletariat. . . .

We Communists will never push aside anyone who is revolutionary; we shall persevere in the united front and practise long-term co-operation with all those classes, strata, political parties and groups and individuals that are willing to fight Japan to the end. But it will not do if certain people want to push aside the Communist Party; it will not do if they want to split the united front. China must keep on fighting Japan, uniting and moving forward, and we cannot tolerate anyone who tries to capitulate, cause splits or move backward.

REFUTATION OF "LEFT" PHRASE-MONGERING

If the capitalist road of bourgeois dictatorship is out of the question, then is it possible to take the socialist road of proletarian dictatorship?

No, that is not possible either.

Without a doubt, the present revolution is the first step, which will develop into the second step, that of socialism, at a later date. And China will attain true happiness only when she enters the socialist era. But today is not yet the time to introduce socialism. The present task of the revolution in China is to fight imperialism and feudalism, and socialism is out of the question until this task is completed. The Chinese revolution cannot avoid taking the two steps, first of New Democracy and then of socialism. Moreover, the first step will need quite a long time and cannot be accomplished overnight. We are not utopians and cannot divorce ourselves from the actual conditions confronting us. . . .

REFUTATION OF THE DIEHARDS

. . . Everybody knows that the Communist Party has an immediate and a future programme, a minimum and a maximum programme, with regard to the social system it advocates. For the present period, New Democracy, and for the future, socialism; these are two parts of an organic whole, guided by one and the same communist ideology. Is it not, therefore, in the highest degree absurd to clamour for communism to be "folded up" on the ground that the Communist Party's minimum programme is in basic agreement with the political tenets of the Three People's Principles? It is precisely because of this basic agreement between the two that we Communists find it possible to recognize "the Three People's Principles as the political basis for the anti-Japanese united front" and to acknowledge that "the Three People's Principles being what China needs today, our Party is ready to fight for their complete realization"; otherwise no such possibility would exist. Here we have a united front between communism and the Three People's Principles in the stage of the democratic revolution, the kind of united front Dr. Sun Yat-sen had in mind when he said: "Communism is the good friend of the Three People's Principles."

THE THREE PEOPLE'S PRINCIPLES, OLD AND NEW

In the first place, the revolutionary, new or genuine Three People's Principles must include alliance with Russia. As things are today, it is perfectly clear that unless there is the policy of alliance with Russia, with the land of socialism, there will inevitably be a policy of alliance with imperialism, with the imperialist powers. Is this not exactly what happened after 1927? . . .

In the second place, the revolutionary, new and genuine Three People's Principles must include co-operation with the Communist Party. Either you co-operate with the Communist Party or you oppose it. . . .

In the third place, the revolutionary, new and genuine Three People's Principles must include the policy of assisting the peasants and workers. Rejection of this policy, failure wholeheartedly to assist the peasants and workers or failure to carry out the behest in Dr. Sun Yat-sen's Testament to "arouse the masses of the people," amounts to preparing the way for the defeat of the revolution, and one's own defeat into the bargain. Stalin has said that "*in essence,* the national question is a peasant question." This means that the Chinese revolution is essentially a peasant revolution and that the resistance to Japan now going on is essentially peasant resistance. Essentially, the politics of New Democracy means giving the peasants their rights. The new and genuine Three People's Principles are essentially the principles of a peasant revolution. Essentially, mass culture means raising the cultural level of the peasants. The anti-Japanese war is essentially a peasant war. We are now living in a time when the "principle of going up into the hills" applies; meetings, work, classes, newspaper publication, the writing of books, theatrical performances—everything is done up in the hills, and all essentially for the sake of the peasants. And essentially it is the peasants who provide everything that sustains the resistance to Japan and keeps us going. By "essentially" we mean basically, not ignoring the other sections of the people, as Stalin himself has explained. As every schoolboy knows, 80 per cent of China's population are peasants. So the peasant problem becomes the basic problem of the Chinese revolution and the strength of the peasants is the main strength of the Chinese revolution. In the Chinese population the workers rank second to the peasants in number. There are several million industrial workers in China and several tens of millions of handicraft workers and agricultural labourers. China cannot live without her workers in the various industries, because they are the producers in the industrial sector of the economy. And the revolution cannot succeed without the modern industrial working class, because it is the leader of the Chinese revolution and is the most revolutionary class. In these circumstances, the revolutionary, new and genuine Three People's Principles must include the policy of assisting the peasants and workers. Any other kind of Three People's Principles which lack this policy, do not give the peasants and workers whole-hearted assistance or do not carry out the behest to "arouse the masses of the people," will certainly perish. . . .

A given culture is the ideological reflection of the politics and economics of a given society. There is in China an imperialist culture which is a reflection of imperialist rule, or partial rule, in the political and economic fields. . . . Imperialist culture and semi-feudal culture are devoted brothers and have formed a reactionary cultural alliance against China's new culture. This kind of reactionary culture serves the imperialists and the feudal class and must be swept away. Unless it is swept away, no new culture of any kind can be built up. There is no construction without destruction, no flowing without damming and no motion without rest; the two are locked in a life-and-death struggle.

As for the new culture, it is the ideological reflection of the new politics and the new economy which it sets out to serve. . . .

THE HISTORICAL CHARACTERISTICS OF CHINA'S CULTURAL REVOLUTION

On the cultural or ideological front, the two periods preceding and following the May 4th Movement form two distinct historical periods.

Before the May 4th Movement, the struggle on China's cultural front was one between the new culture of the bourgeoisie and the old culture of the feudal class. The struggles between the modern school system and the imperial examination system, between the new learning and the old learning, and between Western learning and Chinese learning, were all of this nature. . . .

Prior to the May 4th Movement, China's new cultural movement, her cultural revolution, was led by the bourgeoisie, which still had a leading role to play. After the May 4th Movement, its culture and ideology became even more backward than its politics and were incapable of playing any leading role; at most, they could serve to a certain extent as an ally during revolutionary periods, while inevitably the responsibility for leading the alliance rested on proletarian culture and ideology. This is an undeniable fact.

The new-democratic culture is the anti-imperialist and anti-feudal culture of the broad masses; today it is the culture of the anti-Japanese united front. The culture can be led only by the culture and ideology of the proletariat, by the ideology of communism, and not by the culture and ideology of any other class. In a word, new-democratic culture is the proletarian-led, anti-imperialist and anti-feudal culture of the broad masses. . . .

SOME WRONG IDEAS ABOUT THE NATURE OF CULTURE

Everything new comes from the forge of hard and bitter struggle. This is also true of the new culture which has followed a zigzag course in the past twenty years, during which both the good and the bad were tested and proved in struggle. . . .

So far as the orientation of our national culture is concerned, communist ideology plays the guiding role, and we should work hard both to disseminate socialism and communism throughout the working class and to educate the peasantry and other sections of the people in socialism properly and step by step. However, our national culture as a whole is not yet socialist.

Because of the leadership of the proletariat, the politics, the economy and the culture of New Democracy all contain an element of socialism, and by no means a mere casual element but one with a decisive role. However, taken as a whole, the political, economic and cultural situation so far is new-democratic and not socialist. For the Chinese revolution in its present stage is not yet a socialist revolution for the overthrow of capitalism but a bourgeois-democratic revolution, its central task being mainly that of combating foreign imperialism and domestic feudalism. . . .

Beyond all doubt, now is the time to spread communist ideas more widely and put more energy into the study of Marxism-Leninism, or otherwise we shall not only be unable to lead the Chinese revolution forward to the future stage of socialism, but shall also be unable to guide the present democratic revolution to victory. However, we must keep the spreading of communist ideas and propaganda about the communist social system distinct from the practical application of the new-democratic programme of action; we must also keep the communist theory and method of investigating problems, undertaking research, handling work and training cadres distinct from the new-democratic line for national culture as a whole. It is undoubtedly inappropriate to mix the two up. . . .

A NATIONAL, SCIENTIFIC AND MASS CULTURE

New-democratic culture is national. It opposes imperialist oppression and upholds the dignity and independence of the

Chinese nation. It belongs to our own nation and bears our own national characteristics. It links up with the socialist and new-democratic cultures of all other nations and they are related in such a way that they can absorb something from each other and help each other to develop, together forming a new world culture; but as a revolutionary national culture it can never link up with any reactionary imperialist culture of whatever nation. To nourish her own culture China needs to assimilate a good deal of foreign progressive culture, not enough of which was done in the past. We should assimilate whatever is useful to us today not only from the present-day socialist and new-democratic cultures but also from the earlier cultures of other nations, for example, from the culture of the various capitalist countries in the Age of Enlightenment. However, we should not gulp any of this foreign material down uncritically, but must treat it as we do our food—first chewing it, then submitting it to the working of the stomach and intestines with their juices and secretions, and separating it into nutriment to be absorbed and waste matter to be discarded—before it can nourish us. To advocate "wholesale westernization" is wrong. China has suffered a great deal from the mechanical absorption of foreign material. Similarly, in applying Marxism to China, Chinese communists must fully and properly integrate the universal truth of Marxism with the concrete practice of the Chinese revolution, or in other words, the universal truth of Marxism must be combined with specific national characteristics and acquire a definite national form if it is to be useful, and in no circumstances can it be applied subjectively as a mere formula. Marxists who make a fetish of formulas are simply playing the fool with Marxism and the Chinese revolution, and there is no room for them in the ranks of the Chinese revolution. Chinese culture should have its own form, its own national form. National in form and new-democratic in content—such is our new culture today. . . .

A spendid old culture was created during the long period of Chinese feudal society. To study the development of this culture, to reject its feudal dross and assimilate its democratic essence is a necessary condition for developing our new national culture and increasing our national self-confidence, but we should never swallow anything and everything uncritically. It is imperative to separate the fine old culture of the people which had a more or less democratic and revolutionary character from all the decadence of the old feudal ruling class. China's present new politics and new economy have developed out of her old politics and old economy, and her present new culture, too, has developed out of her old culture; therefore, we must respect our own history and must not lop it off. However, respect for history means giving it its proper place as a science, respecting its dialectical development, and not eulogizing the past at the expense of the present or praising every drop of feudal poison. As far as the masses and the young students are concerned, the essential thing is to guide them to look forward and not backward.

New-democratic culture belongs to the broad masses and is therefore democratic. It should serve the toiling masses of workers and peasants who make up more than 90 per cent of the nation's population and should gradually become their very own. There is a difference of degree, as well as a close link, between the knowledge imparted to the revolutionary cadres and the knowledge imparted to the revolutionary masses, between the raising of cultural standards and popularization. Revolutionary culture is a powerful revolutionary weapon for the broad masses of the people. It prepares the ground ideologically before the revolution comes and is an important, indeed essential, fighting front in the general revolutionary front during the revolution. People engaged in revolutionary cultural work are the commanders at various levels on this cultural front. "Without revolutionary theory there can be no revolutionary movement," one can thus see how important the cultural movement is for the practical revolutionary movement. Both the cultural and practical movements must be of the masses. Therefore all progressive cultural workers in the anti-Japanese war must have their own cultural battalions, that is, the broad masses. A revolutionary cultural worker who is not close to the people is a commander without an army, whose fire-power cannot bring the enemy down. To attain this objective, written Chinese must be reformed, given the requisite conditions, and our spoken language brought closer to that of the people, for the people, it must be stressed, are the inexhaustible source of our revolutionary culture.

A national, scientific and mass culture—such is the anti-imperialist and anti-feudal culture of the people, the culture of New Democracy, the new culture of the Chinese nation.

Combine the politics, the economy and the culture of New Democracy, and you have the new-democratic republic, the Republic of China both in name and in reality, the new China we want to create.

Behold, New China is within sight. Let us all hail her!

Her masts have already risen above the horizon. Let us all cheer in welcome!

Raise both your hands. New China is ours!

The Party of the War Bases*

THE YEAR 1937 is a sharp line of demarcation in the history of the Chinese Communist Party. The overwhelming event of that year was the full-scale outbreak of the Japanese war and the formation of the United Front between the Kuomintang and the Communist Party. Party policy was riveted to these facts for eight years. A second factor was the post-1937 development of the Anti-Japanese War Bases. A final fact was the explosive expansion in Party membership after 1937 and the growth of a new Party organization under Mao Tse-tung's sole leadership.

WAR AND THE UNITED FRONT

Two Chinas fought Japan. There is no point in continuing the argument here as to which fought harder or more effectively. More important is the fact that two types of warfare were waged on two different battlegrounds. Nationalist armies fought from a unified region while the Kuomintang and its government rotted. The Communist Party fought from a patchwork of unstable War Bases and grew enormously. For the first two years of Japanese aggression, the United Front promised to weld the traditional enemies into close alliance, but 1945 ended with the virtual certainty of civil war.

The United Front agreements were concluded in September, 1937, five years after the Communist Party of China first declared war on Japan and demanded an anti-Japanese alliance. Agreement was finally forced on the Kuomintang by the Sian Incident of 1936 and the pervasive nationalism of the period. The initial success of the 1937 alliance should be attributed more to the enthusiastic spirit of resistance which permeated China than to a detailed working out of common problems; agreement remained in principle and on paper.

* Introduction, pp. xvi–xxxix, reprinted from MAO'S CHINA: PARTY REFORM DOCUMENTS, 1942–1944, trans. by Boyd Compton. Copyright, 1952. By permission of University of Washington Press. All rights reserved.

Communists agreed not to undermine the Kuomintang-directed government, but to work instead for united resistance and the realization of the ambiguous Three People's Principles. The Red Army lost its name and became the Eighth Route Army, accepting formal allegiance to the National Military Council. Communist areas growing in the northern provinces were designated special administrative regions under the national government. In return, the Kuomintang promised to turn its eyes from "bandit-suppression" to war with Japan. The Communist Party was once again legally free to organize. Although the pact of alliance immediately became a symbol of unity, it was soon shown to be more a truce than a settlement.

A semblance of unity was displayed at higher levels throughout the war; it was at the lower levels of contact that friction first appeared. A typical clash came in southern Hopei when the Kuomintang dispatched Lu Chung-lin to act as governor in an area already organized behind Japanese lines by a Peking professor, Yang Hsiu-feng. Lu immediately proposed changes in administration and policy which Yang could not accept, then proceeded to set up a parallel administration of his own. Through the middle of 1939 two governments worked side by side—one Kuomintang, the other drawing closer and closer to Communist policy and the Red military forces operating in the area. The issue was finally decided when a section of Lu's troops went over to the Japanese and his government disintegrated.

The Hopei case was typical of the United Front as a whole. Conflict was rooted in suspicions and fundamental policy differences which had been glossed over by the 1937 agreements. Only the problem of jurisdiction was solved in Hopei. No concrete plan for cooperation was even considered. In 1939 and 1940 the Kuomintang and Communist Party squabbled and drew steadily apart. In the New Fourth Army Incident of early 1941, open warfare nearly cracked the partnership. The barrier of Nationalist troops thrown across the Red southern flank now became a blockade. The further development of the Anti-Japanese War Bases took place behind a joined screen of Kuomintang and Japanese troops.

No renunciation of the United Front was issued by either side, despite mounting accusations of violation and lack of faith. Chungking admitted Communist negotiators and allowed the publication of the *Hsin Hua Jih Pao*, a Communist daily. Kuomintang members participated in the local administrations of Communist regions, though they did not represent a regularly functioning Party organization. The Kuomintang group in Shansi-Chahar-Hopei was finally disowned by Chungking for straying to the left. The over-all picture was not one of United Front, but of two jurisdictions which corresponded to areas of Kuomintang and Communist military supremacy. In each area, policy formation was a Party monopoly.

THE ANTI-JAPANESE WAR BASES

In 1937 the Communist Party was dominant in only the barren Shensi-Kansu-Ninghsia Border Region, where remnants of the Long March from the south had consolidated two years earlier with local forces under Liu Tzu-tan. The coming of war created an unequaled opportunity for the Party to expand its core of 80,000 battle-toughened veterans. While Shen-Kan-Ning remained a party nerve center, by far the most important fields for military and revolutionary activity were to the east behind Japanese lines. There, at the enemy's back and between his lines of control, the Party took root again and began to develop compartments of resistance.

The War Bases grew up under two pressures: (1) the spontaneous development of local resistance groups behind Japanese lines, and (2) Communist organizing activities carried into resistance areas by Red military forces and their political organizers. Neither pressure should be undervalued.

The first base formed was the Shansi-Chahar-Hopei Border Region (Chin-Cha-Chi), established in 1938 at the Fuping Conference, and eventually including a population of 20,-000,000. The same year Liu Po-ch'eng's 129th Division swept south and east from the Shansi hills onto the North China plain, then into Shantung and to the China Sea. As it traveled, it dispersed into small units which organized new centers of resistance or coordinated the activities of resistance groups already operating. In southern Hopei they found Professor Yang Hsiu-feng working as head of an administrative office for thirty hsien. Guerrilla units were already operating independently in many other areas covered by Liu's 6,000 troops. The effect of Communist leadership and policy was soon seen in the tendency of guerrilla bands to unite and form military-political administrations. In 1941 nearly the entire hill and plain region was unified in the Shansi-Hopei-Honan-Shantung Border Region.

The process was repeated elsewhere. In Central China eight smaller bases grew up around the New Fourth Army. By 1945, nineteen Anti-Japanese War Bases with an estimated population of 90,000,000 were sandwiched in between the Japanese garrisons and points of control in North and Central China.

Red China grew slowly. Its form was dictated by the conditions of war, but its lifeblood was the nationalism and unrest of the millions in the battle area.

The existence of the War Bases depended upon the one condition which made their administration most difficult. As their double and triple names indicate, they were border regions—areas which straddled mountainous provincial boundaries or spread through nearly inaccessible backlands. They maintained a measure of stability through their isolation from key cities and arteries controlled by the Japanese. In Chinese history, these areas of divided jurisdiction have been natural trouble spots. The rampaging Ming Dynasty bandits, Li Tsuch'eng and Chang Hsien-chung, both operated in the Shensi hills near Yenan; the center of the nineteenth-century Nien Rebellion coincided with the Shansi-Hopei-Honan-Shantung Border Region. The isolation and poor communications which protected these in-between areas made the coordination of military and administrative functions immensely difficult.

The problem of coordination between the compartments of resistance was even more challenging than the problem of joint action and liaison within. As the war progressed, it became increasingly difficult to break across the Japanese moat and blockhouse system. Chiang Kai-shek's armies had utilized this system in 1934 to destroy Communist bases in Kiangsi; the Japanese now followed his earlier lead and succeeded in pushing the War Bases into virtual isolation. The result was the single fact which dominated War Base political life: at no time during the war was there a central government or administration for the separate regions of Communist China. The task of over-all unification fell to the Communist Party.

Communist troops and political organizers fought two campaigns behind Japanese lines: one with weapons, the other with slogans. War was superimposed on revolution. The development of the War Bases into bastions of both military and political support would have been inconceivable without a Party program capable of sprouting simple slogans with broad appeal. During the war, the Chinese Communists compared the Party to a fish and the people to the water. The engulfing masses could be hostile, disinterested, or friendly; the greatest Party asset was a systematic program which answered local problems, adapted itself to local needs, and gained the active friendship of the greater part of the War Base population.

In its broad outlines, Party policy was in keeping with the United Front policy handed down by the Seventh Congress of the Comintern in 1935. But it is also true and perhaps more important that a great part of Comintern policy was in line with the Chinese Communist statements which accompanied the declaration of war against Japan in 1932. The complicated policy line from Comintern to Chinese Party cannot be analyzed here; it is enough to say that the general policy of the United Front was not channeled to the Chinese Communist Party from a Comintern source, but grew as a response to national conditions. After the Seventh Congress, Communist United Front overtures to the Kuomintang were more systematic and offered a change in basic revolutionary policy. On August 1, 1935, the Central Committee called for war and political coalition, renouncing its extreme policy of land confiscation and agrarian revolution. As Communist areas expanded and administrative problems multiplied, general policy was given a more concrete form which can be broken down under three slogans.

"Exterminate the Japanese Aggressor." Undoubtedly, the most effective Party slogans were military and nationalistic. The prestige of early and consistent pleas for resistance to Japan had already won the Party wide support when war came. This stand was particularly telling in winning the support of middle groups and the university intellectuals who fled to liberated areas. With bold and timely slogans, the Party took its first real slice of Kuomintang support before war came.

When the fighting started, Party life in the War Bases became almost completely militarized, for no area of activity was free from Japanese attack. War Base military forces formed a pyramid with three levels. (1) Communist troops (80,000 in 1937, 910,000 in 1945) of the Eighth Route Army and New Fourth Army were divided into Main Forces, for general operational movements, and Regional Forces, for guerrilla operations. (2) The People's Militia (over 2,000,000 in 1945) consisted of village volunteers; service was part-time and the forces corresponded roughly to the National Guard in the American states in that normal command rested with local government but special conditions would place militia units under regular army commanders. (3) The Self-Defense Corps included all young, middle-aged, and even old men and women . . . voluntarily, democratically organized . . . ," according to Mao Tse-tung. This supposedly democratic group was as important in the organization of production as it was in strictly military activities.

Armaments in the military pyramid ranged from a few rifles and many spears in the Self-Defense Corps to a fairly adequate supply of captured rifles and small arms in the Eighth Route and New Fourth Armies. The three steps in organization were progressive; the best Self-Defense units graduated to militia status, and militia units were pulled into the regular forces in increasing numbers toward the end of the war. This graduation process would explain the fact that regular Communist forces doubled in size in 1944–45.

The dispersed regular forces under Red command succeeded in gaining powerful popular support in their command areas. Strategy had split the military forces and placed them close to village life; farsighted policy made this potentially dangerous position not only tenable but advantageous. Orders demanded that Communist troops pay for supplies, engage in production when not fighting, respect local organizations, and in general "love the people." Small unit warfare also demanded that they live with and not on the people, for it was the village which fed, hid, and clothed the army, provided spies, informants, replacements, and recruits. The success of Communist policy —coupled with the absence of large-unit positional warfare— made conscription unnecessary. Substantial mass support and participation was a pivotal factor in the enlargement of the Anti-Japanese War Bases and the later victory in the Civil War.

"Reduce Rent. Reduce Interest. Guarantee Rent. Guarantee Interest." The moderation of the economic and political program which the Communists carried into the War Bases won them the title "agrarian reformers." The name is correctly given for the United Front period. Compromise remained the Party tactic until 1946. The heart of economic policy was the reduction of exorbitant rent and interest rates and the rationalization of the confused tax system. A 1942 Central Committee resolution called for a blanket 25 per cent reduction in rent. Interest rates were set at 1½ per cent. Taxation was to be progressive and greatly simplified. The rural proletariat could only accept a rain check on its hopes for land; no large-scale redistribution was ordered until after the war. Tenancy remained, the landlord was guaranteed his rent and the usurer his interest. In short, each class heard a promise. The degree of fulfillment was evidently impressive in the more stable areas.

The Communist economic policy was effective because it was simple. It satisfied neither the very rich nor the very poor, yet an extreme policy would have been impossible under conditions of war. A middle-ground tactic was obviously necessary. The problem of training and indoctrination was to obtain unanimous and effective support for the reformist program from hundreds of thousands of radical and enthusiastic Party recruits. Mao Tse-tung and Liu Shao-ch'i vigorously condemn the new Party members' errors of extremism and independent action in *Reform Documents*. It was no simple matter for the Party to put the brakes on the force of revolution.

"Establish a Democratic Coalition Government." Party political policy appeared democratic during the war; it called for the election of all officials directing administrative offices in the Anti-Japanese War Bases. Suffrage was universal, with some exceptions. A broad group defined as "workers, peasants, anti-Japanese intellectuals, and those who are not opposed to the mass-movement" could hold office. At the top of the governmental hierarchy was the Regional Assembly with its administrative standing committee, then in order, the administrations of the sub-region (for most bases), prefecture (*chuan chu*), county (*hsien*), district (*chu*), and village. . . .

The model for this elective system was obviously the democratic-centralism of Soviet Russia, under which the general content as well as the form of political action is prescribed. Yet within the narrow limits of democratic-centralism, Party policy succeeded in bringing a new experience in political participation to millions—in itself a political revolution of immense significance.

At the district level, Party, army, and government shared political power with various legally recognized "mass organizations." These included trade unions, women's associations, cooperatives, and Peasant Salvation Associations. When the latter became the chief weapon of the 1946–47 land revolution, it was said, "The government has the right; the Salvation Association has the power." The associations apparently represented an independent power at the local level as early as 1943, when the Central Committee warned them against "taking over administrative functions from the government in making arrests, examinations, and judgments. . . ." The Party achieved leadership in mass organizations through the work of its Party groups (*tang t'uan*). As in government, the Party was leader; complete organizational independence was not even pretended. But mass organizations possessed wide areas of operational independence and acted as the most important sounding boards for popular sentiments.

Other slogans concerned women's rights, education, labor, and traitors. The program was broad and timely and allowed the Communists to rally the War Base masses in support of both the war and the Party. A devastating comparison could be made with Kuomintang regions, where conscription was a tragedy to the tenant and a joke to the landlord, where taxes, rents, and corruption mounted incessantly, and where the promises of the ruling party's platform remained on paper.

Successful as these slogans were, they could not eliminate several basic Party problems:

(1) Foremost was the difficulty in coordination and liaison within and between bases, a problem originating in geography, poor communications, and the unstable conditions of guerrilla warfare. These, plus the absence of a central government for Red China, threw the task of over-all unification to the Communist Party: it had to function not only through government, but as government. No matter what steps the Party might have taken in this role to tie units and areas together, decentralization and segmentation remained a fact. Considerable areas of local Party initiative existed throughout the war. In this setting, uniformity of action could not be forced on the scattered Party units. It would have been impossible to set up a system of close central inspection. The Party answered its challenge through an intensive program of indoctrination and training which culminated in the Cheng Feng Movement.

(2) A second problem was the need to strike a balance between Party control and mass support. In Russia, internal stability and a state monopoly of force have allowed the importance of popular support to be minimized and controls magnified when quick and decisive action is imperative. An example is the expropriation of the kulaks in 1929–30. The position of the Chinese Communist Party in the War Bases was precarious in comparison. No major opposition or challenge appeared from within, but with frequent and sudden Japanese attacks, the existence of the Party and its armies depended entirely on the friendship and active cooperation of the village peasants. Still more important, the peasants were armed in the People's Militia and Self-Defense Corps. Village arms were inferior and regular Red armies could undoubtedly have maintained order, but the Party could not afford disorder of any type. The support and cooperation of the armed village was the Party's margin of survival.

The Party had no strangle hold on the War Bases. It was leader and policy maker, but its power was limited by the necessity for active popular support. This did not lead to a western-type democratic rule in War Base organizations. It did, however, call for the maximum use of persuasion rather than force, and indirect controls rather than a system of dictation. Throughout the War Base period, the Party stumbled over the formal structural balance it had created in the "three-thirds" system and the triple military force. The Party could only attain its ends with an adaptable organization and strong discipline.

(3) A third set of problems sprang from the low educational level of the agrarian backlands. Slogans could be passed verbally or acted out in the Yang-ko dramas, but widespread illiteracy and lack of education were recognized as decisive barriers to Party policy. The Communists answered this problem energetically in the ingenious makeshift school system Lindsay describes in his *Notes on Educational Policy in Communist China*. The general problem of education in the Anti-Japanese War Bases was also a Party problem, for the hundreds of thousands of new Party members came principally from the agrarian poor. It is not surprising that the principal focus of the Cheng Feng Reform Movement was education and individual training.

After 1937, war and the War Bases produced a Chinese Communist Party which was new in membership and composition. The Party had been virtually destroyed twice in fifteen years, first in the debacle of 1927 and later in the fall of the Kiangsi Soviets in 1934. The Long March, which lasted 8,000 miles and ended in Shensi in 1935, was a symbol of both heroism and defeat. Wang Ming certainly exaggerated in claiming a Party membership of "hundreds of thousands" for the following year. Mao had claimed a Party membership of 40,000 for 1937. A rapid expansion followed:

1937	40,000	Mao Tse-tung
1938	200,000	Nym Wales
1942	"Several Hundred Thousand"	Mao Tse-tung
1943	800,000	Chou En-lai
1945	1,200,000	Mao Tse-tung

This twelve-fold expansion made the Chinese Communist Party the world's second largest at the end of the war. The social background and educational level of the new members was as great a problem to the Party as was their numbers.

The concept of the multiclass New Democratic revolution demanded that the Party draw its recruits from many sources in society. A key to the Party's preferences was the length of the probation period required of members from various classes. No probation period was required of the urban worker or the hired farm hand. This source was limited, however, by the underdevelopment of War Base industry and the predominance of individual land ownership. The poor peasantry was by all odds the largest source. According to Po I-po, the Shansi-Hopei-Honan-Shantung Border Region, with a population of 30,000,000 had only one city with over 100,000 and eight or nine with between forty and fifty thousand. The Party therefore drew the great bulk of its wartime recruits from a reservoir of small farmers who served a one-month probation period. Middle Peasants were classified with petty bourgeois groups and served three months' probation. A final source was the group of intellectuals who fled the coastal cities to fight in the War Bases. The Party faced a staggering problem in attempting to creat a minimum uniformity of thought and action among these different segments of its membership.

So it was anything but a Party of the proletariat which emerged from the War Bases. It did not claim to be. According to Liu Shao-ch'i, the "errors" attacked in the Cheng Feng Movement were rooted in the nonproletarian outlooks of the majority of the million Chinese who joined the Party from 1937 to 1945:

The Party and the proletariat have been constantly encircled by the power of the nonproletarian classes. . . . Unstable elements, having passed into the Party and the proletariat and penetrated to their heart, have constantly influenced them in ideology, living habits, theory and action. This is the source of all undesirable, mistaken tendencies within the Party.

Significantly, the most serious errors were attributed not to the conservatism of the peasantry, but to the extremism of the petty bourgeois intellectuals the Party was so eager to absorb. The enemy of the Cheng Feng Movement, however, was not a particular type of unorthodox thinking. It was heterodoxy in general. Cheng Feng was a strict diet concocted to regulate rapid Party growth, rather than an antidote for a specific ailment.

Wartime problems demanded a strong, flexible Party structure, as well as a correct line of thought. The Party pyramid did not differ basically from that of the Russian Party. The striking difference was the absence of a central government through which the Party could work its policy. Contact between Party and government began on the regional level. The levels of Party administrative organs in descending order were:

> Central Committee
> Central Committee Regional Department
> Border Region or Provincial Committee
> Area Committee
> Municipal or Country Committee
> District Committee

Branch

Sub-branch

According to the Party Regulations adopted at the 1945 Congress, each of these organs was to be elected by a conference or congress at the same level and approved by the next higher organ. The standard Bolshevik organizational principles were acknowledged: democratic-centralism, iron discipline, self-criticism, and perpetual study and training.

The Central Committee worked in Yenan under Chairman Mao's increasingly strong leadership. As in the Russian Party, its principal organ was a Politburo which held actual power of decision. Under the seven-man Politburo came the Propaganda Bureau, Organization Bureau, United Front Bureau, and Military Affairs Committee. The Central Committee also included committees and sections for labor, culture, youth, and women's affairs.

An outstanding feature of the new Party which grew in Yenan and the War Bases was the central educational apparatus which functioned under the Central Committee. Before 1935, selected cadres from the various national parties went to Moscow's Lenin Institute for their training; after 1935 there was increasing emphasis on the development of Party schools in all countries. In Red China, these included the Central Party School, Yenan University (Yenta), the Lu Hsün Academy, a Natural Science Academy, and a Central Research Institute. The thousands of students who passed through these schools and returned to the War Bases were a powerful unifying factor in the Party.

Another distinctive feature of the wartime Party was the importance of the Central Committee's regional departments. Beyond the barriers of Japanese troops, the Northwest, North China, and Central China Bureaus carried on the Central Committee's work in the War Base areas, apparently serving as miniature central committees with their own organs and schools. It can be assumed that similar departments functioned underground in south and east China. The importance of the departments can be disputed, but 1950 finds six regional bureaus of the Central Committee with great power and some independence.

Within the Border Regions, the Party came directly in contact with the areas it controlled. In general, the structure of the Party down to the district (*chu*) duplicated the structure of the government, the various mass organizations, and the military forces. A diagram would show four nearly identical pyramids. Party control of these groups was assured by a number of factors. First was Party prestige and the mere fact of Party participation. More direct guidance was attained through what amounted to a "double-squeeze": (1) The highest levels of non-Party organizations were Party dominated. It was Party policy which came down from the top in each. (2) At each level, the subdivisions of each non-Party organization were guided by groups (*t'uan*) from the same level in the Party pyramid. The method can be seen clearly in the armed forces and mass organizations.

The top generals in the Eighth Route and New Fourth Armies—Liu Po-ch'eng, Lin Piao, Ch'en Yi, Nieh Jung-chen —were high ranking Party members. As a result, military policy came directly from the Party's Central Committee. Supplementary to this control was the work of the political commissioners attached to army units at the divisional, regimental, and battalion level. The commissioner functioned both as teacher and leader. As teacher, he was responsible for the political indoctrination and organization of the unit's troops. As leader, he divided responsibility with the military commander and passed on all military decisions of possible political significance. Anxious to strengthen Party leadership in the armed forces, the Central Committee ruled in 1943 that the jobs of political commissioner in garrison regiments and battalions were to be held by the secretaries of area and district Party committees. Through the efforts of these commissioners and Party branches organized at the lowest levels, the Red armies became effective political as well as military forces.

Double Party control was also exercised in most of the so-called mass organizations. For example, the leader of the "non-Party" All-China Federation of Labor was Central Committeeman Liu Shao-ch'i. As in the school system, women's groups, and peasants' associations, policy-making was an unofficial Party monopoly. A second check was provided at each level in these organizations by Party groups (*t'uan*) responsible to Party committees or branches. Policy was controlled from above; work was guided and checked by lower-level Party units. Obviously, this pattern could not be applied everywhere; wartime confusion demanded wide local initiative in both Party and non-Party groups. The peasant associations in the villages were evidently the most difficult to keep in check.

Party guidance was less direct in government, where the Party saw its problem as one of salesmanship rather than control. Limited to one-third of all elective officers, the Party had to rely on the discipline and organization of the groups it had working in civil administration from the Border Region down to the district. There are actually instances, though only a few, in which points of Party policy were actually voted down by non-Communist majorities. But with the advantages of prestige, political organization, and an army, the Party was able to achieve a fairly uniform adoption of its United Front Program.

As guerrilla areas and compartments of resistance combined to form War Bases, the Party saw a major problem in co-ordination at the Border Region level. Its answer came in 1943 with the creation of Unified Leadership Committees of representatives from the Party, army, government, and mass organizations. Little is known about their actual functioning, but their mere existence indicates the difficulty met by the Party in guiding the various non-Party organizations through the normal Party structure. On paper the committees appear to have been unofficial ruling organs more easily subject to Party control than the regular governmental offices.

There is no doubt that the Chinese Communist Party of the War Bases organized itself with the Communist Party of the Soviet Union as a model. Party leaders could not, however, control their environment. At the highest levels, war and de-centralization combined to produce several unique organiza-tional features: the absence of a central government, the importance of the Central Committee's regional departments, and the Unified Leadership Committees. At the lowest level of organization, the *Chih Pu* or Party branch, rapid expan-sion and wartime chaos created a constant test of Party dis-cipline and indoctrination. Mao and his lieutenants faced a staggering task in welding this organization together for war and revolution. Their answer was the Cheng Feng Movement of 1942-44.

THE REFORM MOVEMENT

More than a thousand Party members crowded a Yenan lecture hall on February 1, 1942, to hear Mao Tse-tung in-augurate the Cheng Feng Reform Movement. In a speaking style close to Stalin's, Mao launched a broad three-front attack on errors in the Party's style of work and thought. He slashed at subjectivism in thought, sectarianism (separation from the masses) in Party relations, and formalism in literature and art. As he ended his speech, Mao advised that the audience and the entire Pary work vigorously to correct their ways of thought and action. An editorial in the *Liberation Daily* the next day claimed, "There is already a new spirit in Yenan." One week later, Mao and propaganda chief K'ai Feng elaborated on the evils of formalism in Party literature and propaganda to an audience of 800. Mao's role as keynote speaker for the Cheng Feng Movement ended there; the reform machinery slowly began to operate.

The first activity noted by the *Liberation Daily* was in the higher-level organs in the Yenan area. An article of February 21 reported that full discussions and investigations had been concluded in committees, organs, and schools directly subordinate to the Central Committee. Editorials and articles indicate increased activity in March as the Political Academy and the Pao An military command reported their reform programs. The Party School was reorganized with Teng Fa as principal, and by the end of the month the movement was in full swing in the Natural Sciences Academy. Finally, on April 3, a formal movement for the entire Party was announced in a bulletin of the Central Committee's Propaganda Bureau.

The Propaganda Bureau communiqué called for a movement in three parts: (1) A period of study and discussion, to last two months for all Party schools and three months for Party organs. At the end of this period, a general examination was to be held on Mao's speeches and twenty other documents. These twenty-two pieces are the core of this volume. (2) A period for the investigation of Party work. The investigations were to be carried out by the organs and schools themselves, and not by a central agency. (3) A final period in which members in the individual organs and schools were to draw conclusions on the quality of their comrades' work, then submit reports to higher levels for approval. Incorrigible comrades were to be dismissed from the Party, but a second and third chance were to be given comrades who confessed and showed willingness to reform. The reform machinery outlined by the Central Committee was thus simple; under war conditions it had to be. Its most striking characteristic was a type of decentralization which matched that of the Party as a whole.

There is too little information on what actually transpired during the Cheng Feng period. The picture can only be pieced together from the scraps of available fact. Reform was evidently carried out through small study groups which worked their way through the maze of standards set in *Reform Documents;* criticism and self-criticism then followed on the basis of these often contradictory standards. Self-criticism meant complete confession and symbolized allegiance to Mao's standards, whatever they might be. . . .

The object of Cheng Feng, however, was not physical control of the Party's members. Its purpose was the type of intensive indoctrination and training which would allow the Party to operate with unanimity in a situation where close administrative control and inspection were out of the question. Nothing was more important in 1942, 1943, and 1944 than the immense amount of time spent up and down the Party hierarchy studying the writings which make up *Reform Documents*. The entire Party went to school.

Was Cheng Feng also a purge? Even in its general outlines, the 1942-44 movement had no close counterpart in Russian experience. It was certainly aimed at a specific group of leaders, but important characteristics of the 1933-35 and 1937 purges in Russia were absent. First, it was not called a purge. No personalities in power at the time were mentioned in *Reform Documents* to dramatize errors; 1942 provided no Trotsky, Zinoviev, Bucharin, or Radek to set up as a symbol of crawling, cunning wickedness. Finally, 1942-44 did not take a 270,000 slice from the membership of the Chinese Communist Party as the 1933-35 cleansing had done in Russia; instead Party membership doubled. The word "purge" in its usual sense should not be used in speaking of the Cheng Feng Movement.

The specific target for Cheng Feng was evidently the important group which centered around Wang Ming, the Party's leading Comintern representative. Wang returned from Moscow schooling in 1930 with twenty-seven comrades. In January of the following year, he, Po Ku, Lo Fu, and Shen Tse-min led the attack on Li Li-san and immediately assumed the leading positions in the Central Committee. They monopolized these posts from 1931 until the ascendancy of Chinese-trained leaders around Mao in 1935-37. The last major appearance of the Wang group as principal bearers of the Party line was in 1939 when Wang Ming and Po Ku wrote articles on the "imperialist" war in Europe and the United Front in China. It is worth noting that none of the Cheng Feng documents written from 1939 to 1943 came from Wang's coterie. They issue rather from the practical workers whose experience had been closer to the day-to-day struggle in China than to Moscow or the Comintern.

Unfortunately, no Ruth Fischer or Leon Trotsky has fled the Chinese Communist Party to write about inner-Party alignments and the struggle for power. We cannot expect the Party itself to tell such a personal story openly. The clearest description we have of the drama is told indirectly in the Cheng Feng documents.

Two articles in this volume seem to attack Wang Ming directly: Mao's "In Opposition to Party Formalism" and Liu Shao-ch'i's "Liquidation of Menshevik Thought." Through the veil of impersonality, Wang can be seen as the foreign formalist and dogmatist that Mao and his spokesman deride. His writings in the *Communist International* and *International Press Correspondence* show dependence on Russian and European examples, an avoidance of practical Chinese problems, and worst of all, lavish praise for Stalin and Dimitrov but few adjectives for Mao. Mao's idea of a real theoretician in 1942 was one who had done as much organizing as he had reading. Wang did not fill the bill. When Mao first rose to practical leadership in the Party during the Kiangsi Soviet period, Wang was with the Central Committee near Shanghai; during the Long March he was in Moscow. Leading policy statements after 1937 came more and more from Mao, Chou En-lai, and rising theoreticians Liu Shao-ch'i, Ch'en, Po-ta, and Ch'en Yün. After the Cheng Feng attack, Wang, Lo Fu, and Po Ku lost their voice.

Cheng Feng represented a final stage in Mao's consolidation of leadership. Mao gained prestige in the twenties, practical leadership of the Party in the middle thirties, and official leadership when he became head of the Politburo in 1937. His only contestant for power. Chang Kuo-t'ao, was actually purged as a traitor in 1938. When Cheng Feng came, the leaders of the "28 from Moscow" were not in any sense purged; Wang lost prestige when demoted to the principalship of a girl's school, but he, Lo Fu, and Po Ku were still Central Committeemen in 1945. What they actually lost was control of the highest Party offices and their positions as principal Party spokesman. The theme of Cheng Feng was the union of "the universal truths of Marxism-Leninism with the concrete reality of the Chinese Revolution." Wang and his group had only theory. They were demoted, passed up by leaders with the practical experience Cheng Feng demanded.

Cheng Feng thus had two major characteristics. A group of high leaders fell from power; to this extent it was a purge. On the other hand, its principal importance to the entire Party was intensive indoctrination and education in the principles of Mao Tse-tung's communism.

The Yenan Period of Chinese Communism was characterized by two objectives: the war against the Japanese and rebuilding the Party and army. From 1927 to 1937 the Communist movement had developed from a minority worker's party following doctrinaire Marxism to a well-seasoned agrarian movement representing a mixture of rural revolution and nationalism. On this base the Communists continued to develop, throughout the period of national resistance to Japanese aggression, a unique Chinese theory and practice of revolution which included community organization, political education, and the mobilization of a unified and egalitarian political party. This is clearly portrayed in the Communist documents of the period. There is a soul-searching analysis of past mistakes, ways in which to rectify them and new lines of exploration. The events, activities and experiences in this period were the formative years of communism in China. The lessons learned during this time laid the ideological and organizational groundwork not only for the consolidation of national power by the Communists but also for the overall pattern of development of a new society since then. The influence of doctrines evolved at that time is clearly indicated by the fact that they are being reprinted and circulated for study today as part of the cultural revolution.

The following documents highlight a number of concerns involving the education of a new Chinese man. In general the opposition is to a type of person and not to people as physical entities. The underlying assumption is that behaviors and attitudes of people can be changed. This, then, becomes the aim of defining certain actions or orientations as enemy traits: in order to rid the Party of them.

Reform in Learning, the Party and Literature*
(February 1, 1942)

. . . WHAT ABOUT the problem of the so-called "intelligentsia"? Because our China is a semi-colonial, semi-feudal country and its culture is undeveloped, the intelligentsia are of special value. According to a resolution of the Central Committee, we must strive for a broad intelligentsia. It is very correct that an attitude of welcome be adopted toward them, if only they are revolutionary and willing to participate in the War of Resistance. But as a result of this attitude, the intelligentsia have been glorified and the local bumpkins are handicapped. We consider it entirely necessary to hold the intelligentsia in esteem,

* Mao-Tse-tung, "Reform in Learning, the Party and Literature," excerpts translated by Boyd Compton in MAO'S CHINA: PARTY REFORM DOCUMENTS, 1942–44, op. cit., pp. 14–22.

for without a revolutionary intelligentsia, the revolution cannot succeed.

However, we know that there are many intellectuals who consider themselves very learned and who make a great display of the knowledge, not realizing that this attitude is harmful and obstructs their progress. One truth that they should realize is that a great many so-called intellectuals are actually exceedingly unlearned, and that the knowledge of the workers and peasants is sometimes somewhat greater than theirs. At this someone may say, "Aha! You're turning this upside down. It's a mass of confused words!" (*Laughter*) But, comrades, don't get excited. What I say is to a certain extent reasonable.

What is knowledge? From ancient times down to the present, there have only been two types of knowledge: one type is knowledge of the struggle in production; the other is knowledge of the class struggle. Knowledge of the national struggle is also included in these. What knowledge is there aside from this? There is none. Natural science and social science are nothing but the crystallization of these two types of knowledge. Philosophy is then a generalization and summary of natural science and social science. Aside from these, there is no other type of knowledge.

Now let us consider those students who graduate and leave their schools where they have been completely isolated from the practical activities of society. In what position do they find themselves? A man studies through from grade school to university, graduates, and is then considered learned. Yet, in the first place, he cannot till the land; second, he has no trade; third, he cannot fight; fourth, he cannot manage a job—in none of these fields is he experienced nor does he have the least practical knowledge. What he possesses is merely book knowledge. Would it be possible to regard such a man as a complete intellectual? It would be very difficult, and at the most I would consider him a half-intellectual, because his knowledge is still incomplete.

What is comparatively complete knowledge? All comparatively complete knowledge is formed in two stages: the first is that of knowledge through immediate perception; the second is knowledge through reason. Knowledge through reason is a higher stage of development of knowledge through immediate perception. In which category does the book knowledge of students fall? Even if we suppose that their knowledge is correct, it is still theory drawn from the experience of their predecessors in the struggle of production and the class struggle, and not knowledge drawn from their own personal experience. It is absolutely necessary that they obtain this [theoretical] knowledge, but they should realize that, for them, this knowledge is inverted, backward, one-sided; it has been proved by others, but still not verified by the students themselves. They should know that it is not at all difficult to obtain this type of knowledge, that it is even extremely easy. In comparison, the cook's task in preparing a meal is difficult. To create something ready to eat, he must use a combination of wood, rice, oil, salt, sauce, vinegar, and other materials. This is certainly not easy, and to cook a good meal is all the more difficult. If we compare the tasks of the cook at the Northwest Restaurant and the cooks in our homes, we find a great difference. If there is too much fire, the food will burn, too much vinegar, and it will be sour. (*Laughter*)

Cooking food and preparing dishes is truly one of the arts. But what about book knowledge? If you do nothing but read, you have only to recognize three to five thousand characters, learn to thumb through a dictionary, hold some book in your hand, and receive millet from the public. Then you nod your head contentedly and start to read. But books cannot walk, and you can open and close a book at will; this is the easiest thing in the world to do, a great deal easier than it is for the cook to prepare a meal, and much easier than it is for him to slaughter a pig. He has to catch the pig . . . the pig can run . . . (*Laughter*) he slaughters him . . . the pig squeals. (*Laughter*) A book placed on a desk cannot run, nor can it squeal. (*Laughter*) You can dispose of it in any manner you wish. Is there anything easier to do? Therefore, I advise those of you who have only book knowledge and as yet no contact with reality, and those who have had few practical experiences, to realize their own shortcomings and make their attitudes a bit more humble.

How can half-intellectuals be transformed into intellectuals with a title corresponding to reality? There is only one way: to see that those with only book knowledge become practical workers engaged in practical tasks, and see that those doing theoretical work turn to practical research. In this way we can reach our goal. . . .

On the other hand, mistakes are also going to be made by those comrades engaged in practical work who made an incorrect application of the experience. It is quite true that such men have had a great deal of experience and should be valued highly. But there is great danger if they are satisfied with their experience. They should realize that greater part of their knowledge is gained from immediate perception and is therefore limited, and that they fall short when it comes to reasoning and universal knowledge, that is to say, they fall short in theory. Thus their knowledge, too, is comparatively incomplete. Yet without comparatively complete knowledge it is impossible to finish the revolution.

Seen in this way, there are two types of incomplete knowledge. One is knowledge taken from books, and I am afraid that even Marxist-Leninist books can leave a man empty in his thinking. Another type of knowledge is overweighted on the side of immediate perception and therefore limited; it has not developed into something rational and universal. Both types are one-sided, and only if they are combined can something worth-while and comparatively complete be produced.

However, if our workers' and peasants' cadres are going to study theory, they must first study culture, for if there were no culture, Marxism-Leninism could not be absorbed. At the appropriate time, after culture has been studied thoroughly, they can study Marxism-Leninism. When I was a youth, I did not attend a Marxist-Leninist school; I studied a mass of things, like "Confucius said, 'Is it not pleasant to study your lessons and practice them constantly?' " (*Laughter*) I learned to read in just this way. For example, I learned the characters for "to study" and can now use them in "studying" Marxism-Leninism. However, people do not study Confucius now, but the new national language, history, geography, and general knowledge in the natural sciences. Studied thoroughly, these cultural lessons are applicable everywhere. Our Party's Central Committee is now vigorously urging the workers' and peasants' cadres to engage in cultural studies, because after these are studied, politics, military affairs, and economics can all be studied. Otherwise, whether they have a wealth of experience or not, the workers' and peasants' cadres will still not have advanced to the stage where theorizing is possible.

Thus if we are antisubjectivist, we must see that the two types described above develop in those spheres where they are deficient; we must see that these two types combine. Only if those with book knowledge develop in practical spheres will it be possible for them to go beyond their books; only then will it be possible for them to avoid the error of dogmatism. Men with working experience have to study theory and realize the value of reading; only then will it be possible for them to raise their experience to the level of reason and synthesis, the level of theory. Only then will it be possible for them to avoid classifying their partial experience as universal truth and avoid the error of empiricism. Dogmatism and empiricism are both forms of subjectivism, though they arise from two different extremes.

There are thus two types of subjectivism in our Party. One type is dogmatism, the other, empiricism. Both errors see only one side and not the entire picture. If you ignore this one-sidedness and fail to understand its shortcomings, and at the same time expect to make progress, it will be easy for you to travel the path of error.

Of these two types of subjectivism in our Party, the more important and dangerous is still dogmatism. Because it easily assumes the guise of Marx-Engels-Lenin-Stalinism, frightens the workers' and peasants' cadres, and captures the local hay-seeds for personal servants, it is difficult for the workers' and peasants' cadres to see through its mask. It can also frighten innocent youths and take them captive. If we conquer dogmatism, we will be able to see that cadres with book knowledge develop a willingness to associate with cadres with experience and engage in the study of practical matters. It will be possible to produce many good workers who combine experience and theory, and it will be possible to produce many true theoreticians. If we conquer dogmatism, comrades with experience can obtain good teachers and rise to the level of theory, thus avoiding the error of empiricism.

In addition to the two vague terms, "theoretician" and "intellectual," there is a phrase we read every day, "the union of theory and practice," which still has a vague meaning for many of our comrades. Every day they speak of "union," but on the contrary actually mean "separation," for they take no steps toward "union." How can Marxist-Leninist theory and the reality of the Chinese Revolution be united? Take the common saying, "To shoot an arrow, have a target" (*yu ti fang shih*). Arrow (*shih*) means arrow (*ch'ien*), and target (*ti*) means target (*pa*). In shooting the arrow, you must have a target to aim at. The relation between Marxism-Leninism and the Chinese Revolution is the same as between the arrow and the target. However, some comrades are shooting arrows without a target, shooting them recklessly. It is easy for them to harm the revolutionary cause.

In addition, there are some comrades who merely take the arrow in hand, twist it back and forth, and say again and again in praise, "excellent arrow, excellent arrow," but are never willing to shoot it. This type of person is a connoisseur of antiques who has hardly any relationship with the revolution. The arrow of Marxism-Leninism must be used to hit the target of the Chinese Revolution. If it were otherwise, why would we want to study Marxism-Leninism? Isn't it because we have not digested our millet that we read a book on the relief of indigestion? Why has our Party School decided to study Marxism-Leninism? If this problem is not clearly understood, the theoretical level of the Party can never be raised and the Chinese Revolution can never succeed.

Our comrades must understand that we do not study Marxism-Leninism because it is pleasing to the eye, or because it has some mystical value, like the doctrines of the Taoist priests who ascend Mao Shan to learn how to subdue devils and evil spirits. Marxism-Leninism has no beauty, nor has it any mystical value. It is only extremely useful. It seems that right up to the present quite a few have regarded Marxism-Leninism as a ready-made panacea; once you have it, you can cure all your ills with little effort. This is a type of childish blindness and we must start a movement to enlighten these people. Those who regard Marxism-Leninism as religious dogma show this type of blind ignorance. We must tell them openly, "Your dogma is of no use," or to use an impolite phrase, "Your dogma is less useful than excrement." We see that dog excrement can fertilize the fields and man's can feed the dog. And dogmas? They can't fertilize the fields, nor can they feed a dog. Of what use are they? (*Laughter*)

Comrades! You know that the object of such talk is to ridicule those who regard Marxism-Leninism as dogma, to frighten and awaken them, to foster a correct attitude toward Marxism-Leninism. Marx, Engels, Lenin, and Stalin have repeatedly said, "Our doctrine is not dogma; it is a guide to action." Of all things, these people forget this most important sentence. Theory and practice can be combined only if men of the Chinese Communist Party take the standpoints, concepts, and methods of Marxism-Leninism, apply them to China, and create a theory from conscientious research on the realities of the Chinese Revolution and Chinese history. If we merely verbalize about union but do not practice union in our actions, we can talk for a hundred years and still not benefit. . . .

> The Chinese Communists, from their wartime days in Yenan, have been engaged in two distinct but more or less simultaneous revolutions. One is the revolution to change the landscape of China: to industrialize, radically improve the conditions of production and create new communities. The other is the revolution to change men's minds: to turn traditional ways of thinking into new and modern channels of thought, and aspirations—the kind that will enable Chinese

society to speed through centuries of progress into the communist future within a matter of decades. This latter revolution (referred to as "thought reform") is as arduous and formidable a task as the former, especially under circumstances in which a number of stages of development are telescoped into one another. It is not simply a matter of transforming a working-class into a socialist community but first (and at the same time) transforming a tradition-bound peasantry into a modern working-class.

The Cheng Feng Movement, initiated in February 1942 (see pp. 267-272 for Mao's opening speech), was the first major effort in the direction of changing basic attitudes and behavior of Party members through a process of "study" and "self-criticism." During the Cheng Feng Reform Period (1942–1944) Liu Shao-ch'i emerged as the leading Party ideologist. With its center of operations in the Yenan hinterland, the Party was engaged in fighting the Japanese and simultaneously preparing itself as an effective instrument for political revolution. In order to achieve that objective Party members had to be drawn away from imitating Russian models, empty theorizing and thrown into a conscious grappling with practical problems. They could not, however, be expected to handle practical problems without also coming to grips with themselves—their own work habits and attitudes.

According to Marxian theory the Communist Party is a proletarian party which qualifies it as vanguard of the revolution. In China, however, the Communist Party of the forties was far removed from any contact with the working-class. Party rank and file were almost entirely drawn from the peasantry or intelligentsia. This created two problems, one theoretical the other practical. The theoretical problem—what made the Party proletarian if it was completely divorced from an urban proletariat?—was ignored. In Liu Shao-ch'i's How To Be a Good Communist, it is flatly asserted that the Chinese Communist Party is the party of the proletariat. Although there is the implication that lan·lless peasantry constitute the rural equivalent of a proletariat, in general there is no acknowledgment of the discrepancy between Marxist ideal and Chinese reality. The Chinese were involved in a revolutionary war and their primary concerns were practical; theory therefore addressed itself to practical problems.

The practical problems stemmed from the fact that the Party had expanded enormously in the preceding period drawing in large numbers of peasants not equipped to lead a modern revolution. Liu Shao-ch'i's How To Be a Good Communist was one of the documents used to educate party members, not only in the tactics of revolutionary organization but in everything from politics to manners. The main concern was that party members acquire a method, an approach to understanding the full picture of events, so that they knew where and how they fit into it. This would secure Party discipline and reliability in the exercise of initiative and making judgments that affected the destiny of the Movement.

The following is a selection from Liu Shao-ch'i's article presenting a model of ideal behavior for a Communist Party member. The Party, as backbone of the revolution, was responsible for training a community of believers. It raised, supported, praised and punished the individuals who would carry forward the revolution and in so doing were forced to discard old ways and learn new ones.

Prior to the recent events of the proletarian cultural revolution Liu Shao-ch'i, as one of the eminent older leaders of the Party, provided basic reading for all Chinese. In recent months he has been discredited and his work withdrawn from the lists of required reading. This adds a special importance to the document not because its subject matter is controversial but for the opposite reason. It indicates that a man's work, no matter how unobjectionable it is intrinsically, is considered part of the entirety of his personality. Liu Shao-ch'i's writings are blacklisted because he has become the symbol of a weakness, a shortcoming in the revolutionary fibre of today's China. His person has not been attacked but his thinking has—his values which are supposed to exhibit bourgeois deviationist traits. As a result Liu Shao-ch'i himself has vanished into the obscurity that has so often marked his political career in the past even while his name receives enormous publicity.

How to Be a Good Communist*

. . . A COMMUNIST must be clear about the correct relationship between personal and Party interests.

The Communist Party is the political party of the proletariat and has no interests of its own other than those of the emancipation of the proletariat. The final emancipation of the prole-

* Liu Shao-ch'i, HOW TO BE A GOOD COMMUNIST (Peking: Foreign Languages Press, 1964) pp. 46–75 (excerpts).

tariat will also inevitably be the final emancipation of all mankind. . . .

The test of a Party member's loyalty to the Party, the revolution and the cause of communism is whether or not he can subordinate his personal interests absolutely and unconditionally to the interests of the Party, whatever the circumstances.

At all times and on all questions, a Party member should give first consideration to the interests of the Party as a whole, and put them in the forefront and place personal matters and interests second. The supremacy of the Party's interests is the highest principle that must govern the thinking and actions of the members of our Party. In accordance with this principle, every Party member must completely identify his personal interests with those of the Party both in his thinking and in his actions. He must be able to yield to the interests of the Party without any hesitation or reluctance and sacrifice his personal interests whenever the two are at variance. Unhesitating readiness to sacrifice personal interests, and even one's life, for the Party and the proletariat and for the emancipation of the nation and of all mankind—this is one expression of what we usually describe as "Party spirit," "Party sense" or "sense of organization." It is the highest expression of communist morality, of the principled nature of the party of the proletariat, and of the purest proletarian class consciousness.

Members of our Party should not have personal aims which are independent of the Party's interests. Their personal aims must harmonize with the Party's interests. . . . Apart from this aim, Party members should have no independent personal motives such as attaining position or fame, or playing the individual hero, otherwise they will depart from the interests of the Party and may even become careerists within the Party.

If a Party member thinks only of the communist interests and aims of the Party, is really selfless and has no personal aims and considerations divorced from those of the Party:

First, he has a high communist morality. Taking a clear-cut, firm proletarian stand, he is able to show loyalty to and love for all comrades, all revolutionaries and working people, help them unreservedly and act towards them as his equals, and he will never allow himself to hurt a single one of them for his own interests. . . . He is "the first to worry and the last to enjoy himself." Whether in the Party or among the people, he is the first to suffer hardship and the last to enjoy comfort; he compares himself with others not with respect to material enjoyment but to the amount of work done for the revolution and the spirit of hard endurance in struggle.

Second, he has the greatest revolutionary courage. Having no selfish motives, he has nothing to fear. Having done nothing to give himself a guilty conscience, he can lay bare and courageously correct his mistakes and shortcomings, which are like "an eclipse of the sun or the moon." . . .

Third, he learns how best to grasp the theory and method of Marxism-Leninism. He is able to apply them in keenly observing problems and in knowing and changing reality. . . .

Fourth, he is the most sincere, most candid and happiest of men. Because he has no private axe to grind, nothing to conceal from the Party and nothing he cannot tell others, he has no problems of personal gain or loss and no personal anxieties other than for the interests of the Party and the revolution. Even when he is working on his own without supervision and is therefore in a position to do something bad, he is just as "watchful over himself when he is alone" and does not do anything harmful. His work bears examination and he is not afraid of having it checked. He does not fear criticism and at the same time is able to criticize others with courage and sincerity.

Fifth, he has the greatest self-respect and self-esteem. For the sake of the Party and the revolution he can be most forbearing and tolerant towards comrades and can suffer wrong in the general interest, even enduring misunderstanding and humiliations without bitterness if the occasion so demands. No personal aims lead him to flatter anyone or to desire flattery from others. When it comes to personal matters, he knows how to conduct himself and has no need to humble himself in order to get help from others. . . .

Ours is a fine morality precisely because it is proletarian and communist. It is founded not on the protection of the interests of individuals or of the exploiting few, but on those of the proletariat and the great mass of working people, of the cause of the final emancipation of all mankind, the liberation of the whole world from the calamities of capitalism, and the building of a happy and beautiful communist world —it is a morality founded on the Marxist-Leninist theory of scientific communism. As we Communists see it, nothing can be more worthless or indefensible than to sacrifice oneself in the interests of an individual or a small minority. But it is the worthiest and justest thing in the world to sacrifice oneself for the Party, for the proletariat, for the emancipation of the nation and of all mankind, for social progress and for the highest interests of the overwhelming majority of the people. . . .

The Communist Party represents the general and long-range interests of the proletariat and all mankind in their struggle for emancipation; the Party's interests are the concentrated expression of this cause. One must never regard the Communist Party as a narrow clique, like a guild pursuing the interests of its members. Anyone who does so is no Communist.

A Party member has interests of his own, which may be inconsistent with or even run counter to the interests of the Party in certain circumstances. Should this happen, it is incumbent on him to sacrifice his personal interests and unconditionally subordinate them to the interests of the Party; under no pretence or excuse may he sacrifice the Party's interests by clinging to his own. . . .

Members of our Party must subordinate personal to Party interests and are required to sacrifice them to Party interests if necessary. But this by no means implies that our Party does not recognize, or brushes aside, the personal interests of its members or that it wants to wipe out their individuality. Party members do have their personal problems to attend to, and, moreover, they should develop themselves according to their individual inclinations and aptitudes. Therefore, so long as the interests of the Party are not violated, a Party member can have his private and family life, and develop his individual inclinations and aptitudes. At the same time, the Party will use every possibility to help members develop their individual inclinations and aptitudes in conformity with its interests, furnish them with suitable work and working conditions and commend and reward them. As far as possible, the Party will attend to and safeguard its members' essential interests; for example, it will give them the opportunity to study and to acquire an education, it will help them cope with health and family problems and, when necessary, it will even give up some of its work in order to preserve comrades working under the rule of reaction. But all this has no other purpose than the over-all interests of the Party. For the fulfilment of its tasks the Party must ensure that members have the conditions necessary for life, work and education so that they can perform their tasks with enthusiasm and without worry. Comrades in responsible Party positions must bear all this in mind when they deal with Party members' problems. . . .

EXAMPLES OF WRONG IDEOLOGY IN THE PARTY

. . . What are the fundamentally wrong ideas to be found among comrades in our Party?

First. The people joining our Party not only differ in class origin and personal class status but also carry with them aims and motives of every description. Many, of course, join the Party in order to bring about communism and attain the great goal of the emancipation of the proletariat and all mankind, but some do so for other reasons and with other aims. For example, some comrades of peasant background used to think that communism meant "expropriation of local tyrants and distribution of the land." . . . A few even join because they count on the Party to get their taxes reduced, or because they hope to "make their mark" some day, or because their relatives or friends have brought them in, etc. . . . Since they bring all sorts of ideas with them into the Party, it is most important that they should be educated and should train and temper themselves. Otherwise, they cannot become revolutionary fighters of the proletariat. . . .

Second. Fairly strong individualism and selfishness are still to be found in some members of our Party. . . .

When it comes to status, material benefits and other questions affecting everyday life, they invariably try to get more than others, compare themselves with those at the top, diligently strive after greater personal benefits and crow when they get them. But when it comes to work, they like to compare themselves with those who are less capable. When there are hardships to bear, they make themselves scarce. In times of danger they want to run away. When it comes to orderlies, they always want more. Their living quarters must be of the best, and they want to show off and to bask in the Party's glory. They want to grab all the good things of life, but when it comes to the "unpleasant things," they think these are for others. . . .

This type of self-seeking individualism often manifests itself inside the Party in unprincipled quarrelling, factional struggle, sectarianism and departmentalism; it manifests itself in disrespect for and wilful violation of Party discipline. Most unprincipled struggles originate in personal interests. Those who go in for factional struggle and are given to sectarianism usually place their own individual interests, or the interests of a small minority, above those of the Party. Often, in their unprincipled factional struggles they deliberately undermine Party organization and discipline, making unprincipled and sometimes calculated attacks on certain people, while contracting unprincipled friendships to avoid giving offence, to cover up for one another, to sing each other's praises, etc. ....

Third. Conceit, the idea of individualistic heroism, ostentatiousness, etc. are still to be found, to a greater or lesser extent, in the minds of quite a few Party comrades. ....

Communists must not be in the least complacent or arrogant. Granted that some comrades are very capable, have done some good work and have to their credit considerable achievements, which may be reckoned "great" and on which they might well preen themselves (for example, our army commanders who have led thousands and tens of thousands of men in battle and won victories, or the leaders of our Party and mass work in various places who have brought about fairly significant changes in the situation). Yet after all, how great are these achievements compared with the communist cause as a whole? And for people with a communist world outlook, what is there worth preening oneself about in these achievements? ....

Therefore, while we are opposed to individualistic heroism and to ostentatiousness, we are certainly not opposed to a spirit of enterprise in the Party members. The desire to make progress in the interests of the people is a most precious quality in a Communist. But the communist, proletarian, spirit of enterprise is entirely different from the individualist "spirit of enterprise." ....

Our comrades must also understand that a member, or a leader and hero, whoever he may be, can only do part of the work, can only carry part of the responsibility, in the communist movement. The communist cause is an undertaking which requires the collective efforts of tens of millions of people over a long period of time, and which cannot be encompassed by any one individual alone. ....

Naturally, in assigning work to members, the Party organization and the responsible Party comrades should, as far as possible, take their individual inclinations and aptitudes into consideration, develop their strong points and stimulate their zeal to go forward. However, no Communist must refuse a Party assignment on the grounds of personal preference.

Fourth. A small number of comrades are deeply imbued with the ideology of the exploiting classes. They are usually unscrupulous in dealing with comrades and in handling problems inside the Party, and are utterly devoid of the great and sincere proletarian communist spirit of mutual help and solidarity. ....

The proletariat must carry the cause of the emancipation of humanity through to the end, fighting step by step for the liberation of all mankind, and there can be no giving up or compromising half-way.

As a result of this objective position occupied by the proletariat, the ideology of the politically conscious workers is the diametrical opposite of that of the exploiters. Communists are vanguard fighters of the proletariat, who arm themselves with Marxism-Leninism and are ruthless towards the people's enemies but never towards the toilers, their class brothers and comrades. They differentiate clearly and sharply between the attitudes and methods to be adopted against the enemy and those to be adopted towards their comrades and friends. They cherish great and sincere friendship, warmth and sympathy for other members of their own class and for all oppressed and exploited working people, towards whom they show a fine spirit of mutual help, firm unity and genuine equality. They are absolutely opposed to privileges of any kind for anyone, consider it impermissible to think in terms of privileges for themselves, and would deem it unthinkable, and indeed a disgrace, to occupy a privileged position among the people. If they themselves are to develop and improve their own status, they must develop others and improve the status of all the working people at the same time. . . . Not harbouring any desire to settle old scores, they can return good for evil to their own comrades and brothers and help them straighten themselves out. They can be strict with themselves and lenient with others. The stand they take is firm, strict and principled, their attitude is frank, upright and responsible, they do not give way on matters of principle, they do not tolerate anyone who harms the Party, they do not permit anyone to insult them and are particularly contemptuous of adulation and flattery as contrary to all principle. They oppose all unprincipled struggles; they do not let themselves become involved in such struggles, and are not so swayed by irresponsible or casual criticism made behind their backs as to depart from principle, become incapable of thinking calmly or lose their composure. Such are the proletarian qualities of mind every Party member must learn to acquire and foster. . . .

Fifth. Pettiness, fussing over trifles and ignoring the general interest are faults still prevalent among some Party members. . . .

There are other people who do not seem to have a clear-cut and definite attitude in their Party life, people who shift and hedge. They are actually of two kinds; for one kind the question is one of understanding, and for the other, of moral character. The latter are always opportunistic in their personal behaviour, curry favour with all sides and try to please everybody. They tailor their words to the person and the circumstances, tack with the wind and show no principle whatsoever. Such are their characteristics. Sometimes, they wait and see what will suit the occasion, . . . and then move over to the winning side. Such double-faced creatures, who are neither fish nor fowl, are not altogether unknown in our ranks. They have the traits of the old-fashioned merchant. In addition, there are some individuals who, unable to resist the lure of the old society's exploiting classes, with their glittering world, their money and their women, begin to waver, go wrong and eventually betray the Party and the revolution. . . .

The newcomers may ask, "Does not the Communist Party stand for all that is just? Are not Communists the finest people? Why are there still such bad people and ugly things in the Communist Party? How strange!" Before joining the Party, some young comrades were bitterly dissatisfied with existing society, saw no way out and turned to the Communist Party as to a beacon of light. They thought that everything would be satisfactory and would work out well once they joined. Yet after doing so, or after arriving in our revolutionary base area, they find there are shortcomings and mistakes in the Party, too, and in real life not everything is satisfactory (much that would satisfy them would not be in the interests of the revolution and the Party), and so they feel that reality is not entirely as they pictured it, and some begin to have doubts and feel puzzled. They ask, "Why are such things to be found in the Communist Party as well?" . . . The reason, I think, is rather simple. Our Party has not fallen from the skies, but has grown out of Chinese society. In general, our Party consists of the finest sons and daughters of our country, the vanguard of the Chinese proletariat, but they come from all strata of the old society, and in China today there still exist exploiting classes and the influence of these classes—selfishness, intrigue, bureaucracy and various other kinds of filth. We have many excellent Party members who are not easily affected by such influences. But is it so strange that certain members unavoidably bring some of the filth of the old society with them into our Party or reflect it there? Is it so strange that a person who has just crawled out of the mud is covered with slime? Of course not. It is only to be expected. It would be strange, and indeed incredible, if the ranks of the Communist Party were absolutely free from such filth. It may be said that so long as such filth exists in society, so long as classes and exploiting class influences exist in society, there is bound to be some filth in the Communist Party. It is precisely because there is such filth in society, and in the Party, that it is the duty of the Communist Party to change existing society, and it is necessary for Communists to remould, cultivate and temper themselves. In addition to carrying on a struggle in society at large against everything evil and backward, it is imperative for us to carry on a struggle inside the Party against every social evil and backward influence as mirrored in the Party by vacillating and unsteady elements. This is the source of inner-Party contradiction and struggle. Through struggle, both inside and outside the Party, we seek to change society and gradually rid it of its evils and backwardness, and at the same time seek to perfect our Party and remould our Party members, and to resolve our inner-Party contradictions, so that our Party and its membership will become healthier and stronger. . . .

There are qualities of twentieth-century communism in China that are similar in ways to nineteenth-century democracy in the United States. There is a dynamic movement, with an expansiveness which is an outgrowth of success; a dazzling combination of pragmatic experimentation and idealistic devotion is in the service of a population bent on building a new and better world in isolation from the rest of the world.

In Communist China today, as in the Communist-dominated areas during the war years, there is a commitment, a sense of common purpose that pervades the social fabric. Enthusiasm is invested in hard work and a fierce determination infuses all aspects of life. Whether it is in agricultural production, a factory assembly-line, in a class-room or a hospital, in painting, writing for films or training for an olympic sport, there is a feeling that everything is an integral part of the whole society—which is on the move. Ideology is the bloodstream of the social organism. It integrates, incorporates and separates the activities and behaviors of people according to certain principles whose application in all spheres provides the standard of evaluation.

Unlike the democratic ideology in the West, however, Communist ideology—in China, the philosophy of Mao Tse-tung—has not yet become fossilized; it remains a phenomenon that grows out of the very pattern of existence that people engage in regularly. It is, therefore, not external to them but addresses itself to their problems as if it were innate. The following document, "Talks at the Yenan Forum on Literature and Art," provides a background for the evolution of this Weltanschauung. First published twenty-four years ago and reprinted as one of the documents of the proletarian cultural revolution, this piece draws the lines of the network linking politics, ideology, art, literature, the class struggle, production and the Party.

A major difference between the overwhelming dominance of the "democratic principle," as de Tocqueville observed it in the New World of 1848, and that of the new China today is the degree of consciousness with which people confront their conditions and tasks. There seems to be a much greater and more generalized articulateness and conscious application of the principle fostered in China today than was the case in nineteenth-century America. Time, historical and geographical accident account for at least part of this difference: Americans could afford the luxury of an extended youth during which time consciousness wastefully indulged the flights of imagination. The Chinese find no time for this indulgence; everyone learns at maximum speed and nothing escapes the totality of sweeping change; literature and art included.

The question is, what constitutes revolutionary literature and art? For whom is it written, under what conditions? The answer is that art to be revolutionary must be written for the masses, by artists who feel themselves a part of the great swell of Chinese people. The criticism of writers and intellectuals is that even while they think they are writing for the ordinary people they are actually addressing each other. Artists seek out people of their own kind instead of living and working among the masses of non-artists and end up by sneering at folk art, the simplicity and primitiveness of the artistic expression of the common man.

It is important in all of Mao Tse-tung's discussion of art and its relationship to Marxism to bear in mind his basically Sino-centric orientation. When he attacks "bourgeois-feudal" art the meaning of the term is circumscribed by his acquaintance with Chinese art—traditional and imitational. It is doubtful (though irrelevant to our discussion) that traditional Chinese art was bourgeois but the fact that Mao calls it that (except for the folk novels) should not obscure the substance of what he objects to and is attempting to change.

Talks at the Yenan Forum on Literature and Art*

INTRODUCTION—MAY 2, 1942

Comrades! You have been invited to this forum today to exchange ideas and examine the relationship between work in the literary and artistic fields and revolutionary work in general. Our aim is to ensure that revolutionary literature and art follow the correct path of development and provide better help to other revolutionary work in facilitating the overthrow of our national enemy and the accomplishment of the task of national liberation.

In our struggle for the liberation of the Chinese people there are various fronts, among which there are the fronts of the pen and of the gun, the cultural and the military fronts. To defeat the enemy we must rely primarily on the army with guns. But this army alone is not enough; we must also have a cultural army, which is absolutely indispensable for uniting our own ranks and defeating the enemy. Since the May 4th Movement [1919] such a cultural army has taken shape in China, and it has helped the Chinese revolution, gradually reduced the domain of China's feudal culture and of the comprador culture which serves imperialist aggression, and weakened their influence. To oppose the new culture the Chinese reactionaries can now only "pit quantity against quality." In other words, reactionaries have money, and though they can produce nothing good, they can go all out and produce in quantity. Literature and art have been an important and successful part of the cultural front since the May 4th Movement. During the ten years' civil war, the revolutionary literature and art movement grew greatly. That movement and the revolutionary war both headed in the same general direction, but these two fraternal armies were not linked together in their practical work because the reactionaries had cut them off from each other. It is very good that since the outbreak of the War of Resistance Against Japan, more and more revolutionary writers and artists have been coming to Yenan and our other anti-Japanese base areas. But it does not necessarily follow

* Mao Tse-tung, excerpts from "Talks at the Yenan Forum on Literature and Art," reprinted in Peking Review, Vol. No. 28, July 8, 1966, pp. 3–16.

that, having come to the base areas, they have already integrated themselves completely with the masses of the people here. The two must be completely integrated if we are to push ahead with our revolutionary work. The purpose of our meeting today is precisely to ensure that literature and art fit well into the whole revolutionary machine as a component part, that they operate as powerful weapons for uniting and educating the people and for attacking and destroying the enemy, and that they help the people fight the enemy with one heart and one mind. What are the problems that must be solved to achieve this objective? I think they are the problems of the class stand of the writers and artists, their attitude, their audience, their work and their study. . . .

Since the audience for our literature and art consists of workers, peasants and soldiers and of their cadres, the problem arises of understanding them and knowing them well. A great deal of work has to be done in order to understand them and know them well, to understand and know well all the different kinds of people and phenomena in the Party and government organizations, in the villages and factories and in the Eighth Route and New Fourth Armies. Our writers and artists have their literary and art work to do, but their primary task is to understand people and know them well. . . . If you want the masses to understand you, if you want to be one with the masses, you must make up your mind to undergo a long and even painful process of tempering. Here I might mention the experience of how my own feelings changed. I began life as a student and at school acquired the ways of a student; I then used to feel it undignified to do even a little manual labour, such as carrying my own luggage in the presence of my fellow students, who were incapable of carrying anything, either on their shoulders or in their hands. At that time I felt that intellectuals were the only clean people in the world, while in comparison workers and peasants were dirty. I did not mind wearing the clothes of other intellectuals, believing them clean, but I would not put on clothes belonging to a worker or peasant, believing them dirty. But after I became a revolutionary and lived with workers and peasants and with soldiers of the revolutionary army, I gradually came to know them well, and they gradually came to know me well too. It was then, and only then, that I fundamentally changed the bourgeois and petty-bourgeois feelings implanted in me in the bourgeois schools. I came to feel that compared with the workers and peasants the unremoulded intellectuals were not clean and that, in the last analysis, the workers and peasants were the cleanest people and, even though their hands were soiled and their feet smeared with cow-dung, they were really cleaner than the bourgeois and petty-bourgeois intellectuals. That is what is meant by a change in feelings, a change from one class to another. If our writers and artists who come from the intelligentsia want their works to be well received by the masses, they must change and remould their thinking and their feelings. Without such a change, without such remoulding, they can do nothing well and will be misfits. . . .

CONCLUSION—MAY 23, 1942

Comrades! Our forum has had three meetings this month. In the pursuit of truth we have carried on spirited debates in which scores of Party and non-Party comrades have spoken, laying bare the issues and making them more concrete. This, I believe, will very much benefit the whole literary and artistic movement.

In discussing a problem, we should start from reality and not from definitions. We would be following a wrong method if we first looked up definitions of literature and art in textbooks and then used them to determine the guiding principles for the present-day literary and artistic movement and to judge the different opinions and controversies that arise today. . . .

I

The first problem is: literature and art for whom?

This problem was solved long ago by Marxists, especially by Lenin. As far back as 1905 Lenin pointed out emphatically that our literature and art should "serve . . . the millions and tens of millions of working people." . . . We should take over the rich legacy and the good traditions in literature and art that have been handed down from past ages in China and foreign countries, but the aim must still be to serve the masses of the people. Nor do we refuse to utilize the literary and artistic forms of the past, but in our hands these old forms, remoulded and infused with new content, also become something revolutionary in the service of the people.

Who, then, are the masses of the people? The broadest sections of the people, constituting more than 90 per cent of our total population, are the workers, peasants, soldiers and urban petty bourgeoisie. Therefore, our literature and art are first for the workers, the class that leads the revolution. Secondly, they are for the peasants, the most numerous and most steadfast of our allies in the revolution. Thirdly, they are for the armed workers and peasants, namely, the Eighth Route and New

Fourth Armies and the other armed units of the people, which are the main forces of the revolutionary war. Fourthly, they are for the labouring masses of the urban petty bourgeoisie and for the petty-bourgeois intellectuals, both of whom are also our allies in the revolution and capable of long-term co-operation with us. These four kinds of people constitute the overwhelming majority of the Chinese nation, the broadest masses of the people.

Our literature and art should be for the four kinds of people we have enumerated. To serve them, we must take the class stand of the proletariat and not that of the petty bourgeoisie ... Coming from the petty bourgeoisie and being themselves intellectuals, many comrades seek friends only among intellectuals and concentrate on studying and describing them. Such study and description are proper if done from a proletarian position. But that is not what they do, or not what they do fully. They take the petty-bourgeois stand and produce works that are the self-expression of the petty bourgeoisie, as can be seen in quite a number of literary and artistic products. Often they show heartfelt sympathy for intellectuals of petty-bourgeois origin, to the extent of sympathizing with or even praising their shortcomings. On the other hand, these comrades seldom come into contact with the masses of workers, peasants and soldiers, do not understand or study them, do not have intimate friends among them and are not good at portraying them; when they do depict them, the clothes are the clothes of working people but the faces are those of petty-bourgeois intellectuals. In certain respects they are fond of the workers, peasants and soldiers and the cadres stemming from them; but there are times when they do not like them and there are some respects in which they do not like them: they do not like their feelings or their manner or their nascent literature and art (the wall newspapers, murals, folk songs, folk tales, etc.). At times they are fond of these things too, but that is when they are hunting for novelty, for something with which to embellish their own works, or even for certain backward features. At other times they openly despise these things and are partial to what belongs to the petty-bourgeois intellectuals or even to the bourgeoisie. These comrades have their feet planted on the side of the petty-bourgeois intellectuals; or, to put it more elegantly, their innermost soul is still a kingdom of the petty-bourgeois intelligentsia. Thus they have not yet solved, or not yet clearly solved, the problem of "for whom"? This applies not only to newcomers to Yenan; even among comrades who have been to the front and worked for a number of years in our base areas and in the Eighth Route and New Fourth Armies, many have not completely solved this problem. It requires a long period of time, at least eight or ten years, to solve it thoroughly. But however long it takes, solve it we must and solve it unequivocally and thoroughly. Our literary and art workers must accomplish this task and shift their stand; they must gradually move their feet over to the side of the workers, peasants and soldiers, to the side of the proletariat, through the process of going into their very midst and into the thick of practical struggles and through the process of studying Marxism and society. Only in this way can we have a literature and art that are truly for the workers, peasants and soldiers, a truly proletarian literature and art. . . .

II

Having settled the problem of whom to serve, we come to the next problem, how to serve. To put it in the words of some of our comrades: should we devote ourselves to raising standards, or should we devote ourselves to popularization?

In the past, some comrades, to a certain or even a serious extent, belittled and neglected popularization and laid undue stress on raising standards. Stress should be laid on raising standards, but to do so one-sidedly and exclusively, to do so excessively, is a mistake. The lack of a clear solution to the problem of "for whom?", which I referred to earlier, also manifests itself in this connection. As these comrades are not clear on the problem of "for whom?", they have no correct criteria for the "raising of standards" and the "popularization" they speak of, and are naturally still less able to find the correct relationship between the two. Since our literature and art are basically for the workers, peasants and soldiers, "popularization" means to popularize among the workers, peasants and soldiers, and "raising standards" means to advance from their present level. . . . We must popularize only what is needed and can be readily accepted by the workers, peasants and soldiers themselves. Consequently, prior to the task of educating the workers, peasants and soldiers, there is the task of learning from them. This is even more true of raising standards. There must be a basis from which to raise. Take a bucket of water, for instance; where is it to be raised from if not from the ground? From mid-air? From what basis, then, are literature and art to be raised? From the basis of the feudal classes? From the basis of the bourgeoisie? From the basis of the petty-bourgeois intellectuals? No, not from any of these; only from the basis of the masses of workers, peasants and soldiers. Nor does this mean raising the workers, peasants and soldiers to the "heights" of the feudal classes, the bourgeoisie or the petty-bourgeois intellectuals; it means raising the level of literature and art in the direction in which the workers, peasants and soldiers are themselves advancing, in the direction in which the proletariat is advancing. . . .

In the last analysis, what is the source of all literature and art? Works of literature and art, as ideological forms, are products of the reflection in the human brain of the life of a given society. Revolutionary literature and art are the products of the reflection of the life of the people in the brains of revolutionary writers and artists. The life of the people is always a mine of the raw materials for literature and art, materials in their natural form, materials that are crude, but most vital, rich and fundamental; they make all literature and art seem pallid by comparison; they provide literature and art an inexhaustible source, their only source. They are the only source, for there can be no other. Some may ask, is there not another source in books, in the literature and art of ancient times and of foreign countries? In fact, the literary and artistic works of the past are not a source but a stream; they were created by our predecessors and the foreigners out of the literary and artistic raw materials they found in the life of the people of their time and place. We must take over all the fine things in our literary and artistic heritage, critically assimilate whatever is beneficial, and use them as examples when we create works out of the literary and artistic raw materials in the life of the people of our own time and place. It makes a difference whether or not we have such examples, the difference between crudeness and refinement, between roughness and polish, between a low and a high level, and between slower and faster work. Therefore, we must on no account reject the legacies of the ancients and the foreigners or refuse to learn from them, even though they are the works of the feudal or bourgeois classes. But taking over legacies and using them as examples must never replace our own creative work; nothing can do that. Uncritical transplantation or copying from the ancients and the foreigners is the most sterile and harmful dogmatism in literature and art. . . .

Although man's social life is the only source of literature and art and is incomparably livelier and richer in content, the people are not satisfied with life alone and demand literature and art as well. Why? Because, while both are beautiful, life as reflected in works of literature and art can and ought to be on a higher plane, more intense, more concentrated, more typical, nearer the ideal, and therefore more universal than actual everyday life. Revolutionary literature and art should create a variety of characters out of real life and help the masses to propel history forward. For example, there is suffering from hunger, cold and oppression on the one hand, and exploitation and oppression of man by man on the other. These facts exist everywhere and people look upon them as commonplace. Writers and artists concentrate such everyday phenomena, typify the contradictions and struggles within them and produce works which awaken the masses, fire them with enthusiasm and impel them to unite and struggle to transform their environment. Without such literature and art, this task could not be fulfilled, or at least not so effectively and speedily.

What is meant by popularizing and by raising standards in works of literature and art? What is the relationship between these two tasks? Popular works are simpler and plainer, and therefore more readily accepted by the broad masses of the people today. Works of a higher quality, being more polished, are more difficult to produce and in general do not circulate so easily and quickly among the masses at present. The problem facing the workers, peasants and soldiers is this: they are now engaged in a bitter and bloody struggle with the enemy but are illiterate and uneducated as a result of long years of rule by the feudal and bourgeois classes, and therefore they are eagerly demanding enlightenment, education and works of literature and art which meet their urgent needs and which are easy to absorb, in order to heighten their enthusiasm in struggle and confidence in victory, strengthen their unity and fight the enemy with one heart and one mind. For them the prime need is not "more flowers on the brocade" but "fuel in snowy weather." In present conditions, therefore, popularization is the more pressing task. It is wrong to belittle or neglect popularization.

Nevertheless, no hard and fast line can be drawn between popularization and the raising of standards. Not only is it possible to popularize some works of higher quality even now, but the cultural level of the broad masses is steadily rising. If popularization remains at the same level for ever, with the same stuff being supplied month after month and year after year, always the same "Little Cowherd" and the same "man, hand, mouth, knife, cow, goat," will not the educators and those being educated be six of one and half a dozen of the other? What would be the sense of such popularization? The people demand popularization and, following that, higher standards; they demand higher standards month by month and year by year. Here popularization means popularizing for the people and raising of standards means raising the level for the people. And such raising is not from mid-air, or behind closed doors, but is actually based on popularization. It is determined by and at the same time guides popularization. In China as a whole the development of the revolution and of revolutionary culture is uneven and their spread is gradual. While in one place there is popularization and then raising of standards on the basis of popularization, in other places popularization has not even begun. Hence good experience in popularization leading to higher standards in one locality can be applied in other localities and serve to guide popularization and the raising of standards there, saving many twists and turns along the road. Internationally, the good experience of foreign countries, and especially Soviet experience, can also serve to guide us. With us, therefore, the raising of standards is based on popularization, while popularization is guided by the raising of standards. Precisely for this reason, so far from being an obstacle to the raising of standards, the work of popularization we are speaking of supplies the basis for the work of raising standards which we are now doing on a limited scale, and prepares the necessary conditions for us to raise standards in the future on a much broader scale.

Besides such raising of standards as meets the needs of the masses directly, there is the kind which meets their needs indirectly, that is, the kind which is needed by the cadres. The cadres are the advanced elements of the masses and generally have received more education; literature and art of a higher level are entirely necessary for them. To ignore this would be a mistake. Whatever is done for the cadres is also entirely for the masses, because it is only through the cadres that we can educate and guide the masses. If we go against this aim, if what we give the cadres cannot help them educate and guide the masses, our work of raising standards will be like shooting at random and will depart from the fundamental principle of serving the masses of the people. . . .

Now that we have settled the problem of the relationship between the raising of standards and popularization, that of the relationship between the specialists and the popularizers can also be settled. Our specialists are not only for the cadres, but also, and indeed chiefly, for the masses. Our specialists in literature should pay attention to the wall newspapers of the masses and the reportage written in the army and the villages. Our specialists in drama should pay attention to the small troupes in the army and the villages. Our specialists in music should pay attention to the songs of the masses. Our specialists in the fine arts should pay attention to the fine arts of the masses. All these comrades should make close contact with comrades engaged in the work of popularizing literature and art among the masses. On the one hand, they should help and guide the popularizers, and on the other, they should learn from these comrades and, through them, draw nourishment from the masses to replenish and enrich themselves so that their specialties do not become "ivory towers," detached from the masses and from reality and devoid of content or life. We should esteem the specialists, for they are very valuable to our cause. But we should tell them that no revolutionary writer or artist can do any meaningful work unless he is closely linked with the masses, gives expression to their thoughts and feelings and serves them as a loyal spokesman. Only by speaking for the masses can he educate them and only by being their pupil can he be their teacher. If he regards himself as their master, as an aristocrat who lords it over the "lower orders," then, no matter how talented he may be, he will not be needed by the masses and his work will have no future. . . .

III

Since our literature and art are for the masses of the people, we can proceed to discuss a problem of inner-Party relations, *i.e.*, the relation between the Party's work in literature and art and the Party's work as a whole, and in addition a problem of the Party's external relations, *i.e.*, the relation between the Party's work in literature and art and the work of non-Party people in this field, a problem of the united front in literary and art circles.

Let us consider the first problem. In the world today all culture, all literature and art belong to definite classes and are geared to definite political lines. There is in fact no such thing as art for art's sake, art that stands above classes or art that is detached from or independent of politics. Proletarian literature and art are part of the whole proletarian revolutionary cause; they are, as Lenin said, cogs and wheels in the whole revolutionary machine. . . . We do not favour overstressing the importance of literature and art, but neither do we favour underestimating their importance. Literature and art are subordinate to politics, but in their turn exert a great influence on politics. Revolutionary literature and art are part of the whole revolutionary cause, they are cogs and wheels in it, and though in comparison with certain other and more important parts they may be less significant and less urgent and may occupy a secondary position, nevertheless, they are indispensable cogs and wheels in the whole machine, an indispensable part of the entire revolutionary cause. If we had no literature and art even in the broadest and most ordinary sense, we could not carry on the revolutionary movement and win victory. . . .

IV

Literary and art criticism is one of the principal methods of struggle in the world of literature and art. It should be developed and, as comrades have rightly pointed out, our past work in this respect has been quite inadequate. Literary and art criticism is a complex question which requires a great deal of special study. Here I shall concentrate only on the basic problem of criteria in criticism. I shall also comment briefly on a few specific problems raised by some comrades and on certain incorrect views.

In literary and art criticism there are two criteria, the political and the artistic. According to the political criterion, everything is good that is helpful to unity and resistance to Japan, that encourages the masses to be of one heart and one mind, that opposes retrogression and promotes progress; on the other hand, everything is bad that is detrimental to unity and resistance to Japan, foments dissension and discord among the masses and opposes progress and drags people back. How can we tell the good from the bad—by the motive (the subjective intention) or by the effect (social practice)? Idealists stress motive and ignore effect, while mechanical materialists stress effect and ignore motive. In contradistinction to both, we dialectical materialists insist on the unity of motive and effect. The motive of serving the masses is inseparably linked with the effect of winning their approval; the two must be united. The motive of serving the individual or a small clique is not good, nor is it good to have the motive of serving the masses without the effect of winning their approval and benefiting them. In examining the subjective intention of a writer or artist, that is, whether his motive is correct and good, we do not judge by his declarations but by the effect of his actions (mainly his works) on the masses in society. The criterion for judging subjective intention or motive is social practice and its effect. . . .

There is the political criterion and there is the artistic criterion; what is the relationship between the two? Politics cannot be equated with art, nor can a general world outlook be equated with a method of artistic creation and criticism. We deny not only that there is an abstract and absolutely unchangeable political criterion, but also that there is an abstract and absolutely unchangeable artistic criterion; each class in every class society has its own political and artistic criteria. But all classes in all class societies invariably put the political criterion first and the artistic criterion second. The bourgeoisie always shuts out proletarian literature and art, however great their artistic merit. . . . What we demand is the unity of politics and art, the unity of content and form, the unity of revolutionary political content and the highest possible perfection of artistic form. Works of art which lack artistic quality have no force, however progressive they are politically. Therefore, we oppose both the tendency to produce works of art with a wrong political viewpoint and the tendency towards the "poster and slogan style" which is correct in political viewpoint but lacking in artistic power. On questions of literature and art we must carry on a struggle on two fronts.

Both these tendencies can be found in the thinking of many comrades. A good number of comrades tend to neglect artistic technique; it is therefore necessary to give attention to the raising of artistic standards. But as I see it, the political side is more of a problem at present. Some comrades lack elementary political knowledge and consequently have all sorts of muddled ideas. Let me cite a few examples from Yenan.

"The theory of human nature." Is there such a thing as human nature? Of course there is. But there is only human nature in the concrete, no human nature in the abstract. In class society there is only human nature of a class character; there is no human nature above classes. We uphold the human nature of the proletariat and of the masses of the people, while the landlord and bourgeois classes uphold the human nature of their own classes, only they do not say so but make it out to be the only human nature in existence. The human nature boosted by certain petty-bourgeois intellectuals is also divorced from or opposed to the masses; what they call human nature is in essence nothing but bourgeois individualism, and so, in their eyes, proletarian human nature is contrary to human nature. "The theory of human nature" which some people in Yenan advocate as the basis of their so-called theory of literature and art puts the matter in just this way and is wholly wrong.

"The fundamental point of departure for literature and art is love, love of humanity." Now love may serve as a point of departure, but there is a more basic one. Love as an idea is a product of objective practice. Fundamentally, we do not start from ideas but from objective practice. Our writers and artists who come from the ranks of the intellectuals love the proletariat because society has made them feel that they and the proletariat share a common fate. We hate Japanese imperialism because Japanese imperialism oppresses us. There is absolutely no such thing in the world as love or hatred without reason or cause. As for the so-called love of humanity, there has been no such all-inclusive love since humanity was divided into classes. All the ruling classes of the past were fond of advocating it, and so were many so-called sages and wise men, but nobody has ever really practised it, because it is impossible in class society. There will be genuine love of humanity—after classes are eliminated all over the world. Classes have split society into many antagonistic groupings; there will be love of all humanity when classes are eliminated, but not now. We cannot love enemies, we cannot love social evils, our aim is to destroy them. This is common sense; can it be that some of our writers and artists still do not understand this? . . .

"The task of literature and art has always been to expose." This assertion, like the previous one, arises from ignorance of the science of history. Literature and art, as we have shown, have never been devoted solely to exposure. For revolutionary writers and artists the targets for exposure can never be the masses, but only the aggressors, exploiters and oppressors and the evil influence they have on the people. The masses too have shortcomings, which should be overcome by criticism and self-criticism within the people's own ranks, and such criticism and self-criticism is also one of the most important tasks of literature and art. But this should not be regarded as any sort of "exposure of the people." As for the people, the question is basically one of education and of raising their level. Only counter-revolutionary writers and artists describe the people as "born fools" and the revolutionary masses as "tyrannical mobs."

"It is not a question of stand; my class stand is correct, my intentions are good and I understand all right, but I am not good at expressing myself and so the effect turns out bad." I have already spoken about the dialectical materialist view of motive and effect. Now I want to ask, is not the question of effect one of stand? A person who acts solely by motive and does not inquire what effect his action will have is like a doctor who merely writes prescriptions but does not care how many patients die of them. Or takes a political party which merely makes declarations but does not care whether they are carried out. It may well be asked, is this a correct stand? And is the intention here good? Of course, mistakes may occur even though the effect has been taken into account beforehand, but is the intention good when one continues in the same old rut after facts have proved that the effect is bad. In judging a party or a doctor, we must look at practice, at the effect. The same applies in judging a writer. A person with truly good intentions must take the effect into account, sum up experience and study the methods or, in creative work, study the technique of expression. A person with truly good intentions must criticize the shortcomings and mistakes in his own work with the utmost candour and resolve to correct them. This is precisely why Communists employ the method of self-criticism. This alone is the correct stand. Only in this process of serious and responsible practice is it possible gradually to understand what the correct stand is and gradually obtain a good grasp of it. If one does not move in this direction in practice, if there is simply the complacent assertion that one "understands all right," then in fact one has not understood at all.

"To call on us to study Marxism is to repeat the mistake of the dialectical materialist creative method, which will harm the creative mood." To study Marxism means to apply the dialectical materialist and historical materialist viewpoint in our observation of the world, of society and of literature and art; it does not mean writing philosophical lectures into our works of literature and art. Marxism embraces but cannot replace realism in literary and artistic creation, just as it embraces but cannot replace the atomic and electronic theories in physics. Empty, dry dogmatic formulas do indeed destroy the creative mood; not only that, they first destroy Marxism. Dogmatic "Marxism" is not Marxism, it is anti-Marxism. Then does not Marxism destroy the creative mood? Yes, it does. It definitely destroys creative moods that are feudal, bourgeois, petty-bourgeois, liberalistic, individualist, nihilist, art-for-art's sake, aristocratic, decadent or pessimistic, and every other creative mood that is alien to the masses of the people and to the proletariat. So far as proletarian writers and artists are concerned, should not these kinds of creative moods be destroyed? I think they should; they should be utterly destroyed. And while they are being destroyed, something new can be constructed.

The problems discussed here exist in our literary and art circles in Yenan. What does that show? It shows that wrong styles of work still exist to a serious extent in our literary and art circles and that there are still many defects among our comrades, such as idealism, dogmatism, empty illusions, empty talk, contempt for practice and aloofness from the masses, all of which call for an effective and serious campaign for rectification.

Because of confusion in their thinking, many of our comrades are not quite able to draw a real distinction between our revolutionary base areas and the Kuomintang areas and they make many mistakes as a consequence. A good number of comrades have come here from the garrets of Shanghai, and in coming from those garrets to the revolutionary base areas, they have passed not only from one kind of place to another but from one historical epoch to another. . . . The past epoch is gone, never to return. Therefore, we must integrate ourselves with the new masses without any hesitation. . . . Intellectuals who want to integrate themselves with the masses, who want to serve the masses, must go through a process in which they and the masses come to know each other well. This process may, and certainly will, involve much pain and friction, but if you have the determination, you will be able to fulfil these requirements.

Today I have discussed only some of the problems of fundamental orientation for our literature and art movement; many specific problems remain which will require further study. I am confident that comrades here are determined to move in the direction indicated. I believe that in the course of the rectification movement and in the long period of study and work to come, you will surely be able to bring about a transformation in yourselves and in your works, to create many fine works which will be warmly welcomed by the masses of the people, and to advance the literature and art movement in the revolutionary base areas and throughout China to a glorious new stage.

Memoranda by Foreign Service Officers in China 1943–1945*

August 3, 1944 (Service)

"THE CHINESE Communist Party claims that it is Marxist. By this the Communists mean that their ideology, their philosophical approach, and their dialectical method are based on Marxist materialism. Marxism thus becomes to them chiefly an attitude and approach to problems. It is a long-term view of

* These extracts from reports by John P. Davies, Jr., Raymond P. Ludden and John Stewart Service, in UNITED STATES RELATIONS WITH CHINA, with Special Reference to the Period 1944–1949 (Washington, D.C.: The Department of State, 1949), pp. 565–565–576.

political and economic development to which all short-term considerations of temporary advantage or premature power are ruthlessly subordinated.

"The Communists actively support the war because this gives them an opportunity to mobilize, organize and indoctrinate the people, and to create and train an efficient army.

"They operate by preference in the areas behind the Japanese lines because there they are relatively free from Kuomintang interference.

"Such policies as the abandonment of land confiscation are useful temporary expedients to help them carry on the war and to win unified popular support in the areas of their operations. It also has strong propaganda appeal in other areas.

"Their espousal of democracy appeals to the great majority of the people of China and is a good club for beating the Kuomintang. They realize that popular support must be their principal weapon against the superior arms of the Kuomintang in any contest of strength.

"Their democratic claims, their engagement in guerrilla warfare behind the enemy lines, and their proclamation of liberal economic policies based on private property are also useful in appealing to foreign sympathy and in winning the foreign support which they realize will be necessary, at least for a time, in the economic rehabilitation and development of China following the war."

3. The Chinese Communists have become the most dynamic force in China and are challenging the Kuomintang for control of the country.

October 9, 1944 (Service)

"Reports of two American officers, several correspondents, and twenty-odd foreign travelers regarding conditions in the areas of North China under Communist control are in striking agreement. This unanimity, based on actual observation, is significant. It forces us to accept certain facts, and to draw from those facts an important conclusion.

"The Japanese are being actively opposed—in spite of the constant warfare and cruel retaliation this imposes on the population. This opposition is gaining in strength. The Japanese can temporarily crush it in a limited area by the concentration of overwhelming force. But it is impossible for them to do this simultaneously over the huge territory the Communists now influence.

"This opposition is possible and successful because it is total guerrilla warfare aggressively waged by a totally mobilized population. In this total mobilization the regular forces

of the Communists, though leaders and organizers, have become subordinate to the vastly more numerous forces of the people themselves. They exist because the people permit, support and wholeheartedly fight with them. There is complete solidarity of Army and people.

"*This total mobilization is based upon and has been made possible by what amounts to an economic, political and social revolution.* This revolution has been moderate and democratic. It has improved the economic condition of the peasants by rent and interest reduction, tax reform and good government. It has given them democratic self-government, political consciousness and a sense of their rights. It has freed them from feudalistic bonds and given them self-respect, self-reliance and a strong feeling of cooperative group interest. *The common people, for the first time, have been given something to fight for.*

"The Japanese are being fought now not merely because they are foreign invaders but because they deny this revolution. *The people will continue to fight any government which limits or deprives them of these newly won gains.*"
November 7, 1944 (Davies)

"The Chinese Communists are so strong between the Great Wall and the Yangtze that they can now look forward to the postwar control of at least North China. They may also continue to hold not only those parts of the Yangtze valley which they now dominate but also new areas in Central and South China. The Communists have fallen heir to these new areas by a process, which has been operating for seven years, whereby Chiang Kai-shek loses his cities and principal lines of communication to the Japanese and the countryside to the Communists.

"The Communists have survived ten years of civil war and seven years of Japanese offensives. They have survived not only more sustained enemy pressure than the Chinese Central Government forces have been subjected to, but also a severe blockade imposed by Chiang.

"They have survived and they have grown. Communist growth since 1937 has been almost geometric in progression. From control of some 100,000 square kilometers with a population of one million and a half they have expanded to about 850,000 square kilometers with a population of approximately 90 million. And they will continue to grow.

"The reason for this phenomenal vitality and strength is simple and fundamental. It is mass support, mass participation. The Communist governments and armies are the first governments and armies in modern Chinese history which have positive and widespread popular support. They have this support because the governments and armies are genuinely of the people. . . ."

The Kuomintang and National Government are disintegrating.

June 20, 1944 (Service)

"B. *The position of the Kuomintang and the Generalissimo is weaker than it has been for the past ten years.*

"China faces economic collapse. This is causing disintegration of the army and the government's administrative apparatus. It is one of the chief causes of growing political unrest. The Generalissimo is losing the support of a China which, by unity in the face of violent aggression, found a new and unexpected strength during the first two years of the war with Japan. Internal weaknesses are becoming accentuated and there is taking place a reversal of the process of unification.

"1. Morale is low and discouragement widespread. There is a general feeling of hopelessness.

"2. The authority of the Central Government is weakening in the areas away from the larger cities. Government mandates and measures of control cannot be enforced and remain ineffective. It is becoming difficult for the Government to collect enough food for its huge army and bureaucracy.

"3. The governmental and military structure is being permeated and demoralized from top to bottom by corruption, unprecedented in scale and openness.

"4. The intellectual and salaried classes, who have suffered the most heavily from inflation, are in danger of liquidation. The academic groups suffer not only the attrition and demoralization of economic stress; the weight of years of political control and repression is robbing them of the intellectual vigor and leadership they once had.

"5. Peasant resentment of the abuses of conscription, tax collection and other arbitrary impositions has been widespread and is growing. The danger is ever-increasing that past sporadic outbreaks of banditry and agrarian unrest may increase in scale and find political motivation.

"6. The provincial groups are making common cause with one another and with other dissident groups, and are actively consolidating their positions. Their continuing strength in the face of the growing weakness of the Central Government is forcing new measures of political appeasement in their favor.

"7. Unrest within the Kuomintang armies is increasing, as shown in one important instance by the 'Young Generals' conspiracy' late in 1943. On a higher plane, the war zone commanders are building up their own spheres of influence and are thus creating a 'new warlordism.'

"8. The break between the Kuomintang and the Communists not only show no signs of being closed, but grows more critical with the passage of time: the inevitability of civil war is now generally accepted.

"9. The Kuomintang is losing the respect and support of the people by its school policies and its refusal to heed progressive criticism. It seems unable to revivify itself with fresh blood, and its unchanging leadership shows a growing ossification and loss of a sense of reality. To combat the dissensions and cliquism within the Party, which grows more rather than less acute, the leadership is turning toward the reactionary and unpopular Chen brothers clique.

"10. The Generalissimo shows a similar loss of realistic flexibility and a hardening of narrowly conservative views. His growing megalomania and his unfortunate attempts to be 'sage' as well as leader—shown, for instance, by 'China's Destiny' and his book on economics—have forfeited the respect of many intellectuals, who enjoy in China a position of unique influence. Criticism of his dictatorship is becoming outspoken.

"In the face of the grave crisis with which it is confronted, the Kuomintang is ceasing to be the unifying and progressive force in Chinese society, the role in which it made its greatest contribution to modern China.

"C. *The Kuomintang is not only proving itself incapable of averting a debacle by its own initiative: on the contrary, its policies are precipitating the crisis.*

"Some war-weariness in China must be expected. But the policies of the Kuomintang under the impact of hyperinflation and in the presence of obvious signs of internal and external weakness must be described as bankrupt. This trait is emphasized by the failure of the Kuomintang to come to grips with the situation during the recently concluded plenary session of the Central Executive Committee.

"1. *On the internal political front the desire of the Kuomintang leaders to perpetuate their own power overrides all other considerations.* The result is the enthronement of reaction.

"The Kuomintang continues to ignore the great political drive within the country for democratic reform. The writings of the Generalissimo and the Party press show that they have no real understanding of that term. Constitutionalism remains an empty promise for which the only 'preparation' is a half-hearted attempt to establish an unpopular and undemocratic system of local self-government based on collective responsibility and given odium by Japanese utilization in Manchuria and other areas under their control.

"Questions basic to the future of democracy such as the form of the Constitution and the composition and election of the National Congress remain the dictation of the Kuomintang. There is no progress toward the fundamental conditions of freedom of expression and recognition of non-Kuomintang groups. Even the educational and political advantages of giving power and democratic character to the existing but impotent Peoples Political Council are ignored.

"The Kuomintang shows no intention of relaxing the authoritarian controls on which its present power depends. Far from discarding or reducing the paraphernalia of a police state—the multiple and omnipresent secret police organizations, the Gendarmerie, and so forth—it continues to strengthen them as its last resort for internal security.

"2. *On the economic front the Kuomintang is unwilling to take any effective steps to check inflation which would injure the landlord-capitalist class.*

"It is directly responsible for the increase of official corruption which is one of the main obstacles to any rational attempt to ameliorate the financial situation. It does nothing to stop large-scale profiteering, hoarding and speculation—all of which are carried on by people either powerful in the Party or with intimate political connections.

"It fails to carry out effective mobilization of resources. Such measures of war-time control as it has promulgated have remained a dead letter or have intensified the problems they were supposedly designed to remedy—as for instance ill-advised and poorly executed attempts at price regulation.

"It passively allows both industrial and the more important handicraft production to run down, as they of course must when it is more profitable for speculators to hold raw materials than to have them go through the normal productive process.

"It fails to carry out rationing except in a very limited way, or to regulate the manufacture and trade of luxury goods, many of which come from areas under Japanese control. It shows little concern that these imports are largely paid for with strategic commodities of value to the enemy.

"It fails to make an effective attempt to reduce the budgetary deficit and increase revenue by tapping such resources as excess profits and incomes of landlords and merchants. It allows its tax-collecting apparatus to bog down in corruption and inefficiency—to the point that possibly not more than one-third of revenues collected reach the government. It continues to spend huge government funds on an idle and useless Party bureaucracy.

"At best, it passively watches inflation gather momentum without even attempting palliative measures available to it, such as the aggressive sale of gold and foreign currency.

"It refuses to attack the fundamental economic problems of China such as the growing concentration of land holdings, extortionate rents and ruinous interest rates, and the impact of inflation.

D. *These apparently suicidal policies of the Kuomintang have their roots in the composition and nature of the Party.*

"In view of the above it becomes pertinent to ask *why* the Kuomintang has lost its power of leadership; *why* it neither wishes actively to wage war against Japan itself nor to co-operate whole-heartedly with the American Army in China; and *why* it has ceased to be capable of unifying the country.

"The answer to all these questions is to be found in the present composition and nature of the Party. Politically, a classical and definitive American description becomes ever more true; the Kuomintang is a congerie of conservative political cliques interested primarily in the preservation of their own power against all outsiders and in jockeying for position among themselves. Economically, the Kuomintang rests on the narrow base of the rural-gentry-landlords and militarists, the higher ranks of the government bureacracy, and merchant bankers having intimate connections with the government bureaucrats. This base has actually contracted during the war. The Kuomintang no longer commands, as it once did, the unequivocal support of China's industrialists, who as a group have been much weakened economically, and hence politically, by the Japanese seizure of the coastal cities.

"The relations of this description of the Kuomintang to the questions propounded above is clear.

"The Kuomintang has lost its leadership because it has lost touch with and is no longer representative of a nation which, through the practical experience of the war, is becoming both more politically conscious and more aware of the Party's selfish shortcomings.

"It cannot fight an effective war because this is impossible without greater reliance upon and support by the people. There must be a release of the national energy such as occurred during the early period of the war. Under present conditions, this can be brought about only by reform of the Party and greater political democracy. What form this democracy takes is not as important as the genuine adoption of a democratic philosophy and attitude; the threat of foreign invasion is no longer enough to stimulate the Chinese people and only real reform can regain their enthusiasm. But the growth of democracy, though basic to China's continuing war effort, would, to the mind of the Kuomintang present leaders, imperil the foundations of the Party's power because it would mean that the conservative cliques would have to give up their closely guarded monopoly. Rather than do this, they prefer to see the war remain in its present state of passive inertia. Thus are they sacrificing China's national interests to their own selfish ends.

"For similar reasons, the Kuomintang is unwilling to give whole-hearted cooperation to the American Army's effort in China. Full cooperation necessarily requires the broad Chinese military effort which the Kuomintang is unable to carry out or make possible. In addition, the Kuomintang fears the large scale widespread and direct contact by Americans with the Chinese war effort will expose its own inactivity and, by example and personal contacts, be a liberalizing influence."

5. The rivalry between these two forces threatens to culminate in a civil war which (a) would hamper the conduct of the war against Japan, (b) would press the Communists back into the arms of the U.S.S.R. and (c) might well lead eventually to American-Soviet involvement and conflict.

January 23, 1943 (Service)

"It is now no longer wondered whether civil war can be avoided, but rather whether it can be delayed at least until after a victory over Japan.

"The dangers and implications of this disunity are obvious and far-reaching. Militarily, the present situation is a great hindrance to any effective war effort by China. Its deterioration into civil war would be disastrous. The situation therefore has direct relationship to our own efforts to defeat Japan.

". . . there can be no denial that civil war in China, or even the continuation after the defeat of Japan of the present deadlock, will greatly impede the return of peaceful conditions. This blocking of the orderly large scale rehabilitation of China will in itself seriously and adversely affect American interests. Even if a conflict is averted, the continuance, or, as is probable in such an event the worsening of the already serious economic strains within the country may result in economic collapse. If there is civil war the likelihood of such an economic collapse is of course greater.

"There is also the possibility that economic difficulties may make the war-weary, over-conscripted and over-taxed farmers fertile ground for Communist propaganda and thus bring about a revolution going beyond the moderate democracy which the Chinese Communists now claim to be seeking. Such a Communist government would probably not be democratic in the American sense. And it is probable, even if the United States did not incur the enmity of the Communists for alleged material or diplomatic support of the Kuomintang, that this Communist government would be more inclined toward friendship and cooperation with Russia than with Great Britain and America."

June 24, 1943 (Davies)

"Basis for Conflict"

"The Kuomintang and Chiang Kai-shek recognize that the Communists, with the popular support which they enjoy and their reputation for administrative reform and honesty, represent a challenge to the Central Government and its spoils system. The Generalissimo cannot admit the seemingly innocent demands of the Communists that their party be legalized and democratic processes be put into practice. To do so would probably mean the abdication of the Kuomintang and the provincial satraps.

"The Communists, on the other hand, dare not accept the Central Government's invitation that they disband their armies and be absorbed in the national body politic. To do so would be to invite extinction.

"This impasse will probably be resolved, American and other foreign observers in Chungking agree, by an attempt by the Central Government to liquidate the Communists. This action may be expected to precipitate a civil war from which one of the two contending factions will emerge dominant. . . ."

June 20, 1944 (Service)

"Obsessed by the growing and potential threat of the Communists, who it fears may attract the popular support its own nature makes impossible, the Kuomintang, despite the pretext —to meet foreign and Chinese criticism—of conducting negotiations with the Communists, continues to adhere to policies and plans which can only result in civil war. In so doing it shows itself blind to the facts: that its internal political and military situation is so weak that success without outside assistance is most problematic; that such a civil war would hasten the process of disintegration and the spread of chaos; that it would prevent the prosecution of any effective war against Japan; and that the only parties to benefit would be Japan immediately and Russia eventually."

December 9, 1944 (Davies)

". . . The Generalissimo realizes that if he accedes to the Communist terms for a coalition government, they will sooner or later dispossess him and his Kuomintang of power. He will therefore not, unless driven to an extremity, form a genuine coalition government. He will seek to retain his present government, passively wait out the war and conserve his strength, knowing that the Communist issue must eventually be joined.

"The Communists, on their part, have no interest in reaching an agreement with the Generalissimo short of a genuine coalition government. They recognize that Chiang's position is crumbling, that they may before long receive substantial Russian support and that if they have patience they will succeed to authority in at least North China. . . ."

6. The Communists would, inevitably, win such a war because the foreign powers, including the United States, which would support the Government, could not feasibly supply enough aid to compensate for the organic weaknesses of the Government.

January 23, 1943 (Service)

". . . Assuming that open hostilities are for the time being averted, the eventual defeat and withdrawal of the Japanese will leave the Kuomintang still confronted with the Communists solidly entrenched in most of North China (East Kansu, North Shensi, Shansi, South Chahar, Hopei, Shantung, North Kiangsu and North Anhwei). In addition the Communists will be in position to move into the vacuum created by the Japanese withdrawal from Suiyan, Jehol and Manchuria, in all of which areas there is already some Communist activity. In the rest of China they will have the sympathy of elements among the liberals, intellectuals, and students.

". . . There is undoubtedly a strong revulsion in the mind of the average, non-party Chinese to the idea of renewed civil war and the Kuomintang may indeed have difficulty with the loyalty and effectiveness of its conscript troops."

October 9, 1944 (Service)

"*Just as the Japanese Army cannot crush these militant people now, so also will Kuomintang force fail in the future.* With their new arms and organization knowledge of their own strength, and determination to keep what they have been fighting for, these people—now some 90 million and certain to be many more before the Kuomintang can reach them—will resist oppression. They are not Communists. They do not want separation or independence. But at present they regard the

Kuomintang—from their own experience—as oppressors; and the Communists as their leaders and benefactors.

"*With this great popular base, the Communists likewise cannot be eliminated.* Kuomintang attempts to do so by force must mean a complete denial of democracy. This will strengthen the ties of the Communists with the people: a Communist victory will be inevitable. . . .

"From the basic fact that the Communists have built up popular support of a magnitude and depth which makes their elimination impossible, *we must draw the conclusion that the Communists will have a certain and important share in China's future* . . . I suggest the future conclusion that unless the Kuomintang goes as far as the Communists in political and economic reform, and otherwise proves itself able to contest this leadership of the people (none of which it yet shows signs of being willing or able to do), the Communists will be the dominant force in China within a comparatively few years."

November 7, 1944 (Davies)

"Only if he is able to enlist foreign intervention on a scale equal to the Japanese invasion of China will Chiang probably be able to crush the Communists. But foreign intervention on such a scale would seem to be unlikely. Relying upon his dispirited shambling legions, his decadent corrupt bureaucracy, his sterile political moralisms and such nervous foreign support as he can muster, the Generalissimo may nevertheless plunge China into civil war. He cannot succeed, however, where the Japanese in more than seven years of determined striving have failed. The Communists are already too strong for him.

"If the Generalissimo neither precipitates a civil war nor reaches an understanding with the Communists, he is still confronted with defeat. Chiang's feudal China can not long coexist alongside a modern dynamic popular government in North China.

"The Communists are in China to stay. And China's destiny is not Chiang's but theirs."

7. In this unhappy dilemma, the United States should attempt to prevent the disaster of a civil war through adjustment of the new alignment of power in China by peaceful processes. The desirable means to this end is to encourage the reform and revitalization of the Kuomintang so that it may survive as a significant force in a coalition government. If this fails, we must limit our involvement with the Kuomintang and must commence some cooperation with the Communists, the force destined to control China, in an effort to influence them further

into an independent position friendly to the United States. We are working against time because, if the U.S.S.R. enters the war against Japan and invades China before either of these alternatives succeeds, the Communists will be captured by the U.S.S.R. and become Soviet satellites.

June 20, 1944 (Service)

"We must seek to contribute toward the reversal of the present movement toward collapse and to the rousing of China from its military inactivity. This can be brought about only by an accelerated movement toward democratic political reform within China. Our part must be that of a catalytic agent in this process of China's democratization. It can be carried out by the careful exertion of our influence, which has so far not been consciously and systematically used.

"This democratic reform does not necessarily mean the overthrow of the Generalissimo or the Kuomintang. On the contrary—if they have the vision to see it—their position will be improved and the stability of the Central Government increased. The democratic forces already existing in China will be strengthened, the reactionary authoritarian trends in the Kuomintang will be modified, and a multi-party United Front Government will probably emerge. It is almost certain that the Generalissimo and the Kuomintang would continue to play a dominant part in such a government.

"It goes without saying that this democratization of China must be brought about by, and depend on, forces within the country. It cannot be enforced by us—or by any foreign nation—

". . . If we come to the rescue of the Kuomintang on its own terms we would be buttressing—but only temporarily—a decadent regime which by its existing composition and program is incapable of solving China's problems. Both China and ourselves would be gaining only a brief respite from the ultimate day of reckoning. . . ."

November 15, 1944 (Davies)

"We should not now abandon Chiang Kai-shek. To do so at this juncture would be to lose more than we could gain. We must for the time being continue recognition of Chiang's Government.

"But we must be realistic. We must not indefinitely underwrite a politically bankrupt regime. And, if the Russians are going to enter the Pacific War, we must make a determined effort to capture politically the Chinese Communists rather than allow them to go by default wholly to the Russians. Furthermore, we must fully understand that by reason of our recognition of the Chiang Kai-shek Government as now constituted we are committed to a steadily decaying regime and severely restricted in working out military and political cooperation with the Chinese Communists.

"A coalition Chinese Government in which the Communists find a satisfactory place is the solution of this impasse most desirable to us. It provides our greatest assurance of a strong united, democratic, independent and friendly China—our basic strategic aim in Asia and the Pacific. If Chiang and the Communists reach a mutually satisfactory agreement, there will have been achieved from our point of view the most desirable possible solution. If Chiang and the Communists are irreconcilable, then we shall have to decide which faction we are going to support.

"In seeking to determine which faction we should support we must keep in mind these basic considerations: Power in China is on the verge of shifting from Chiang to the Communists.

"If the Russians enter North China and Manchuria, we obviously cannot hope to win the Communists entirely over to us, but we can through control of supplies and post-war aid expect to exert considerable influence in the direction of Chinese nationalism and independence from Soviet control."

8. A policy of this description would also—and this is a decisive consideration in the war against Japan—measurably aid our war effort.

December 12, 1944 (Davies)

"The negotiations looking to an agreement between the Generalissimo and the Chinese Communists have failed. It is not impossible, however, that one or the other side may in the near future revive the negotiations with a new proposal.

"So long as the deadlock exists, or new negotiations drag on, it is reasonable to assume that the Generalissimo will continue to refuse us permission to exploit militarily the Chinese Communist position extending into the geographical center of Japan's inner zone. With the war against Japan proving so costly to us we can ill afford to continue denying ourselves positive assistance and strategically valuable positions.

"It is time that we unequivocally told Chiang Kai-shek that we will work with and, within our discretion, supply whatever Chinese forces we believe can contribute most to the war against Japan. We should tell him that we will not work with or supply any Chinese unit, whether Central Government, Provincial or Communist, which shows any inclination toward precipitating civil conflict. We should tell him that we propose to keep him, as head of the recognized government, informed of what supplies we give the various Chinese forces.

"It is time that we make it clear to Chiang Kai-shek that we expect the Chinese to settle their own political differences; that we refuse to become further involved in and party to Chinese domestic political disputes. We greatly hope and desire that China will emerge from this war unified, democratic, independent and strong. We feel that this goal is to be achieved most expeditiously and with the least possible expenditure of Chinese and American blood and treasure if the United States bends its efforts in China primarily toward working with and assisting whatever elements can contribute most to the speedy defeat of Japan."

February 14, 1945 (Ludden and Service)

"American policy in the Far East can have but one immediate objective: the defeat of Japan in the shortest possible time with the least expenditure of American lives. To the attainment of this objective all other considerations should be subordinate.

"The attainment of this objective demands the effective mobilization of China in the war against Japan. Operating as we are in a land theater at the end of a supply line many thousands of miles in length, the human and economic resources of China increase in importance as we draw closer to Japan's inner zone of defense. Denied the effective use of these resources the attainment of our primary objective will be unnecessarily delayed.

"There is ample evidence to show that to the present Kuomintang Government the war against Japan is secondary in importance to its own preservation in power. China's military failure is due in large part to internal political disunity and the Kuomintang's desire to conserve such military force as it has for utilization in the maintenance of its political power. The intention of the Generalissimo to eliminate all political opposition, by force of arms if necessary, has not been abandoned. In the present situation in China, where power or self-preservation depend upon the possession of military force, neither the Kuomintang nor opposition groups are willing to expend their military resources against the Japanese through fear that it will then *vis-à-vis* other groups.

"The aim of American policy as indicated clearly by official statements in the United States is the establishment of political unity in China as the indispensable preliminary to China's effective military mobilization. The execution of our policy has not contributed to the achievement of this publicly stated aim. On the contrary, it has retarded its effect because our statements and actions in China have convinced the Kuomintang Government that we will continue to support it and it alone. The Kuomintang Government believes that it will receive an increasing flow of American military and related supplies which, if past experience is any guide, it will commit against the enemy only with great reluctance, if at all.

"We cannot hope for any improvement in this situation unless we understand the objectives of the Kuomintang Government and throw our considerable influence upon it in the direction of internal unity. We should be convinced by this time that the effort to solve the Kuomintang-Communist differences by diplomatic means has failed; . . .

"At present there exists in China a situation closely paralleling that which existed in Yogoslavia prior to Prime Minister Churchill's declaration of support for Marshal Tito. That statement was as follows:

" 'The sanest and safest course for us to follow is to judge all parties and factions dispassionately by the test of their readiness to fight the Germans and thus lighten the burden of Allied troops. This is not a time for ideological preferences for one side or the other.'

"A similar public statement issued by the Commander in Chief with regard to China would not mean the withdrawal of recognition or the cessation of military aid to the Central Government; that would be both unnecessary and unwise. It would serve notice, however, of our preparation to make use of all available means to achieve our primary objective. It would supply for all Chinese a firm rallying point which has thus far been lacking. The internal effect in China would be so profound that the Generalissimo would be forced to make concessions of power and permit united-front coalition. The present opposition groups no longer under the prime necessity of safeguarding themselves, would be won wholeheartedly to our side and we would have in China, for the first time, a united ally."

Joseph Stilwell on Chiang Kai-shek*

CHIANG KAI-SHEK has been boss so long and has so many yes-men around him that he has the idea he is infallible on any subject. He is, however, determined and forceful, and wants to get on with the war. He is not mentally stable, and he will say many things to your face that he doesn't mean fully or exactly. My only concern is to tell him the truth and go about my business. If I can't get by that way, the hell with it: it is patently impossible for me to compete with the swarms of parasites and sycophants that surround him.

* * *

CHIANG KAI-SHEK   I never heard Chiang Kai-shek say a single thing that indicated gratitude to the President or to our country for the help we were extending to him. Invariably, when anything was promised, he would want more. Invariably, he would complain about the small amount of material that was being furnished. He would make comparisons between the huge amounts of Lend-Lease supplies going to Great Britain and Russia with the meager trickle going to China. He would complain that the Chinese had been fighting for six or seven years and yet we gave them practically nothing. It would of course have been undiplomatic to go into the nature of the military effort Chiang Kai-shek had made since 1938. It was practically zero.

Whether or not he was grateful was a small matter. The regrettable part of it was that there was no quid pro quo. We did what we could, furnished what was available, without being allowed to first ask what he would do, etc. The result was that we were continuously on the defensive and he could obstruct and delay any of our plans without being penalized.

[I have] faith in Chinese soldiers and Chinese people: fundamentally great, democratic, misgoverned. No bars of caste or religion. . . . Honest, frugal, industrious, cheerful, independent, tolerant, friendly, courteous.

I judge Kuomintang and Kungchantang [Communist party] by what I saw:

* From pp. 80, 315–321, 340–341, in THE STILWELL PAPERS by Joseph Stilwell, arranged and edited by Theodore H. White (William Sloane Associates, Inc., 1948). Reprinted by permission of William Morrow and Co., Inc. Copyright © 1948 by Winifred A. Stilwell.

[KMT] Corruption, neglect, chaos, economy, taxes, words and deeds. Hoarding, black market, trading with enemy.

Communist program . . . reduce taxes, rents, interest. Raise production, and standard of living. Participate in government. Practice what they preach.

CHINESE ARMY   In 1944, on paper, the Chinese Army consisted of 324 divisions, 60-odd brigades and 89 so-called guerrilla units of about 2,000 men each. This looks formidable on paper, till you go into it closely. Then you find:

1. That the average strength per division instead of 10,000 is not more than 5,000.
2. That the troops are unpaid, unfed, shot with sickness and malnutrition.
3. That equipment is old, inadequate, and unserviceable.
4. That training is nonexistent.
5. That there is no artillery, transport, medical service, etc., etc.
7. That conscription is so-and-so.
8. That business is the principal occupation. How else live? How would you start to make such an army effective?

Chiang Kai-shek is confronted with an idea, and that defeats him. He is bewildered by the spread of Communist influence. He can't see that the mass of Chinese people welcome the Reds as being the only visible hope of relief from crushing taxation, the abuses of the Army and [the terror of] Tai Li's Gestapo. Under Chiang Kai-shek they now begin to see what they may expect. Greed, corruption, favoritism, more taxes, a ruined currency, terrible waste of life, callous disregard of all the rights of men.

[An Undated Paper, on the dominant military doctrine of the Chinese Army.]

In time of war you have to take your allies as you find them. We were fighting Germany to tear down the Nazi system—one-party government, supported by the Gestapo and headed by an unbalanced man with little education. We had plenty to say against such a system. China, our ally, was being run by a one-party government (the Kuomintang), supported by a Gestapo (Tai Li's organization) and headed by an unbalanced man with little education. This government, however, had the prestige of the possession of power—it was opposing Japan, and its titular head had been built up by propaganda in America out of all proportion to his deserts and accomplishments. We had to back the existing regime in order to have any chance of getting China to pull her weight. To change the structure during the emergency would have been next to impossible. All through the Chinese machinery of government there are interlocking ties of interest . . . family, financial, political, etc. No man, no matter how efficient, can hope for a position of authority on account of being the man best qualified for the job: he simply must have other backing. To reform such a system, it must be torn to pieces. You build a framework to grow grapevines on: in the course of time, the vines grow all over it, twisting in and out and around and pretty soon the frame is so tightly held by vines that if you start pulling them out, you will tear the frames to pieces. We could not risk it, we had to take the instrument as we found it and do the best we could. But because it was expedient to back this government to get action against Japan, it was not necessarily advisable to endorse its methods and policies. We could have required some return for our help.

Chiang Kai-shek made a great point of how badly the U.S.A. had neglected China, who had been fighting desperately for so long, while Lend-Lease materials had been poured into Great Britain and Russia by the billion. His case was that we owed him a great debt and that it was a crying shame that we didn't do more to discharge it. This attitude met with sympathy in the U.S. It was true that large quantities of Lend-Lease materials were going to Russia and Great Britain. It was also true that Russia and Great Britain, particularly Russia, were making good use of this material against Germany. It was also true that there was no possible way of delivering the goods to Chiang Kai-shek unless he made an effort on his part to help break the blockade. It seemed reasonable to expect Great Britain to use the huge Indian Army for the purpose. The U.S. was fighting Germany in Europe, and Japan in the Pacific. She was supplying enormous quantities of munitions and food to all the Allies. Under the circumstances it seemed reasonable for somebody else to display a little energy in Burma.

To keep the show going, I had to overlook some of these incongruities and pretend, like the other players. If not, the critics would say it was a bum show, and we are very much afraid of the critics in our show.

[This paper was never finished.]

[UNDATED] Chiang Kai-shek is the head of a one-party government supported by a Gestapo and a party secret service. He is now organizing an S.S. of 100,000 members.

[He] hates the so-called Communists. He intends to crush them by keeping any munitions furnished him and by occupying their territory as the Japs retire.

[He] will not make an effort to fight seriously. He wants to finish the war coasting, with a big supply of material, so as to perpetuate his regime. He has blocked us for three years and will continue to do so. He has failed to keep his agreements.

[He] has spoken contemptuously of American efforts and has never said one word to express gratitude for our help, except in one message to the President, in which he attacked me.

[He] is responsible for major disasters of the war. Nanking, Lan Fang. Changsha and Hengyang. Kweilin and Liuchow. Red blockade.

But [he] is the titular head of China and has marked me as *persona non grata*.

Therefore I cannot operate in the China theater while he is in power—unless it is made clear to him that I was not responsible for the September 19 note, and that the U.S. will pull out unless he will play ball.

U.S. RELATIONS WITH CHINA

After the attack on Pearl Harbor in 1941, U.S. activities in the Far East were primarily focused on the defeat of Japan. There was a great deal of ignorance of the Orient, generally, on the part of Americans, and the process of learning about Chinese society, at a time when Chiang Kai-shek and the Kuomintang had badly deteriorated and the Chinese Communists controlled a large portion of China, was too great a task. General Stilwell, during the war, had made some telling if blunt remarks on the nature of the Kuomintang and the Chinese situation but these were hardly considered seriously. They were attributed to the personal animosity of the General to Chiang Kai-shek.

Who, after all, could be said to understand the Chinese? Americans did not trust other Americans to comprehend that elusive phenomenon, the inscrutable Oriental. A mixture of racial superiority, guilt over it and widespread ignorance interfered in the policy-making machinery, propelling Americans to a greater and greater involvement in China without any control over the effects or consequences of such involvement. Until the conclusion of the war against Japan, the U.S. supported Chiang Kai-shek. After the war, George Marshall was despatched to China to make peace between the Communists and the Kuomintang. When this failed Americans were surprised and disillusioned with the outcome.

The Marshall Report (in the following selection) is still in the American spirit of disinterested concern. He seeks, in his investigation, to comprehend the source of the civil war and the failure of both sides to come to terms that would ensure a peaceful, unified and democratic China. This failure is attributed to the mutual mistrust of the two sides and their different interpretative schemes. There is implicit in Marshall's analysis the judgment that both the Communist Party and the Kuomintang, regardless of their distinctive ideologies, consisted of sincere men desirous of peace for China. Where he erred was in his assumption (naive, in the context of the entire development of the rift between Chinese Communism and the Kuomintang regime) that compromise between the two was realistically feasible without spelling the defeat of either one or the other side's raison d'etre. Naive as this may be, however, it does not reflect a preconceived picture of a world caught in the grips of a life and death struggle between the forces of good and evil. It is still predicated on the assumption that Communists (Chinese, in this instance) are human beings with certain objectives and a way of understanding reality and truth that differs widely from our own.

By the time Wedemeyer presents his report on China we can already read a new American orientation, the Cold War objectives. United States policy is no longer disinterested; it has settled on a new course in foreign policy: to contain and/or combat communism in the world wherever it may be encountered.

Personal Statement by the Special Representative of the President (Marshall), January 7, 1947*

THE PRESIDENT has recently given a summary of the developments in China during the past year and the position of the American Government toward China. Circumstances now dictate that I should supplement this with impressions gained at first hand.

In this intricate and confused situation, I shall merely endeavor here to touch on some of the more important considerations—as they appeared to me—during my connection with the negotiations to bring about peace in China and a stable democratic form of government.

* State Department White Paper, UNITED STATES RELATIONS WITH CHINA, with Special Reference to the Period 1944–1949, op. cit., pp. 686–689.

In the first place, the greatest obstacle to peace has been the complete, almost overwhelming suspicion with which the Chinese Communist Party and the Kuomintang regard each other.

On the one hand, the leaders of the Government are strongly opposed to a communistic form of government. On the other, the Communists frankly state that they are Marxists and intend to work toward establishing a communistic form of government in China, though first advancing through the medium of a democratic form of government of the American or British type. . . .

Combined with this mutual deep distrust was the conspicuous error by both parties of ignoring the effect of the fears and suspicions of the other party in estimating the reason for proposals or opposition regarding the settlement of various matters under negotiation. They each sought only to take counsel of their own fears. They both, therefore, to that extent took a rather lopsided view of each situation and were susceptible to every evil suggestion of possibility. This complication was exaggerated to an explosive degree by the confused reports of fighting on the distant and tremendous fronts of hostile military contact. Patrol clashes were deliberately magnified into large offensive actions. The distortion of the facts was utilized by both sides to heap condemnation on the other. It was only through the reports of American officers in the field teams from Executive Headquarters that I could get even a partial idea of what was actually happening and the incidents were too numerous and the distances too great for the American personnel to cover all of the ground. . . .

I think the most important factors involved in the recent breakdown of negotiations are these: On the side of the National Government, which is in effect the Kuomintang, there is a dominant group of reactionaries who have been opposed, in my opinion, to almost every effort I have made to influence the formation of a genuine coalition government. This has usually been under the cover of political or party action, but since the Party was the Government, this action, though subtle or indirect, has been devastating in its effect. They were quite frank in publicly stating their belief that cooperation by the Chinese Communist Party in the government was inconceivable and that only a policy of force could definitely settle the issue. This group includes military as well as political leaders.

On the side of the Chinese Communist Party there are, I believe, liberals as well as radicals, though this view is vigorously opposed by many who believe that the Chinese Communist Party discipline is too rigidly enforced to admit of such differences of viewpoint. Nevertheless, it has appeared to me that there is a definite liberal group among the Communists, especially of young men who have turned to the Communists in disgust at the corruption evident in the local governments— men who would put the interest of the Chinese people above ruthless measures to establish a Communist ideology in the immediate future. The dyed-in-the-wool Communists do not hesitate at the most drastic measures to gain their end as, for instance, the destruction of communications in order to wreck the economy of China and produce a situation that would facilitate the overthrow or collapse of the Government, without any regard to the immediate suffering of the people involved. They completely distrust the leaders of the Kuomintang and appear convinced that every Government proposal is designed to crush the Chinese Communist Party. I must say that the quite evidently inspired mob actions of last February and March, some within a few blocks of where I was then engaged in completing negotiations, gave the Communists good excuse for such suspicions.

However, a very harmful and immensely provocative phase of the Chinese Communist Party procedure has been in the character of its propaganda. I wish to state to the American people that in the deliberate misrepresentation and abuse of the action, policies and purposes of our Government this propaganda has been without regard for the truth, without any regard whatsoever for the facts, and has given plain evidence of a determined purpose to mislead the Chinese people and the world and to arouse a bitter hatred of Americans. . . .

Sincere efforts to achieve settlement have been frustrated time and again by extremist elements of both sides. The agreements reached by the Political Consultative Conference a year ago were a liberal and forward-looking charter which then offered China a basis for peace and reconstruction. However, irreconcilable groups within the Kuomintang, interested in the preservation of their own feudal control of China, evidently had no real intention of implementing them. Though I speak as a soldier, I must here also deplore the dominating influence of the military. Their dominance accentuates the weakness of civil government in China. At the same time, in pondering the situation in China, one must have clearly in mind not the workings of small Communist groups or committees to which we are accustomed in America, but rather of millions of people and an army of more than a million men. . . .

Between this dominant reactionary group in the Government

and the irreconcilable Communists who, I must state, did not so appear last February, lies the problem of how peace and well-being are to be brought to the long-suffering and presently inarticulate mass of the people of China. The reactionaries in the Government have evidently counted on substantial American support regardless of their actions. The Communists by their unwillingness to compromise in the national interest are evidently counting on an economic collapse to bring about the fall of the Government, accelerated by extensive guerrilla action against the long lines of rail communications—regardless of the cost in suffering to the Chinese people.

The salvation of the situation, as I see it, would be the assumption of leadership by the liberals in the Government and in the minority parties, a splendid group of men, but who as yet lack the political power to exercise a controlling influence. Successful action on their part under the leadership of Generalissimo Chiang Kai-shek would, I believe, lead to unity through good government.

In fact, the National Assembly has adopted a democratic constitution which in all major respects is in accordance with the principles laid down by the all-party Political Consultative Conference of last January. It is unfortunate that the Communists did not see fit to participate in the Assembly since the constitution that has been adopted seems to include every major point that they wanted.

Soon the Government in China will undergo major reorganization pending the coming into force of the constitution following elections to be completed before Christmas Day 1947. Now that the form for a democratic China has been laid down by the newly adopted constitution, practical measures will be the test. It remains to be seen to what extent the Government will give substance to the form by a genuine welcome of all groups actively to share in the responsibility of government.

The first step will be the reorganization of the State Council and the executive branch of Government to carry on administration pending the enforcement of the constitution. The manner in which this is done and the amount of representation accorded to liberals and to non-Kuomintang members will be significant.

Report to the President on China
from General Wedemeyer*

CHINA

PART I—GENERAL STATEMENT

... Notwithstanding all the corruption and incompetence that one notes in China, it is a certainty that the bulk of the people are not disposed to a Communist political and economic structure. Some have become affiliated with Communism in indignant protest against oppressive police measures, corrupt practices and mal-administration of National Government officials. Some have lost all hope for China under existing leadership and turn to the Communists in despair. Some accept a new leadership by mere inertia. . . .

The economic deterioration and the incompetence and corruption in the political and military organizations in China should be considered against an all-inclusive background lest there be disproportionate emphasis upon defense. Comity requires that cognizance be taken of the following:

Unlike other Powers since V-J Day, China has never been free to devote full attention to internal problems that were greatly confounded by eight years of war. The current civil war has imposed an overwhelming financial and economic burden at a time when resources and energies have been dissipated and when, in any event, they would have been strained to the utmost to meet the problems of recovery.

The National Government has consistently, since 1927, opposed Communism. Today the same political leader and same civil and military officials are determined to prevent their country from becoming a Communist-dominated State or Soviet satellite.

Although the Japanese offered increasingly favorable surrender terms during the course of the war, China elected to remain steadfast with her Allies. If China had accepted surrender terms, approximately a million Japanese would have

---

* Excerpts from Report to President Truman by Lieutenant General Albert C. Wedemeyer, U.S. Army, in U.S. Relations with China, op. cit., pp. 766–773. (All references to Korea were deleted from the White Paper as irrelevant.)

been released for employment against American forces in the Pacific.

I was assured by the Generalissimo that China would support to the limit of her ability an American program for the stabilization of the Far East. He stated categorically that, regardless of moral encouragement or material aid received from the United States, he is determined to oppose Communism and to create a democratic form of government in consonance with Doctor Sun Yat-sen's principles. He stated further that he plans to make sweeping reform in the government including the removal of incompetent and corrupt officials. He stated that some progress has been made along these lines but, with spiraling inflation, economic distress and civil war, it has been difficult to accomplish fully these objectives. He emphasized that, when the Communist problem is solved, he could drastically reduce the Army and concentrate upon political and economic reforms. I retain the conviction that the Generalissimo is sincere in his desire to attain these objectives. I am not certain that he has today sufficient determination to do so if this requires absolute overruling of the political and military cliques surrounding him. Yet, if realistic United States aid is to prove effective in stabilizing the situation in China and in coping with the dangerous expansion of Communism, that determination must be established. . . .

PART II—CHINA

Political

Although the Chinese people are unanimous in their desire for peace at almost any cost, there seems to be no possibility of its realization under existing circumstances. On one side is the Kuomintang, whose reactionary leadership, repression and corruption have caused a loss of popular faith in the Government. On the other side, bound ideologically to the Soviet Union, are the Chinese Communists, whose eventual aim is admittedly a Communist state in China. Some reports indicate that Communist measures of land reform have gained for them the support of the majority of peasants in areas under their control, while the others indicate that their ruthless tactics of land distribution and terrorism have alienated the majority of such peasants. They have, however, successfully organized many rural areas against the National Government. Moderate groups are caught between Kuomintang misrule and repression and ruthless Communist totalitarianism. Minority parties lack dynamic leadership and sizable following. Neither the moderates, many of whom are in the Kuomintang, nor the minority parties are able to make their influence felt because of National Government repression. Existing provincial opposition leading to possible separatist movements would probably crystallize only if collapse of the Government were imminent.

Soviet actions, contrary to the letter and spirit of the Sino-Soviet Treaty of 1945 and its related documents, have strengthened the Chinese Communist position in Manchuria, with political, economic and military repercussions on the National Government's position both in Manchuria and in China proper, and have made more difficult peace and stability in China. The present trend points toward a gradual disintegration of the National Government's control, with the ultimate possibility of a Communist-dominated China. . . .

Economic

Under the impact of civil strife and inflation, the Chinese economy is disintegrating. The most probable outcome of present trends would be, not sudden collapse, but a continued and creeping paralysis and consequent decline in the authority and power of the National Government. The past ten years of war have caused serious deterioration of transportation and communication facilities, mines, utilities and industries. Notwithstanding some commendable efforts and large amounts of economic aid, their overall capabilities are scarcely half those of the pre-war period. With disruption of transportation facilities and the loss of much of North China and Manchuria, important resources of those rich areas are no longer available for the rehabilitation and support of China's economy. . . .

Under inflationary conditions, long-term investment is unattractive for both Chinese and foreign capital. Private Chinese funds tend to go into short-term advances, hoarding of commodities, and capital flight. The entire psychology is speculative and inflationary, preventing ordinary business planning and handicapping industrial recovery. . . .

Social—Cultural

Public education has been one of the chief victims of war, and social and economic disruption. Schoolhouses, textbooks and other equipment have been destroyed and the cost of replacing any considerable portion cannot now be met. Teachers, like other public servants, have seen the purchasing power of a month's salary shrink to the market value of a few days' rice ration. . . . The universities have suffered in an additional and no less serious respect—traditional academic freedom. Students participating in protest demonstrations have been severely and at times brutally punished by National Government agents without pretense of trial or public evidence of the sedition charged. Faculty members have often been dismissed or refused employment with no evidence of professional unfitness, patently because they were politically objectionable to government officials. Somewhat similarly, periodicals have been closed down "for reasons of military security" without stated charges, and permitted to reopen only after new managements have been imposed. . . .

PART IV—CONCLUSIONS

China

The spreading internecine struggle within China threatens world peace. Repeated American efforts to mediate have proved unavailing. It it apparent that positive steps are required to end hostilities immediately. The most logical approach to this very complex and ominous situation would be to refer the matter to the United Nations.

A China dominated by Chinese Communists would be inimical to the interests of the United States, in view of their openly expressed hostility and active opposition to those principles which the United States regards as vital to the peace of the world.

The Communists have the tactical initiative in the overall military situation. The Nationalist position in Manchuria is precarious, and in Shantung and Hopei Provinces strongly disputed. Continued deterioration of the situation may result in the early establishment of a Soviet satellite government in Manchuria and ultimately in the evolution of a Communist-dominated China.

China is suffering increasingly from disintegration. Her requirements for rehabilitation are large. Her most urgent needs include governmental reorganization and reforms, reduction of the military budget and external assistance.

A program of aid, if effectively employed, would bolster opposition to Communist expansion, and would contribute to gradual development of stability in China.

Due to excesses and oppressions by government police agencies basic freedoms of the people are being jeopardized.

Maladministration and corruption cause a loss of confidence in the Government. Until drastic political and economic reforms are undertaken United States aid can not accomplish its purpose. . . .

5

CONSOLIDATION OF COMMUNIST RULE

WHEN THE victorious Communists marched into Peking they were enthusiastically welcomed. Not only success but a reputation for justice, efficiency and incorruptibility had preceded them, and even those who mistrusted their ideological commitments reserved judgment allowing the Communists the benefit of the doubt. By 1949, disillusionment with Chiang K'ai-shek and the Kuomintang had become so total and the ravages of war and dislocation so devastating that for the majority of Chinese there was literally nothing to lose and everything to gain from Communist reconstruction.

The first steps toward a consolidation of law and order under communist rule were sufficient to convince the skeptics of the exemplary behavior of their new rulers. They restored stability to the economy by redistributing land among landless peasants, controlling prices, relieving famine and ending speculation. They took over enterprises and set up state-owned companies to handle distribution. They turned prisons into schools emphasizing the possibility of reform through study and self-criticism and meted out punishment through mass trials for individuals who had exploited economic dislocation to enrich their own coffers at the expense of the poor and disadvantaged. Between 1949 and 1952 the Communists succeeded in restoring food, hope and pride to war-torn China. This was, however, only the end of an era; the beginning of a new one had yet to take root.

Once having assumed political control over all of China and brought the entire productive process back into working order, the Communists faced a new set of problems. With economic recovery to pre-war levels of production, the serious task of large-scale industrial development and building a new society commenced. The dilemma was how to create a modern industrial sector on a weak base while simultaneously raising the level of agricultural output high enough to support both the population and the burden of financing such industrial development. The first Five-Year Plan, put into effect between 1953–1957, had as its objective rapid industrialization with special emphasis on heavy industry. During this period the Chinese relied upon Soviet aid and technical assistance and looked upon the Soviet experience as a model. Agriculture was slighted with only those developments fostered that necessitated small financial investments such as land reclamation, flood control projects, repairing irrigation systems, and encouraging homesteading in Manchuria and the Northwest. Collectivization of agriculture proceeded slowly from mutual-aid teams to semi-cooperatives and then cooperatives. In 1953–54 there was strict rationing of food to prevent withholding of grain which was being exported to the U.S.S.R. in exchange for industrial equipment.

There has been some difficulty, especially in light of later events, in evaluating the significance of the Soviet contribution to China's initial development. A number of reliable observers have concluded, however, that technical assistance of the scope rendered (which cannot be measured strictly in financial terms) must have contributed substantially to the *efficiency* of investment in this period. "But the fact remains," as Choh-Ming Li points out, "that for the five-year period, 97 per cent of the investment for basic development came from the Chinese people themselves." (Choh-Ming Li, "Economic Development in the First Decade," THE CHINA QUARTERLY, p. 39)

In 1958 the Chinese reversed their policy. They adopted a self-reliant course by attempting to solve their problems of economic development on their own. The road was a difficult one to follow for there were few reliable guidelines, and the Soviet Union was not one of them. Although the Soviet Union had started out with similarly underdeveloped resources and managed to industrialize in a miraculously short time China could not duplicate the process. There were too many differences in the circumstances and objectives in the two situations. As a result, since 1958 the Chinese have utilized the Soviet Union more as a model of what *not* to do. The leadership of new China once again expressed a long-standing determination of theirs: that China would develop in a uniquely independent and Chinese way.

What has made this pattern of Chinese economic and social development unique is its dialectical movement. First one extreme is pursued and then its opposite, resulting in a shifting policy that has variously been referred to as a "zig-zag" pattern or the fluctuations of an "ideology versus rationality

pendulum." The policy before 1957 stressed economic efficiency, centralization of planning and control, resort to material incentives and recognition of the superiority of expertise
and "technique" over strictly ideological or political criteria.
Technicians and intellectuals formerly loyal to the Kuomintang were treated with diffidence and their skills rewarded so
long as they agreed to the minimum political requirements of
study and reform. Loyal Communist Party cadres, on the
other hand, were urged to be conscious of their technical
insufficiencies and "understanding" of the ideological weaknesses of the "experts."

In 1958 with the Great Leap Forward there was a nation-
wide policy swing in the opposite direction. China embarked
on a startling series of revolutionary experiments aimed at
drastically increasing both agricultural and industrial production in unexpected ways. The sober respect for economic
rationality was overturned in favor of spontaneous and hitherto unconventional means of organizing production. Decentralization of economic activities, including planning and control,
was vigorously promoted. In line with this, small and medium
scale industries were constructed, back-yard steel furnaces
were built, and the masses of Chinese were exhorted to im-
provise at any and all forms of production utilizing *local*
initiative, capital, resources and ingenuity. A new and unique
form of social organization, the commune, was the permanent
outgrowth of this upheaval with continued ramifications for
social change.

The dominant characteristics of the Great Leap Forward
were a heady optimism: an overwhelming concern with ideological purity as opposed to technological expertise and the
stringent application of an equalitarian ethic. In a similar
direction there were attempts at breaching the distance between rural and urban areas. Party, government, and urban
workers were transferred to the countryside to participate in
agriculture, and students were required to put in specified
stints at manual labor. The primitive nature of most of these
endeavors—the steel was inferior in quality, the agricultural
output was overestimated, etc.—was not as significant a factor
for the entire long-run development of China as the approach
itself in which people were encouraged to assume initiative in
making decisions. The experiment with localized responsibility
was an important lesson in what might turn out to be a new
form of participatory democracy.

By 1962 this policy had run its course and there was relaxation again in the direction of greater economic rationality,

more realistic projections, and reasonable demands on the population. Although at the time this relaxation or back swing of the policy pendulum was attributed by western scholars to the failures of the Great Leap, from today's perspective, in the light of the recent ideological upheavals this explanation is inadequate. It is more fruitful, it seems to me, to hypothesize that this swinging motion is a manifestation or expression of basic objectives, at least consciously encouraged if not provoked by the aspirations of the leadership.

The Chinese Communists are pursuing something more than economic development through industrialization and modernization. Their objective is not simply to raise the standard of living but also to create a new society. The problem is to modernize without westernizing. Instead of allowing the introduction of those values that accompanied modernization in the west (including the Soviet Union), the Chinese are trying to combine industrial development which is based on hard work and self-sacrifice with the new values of a future Communist society. This necessitates the creation of a new man in China, the radical transformation of people from old ways of thinking, i.e., in distinctions of class, status, occupation, age, etc. to new habits, ideas and possibilities. Social change of this magnitude can only hope to be achieved through massive education.

Possibly nowhere else in the world does such a profound respect for and belief in education characterize an entire people. Along with the eradication of capitalist enterprise, the collectivization of agriculture in the form of communes and the study of scientific techniques of one sort or another, there is a complex and intensive "socialist education." Everyone in China studies. Learning how to read and write or learning a trade or profession is not enough; one learns values—a whole range of attitudes—and all from "the thought of Mao Tsetung." In establishing a new society, a socialist society, in China the primary emphasis is on re-educating those whose ideas stem from an earlier epoch and educating youngsters in the ways of thinking and behaving that will best serve to renew the vigor and enthusiasm of a rapidly developing society. The workers and peasants learn not only basic skills for production but also political concepts, and a new morality. Students learn not only technical subjects like math and physics but also political *behavior* (they must learn to go out into the world just as the peasant must learn as a supplement to *his* activities, book-studies) for which they are sent out into the countryside to harvest or into the factory to produce on the assembly-line.

One of the major aspects of education in China is the

"spare-time" program. People past school age cannot afford to go to school full-time, so educational facilities must be conveniently made available to them where they work as a supplement to their jobs. In this way older people can learn as well as youth, thus, helping to eradicate illiteracy. The Chinese aim to produce a socialist society through education and not simply through industrialization and the production of consumers' goods. Their premise seems to be that the socialist man cannot be assumed to be a natural or automatic outgrowth of machines and modernization but must be nurtured through education—the changing of men's minds. In recent years in the western world the idea of changing men's minds has assumed undesirable overtones, but the Chinese going through their own "Enlightenment" fervently believe in man's potential to perfect himself through a combination of hard work and learning. Improving man's mind, for the Chinese, is still a worthwhile goal, and the state encourages men to value it as well as achieve it. Perhaps the enormous optimism of the Chinese derives from their successes in the past when so often, contrary to all expectations, they turned out to be right in their predictions and effective in their actions.

On the whole, national policy in China since 1952 is characterized by both more organization (rational planning) and less rigidity than most westerners can conceive. By this I mean that the leadership appears to be conscious throughout, of the central long-range problems that they face in pursuing their objectives and choose a highly flexible and experimental means of achieving them. In their handling of the short-run problems it is somewhat like a juggling act. At any point in time there is a concentration on one problem while the others are suspended in time later to fall into focus of their own momentum. First, they organize a campaign against over-centralization by arousing mass participation in any number of unusual ways. Once having aroused lower levels of popular involvement (which under some conditions necessitates exaggerated emphasis) the movement is curtailed by a shift, often radical, to another problem or aspect of the problem.

From this perspective the Marxism of Mao Tse-tung is much more than an accidental affectation. As the Bard will have it, "Though this be madness, yet there is method to 't." The method, dialectics, is a useful way of structuring problems of organization, in terms of their polar aspects: centralization vs. decentralization, ideological purity vs. technical skills, youth vs. experience. The basic objectives of the Communist revolution, while they *ultimately* complement one another, remain for the short-run duration contradictory in their effects. It is this that makes Marxism-Leninism in Mao's formulation of it a vital and constructive force for the Chinese.

From the American perspective, what appeared as disaster— the downfall of Chiang Kai-shek—was to the Chinese the beginning of a new era. The following selection is the fade-out not only on the Kuomintang but on the U.S. presence in China. It is the American ambassador's prognostication in 1948 of a Communist victory. It is the fade-out that ushers in new China which is documented in the succeeding selections.

The two selections by Joan Robinson present a westerner's perceptions of early changes in new China and a discussion of the communes which constitute the basic form of social organization in China today. The final selection is an overall evaluation of the state of technological development as seen through the eyes of a Japanese, Genko Uchida.

THE AMBASSADOR IN CHINA (STUART)
TO SECRETARY MARSHALL*

NANKING, *August 10, 1948*

1. MILITARY: The Communists continue to win the civil war. They have retained the initiative with all the advantage given by the offensive and government troops just do not seem to have the will or the ability to fight. There are many reports of defections to the Communists but none from Communist ranks. Occupying as they do most of north China east of Sian and north of the Yangtze River except for a few scattered urban centers such as Peiping and Tientsin and certain lines of communication the Communists now appear intent on removing the last vestiges of government strength from Shantung Province, a prelude possibly to full-scale attack south to Nanking or possibly to an all-out attack on Peiping-Tientsin area. In Central China south of the Yangtze scattered Communist bands operate throughout the countryside creating confusion and disorder with the obvious intent of further weakening the

* U.S. RELATIONS WITH CHINA, *ibid.*, pp. 885–886.

government and preparing the way for some future large-scale operation. In South China though less active Communist guerrilla units operate more or less at will and the government has no forces to employ against them.

It is a gloomy picture and one would expect the government to clutch at any means of improving the situation. Nevertheless it ignores competent military advice and fails to take advantage of military opportunities offered. This is due in large part to the fact that government and military leadership continue to deteriorate as the Generalissimo selects men on the basis of personal reliability rather than military competence. In the distribution of desperately needed military supplies men of proven military competence such as Fu Tso-yi are given low priority and are almost left to fend for themselves. Long contemplated plans for training new armies and replacements are not being implemented or are moving too slowly materially to affect the situation in the coming desperate months. There is an awareness of the desperateness of the military situation yet no evidence of a will or capability to cope with it.

2. Economic: The inflationary spiral continues at an accelerated pace. Prices have become astronomical and their rise so rapid that the government has been unable to print sufficient money to meet day-by-day needs with the result that barter is becoming more and more the rule. Prices increasingly are quoted either in US dollars, silver or gold. In the interior silver dollars are coming back to use. Thus government has introduced measures to control inflation but the effects have been only temporary and palliative. The fact is that the government in the absence of assured continuing and massive loans from the United States cannot hope to find an answer as long as circumstances require the maintenance of the present military establishment. A renewed and concerted attack on the periphery of the central problem now impends but at best it can only provide a breathing spell.

3. Psychological: After years of war and destruction the all-consuming urge of the people today, and this includes both low and high ranking members of the government and Communist areas as well, is for peace. This urge becomes all the more insistent as most people can see no ray of hope under present conditions. A spirit of defeatism is prevalent throughout the country reaching even men of cabinet rank. Almost without exception there is no longer faith that the present government can bring a return to even a bearable standard of living without some radical reorganization. With this frame of mind a cessation of hostilities is desired at almost any price.

There is an overwhelming desire for peace yet the Generalissimo wants only military victory over the Communists and no one has yet found a way to surmount the Generalissimo's objections and win out to peace.

4. The Generalissimo himself: Universally the Generalissimo is criticized for his ineffective leadership and universally no one can suggest any one to take his place. He is the one who holds this vast country together. Without him disintegration seems inevitable yet long experience with him suggests that he is no longer capable of changing and reforming or of discarding inefficient associates in favor of competent ones and unless he can summon the resources to reverse the present trend he will inevitably and in time be discarded. . . .

A Western Visitor's Impressions of China* in the Early Days After Revolution

JOAN ROBINSON

Joan Robinson is professor of Economics at Cambridge University, England. She is the author, among other noted works, of Economic Philosophy and Essays in the Theory of Economic Growth. Although Miss Robinson makes no claim to be an expert on China she has had the opportunity to visit China on three separate occasions, 1953, 1957 and 1963, and was engaged in more intensive study than is possible on the usual tours. Her observations, therefore, combine a scholarly familiarity with problems of economic development and an invaluable first-hand experience with conditions in China. The following two selections give us some indication of the ways in which traditional patterns have been and continue to be transformed in the process of modernization. In the first selection, written in 1953, there are some impressions of life in China gathered in the early days after the revolution. In the second selection Joan Robinson describes the principles on which the communes are organized based on her trip to various communes in different parts of China in the summer of 1963.

. . . EVERY SUNDAY is a Bank holiday for crowds in the parks and palaces of Peking, yet never a scrap of litter. But people

* Excerpts from Joan Robinson, LETTERS FROM A VISITOR TO CHINA (Students' Bookshops Ltd, 21, Silver St., Cambridge, England, 1954), pp. 4–7, 30–33. By permission.

evidently have to learn one thing at a time: they have not yet mastered the habit of hawking and spitting all over the place.

It is also true that China has turned honest. People leave property about in public places without any fear (but I did hear of a dynamo being stolen off a bicycle in the Legation Quarter); there are fixed prices in all the shops—even the curio and junk dealers in a sort of Caledonian Market—and foreigners fumbling with notes, still in confusingly astronomical denominations since the inflation, can rely on being given the right change. A resident Englishman told me that he dropped a wad of money in the bazaar without noticing and had it given back to him a week later when he happened to go down the same alley. A curio dealer—a profession that one would not expect to be particularly enthusiastic about New China—when asked how he finds things after the Liberation, said that it saved him money; his shop has three doors, and formerly he had to have three assistants to stop pilfering; now he can manage single handed. The respect for public property is such as exists nowhere else. I wonder if even in Denmark the railways could provide bedroom slippers in the sleeping cars without fear that passengers would take them for keeps? As for large-scale crookery, everyone, even the least sympathetic foreign observer, agrees that it has been totally abolished.

It may seem tiresome to harp upon the clean-and-honest theme. But it is something new to meet a people who combine the boring though necessary Protestant virtues with the light touch, the sensibility and the flair for enjoying life of the Chinese.

Besides, the high public morality is the "outward and visible sign" of a very remarkable phenomenon—the state of mind of the people. Chinese themselves are amazed and ask each other: How is it that we can perform miracles? Changes in social habits—the freeing of women, economic achievements like the stabilization of prices, feats of construction like the great river barrages, which might reasonably be expected to take ten or twenty years of struggle and experiment, smoothly accomplished in two or three.

The secret lies partly, I believe, in the technique of "criticism and self-criticism" as it has been developed in China. Before I came here I thought of it as something like the Group Movement or a Dostoevskyish wallowing in repentance, but it is nothing of the kind. I get an impression of how it works from one or two Chinese friends with whom I am on terms to discuss intimate questions and from a number of foreigners who are working here and who are put through it like everyone else.

Each office or group such as a university faculty or the staff of a newspaper is constantly reviewing its work and discussing how to improve it. Everyone, beginning with the boss, is criticised but it is against the spirit of the thing to introduce a personal note—all is concentrated on how to do the job better. The individual has to examine himself to see why he fails in this or that way to help the work as well as he might. It is not required of people who cannot take it—an old fogey who really hasn't a clue is allowed just to run on, and anyone who has the misfortune to have an incurably sensitive temperament is dealt with gently. The more "advanced" the person is, the more frankly he is discussed.

Short-comings are diagnosed as due to one or other of the recognised propensities, such as "commandism," "individual heroism," "hard bureaucracy" (red-tapery) or "soft bureaucracy" (letting things slide) and when the patient has agreed to the diagnosis, the group helps him to get over the complaint.

H., whom you remember as a rather ivory-tower intellectual at Cambridge (he is very happy and completely absorbed in the New China without his delicate charm having been at all coarsened by it), said to me: "At first when I was not sure of myself I used to agree to criticism without really accepting it. Of course in the long run that would have heaped up inward resentment that would have ended by exploding. But now I realise that you must stick to your opinions and argue a question out to a genuine agreement."

The result is not to make people uneasy and self-conscious, but, on the contrary, to build up confidence. With all the tasks that have to be done, half the jobs are filled by people too inexperienced for them, by any ordinary standard, and the knowledge that they will not be allowed to go wrong prevents them from getting into a state of feeling helpless and inadequate. It is natural enough for young people to take to this way of life—after all it is very much how we treated each other as undergraduates (though we were more catty withal); what impresses me is the way that middle-aged people whom I have talked to have evidently been re-vitalised by it. Here the adage that everyone over forty is a scoundrel no longer applies.

On the various visits which I have made to schools, co-operatives, a hospital, a prison, the spokesmen who explained the methods of work and the results achieved (particularly the women) had an air of assurance and unegotistical pride in what was being done. In this half of the world you always join in clapping yourself, to show that you do not take applause personally. That spirit runs through everything.

I came across one or two slogan bores, who could not go beyond saying the correct thing, refusing to admit any drawbacks or shortcomings, and they seemed to me precisely people who lacked inner conviction, who were resolved to be on the safe side when speaking to a foreigner or who perhaps needed to reassure themselves of their own orthodoxy.

The Chinese must have been well prepared for the new life by their old tradition of education. They have smooth unneurotic faces and calm gestures. (In this, a foreigner who lived under the occupation remarked, the Japanese were just the reverse, going about frowning and muttering to themselves, looking like so many psycho-pathic cases.) I noticed long ago that Chinese students were remarkably free from the mental egoism and desire to show off that make so many young men tiresome to try to teach. But whatever the ancient foundation, the present state of mind is something new and powerful. It is like a great technical discovery—a source of energy hitherto unknown.

The clean and honest phenomenon illustrates another point: the leap-frog principle, by which the most backward economy, when it begins to move, jumps ahead of the formerly most advanced. Chinese towns used to be, I suppose, as filthy as, say, Bangkok is today. Formerly highway robbery was too common to be worth mentioning. And China was a country where dishonesty was not confined to crooks. Every decent man felt it a duty to scrounge and wangle for the benefit of his family.

Another thing about it is that I already feel that when I get home I shall begin to wonder if I have not really been visiting Erewhon backwards. But one must face facts, and the absence of flies and of swindlers are solid facts, which no one denies and which have to be accounted for somehow.

MARX-LENINISM

What has all this got to do with Marxism? The importance of a doctrine lies in what it denies. For the Chinese, Marx-Leninism is denying the complex of ideas and attitudes which they call Feudal. It means that children must not be sold to pay the rent. It means that widows can re-marry and young people betroth themselves. It means that the police must treat everyone alike and everyone helpfully, instead of kicking the poor and fawning on the rich. It has brought a release of creative energy by teaching people to look towards the future that they are building instead of regarding the present as a state of degeneracy from a pre-Confucian golden age. What have long been commonplaces to us are new revelations to China, and Marx-Leninism gets the credit since it was the medium through which the revelation came.

It means, also, denying the sophistries of classical economics by which the doctrine of comparative advantages was used to justify the foisting of a permanent colonial status on the primary-producing countries, and has revealed to China that she can become a great industrial nation.

It does not mean a root-and-branch objection to capitalism as such. Private capitalism in all but the key positions of transport and heavy industry is being fostered and encouraged to make a contribution to industrialisation, and so is handicraft production, which is still a very important element in the Chinese economy. The present position is often compared to the N.E.P. but there is an important difference; N.E.P. in Russia was a step back from an over-hasty rush towards socialism. The present phase in China is intended to lead smoothly into socialism without wasting any scrap of useful resources meanwhile. (The Old China Hands complain, with some justification from their point of view, that their goodwill and know-how was scrapped wantonly; but perhaps that was a necessary element in the revolt against colonialism.)

On the intellectual plane Feudalism means scholasticism and respect for authority, so that Marxism, in denying it, imports the scientific, empirical spirit and respect for results. . . .

DEMOGRAPHY

China is bubbling over with babies. In Canton the women, who work in the fields and on the boats, carry their babies in a scarf on their backs (imagine never being able to lean back all day!). On the river it is a common sight to see four or five children in a small boat, their only home, the baby on the mother's back and the next youngest tied by a string to stop him falling into the water. (There are schools afloat now, as the river children would not go ashore.)

Round Peking, women work less (one of the new rights the village woman was rejoicing in was being allowed to work out of doors) and the baby-minding is done by elder children. In the city you often see a man carrying a baby, and there are a few low double prams in wickerwork (wasteful in a Chinese family to have a pram for one). The streets are lined with toddlers playing about, very free and chirpy.

The first complete census ever to be taken is now being prepared in connection with the forthcoming elections. People are speculating as to whether the population will not be nearer to 600 million than to the traditional figure of 400 million.

The death-rate, particularly infant and maternal deaths, has fallen sharply with the new health measures and there are no signs of the birth-rate having fallen, so that natural increase must have risen with a bound; there is also a trickle of immigration of overseas Chinese (we travelled with a train load from the frontier, looking wayworn and grubby compared to the New Chinese).

No one will hear of Malthus. Birth control is too much associated with a pessimistic, defeatist, anti-Marxist view of life; they say that the cultivable area of China can be doubled (of mere space there is no lack, as the train journey through the North East and into Inner Mongolia brought home to me) and yields can be increased on existing land by scientific farming. But this is only to meet the Malthusian argument in its crudest form. It does not counter what seems to me the most cogent point, that the standard of life in physical consumption and in culture and amenities can be raised the faster the more investment goes into raising capital per head, as opposed to catering for more heads.

There is a boundless internal reserve of labour waiting to be released by submitting capital equipment for the fantastically man-power-using methods of production now in operation, so that there can be no question of not having enough people to utilise the natural resources of China.

But it is of no use to argue with the economists. No doubt in time the universal unofficial trade union of women will take the matter in hand.

ECONOMIC DISCIPLINE

Railways and the bulk of heavy industry are nationalised; there is quite a large area of pure private enterprise in miscellaneous industry and trade. The mixed part of the economy, in staple products, is controlled through state wholesaling. The major part of all the main crops is bought from the peasantry (apart from the portion contributed as taxation) by a network of Supply and Marketing Co-operatives and sold to government corporations. Prices are fixed by the corporations, price ratios being calculated to give an incentive to produce industrial crops such as cotton and tobacco (in both of which China has changed since Liberation from an importer to an exporter).

Raw materials are partly sold to private industrialists, partly manufactured by them on commission and partly used in government factories. Staple manufactures (cloth, soap, fertilisers) are also partly wholesaled by the corporations. Retailing in towns is predominantly private enterprise, but there are enough state department stores and urban consumer co-operatives to keep margins within bounds and set standards of quality. Retailing in the villages is more and more becoming dominated by the Supply and Marketing Co-ops. There are also a growing number of handicraft Co-operatives beginning to organise the great mass of artisan production.

The system depends on carrying sufficient stocks to be able to kill speculation. Under this method of control there is no need for price regulation by decree and no scope for a black market.

The inflation was mastered in March 1950 and prices have been substantially stable ever since.

We hear some echoes of the great drive against the Five Vices and the Three Evils. This, like Land Reform, was a hurricane that has blown over. The Five Vices of private enterprise were bribery, tax evasion, theft of state property, cheating on government contracts, and stealing information for private speculation. Accusations were brought by the workers against their employers and in the prolonged investigations there were many suicides, not so much from fear of the consequences of conviction as from shame at exposure.

An English industrialist who had been through it told me that the trade unions, as might be expected, showed excessive zeal in making accusations and were rough and high handed. He himself had had some pretty nasty moments, and every business lost money during the paralysis of trade while the hurricane was blowing, but a man with patience and a clear conscience got pretty fair treatment in the end.

There is no suggestion that malpractices have crept back to any appreciable extent; the trade unions are on the look out, though co-operation between labour and management for the sake of production is now the watchword.

The affair provides a commentary on the old liberal adage that light is the best antiseptic. We know what that amounts to when the light flickers from a Royal Commission once in twenty years; to have it turned on permanently from below is a very different matter.

The Three Evils among Government employees were corruption, waste, and bureaucracy. These also were hunted out to the smallest detail. There is a new drive against bureaucracy going on now, which entails civil servants spending a certain proportion of their time in the field to learn the reality of what they deal with on paper.

The anti-bureaucracy campaign is a necessary corrective to the Chinese passion for exact detail. The by-word for a bureaucrat is the man who ordered the mosquitoes to be counted.

TECHNOLOGY

On the way up I visited an exhibition at Mukden of local industrial products. The display of machine tools was impressive; all the more so when you consider that these massive docile robots will be for many years fellow producers with the little sweating blacksmiths of Peking.

China is a wonderful museum of economic history. A foreign engineer told me that he was startled to recognise a cupola from the first chapter of the text book of his student days illustrating how pig iron was made 2,000 years ago, working next door to a huge automatic steel mill of the very latest design.

Another feature of the exhibition was a number of inventions made by miners and steel workers. One was a seamless chain (for greater strength) the links cut out from a solid bar of iron on the same principle that chains are made from jade.

An architect told me of numerous devices for speeding up construction that building workers have introduced (I leave you to draw the moral).

TRAVEL DIARY

Well there you are. I have had a little glimpse at this huge event and I tell you what I can. It does not add up to a great deal, but in the prevailing state of ignorance at home I feel that any crumb of information is worth sharing.

To end, I will give you an outline of my journey, so that you can see how these snippets fit together.

I went to China with a group of business men organised by the British Council for the Promotion of International Trade. As I had no business to do, I attended only the formal meetings and banquets and some group expeditions. Most of the time I was scouting around on my own, and I am travelling back alone. . . .

China, 1963: the Communes*

JOAN ROBINSON

THE HEADY enthusiasm of the Great Leap Forward in China has given way to a mood of sober satisfaction at having come through. The leap itself created some difficulties, though great achievements remain solid. Too many projects were started at once in 1958; there was too much in the pipe line and not enough coming out; labour was drawn out of agriculture into industry, and in the countryside too much went into the drive for steel, which over-strained the transport system and took time from cultivation.

In the normal way, all this would have been corrected and balance soon restored; but '59, '60 and '61 were bitter years. 'Natural disasters' are endemic in China, but those three years saw a concentration of drought in the North, floods in the South, and typhoons in the East to beat the records of a century. Much of the irrigation work carried out in the Great Leap was frustrated. The Yellow River was reduced to a trickle that motor cars could drive through. The great reservoir behind the Three Gates dam had not had time to fill up and was useless to combat the drought.

In the midst of all this, in July 1960, came the fantastic episode of the withdrawal of the Soviet technicians (who took with them the blue-prints of half-finished projects) and the cancellation of contracts for equipment. (At the same time the Soviet Government exacted repayment of the Korean-war loan, on top of commercial repayments which were being fully honoured.) The technicians (who were given three days to quit) were bewildered and dismayed. Some who expected to stay for two years had been only a few weeks in the country. Their Chinese colleagues saw them off with farewell dinners, and the Russians parted from them, often with tears. Chinese technicians have cracked some of the problems since, but many plants are still idle and shells of factories empty. Nothing was said officially about this affair; it was too shaming for the Communist cause, and too shocking for the public at large, though city dwellers saw it with their own eyes. Now that it is brought into the open in the course of bitter mutual recrim-

* From COLLECTED ECONOMIC PAPERS, Volume 3 (1965) by Joan Robinson, by permission of Basil Blackwell, Oxford. Pp. 192–206.

inations with the Soviets, many people will dismiss it as a fabrication.

Through all this the government kept its head and the people kept their nerve. No one starved. This was an experience much more completely unprecedented than the natural disasters. The stricken areas were supplied. In the cities rations were tight, but they were always honoured. There was no inflation, and apparently, scarcely any black market.

Foreigners who lived through those years pay tribute (enthusiastic or grudging according to their point of view) to the high morale and good conduct of the public. But morale alone will not check inflation in a time of scarcity, and nor can the police. The secret, it seems, lay in sensible policy and incorruptible administration. The staples—grain, vegetable oil and cotton cloth—are dealt in exclusively by government agents. This makes it next to impossible for a black market to develop in those commodities, when the public is backing up the administration, for no unauthorized person dares to be seen moving them. For these commodities there were specific rations. Other things were on coupons, on a point system covering everything from eggs to bicycles. The prices of the three staples were held constant. (They have been substantially constant ever since the currency stabilization in 1950.) The official prices of luxury goods and consumer durables were set very high, to mop up purchasing power. (An overcoat of foreign cloth still costs £60.) In the free market, which is permitted on the fringes of the state trading system, some off-coupon items could be had at free-market prices. (Though it seems that even in this sector there was some check on profiteering.)

In the cities, the winter of 1960–61 was the worst. Grain rations were barely enough. Extras were hard to come by. Tobacco was diluted. People grew haggard and shabby. Party members, to set a good example, gave up eating meat, and would not accept invitations from their pampered foreign colleagues. By the summer of '61 rations began to be increased (by way of supplements for various categories of consumers) and points and prices for one thing or another began to be reduced. Now the grain ration is more than ample. Nearly everything except meat is off coupons. The cotton ration is very tight, but substitutes can be had. The street crowds have bonny faces again and neat clothes. With the summer flush, there is a positive glut of vegetables and fruit; in many cities the free-market price has fallen below the official price, itself reduced.

In easing the country through this narrow strait, the Communes played an important role.

I

This method of organizing agriculture was not thought out in advance; it was evolved by a gradual process, though all the stages were run through at vertiginous speed.

During the civil war, when the Communists took over a district, they merely freed the bondsmen and reduced rent and interest. (This is the stage that Tibet is now at, apart from confiscated rebel estates.) After the creation of the People's Republic in 1949, the land reform was set going; by 1952 it had covered the whole country except for some of the National Minority areas.

The land reform was preceded, in every village, by an analysis of the land/labour ratio of each family. Landlords did little or no work and drew their income from rent, usury and other exactions. Rich peasants worked but had more than enough land in their family's labour force. Middle peasants neither hired labour nor worked for others; this class was divided into an upper section, not too badly off and a lower, on the brink of misery. Poor peasants were obliged to work for others and lived in misery indeed. At the land reform, the rich and middle peasants became free-holders of what they had; the landlords' houses and fields were confiscated and distributed, so much per head, amongst the landless families, including their own. The holdings so created were tiny; no basis for efficient agriculture.

The process of collectivization started very gently. A network of Supply and Marketing Co-operatives assisted the peasants in trade with cities. Mutual-aid teams were encouraged—first just a group of families helping each other at the harvest, then all-the-year-round teams; their 'lower form co-operatives' in which families pooled land and beasts to work together, drawing a share of the proceeds both for the property and for the work put in. A few 'higher-form co-operatives,' in which distribution was only for work, were formed early, but very few. I remember (it seems ironic now) discussing the position in 1953 with a Russian expert who was wagging his head over the Chinese, wondering when they are going to make a serious start on collectivization. At first the doctrine prevailed that there is no point in enlarging the scale of agriculture until it can be mechanized. Experience and reflection, however, showed that, in Chinese conditions, just the reverse is true. Without mechanization, the only hope of progress lay in mobilizing labour in large units. The 'high tide of the socialism' carried almost the whole countryside into higher-form co-operatives in 1956. Watching developments and analysing experience, it seems that the authorities formed the view that the co-operatives were too large for good management, and they began to be reorganized in that sense. But during the Great Leap in 1958 a group of co-operatives in Honan decided to work together on some irrigation schemes too large to be tackled individually. The idea seemed reasonable. After the usual debate, the Party adopted it, and communes spread like wild fire over the whole country.

Battered, sifted and reorganized in the bad years, they have emerged as a stable framework within which it is intended to let agriculture evolve for a long run of years.

II

The organization, as it now exists, is in three tiers, the Commune, the Brigade and the Team.

The team is the unit in which day-to-day work is organized. It commands 'the four fixed,' that is productive resources that cannot be alienated; the labour force, the animals, the farm implements, carts and so forth (tools are owned by individuals) and the land allotted to it for cultivation. The team consists of the workers from thirty or forty neighbour families, usually cultivating the very land that they have always worked. Generally speaking, there are not supposed to be more than ten teams in a brigade, but this, like all such rules, is subject to exceptions in special cases.

There are usually several teams in a village. Where the villages are large, the brigade coincides with a village. In hilly areas with small villages and hamlets, a dozen or more may be in a single brigade. To the peasants, the village is the real, human, historical unit—the stem on to which the new system is grafted.

The brigade is the primary unit for planning the crop programme. Each year it sketches out the next year's plan, in consultation with its teams. The draft plan is sent up, through the commune, to the county authorities, who return it with amendments. After some to and fro, a detailed plan is submitted and comes back to the brigade as a binding agreement. ('Two ups and two downs.') The brigade then allocates work to the teams.

The commune comprises a dozen or two of brigades. There are between sixty and seventy thousand communes, covering the whole country, apart from Minority areas which are at a less advanced stage of organization. A commune may cover anything from one to fifty thousand acres, according to the nature of the terrain. It has taken over the functions of the smallest unit of the old district administration, concerned with such things as registration of births, deaths and marriages, civil disputes, and command of the local militia. (Police, law courts and recruitment to the army are under the county authorities.) The commune directorate, with a staff of ten to twenty members, is generally responsible for the external financial and commercial relations of its brigades, for assisting and co-ordinating brigade plans, for organizing schemes of investment and operating enterprises that require a larger scale than the old co-operatives, for running schools and hospitals, for entertainments, such as film projection teams, for analysing experience and spreading improved technique and for generally keeping the whole affair jollied along.

The establishment of the 'basic accounting unit' is an important matter. To this group accrues income in cash and kind to be distributed amongst its members. Thus, where there is a dispersion in earnings, for whatever reason, the wider is the group the more are the higher earnings diluted in the average. The smaller the group, the closer and the more visible is the connection between one's own effort and one's income; the more conspicuous would be slacking or malingering. It was a concession to realism from the Utopian conceptions of the Great Leap to make the team, rather than the whole co-operative, the accounting unit. This is now the commonest case. Here and there, however, brigades are established in the role. When the brigade is the accounting unit it controls the 'four fixed' but still allocates the land to teams as operational units. Sometimes there is one such brigade in a commune, while the rest have not yet got beyond the stage of teams as basic units. In a few cases, amongst the prosperous, highly organized market gardens around Peking, the unit is the whole commune.

III

From another angle, the family is still the basic economic entity. Commonly three generations pool their earnings and share a house. (The horror-comic story, now being repeated in Russia, about 'dormitories' was fabricated from a mistaken translation of 'room' or more exactly 'dwelling unit.') There must be a few families (not counting ex-landlords) in every neighborhood who were formerly better off in terms of income, though not in terms of social security, insurance against disaster and educational opportunities. Every one has the legal right still to reclaim an equivalent of his own original land. During the bad years it was not unknown for individuals to insist on doing so. One of the duties of the Party members in the communes is to keep an eye open for signs of 'the spontaneous development of capitalism' and nip it in the bud. It is said that not only ex-landlords are apt to be idle or to attempt speculation (buying cheaper to sell dearer). Sometimes ex-poor peasants are the worst. But the offenders are a tiny handful, in well-run communes, not more than one or two in a team, and the rest keep them up to the mark. There must be some bad patches, of course. A small minority of communes, it is said, are not doing well at all, and there have been scandals. For this the blame is put on the Party workers, not on the peasants.

A private plot is allocated by the team or brigade for the use of a family according to the number of its members, property in the land being retained as part of the 'four fixed.' The plots are very small; there is a general rule that the area set aside for them must not exceed 5 or 7 per cent of the whole. A family of six may have one fifth, or sometimes one tenth, of an acre. Apart from their plots, many families have made small vegetable gardens in their courtyards, with vines or fruit trees. Most keep a few chickens; many are fattening a pig, or milking a goat bred for them by the brigade. Where cotton is grown, members can have some to spin and weave for their own use. There is a co-operative organization for handicrafts, interpenetrating the communes, and the Supply and Marketing Co-operative, which runs shops in the villages and moves produce into town, can buy from individuals as well as from teams or brigades. Finally, periodic fairs are held, to which grandpa can be sent to sell a dozen eggs or a handful of tobacco leaves. Family production is important to the family but (in contrast to the situation in U.S.S.R.) it is reckoned to contribute less than 10 per cent to national supplies.

IV

The three-tiered frame-work of team, brigade and commune, is highly flexible. Dipping at random in three northern provinces we find a great variety of types.

In one the upper layers are still embryonic. The teams correspond to old lower-form co-operatives, and remain the centre of all economic activity, including the upkeep of elementary schools. The brigades are inserted merely for the sake of conforming to the national pattern, and the commune, apart from sharing with two others in a small irrigation scheme, functions merely in its capacity as the organ of local government. Here, apart from grain and fodder for man and beast, the whole cultivated area is under cotton, and the cash income of members is exceptionally high.

At another place, while the team is the accounting unit, the brigades and the commune are full of activity. The commune had organized a drainage scheme, requiring a canal of 20 kilometers. The cost was borne by teams according to the area benefited, and labour supplied in proportion to the labour force of each. The commune had brought in the high-voltage cable to electrify the villages, the brigades being responsible for the distribution cables. Most of the houses have light; the commune pays the monthly bill and divides it between households at so much per lamp. The commune operates a manufacturing and repair shop for tools, complete with miniature iron foundry. It breeds draft animals to supply to teams, as well as pigs. The brigades sell piglets to be reared by households. Brigades operate smaller-scale enterprises, such as a brick kiln. They grind the members' grain for a small fee, and sell noodles. There is a hospital and three clinics. The teachers for the secondary school are paid by the government, while the brigades provide the primary schools, with a subsidy. (Everywhere nowadays it is claimed that all children of primary-school age are going to school; a good proportion attend secondary schools, and many communes boast of members who are away at college.)

In another commune there is one large brigade that is the centre of life (the other brigades are smaller and less developed). Here a higher-form co-operative was set up earlier than most, and since it was satisfactorily established, it carried on as before in the new setting. In such a case, the main task of the commune is to nurse the other teams up to the same standard.

Further examples conform more or less to one or the other of these three types.

V

Receiving visitors has its own ritual. When we picked on a commune that had never had a visit before, they hastily boned up from the county offices on proper procedure.

The commune office is sometimes in a new building in the old style (mud bricks and unglazed tiles), sometimes a room in an ex-landlord's compound or the court of a temple. (The gods are much out of fashion, but in some houses a little image in a niche in the wall is still being honoured with paper offerings.) The foreigners, with their escort of hardly less foreign city folk, sit round the large table; they are served tea, or more often hot water as a symbol of tea, and heaps of delicious fruits fresh from the trees. The spokesman is sometimes the director of the commune, sometimes a brigade leader or a Party secretary—an old peasant with beady eyes in his walnut-wrinkled face; a married woman, still handsome; an ex-school teacher with the indefinable cast of book education faintly showing in his countenance. No matter who, unflurried, easy courtesy prevails. We are a little off the beaten track: 'Do you often have foreign visitors'? 'Oh yes, last year there were some Koreans.'

The spokesman, with a little notebook, gives us the main figures—area, numbers, income per capita, yields per mou (they are strong on averages); then the horses, carts and pigs; the main investment schemes; the number of electrified pumps, grinders and chaff-cutters that have been installed. Questions are frankly answered (including a little tease about 'the spontaneous development of capitalism'). There is no dodging for cover behind phrases (as sometimes happens in the city) about the leadership of the Party and the Three Red Banners. Figures do not mean much unless one knows exactly how they are calculated, but the variations in the pattern of organization and in the achievements claimed is very instructive.

After the introductory session we step out to see the dam, the pumps, the tool shop, the noodle makers; and visit some houses, where grandma is usually at home with the babies, and hurries to pour us more cups of hot water. Some families sleep four or five on one kang. Some enjoy a room each. The mud floor is perfectly clean. The high rafters keep us cooler than in the hotel rooms we have come from. The walls are pasted over with colour prints of scenes from operas or patriotic posters. There is the store of grain, and there is the bicycle.

After a few visits, the brigade leader takes us to his own house, where tables and stools are set out under the vine that shades his courtyard, ready for a delicious meal of noodles, vegetables and eggs. A little rest after lunch is the custom. At two we sally out again to see a school, the hospital, the orchards; then reassemble for the questions we forgot in the morning, and so goodbye.

VI

Taking the second example described above as the representative case, we can trace the flows of transactions involved in it.

The main income accrues to the team in the form of its

crops. Of cash crops, such as cotton, practically the whole is handed over to the government buying station. The amount of grain to be sold is settled in the annual plan. Sales above the agreed quota are welcomed. A short-fall, in the ordinary way, will not occur, as the quota is calculated after allowing for costs (seed, fodder, etc.), and an adequate allowance for feeding the member families. The brunt of a deficiency falls on home consumption. But in case of a short-fall due to natural disasters, the quota is reduced or waived, without any obligation being carried forward. Vegetables and other subsidiary products are sold under contract between the team and the government purchasing agency or city co-operatives.

Thus the team has a certain annual gross income, the crops retained for home consumption being put into the account at the government purchase price. From this there are four deductions.

First, the agricultural tax. It is assessed on a notional normal output of each parcel of land. The tax, at 11–13 per cent of notional output, is sometimes as low as 4 per cent of actual output, where productivity has been rising. Slack production is penalized correspondingly by a higher tax ratio. An actual rate of tax as high as 14 per cent is said to be very rare. In case of natural disasters the tax is remitted.

The second deduction is for costs—seed, fertilizers, insecticides and so forth. Presumably repair of machinery comes under this head, as well as payments to a neighbouring state farm or tractor station for contract ploughing; notions of depreciation are somewhat vague, but in any case the distinction between depreciation and accumulation is not important so long as net accumulation is going on.

The third deduction is for accumulation. The accumulation fund belongs to the team, but its use for any large scheme has to be sanctioned by the Commune.

The fourth deduction is 1 or 2 per cent for the welfare fund, which is used to help out families without adequate earning power, provide for old people with no relatives, etc., and to contribute to the cost of schools and clinics.

These deductions normally amount to something like 40 per cent of gross income; 60 per cent remains to be distributed.

The famous scheme for 'free food,' which caused so much stir when the first reports of the communes came out, was as follows: a ration of grain was calculated for a worker, a child, etc., and the quantity required to provide rations for all the families was deducted from the distributable income. Each individual drew his appropriate daily ration, to cook at home or eat in the communal dining room. The remainder of the distributable income was then allocated according to work performed.

This system was dropped in 1960. Now the whole distributable income is shared out at so much per labour day. The job-evaluation for various tasks is agreed by the team as a whole. Family earnings depend on work performed, with the exception of the hard cases looked after by the welfare fund. The communal dining rooms have gone out of fashion and are now used only for convenience in the rush seasons. Advances of estimated earnings are paid out over the first three-quarters of the year, with a grand annual settlement after the harvest.

The staff of a brigade—the director, the deputy director, the accountant, the Party secretary and so forth—are team members elevated to these posts by election. They earn labour days like any one else, time spent in meetings and so forth being evaluated like any other job. The Brigade employs whole-time wage workers, for instance in a brick kiln, and sells the products to teams or families. It may amass an accumulation fund from the proceeds, or in some cases, it may make a levy on the accumulation fund of teams.

Three, sometimes more, of the commune staff are paid by the county, in respect of their local-government functions. The rest earn labour days with allowances (which must not exceed 2 per cent of a team's labour time) for their administrative work. The enterprises run by the commune are profitable, and the commune may also take a levy from the teams. The levies of brigade and commune together must not exceed 20 per cent of the teams' accumulation funds.

Adding transactions between the Supply and Marketing Co-operative and household, team, brigade and commune; transactions with the county authorities; and the minuscule trade of the families, there is a highly intricate network of payments and receipts. The commune is a microcosmic economy, comprising a major socialist and a minor private sector, with its budget, its balance of payments, and its planned allocation of resources between consumption, investment and liquid reserves. The price level in money terms is governed by the fixed purchase prices in its external trade. These determine the money value of labour time, and so all internal costs. The profit margins in commune enterprises are limited by the state selling prices for comparable goods and services.

The team is small enough to bring individualistic economic incentives into play. The commune is large enough to exhibit the visible benefits of collective organization. Economic incentives are not everything; the authorities are much concerned to keep morale high, but they are careful not to put any more weight on it than it can bear. For instance, during the bad years, in a district that had not suffered and was enjoying relative plenty, sales of grain above quota were encouraged, but the quota itself was not raised.

VII

Of the physical, visible effects of collective work, the greatest is saving and creating land. In the crumbling loess zone for instance, along whole valleys the soil has been tethered to the hill-sides in neat 'fish-scale' terraces, with properly placed water-vents, besides pine groves and orchards (the oldest now beginning to bear) and drainage in the wet bottoms. This work is carried out, with the advice of experts from the local Agricultural College or Technique Popularization Station, by mutual help between brigades, each keeping the cultivable land created in its own territory as a permanent addition to its 'four fixed.' To the peasants, this is something for nothing; the idea is free and the labour time would only have leaked away in vacancy during the slack of the agricultural year.

In a way, perhaps, an even more striking tribute to the collective aspect of the micro-economy is the fact that the lanes in the villages are perfectly clean.

Under the individualistic aspect, the greatest benefit, of course, outweighing all else, is two good meals a day, with the comfortable feeling of stocks to fall back on as well. Besides this, every family has some kind of roof over its head (which very many poor peasants somehow lived without). There has been a lot of building, with local materials in traditional style. This is something for not very much more than nothing. Consumer durables are gradually trickling in. The brigade leader recounts with touching pride: Everyone now has thermos flasks and rubber boots; there is a bicycle in half the households; so and so many radio sets; so many sewing machines. His pride gathers up personal possessions into collective achievement, and makes them not purely individualistic after all.

VIII

The Chinese symbolism of Yin and Yang has absorbed the dialectical concept of the interpenetration of opposites. In the communes government interpenetrates the co-operatives; authority, democracy; planning, initiative.

'Under the leadership of Chairman Mao and the Communist Party' is not a mere slogan. Policy is formed at the centre and transmitted to the nerve-endings through the communes. But policy is not arbitrary, it is distilled from experience.

During 1959 the authorities woke up to the fact that the limit upon the development of industry is set by the marketed surplus from agriculture. It needed a strong intellectual effort to throw off the dogma, learned from the Russians, that the first law of socialist development is the permanent priority of heavy industry. After scrambling through the bad years, the new policy was formulated in 1962: Agriculture the foundation; industry the leading factor.

The proportion of state investment allotted to agriculture was stepped up; industrial investment was deflected towards the needs of agriculture—tractors, farm machinery, fertilizers; for scarce consumer goods the country is given an advantage over the town. In 1963, as things grow a little easier, the Party watchword is: It is not yet time to relax. The policy is to increase output and to draw off the surplus smoothly without having to turn the screw on the peasants.

From one side, the communes are the means of imposing government policy. From the other side, they are highly democratic.

Formal democracy, within the micro-economy, is represented by the election of the director of the commune, the brigade and team leaders and accountants. The representative council of the commune meets once a quarter and of the brigades once a month. The team calls a full meeting of all members when required by current problems. Women have an organization to deal with family affairs, apart from participating as workers in team, brigade and Party.

Formal democracy, however, is interpenetrated at each level by the Party organization, which owes its loyalty outside. What gives reality to democracy is the economic situation. The peasant commands his own food supply; daily wants can be met by traditional crafts; the radio and the bicycle could very well be postponed. The town needs the peasant far more than the peasant needs the town. The leading characters in every district are old guerrillas, and the young people are learning rifle-shooting in the militia. If the peasants once turned sulky, the commune leaders would be helpless. It is this, with the Russian example before the eyes, that 'Chairman Mao and the Communist Party' must at all costs avoid. Direction from the top is controlled by good-will from below.

IX

What of the prospects? There is a complete statistical blackout in China at present, connected with the quarrel with the Soviets. One can only guess, from the behaviour of rations and prices, and from the impressionistic evidence of talks in communes, that the grain output is now well above the level of 1957 (the exaggerations of 1958 are tacitly passed over on both sides), that current consumption is adequate, but that stocks have to be built up.

There seems to be good ground to hope for a continuing rise in output over the current five-year plan (which has not yet been formulated) for a simple reason—hitherto, the use of artificial fertilizers has been at a low level. Now, with the extension of irrigation and of the education of the peasants, the country is ready to absorb artificials to the Japanese standard. Production has been held up because a vital component in the equipment is on the embargo list for the capitalist countries and has been withheld by the socialist countries. Chinese engineers have now mastered the technology and a number of large-scale plants are being set up. This, with other improvements such as better seed, means that there is a great potential rise in yields waiting to be realized. As yields on wet land rise, the poorest and most awkward dry land can be released from cultivation and put to forest. Thus output per man can be raised along with output per acre. At the same time empty lands in the North and West are being peopled. Once the agricultural surplus is secure, the rhythm of development in industry will pick up again.

But there is a heavy drag on progress—growing population. The statistical blackout covers demography, but we are allowed to know that overall numbers have not yet touched 700 million but soon will. Later marriages and birth control are being plugged. The situation seems to be about at the stage of England fifty years ago. Sophisticated people have two children, and the rest what God sends. A safe, foolproof and inoffensive contraceptive would make a big difference. But even if the rate of increase were checked tomorrow, a formidable problem would remain.

The restoration of law and order, and an upward bound in hygiene, following long years of chaos and misery, brought a huge bulge in the population after 1949. In the next fifteen years there will be a formidable increase in the numbers requiring adult rations and needing to be supplied with means of production. Certainly it is not yet time to relax.

It is rare for a westerner to have any first-hand experience with life in China today. For visitors, no matter how extensive their tour, there is only a fleeting glance. The Chinese, on the other hand, though cordial to westerners are self-absorbed. For this reason alone the book, The First Years of Yangyi Commune, written by Isabel and David Crook is an invaluable contribution to the westerner's understanding of events in China.

David Crook, born in London, was educated in Britain and the United States and has spent a good part of his life working and studying in China. His wife was born in China and except for a stint in London during the Second World War has spent most of her life there. The authors lived in Yangyi Commune for a year after an earlier sojourn in one of the villages incorporated into the commune. On the basis of this they have described the origins of this particular commune in 1958, and how it developed during the natural disasters of 1959–1961, drawing on case histories to illustrate both problems and the devices used to solve them. The following selection from their account highlights the attitudes, resources and difficulties of the individual participants of a commune thereby adding a personal dimension to the previous discussions of the commune which presented a birdseye perspective.

An on-the-Spot Investigation of a People's Commune*

ISABEL AND DAVID CROOK

MIXED FEELINGS

THE SHAPING of its administrative set-up and working systems, as well as major large-scale efforts in irrigation, changes in farming technique (which had previously altered little in the course of centuries) all took place in the first year or so of the commune's existence.

These social and technical changes touched almost every aspect of life. Many had proved successful, a few had been failures, some were still debatable. Reactions to the changes were varied. Many commune members tended to judge the developments of the year according to certain limited, specific features

* From THE FIRST YEARS OF YANGYI COMMUNE by Isabel and David Crook, Routledge and Kegan Paul, Ltd., 1966. New York: Humanities Press, Inc., 1966. Reprinted by permission.

with which they came into closest contact and which affected them most personally.

The young people who had 'tempered themselves as they tempered the steel' felt that with the commune behind them and the Party to lead them there was nothing they could not do. It was the same with the youth 'shock teams' who had made bold and successful experiments in carrying out the Eight Point Charter. They were breaking with the traditional hankering of young people to leave the countryside for the cities the moment they became literate. Exciting prospects opened up by the commune stretched before them in the countryside. Inspired by the whitewashed slogan on their own mudbrick walls: 'Three years of bitter struggle! Ten thousand years of joy!' they were prepared to work night and day to bring Communism nearer.

This was true not only of the youth. One 75-year-old man said: 'I'd rather lose a pound of my flesh than a pound in the yield of grain.' And he worked with youthful zest.

But others struck a different note. 'All this leaping forward takes it out of you,' one man complained.

Still others stood between these two extremes. They supported the commune on the whole but were critical of some aspect or other of its growth.

Most people, for instance, were proud of the results of the steel campaign. Yet some felt it had its flaws. Almost all the most energetic young people had been drawn into it, they pointed out. As a result, the harvesting had been rather slapdash. With a shortage of field hands at the crucial moment, some fields had been reaped too fast, others too late. So some grain was lost. To those who had suffered from famine in the past, wasting grain was a crime.

The bumper crops of 1958 and the records set on experimental plots had inspired exuberant murals on the village walls, showing sky high piles of golden grain. Now some said: 'We grow more grain all right. But where does it go? The more we grow, the more they take.' This referred to the government's regulation for the planned purchase and supply of grain, aimed at guaranteeing food for the cities, building up reserves and preventing speculation.

As to the community dining-rooms, while one woman exclaimed that it was 'like heaven' to be freed from cooking, some people complained that the canteen food was 'always the same old stuff' and that you could not 'eat what you like and when you like, the way you could at home.' Others worried about waste or extravagance in the running of the canteens.

Many were convinced that the commune would carry them rapidly to industrialization and the material and cultural advantages that went with it. In fact, among the painters of village murals and the composers of the poems on village walls, the favourite symbol for the commune was a railway engine racing across the countryside. Yet at the same time there were people who found the speed unsettling, who would have preferred the spartan 'prosperity' already achieved, to constantly striving for something better. Let well enough alone, they urged. Others, alarmed by the period when the 'winds of communism blew too hard,' also favoured putting on the brakes.

The Commune Council and the brigade cadres found that the larger scale and scope of the commune placed heavy responsibilities on them. 'It's harder to lead a brigade than it was to lead a high-level co-op, even though both may have been formed out of the same village,' said one of the commune leaders. 'Cadres who did quite a good job leading a socialist co-op soon find out that it's not enough to rely on their old experience. Something more is called for when you not only go in for farming, but run industry, trade and education and organize defence and social services too.' Some cadres found it hard to measure up to all these tasks and so fell short of the demands of their brigade and work team members.

Mixed feelings about the events of the first year of the commune were not confined to the rank-and-file. Some cadres, carried away by what they saw ahead, made light of problems and difficulties. Their reports to the higher levels stressed successes. Problems and difficulties were hardly mentioned.

In the eyes of other cadres, problems and difficulties loomed large. Mass movements, for instance, had characterized the main events of the year, including the setting up of the commune. But when the winds of communism blew too hard these cadres began to question mass movements in general. Once you launch a mass movement, they reasoned, things get out of hand and mistakes are made. Their conclusion was: the locomotive of socialism should go ahead slowly but surely, with experienced cadres at the controls. Leaving too much to the rank-and-file could cause accidents or even create chaos.

These varied views arose from the changes brought about by the General Line for socialist construction, the Great Leap in steel and farm production and above all by the shaping of the commune itself.

This was how things stood in Yangyi Commune in August 1959, when the Central Committee of the Chinese Communist Party held its Eighth Plenary Session. . . .

'RECTIFICATION' (WINTER, 1959–60)

When the autumn harvest had been brought in and the ploughing and sowing of the winter crops was done, there was time to tackle the tasks set by the Central Committee of: 'correcting shortcomings in work, overcoming Right opportunist sentiments among unstable elements, striking telling blows against the disruptive activities of anti-socialist elements.' And in mid-October 1959, a 'Rectification and Socialist Education Campaign' was launched in Yangyi. . . .

RECTIFICATION AND UPGRADING OF PARTY
MEMBERS AND CADRES

The movement combined the study of Marxist theory and current policies with a down-to-earth examination of the leadership each Party Branch had given, of the activities and attitudes of all Party members and cadres. How had they analysed the situation in the commune and the brigade? How had they assessed results? . . .

The main targets of criticism were 'bureaucracy, sectarianism and subjectivism.'

These high-sounding terms referred to very ordinary, everyday shortcomings. Bureaucracy, which at different times and places has different forms and roots, here was mainly of the type known as 'having-a-hard-time-of-it' bureaucracy. The 'bureaucrats' were as a rule well-intentioned, hard-working, plain-living, self-sacrificing men or women, but they were shouldering jobs they had never done before and for which they had little or no training or experience. Not always knowing how to single out the key problems from among the complex new tasks facing them, they tended to be run off their feet trying to keep up with developments. As a result they found no time to investigate matters carefully enough to make considered judgements. They grappled with many problems but solved few. And some, when distraught, became short-tempered. Thus friction and even antagonism appeared and began to drive a wedge between such cadres and the people.

There was also a second type of bureaucracy to be found, which did not simply reflect a cadre's failure to master his job. It reflected rather the old attitude that those in positions of leadership were above manual work and those who did it. The farmers spoke of such bureaucrats as 'four-armed' cadres —for they went to the fields to give directions, their jackets slung over their shoulders like capes. The limply dangling empty jacket sleeves—the extra arms—were a symbol of their

not the only case of this sort. Until staple food
ant nearly every housewife needed to plan consump-
last grain. Quite a number lacked this ability.
xamining the situation in different households the
ched the conclusion that it had not looked at things
ss standpoint. The canteens, they decided, had had
ts, due to the inexperience of the managers and the
ides, people could not get used to them immediately.
ormer poor and middle peasants who formed the
ad not wanted the canteens closed down, but im-
he well-to-do middle farmers did eat better at home
improved management and cooking the canteens
able to offer better food than the vast majority coul
home.
up and consolidating canteens, the branch affirmed
s stage part of the battle for higher production an
ng. With shortage of labour preventing bigger a
production, canteens could play a key role, both
women for farm work and by helping everyo
rk on time.
ight of this conclusion the Party and also the You
embers decided to examine their own attitudes
ing in community dining-rooms.
the canteens were set up, according to custom, peo
their bowls of cereal, frugally trimmed with ve
to their front doorstep and had stood or squat
d chatting with their neighbours. Meals were a fi
affair (except for the housewife) with no fixed ti
ompany. The community dining-rooms were differ
a few of the Communist Youth League meml
hard to get used to them.
uth League Branch Committee, therefore, posed
'How should a League member look at the din
he conclusion reached was: In the long run the
way of life is not dependable. It offers no securit
le prospect. Only the collective can bring the pe
and well-being and accord with the League's ai
or communism. So the old way of eating belon

hat the Party and Youth League members were
at running canteens was part of 'the struggle bet
roads,' they decided to launch a broad publi
s a form of socialist education. The questions the
re canteens a good thing? Shall we have some i

non-participation in field work. A few cadres did not even get as far as the fields. These were described as 'talking a lot but never going to the masses to help them solve their problems.'

Sectarianism, too, has various forms. Here it generally took the form of 'localism'—of being narrowly absorbed in the interests of one's own brigade or work team and determined to make it succeed regardless of how others fared. This might be practised by cadres or rank-and-filers who disregarded their personal interests or ambitions, but when it came to any project involving their brigade or team were calculating in the extreme, working out the balance sheet again and again to make sure that their own group came out best. This was an old problem which in the co-operative period had taken the form of the pulling up a neighbour's sorghum stalks when they threatened the peanuts of one's own co-operative; or in surreptitiously moving a boundary stone to straighten out a furrow.

Subjectivism was mainly a matter of jumping to conclusions, of seeing only what fitted one's preconceived ideas, instead of investigating, weighing all the factors or hearing all sides of a case. And with the commune—a more complex social unit than had existed in the countryside before—there were more factors to weigh and more sides to hear than ever.

The Party Secretary of the Shidong District, to which Ten Mile Inn belonged, for instance, was criticized for the way in which time limits were set for the sowing of winter wheat. One brigade had been given seven days. But at the end of that time it had only half finished the job; so its cadres and members were publicly criticized. When the commune leadership looked into the matter, however, it found that the brigade had worked very hard. But they had not enough draught animals and it was unrealistic to expect them to finish in a week without providing any. Once arrangements were made for them to borrow animals from other brigades they soon finished the sowing. The District cadre had not taken the trouble to investigate carefully and weigh things up before setting the targets and meting out criticism. He had been subjective.

Through the thrashing out of such problems and the examination of individual actions it was possible for the Party members and cadres throughout the commune to improve their leadership. Commune leadership was a complex task. It involved keeping close to reality, knowing an immense number of facts and at the same time being able to sort out the major points from the minor ones. It demanded the ability to analyse matters from a class standpoint, instead of being influenced or befuddled by personal relations, the overcoming of any tendency to magnify problems or to under-estimate them.

Any of these defects would lead to decisions adversely affecting the lives of the commune members and thereby setting up a barrier between cadres and rank-and-file. Each mistake examined, each weakness overcome removed a barrier and strengthened unity.

This was one of the purposes of the rectification campaign. But in the course of it, in some villages, problems of a deeper nature were brought to light. . . .

RECTIFICATION AND CANTEENS IN TEN MILE INN

In Ten Mile Inn the Party branch made a searching examination of production. Had it gone up as much and as fast as it could? It had certainly gone up, but not as fast as in Little Yetao, for instance. Why not? The branch members went over in detail the records of the various crops and even of the different fields. In certain fields the crops had not been put in early enough to achieve the best results. In others, through late hoeing, not enough rain had been absorbed. With spring and autumn rain so precious, why was it wasted? The answer was: shortage of labour.

Work team records revealed that although there were 480 able-bodied men and women in the village, the average daily working-force had been only 290. A number, of course, had been off on such jobs as railway building; and others were engaged in commune industry or construction. These undertakings were necessary and in the long run would benefit the brigade.

But there were two ways in which much time and labour was being wasted.

Each day some families had already finished their breakfast when others were just starting it. It was the same with the midday meal. By the time all the members of a team had assembled and work had been allocated, valuable time had been lost.

This state of affairs was hardly surprising. Living as they did in a society still in the early stages of industrialization clocks and watches played little part in their daily life. So long as the household was the unit of production such lack of precision and punctuality had presented no great problem. But with a larger organization, such as the work team, involving the co-ordinated efforts of dozens of people, losses of

time were multiplied. Minutes grew of work time frittered away.

Housework, too, in such a society onerous. Water had to be fetched a outskirts of the village; grain had to turned by a donkey or by the hou be gathered from the hills; clothes hand; vegetables pickled, or slice winter months. What with all this o washing, few women could be count for work in the fields. Most of thos late and left early, putting in only a

The solution to this problem, p setting up of the commune, had be cooking made it possible to save m before the introduction of running w electric stoves; at the same time it improvements. Now, one of the fir Ten Mile Inn Party branch during t did we close the canteens?'

In 1959, soon after the April ch been set up. This was during the su per cent of the brigade's families h community dining-rooms. In the au branch and village cadres knew th such as: 'The food's no good,' 'Al and 'You can't eat what you want on knew, too, that in some other villag teens had already been closed. So the conclusion that the people of Ten M for this step towards collective livin closed (though grain was still issue

Now the branch considered wheth correct. Just how widespread was th no good' and that it was 'always th vestigation was made. It showed that and most of the ex-middle peasants majority of the diners, found the f than they had at home. One man, c he food satisfactory but found pea In the canteen, for his wife was a p uch generous meals at the beginnin had to borrow grain at the end of hifted to the shoulders of the dining rom this worry. When the cantee

Fu's was was abund tion to th

After e branch rea from a cla their defe cooks; bes But the f majority proved. T but with would be provide a

Setting was at thi better livi vances in releasing get to wo

In the League n wards ea

Before had taken table, ou eating an and-easy place or and even found it

The Y question : rooms?' dividual worthwh happiness fighting f the past.

Now t vinced th the two cussion a were: 'A brigade?'

These questions were discussed throughout the village and the advantages and shortcomings of the defunct canteens were weighed up.

Criticisms fell into two different categories. A large number were the complaints of people unaccustomed to eating in any sort of canteen or at any fixed time and place. They were bound to arise, unless each individual weighed up the disruption of his old habits against the advantages he gained from speeding the advance in general prosperity; in other words against his rising income in terms of food, clothing, thermos flasks, torches, bicycles and so on. As a result of the discussion most people came to the conclusion that the advantages of the canteens might well outweigh their inconveniences. And they voted to give them another try.

The second main category of criticism concerned defects in management and in cooking. As to cooking, there were complaints of grit in the grain, of flavourless food, of buns not cooked through, of unvarying menus. Defects in management included not keeping the accounts clear, up-to-date and regularly posted where everyone could see them. There were also complaints of some waste and extravagance.

Such criticisms were generally felt to be well founded. The solution proposed was to elect the best possible team of cooks and managers for the canteens, instead of just picking those who could best be spared from field work, as had tended to be the case in the past.

There was, however, a third category of criticism.

In the course of the discussion and the sorting out of the problems, some of the villagers became increasingly indignant with two men who, they suspected, had been consciously undermining the canteens by exaggerating defects that did exist and inventing others that did not. These two men were both former Kuomintang officials who had been 'struggled against' during the land reform, but who later had been admitted on sufferance first into the socialist co-operatives and then into the commune.

One of these was Wang Dian-yuan, son of Ten Mile Inn's once most feared and hated landlord, Wang Ban-yen. The latter had been a Kuomintang official, and a local tyrant guilty of more than one capital crime. He was put to death by peasants during the land reform. Wang Dian-yuan himself, who had also been a Kuomintang official, had been fined for tax evasion during the land reform and had not qualified for membership in the semi-socialist co-operative.

Of the same type was the former rich peasant Wang Jia-wen.

He too had served the Kuomintang and later been penalized for opposing the land reform. He had then left home, returning only in 1949 when he felt things had quietened down.

When the discussion on canteens was being wound up, these two men, in line with the policy of 'striking blows against the disruptive activities of anti-socialist elements,' were singled out for public reprimand.

Meanwhile, when everyone had had ample chance to air their views, a summary was made. The consensus was that the canteens had six important advantages—and that they should be given another try. The six advantages of the canteens were:

1. They enable us all to go to the fields and come back from them at the same time; to have unified, collective action. Without them it's come and go as you please.
2. They take a great load off the minds of those people who don't know how to plan and budget properly and so are always finding themselves in a fix.
3. They free women from household chores and so bring a big increase to the working force in the fields.
4. They free people living on their own from having to start carrying water, lighting fires and cooking at the end of a hard day's work.
5. They permit a great saving in overhead expenses on fuel, oil, seasoning and so on.
6. They strengthen the spirit of collectivism.

Following this summing-up the Party and Youth League members called on all the teams to set up their own canteens. Eighteen of them were soon established and, though some people later dropped out, in the high tide of enthusiasm which followed this discussion, everyone in Ten Mile Inn applied to join, including the two former Kuomintang officials.

Wang Dian-yuan, in fact, had little choice, since his wife and daughter-in-law both applied and it was they who had always done the cooking at Wang's home. When it came to a choice between cooking for himself and eating in a community dining-room, even he saw the advantages of collectivism. Wang Jia-wen was less fortunate. The members of his work team, angered at what they considered his undermining of the canteen in its early days, refused to accept him. But they did accept the nephew and niece with whom he lived. So Wang Jia-wen had to do his own cooking, day in and day out, after working in the fields. Again and again he went to the brigade office and pleaded with the Party Secretary to intercede for him. But it was a good two months before his team-mates grudgingly permitted him to eat in their new canteen.

The analysing of the canteen problem—first inside the Party, then in broad, public discussion—was only one of the matters dealt with during the campaign for 'rectification and socialist education.' The chief lessons which the Ten Mile Inn Party branch members felt they learnt from it were: the need for finding out all the main facts instead of jumping to conclusions on the basis of a few complaints; and the need to 'subject the facts to a class analysis, not to give equal weight to all views regardless of their origin.' In this case a class analysis meant looking at the canteens with the eyes of the majority—that is, of the poor peasants and most of the former middle peasants—not with the eyes of a handful of well-to-do farmers; still less with those of ex-landlord and rich peasant Kuomintang officials such as Wang Dian-yuan and Wang Jia-wen.

> While China's last dynasty was crumbling under western impact, Japan was rapidly absorbing western knowledge in order to industrialize on her own. By the end of the First World War, she had joined the imperialist powers in their plunder of China only to out-distance them prior to the Second World War. Today, after her defeat in the Second World War, Japan has resumed her traditional interests in China despite United States disapproval. In light of Japan's proximity to China, and her parallel if more "successful" experiences with industrialization and westernization, it is extraordinarily instructive to observe China's current technological programs through the eyes of a Japanese familiar with the problems involved. The following article is written by Genko Uchida who is international economic secretary in the Ministry of International Trade and Industry of Japan. A number of years ago he initiated a study of science and technology in China as part of the Ministry's China Study Group. Uchida has engaged in studies both in London and the United States, visiting the latter country in 1958 with a Japanese group studying automation.

Technology in China*

GENKO UCHIDA

WHAT PROGRESS are the Chinese making in technology and industrialization? The fact that mainland China accounts for

* Genko Uchida, "Technology in China," *Scientific American*, CCXV, 5 (Nov. 1966), pp. 37–45. Copyright © 1966 by Scientific American, Inc. All rights reserved. Reprinted with permission.

a fifth of the world's population is sufficient reason for world-wide interest in this question. As next-door neighbors of China we in Japan of course are more interested than most people. Three years ago I began a systematic study with the object of obtaining a detailed estimate of China's technical development. Measuring a nation's technical progress is at best a difficult problem. In China's case the immensity of the country and the secretiveness of her government magnify the difficulty; the task seems comparable to trying to guess the number of beans in an opaque bottle. The problem is not, however, completely unsolvable. China's own statements and her intercourse with the industrial world outside provide enough clues to allow a well-based appraisal of the state of her technology.

We Japanese are in a particularly good position to measure China's progress because in the past 20 years we traveled the road over which China is now laboring. Twenty years ago Japan was a backward country with a per capita income of less than $100; today our per capita income is well over $500 —the milestone that divides the advanced countries from the backward—and Japan is recognized as one of the world's most modern industrialized nations. By comparing China's present development in various sectors with the stages in our own history we can estimate how far China has come along the road.

I shall present here a brief review of China's stated technical goals and policies, her problems and the extent of her advancement in key industries. I must emphasize that my conclusions are only estimates derived from fragmentary information, not the kind of precise evaluation that is possible in countries where the essential technological and economic facts are fully known.

One should understand at the outset that, although the most conspicuous aspect of modern China is her system of communistic control, in a fundamental sense she is more a "developing" country than a communistic one. That is to say, her economic policies are rooted primarily in her needs as a still poor, backward nation. This may help to explain why her views on Marxism and communism differ in some respects from those of the more advanced U.S.S.R. It also accounts for the extremely aggressive, evangelistic role adopted by the Chinese central government in directing the development of the national economy. In a country seeking to transform itself rapidly from the primitive, impoverished state to a modern industrial power, patriotic zeal and strong central control over the economy are indispensable.

Naturally zeal has tended to run far ahead of capability. Under the lash of experience the overall approach of China's leaders toward industrialization has undergone an evolution that is subtly reflected in the changing slogans they have used to exhort the people. They began with a simple appeal: "Catch up and overtake." They believed that by heroic efforts their immense, determined country could soon establish a modern industrial economy and outdo the advanced nations of the West. To that end they threw all the capital and labor they could command into the industrialization sector. They soon learned that this was a self-defeating policy. It took too much labor and capital from the agricultural sector and thus left the population intolerably short of food. Furthermore, the Chinese leaders (like the politically oriented leaders in most developing countries) had underestimated the importance of technical know-how. They had failed to realize that industrialization requires not only capital and a work force but also an adequate staff of technically trained personnel who understand the machines. Without this third essential element much of the capital and labor was wasted.

The agricultural problem was compounded by three years of bad weather (between 1959 and 1962) that ruined crops. The Chinese government shifted to greater emphasis on the agricultural sector and introduced a new slogan: "Stable production and more crops." Meanwhile China had been hit by another unexpected setback. As a result of the Chinese criticisms of Russian leadership, the U.S.S.R. suddenly withdrew its technical advisers and workers from China in August, 1960. The factories under construction and those already in operation were left without skilled personnel. Faced with the necessity of training her own people to complete the construction projects and run the factories, the Chinese government issued a new slogan: "Self-development." From 1960 on China depended largely on her own resources for training engineers, technicians and researchers.

She became timid and notably suspicious in her dealings with other countries, Communist or non-Communist, friendly or unfriendly. Her feeling was that those with whom she could trade were out to "pick her clean." For this feeling there was some justification, as some of the equipment China had bought from Communist countries turned out to be obsolescent. The Chinese government in recent years has insisted on buying only the latest models of equipment, often overlooking the fact that the newest models are not necessarily the best for China's own needs. The Chinese also ask for a two-year or three-year supply of spare parts for the equipment, fearing that in the event of an increase in international tension the suppliers might refuse to deliver parts. All in all, the Chinese suspicion of foreigners is so strong and the drive for self-reliance so determined that there is a general reluctance to use foreign machinery at all.

China today has a well-organized establishment for the direction of science and technology. At the policy level it is headed by a Science and Technology Commission in the Chinese Department of State. Under this commission are many bureaus, bearing names such as the General Agency, the International Cooperation Bureau, the Standards Bureau and the Fourth Bureau, whose responsibility is the needs of the manufacturing industries. The control of research work itself is centered in the National Science Department, the Chinese version of the U.S.S.R.'s Academy of Sciences. This department maintains about 100 research institutes, employing a total of about 7,000 investigators who work on research projects assigned by the government. The department's head is Kou Mo-jo; he is also president of the National Institute of Science and Technology, which was established for the education of engineers, particularly in the fields of atomic research and electronics.

The new generation of engineers that China is producing is an impressive national asset. The profession is not limited to men; it is attracting increasing numbers of women. China's young engineers are confident, ambitious, eager to learn. They are acquiring, mainly from foreign publications, a detailed theoretical knowledge of the latest advances in technology. The Chinese engineering establishment is still weak, however, in two crucial requirements: seasoned leadership and the resourcefulness that can come only from practical experience. In an industrialized country the engineers are imbued by education and job experience with a generalized expertise that enables them to cope with a wide range of tasks and with new problems as they arise. In addition to their specific training they have automatically absorbed a fund of basic knowledge and skills—one may call it a common sense—that is the heritage of the nation's industrial traditions. China of course lacks such traditions or such a "common sense." Her engineers' knowledge is largely theoretical; the questions they ask of foreign engineers often betray a naïveté that shows lack of experience in applying the theories. The lack of practical experience has led China's leaders into some serious errors in industrial policy.

Let me cite a few errors that we Japanese can appreciate because they repeat lessons we learned ourselves on the road to industrialization. One lesson has to do with imitation. It is natural, and indeed inevitable, for a developing country to begin by copying the products of advanced industrial countries. Unfortunately there are grave pitfalls in such a policy. First of all, one had better be careful about what one selects for copying. A case in point is an agricultural machine China began to produce a few years ago. It was copied from a machine that had been designed and produced by a small manufacturer in Japan. After a year or so the Chinese found that the machine was poorly designed—and that the Japanese manufacturer who had produced it had gone into bankruptcy. China lacked this automatic corrective; once the model was put on the production line, politics and bureaucracy made it very difficult to stop. Other instances of unwise imitation can be cited. A Chinese instrument-producing plant lavished great care on the production of a laboratory oscillograph it had copied from a foreign make, but all efforts to get the instrument to work well failed because it was badly designed. At a trade show in Tokyo the Chinese displayed an automobile they had copied from a 20-year-old model of a Western car; by loading it with air conditioning and other new equipment, they had made the sedan as heavy as a small dump truck!

Another pitfall inherent in imitation is that it retards the development of a capability for design. China requires detailed designs to accompany all the equipment she buys from foreign countries so that she can copy the equipment in her own factories. She has succeeded in copying many sophisticated machine tools of the U.S.S.R., Germany, the U.S., Switzerland and Japan. This itself is no small achievement. Yet although China has developed high skill in copying designs, she has not developed much ability to improve on them or to design new machinery of her own. Indeed, I have seen no evidence that any factory in China has a research and development division for the design of new products.

Japan herself went through a period of industrial copying that gave her the reputation of being an "imitator." She soon recognized, however, that the development of a technology of design was itself an essential step toward full industrialization, and she hastened this stage by purchasing expertise from abroad. China now seems to be coming to the same realization; she has begun to seek technical assistance and knowledge from non-Communist countries.

A second mistake in policy that has victimized China is the

"production first" slogan, or what is called in the U.S. the "crash program." This is the policy of putting all the available resources to work at any cost to turn out some article for which there is an urgent need. For example, the Chinese at one point found there was an acute shortage of steel angle irons for agricultural development, and all the steel factories were therefore ordered to make angle irons, whether or not they had efficient equipment for doing so. The result was a deluge of angle irons and a sharp reduction in the country's total industrial output. This lack of balance or planned programming has been characteristic of Chinese factories and of the overall economy. Japan learned the necessity of harmonizing production in the various sectors of the economy 20 years ago. It appears that the leaders of China have now learned the same lesson and are beginning to apply it.

Chinese technology shows many signs of severe imbalance. For example, the country is mass-producing agricultural machinery but has not yet persuaded the farmers to make full use of it. China is building many dams and hydroelectric plants; however, because she has not mastered the technology of control of river systems, there are often harmful repercussions upstream from the dams. China's factories are producing machine tools of excellent design but so poor in the quality of the materials that their reliability is far below standard.

The manufacturing industry as a whole is backward in the sense that it lacks the base of feeder industries for making parts and components. The plants producing final products (for instance the leading factory for building trucks) must make their own nuts and bolts. A factory that makes electrical measuring instruments assigns a considerable proportion of its 4,000 workers to turning out precision screws on bench lathes and to die-casting metal parts. A plant that produces testing machines must build its own oil pumps. In short, the unorganized structure of China's industry and technology is a severe obstacle to the development of high special skills and efficient production. Chinese industrial leaders are now taking steps toward establishment of a parts industry: they have built a pilot project in the Shenyang area of Manchuria around heavy-machinery and machine-tool factories. From Japan's experience it must be said that the full integration of satellite parts plants into the industrial system as a whole will take a long time.

To round off this discussion of general approach and policies, I shall merely mention one other simple but fundamental lesson that Japan learned some time ago and that China's leaders now begin to show signs of appreciating. A populous country is tempted to believe any project, however formidable, can be accomplished if one only puts enough people to work on it—the "human sea" idea. This method has been demonstrated as working wonders in circumstances such as the restoration of a bombed road in wartime with only human hands as tools, but it is certainly an unsound one for building an industrial system or a modern civilized society. Man is not an ant. China, with all her hundreds of millions of people, is now turning to emphasis on modern tools—mechanization and automation—for building her society.

For the specific measurement of China's technical progress so far, let us look at three basic industries: (1) iron and steel, (2) chemicals and (3) machinery, including consumer machines such as automobiles and electronic devices. I wish to remark here that in this evaluation we cannot take production figures alone as our guide. In China the rate of industrial production is heavily conditioned by the structure and quality of management and by the prevailing attitude toward productivity, which are still in a highly primitive stage. Each factory is more or less autonomous, and the plant is run by a quadrumvirate consisting of the manager, the chief engineer, the workers' labor union and a Communist party representative who is responsible for education of the workers. Thus the plant management is democratic but not particularly conducive to rapid decisions, flexibility in innovation or efficiency of operation. The manager usually has little training in the special techniques of management. Moreover, Chinese policies have given scant regard to production efficiency. The net result is that the productivity of labor in China's industries is very low. it averages only about a tenth to a fifth of the productivity of workers in Japan. Presumably the skill of management and production efficiency in China will grow as her industries advance in size and sophistication. In any case, what we are concerned with here is not the question of efficiency but the state of China's industrial techniques, or engineering, as the measure of her technological progress.

China's iron and steel industry is a mixture of large-scale and small-scale operations, of modern methods and primitive ones. In her hurry to industrialize, the new Chinese nation urged the farmers to turn to making iron and steel in their spare time. Some 400,000 small shops, hardly more than smelting sheds, sprouted all over the country. This effort proved to be so inefficient and so injurious to agriculture that only about 300 of the small mills are still operating. They supply, however, about a third of China's pig iron and steel, and they remain politically important because they enable farmers to contribute to the nation's industrialization.

Before World War II China had five large steel plants, located in Shanghai, Tientsin, Dairen and two other cities in Manchuria near Dairen. These five accounted for nearly 90 percent of the country's iron and steel production. Today there are 20 large iron and steel combines, or producing centers, distributed in central and southern China as well as in the northeast. Their blast furnaces for iron production are large, but they do not employ the high-pressure oxygen technique of the most modern furnaces. In the production of steel the Chinese mills are limited to the open-hearth-furnace technique without oxygen; they have not yet come to the liquid-oxygen converters or the large electric furnaces that are now being installed in advanced countries. China's rolling mills for processing steel are mostly imports from the U.S.S.R. and East Germany that are not up to date and are operated by control instruments that had to be improvised by Chinese engineers, since the Russian technicians left in the midst of the installation of the mill machinery. The Chinese plants have no strip-milling equipment. Nor are they yet able to produce or process high-grade special steels (such as stainless steel) in any substantial quantity.

On the whole I estimate that in steel technology China today is about 15 years behind Japan (which is the world's third-largest producer of iron and steel, behind the U.S. and the U.S.S.R.). It is quite possible that China, as a larger country, will achieve her goal of passing Japan and becoming third in total steel production by 1973, but that does not mean she will have caught up in technology. If she depends only on her own resources, it will take her considerably more than six years to develop her own strip mills and reach the present world standards in modernization of steelmaking. In this connection it should be remarked that China has recently signed a contract with several companies in West Germany to obtain a complete rolling mill for the production of thick steel plates.

In chemical technology also China is about 15 years behind. There too her development is repeating Japan's history. In a developing country the first chemical industries to receive attention are those required for the production of fertilizers, acids (principally sulfuric acid for fertilizers) and alkalis (comprising two main industries: soap and detergents and soda, which supplies raw materials for glass). China's fertilizer industry is already sizable: she produces some 7.5 million tons of chemical fertilizer a year. This is still far short of her needs, however. Although she adds to her own production by importing upward of four million tons a year (which makes her the world's largest importer of fertilizer), her total supply amounts to only 12 pounds per acre of cultivated land—about a tenth of the amount used per acre in Japan. Moreover, her production consists mostly of ammonium sulfate and includes only negligible amounts of urea and high-grade compound fertilizers that are now in common use in Western countries. It appears that unless China obtains substantial help from outside it will take at least five to 10 years to raise her agricultural productivity to a level at which it can provide her with sufficient capital for a major breakthrough in industrialization.

From Japan's experience it can be predicted that China's next stage in the development of chemical industries will be based principally on the extraction of products from coal tar. Like prewar Japan, China still depends on coal as her main fuel (although large oil fields are reported to have been discovered recently in Manchuria). From coal tar the principal products one can obtain are dyestuffs, drugs and gunpowder. There is evidence that China is already launched on the "tar age" in chemical production. She has begun to produce pesticides in substantial quantities for her agriculture, and we can reasonably guess, even without specific information, that she is not neglecting explosives production.

After the tar age comes the age of synthesis, meaning the production of new chemicals from basic raw materials. Japan entered this stage only 20 years ago, after World War II. China, although still in the early phases of the tar age, has made a beginning in the establishment of synthetics industries. She has been able to do this by importing complete plants from abroad. The Chinese chemical industry is now producing perhaps 60,000 to 70,000 tons of plastics a year, including some 25,000 tons of vinyl chloride and small amounts of synthetic fibers such as rayon and nylon. China does not have a synthetic rubber industry of any consequence, partly because she readily obtains natural rubber from Indonesia and Malaysia and partly because her total use of rubber (about 1.5 million tons a year) is still relatively small, only about half the amount used in Japan.

In oil refining and the production of petrochemicals China is held back, as are all but the most advanced countries, by the fact that modern, large-scale operation in this field depends entirely on automation. Like some other developing countries, however, China has recently made a beginning by entering into contracts to buy oil refining plants (from Italy, West Germany and France in her case).

China is making an effort to speed up development of a wide spectrum of chemical industries by buying plants of various types from Japan, Italy, the United Kingdom, France, the Netherlands and West Germany. Experience has shown, however, that a country cannot make great progress in industrialization until it has acquired the ability to build its own equipment. Japan reached that stage a decade ago and has since become the world's third-largest producer of synthetic fibers, oil refinery products and petrochemicals. China is now taking the first steps toward such self-reliance in chemical technology. For a vinyl chloride factory in Peking the Chinese constructed the carbide electric furnaces, electrolytic chlorine cells, equipment for the synthesis of chloric acid and equipment for the synthesis and refining of the monomers that are linked to make vinyl chloride. They had to import from West Germany, however, the polymerization equipment that joins the monomers into the final product. The polymerization division has 2,700 employees, which seems a very large number, but the management explains that most of them are trainees who will staff new plants to be built soon.

Obviously the clearest index to a nation's industrial development is the state of its machinery industry, because this must supply the tools for all other industries. In the production of machines China presents a mixed picture: she is well advanced in some fields, far behind in others.

As in the chemical industry, in launching a machinery industry a developing country's first concern must be the needs of agriculture. The Chinese have put great emphasis on the production of farm tractors. A single large factory in Loyang is turning out 300 to 400 45-horsepower tractors a month, plus some power shovels and graders. The production cost of the tractors is reported to be about $10,000 apiece—30 to 40 percent higher than the standard in industrialized countries. To Japan, which produces tractors mainly for construction jobs rather than for agriculture, China's investment in tractor production seems disproportionately large, since labor-saving in farming is less urgent than increasing the productivity of the soil.

In addition to her tractor factories China has a great number of small factories throughout the country producing other agricultural machines and implements. She has also developed a substantial industry in the manufacture of pumps, which are used to a large extent for agriculture. A pump factory in Shanghai is mass-producing about 2,000 rotary pumps a month. In size (up to 1,600 millimeters in diameter) and design (applying the latest hydrodynamic theories) the pumps are quite modern, and so is the equipment employed in producing them, except for the final testing instruments.

One of the early requirements for an industrializing country is the production of machinery for transporation—a vital necessity for the exchange of products between the agricultural and industrial sectors. When Japan started to produce railroad rolling stock some 90 years ago, it took her nearly 20 years to reach the industrial nations' technical level in this field at the time. China began to build locomotives 15 years ago and is now reported to be producing almost all her supply of these machines in her own shops. In shipbuilding, an industry Japan developed within 20 years in the 19th century, China lags, primarily because she has relatively little foreign trade and depends mainly on overland and inland-waterway transport within her own country. She has no facilities yet for building a ship of more than 12,000 tons and lacks modern techniques such as the block-building system of construction of giant tankers.

Transport machinery in a modern industrial system also includes trucks and automobiles, but this industry requires a higher level of development. China does not yet have an automotive industry in the modern sense.

After the initial development of elementary machines for agriculture and transport, the next stage for an industrializing country is the production of machine tools and major power sources, which entails the making of boilers, turbines and heavy electrical machinery. China has entered this second stage. As I have mentioned, many of her factories are equipped with modern machine tools that were imported from various countries: East Germany, Czechoslovakia, Switzerland, West Germany, the United Kingdom, France and Japan. China herself is only beginning, however, to produce machine tools of her own, and her progress so fas is very uneven. Her output of tools of the grinding class, for example, is good, but her boring tools are far below standard. We can estimate the level of the Chinese machine-tool industry by noting that it does not produce transfer machines, roll grinders or jig borers and it cannot turn out really large machines; the boring machines are limited to 150 millimeters (about six inches), hobbing machines to 2,500 millimeters, vertical boring and turning lathes to 6,000 millimeters and planomillers to 3,000 millimeters.

China's dependence on foreign machine tools has held back

her own education and practice in the design of such tools, but on the other hand it bestows the advantage that her engineers are not inhibited by experience. They can boldly explore unorthodox approaches. For example, in a machine-tool factory in Shanghai they have put all the operations, from machining of the various parts to final assembly, in one huge, temperature-controlled room—perhaps the largest room in the world for making machine tools. With increasing sophistication in the techniques and synthesis of the various operations, this room might eventually turn out the world's best machine tools.

Judging from the history of our own machine-tool industry in Japan, we can estimate that China is about 15 years behind in this field, but with the importation of foreign know-how she might easily catch up in a decade. Much the same conclusion applies to her production of heavy electrical machinery. China has built a turbogenerator of the high-temperature, high-pressure type with a capacity of 30,000 kilowatts—a position Japan reached 15 years ago. We are now building 500,000-kilowatt generators; presumably it will take China a similar period to reach that level.

The production of automobiles requires not only a high level of specific techniques for their fabrication but also a highly integrated industrial structure bringing together a diversity of industries. Many different enterprises contribute to the making and running of an automobile: a wide variety of materials (including fuel) and of parts (including many specialized instruments). All of these must be supplied in reliable quantity and quality. Presumably the lack of such diversity and industrial organization is the main reason China has not yet even attempted to create an automotive industry. She has only one mass-production plant in this field: a factory in Changchun that turns out 2,000 trucks a month. It can be estimated that from this infant stage it will take China more than 20 years to develop an industry capable of producing automobiles comparable to those of the advanced countries. The same is true of her production of aircraft. She has begun to produce small planes by herself, but almost all are complete copies of Russian models.

In electronics, a field in which Chinese leaders are now showing keen interest, China has not yet gone much further than investigations in the laboratory. About the only device she has put into production is a transistor radio incorporating low-grade germanium transistors. She is not far advanced in research on the technology of digital computers, but it is reported that her laboratories have recently built some analogue computers. No doubt China will give increasing attention to electronics in the coming years, because of its great importance from the standpoint of automating her industries and developing communications over her large territory.

If we take Japan to be typical of the modern industrialized country, then by nearly all the indexes China is 10 to 15 years behind in technology. It is a striking fact that the Japanese engineers who have visited China recently have in almost every case found Chinese engineers today confronted by the same problems Japan attacked about 15 years ago. Since China seems to be repeating our history technologically, we can perhaps also make a forecast of her likely development in economic terms.

In 1950 Japan's income as a nation was $9.3 billion, amounting to $93 per capita. She soon passed the level of $100 per capita, and thereafter she was able to devote an average of about 30 percent of her annual gross national product to capital investment; in 1961 she actually allocated 43 percent of her G.N.P. to expanding her productive capacity. This high rate of investment enabled the nation to generate a growth rate of 10 to 20 percent a year in G.N.P. By 1965 her national income had risen to $62 billion, or $620 per capita. In 15 years it had multiplied sevenfold.

China's present national income is estimated to be about $100 per capita, or $60 billion in total for her estimated 600 million population. Most of that income of course comes from agriculture. She has emerged from the "takeoff" stage (to borrow a term from the U.S. economist W. W. Rostow) and entered the industrialization stage. If she follows the experience of Japan, she will soon accumulate enough technical knowledge and capital to make a breakthrough into a period of rapid economic growth, a growth that is driven by industrial investment. In 10 to 15 years she might attain a per capita income equal to Japan's present figure ($620). In that case China's gross national income would be about 70 percent as large as that of the U.S.

How far off is the impending breakthrough for China? My own estimate is five to 10 years. One may wonder, of course, whether recent political events in China, apparent to the outside world largely in the activities of the so-called "Red Guards," will affect this timetable. In this connection I shall observe that Japan suffered from similar political instability in the years before World War II. Thereafter the pace of her progress toward industrialization was quicker.

6

CHINA'S FOREIGN POLICY

POLICIES ARE OFTEN adjudged "irrational" when we assume they are means to some end other than the one they were designed to achieve. This is particularly true of an area like foreign policy where full and accurate information is notoriously hard to come by. It is difficult enough speculating on the foreign policy objectives of our own government, how much more difficult to speak knowledgeably of China's! Official Chinese policy is accessible but, as with all policy declarations, stands in need of interpretation. When the Chinese proclaim, for example, that "United States imperialism must be firmly opposed by all peace-loving peoples in the world," does it mean that the Chinese intend to send troops clear around the globe? or to Vietnam? Or does it mean that the Chinese want the Vietnamese, the Arab nationalists, etc. to fight United States imperialism but to do the fighting themselves? What the official statement of Chinese policy objectives means *to us* depends on the assumptions and inferences *we* draw from the information. An interpretation of other people's actions is always in danger of foundering not only on faulty information but on delusions or mistaken assumptions about the meaning of their behavior.

This danger is not peculiar to the average citizen, but the pitfall equally of "experts" and policy-makers with far greater consequences for the destiny and welfare of all mankind. Tragically, such consequences are not necessarily borne of evil intent. It is impossible to comprehend the foreign policy of another nation without seeing its national interest from *its own point of view*. While this is expectedly difficult (if not impossible) for both the layman without adequate information and his government, presumably with information, it is equally unlikely for the so-called knowledgeable, disinterested outsider, the scholar. He, too, uses his own assumptions in the interpretation of human events, his proper precautions to ensure objectivity notwithstanding.

This was particularly evident in the reactions of western scholars to China's vilification of the Soviet Union. An early response to China's vehement attacks on her former partner was to label it "irrational" on the assumption that the Soviet Union was the only nation in a position to provide needed "help." From the point of view of Chinese leaders, however, Soviet aid entailed gratuitous restrictions. Perhaps to avoid these, China's foreign policy exhibits an overzealous protectiveness of her national independence and freedom of expression and development. It is by no means an "irrational" policy for a society whose century-long subservience to powerful outside forces ended less than twenty years ago. There is a parallel in the rebuke of reasonable white people in the U.S. of "black power" advocates. They, too, decry this black independence of white "aid" as "irrational," failing to sense the "rational" significance of it in social-psychological terms. Under certain conditions an understanding of human behavior, as well as the behavior of nation-states, is attained through a form of empathy.

This section is based on two premises: first, there is nothing accidental about China's foreign policy; second, China's foreign policy can be appreciated as an outgrowth of her domestic needs and experiences. A combination of national interests and long-range aspirations expressed through the ideology of Maoism goes a long way in explaining the vicissitudes of China's foreign relationships. Despite obstacles, I suggest it *is* possible to make sense of the Chinese policies provided we take her real motives into account. Shifts in policy and decisions which on the surface appear contradictory can yield new insights if we suspend ordinarily-held assumptions and adopt a perspective that derives from China's history. Regardless of how we think the Chinese ought to feel and before we are in any position to properly evaluate the consequences of it we must investigate their side of the story, subjectively as it were. It is in this context that many of the documents in this chapter have been selected.

After 1949 when the Chinese Communists were consolidating their power, they followed a moderate domestic and foreign policy modeled to a great extent on the Soviet Union. Not only did the Soviet Union figure significantly in the calculations of men and material needed for internal development, but this reliance was reflected in a foreign policy of "leaning to one side." The world was assumed to be divided into two armed camps, the Soviet Union presiding over and protecting the socialist camp and the U.S. heading the "gang" of imperialists, with no space in-between. Friendly relations with the U.S.S.R. were a matter of course for the newly-established regime, assuring nuclear protection for new China in exchange for junior partnership in world affairs. This policy lasted until 1957 when a new temper seemed to propel China toward an increasingly autonomous role.

This new course in foreign policy was an outgrowth of experimental experiences that convinced the Chinese of the feasibility of pursuing a radically independent course of action. Between 1952 and 1957 China went through a transitional phase of testing out her strength, attempting to forge alliances with "neutralist" countries in Asia and Africa and, within the avowed framework of mutual hostility with the U.S., adopting a statesmanlike stance of accommodation to power politics. At the Geneva Conference in 1954 and a year later at the Bandung Conference of Afro-Asian nations. Chou En-lai, representing China, appeared conciliatory. He offered to negotiate problems that were sources of friction provided, of course, that China's interests would be taken into account: China was ready to settle with any Asian nation the problems of status of the overseas Chinese and was even willing to negotiate with the U.S. over Formosa in order to relieve world tensions. The major tactic during this period was to play down China's millennial revolutionary role in the world, the objective being to champion the cause of *all* nations desiring independent development free of the pressures of the Great Power disputes.

Although, as far as the Chinese are concerned, this objective has never been altered, the tactics have exhibited considerable variation. By 1959 China was bridling at the external restraints on her world power status. Reliance on the U.S.S.R. was bearing a higher price tag than China had bargained for or at least was willing to pay, and in 1960 the rupture between the two was symbolically, as well as materially, finalized by the disastrously abrupt withdrawal of Soviet aid and technicians from China. It was borne home to the Chinese once again that there was no feasible alternative to self-reliance.

As, internally, the Chinese practised standing on their own feet and experimenting with new approaches to economic development and new forms of organization, they reflected this initiative in a foreign policy declaration of independence from the Soviet Union—just as in another century the U.S. had similarly forged for itself a new path. China, with a puritanical fervor reminiscent of New England, divorced herself from the corruption of the "old world" to which she now added her erstwhile partner, the Soviet Union.

Since 1960 China has been dependent almost entirely on her own resources with which she is not only paying for rapid industrialization, but also an advanced weapons program to provide for her own defense. By all appearances she has now successfully passed through the developmental stage of the latter, and the latest nuclear test indicates an ability to produce thermonuclear devices at least in limited quantity. With this indisputable symbol of its independent power, China feels free to direct her own course in the shifting undercurrents of international waters. Pursuit of that invaluable commodity, national integrity, has paid off, success being ample proof for the Chinese of the "correctness" of their position and adding a sanctimonious air to official pronouncements.

But the spectacular reversal of the earlier friendship between the Soviet Union and China, accompanied though it is by a continuing barrage of vitriolic rhetoric, is no indication that war between them is imminent. It is, in fact, a remote possibility. The Soviet Union and China are historical kin much as England and the U.S., which accounts for the bitterness with which the Chinese rebuke the Russians for their "revisionism." Perhaps, as some have suggested, the Chinese feel they can exercise some influence to reverse the trend within the Societ Union. More likely, their extreme antagonism towards the Soviet Union derives from their fear of a détente between the U.S. and the U.S.S.R.

Such a convergence of interests is more than a xenophobic fantasy on the part of the Chinese. Their historical experiences with communism taught them to understand it as a *national* phenomenon. Far from transcending the self-interest of nation-states, the international communist movement has been compromised time and again by its use as a tool to serve the national interests of the Soviet Union. Thus the Chinese find it "natural" (even though they decry it as a departure) for the Soviet Union to seek an accommodation with the U.S. The net effect of this threatens *Chinese national* interest, in addition to thwarting the remaining have-not nations in their struggles for a future of their own.

An added perspective on this situation is obtained by thinking in terms of a distinction between word and deed. While China is verbally bellicose she is reserved in her actions. Lin Piao's statement on People's War (see pp. 480-490) makes this point explicit. It is, in effect, a *moral* commitment to oppressed peoples in the world but it urges them to fight their own wars of liberation. The Chinese pursue *in practice* what they attack the Soviet Union for *in theory*: encouraging revolutionary wars without paying for them. But the Chinese pride themselves on their lack of hypocrisy; they feel they more genuinely and sincerely address themselves to the needs of the "third world" without making promises that will be broken or raising needless anxieties about Chinese expansionism. They believe this position, unlike the Soviet Union's, is not a betrayal of their own avowed principles but rather an extension of them and far less risky internationally (they point to the Cuban crisis to illustrate the contention).

Many of the ideological differences between the Soviet Union and China are attributable to the fact that the two countries are at different stages in their internal development —where their real national and international interests conflict. In addition they have pursued different solutions to similar problems, thereby vying with each other as a model for the poor nations of the world to follow. In this competition the Russians are hardly less acrimonious in their denunciations than the Chinese. Less ideologically inclined, their portentous exaggerations of Chinese aggressiveness sometimes exhibit racial overtones. This is not as apparent in the official repartee we have access to in the daily press as it is in the informal conversational circles of the Russian intelligentsia of which Feifer reports (see pp. 409-419).

Irrespective of ideology, the major foreign policy objective of China is protection of her national interest, the foremost threat to which is the U.S. China would like to eliminate U.S. power in Asia, which part of the world she sees very much like the U.S. saw the western hemisphere in the early part of the nineteenth century. The parallel is misleading, however, for in reality the U.S. in 1823, when the Monroe Doctrine was articulated, was not as visibly encircled as China finds herself today. The U.S. now holds all points of power formerly controlled by Japan. From these points China was invaded by Japan and the U.S., with its vastly more powerful control over the air and sea surrounding China, is capable of far greater destruction than China's past enemies. But in her action China seems aware of the futility of confronting the "paper tiger" and satisfies herself with flinging epithets and preparing an adequate defense.

The Chinese have charted a map of the international social order in three dimensions. Horizontally they think in terms of geography, technology, the nation-state and power politics. Vertically, they divide the world into have and have-not peo-

fringe benefits in the form of better working conditions, material incentives and holidays and the survival of elements of private enterprise in the countryside with an orientation towards recognition of the peasant household as the basic unit of rural economic and social life.

The Chinese Communists are presently trying to avert this Soviet experience. They are purists, vociferously opposed to "revisionism," in their determination to avoid what they regard as the pitfalls of modernization under conditions of backwardness. Their alternative to material incentives and a new stratification is an inflated ideological currency, the stability of which remains to be tested over time. This, then, accounts for part of the enormous hostility between the two major socialist nations of the world.

The Embourgeoisement of the Soviet Union and the Proletarianization of Communist China*

T. H. RIGBY

IT IS NOW clear that, despite a high level of coincidence between the interests and outlook of the U.S.S.R. and the Chinese People's Republic, differences nevertheless exist. Most discussions of this question has focused on six main groups of issues:

1. Status within the bloc and authority in the international Communist movement.

2. Competition for influence in the uncommitted countries.

3. How far the Chinese path to Communism may properly stray from the Soviet model.

4. Different views over the possibility and desirability of improving relations with the imperialists and avoiding war.

5. The amount and timing of Soviet economic aid.

6. Border areas—Sinkiang, Mongolian People's Republic, etc.

There are, moreover, strong indications that each of these groups of issues has contributed to tension between the two allies at some stage or other of their ten-year-old alliance.

There is another series of factors which, I believe, are already exercising an influence upon Sino-Soviet relations, and whose influence will probably grow during the next two decades. These are factors deriving from differences in the

* FROM UNITY AND CONTRADICTION, pp. 19–36 edited by Kurt London (N.Y.: Frederick A. Praeger, 1962). Reprinted by permission of Frederick A. Praeger, Inc.

character of the two societies—factors that I have alluded to in pseudo-Marxian terms in my title.

Industrialization in all societies involves recruitment of a new wage-earning class from other classes existing in pre-industrial society, primarily from the peasantry and petty bourgeoisie of artisans and shopkeepers. For most individuals, the change of class is accompanied by some or all of the following consequences: a real or apparent worsening of material living conditions, at least in certain basic aspects; subjection to an unwonted and often harsh labor discipline; loss of the standing and satisfactions that go with independence and traditional skills; uprooting from a local community in which the individual's behavior was clearly prescribed for all common circumstances of life.

These objective and subjective deprivations tend to alienate the new wage worker from society at large, and this is what is meant here by proletarianization. The classical description of the proletarian given by Marx and Engels in the *Communist Manifesto* pictures him as possessing "nothing to lose but his chains"; his wages are sufficient only "to prolong and reproduce mere existence"; "modern industrial labor . . . has stripped him of every trace of national character. Law, morality, religion are to him so many bourgeois prejudices, behind which lurk in ambush just as many bourgeois interests."

Of course, no proletariat has ever fully conformed to the *Manifesto* pattern. Before the factors making for the proletarianization of the new worker have taken full effect, new processes are under way tending to integrate him into society at a new level. Even in England, which provided the chief model for the *Manifesto* proletarian, influences as varied as the Wesleyan chapels, the mutual-aid societies, and the mechanics' institutes were early at work to render the working man less of an outcast and to link him up with the emerging urban community in which he found himself. At a later stage, working-class organizations ostensibly directed against the existing order—trade unions and socialist political parties—to the extent that they were legally tolerated, themselves became potent forces integrating the industrial workers in the nation and the state. Alongside psychic factors tending to moderate the proletarianization of the wage earner, material factors soon made themselves felt. As the first rigors of early industrialization passed and the capital created thereby began to be reflected in a rising per capita national income, benefits started trickling down to the workers in the form of improved working conditions, housing, community services, more leisure, and, most important of all, consumption levels rising above mere subsistence and permitting the accumulation of a modest store of personal and family property. One must not minimize the importance of the psychic factors, but their impact would probably have remained very limited without the driving force of improving material conditions; the two acting together constituted a process of deproletarianization which assumed growing importance in the maturing industrial society.

These two overlapping processes of proletarianization and deproletarianization of the new wage-earning class are aspects of the adaptation of traditional societies to industrialization. The timing and intensity of the various factors contributing to these processes varied greatly from country to country, and also between different sections of the working class within particular countries. Their political expression also took various forms. However, the usual pattern showed a greater or lesser degree of intensification and radicalization of working-class politics in the earlier decades of industrialization, with more or less violent movements of protest, followed by a period of increasing regularization, institutionalization, and moderation (in which, however, established radical traditions continued to receive lip service, and sometimes influenced action when war or recession brought psychic disturbance or a worsening of material conditions).

THE PROLETARIANIZATION OF RUSSIA

The beginnings of modern factory production in Russia can be traced back well into the eighteenth century, with serfdom and the Czarist autocracy producing some interesting distortions of Western European models—notably the assignment of families or whole villages of state peasants as hereditary labor in particular enterprises. However, the influence of these early feudal elements in the Russian factory should not be exaggerated, and in particular, left no great legacy of paternalism in employer-worker relations, such as that which in Japan, for instance, exercised such a profound influence upon the social and political effects of industrialization. It was in the eighteen-sixties that industrialization got under way, with the stimulus of the liberation of the serfs and the building of railways. By the nineties, it was proceeding apace (pig-iron production trebled between 1886 and 1896), and on the eve of World War I, Russia had a substantial class of wage earners in industry, transport, mining, and construction, amounting to over 10 per cent of the employed population.

This was a proletariat par excellence. All the ingredients

were there: the exchange of traditional village life—with its omnipresent spiritual and secular authorities and the built-in social insurance of household and commune—for the squalor, insecurity, and confusion of the industrial center—with low wages, long hours, and often appalling working conditions. Hence, the radical moods of this class, which erupted in the great strikes of the nineties and played a prominent part in the revolutions of 1905 and March, 1917.

The Russian proletariat was also *one* of the instruments of the Communists in the "proletarian revolution" of November, 1917, and in the Civil War that followed. Consequently, alongside the populist slogan of "land to the tillers," Bolshevik tactics found a place for the syndicalist slogan of "workers' control." The contrast between urban-based Russian Communism and village-based Chinese Communism can be exaggerated; it is probably true that the Bolshevik victory in the Civil War was ultimately due to the fact that for the majority of peasants, the Reds seemed the lesser evil, since a White victory threatened loss of their new-won acres. Nevertheless, working-class participation was undoubtedly a much greater factor in the Russian Revolution than in the Chinese. This lends special significance and irony to the fact that while the final victory of the Bolsheviks entailed for the peasants satisfaction of their basic grievances, it brought for the workers merely confirmation of their proletarian status. The collapse of the syndicalist dreams of workers' control and equality played a part in the Kronstadt revolt and in the "workers' opposition" within the party. This disappointment, together with the disillusioning experience of the New Economic Policy, help to explain the persistence of proletarian attitudes of mind among the Soviet working class and their alienation from the "workers' state."

On the eve of the First Five-Year Plan, this still essentially proletarian working class constituted some 10 per cent of those employed. Eighty per cent were peasants—most of them now independent proprietors. The next ten years saw the proletarianization of this peasant mass. On the one hand, there was a resumption of large-scale industrialization, which had been interrupted by fourteen years of war, civil war, and rehabilitation, and by 1937, nearly a third of the peasants had been shifted into wage-earning jobs. These Russian peasants entering industry in the thirties were subjected to essentially the same proletarianizing pressures, material and psychic, as had been their predecessors of forty years earlier.

On the other hand, a frontal attack was made on the petty-bourgeois character of peasant life itself. A minority of peasants were converted directly into wage workers (State Farms and Machine-Tractor Stations provided less than ten per cent of rural employment in 1940), while the majority were dragooned into "collective farms," which were in form voluntary co-operatives. The distinctions between the two, though invested with great legal and theoretical significance by Communist writers, are of secondary importance for our present purposes. The collective farmers, too, were deprived of their family enterprises and set to work in the "public" sector, where they were directed by management chosen by the local Party and Government authorities, allotted targets under the state plan, and paid according to "the amount and quality of work done" out of profits primarily determined by state-fixed prices.

Thus, between 1928 and 1933, the petty-bourgeois masses of Russia were converted into employees of enterprises directly or indirectly controlled by the state. At the same time, there was a drastic decline in their material living standards. According to one estimate, workers' real wages, even in 1938, averaged 57.5 per cent of their 1928 levels. In the countryside, the decline in consumption levels reached famine proportions in some areas during the early years of collectivization and it was probably only in the nineteen-fifties that the standards of the twenties were regained. The social transformation effected during these years has often been described as a "revolution from above." The ironically minded might call it a "proletarian revolution from above"—but one made to *create,* not to emancipate, a proletariat. Politically the conversion of the bulk of the Soviet population into proletarians had the same consequences as similar transformations elsewhere—the alienation of the proletarianized masses from society and the regime.

The proletarianization of Soviet society was never complete. It was limited by the following three factors:

1. Creation of privileged strata. Marxist writers, in seeking to explain the failure of the population in capitalist countries to behave in a revolutionary fashion, have often pointed to the "bribing" (a) of the managerial-technical-clerical strata, which are given material and status privileges and encouraged to orient themselves toward the employers rather than the workers, and (b) of sections of the working class itself (the phrase "aristocracy of the proletariat" was once popular), who are given higher wages and encouraged to lead the workers in a conciliatory and reformist direction. In the Soviet Union, the "bribery" of these two groups was undertaken as a part of Party policy and opposition to it labeled "petty-bourgeois

egalitarianism." During the First Five-Year Plan, income differentials were radically widened so as to create relatively high rewards for the managerial-technical intelligentsia, and also (by virtue of wide margins for skill and often steeply progressive piece rates) for a section of the industrial workers themselves. The creation of this privileged intelligentsia and of the Stakhanovite aristocracy of the proletariat tended to behead any potential movement of protest.

2. Granting of fringe benefits. In the early decades of industrialization in England, when real wages were at their lowest, other determinants of working-class living standards (conditions of work, social protection, etc.) were also at their most unfavorable. In Germany and some other countries where industrialization came later, the debasement of working-class conditions was soon significantly mitigated by social legislation. In the Soviet Union, such social legislation assumed a scale unprecedented in any country at a similar stage of industrialization. Hours of work were limited to 48 in 1940, cut to 46 in 1956, and are currently being reduced to 40, with a further reduction to 36 promised in the next few years. Regular holidays, pensions, and protection from arbitrary punishment and dismissal were provided, and the workers and their families were included in ambitious state education and health programs.

3. Survival of elements of private enterprise in the countryside. The attempt in the early stages of collectivization to concentrate all production in the public sector and eliminate the peasant household altogether as an economic unit was soon discontinued, and by 1935, the right of each household to its auxiliary plot and a small amount of livestock was confirmed. The produce of these plots was not restricted to consumption by the household, but might be traded in the collective-farm markets. Due partly to Government price policies, which often rendered the return from work on the public sector negligible, and partly to the power of traditional attitudes toward property, the peasants tended to be oriented primarily toward their private plots, and the peasant household remained, as it had been for centuries, the basic unit of rural economic and social life, while work on the collective sector was widely regarded as a sort of *corvée*. Thus, strong petty bourgeois elements remained to moderate the proletarianization of the peasantry.

These three factors limiting the proletarianization of the Soviet population also clearly moderated its political effects. The compromise permitting the peasants to retain their private plots took some of the fire out of their hostility, which had reached such desperate proportions at the beginning of the collectivization era. Fringe benefits narrowed the resentment of the urban working class. The "bribery" of the managerial-technical intelligentsia and the Stakhanovite aristocracy of the proletariat meant that the most able and energetic tended to do relatively well under the regime and were thus inclined to identify their interests with *its* rather than with those of the masses.

Nevertheless, by the nineteen-thirties, substantial sections of the proletarianized population of the U.S.S.R. appear to have become politically and socially alienated from the regime, and, as has happened in other industrializing countries, this found expression in more or less violent movements of protest. These took such varied forms of spontaneous strikes during the early thirties, the destruction of property and assassination of Communists by the peasants at the time of collectivization, and the Vlasov movement and other anti-Soviet manifestations during World War II. That protest movements did not consume such proportions as to overwhelm the regime was of course due to the strength of Soviet physical, organizational, and ideological controls.

The aggravation of internal-security problems characteristically accompanying industrialization has usually been met by intensified police and often internal military controls. Nowhere has this been truer than in the Soviet Union. But, as was mentioned, it is also characteristic for the proletariat to generate its own organizational and psychic links with society, which tend ultimately to moderate this alienation and the security problems arising therefrom. In the Soviet Union, such links were a deliberate creation of the regime. The Soviet regime sought to involve the masses organizationally and ideologically to a degree unprecedented in the world, though subsequently surpassed in China. In this way, they strove to direct resentments and political and intellectual energies in to safe channels. A central part in this involvement was played by a mythological world view, to whose demands Marxist theory, history, science, journalism, and the arts were all subordinated, and whose dominant expression was the cult of the God-King Stalin.

THE EMBOURGEOISEMENT OF RUSSIA

The embourgeoisement of the working class in developed capitalist countries has sometimes been understood in terms of property rights. Workers become house-owners, have savings-bank deposits and perhaps other investments, and consequently develop the bourgeois outlook of men of property. It is, however, now clear that the emphasis should rather be placed upon consumption in a wider sense. As the real wages of the working class increase, are they used to create a distinctive working-class material style of life? Rarely to any significant extent, and never for long. On the contrary, the workers' increasing income is applied to emulate bourgeois standards of dress, house-furnishing, and decoration, and the workers soon show themselves as anxious as their middle-class fellow citizen to keep up with the Joneses in the acquisition of cars, television sets, and refrigerators.

The political consequences of embourgeoisement are a matter of common experience. The working-class movement ceases to be millennarian, ceases to be revolutionary, becomes reformist, and ultimately becomes geared to the attainment of small specific material benefits within the existing socioeconomic system. This reflects the transformation of the outlook of the individual worker. No longer required to concentrate all his efforts on attaining mere subsistence, with no prospect of improving his position so long as society is organized as it is and his place in it remains unchanged, he now finds his basic needs guaranteed, and his aspirations are turned toward the "extras," toward material luxuries, and the existing system seems to promise him a grown share of these. In capitalist countries, this does not mean that the workers necessarily become advocates of capitalism. But they can no longer be seriously interested in radical measures to change the system. Like the middle classes before them, they are now basically oriented toward stability.

In the Soviet Union, embourgeoisement is implicit in the very policy of material incentives, said to be the main distinctive feature of socialism, the lower stage of Communism— "from each according to his ability, to each according to his work." It might be recalled that Lenin pointed out in *The State and Revolution* that payment in proportion to work done implies the persistence of "bourgeois right" in the domain of distribution. My argument here, however, rests not upon Marxist theory but upon the consequences of the policy of incentives in practice. The additional income of those who have benefited from this policy has been applied, not to the creation of a distinctive socialist material culture, but, no less than in the case of the working class in capitalist countries, ot the emulation of bourgeois standards of consumption. Modest and discreet at first (up to the mid-thirties, even Politburo members wore cloth caps), it became increasingly open and blatant, following the replacement of the Old Bolsheviks by Soviet-bred "organization men" during the Great Purge. As a reward for helping to build a socialist society, Soviet citizens are encouraged to build a bourgeois personal life.

Until recently, embourgeoisement was limited to the "bribed" categories of managerial-technical intelligentsia and Stakhanovite aristocracy of the proletariat. The great social change that is now taking place in the Soviet Union is the extension of this process to wider and wider sections of the population. As in other countries, marginal social benefits and ideological factors were not in Russia sufficient to eliminate the essentially proletarian character of the masses so long as their material standards remained at about subsistence level. It is the achievement of relatively high and rising real income that is now carrying the Soviet masses through the process of deproletarianization on to embourgeoisement.

This is true even though we cannot say with too much confidence just how high this real income is and how fast it is rising. There would be general agreement that average real income, after a catastrophic fall during the First Five-Year Plan, a gradual rise during the thirties, and a further drastic setback during the War, did not regain the levels of the late twenties until around 1950. Since then, the official claim is that between 1950 and 1958, the real income of workers and white-collar employeees rose by 55 per cent and of peasants by 85 per cent. This claim is probably exaggerated, but not wholly misleading. Money wages at present appear to average about eighty rubles a month. Though comparisons of this kind are notoriously treacherous, we would probably not be too far wrong in suggesting that these eighty rubles will purchase food, drink, clothing, and household goods and furniture equivalent to about one-third of those currently purchasable by one month's average wages in Great Britain, and no more than a quarter of what may be bought with a month's average wages in the United States. But one must also take into account the far lower cost of housing in the U.S.S.R., the scale of publicly provided services (comparable with those provided in Great Britain and considerably greater than in the United States), and the fact that in the overwhelming majority of Soviet families, both husband and wife have full-time jobs. In short, though real wages in the Soviet Union are still well below Western European, let alone Northern American standards, these have now ceased to be quite absurd as a basis for comparison.

Reverting to the official figures, the physical volume of Soviet retail trade is said to have more than doubled between 1950 and 1958. Sales of meat, butter, and eggs—crucial items where living standards are advancing from subsistence levels —increased two and a half or three times. The expansion of clothing and footwear sales was on the same level. Turning to consumer durables, a more telling case for the purposes of our thesis, we get the following picture: In the same years, 1950– 58, sales of radios rose from under a million to 3.67 million, of sewing machines from 500,000 to nearly 3 million, of bicycles from 650,000 to nearly 3 million, of television sets from 12,000 to nearly a million, refrigerators from 1,000 to 330,000, washing machines from 280 to 500,000, of vacuum cleaners from 6,000 to 250,000. The number of passenger cars produced rose from 60,000 to 120,000, and of motorcycles from 120,000 to 400,000. There is, so far as I know, no reason to think these figures seriously misleading. What they show is this: Although many items that have been standard home equipment in the more prosperous capitalist countries for a quarter century or more are only now becoming available to the general public in the U.S.S.R., and other items that are *becoming* or have just become standard equipment in the former are still limited to a small minority in the latter, the Soviet Union has nevertheless now entered the era of the mass consumption of durable consumer goods. In this respect, it is probably at a stage comparable with Western Europe between the wars. The progress, however, is quite rapid, and there is probably nothing fantastic in the aim to increase real income per head by forty per cent during the current Seven-Year Plan. Whatever the exact rate may be, each year extends the availability of many important items several rungs down the social scale. And by now, almost the whole population is involved to a greater or lesser extent in this process.

This applies even in the countryside. The official estimates that the value of the labor day trebled between 1953 and 1957, while the average money income of the kolkhoznik more than doubled between 1952 and 1957, are probably not too far from the facts. Here a complex social process is going on. Despite the removal of the tax on the products of the private plots and the lifting of other restrictions on the peasants' "private enterprise," there is a general cautious move toward limiting the role of the latter (cutting down and consolidating plots, raising the compulsory minimum of work on the "public" sector, sale of kolkhozniks' cows to the collective, and so on). The most important factor has been the change in price policy, which has made work on the "public" sector a paying proposition, and it should not be long before the peasants are relying on this as their main source of income. These trends indicate a decline of the petty-bourgeois element in peasant life. However, it is clear that the peasants will never be proletarianized, as they are now being caught up in the nationwide process of embourgeoisement in the area of consumption.

I believe that all this is effecting a profound change in the outlook and mentality of the Russians. One American writer has described this as the coming of the "consumer ethic." Since "bourgeois right" reigns in the area of consumption, and Soviet consumer standards are a direct reflection of those of bourgeois Europe and America, we can also regard this as the era of the embourgeoisement of Russia.

This process has only recently begun and will really get under way during the next decade. Present plans provide for the rehousing of the bulk of the population from single rooms in "communal" flats to small family flats during this period. Even if construction plans fall well below present targets, it is clear that for a large part of the Soviet people, the next few years will see the great undertaking of furnishing and equipping their new-won living space. The spreading of high levels of mass consumption has a peculiar excitement and adventurous quality to it which, I think, is beginning to infect the atmosphere in the Soviet Union. The new concern shown by the top leadership with the retail-trade mechanism is symptomatic of this, and has found such varied expressions as experiments in the introduction of self-service, the establishment of installment-buying arrangements, and the 1960 decisions on internal trade, which, among other things, provide for a great expansion in retailing facilities.

Anyone who has spent much time talking to Soviet people recently must have been impressed by the way individuals in all social classes and in all areas are taken up with saving for and acquiring luxuries: clothes in fashionable styles and good materials, furniture, household appliances, cars. Resentment tends to be directed no longer against the system as a whole, or against some scapegoat such as the internal or external enemy or the backward past, but against shortages or poor quality in the ranges of durable consumer goods into which the individual has now moved.

This is obviously fraught with great political implications, perhaps not dissimilar in certain important respects to those produced by the embourgeoisement of the working class in capitalist countries. In the view of the present writer, the underlying alienation of the bulk of the Soviet population from the Soviet system is passing. It is being replaced, not by a militant dedication to the official ideology, but merely by an acceptance of existing society as normal, as providing for their interests, and not fundamentally a conspiracy against them. The existing order seems to promise satisfaction of their current aspirations for durable consumer goods, and the opening up of ever-new possibilities beyond these. Thus, like the masses in the more prosperous capitalist countries and like their own privileged sections in the past, the Soviet masses have now acquired a vested interest in stability. In the past, a *section* of society was "bribed" by material incentives to support the regime's exploitation of the masses. Now everyone is "bribed" to accept the existing order. The antagonism between privileged and underprivileged is therefore undermined, and the way opened up for a new consensus in Russian society, based on the maintenance of ever rising consumption standards for all classes.

This involves a fundamental change in the security problem. Formerly, the proletarianized condition of the masses produced such powerful pressures toward protest that the system could only be maintained by means of the most elaborate and violent physical and ideological counterpressures. These counterpressures can now be eased. Hence, developments varying from a curtailment of the powers and activities of the police to a certain modification of the mythological character of the official world view.

THE PROLETARIANIZATION OF CHINA

No one would question the historical fact of the proletarianization of China, as the term is here defined. What should be noted is that it seems to be going further, and promises to last longer, than in Russia.

Communist China began its industrialization efforts with a far smaller industrial base in proportion to population, and with lower mass-consumption levels, than did the Soviet Union. The road to the achievement of high average levels of real income is proportionately longer and more difficult to traverse. It is not surprising that the Chinese Communist leaders have sought so diligently for short cuts. What they have found are various ways of maximizing production effort and minimizing current consumption, and of reinforcing physical and ideological controls to counter the resentments so caused.

In considering the impact of the changes wrought on Chinese society since 1949, one should not forget the relative strength of petty-bourgeois elements in the old China. Without romancing about the sturdy independent peasant or minimizing the role of landlordism, one cannot but be impressed by the firm place traditionally occupied by the peasant family holding as an economic unit, as compared, for instance, with the Russian peasant household, whose role was for so long distorted by the authority of the commune (*obshchina*) and the centuries of serfdom. Chinese towns, too, were still strongholds of the trading and artisan classes, which in early-twentieth-century Russia were already largely overshadowed by the new factory proletariat. Commercial values seem to have enjoyed an acceptance in China which they were always denied in Russia. Chinese society, therefore, would appear to have been far worse prepared than Russian society to undergo the experience of total proletarianization.

Up to 1958, the Chinese Communists nevertheless contrived to proletarianize their country in a more gradual, less cataclysmic manner than had their Soviet comrades. Collectivization of the peasantry was approached through graded steps of mutual aid and co-operation and, when completed in 1955–56, contained concessions to family holdings such as were not granted in Russia until after the first crisis of collectivitization was past. Expropriation of industrialists and traders in the towns was also eased by intermediate stages of mixed ownership and participation in management. Rationality and moderation, however, were completely overwhelmed by the tidal wave of communization that swept over the country in the second half of 1958.

The communes have brought changes in the domains of both production and consumption which carry proletarianization in China beyond Soviet levels. Despite the partial reversal in December, 1958, of the policy of totally eliminating the peasant family enterprise by confiscating private plots, livestock, and implements, the private economy of the peasantry appears destined to play a far more subordinate role in the Chinese rural scene than it has so far in Russia. In the time that remains after they have cultivated the communal fields, the peasants are required to devote their energies to communal industrial undertakings or public works rather than their private plots.

If the communes have restricted and threatened the existence of petty-bourgeois elements in agricultural production, they have done the same thing for the "bourgeois right" in the area of distribution and consumption. It is true that the principle of material incentives, of "to each according to his work," has never been discarded (though sometimes treated cavalierly or with impatience), and sections of the population are "bribed" by fairly wide wage differentials and discriminatory rationing procedures. However, the impact of material incentives is severely limited under commune conditions. Although there has been a retreat from the immediate pooling of personal and family property and even dwellings, the atmosphere in the communes is clearly hostile to the private accumulation of luxuries, and the cadres and other relatively privileged strata as expected to set an example in austerity. Communal mess halls and care of old people and children—practices whose primary aim is no doubt the release of women for "production"—and the system of free supply (now rather in abeyance), have the effect of minimizing the role of the family as a consumption unit.

These are the main distinguishing features of the Chinese experience of proletarianization. Comparison of actual material living standards with those prevailing in Russia at a similar stage of development can have little relevance. What is, perhaps, worth noting is that China is incapable of supporting a program of social services and other fringe benefits that mitigate the effects of proletarianization comparable with those provided in the Soviet Union even during the thirties. The Chinese worker, urban or rural, seems to have little defense against arbitrary disciplinary measures by his superiors, and extremely long hours of work appear typical.

Such an extreme form of proletarianization as has been imposed upon the population of China gives rise to pressures which could assume explosive force if not subdued by commensurate counter-pressures generated by the regime. The CCP leadership has made ample use of internal police and military controls and of mass-communication media, but has made to this stock in trade of all totalitarian states some additions of its own. In this connection, the militarization of rural commune life may be mentioned, in its aspects both of organization of the "people's militia" and of regimentation of work activities. Even more important, however, is the control exercised over every individual through his work-study group. The universal obligation to engage in regular directed "study" and "discussion" requires the rank-and-file worker to remold his attitudes and actively commit himself to a degree that in the Soviet Union is expected only of Party members.

IMPLICATIONS

It has been argued that in certain fundamental respects, the societies of China and the Soviet Union are diverging radically in their character at the present time. These divergent social trends will tend to produce certain political consequences, both within the two countries themselves and in their relations with each other and with other states. Nevertheless, it is obvious that they constitute only one factor among the many influencing political behavior. All I shall do here is to suggest the direction of pressures arising from this particular factor, without attempting to estimate how effective these pressures might be expected to be.

One would expect it to produce, I think, a growing mutual irritation and difficulty of communication, arising from the sharp contrast in the tone and atmosphere—one might almost say the rationale—of life in the two societies. Let us look at one or two points that highlight this contrast.

Since 1958, the Chinese Communists have been engaged in attempting to supplant the family cooking stove, as far as possible, by communal mess halls. Meanwhile, in the Soviet Union, a great housing program is in progress, aiming (among other things) at providing family kitchens for millions who formerly shared their cooking facilities with others in "communal" flats. The striving for cozy and "cultured" family living conditions is a natural and long-accepted corollary of Soviet policy on material incentives, but it seems quite alien to current Chinese ideas on how to move toward Communism.

The last few years have seen a growing respect for hard facts in the Soviet intellectual sphere, and an increasing concern to relate plans consistently to objective reality. In China, on the other hand, the tendency has been in favor of subjective against objective factors, excessive concern with the latter even becoming one of the criteria of "rightist opportunism." The Chinese taste for "letting politics take command" accords ill with the current Soviet stress on practical economic studies as the dominant element in Party education. Connected with this is the Chinese attitude on incentives. Relying on incentives has been vigorously attacked in China as another of the errors of the "rightist opportunists," whereas, in Russia, their central importance has never been called in question, and at no time more than the present has greater reliance been placed on material incentives as a built-in stimulus to production, overshadowing the role of all external organizational and ideological pressures.

In such ways, the two societies are becoming remote and, I should say, out of sympathy with each other. Soviet administrators and executives, not to mention more ordinary citizens, may increasingly find it easier to establish a rapport with, for instance, Americans than with Chinese Communists.

It might be objected here that all this, whether right or wrong, has no bearing on international relations, which are decided by a few individuals at the top. But these few do not move in a vacuum. While largely molding the societies around them, they are to some extent molded in their turn by the societies. Attention has been drawn to the contrast in the atmosphere and tone of life between present-day China and Russia. But the leaders of both are very much in tune with the current tone and atmosphere of their countries. No one who has studied Khrushchev carefully over the past seven years could seriously doubt his involvement in the enterprise of raising mass-consumption levels. Nor is it likely that the commune, "leap forward," and "walking on two legs" mentality is merely manipulated by the Chinese leadership without its infecting them, too.

No little importance here attaches to the upper- and middle-level officials, who form the human environment within which these top leaders move. In China, these are predominantly old, pre-1949 cadres, whose administrative apprenticeship was served under harsh material circumstances and military conditions. For them, the austerity of extreme proletarianization, the regimentation, improvisation, and reliance on organization and propaganda rather than objective conditions must appear natural features of the struggle for Communism. Their opposite numbers in Russia, in their overwhelming majority, are anything but revolutionaries, but are drawn from the pioneers of embourgeoisement in the U.S.S.R.——members of the new technical-managerial intelligentsia who were placed on the power escalator by Stalin's purging of the Civil War generation of cadres. For these men, career-making in the Party, administrative, or managerial hierarchy has meant constantly raising the levels of family consumption, acquiring a comfortable, well-furnished multiroom flat, a nice *dacha*, expensive holidays. Nothing could be more natural for *them* than to equate the spread of ever higher consumption levels with progress and the march toward Communism. What is of particular interest to note is that not only is China not administered by such people *now*, but, if it turns out that the more ambitious forms of communization are established, she never will have such a group as administrators. The road to Communism in Russia has been via embourgeoisement. If China attempts to avoid this path, the end result in the two cases may be very different.

The implications of all this for relations with the "imperialists" seem fairly plain. The notion of achieving victory over capitalism in peaceful economic competition, with the population of capitalist countries "choosing" Communism when they realize what high living standards it opens up, is obviously very congenial to the present state of mind among Russians. At the same time, the idea of a destructive war, robbing them of the comforts they have so long been deprived of and are now beginning to enjoy, is deeply repugnant, and I believe this repugnance reaches very high into the Soviet hierarchy. In China, tension is needed to support the mythological world view which the regime requires to control its proletarianized population. The threat of "imperialist" attack in an integral part of this (compare the "capitalist encirclement" in Stalin's Russia), essential to justify austerities, hard work, and regimentation as well as that Iron Curtain without which the mythology could not survive. International tension is no longer necessary to the Soviet leadership in the same way to ensure internal control. But the contrast goes further than this. Atomic war would render meaningless the strivings and achievements of Soviet society over the last thirty years; this is not true of the proletarianized society of China, which has nothing to lose but its chains.

Chinese Comment on the Open Letter of the Central Committee of the Communist Party of the Soviet Union, March 31, 1964*

PEOPLE'S DAILY; RED FLAG

THE PRESENT article will discuss the familiar question of "peaceful transition". It has become familiar and has attracted everybody's attention because Khrushchov raised it at the 20th Congress of the CPSU and rounded it into a complete system in the form of a programme at the 22nd Congress, where he pitted his revisionist views against the Marxist-Leninist views. The Open Letter of the Central Committee of the CPSU of July 14, 1963 once again struck up this old tune. . . .

* THE PROLETARIAN REVOLUTION AND KHRUSHCHEV'S REVISIONISM (Peking: Foreign Languages Press, 1964) pp. 13–22, 37–48 (excerpts).

At the time of the meeting of representatives of the Communist and Workers' Parties in 1957, the delegation of the CPC engaged in a sharp debate with the delegation of the CPSU on the question of the transition from capitalism to socialism.

In the first draft for the Declaration which it proposed during the preparations for the Moscow meeting, the Central Committee of the CPSU referred only to the possibility of peaceful transition and said nothing about the possibility of non-peaceful transition; it referred only to the parliamentary road and said nothing about other means of struggle, and at the same time pinned hopes for the winning of state power through the parliamentary road on "the concerted actions of Communists and socialists." Naturally the Central Committee of the CPC could not agree to these wrong views, which depart from Marxism-Leninism, being written into the programmatic document of all the Communist and Workers' Parties. . . .

The delegation of the CPC expressed its disagreement with these erroneous views in clear terms. On November 10, 1957 it systematically explained its own views on the question of the transition from capitalism to socialism to the Central Committee of the CPSU, to which it also presented a written outline.

The main points made in our written outline are summarized below.

It is advantageous from the point of view of tactics to refer to the desire for peaceful transition, but it would be inappropriate to over-emphasize the possibility of peaceful transition. It is necessary to be prepared at all times to repulse counter-revolutionary attacks and, at the critical juncture of the revolution when the working class is seizing state power, to overthrow the bourgeoisie by armed force if it uses armed force to suppress the people's revolution (generally speaking, it is inevitable that the bourgeoisie will do so).

The parliamentary form of struggle must be fully utilized, but its role is limited. What is most important is to proceed with the hard work of accumulating revolutionary strength; peaceful transition should not be interpreted in such a way as solely to mean transition through a parliamentary majority. The main question is that of the state machinery, namely, the smashing of the old state machinery (chiefly the armed forces) and the establishment of the new state machinery (chiefly the armed forces).

The social democratic parties are not parties of socialism; with the exception of certain Left wings, they are a variant of bourgeois political parties. On the question of socialist revolution, our position is fundamentally different from that of the social democratic parties. This distinction must not be obscured.

These views of ours are in full accord with Marxism-Leninism.

The comrades of the delegation of the Central Committee of the CPSU were unable to argue against them, but they repeatedly asked us to make allowances for their internal needs, expressing the hope that the formulation of this question in the draft Declaration might show some connection with its formulation by the 20th Congress of the CPSU.

We had refuted the wrong views of the leadership of the CPSU and put forward a written outline of our own views. For this reason and for the sake of the common struggle against the enemy, the delegation of the CPC decided to meet the repeated wishes of the comrades of the CPSU and agreed to take the draft of the Central Committee of the CPSU on this question as the basis, while suggesting amendments in only a few places.

We hoped that through this debate the comrades of the CPSU would awaken to their errors and correct them. But contrary to our hopes, the leaders of the CPSU did not do so.

At the meeting of fraternal Parties in 1960, the delegation of the CPC again engaged in repeated sharp debates with the delegation of the CPSU on the question of the transition from capitalism to socialism, and thoroughly exposed and criticized Khrushchov's revisionist views. During the meeting, the Chinese and the Soviet sides each adhered to its own position, and no agreement could be reached. In view of the general wish of fraternal Parties that a common document should be hammered out at the meeting, the delegation of the CPC finally made a concession on this question again and agreed to the verbatim transcription of the relevant passages in the 1957 Declaration into the 1960 Statement, again out of consideration for the needs of the leaders of the CPSU. At the same time, during this meeting we distributed the Outline of Views on the Question of Peaceful Transition put forward by the Chinese Communist Party on November 10, 1957, and made it clear that we were giving consideration to the leadership of the CPSU on this issue for the last time, and would not do so again.

If comrades now make the criticism that we were wrong in giving this consideration to the leaders of the CPSU, we are quite ready to accept this criticism. . . .

SOPHISTRY CANNOT ALTER HISTORY

The leaders of the CPSU openly distort the works of Marx and Lenin and distort history too to cover up their betrayal of Marxism-Leninism and justify their revisionist line.

They argue: Did not Marx "admit such a possibility [peaceful transition] for England and America"?

It is true that in the 1870's Marx said that in countries like the United States and Britain "the workers can reach their goal by peaceful means." But at the same time he stressed that this possibility was an exception. He said that "even if this be so, we must also recognize that in the majority of countries on the continent force must serve as the lever of our revolution." ("On the Hague Congress." Speech at a Mass Meeting in Amsterdam, *Collected Works of Marx and Engels*, 2nd Russian ed., Moscow, Vol. 18, p. 154.) What is more, he pointed out,

The English bourgeoisie has always shown its readiness to accept the decision of the majority, so long as it has the monopoly of the suffrage. But believe me, at the moment when it finds itself in the minority on questions which it considers vitally important, we will have a new slave-holders' war here. ("Record of a Talk Between K. Marx and the Correspondent of *The World*," *Collected Works of Marx and Engels*, 2nd Russian ed., Moscow, Vol. 17, p. 637.) . . .

When we point out that world history has thus far produced no precedent for peaceful transition from capitalism to socialism, the leaders of the CPSU quibble, saying that "practical experience exists of the achievement of the socialist revolution in peaceful form." And shutting their eyes to all the facts, they state, "In Hungary in 1919, the dictatorship of the proletariat was established by peaceful means." . . . The leaders of the CPSU are telling a glaring lie when they say that the Hungarian revolution was an example of peaceful transition.

It is alleged in the Soviet press that the Hungarian bourgeois government "voluntarily resigned," and this is probably the only ground the leaders of the CPSU base themselves on. But what were the facts?

Karolyi, the head of the Hungarian bourgeois government at the time, was quite explicit on this point. He declared:

I signed a proclamation concerning my own resignation and the transfer of power to the proletariat, which in reality

had already taken over and proclaimed power earlier . . .
*I did not hand over power to the proletariat, as it had
already won it earlier, thanks to its planned creation of a
socialist army.*

For this reason, Bela Kun pointed out that to say the bourgeoisie voluntarily handed political power over to the proletariat was a deceptive "legend." (Bela Kun, *Lessons of the
Proletarian Revolution in Hungary,* Russian ed., Moscow,
1960, p. 49.) . . .

LIES CANNOT COVER UP REALITY

The principal argument used by the leaders of the CPSU
to justify their anti-revolutionary line of "peaceful transition"
is that historical conditions have changed.

With regard to the appraisal of the changes in historical
conditions since World War II and the conclusions to be drawn
from them, Marxist-Leninists hold entirely different views
from those of Khrushchov. . . .

Marxist-Leninists base themselves on the fact that the
changes in post-war conditions have become increasingly
favourable for revolution and on the law that imperialism
and reaction will never change their nature. Therefore they
draw the conclusion that revolution must be promoted, and
they hold that full use must be made of this very favourable
situation and that in the light of the specific conditions in
different countries the development of revolutionary struggles
must be actively promoted and preparations must be made to
seize victory in the revolution.

On the other hand, using the pretext of these very changes
in post-war conditions, Khrushchov draws the conclusion that
revolution must be opposed and repudiated, and he holds that
as a result of the changes in the world balance of forces imperialism and reaction have changed their nature, the law of
class struggle has changed, and the common road of the
October Revolution and the Marxist-Leninist theory of proletarian revolution have become outmoded.

REFUTATION OF "OPPOSITION TO LEFT OPPORTUNISM"

The Open Letter of the Central Committee of the CPSU
fabricates a tissue of lies in its treatment of the question of
proletarian revolution. It asserts that the Chinese Communist
Party favours "advancing the slogan of immediate proletarian
revolution" even in the absence of a revolutionary situation,
that it stands for abandoning "the struggle for the democratic
rights and vital interests of the working people in capitalist

countries," that it makes armed struggle "absolute," and so on. They frequently pin such labels as "Left opportunism," "Left adventurism" and "Trotskyism" on the Chinese Communist Party. . . .

We have always maintained that a revolution cannot be made at will and is impossible unless a revolutionary situation objectively exists. But the outbreak and the victory of revolution depend not only on the existence of a revolutionary situation but also on the preparations and efforts made by the subjective revolutionary forces.

It is "Left" adventurism if the party of the proletariat does not accurately appraise both the objective conditions and subjective forces making for revolution and if it rashly launches a revolution before the conditions are ripe. But it is Right opportunism, or revisionism, if the proletarian party makes no active preparations for revolution before the conditions are ripe, or dare not lead a revolution and seize state power when a revolutionary situation exists and the conditions are ripe.

Until the time arrives for seizing state power, the fundamental and most important task for the proletarian party is to concentrate on the painstaking work of accumulating revolutionary strength. The active leadership given in day-to-day struggle must have as its central aim the building up of revolutionary strength and the preparations for seizing victory in the revolution when the conditions are ripe. The proletarian party should use the various forms of day-to-day struggle to raise the political consciousness of the proletariat and the masses of the people, to train its own class forces, to temper its fighting capacity and to prepare for revolution ideologically, politically, organizationally and militarily. It is only in this way that it will not miss the opportunity of seizing victory when the conditions for revolution are ripe. Otherwise, the proletarian party will simply let the opportunity of making revolution slip by even when a revolutionary situation objectively exists. . . .

From its long practical experience, the Chinese Communist Party is fully aware that it is wrong to reject legal struggle, to restrict the Party's work within narrow confines and thereby to alienate itself from the masses. But one should never tolerate the legalism peddled by the revisionists. The revisionists reject armed struggle and all other illegal struggle, engage only in legal struggle and activity and confine the Party's activities and mass struggles within the framework allowed by the ruling classes. . . .

TWO DIFFERENT LINES, TWO DIFFERENT RESULTS

History is the most telling witness. Rich experience has been gained since World War II both in the international communist movement and in the peoples' revolutionary struggles. There has been successful as well as unsuccessful experience. Communists and the revolutionary people of all countries need to draw the right conclusions from this historical experience.

The countries in Eastern Europe, Asia and Latin America which have succeeded in making a socialist revolution since the War have done so by following the revolutionary Marxist-Leninist line and the road of the October Revolution. Now, in addition to the experience of the October Revolution, there is the experience of the revolutions of China, the socialist countries in Eastern Europe, Korea, Viet Nam and Cuba. The victorious revolutions in these countries have enriched and developed Marxism-Leninism and the experience of the October Revolution.

From China to Cuba, all these revolutions without exception were won by armed struggle and by fighting against armed imperialist aggression and intervention.

The Chinese people were victorious in their revolution after waging revolutionary wars for twenty-two years, including the three years of the People's Liberation War, in which they thoroughly defeated the Chiang Kai-shek reactionaries who were backed up to the hilt by U.S. imperialism.

The Korean people carried on fifteen years of revolutionary armed struggle against Japanese imperialism beginning in the 1930's, built up and expanded their revolutionary armed forces, and finally achieved victory with the help of the Soviet Army. After the founding of the Democratic People's Republic of Korea, it took another three years of war against U.S. imperialist armed aggression before the victory of their revolution could be consolidated.

The Vietnamese people seized state power by the armed uprising of August 1945. Immediately afterwards, they had to begin fighting a war of national liberation lasting eight years against French imperialism and to defeat the U.S. imperialist military intervention, and only then did they triumph in northern Viet Nam. The people of southern Viet Nam are still waging a heroic struggle against U.S. imperialist armed aggression.

The Cuban people started their armed uprising in 1953, and later it took more than two years of people's revolutionary war before they overthrew the rule of U.S. imperialism and its Cuban puppet, Batista. After their victorious revolution, the Cuban people smashed armed invasions by U.S. imperialist mercenaries and safeguarded the fruits of revolution.

The other socialist countries too were all established through armed struggle.

What are the main lessons of the successful proletarian revolutions in the countries extending from China to Cuba after World War II?

1. Violent revolution is a universal law of proletarian revolution. To realize the transition to socialism, the proletariat must wage armed struggle, smash the old state machine and establish the dictatorship of the proletariat.

2. The peasants are the most dependable allies of the proletariat. The proletariat must closely rely on the peasants, establish a broad united front based on the worker-peasant alliance, and insist upon proletarian leadership in the revolution.

3. U.S. imperialism is the arch enemy of people's revolution in all countries. The proletariat must hold high the national banner of opposition to U.S. imperialism and have the courage to fight with firm resolve against the U.S. imperialists and their lackeys in its own country.

4. The revolution of the oppressed nations is an indispensable ally of the proletarian revolution. The workers of all countries must unite, and they must unite with all the oppressed nations and all the forces opposed to imperialism and its lackeys to form a broad international united front.

5. To make a revolution, it is essential to have a revolutionary party. The triumph of the proletarian revolution and the triumph of the dictatorship of the proletariat are impossible without a revolutionary proletarian party established in accordance with the revolutionary theory and style of Marxism-Leninism, a party which is irreconcilable towards revisionism and opportunism and which takes a revolutionary attitude towards the reactionary ruling classes and their state power.

To insist on revolutionary armed struggle is of primary importance not only to the proletarian revolution but also to the national democratic revolution of the oppressed nations. The victory of the Algerian national liberation war has set a good example in this respect.

The whole history of the proletarian parties since the War has shown that those parties which have followed the line of revolution, adopted the correct strategy and tactics and actively led the masses in revolutionary struggle are able to lead the revolutionary cause forward step by step to victory and grow vigorously in strength. . . .

Refutation of the New Leaders of the CPSU on "United Action"*

PEOPLE'S DAILY; RED FLAG

. . . THE ANTAGONISM between Marxism-Leninism and Khrushchov revisionism is a class antagonism between the proletariat and the bourgeoisie; it is the antagonism between the socialist and the capitalist roads and between the line of opposing imperialism and that of surrendering to it. It is an irreconcilable antagonism.

As Lenin said, "Unity is a great thing and a great slogan. But what the workers' cause needs is the *unity of Marxists,* not unity between Marxists, and opponents and distorters of Marxism."

The new leaders of the CPSU argue that even if there are differences of theory and line, these can be put aside and that "united action" should be taken and "unity against the enemy" achieved in practical struggle against imperialism.

The sharpest difference of theory and line between Marxism-Leninism and Khrushchov revisionism concerns precisely the question of handling our relations with enemies and friends, in other words, the question of whether to oppose or unite with imperialism, and above all the question of whether to oppose or unite with U.S. imperialism. This difference is decisive for all the most important practical actions in the international class struggle. How can it possibly be put aside in favour of an unprincipled unity that does not distinguish between enemies and friends? . . .

On April 7 this year, together with his proposal for "unconditional discussions" on the question of Viet Nam, Johnson publicized the scheme for "the international development of Southeast Asia" in order to undermine the struggle against U.S. imperialism waged by the people of Viet Nam and the other Southeast Asian countries and to step up economic infiltration, and he expressed the hope that the Soviet Union would join in. The United States regards the establishment

* REFUTATION OF THE NEW LEADERS OF THE CPSU ON "UNITED ACTION" (Peking: Foreign Languages Press, 1965) excerpts.

of the "Asian Development Bank" as a means of putting this scheme into practice. In response to Johnson's call, the new leaders of the CPSU went so far as to send a delegation to Bangkok in October to sit together with delegations from the United States, Japan, and such puppet cliques as the Chiang Kai-shek gang, South Korean and "Malaysia" and take an active part in preparing for the establishment of the "Asian Development Bank." Such is the ardour of the new leaders of the CPSU for united action with U.S. imperialism. . . .

The new leaders of the CPSU are able to deceive people because they sometimes make a few verbal attacks on U.S. imperialism. Why do they have to do this? The answer is that this meets the need of the U.S. imperialists as well as the revisionists themselves. The Khrushchov revisionists have to give the appearance of opposing the United States in order to render effective help to U.S. imperialism, hoodwink the masses and sabotage revolution. Otherwise, they could not play this deceptive role, and that would not be to the advantage of U.S. imperialism. Minor attacks in words but major help in deeds—such is the way the new leaders of the CPSU serve U.S. imperialism.

Some people ask, why is it that the Marxist-Leninists and the revolutionary people cannot take united action with the new leaders of the CPSU, yet can unite with personages from the upper strata in the nationalist countries, and strive for united action with them in the anti-imperialist struggle, and can even exploit the contradictions among the imperialist countries in the struggle against the United States?

The reason is that in the contemporary world opposition to or alliance with U.S. imperialism constitutes the hallmark for deciding whether or not a political force can be included in the united front against the United States.

In Asia, Africa and Latin America, with the exception of the lackeys of imperialism, personages from the upper strata in many nationalist countries desire in varying degrees to oppose imperialism, colonialism and neo-colonialism headed by the United States. We should co-operate with them in the anti-imperialist struggle.

In the imperialist countries which are in sharp contradiction with the United States, some monopoly capitalists follow the U.S. imperialists, but there are also others who desire in varying degrees to oppose the United States. In the struggle against the United States, the people of the world can take united action with the latter on some questions and to a certain degree.

The crux of the matter is that, so far from opposing U.S. imperialism, the new leaders of the CPSU are allying themselves and collaborating with it to dominate the world. They have thus set themselves in opposition to the united front against U.S. imperialism. If they really opposed U.S. imperialism and did so by actual deeds, we would readily take united action with them. But their so-called opposition to U.S. imperialism is only verbal and not genuine. We must tell them the truth: So long as their line of Soviet-U.S. collaboration against world revolution remains unchanged, and so long as they do not abandon their alliance with U.S. imperialism and reaction, we absolutely refuse to take any "united action" with them. We absolutely refuse to serve as a pawn in their secret diplomacy with U.S. imperialism or help them cover up their assistance to U.S. imperialism in suppressing the peoples' revolution in various countries. . . .

> Within the Soviet Union there has been mounting anti-Chinese sentiment fostered by press, radio and television. As the following selection by George Feifer reports, the Russians, though fundamentally apathetic to questions of politics (foreign policy included), share a set of attitudes towards the Chinese that coincides with their government's position abroad.
>
> It is interesting to note that Soviet citizens who have never been to China share a great deal with Americans in the same position. They are largely ignorant of historical facts relating to China; they are prone to resent the lack of Chinese gratitude for Soviet aid and they are predisposed to react to the Chinese as "oriental," somehow intrinsically outside the mainstream of civilization (assumed to be western).

Russia—Da
China—Nyet*

GEORGE FEIFER

LATE LAST August, two weeks after the last plenum of the Central Committee of the Chinese Communist party had met in Peking and some four months after the launching of the "great proletarian cultural revolution," a new attitude toward China was struck, officially and publicly, in the Soviet Union. After almost two years of relative restraint in the face of

* From The New York Times Magazine, December 4, 1966. © 1966 by The New York Times Company. Reprinted by permission.

Chinese attacks on the Soviet leadership (a rotten, "revisionist" leadership, said the Chinese, which was betraying Marxism-Leninism by restoring private enterprise at home and selling out to American imperialism abroad), the Russians responded with notes and declarations which, as a correspondent here observed, might have been dispatched by a government to its sworn adversary. The Soviet Union formally opened its cold war on a second front.

The contents of the official Soviet notes and declarations to Peking (the Russians were particularly outraged by verbal and physical abuse suffered by their diplomatic personnel during anti-Soviet demonstrations in the Chinese capital) are well-known. Less well-known are the contents of the campaign in the Soviet press which has accompanied the diplomatic offensive. Hardly a day passed since late August without an account from Peking about the frightening situation in China, an analysis of the effects of the Chinese disaster, or republication of an aggrieved statement by a foreign Communist party condemning the Chinese for wreaking grave damage on the Marxist-Leninist cause.

In this campaign, which extends to radio, television and magazines, China is portrayed as a country suffering an Orwellian nightmare. Chilling pronouncements of the Chinese Communist party—about the need to purify the country of the dangers of Beethoven, Tolstoy and similar "bourgeois" influences—are reproduced without comment. Scenes of Red Guards attacking the homes of people suspected of less than fanatical devotion to Mao and assaulting the persons of those wearing lipstick or colorful clothes are described with a sense of horror. "Outrages" and "violations of elementary principles of law"—ransackings, beatings, torture and murder of innocent Chinese citizens—are chronicled in grim detail. Purges, book burnings and terror are dutifully recorded, and the cult of Mao portrayed as a fearful sickness.

One article told the story of a worker who was beaten because he happened to be in a room where the portrait of Mao was enclosed in a cracked frame. Another reproduced a statement by a Red Guard organization that no one in the country was to be trusted except the Central Committee and Mao—and not even the members of the Central Committee were beyond suspicion. A third quoted the winner of a national table-tennis championship attributing his victory to intensive readings of Comrade Mao's works.

China, in short, is presented as a land of totalitarian terror, where all semblance of common sense and normal life have succumbed to the mystifying, crippling, terrifying designs of a leadership which has lost its reason. The ultimate proof of the Chinese leadership's affliction is said to be its betrayal of genuine Marxism-Leninism. Not only does the "great proletarian cultural revolution" have nothing to do with proletarianism, culture or revolution, write Russian correspondents, but it has led to insane attacks, physical as well as ideological, on devoted Communists. Komsomol leaders are listed as "black elements" by ruthless, uncontrolled Red Guards; old-time party officials are humiliated and beaten by youths who accuse them of hiding "capitalistic attitudes," and Red Guard battle groups actually storm, seize and close local party offices. And, warns the Soviet press, the Red Guards are intent on spreading (to the Soviet Union?) their "extreme and dogmatic" theories.

This is the spirit of the China-gone-mad campaign, unique in Soviet history. What do Russians think of it? And of China itself? And of the Sino-Soviet cold war? The questions require somewhat more complex answers than might appear at first sight.

One is struck first when listening to Russians (I have in mind principally members of the Moscow intelligentsia, with whom I spend most of my time in Russia) by the curious circumstance that they think very little either of China or of the momentous change in the official Soviet portrayal of it. Considering the importance of the "Chinese question" in terms of Russia's future, talk about it is remarkably rare in Moscow. One hears occasional jokes about the Chinese, and offhand mention of the "revolutionary" absurdities reported in the newspapers, but almost nothing of the kind of observation, commentary and analysis customary among, say, the New York intelligentsia. China is seldom a subject for casual conversation here.

Why this is so is a matter for speculation. My feeling is that China is rarely mentioned because foreign affairs generally are scarcely discussed. Most Russians are avidly interested in what is happening abroad, especially in the West, and especially in the area of new trends in art and fashion. At the same time, they are only mildly curious, if at all, about foreign affairs, meaning the conduct of politics in other countries and between states. Such matters are rarely discussed in any depth, or with any sense of personal interest or involvement.

An American making his first visit to Russia may easily be misled about this, for he is certain to be questioned—especially when meeting Russians for the first time, and especially

Russians who occupy official positions—about Vietnam. But among themselves Russians rarely mention Vietnam. In the course of five months in Moscow this year and last, I have never heard a serious discussion of the situation there in a Russian home.

Even in the company of Americans they know well, most Russians exhibit only an idle interest in the war. "What are you really doing there"? they are likely to ask, more puzzled and disappointed than curious or angered. "What can you expect to gain by that massive effort? Is it really necessary to fight such a destructive war against peasants? Don't you realize the war is preventing America and Russia from becoming more friendly"?

The only aspect of the Vietnamese war that concerns Russians personally and deeply is the possibility that it may lead to a general conflagration. The thought of a world war, especially war against America, is genuinely terrifying to Russians, who—this cannot be repeated too often—are still suffering, materially and psychologically, from the grievous harm of the last one.

Why Russians are so little interested in foreign affairs generally is also a matter for speculation. One can theorize in terms of Russia's traditional isolation: the isolation imposed by space, climate, inadequate transportation and communications and, above all, by the restrictions of suspicious, dictatorial and slightly xenophobic governments. One feels this isolation—indeed, one is overwhelmed by a sense of being cut off—even today. Unless contact is maintained with the foreign colony in Moscow, one lives in a walled, Russian-Soviet world, where news of the outside is severely limited and interpreted in a manner distinctly unlike that of any political grouping anywhere in the West.

My feeling, however, is that the relative uninterest of Russians in international affairs is best explained by another, although closely related, circumstance: Russians hardly discuss foreign affairs because they hardly discuss politics of any sort, foreign or domestic. The kinds of people who, in the course of a dinner party in New York, would be certain to trade opinions about the pressing domestic and international issues of the day demonstrate, in Russia, scarcely any interest in similar matters.

Russians talk enthusiastically about art, love affairs, the mushroom season, the nature of the soul, the merits of herring and potatoes, the appearance of English boots in a new shoe shop—about everything except governmental affairs. In this most political of nations where, according to Marxist-Leninist theory and the exhortations of all media of public communications, everything from tennis to clothing styles, genetics to whaling, is imbued with political purpose and meaning—the building of Communism, the demonstration of socialism's superiority over capitalism, the proof of Russia's energy, talents and achievements—in this most political of worlds, almost no one talks about politics of any kind. It is paradoxical (or logical?) that the Moscow intelligentsia are preoccupied almost entirely with matters in which they are *personally* involved: their work, their family and friends, their material comfort and intellectual stimulation—their private lives in their intensely private worlds.

Why this is so is once more a matter of speculation. Again, one can seek an explanation in terms of the Russian character: Russians have traditionally valued personal relationships, human contact, involvement in the loves of close ones, more than anything else. And they have never developed a tradition of political involvement, a tradition which evolved as a matter of course in Western countries, where participation in politics (in the kind of political processes that never existed in Russia) was possible and meaningful, to however limited a degree.

But my own feeling is that this phenomenon is best explained by another, although again related, circumstance. Russians are uninterested in politics, I think, because the kinds of information, debate and excitement—the political give-and-take which presupposes a public conflict of parties, points of view and interests—which make the stuff of politics in the West are lacking in the Soviet Union.

Politics are dull when but a single point of view is publicized. They are meaningless to citizens who play no role whatsoever in their determination. (Why is it, I often ask Russians, there is so little interest in the relations between Kosygin and Brezhnev, and in who will succeed them? "What's the use of interest," is the usual answer, "when we're told nothing of what goes on at the top and have no control at all about what happens there? There could be a new leader tomorrow, and we might never know how and why it happened, much less have some say in it. That's why no one cares.") And politics are distasteful when this single point of view is preached relentlessly, every day in every way, as gospel.

"The Moscow intelligentsia are now undergoing a crisis in their attitude toward politics," I was told by a successful novelist, "and this crisis takes the form of complete withdrawal. We are probably the most apolitical—no, antipolitical—people in

Europe. We're sick to death of anything smacking of propaganda or ideology. We want to be left alone, to live our own lives, to be free of any and all 'lines.' This doesn't mean we don't approve of the new leadership (we do) or don't believe in socialism (we do believe in it). But we've been politicized to the point where we don't hear anything that's said about politics and we don't want to hear. That's why it's considered somewhat *mauvais ton* to talk politics with your friends. And that's why we're so politically passive."

It would be wrong, in short, to assume that the Chinese question burns in the minds of the Soviet intelligentsia. But if an outsider steers the conversation toward foreign affairs, China is invariably the predominant subject. The comments then expressed are a widely spread, generally shared set of attitudes which offer some insight into the Soviet state of mind.

At the core of this generally shared set of attitudes are a deep dislike and distrust of China and the Chinese. Comments about both among the Moscow intelligentsia are varied but, in one way or another, they make the same points. The Chinese have gone crazy. They are a menace to themselves and the world. They are to be laughed at and ridiculed and, above all, to be kept under watch and in their place. "Idiocy! Lunacy! Fanaticism! . . . But there are 700-million of them! It's madness, isn't it? It's the coolie mentality. They're miserable types. They're not even *people!*"

A mention of China in Moscow this fall almost unfailingly inspires hostility and contempt. (An exception is provided by the Soviet scientists and engineers who served in China in the nineteen-fifties. They speak fondly of China, and seem unwilling to believe that the country they enjoyed so much has lost its delicate charm. Other Russians explain their attitude in terms of the large salaries they earned while in China, or the great respect and deference accorded them by the Chinese.)

The tone of the intelligentsia's comments ranges from jeering derision—as when they talk of the proposal to change the "go" traffic signal to a "revolutionary" red in China—to sharp belligerence—as when they talk of Chinese divisions poised on, and shooting across the Siberian frontier. The tone is rarely one of sympathy for the Chinese people, for Russians tend to feel that the Chinese are getting what they deserve, that the sad present state of affairs in China is a reflection of the robot-like Chinese national character. Hate is perhaps too strong a word to describe the Russian feeling, but it is not an outrageous exaggeration.

The causes of this animosity toward China are not apparent

from a reading of the official Soviet condemnations of Peking. In these official declarations, the central theme is that China has strayed from the true Marxist-Leninist lines, established by the Soviet Union and the vast majority of foreign Communist parties—indeed, that China is causing grave harm to the building of socialism in all parts of the world and the common fight against American imperialism. Ideology, in other words, is paramount here. It may be that considerations of this sort play a role in the thinking of the Soviet leadership, but in the conversations I have heard, including some by rather highly placed party officials, ideology was never mentioned. Far simpler, more straightforward grievances were at work.

For one thing, Russians are sore because the huge sums of foreign aid pumped into China during the nineteen-fifties—no one here knows the figures, but they are assumed to be very large—were wasted in terms of benefit to Russia. "We didn't expect them to kiss our feet in gratitude," said a young geologist, "but this is really too much. We send them billions, and they kick us in the teeth. What kind of animals are these"?

There is a vague uneasiness in Moscow about foreign aid in general: Many Russians resent the sacrifices required to help underdeveloped countries while their own country is still underdeveloped in living standards. This sense of misgiving, usually mild and unarticulated, can erupt into sharp resentment when China is mentioned: "We went without this, went without that, sent them all kinds of valuable equipment and specialists that were desperately needed here—and those Chinese bastards repay us with vicious attacks that are far worse than anything from the West. The Voice of America, for example, is a true and blue pro-Soviet organ compared with Radio Peking."

Russians are sore also because they see nothing but jealousy and fanaticism in the motives for China's attacks. "What do they have against us, those wild men? What, really? Only that we live better than they do, and want to live still better. Well, we know that Westerners live better than we do, and we don't attack them for that. The Chinese are simply insanely jealous and fanatic; they want the rest of the world, and especially us, to become drones like them. They won't be happy unless everyone dresses in cotton uniforms and eats boiled rice.

"Well, that's not the Russian style of life, or the Russian idea of Communism. We're on the way to living decently here at last, and the Chinese couldn't forgive us for that. To hell with their obsession with revolution and sacrifice; Russians have made enough sacrifices for one century."

To Russians, who are preoccupied now not at all with sacrifice, revolution, or class or national struggle, but with improving their food, clothing and living quarters, the Chinese interpretation of Marxism-Leninism is anathema. "Book burning, purges, denunciations, terror and fear—it's all too reminiscent of the Stalin period," said an elderly librarian. "Mind you, I think the Chinese are far worse: Even in the darkest days of the thirties, no one here tried to stop women from wearing lipstick or trying to dress decently. No one wanted to eradicate all individuality, maybe because we're Russians and not Chinese. Still, what's happening now in China is too close to our own past for comfort. We've lived through that kind of hell, and that's why it repels us. That's why we want to stay as far away from China as we can."

Another experience in the recent Soviet past serves to feed Russians' hostility against China: World War II, which is still the most traumatic episode in the lives of most Russians. The Chinese theory (as it is known in Moscow) that a nuclear conflagration which would cause millions of deaths would not be a catastrophe for world history shocks and appalls every Russian over 25. "Of all the Chinese madness, this is the worst," one said. "When they say that a general war would not be terrible for the world because socialism would emerge with the greatest number of survivors and therefore victorious, that is sheer horror for Russians. We know what millions of casualties mean; 20 million of us were killed 20 years ago. I don't mind what the Chinese do to themselves, but this world war concerns *us*. What's more, I think they want to start the next war *against* us; they're already shooting across our borders. God save us from such people!"

The Chinese attitude toward sacrifice and war is occasionally the subject for satire in Moscow. A wildly funny underground song popular last year, for example, described two simple Russian workmen during a smoke break at their factory, explaining why, in spite of all the hardships of life, they want to continue living. But war is not usually a laughing matter for Russians.

These are major items on the Russians' bill of particulars against the Chinese. (I have not mentioned the racial factor because it is difficult to appraise. It is true than strong racial feelings against African students have emerged in Moscow in recent years: Taxi drivers, barbers and salesgirls are likely to tell one, gratuitously, why they "can't stand those disgusting blacks." On the other hand, there seems to be no racial prejudice whatsoever against Asians—Mongolians, Uzbeks, Tatars and others—who are Soviet citizens. One sometimes hears disparaging remarks against the Chinese, cast in terms of those "little yellow coolies," but I do not think racial prejudice is a significant cause of Russian antagonism toward China.)

But there is a deeper, more general cause of Russian dislike for China which, although Russians themselves do not speak of it, seems to me to explain the Russian attitude more meaningfully than the sum of the particular grievances. Russians, and especially the Russian intelligentsia, want to be Western—that is to say, their sympathies, interests and inclinations are occidental, not oriental. They want Russia to be associated with Europe, not Asia.

This is not at all a new phenomenon. Since even before Peter the Great, Russians who had any education at all have looked westward, read Western literature, copied Western styles and ideas. They have felt, and feel now, very little affinity with the East and a vast attraction to the West. They have believed, and believe now, that the question of whether Russia is a European or an Asian nation is academic: Russia is Western and must become more so.

Consciously or unconsciously, therefore, Russians feel that the period of close cooperation with China was an aberration, an unnatural alliance that was pulling Russia the wrong way. Their uneasiness with their Chinese comrades was all the stronger, of course, precisely because Russia has always been subject to Eastern as well as Western influences and now, again, they felt a real danger that the Eastern wind would prevail. They were apprehensive, when China was Russia's official sister country, about intimate contacts with a culture that was alien and, in terms of Russia's destiny, regressive. If Communism meant that Russia was to be closely allied with agrarian, underdeveloped Asia and estranged from liberal, literate Europe, there was something wrong with Communism. In tone, style, manners, taste, customs, habits, standards of behavior and living, Russia should be more like France, England and America, not like China.

This is why, I think, there is a deep distaste for China in Moscow and relief that the long romance with it has (permanently, Russians hope) ended. This is why there were never, even during the period of closest official cooperation, strong feelings of comradeship with or sympathy for China, or pride in the alliance. (In 1959, well before Russians suspected the alliance might crack, Chinese students in Moscow were among the most popular subjects for jokes. Russians mocked them, often maliciously, because they were methodical and industrious, frugal, humorless, disciplined, ascetic—because they never relaxed, splurged or got drunk; they were not like *us*. I have not heard similar jokes about Westerners.) This is why there is an almost unanimous feeling that it is *natural* that China and Russia be separated—even estranged.

And this is why Russians are now pleased to be saying something like this: "We do not want war, with the Chinese or anyone else, but it has somehow become clear in the last year or two that, if we fight anyone, it's not going to be America, but China. And thank God! If there is one people with whom we want to be close, it's the Americans. If there's one people we can't stomach at the moment, it's the Chinese. The only thing to be said for them is that they may force us into an alliance with America again, as Hitler did in World War II. That is worth hoping for."

There is no sorrow in Moscow that the Sino-Soviet axis has collapsed, and no feeling of loss over the damage to international proletarianism. On the contrary, Russians never cared for international proletarianism—not, anyway, with the Chinese.

There was no sure way of predicting the Sino-Soviet split, but an acquaintance with the intellectual and emotional instincts of the Moscow intelligentsia makes one fairly confident that friendship between the two countries will not soon be re-established, at least from the Russian side. Russians yearn for closer contact with the West and dissociation from the cultural and ideological influences represented by China. These are deep, historically conditioned instincts which the Russians feel in their bones.

So much for the intelligentsia. What does the Russian worker feel? "What does Ivan Ivanovich think about China"? reflected an intense young historian. "Let me put it this way, so you'll understand: If the party finally decides to break fully with China—'To hell with China, comrades, China is not our friend; we've wiped Chinese spit off our faces long enough; there's a point when even Russians lose their patience'—if the party finally decides to announce openly that China is really our enemy, and our most dangerous one, then you will hear a roar of approval all over this country, from Brest to Vladivostok, such as you haven't heard since Berlin fell. The Russian people will stand up to a man, to the last man, and shout themselves hoarse. The masses will bless the party because the masses can't stand the Chinese. It will be the most popular decision taken here in a long, long time.

My friend, it seemed to me, was somewhat carried away. Roars of approval about anything other than a sudden, dramatic improvement in living standards are not likely to be heard soon in Russia, certainly not about anything political. But I think the young historian did capture the essence of the popular Soviet attitude toward China.

Russians do not like China. They feel that the Chinese are more natural enemies than natural friends. They would welcome a complete break, especially if it were accompanied by further *rapprochement* with the West.

A saleswoman in a new department store put the working-class attitude more simply and perhaps more representatively: "The Chinese are crazy. Why did we ever get mixed up with them in the first place? We've got to watch them. They can make fanatics and robots of themselves if they like, but the thing is, those little yellow people want to make fanatics and robots of *us*."

> The westerner has always exhibited a feeling of superiority towards the Chinese—a contempt which in the words of one writer "is sometimes kindly but never tolerant." This led him at times to err in his estimations of Chinese acuity and strength. In the Boxer Rebellion, when the western powers prepared to use an expeditionary force to rescue their legations in Peking from the siege, this was a characteristic element in the decisions of the leaders:

> Since they dropped anchor off Taku, the commanders of the foreign squadrons had done little save discuss the action to be taken if the situation in Peking got out of control. It had occurred to none of them . . . that there was any alternative to an immediate dash to Peking with the strongest forces they could scrape together. They discerned no great hazards in the operation; the officers took their full-dress uniforms with them. They were acting on what The Spectator, on the day before they set out, called the assumption that any force of Europeans however small can beat any force of Chinamen however large. (P. Fleming, *The Siege at Peking*)

> What is particularly noteworthy about this is its contemporaneous flavor. The feeling, for the most part unconsciously expressed, that orientals in accordance with their size must be weaker and no match for the westerner was held during the Second World War just as it seemed to characterize the beliefs of American soldiers in the Korean War and presently in the U.S. war in Vietnam.

When the Boxers surprised their European foes by their

courage, there were westerners who reversed their opinions to the opposite but equally irrelevant extreme, concluding that the Chinese were a shrewd and invincible people. There seems to be a similarly swift pendulum response that characterizes American attitudes towards China today. If the Chinese are not believed to be easily vanquished then they are attributed with inscrutability and omnipotence. An overestimation not validated in reality turns into a mystically powerful force. Though this is by no means the only reaction to China's position in the contemporary world, it is one of frequent enough expression to warrant attention.

At a time when the U.S. is preparing to build a defense system against nuclear attack by China, it can only be observed that fundamental U.S. policy has not changed, despite prognostications to the contrary. The following selections provide the official policy positions of the U.S. and China with respect to each other's intentions. An official memorandum on China policy was issued to all U.S. diplomatic missions abroad by the U.S. Department of State in August 1958. The first selection below consists of excerpts from the pamphlet later published of this document. The second selection (pp. 428-433) is an analysis of the strains and stresses of U.S. policy by Hans Morgenthau, which is followed by excerpts from a speech by President Johnson made in July 1966 (pp. 434-437). And Premier Chou En-lai presents a succinct summary of China's official policy in selection 8.

America's Policy Toward the Chinese People
August 11, 1958*

U.S. DEPT. OF STATE

POLICY TOWARDS Communist China has been an important issue since the Communists came to power there, and it is of critical significance to the United States and the Free World today. In the United States the issue is a very real one to the vast majority of the people. As a result of Korean and Chinese Communist aggression in Korea, the United States suffered 142,000 casualties, bringing tragedy to communities all over the country. Nevertheless, despite the emotions thus engendered and the abhorrence of the American people for the

* AMERICA'S POLICY TOWARD THE CHINESE PEOPLE, (n.p.,n.d.) pp. 1-9.

brutality and utter lack of morality of Communist systems, the policy of the United States Government towards China has necessarily been based on objective considerations of national interest. It also reflects a continuing appraisal of all available facts.

Basically the United States policy of not extending diplomatic recognition to the Communist regime in China proceeds from the conviction that such recognition would produce no tangible benefits to the United States or to the Free World as a whole and would be of material assistance to Chinese Communist attempts to extend Communist dominion throughout Asia. It is not an "inflexible" policy which cannot be altered to meet changed conditions. If the situation in the Far East were so to change in its basic elements as to call for a radically different evaluation of the threat Chinese Communist policies pose to United States and Free World security interests, the United States would of course readjust its present policies. However, the course of events in the Far East since the establishment of the Chinese Communist regime in 1949 has thus far confirmed the United States view that its interests and those of the Free World are best served by withholding diplomatic recognition from the regime in Peiping.

The basic considerations on which United States policy toward China rests are twofold. First, the Soviet bloc, of which Communist China is an important part, is engaged in a long-range struggle to destroy the way of life of the free countries of the world and bring about the global dominion of Communism. The Chinese Communist regime has made no secret of its fundamental hostility to the United States and the Free World as a whole nor of its avowed intention to effect their downfall. Today its defiance of and attacks on the non-Communist world have reached a level of intensity that has not been witnessed since the Korean War. The second basic factor is that East Asia is peculiarly vulnerable to the Communist offensive because of the proximity of the free countries of that area to Communist China, the inexperience in self-government of those which have recently won their independence, their suspicions of the West inherited from their colonial past, and the social, political and economic changes which inevitably accompany their drive toward modernization.

The Chinese Communists see the victory of Communism in Asia as inevitable; and now that they control the vast population and territory of mainland China they are utilizing the advantages these give to encompass their ends. Chinese Communist leaders have shown by their words and acts that they are not primarily interested in promoting the welfare of their people while living at peace with their neighbors. Their primary purpose is to extend the Communist revolution beyond their borders to the rest of Asia and thence to the rest of the world. . . .

United States policy in Asia, as elsewhere in the world, is to promote the domestic welfare and to strengthen the independence of free nations. Because of the proximity of many Asian nations to mainland China and the disparity in size and power between them and Communist China, this can be done only if the Communist threat is neutralized. The first need of United States policy in the Far East is to deter Communist aggression, else the free nations would be in grave danger of succumbing to Communist pressures before they had gathered the strength with which to resist them. The United States has sought to accomplish this by military assistance to the nations directly in the path of Chinese Communist expansion—Korea, Taiwan, and Vietnam—and by a system of mutual defense arrangements with other nations of the area. We have been successful in this effort and since 1954 the Chinese Communists have not been able to make further gains through the open use of military force. . . .

In the effort to block Peiping's attempts to extend Communist rule in Asia the withholding of diplomatic recognition is an important factor. The extension of diplomatic recognition by a great power normally carries with it not only increased access to international councils but enhanced international standing and prestige as well. Denial of recognition on the other hand is a positive handicap to the regime affected and one which makes it that much the more difficult for it to pursue its foreign policies with success. One basic purpose of United States non-recognition of Communist China is to deny it these advantages and to that extent limit its ability to threaten the security of the area.

In the case of China there are special considerations which influence United States policy with regard to recognition. For one thing, although the Chinese Communists have seized the preponderant bulk of China, they have not completed their conquest of the country. The generally recognized legitimate government of China continues to exist and in Taiwan is steadily developing its political, economic and military strength. The government of the Republic of China controls the strategic island of Taiwan and through its possession of a sizable military force—one of the largest on the side of the Free World in Asia—presents a significant deterrent to renewed

Chinese Communist aggression. Recognition of Communist China by the United States would seriously cripple, if not destroy altogether, that government. On the other hand, continued United States recognition and support of the Republic of China enables it to challenge the claim of the Chinese Communists to represent the Chinese people and keeps alive the hopes of those Chinese who are determined eventually to free their country of Communist rule. . . .

Another special consideration in the case of China is that large and influential "overseas" Chinese communities exist in most of the countries of Southeast Asia.

The efforts of these countries to build healthy free societies and to develop their economies would be seriously retarded if these communities were to fall under the sway of the Chinese Communists; and a grave threat of Communist subversion through those overseas communities would arise. Recognition of Communist China by the United States and the decline in the fortunes of the Republic of China which would inevitably result, would have such a profound psychological effect on the overseas Chinese that it would make inevitable the transfer of the loyalties of large numbers to the Communist side. This in turn would undermine the ability of the host countries to resist the pressures tending to promote the expansion of Chinese Communist influence and power.

Still another factor which must be considered in the case of China is the effect which recognition of the Communist regime would have on the United Nations. Recognition of Peiping by the United States would inevitably lead to the seating of Peiping in that body. In the view of the United States this would vitiate, if not destroy, the United Nations as an instrument for the maintenance of international peace. The Korean War was the first and most important effort to halt aggression through collective action in the United Nations. For Communist China, one of the parties against which the effort of the United Nations was directed, to be seated in the United Nations while still unpurged of its aggression and defying the will of the United Nations in Korea, would amount to a confession of failure on the part of the United Nations and would greatly reduce the prospects for future successful action by the United Nations against aggression. Moreover, the Republic of China is a charter member in good standing of the United Nations and its representatives there have contributed importantly to the constructive work of that organization. If the representatives of the Chinese Communist regime were to be seated in their place and given China's veto in the

Security Council, the ability of that body in the future to discharge the responsibility it has under the charter for the maintaining international peace and security would be seriously impaired.

Those who advocate recognition of the Chinese Communists often assume that by the standards of international law applied to such cases the Peiping regime is "entitled" to diplomatic recognition. In the view of the United States diplomatic recognition is a privilege and not a right. Moreover, the United States considers that diplomatic recognition is an instrument of national policy which it is both its right and its duty to use in the enlightened self-interest of the nation. However, there is reason to doubt that even by the tests often cited in international law the Chinese Communist regime qualifies for diplomatic recognition. It does not rule all China, and there is a substantial force in being which contests its claim to do so. The Chinese Communist Party which holds mainland China in its grip is a tiny minority comprising less than two percent of the Chinese people, and the regimentation, brutal repression, and forced sacrifices that have characterized its rule have resulted in extensive popular unrest. To paraphrase Thomas Jefferson's dictum, this regime certainly does not represent "the will of the populace, substantially declared." Finally, it has shown no intention to honor its international obligations. One of its first acts was to abrogate the treaties of the Republic of China except those it chose to continue. On assuming power it carried out a virtual confiscation without compensation of the properties of foreign nationals, including immense British investments notwithstanding the United Kingdom's prompt recognition of it. It has failed to honor various commitments entered into since, including various provisions of the Korean Armistice and the Geneva Accord on Viet-nam and Laos as well as the "agreed" announcement of September, 1955, by which it pledged itself to permit all Americans and China to return home "expeditiously."

The United States policy toward recognition of Communist China is then based on a carefully considered judgment of the nationalist interest. Non-recognition of Peiping coupled with continued recognition and support of the Republic of China facilitates the accomplishment of United States policy objectives in the Far East. Recognition of Peiping would seriously hinder accomplishment of these objectives and would facilitate the advance of Communist power in Asia.

In the process of determining its policy toward China the United States has taken into account the various statements and arguments advanced by proponents of extending diplomatic recognition to Peiping. One of the most commonly advanced reasons for recognition is that reality must be "recognized" and 600 million people cannot be "ignored." While superficially appealing both statements themselves overlook the realities of the situation. United States policy is, of course, based on full appreciation of the fact that the Chinese Communist regime is currently in control of mainland China. However, it is not necessary to have diplomatic relations with a regime in order to deal with it. Without extending diplomatic recognition the United States has participated in extended negotiations with Chinese Communist representatives, in the Korean and Indochina armistice negotiations and more recently in the ambassadorial talks in Geneva. Similarly, United States policy in no sense "ignores" the existence and the aspirations of the Chinese people. Its attitude toward the people of China remains what it historically has been, one of friendship and sympathetic understanding. It is nonetheless clear that our friendship for the Chinese people must not be permitted to blind us to the threat to our security which the Communist regime in China now presents. Moreover, the United States is convinced that the Chinese Communist regime does not represent the true will or aspirations of the Chinese people and that our policy of withholding recognition from it is in actuality in their ultimate interest.

It is sometimes contended that by recognition of Communist China it would be possible to exert leverage on the Peiping regime which might ultimately be successful in weakening or even breaking the bond with Moscow. Unfortunately, there is no evidence to support this belief and there are important reasons why it is unlikely; the alliance between Moscow and Peiping is one of long standing; it traces its origin to the very founding of the Chinese Communist Party in 1921, in which representatives of the Comintern played an important role.

It is based on a common ideology and on mutually-held objectives with respect to the non-Communist world. All recent evidence points to the closeness of the tie between the Chinese Communists and the USSR rather than in the other direction. . . .

Furthermore, the alliance with the USSR has a special importance for the Chinese Communists since it provides them with a dependable source of arms and military supplies. The Chinese Communist leaders, including Mao Tse-tung himself, came to power through their command of military force. They are therefore keenly conscious of the importance of military force to keep themselves in power against domestic and external opposition and to achieve the goals of their foreign policy. It is scarcely credible that they would dare risk any course of action which could lead to loss of their source of military supplies. For this reason alone, it would seem unrealistic to believe that recognition of Peiping by the United States or any other leading nation would have the effect of tempting the Chinese Communists to play a "Titoist" role.

In fact the opposite is quite likely to be the result. Were the United States to grant diplomatic recognition to Peiping—with all that this would entail by way of enhanced international prestige—its leaders would most likely feel confirmed in the correctness of their policies and the advantages of continued close cooperation with Moscow.

It is often alleged that recognition of Communist China is a necessary step in expanding trade relations with that country. For the United States this is of course not a consideration, since the United States embargoes trade with Peiping under the Trading with the Enemy Act as a result of the Korean War. But even for countries which do desire to expand trade with mainland China, the facts do not support the contention that trade is dependent on recognition. To the contrary, Great Britain, which recognized Communist China in 1950, has found that she buys more goods from Communist China than Communist China buys from her. West Germany on the other hand does not recognize Peiping and enjoys a favorable trade balance with the mainland China. In any case, trade opportunities with Communist China are severely limited by a shortage of foreign exchange which is likely to persist for many years to come. Moreover, such trade would always be at the mercy of Communist policies. Peiping uses trade as a means of exerting pressure on the trading partner whenever it deems this to be expedient. . . .

An argument often heard is that the Chinese Communists are here "to stay;" that they will have to be recognized sooner or later; and that it would be the course of wisdom to bow to the inevitable now rather than be forced to do so ungracefully at a later date. It is true that there is no reason to believe that the Chinese Communist regime is on the verge of collapse; but there is equally no reason to accept its present rule in mainland China as permanent. In fact, unmistakable signs of dissatisfaction and unrest in Communist China have appeared in the "ideological remoulding" and the mass campaign against "rightists" which have been in progress during the past year. Dictatorships often create an illusion of permanence from the very fact that they suppress and still all opposition and that of the Chinese Communists is no exception to this rule. The United States holds the view that Communism's rule in China is not permanent and that it one day will pass. By withholding diplomatic recognition from Peiping it seeks to hasten that passing.

In public discussions of China policy one of the proposals that has attracted widest attention is that known as the "Two Chinas Solution." Briefly, advocates of this arrangement propose that the Chinese Communist regime be recognized as the government of mainland China while the government at Taipei remains as the legal government of Taiwan. They argue that this approach to the Chinese problem has the merit of granting the Communists only what they already control while retaining for the Free World the militarily strategic bastion of Taiwan. However, it overlooks or ignores certain facts of basic importance. The Republic of China would not accept any diminution of its sovereignty over China and could be expected to resist such an arrangement with all the means at its disposal. If a "Two Chinas Solution" were to be forcefully imposed against its will, that government's effectiveness as a loyal ally to the Free World cause would be destroyed. Peiping too would reject such an arrangement. In fact over the past year Chinese Communist propaganda has repeatedly and stridently denounced the "Two Chinas" concept and, ironically, has been accusing the United States government of attempting to put it into effect. Peiping attaches great importance to the eventual acquisition of Taiwan and has consistently reserved what it calls its "right" to seize Taiwan by force if other means fail. There is no prospect that it would ever acquiesce in any arrangement which would lead to the permanent detachment of Taiwan from China. . . .

It is sometimes said that non-recognition of Peiping tends to martyrize the Chinese Communists, thereby enabling them to pose, especially before Asian neutralists, as an innocent and injured party. It would be impossible to deny that there is some truth in this. But this disadvantage is far outweighed by the opposite course. It is surely better that some neutralists, who are either unable or unwilling to comprehend the threat inherent in Chinese Communist policies, mistakenly consider Peiping unjustly treated than that the allies of the United States in Asia, who are the first line of defense against Chinese Communist expansion, should be confused and demoralized by what to them could only appear to be a betrayal of the common sense. . . .

Contradictions in U. S. China Policy*

HANS MORGENTHAU

IN ORDER TO understand the policy of the United States toward China it is necessary to ask, first, what has been the situation in China which led to the present Communist regime and, second, what are the basic assumptions upon which the China policy of the United States has been based.

The domestic history of China has been for three centuries a story of civil war, of abortive or successful revolution. Most reigns during that period were established not through constitutional succession to the throne but through some form of violence. Sun Yat-sen's overthrow of the Manchu dynasty in 1911 was his eleventh attempt at revolution since 1895, yet in 1913 Sun Yat-sen as head of the Kuomintang, or Nationalist party, started an unsuccessful revolution against the very republic he had founded.

There is no space here to recount all the revolts, revolutions and civil wars that have followed one against the other virtually without interruption since the first World War. After a long period of anarchy during which the central government was a mere shadow without effective powers, popular loyalty centered from 1927 onward in the Kuomintang under Chiang Kai-shek on the one hand and in the Communists under Mao Tse-tung on the other. All the Japanese imperialism threatening Communists and Nationalists alike brought about the temporary unification of the country under Chiang Kai-shek. It is hardly surprising that with the removal of that threat at the end of the second World War the old cleavage should recur with both sides trying to fill the power vacuum left by the defeated Japanese.

Faced with the inevitability of civil war between the Chinese Communists and Nationalists the United States had to ask itself which side it wanted the victory to fall to in view of the American national interest in seeing the balance of power in Asia maintained. Since the Communists, if they should win control of all of China, were most likely to throw the weight of China to the side of the Soviet Union, the United States was bound

* In FOUNDATIONS OF U.S. CHINA POLICY, edited by Urban G. Whitaker, a transcript of a radio program produced by Pacifica Foundation (Berkeley, California, January 10, 1959), pp. 98–105. By permission of Pacifica Foundation.

to wish for the triumph of the Nationalists. The next question was what it could do to insure the victory of the Nationalists. As long as the war against Japan was in progress we did, and perhaps could do, but little to aid effectively those whom we wanted to control China when the war was over.

As elsewhere, we were only too ready to deceive ourselves about the nature of Communism and to believe that the Communists, like ourselves, had only one ultimate aim, the military defeat of the Axis powers. As elsewhere, we refused to concern ourselves with preparing a new balance of power upon which a stable postwar world was to be built of and for which the groundwork had to be laid while the war was still in progress. We wanted total victory through unconditional surrender and nothing more. When the victory was won, we gave military support to the Kuomintang. Yet then it was too late for the kind of military support we were willing and able to give to be effective in the struggle with Communism.

If the Chinese Communists had been nothing but the stooges of the Kremlin doing the bidding of their masters after the model of the Greek guerrillas or the Communists of North Korea and Eastern Europe, a large-scale police action supported by American arms and advice might have crushed them; but if there existed in China, as there actually did, a revolutionary situation derived from long-smouldering, widespread popular discontent against the inefficiency and corruption of the Nationalist regime, no mere aid in repression, but, short of all-out intervention, only social and political reform could forestall the overthrow of the Nationalists by the people. The Communists were able to win the politically conscious masses of the Chinese people to their side by promising, and in some measure carrying through, the social and political reforms the people demanded.

It is at this point that the confusion over the real issue obscured the thinking and frustrated the policies of the United States. When it became obvious that the Nationalist regime was unable to cope with the revolutionary situation even if supported by American arms and advice, only two courses which General Wedemeyer's report of 1947 clearly envisaged were logically open to American policy. One was military intervention on such a scale as to be sufficient not only to crush the Communist armies but also to keep discontent permanently in check. Military intervention of this kind would have entailed military and political commitments of incalculable magnitude. This course of action was rejected by the framers of our foreign policy on the advice, among others, of the then Secretary of State, George Marshall.

Our other course of action was predicated on the assumption that the triumph of the Communist revolution in China was inevitable. It would then have been incumbent upon American policy to reconcile itself to the inevitable as policy, being the art of the possible, frequently must, and to exploit whatever potentialities there were for the promotion of American interests for, while Chinese Communism is the ideological ally of Moscow, its rise to power owes little to Russia nor will it need to rely on Russian support to maintain itself in power.

This fundamental difference between Chinese Communism and the Communist regimes of Eastern Europe, which would not have come to power nor could have stayed in power without Russian support, allows the Communist government of China a freedom of action in international affairs which the Communist governments of Eastern Europe almost completely lack. Consequently, the Communist government of China can if it chooses pursue a course in foreign policy which is determined not by the interests of the Soviet Union expressed in orders from Moscow, but by the traditional interests of China. So the interests may or may not coincide with the interests of the Soviet Union and Chinese and Russian policies may or may not run parallel.

It must be remembered that the traditional objectives of Russia in the Far East have more often than not been at odds with the traditional objectives of China. Furthermore, and more importantly, the Soviet Union cannot look with equanimity at the economic and military development of Communist China for if Communist China should add to its enormous superiority in manpower the achievements of modern technology under the firm political direction of the Chinese Communist party, it would then become of necessity the most powerful nation on earth, overshadowing by far the Soviet Union. The rulers of the Kremlin, considering their precarious situation at home and their uncertain relations with the satellites of Eastern Europe, must also fear and probably already have reason to fear the influence which China can exert in the struggle for power within the ruling group of the Soviet Union and the struggle for a certain measure of independence which the satellite nations are waging against Moscow. Whether there will be further coincidence or divergence of Russian or Chinese interests and policies will depend in good measure upon the policies of the non-Communist nations.

There was the chance for the United States to pursue a policy which, although difficult to explain to the general public and necessarily devoid of spectacular short-run successes, offered the only chance, granted the inevitability of the Communist dominion of China, to further the traditional American interests in the maintenance of the balance of power in Asia. The United States chose neither of the two courses open to it or, rather, it chose both of them, pursuing them sometimes simultaneously, sometimes alternately, but always half-heartedly and without consistency.

During the civil war we intervened on the side of the Nationalists but limited our commitments in material and men so strictly as to preclude any chance of success. Simultaneously, we tried to bring about a coalition between the Nationalists and Communists which, if it had succeeded, would, of necessity, have led to the absorption of the former by the latter.

General Marshall's attempt in 1946 to end the civil war by forming a coalition government of Communists and Nationalists partook of the same underestimation of Nationalist weakness which underlay all of American policy in the immediate postwar years and compounded it by misunderstanding the character of Chinese Communism. It was grounded in two false assumptions. One was that the Chinese Communists were really agrarian reformers at heart using Marxist slogans without believing them. The other was a misplaced faith in the Nationalist regime as an efficient and reliable machine of government. Actually it had become impossible at that stage to do business with Chiang Kai-shek with any expectation of future efficient and honest performance, and it was to misunderstand completely the nature of Communism, as it manifests itself in China and elsewhere, to disregard its necessary aspirations for total power as a means to realize the truth of Marxism.

After the end of the civil war we continued this essentially contradictory and indecisive policy. Under the impact of the Chinese intervention in the Korean war and influenced by domestic politics, we drifted into a policy of counterrevolution, *per se*. That is to say, we have refused to recognize the Communist regime as a legitimate government of China and have denied its right to represent China in the United Nations. On the other hand, we have continued to recognize the Chiang Kai-shek regime of Formosa as the only authentic voice of all China. We have given it political, economic, moral and military support, assuring its very existence through the commitment of the armed forces of the United States. We have countenanced small scale operations of the Chiang Kai-shek forces against the Chinese mainland and we have given our active military support to a Nationalist defense of the offshore islands.

The result of this policy has been inconclusive in terms of the very assumptions upon which that policy is based. For while that policy has strengthened the Nationalist forces on Formosa, that policy being the very precondition for their survival, it has done virtually nothing to weaken the Communist domination of the Chinese mainland.

Thus, on the one hand, we refuse to recognize that the Chinese Communists are here to stay, and on the other hand, we have done nothing to dislodge that regime by counterrevolutionary measures. We have done nothing effective because there is nothing we can do short of an all-out war against China which we fear will degenerate into an all-out world war destroying us and our enemies.

This policy has had one positive result: it has kept Formosa out of the hands of the Communists. It has had two major negative results: it has isolated us completely from our allies and it has lost us the support of public opinion throughout the world. The Chinese Communists have not been slow to exploit the difficult position in which the United States finds itself today by virtue of its own policy.

While the United States has tried to extricate itself from the impasse of its Far Eastern policy, the Chinese Communists have refused to lend a helping hand. From their point of view it is much more advantageous to let the United States remain entangled in a web of self-created contradictions, unable to advance or retreat, than to co-operate with the United States in the search for a compromise settlement. The Chinese Communists are aware of the difficult American position and they also know that time is on their side, for the balance of military power is bound to be more and more towards the Chinese side. Communist China will become an independent military factor in world politics, and the world-wide opposition to American policy towards China will grow stronger as America's military position grows weaker.

Thus, paradoxically enough, the main issue is today no longer whether or not the United States wants to recognize Communist China. The issue is, rather, whether Communist Chine wants to be recognized by the United States, and obviously it does not want to be recognized if it is to pay the price of recognizing the *status quo* in the Formosa Straits.

What is the rationale of the Far Eastern policy of the United States which has led to such unfortunate results? That policy is based upon two fundamental assumptions. First, the use of force as an instrument of national policy cannot be countenanced anywhere in the world and, second, the policy of containment can be successfully applied to the Far East. The first assumption derives from the fear that the use of violence, however limited, may leap by stages to the use of nuclear weapons and to the destruction of civilization itself. A policy derived from this assumption, however, requires the existence of a *status quo* which is reasonably acceptable to all concerned and therefore does not offer an incentive to change it by violent means. This condition does not prevail at present in the Far East. The other assumption holds that the threat that confronts us around the world is primarily military in nature and therefore must be countered primarily by military means. The policy of military containment, eminently successful in Europe where it originated, must then be applied around the world. (More particularly to the Middle East than the Far East, and it may be expected there to have the same beneficial results it had in Europe.) The correctness of this assumption is subject to very serious doubt. What threatens us in Asia is not primarily military aggression but political aggression and, more particularly, a slow and insidious shift of the allegiance of hundreds of millions of people to Russian and Chinese Communism. To try to stem this tide by military means is likely not only to be useless but also to be self-defeating. Furthermore, even if the threat emanating from Communist China were primarily of a military nature, our military policy in the Far East would be inadequate.

The balance of military power between Communist China and the United States is quite different from that between the United States and the Soviet Union in Europe. The Soviet Union has thus far been deterred by the retaliatory nuclear power of the United States, but could China, with its particular tactics, have been so deterred? In terms of conventional war a strong China is as superior to Southeast Asia as is the United States to Central America. Southeast Asia has been the traditional sphere of influence of a strong China. In order to deny that region to China peripheral military measures will not suffice. Whoever wants to contain a strong China must strike at the center of that power. We have never been willing, and for good reasons, to contemplate such a strike. Thus the United States has been caught in a contradiction between what it wants to achieve and the measures it is willing and able to apply in order to achieve it. Only a radical revision of the very assumptions upon which its China policy is based will extricate it from that contradiction.

Four Essentials for Peace in Asia
(July 12, 1965)

Address by President Johnson*

. . . NOWHERE ARE THE stakes higher than in Asia. So I want to talk to you tonight about Asia and about peace in Asia. Asia is now the crucial arena of man's striving for independence and order, and for life itself.

This is true because three out of every five people in all this world live in Asia tonight. This is true because hundreds of millions of them exist on less than 25 cents a day.

This is true because Communists in Asia tonight still believe in force in order to achieve their Communist goals.

So if enduring peace can ever come to Asia, all mankind will benefit. But if peace fails there, nowhere else will our achievements really be secure.

By peace in Asia I do not mean simply the absence of armed hostilities. For wherever men hunger and hate, there can really be no peace.

I do not mean the peace of conquest. For humiliation can be the seedbed of war.

I do not mean simply the peace of the conference table. For peace is not really written merely in the words of treaties, but peace is the day-by-day work of builders.

The peace we seek in Asia is a peace of conciliation between Communist states and their non-Communist neighbors, between rich nations and poor, between small nations and large, between men whose skins are brown and black and yellow and white, between Hindus and Moslems and Buddhists and Christians.

It is a peace that can only be sustained through the durable bonds of peace: through international trade, through the free flow of people and ideas, through full participation by all nations in an international community under law, and through a common dedication to the great task of human progress and economic development.

* Made from the White House on nationwide radio and television to the American Alumni Council on July 12 (White House press release), reprinted in THE DEPARTMENT OF STATE BULLETIN, Vol. LV, No. 1414, August 1, 1966, pp. 158–162, excerpts.

U.S. OBLIGATIONS IN ASIA

Is such a peace possible?

With all my heart I believe it is. We are not there yet. We have a long way to journey. But the foundations for such a peace in Asia are being laid tonight as never before. They must be built on these essentials:

First is the determination of the United States to meet our obligations in Asia as a Pacific power.

You have heard arguments the other way. They are built on the old belief that "East is East, and West is West, and never the twain shall meet."

—that we have no business but business interests in Asia;

—that Europe, not the Far East, is really our proper sphere of interest;

—that our commitments in Asia are not worth the resources they require;

—that the ocean is vast, the cultures alien, the languages strange, and the races different;

—that these really are not our kind of people.

But all of these arguments have been thoroughly tested. All of them, I think, really have been found wanting.

They do not stand the test of geography because we are bounded not by one but by two oceans. Whether by aircraft or ship, by satellite or missile, the Pacific is as crossable as the Atlantic.

They do not stand the test of common sense. The economic network of this shrinking globe is too intertwined, the basic hopes of men are too interrelated, the possibility of common disaster is too real for us to ever ignore threats to peace in Asia.

They do not stand the test of human concern, either. The people of Asia do matter. We share with them many things in common. We are all persons. We are all human beings.

And they do not stand the test of reality, either. Asia is no longer sitting outside the door of the 20th century. She is here, in the same world with all of us, to be either our partner or our problem.

Americans entered this century believing that our own security had no foundation outside our own continent. Twice we mistook our sheltered position for safety. Twice we were dead wrong.

If we are wise now, we will not repeat our mistakes of the past. We will not retreat from the obligations of freedom and security in Asia.

MAKING AGGRESSION A "LOSING GAME"

The second essential for peace in Asia is this: to prove to aggressive nations that the use of force to conquer others is a losing game.

There is no more difficult task, really, in a world of revolutionary change, where the rewards of conquest tempt ambitious appetites. . . .

BUILDING ASIA'S ECONOMIC PROGRESS

The third essential is the building of political and economic strength among the nations of free Asia.

For years they have been working at that task. And the untold story of 1966 is the story of what free Asians have done for themselves, and with the help of others, while South Viet-Nam and her allies have been busy holding aggression at bay.

Many of you can recall our faith in the future of Europe at the end of World War II, when we began the Marshall Plan. We backed that faith with all the aid and compassion we could muster.

Our faith in Asia at this time is just as great. And that faith is backed by judgment and reason. For if we stand firm in Viet-Nam against military conquest, we truly believe the emerging order of hope and progress in Asia will continue to grow and to grow. . . .

U.S. POLICY TOWARD COMMUNIST CHINA

There is a fourth essential for peace in Asia which may seem the most difficult of all: reconciliation between nations that now call themselves enemies.

A peaceful mainland China is central to a peaceful Asia.

A hostile China must be discouraged from aggression. A misguided China must be encouraged toward understanding of the outside world and toward policies of peaceful cooperation. For lasting peace can never come to Asia as long as the 700 million people of mainland China are isolated by their rulers from the outside world.

We have learned in our relations with other such states that the weakness of neighbors is a temptation, and only firmness, backed by power, can really deter power that is backed by ambition. But we have also learned that the greatest force for opening closed minds and closed societies is the free flow of ideas and people and goods.

For many years, now, the United States has attempted in vain to persuade the Chinese Communists to agree to an ex-

change of newsmen as one of the first steps to increased understanding between our people.

More recently, we have taken steps to permit American
scholars, experts in medicine and public health, and other
specialists to travel to Communist China. Only today we have
here in the Government cleared a passport for a leading
American businessman to exchange knowledge with Chinese
mainland leaders in Red China.

All of these initiatives have been rejected, except the action
today, by Communist China.

We persist because we know that hunger and disease, ignorance and poverty, recognize no boundaries of either creed or
class or country.

We persist because we believe that even the most rigid
societies will one day awaken to the rich possibilities of a
diverse world.

And we continue because we believe that cooperation, not
hostility, is really the way of the future in the 20th century.

That day is not yet here. It may be long in coming, but I
tell you it is clearly on its way, because come it must.

Earlier this year the Foreign Minister of Singapore said that
if the nations of the world could learn to build a truly world
civilization in the Pacific through cooperation and peaceful
competition, then, as our great President Theodore Roosevelt
once remarked, this may be the greatest of all human eras—
the Pacific era.

As a Pacific power, we must help achieve that outcome.
Because it is a goal worthy of our American dreams, and it
is a goal that is worthy of the deeds of our brave men who
are dying for us tonight.

So I say to you and I pledge to all those who are counting
on us: You can depend upon us, because all Americans will
do their part.

Premier Chou's Four-Point Statement on China's Policy Toward U. S.*

(1) CHINA WILL NOT take the initiative to provoke a war with
the United States. China has not sent any troops to Hawaii;
it is the United States that has occupied China's territory of

* On April 10, 1966 Premier Chou En-lai made a four-point statement on China's policy towards the United States. The full text was
reprinted in *Peking Review*, Vol. 9, No. 20, May 13, 1966, p. 5.

Taiwan Province. Nevertheless, China has been making efforts in demanding, through negotiations, that the United States withdraw all its armed forces from Taiwan Province and the Taiwan Straits, and she has held talks with the United States for more than ten years, first in Geneva and then in Warsaw, on this question of principle, which admits of no concession whatsoever. All this serves as a very good proof.

(2) The Chinese mean what they say. In other words, if any country in Asia, Africa or elsewhere meets with aggression by the imperialists headed by the United States, the Chinese Government and people definitely will give it support and help. Should such just action bring on U.S. aggression against China, we will unhesitatingly rise in resistance and fight to the end.

(3) China is prepared. Should the United States impose a war on China, it can be said with certainty that, once in China, the United States will not be able to pull out, however many men it may send over and whatever weapons it may use, nuclear weapons included. Since the 14 million people of southern Vietnam can cope with over 200,000 U.S. troops, the 650 million people of China can undoubtedly cope with 10 million of them. No matter how many U.S. aggressor troops may come, they will certainly be annihilated in China.

(4) Once the war breaks out, it will have no boundaries. Some U.S. strategists want to bombard China by relying on their air and naval superiority and avoid a ground war. This is wishful thinking. Once the war gets started with air or sea action, it will not be for the United States alone to decide how the war will continue. If you can come from the sky, why can't we fight back on the ground? That is why we say the war will have no boundaries once it breaks out.

Testimony to Senate Foreign Relations Committee, 1966, on the Question of Vietnam and Chinese Aggressiveness*

JAMES M. GAVIN

SENATOR CHURCH. Now, if the war continues to spread northward and westward toward the Chinese frontiers, and if

* Excerpts from Hearings before the Committee on Foreign Relations, U.S. Senate, on Supplemental Foreign Assistance Fiscal Year 1966—Vietnam (Washington, D.C.: Government Printing Office, 1966) pp. 267–8, 284–6.

the Chinese intervene and come down into Vietnam, as they did in Korea, in your opinion, General, could we then stop the Chinese from the air, that is to say, by relying on our naval and aerial power to stop them through bombing?

General GAVIN. No, they could not be stopped from the air. Incidentally, you could not do that in North Korea either.

Senator CHURCH. That is right. If they were to be stopped at all, they would have to be stopped on the ground.

General GAVIN. In my opinion; yes, sir.

Senator CHURCH. Now, with respect to China itself, should we find ourselves locked in a war with China, is it your opinion, General, that we could subdue China by an all-out bombing attack against them?

General GAVIN. Nuclear bombing.

Senator CHURCH. Well, let us say, first of all, conventional bombing.

General GAVIN. In my opinion, it would take nuclear bombs anyway, and there is no question about it, if we were to elect to use nuclear weapons the devastation would be incredible that we could inflict on any nation. Our stockpile is tremendous, and the devastation would be beyond understanding.

Senator CHURCH. Beyond imagination?

General GAVIN. Oh, yes.

Senator CHURCH. But even if we were to spread such an incredible desolation through the use of nuclear weapons, do you think it would require a physical occupation of China by American land forces to effect a conquest of China itself?

General GAVIN. If you seek conquest, yes. Certainly not of all of the real estate, but of all of the key areas.

Senator CHURCH. How many American troops, in your judgment, would that require.

General GAVIN. Gee, I do not know, sir. I am sorry, I would be guessing.

Senator CHURCH. But it would require, even according to the most conservative guess, many millions, would it not?

General GAVIN. Yes. You are dealing here with something that would be an awful thing, because we have global commitments that would require us to meet NATO and SEATO and many bilaterals, and this would be an exceedingly difficult thing to do.

Senator CHURCH. At the time that General Ridgway, fresh from his Korean experience, advised strongly against intervention in Indochina, he considered, you will remember, the possibility of a war with China itself.

General GAVIN. Yes, he did.

Senator CHURCH. And I think, in that regard it might be profitable to read one paragraph that Ridgway wrote. It reads as follows:

But I challenge any thesis that destroying the military might of Red China would be in our own long-range interest. We could create there, by military means, a great power vacuum. Then we would have to go in there with hundreds of thousands of men to fill that vacuum—which would bring us face to face with Russia along a 7,000-mile frontier. If we failed to go in, then Russia herself would fill it, and the threat to our own security would not have been abated one iota.

Are you in general agreement?

General GAVIN. Yes, I am.

The CHAIRMAN. General, I understood you to say in the course of one of the questions—I forgot who asked you— that the Chinese are quite aggressive in what they are doing. I wish you would elaborate a bit. In what respect are they very aggressive, contrasting what they are saying to what they are doing?

General GAVIN. Yes. In the first place I have been exposed to, as many Americans, to the filmed reports coming out of China of their militancy, of their training of their youth and their industrial workers and their people in the use of arms, in the military tactics and so on. There is a widespread national program I am led to believe to train their people for military operations.

The CHAIRMAN. Do you consider that aggressive necessarily?

General GAVIN. Not necessarily.

The CHAIRMAN. Per se?

General GAVIN. No. I would like to go on beyond that. But this basic militancy I think exists in their society. I am well aware of the penetrations they have made into North Korea and how costly they were to us. They were certainly aggressive then. . . .

The CHAIRMAN. Do you mean that training of their troops internally is an act of aggression?

General GAVIN. Their movement of troops deep into Korea was.

The CHAIRMAN. No; now I was passing on to their internal training—that is, the training of troops within China. Is that an act of aggression?

General GAVIN. No, no. No, no.

The CHAIRMAN. Well, is there any evidence that they moved troops into South Vietnam or North Vietnam?

General GAVIN. There is not at this time, although some people have been there, who have been to Vietnam, told me that there are Chinese trainers and technical people there, and the Chinese I believe themselves have alleged that volunteers would participate if necessary, and they have also been reported in the press as stating flatly that if we think that we can get away with our efforts in Vietnam without Korea being reopened, we are badly mistaken.

The CHAIRMAN. I understand they have made many threats.

General GAVIN. Yes.

The CHAIRMAN. Of much graver import than that as far as threats go. I was trying to elucidate just how far they have aggressed in recent years actively and by force. Normally we use the word "aggression," I will admit, very loosely.

General GAVIN. Yes.

The CHAIRMAN. But normally it means some action.

General GAVIN. Yes.

The CHAIRMAN. As distinguished from a word or a statement or a threat, doesn't it?

General GAVIN. Yes. Mr. Chairman, if I understand what you are getting at, they haven't made any major forays out of China itself, going after other peoples.

The CHAIRMAN. Do they have any troops outside of their own borders that you know of at the present time?

General GAVIN. Except perhaps those on the northeast Indian frontier. I am not sure of the state of affairs there now, but of course they were into India at one time.

The CHAIRMAN. That was the border incident you are speaking of in 1962?

General GAVIN. Yes, that is correct.

The CHAIRMAN. You will recall—I believe I have the statement of General Taylor—he made a statement before the Appropriations Committee that the Indians precipitated that particular incident, did he not? Do you recall that?

General GAVIN. I don't recall that, Mr. Chairman.

The CHAIRMAN. I will ask the staff to get that statement and put it in the record with regard to that specific incident.

General GAVIN. Yes.

(The information referred to follows:)

(Source: Department of Defense appropriations for 1964 hearings before a subcommittee of the Committee on Appropriations, House of Representatives, 88th Cong., 1st sess., part 2, Thursday, Feb. 14, 1963 (pp. 9–10).)

Mr. SIKES. Let me talk about Red China and the Indian operation. Did the Indians actually start this military operation?

General TAYLOR. They were edging forward in the disputed area; yes, sir.

Mr. SIKES. Is the area of the neutral zone on territory that was formerly claimed by India or claimed by China?

General TAYLOR. In most cases claimed by both.

Mr. SIKES. Where is it with relation to the generally accepted international boundary?

General TAYLOR. That is hard to say because there is no generally accepted international boundary. I am sorry to be vague about this, but I can assure you that I spent hours trying to find out where the McMahon line is. Actually, you find the maps differ on this. The terrain is so terribly rugged, there has been no accurate mapping and no accurate boundary lines or markers placed.

Mr. SIKES. Is the proposed neutral zone generally within territory which was occupied prior to all of this activity by Indian or Chinese forces?

General TAYLOR. Most of it was unoccupied by anybody.
General Hall, are you an expert on this subject?

General HALL. Yes, sir. I would say in general it was occupied by neither force, but that the NEFA was occupied predominantly by Indian forces. One thing I think is very important to point out is that the Chinese Nationalists, when they were in control of China, did not recognize this line either. So it is not a question of the fact it is a Chinese Communist line vis-a-vis an Indian line. It is an Indian line that has never been recognized by either the Chinese Communists or the Nationalists.

Mr. SIKES. Generally the neutral zone is in territory which was claimed by both?

General HALL. Claimed by both; yes, sir.

The CHAIRMAN. I think I recall that in testimony before the Appropriations Committee General Taylor made such a statement. I could be wrong. I think I have it somewhere in my files.

There was a very interesting article in a small provincial paper, the New York Times, on last Sunday, February 5, by Seymour Topping.

The whole purport of that—this is from Hong Kong—is that the Chinese are alleging that they are being encircled. In answer to Senator Hickenlooper, he advanced I believe the thesis that if we didn't stop the Chinese here, that we would be encircled. Now who is encircling whom at the present time?

General GAVIN. I would be inclined to believe that the Chinese think that they are being pretty well hemmed in.

The CHAIRMAN. Is it a fact, do you think, that relatively speaking they are more encircled today than we are?

General GAVIN. There is no question about that.

The CHAIRMAN. Do you think it is reasonable for them to feel that they are being encircled?

General GAVIN. I think in their position I would feel that way.

Testimony presented to Senate Foreign Relations Committee, 1966*

GEORGE F. KENNAN

AGGRESSIVE NATURE OF CHINA

The CHAIRMAN. . . . Now, as a historian, is it your impression that China, when she was a strong country in the past, has been inclined to military aggressiveness such as was characteristic of Germany in two instances recently and other countries from time to time?

Mr. KENNAN. No. It is my impression that the Chinese are tremendously preoccupied with what used to be called "face"— with prestige—with the outward aspects of authority and respect; and that sometimes, as in the present situation, their language can be very violent, and extreme, but that by and large they are very prudent people when it comes to military action.

* * *

The CHAIRMAN. More recently, a statement was made the other day and was this morning referred to during discussion of the Indian matter. . . . But it strikes me to say or to use this as an example of an aggression is rather tenuous. And with regard to Tibet, has not the status of Tibet been a matter of considerable controversy for a long time?

Mr. KENNAN. Yes, of course it has, and the Chinese did regard it as part of their area of sovereignty. I don't say this excuses what they did there. It puts it in a different category.

The CHAIRMAN. But I mean a long time ago, and not just by the Communist Chinese.

Mr. KENNAN. Yes.

The CHAIRMAN. Is it not true that the Nationalist Chinese regarded Tibet as a part of China, not since Mao Tse-tung came in.

Mr. KENNAN. Senator Fulbright, there have been very few of the troubles we have been having in the last few years which we would not have had with any other Chinese regime. A lot of this is national.

REASONS FOR CHINA'S BEHAVIOR

The CHAIRMAN. I don't wish to overplay this but I think when we look at specific cases and examine the circumstances

* Excerpts from Senate Hearings, *Ibid.*, pp. 391–393.

surrounding them, their actions as distinguished from their words have not been unusually aggressive or even as aggressive as many of our Western countries. In view of the history of China during the last century beginning with the opium wars, running up to the Second World War, would you not say there was considerable reason for their having some dislike to Western nations?

Mr. KENNAN. Yes.

I think we have to remember that we deal with the Chinese today at the end of a century in which they had very, very unhappy experiences with Western powers generally. I don't think that the blame for this was entirely on the Western powers. There was usually a good deal of connivance on the Chinese side at these relationships of imperialism.

But, by and large, these were very unhappy experiences. They were humiliating to the Chinese people, and there has accumulated a fund here of sensitivity and resentment which we are probably harvesting today. We have to bear that in mind.

* * *

7

CHINA IN THE SIXTIES—POLITICS AS MORALITY

THERE IS A tendency for "China analysts" to come from two distinct backgrounds. Some have spent their apprenticeship in China studies and are sensitive to the continuities in Chinese history. They emphasize historical parallels pointing out the recurrences of age-old patterns in contemporary events. Other China-watchers base their expertise on a knowledge of "communism" in the Soviet Union. The Sovietologists interpret events in China through their understanding of history in the Soviet Union. But Mao Tse-tung and the Chinese revolution owe far less to the Russian experience than they do to their own tortuous revolutionary development in the hinterland of China. In isolation from the rest of the world, the Chinese Communists elaborated strategies for both remaking society and winning a civil war. These strategies, and the ideals that inspired them, are monuments to their ingenuity. If we are to understand China in the 1960's we must approach her policies as distinctively Chinese *and* 20th century in origin.

The tide-like strategy that was adhered to by the Chinese Communists in winning a civil war against superior force of arms was part of a basic Weltanschauung. It was used not only to baffle the military enemy but as a basic tool of social change. The ebb and flow, fight and fend technique of launching an offensive (if warranted) against the enemy and then switching to the defensive to evade him, has been applied in other areas. Thought reform, the major re-education of the Chinese population which started back in the days of the Kiangsi Republic, has followed this pattern. It is initiated by the leadership in establishing rapport with the people. They learn *from* them, listen and address themselves to the needs of ordinary people so they will be accepted as trusted friends rather than eyed as suspicious "outsiders." At this stage in the process there are enormous pressures on the cadres for self-evaluation and living up to the *spirit* and not only the letter of the "law."

This groundwork laid, a major onslaught against some common weakness or shortcoming is undertaken. It can be a failure in attitude, false motives or harmful behavior on the part of either ordinary villagers or Party cadres. Following a concentrated bombardment of such errors, usually in the form of study-group discussions, there is a relaxation of pressure, an incubation period after which another struggle begins and so on. The procedure is actually a time-honored one in the texts of educators and it is surprising, sometimes, to find China scholars engaging in complicated analyses of it in terms of "de-Stalinization" or Stalinist orthodoxy.

When the "Hundred Flowers Bloom" campaign was launched in 1957, it was generally heralded in the West as a movement akin to "de-Stalinization" in the Soviet Union. When it abruptly dovetailed into a new rectification campaign in which intellectuals who had sharply criticized the regime in the earlier phase were subjected to attack and reform, western observers were quick to draw invidious comparisons with the continuing "thaw" in the Soviet Union. But they are very different phenomena. One is a product of relative affluence and the dissolution of an outmoded disciplinary code identified with the Stalinist period of hardship; the other is part of a more sophisticated Chinese substitute for Stalinism.

The succession of attacks and retreats in the Chinese handling of popular (or intellectual) discontent is not simply a means of protecting the regime from opposition. It is a plan consciously pursued for a more positive purpose: to sustain a vital, revolutionary momentum. It is crucial for the vast number of Chinese to be constantly reminded of the struggle that their drive toward modernization and "the good society" requires. The aim is similar to that of sounding foghorn-warnings at irregular intervals: to keep those on watch alert when things would otherwise "settle down" to a slumbering pace. Although the desirability of this technique in provoking continual efforts at social change was probably suggested by Soviet experience, Chinese history provides sufficient warning of what happens when regimes slacken their vigilance: a traditional gulf emerges between rulers and ruled, a traditional assortment of bureaucratic mannerisms stultify change, and a traditional passivity overtakes the masses reducing participation in affairs once removed from their immediate circle of necessity. These were and continue to be the main targets of attack in an ongoing process of destroying the traditional order of stratification and creating in its midst a new (hopefully non-stratified) society.

The emergence of a new society in China involves two distinct but related developments. One is modernization or "democratization." This refers to the loosening of traditional social bonds, the formation of new relationships and the expression of new needs. Women are encouraged to get out from under their traditional subservience to men. They are urged to assume equal status, express themselves vocally *as individuals* and carry responsibility for participating in community decisions. Children are inculcated with the idea of declaring independence from their parents' needs. In the past, children were expected to sacrifice their opportunities and very often themselves in order to provide for an extended family, especially their elders. Now the community makes arrangements for the welfare of the elderly, the sick and the children thereby releasing younger people from their former obligations.

These changes are part of the industrialization process. We have seen such transformations wherever a modern industrial society has taken root. There are new roles and new skills developed as peasants become literate urban workers. Individuals lose their earlier attachments freeing themselves of the restrictions of commitments to family as more space is created for individual mobility. An accompanying phenomenon in China is mass participation in the activities of society in *all* areas, not just the economic. Everyone is expected to be "political", to express his views publicly by speaking up at meetings, to assume active roles by criticizing as well as praising the behavior of others and himself. The latter—self-criticism—has a special significance in the context of Chinese culture. To talk openly about one's feelings has always been considered inappropriate. Confucian society, with its emphasis on social harmony, produced a culture in which direct confrontation of human emotions was avoided. In attempting to eliminate this social pattern, the Communists exaggerate its opposite. They make it possible (often through making it mandatory) for people to express things about themselves *in public* by ritualizing the format of such expression in "self-criticism" sessions. The language is formulistic, everyone has his turn to expose his past and his feelings; the result is contrary to the expectation of severe censure, one which dispels ingrained fears.

The second aspect of China's transformation is communization. The policies pursued by the regime indicate that the goal of modernization goes hand in hand with the goal of fashioning an equalitarian society. Unfortunately, trying to achieve both of these goals simultaneously is harder and more costly than simply industrializing. It means not only going against the grain of a traditional *agricultural* society but rejecting the experiences of all industrialized societies as well. In addition to the virtues of hard work, sacrifice, initiative and self-reliance, the Chinese Communists are bent on inculcating attitudes and behaviors identified with Marx's vision of the communist society. Instead of money, people should be motivated by work and fulfillment. In place of invidious distinctions —whether of class, status or occupation—which are barriers to mobility, there should be no structural ranking of individuals as having different worth. As an administrator of Peking University explained: "We want to eliminate the three differences, the difference between mental and manual labor, the difference between industry and agriculture and the difference between town and country." No individual achievement should be intrinsically more valuable than any other. Thus regulations require students to take part in physical labor just as manual laborers are compelled to study book-learning. Achievements that add to the community's welfare, however small or great, are honored while scorn is especially heaped on those activities that are rewarding to the individual in material terms.

The pursuit of each of these goals—modernization and communization—interferes with the smooth progress towards the other. The regime acknowledges this dilemma without settling for either one at the expense of the other. Its intent is to accomplish both utilizing a "dialectical" scheme. Policy directs attention to first one, then the other, in a precarious juggling act. The success of the act depends on the readiness with which the society as a whole can rapidly respond by shifting back and forth (within the span of a few years) among the conflicting poles of "expert" and "Red." The result is a succession of extremes which the leadership hopes will end in a synthesis.

The latest stage in this process is the "cultural revolution." There was surprise among western observers when, in the Spring of 1966, news of the cultural revolution swept aside the more sober statements of Chinese leaders in the official press concerning the importance of securing continued economic progress. Chinese leadership appeared to be forsaking a rational economic policy for an outburst of ideological madness. In the name of the "cultural revolution," a flood of criticism was unleashed against the "opponents of Mao Tsetung." The cultural revolution fomented conflict, disrupted stable productive processes in some areas and even invited civil strife. All of this was reported in official sources. Was there an organized opposition to the leadership of Mao, as patriotic Red Guards claimed? What was the significance of these events for the internal development of China?

There is no reliable evidence to indicate any large-scale *organized* opposition. We only hear of the "bandits" and "traitors" who betray Mao Tse-tung from those who attack them. There are no opposition voices that speak for themselves, no appeals for help, no opposition manifestoes or pirate radio stations. It is possible, therefore, that the so-called Maoists are deliberately exaggerating the nature and strength of their "enemies."

There is some evidence to indicate that the diverse activities fostered under the rubric of the "cultural revolution" can best be explained as part of the process of "inspired" social change that we have already described. It is an offensive against the inertia that invariably sets in with the normalization of conditions. As such it is by its very nature an exaggeration. To maintain the momentum necessary for China's modernization and her transformation into a new society, the leadership stays one step ahead of everyone in anticipating the problems this poses. Before some officials get a chance to quietly secure a privileged position in the bureaucracy, they must be made visible and accountable to some public. Before the grumbling and petty discontents of people at all levels dissipate the enthusiastic commitment to a vision of the future, their gripes and grievances must be aired. Before youth revolts against the restrictions that limit its naturally boundless energy and urge to expression, it must be encouraged to channel it in useful directions.

I am suggesting that the "cultural revolution" tackles these problems. It has enabled the Party to oust powerful members of its bureaucracy who were considered detrimental to the further development of the revolution. It has directly called on the masses to fight entrenched power interests within the Party thus appealing to non-Party people—those who formerly were and to some extent still feel at the bottom of the social pile—to criticize members of the power elite in China. And it has permitted youth to feel its own weight, to express its militance, its energetic idealism and its importance. In its unprecedented support of young peoples' rebellion, the "cultural revolution" in China has experimented with a solution closely related to the "problem" of youth in the U.S. The most far-reaching aspect of the developments in China is that young people have been taken seriously and have been allowed to exercise considerable power in their society.

In carrying through a social revolution, there are a number of stages reached when people have to make a decisive break with the habits of thought implanted by the old society. In practice the battle between the new outlook and the old may also be a conflict between two policies, both claiming to be working towards the same goal. This was how it happened when the cultural revolution mushroomed into national prominence. Throughout the Spring and Summer of 1966 there were attacks on officials accused of being "anti-Party" and "anti-socialist monsters" who had insinuated themselves into positions of power in the Party. With great fanfare the official news media publicized the formation of "Red Guards" as a new youth movement to defend Mao Tse-tung and further the study of "the thought of Mao Tse-tung." The schools were closed and while the curriculum was being revamped, bands of youngsters, with red armbands designating them as Red Guards, roved around the countryside and into the cities organizing rallies. They stirred up popular sentiments with their outspoken attacks on any deviations from the purity of their ideals, symbolized for them by the thought of Mao Tse-tung. Eventually what had started as a series of denunciations of lower-level officials in the Party bureaucracy spread during 1967 to upper echelons and Liu Shao-ch'i became the national symbol of "opposition" to Mao Tse-tung and the outstanding example of "bourgeois revisionism." He was accused of being one of a number of officials who were "taking the capitalist road." The officials were "purged" i.e., dismissed from their positions of power, and although they probably live in secluded protection somewhere drawing their salaries, their names and "crimes" have become stigmata.

The eleventh Plenary Session of the Communist Party held in August, 1966, gave its official blessing to the "great proletarian cultural revolution" hailing it as "an extensive Socialist education movement." A communiqué issued by the Central Committee of the Party described it as an outgrowth of the victories achieved in the preceding period between 1962 and 1966. A stabilization of the economy, advances in industrial production, good harvests in four successive years and new successes in scientific experimentation have augured a new leap forward. The decision heralds a mass movement to stimulate the creative study and application of Mao Tse-tung's works by *all* people.

There is the leadership's point of view just as there are

innumerable individuals' points of view. The functions of the cultural revolution from the perspective of the leadership is presented straightforwardly in the Party decision and attributed to the policies "brilliantly put forward by Mao Tse-tung": (1) developing the mass line (having faith in the masses and cultivating their participation), (2) raising and training successors in the proletarian revolutionary cause, (3) strengthening political ideological work to provide direct inspiration and incentive for greater productive efforts, (4) preparing for war and natural calamities to protect the people, (5) breaking down foreign conventions and "following our own road of industrial development," (6) breaking down the lines between military and political specialization, making everybody a soldier, (7) planning for the gradual mechanization of agriculture and (8) calling on *all organizations* from the army, schools, and factories to the Party and Government to become "great schools of revolution."

One of the main concerns of the cultural revolution is ensuring ideological unification. Just as in Ch'in times with the burning of the books, the Chinese today with "the thought of Mao" are straining to secure a unity of thought (and allegiance) *before* they have the wherewithal to be certain of a unity based on material prosperity. The worry that China will break apart under stress is reflected in Lin Piao's statement:

Our country is a big nation of 700 million people and it is necessary for the whole country to have unified thinking. Only when it is unified by Mao Tse-Tung's thought can there be unified action. Without unified thinking a big country of 700 million people will still be like loose sand. The thinking of the people of the entire country can be unified only with the great power of Mao Tse-tung's thought.

At the core of the ideological upheaval is the exhortation to rely on and apply the "thought of Mao Tse-tung." This is not as singularly a cult-ritual as saluting the flag. The substance of Mao's writings, as should by now be apparent, ranges broadly over many topics. It provides a scientific method for people with only primitive tools and traditional know-how at their disposal. It provides a new style of thought, a psychological disposition and a common standard of evaluation with which to confront a multiplicity of situations. In this respect it is the equivalent of the early American ideology with its frontier wisdom; people learned a set of attitudes and beliefs like rugged individualism, hard work, equality and competition which sustained their efforts at community and construction.

The language of Maoism is politics. The slogan "politics in command," however, is meaningless unless we realize that the content of politics is morality. Technical expertise does not automatically endow people with a sense of right and wrong; a social conscience must therefore be superimposed on human beings' mechanical adaptation to industrialization. This concern is illustrated in the cultural revolution's deprecation of specialization at the expense of politics and ideology:

Comrades working in the P. L. A. (People's Liberation Army) must resolutely oppose the tendency to engage solely in military affairs, in specialized work and techniques, while neglecting politics and ideology. How can we do specialized work well? How can we raise the level of work? The only way is to change the mental outlook of people.

The cultural revolution is in a sense a self-conscious reminder of the social (moral) significance of work. The "humiliation" of people paraded through the streets in dunce caps, the public trials and "confessions" of "bourgeois revisionists" are repetitions of a morality play. Through their ritual enactment of good and evil, people learn to identify the moral implications of their behavior.

Another function of the cultural revolution is to ensure the continued commitment of young people to the long-range goals of the revolution. This requires that youngsters' experiences be assimilated to the ruggedness and perseverance of the old guard. Today's adolescents (whose special designation as Red Guards endows them with special importance) were born at the time of or after the revolution of 1949. They have no living memory of the early trials, betrayals, long marches and decades of revolutionary struggling. They have no built-in *esprit de corps* that binds them together across geographical and circumstantial differences. And their childhoods have been filled with hope and promises of a great future; that dream of tomorrow though visible to the old people who remember the days of starvation must still be sacrificed for today by the young people as well. In preparation for their role in perpetuating the revolution, young people undergo in simulated form the "steeling in struggle" their parents actually lived through.

What the May Fourth Movement was to Mao Tse-tung's generation, the cultural revolution is for the present generation of students. It inspires in them a sense of urgency and an intense involvement in national affairs that *counts*. It teaches them a sense of accomplishment that comes from "braving storm and stress" thus assuring a continuity in perspective. In a speech by Chen Po-ta on August 16, 1966 at a mass meeting of students who had traveled to Peking from all over China, the intent is clearly depicted:

Revolutionaries cannot grow up in hot-houses; they must grow up braving storm and stress. We must temper ourselves in the crucible of revolution, to the fount of the great proletarian cultural revolution, you have gone through much hardship, unafraid of storm and stress. . . . Your actions and your struggles show promise, show that you can really become Chairman Mao's worthy students, that you can be successors to the cause of the proletarian revolution. . . . However, this is only the initial test. You have yet to undergo countless tests, tests over long periods of time. You must live and breathe with the masses, get covered with mud and grease with them over and over again and turn yourselves into revolutionaries struggling for the people, for socialism and communism.

This ties youth directly to the older revolutionaries—through their loyalty to Mao Tse-tung—prevails on them to study, follow and move with the masses and be able to withstand adversity, so that by their own action they assure the final victory of a new society (and the destruction of the old). The problem has been maintaining a balance between youthful revolutionary ardor and its excesses with their disturbing consequences.

The Chinese have a way of writing the word "crisis" that incorporates two characters: one signifies "danger," the other "opportunity." This basic contradiction is at the core of communism in China; it is the driving force of an idea and the colossal human effort expended in realizing it. The reflection of this conflict between "danger" and "opportunity" is apparent in the ambivalence that characterizes the government's policy: to exploit human resources without exploitation, to work towards communism through nationalism, to centralize at the same time as decentralizing, to modernize and yet respect the traditional in those areas in which it is useful, to overturn the authority of older generations (who represent bourgeois attitudes) and yet prevent youthful rebellion against *all* authority, to industrialize and yet fulfill the agricultural needs of a pressingly large population. The Chinese are attempting to change the social organization and men's ways of thinking *before* material prosperity makes it desirable. The result is a totally politicized community in which politics is the substance of morality and not just a specialized private occupation. If China can work through the contradiction of her precocity she will equal the United States in her dizzying ascent to greatness.

In order to understand present-day China one has constantly
to recall her history. The characteristic theme today is "structure and change." The importance of unity for China remains
paramount and structures for governing, producing and distributing must operate within some framework of unity and
coordination. On the other hand, change is, in and of itself,
an extremely compelling goal for the Chinese and one which
very often interferes with the smooth functioning of established
structures.

The following article by Franz Schurmann is valuable for
its insights into the importance of organization and ideology
in the modus operandi of the Chinese Communists. There is
an emphasis, it should be noted, on the uses of ideology not
merely as ritual but as a set of tools with which to creatively
confront innumerable problems. It is a necessity, as the Chinese Communists have always recognized, for people to inter-
nalize the ideology, not simply to mouth the words, so as to
be able to apply it as a method in decision-making on any
number of levels.

Organisational Principles of the Chinese Communists*

FRANZ SCHURMANN

THE COUNTRIES of Asia and Africa have seen the rise of
numerous and powerful socio-political movements during the
past few decades, movements which have shaken existing
orders and have launched these nations on the road of mod-
ernisation. Although these movements have almost always
been nationalist in character during the early phases of revolution, subsequently leftist radical movements have arisen,
most of these have been Communist.

Both the nationalists and the Communists have shown
themselves capable of eliciting great collective response from
the peoples on whom they have acted. But in regard to one
essential mechanism of political action, the nationalists have
shown themselves far weaker and less adept than the Communists. That mechanism is *organisation*.

Almost without exception, where the Communists have

* Article by H. F. Schurmann in The China Quarterly, No. 2
(April–June 1960), pp. 47–58. By permission of The China Quarterly.

arisen, they have established disciplined, effective, structured movements, capable of quick and sustained political action, and, perhaps of even more importance, of moving in and mobilising inert masses of people. In those countries of Asia in which the Communists have seized power (China and her smaller neighbours, North Korea and North Vietnam), they have even further extended this propensity for organisation.

The case of Communist China is perhaps the most extraordinary of all. At the moment of victory, the Chinese Communists were in possession of a powerful, battle-tested army and a highly disciplined party. But they also faced a huge land area, wracked by almost a half-century of war, a poverty-stricken population, disorganised masses of people, and the total collapse of government. Within ten years, Communist China has become one of the most powerful nations on the globe. A programme of rapid industrialisation has been launched. Disorganised masses have been transformed into organised masses toiling at monumental construction projects. And, negatively speaking, there is not the slightest indication that the iron grip of the régime is seriously threatened by internal rifts or internal protest.

If one were asked for the magic key to this phenomenal feat, the answer would have to be *organisation*: the ordered mobilisation, control, and manipulation of people for certain ends. Not only organisation in a limited sense, but *total organisation*: the spread of a tight web of organisation over a land of 650,000,000 people. In this article, we shall examine some of the central principles of organisation of the Chinese Communists, principles which might be termed a practical ideology of organisation.

Despite the massive nature and far-reaching extent of organisation in Communist China, there exists a remarkable uniformity in this great structure, a uniformity possible only in a totalitarian society. This uniformity results not only from the persistence of established structures, but through the operation of certain basic organisational principles. These organisational principles derive from the organisational theories and practices of Lenin and the Bolsheviks. However, there are elements in these principles that are distinctly Chinese, elements which were infused as a result of the concrete experiences of the Chinese Communists during the pre-1949 period when they were the leaders only of a revolutionary movement.

There are two elements which are central to the practical ideology of the Chinese Communists: (1) the theory of contradictions, and (2) the theory of democratic centralism. The theory of contradictions has been elevated to the level of supreme dogma in Communist China. It is regarded as the key to the proper understanding of all phenomena. Chinese Communist theoreticians lay more emphasis than their Russian colleagues on the all-pervasive nature of contradictions in the world. They see action and behaviour as the result of the resolution of these contradictions. The principle of democratic centralism is treated as a derivative of the theory of contradictions. It is the theory of the "contradictory" principles of democracy *and* centralism. The theory of democratic centralism finds direct expression in the organisational structure of Communist China. If the theory of contradictions represents what one might call a metaphysics of organisation, the theory of democratic centralism is the basic theory of organisation itself.

THE THEORY OF CONTRADICTIONS

The theory of contradictions has played a prominent part in the official ideology of the Chinese Communists since the publication of Mao Tse-tung's famous article *On Contradiction*. This article became supremely important in Chinese Communist ideology after the publication of Mao-Tse-tung's February 1957 speech *On the Correct Resolution of Contradictions among the People* [NCNA, June 18, 1957]. The reasons behind the original formulation of the theory of contradictions undoubtedly related to the real contradictions which the Communists faced during the early years of their nationalistic United Front policy—contradictions between the radical revolutionary aims and actions of the Party and the call for a class-transcending alliance against the Japanese.

However, as one reads the literature on organisation which began to appear in China during the Yenan period, in particular the writings of Liu Shao-ch'i, who, much more than Mao himself, deals explicitly with the theory and practice of organisation, it emerges that the theory of contradictions gradually became a device—an ideological device—out of which a complex but highly practical theory of organisation was created. This theory, in almost all essential respects, anticipates the definitive formulation of the theory in the February 1957 speech. There were definite practical considerations —the Hungarian Revolt and the need for a new "rectification" movement—which prompted Mao to make that speech then. But in essence the speech simply outlined in clear-cut terms a theory which had become deeply rooted in Chinese Communist thinking long before that.

Mao stated in the speech that there were two types of contradictions, antagonistic and non-antagonistic. The former are the classic contradictions of Marxist ideology, contradictions between hostile classes and hostile social systems, "the contradictions between the enemy and ourselves." These contradictions cannot be resolved except by force; these contradictions are the very substance of the inexorable process of history.

But non-antagonistic contradictions are of a different sort. They occur within Socialist society. In fact, although this is not stated explicitly, they seem to be a part of the very fabric of Socialist society. For Stalin, the so-called non-antagonistic contradictions were basically technological in nature, contradictions which arose out of discrepancies between the "relations of production" and "the productive forces of society," in other words contradictions due to the "advanced nature" of the Soviet social system and the "backward nature" of its economic structure.

However, the non-antagonistic contradictions of the Chinese Communists are much more than mere technological discrepancies. They are, as Mao puts it, "the contradictions between the interests of the nation and the collective on the one hand, and those of individuals on the other, the contradictions of democracy and centralism, the contradictions between leaders and led, between the bureaucratic tendencies of cetrain individuals who work in the bureaucracy and the masses."

Contradictions, in the Hegelian-Marxian scheme, demand resolution, and the lineal progression of contradiction—resolution—contradiction makes up the process of history. The mode of resolution for each of these two contradictions is different. For the former—antagonistic—it is essentially violent. For the latter—non-antagonistic—it is essentially non-violent, through the process of "discussion, criticism, and education."

There is no question that the timing and the substance of Mao's speech on contradictions related to certain practical problems which had arisen. As we now know, the Hungarian Revolt made a deep impression on the Chinese, particularly the intellectuals, and had led to serious questions being raised on the relations of the leadership to the masses in Communist society. Furthermore, the old, recurrent organisational enemy "bureaucratism" had again shown itself. The beginnings of a "rectification" movement were already apparent in the widespread movement for the decentralisation of cadres (the *hsia-fang*) movement—a movement to transfer urban cadres to rural areas.

But aside from the practical significance of the speech, it also had great theoretical importance, for it expressed formally a mode of thinking already basic to practice. This mode of thinking is perhaps nowhere more clearly expressed than in the writings of Liu Shao-ch'i. In a talk given some time between 1941 and 1945, Liu began a long and detailed explication of principles of organisation and discipline with the statements: "What is the organisational structure of the Party? As with other things, it is a contradictory structure, it is a contradictory unity. . . ." In this speech, Liu applies the dialectic to an analysis of the internal structure and functioning of the Party. The basic contradictory polarisation in Party organisation, he maintains, is that between "centralism" and "democracy," between the leaders and the led. Correct resolution of the contradictions which therefore arise gives life and lineal development to the organisation. Incorrect resolutions—incorrect intra-party struggles, so to speak—would lead to its destruction. The theory of contradictions as applied to organisation thus presupposes a precarious structure in which the opposition of forces and counter-forces produces tension. The structure can only be maintained by a continuous process of correct resolution of the contradictions and removal of the tensions.

Mao Tse-tung entitled his speech *On the Correct Resolution of Contradictions among the People.* We have already spoken of contradictions and resolution, but the word "correct" must not be overlooked. For every contradiction, there can only be a single correct resolution, for the contradictions are objective and the laws of history are objective. Of course, what seems correct today may, in the light of a more exact analysis of the laws of history, prove incorrect tomorrow. Such correctness not only springs out of metaphysical determinedness, but more specifically out of what Mao calls "the fundamental consensus as to the interests of the People." But what is this consensus? It is consciousness of the true interests of the People. Given the Leninist theory of the vanguard, to which the Chinese Communists undeviatingly adhere, it is the Party which emerges as the infallible and supremely competent interpreter of this consensus. The "correctness" of the resolution thus relates to the role of absolute and supreme authority held by the Party. It is natural for contradictions to seek resolution, but only the Party can guarantee correctness.

This syndrome of interacting and counteracting forces in a

context of absolute authority is perhaps the most important aspect of the organisational model of the Chinese Communists. It is this syndrome which gives Chinese Communist organisation both flexibility and rigidity, which at times makes it appear monolithic and at other times dynamic. It is an organisational model which expects simultaneously abject submission from all echelons and along with this spontaneity and creativity. In its structure it is dialectical, for it is "contradictory," as Liu Shao-ch'i says. And as such it produces tensions, the benign contradictions of the "non-antagonistic" sort. These contradictions find resolution in the various rectifying actions instituted by the Absolute Authority: mass movements, criticism and self-criticism, "rectification" movements and so on. If in the above sections we have dealt with what may be called the ideology of organisation, we must now proceed to organisation itself. And here the two crucial principles are "democratic centralism." We say two because in the Chinese context "democratic centralism" becomes two nouns, "democracy and centralism," the two contradictory principles of democracy and centralism, as Liu Shao-ch'i says. We must further, in order to understand properly the operations of organisation here, completely lay aside any notions we have as to the meaning of the word "democracy." For the Chinese Communists, "democracy" has real and important meaning, albeit a meaning which has nothing to do with what is understood by this term in the West. For the Chinese Communists, all organisational structure and function must operate according to the principles of democracy and centralism. Let us first discuss centralism, familiar enough in its Soviet context.

CENTRALISM

The operation of the principle of centralism has seen the creation of a web of organisation with vertical chains of command which ultimately merge, like the apex of a pyramid, at the very top. Although at a few key points, a certain form of horizontal contact and communication can and does occur, for the most part commands move downward and information moves upward, all along vertical lines. Organisational charts give a graphic picture of the web of organisation for the country as a whole, but the actual operation of centralism may perhaps be seen most easily on the lowest level of organisation, at the point where organisation is in direct contact with the masses. For this purpose, let us consider the organisational structure and function of a "party primary group"—the most basic nucleus of party organisation—in an hypothetical factory. The Chinese Communists (like the Russians) place their nuclei of organisation in some existing organisation, whether social, economic, ecological or other, such as a factory, a school, a military unit, a village and so on. These are known as "primary units of production or territory." Thus in the case of our hypothetical factory, the party primary organisation (also so called in the U.S.S.R.) exists only in the factory; its members are drawn from the factory alone and its activities relate only to the factory. Aside from intra-unit communication, its only official contacts are with higher party echelons.

In a large industrial unit, the party primary group may consist of enough members so that there will be some structuring along echelon lines within the primary group. Such structuring will always follow the principle of centralism. Party branches will be set up in each of the "shops"—below the branches there will be the party small groups, the most basic of all organisational groups. A series of such shop branches will be under the control of a general branch. The cadres of the general branch form the members of the executive committee of the party primary group. Within the party organisation in the factory, supreme control rests in this committee, and ultimately in the hands of the party secretary. The only real decision-making power within the context of the party primary group rests with the executive committee. Party rules and organisational handbooks specify periodic delegate meetings at various higher levels. Although there is every reason to believe that no important decisions are made at these meetings, there is also every reason to believe that these meetings, like mass meetings in general, have other important organisational functions.

If hierarchical structuring is crucial to centralism at all levels, there is another dimension to centralism which is of great importance: leadership. Few organisational problems have been discussed more seriously in Chinese Communist literature than the problem of leadership. No society can undergo rapid change without a great corps of leaders to direct and carry out changes. Leaders may be born, but the Chinese Communists operate with the conviction that they can be made. Leadership ability is one of the requisites for membership in the party. Prospective members and candidate members must have demonstrated not only absolute political loyalty, but leadership ability. They must be able to influence and lead the masses in practical tasks such as mass movements, propaganda and agitation, work brigades and so on. The term *kanpu*—cadre—means, in fact, a leader, an organiser, a person who holds command and authority in a given organisational setting. Liu Shao-ch'i has spoken and written at length on "training for leadership." In the specific context of our hypothetical party group, the principle of leadership demands that each party grouping, whatever small group or branch or committee at whatever level, be headed by a defined leader. There must be collective leadership, say the Communists, but there must also be individual responsibility. The group leader is the direct link in the chain between the group and higher echelons. It is from him that higher party directives are transmitted to the group members. As leader and as crucial link in the chain, the group leader possesses immense authority. It is through his authority and through the more "positive" elements around him that control from above extends downward. But, as we shall show, there is a control from below, control of a certain and limited type, of course.

During the early years, both before and after victory, cadres were divided into party and non-party cadres. A large segment of party membership consisted of peasants of low literacy and no technical competence. As a result, the régime was compelled to make wide use of individuals who possessed the requisite competence to act as organisational leaders, but who were not party members. However, through training and education, and through selective recruitment, the general qualitative level of party members has been considerably raised over the past ten years. Therefore, the ratio of non-party to party cadres has been declining. More and more of the top bureaucrats in industry are now party members. The tolerance of minority parties does not seem to involve tolerance of a vast non-party cadre group in the country, such as the technocratic group in the U.S.S.R.

Another example of the tendency to merge organisational cadre with party membership may be cited. When the communes were formed, instructions were issued to place party members in key cadre positions or to recruit leadership personnel into the party. However, this does not mean that in a factory, for example, the director is also head of the party unit. Judging from scattered information, the party secretary usually has a full-time job, and is usually distinct from the directors, either of management or of the "trade union." However, inasmuch as the top people of management and the union are party members, they participate—and in a most important way—in party meetings. Thus, on the one hand, the party maintains an organisation separate from and parallel with the organisational lines of management (which are subordinate to the relevant ministry) and with the unions (which are linked with a given "industrial union"); but on the other hand, the frequency of what the Chinese Communists call "double roles" (holding party membership and at the same time some other position in organisation) has brought about an important meshing of the three organisational sectors of our hypothetical factory. It is in the party meeting that top party people, top management people, and top union people meet together. It is undoubtedly at such meetings that the most important decisions are made.

DEMOCRACY

If the operation of the principle of centralism has created hierarchical structurings with defined leadership at all levels— the skeletal framework of a totalitarian society—the dialectical opposite of centralism, "democracy," also has great organisational functions. As a whole, in the organisational handbooks, a straightforward definition of "democracy" is avoided in favour of a more elliptical treatment in terms of yet another duality of principles: "centralism on a democratic basis" and "democracy under centralised leadership." This, of course, avoids the obvious embarrassment of dealing with "freedom" without the qualification of "necessity." However, despite the tortuous road which the Communist ideologues follow in treating these principles, "democracy" plays an important part in Chinese Communist organisational thinking and practice.

In one organisational handbook, three important functions of active intra-party democracy are singled out. First, sufficiently broad intra-party democracy will permit individual party members and local party organisations to develop "positivism" and "creativity." The development of these qualities is important for they are requisites for leadership capacity. Secondly, the broad development of intra-party democracy will strengthen ties between the party and the masses. If the active participation of all party members in party life is assured, in particular if "criticism" of party cadres is permitted, then this will act to counter the tendencies of "subjectivism" and "bureaucratism." Furthermore, such close ties between party and masses will assure that the "opinions and demands" of the masses are "reflected" at all times to the party organisation. Thirdly, broadening of intra-party democracy permits regional party organisations to solve problems "according to the special conditions in their own particular work areas." This independent problem-solving makes it possible to adapt party directives "to all kinds of dissimilar conditions of time, place, and circumstance."

In a typically concise way, the organisational handbook has explained the three major functions of "democracy." Before going on to an analysis of the actual nature of "democracy," let us consider these three functions. "Positivism" and "creativity" are favourite terms in organisational literature. "Positivism" in many ways is the Chinese counterpart of the Soviet *aktivnost.*" However, there seem to be differences, which become more apparent when one considers the paired term "creativity." "Positivism" and "creativity" demand not only enthusiastic, absolute obedience from individuals, but demand what might be called creative obedience, the capacity to make decisions of an independent nature but absolutely in accord with the intent of a party resolution. In other words, initiative, spontaneity, willingness to make decisions are attributes of "positivism" and "creativity." Blind obedience, as Liu Shao-ch'i has stated, is not what the party expects from its members.

The second point stresses participation in party life and criticism of cadres as important mechanisms for combating "bureaucratism." In a sense, every one of the party's many "rectification" movements has been directed to the problem of "bureaucratism." Bureaucratism may be described as the over-perfect functioning of centralised control—excessive centralism as it has been described in the literature. The party bureaucrat functions in perfect accord with the directives of the party, but in the process his work becomes mere routine and he loses his ability to make independent decisions. He depends increasingly on his position of power and on the formal rules of his office to enforce his will.

In such situations, the party senses trouble: alienation of the party from the masses, stagnation of party work and so on. Through clever manipulation, a programme of "criticism and self-criticism" is launched against the offending bureaucrat. In the regularly scheduled party meetings, certain individuals will arise and commence the criticism. Usually, the target will know that the criticism has been arranged. He cannot fight it, not only because the party at higher echelons is immediately behind it, but because criticism and self-criticism are legitimate institutions within the system ("everybody is subject to criticism"). The process of criticism may proceed for a short or long period. Either the critics will be able to arouse their target from his bureaucratic stupor and reinvigorate him with the spirit of "positivism" and "creativity"; or the erring bureaucrat will be dismissed. Though the Chinese Communists have never been involved in the bloody purges of party and bureaucracy which were instituted in the U.S.S.R. in the 1930s, in a sense a continuous purge goes on all the time. These are periodically interspersed with large-scale purge movements, the so-called "rectification" movements. Though rectification sometimes aims at cleaning out politically unreliable elements, more often its aim is to stir up bureaucracies become stagnant through routine.

The third point made by the handbook stresses the importance of "democracy" in allowing regional and local party organisations to make independent decisions in the framework of the particular problems which they encounter. Here again, not "blind obedience," but initiative, is demanded from party cadres.

One of the extraordinary characteristics of organisation in Communist China has been its flexibility, a flexibility apparently greater than that in the bureaucracies of the U.S.S.R. The source of this flexibility is "democracy," just as "centralism" is the source of rigidity. This flexibility manifests itself in the expectation of considerable independence on the part of local cadres, though, of course, on a basis of absolute commitment to the party. The Communists stress that "democracy" means the rights of individual organisation members to express their opinions, to criticise, to participate in party meetings, to take part in collective decision-making and so on. The common thread which runs through all these "rights" is the "right" to participate, to be present at all meetings. This is in fact the crucial requisite of "democracy." For it is through participation that the full effect of indoctrination, group pressure, involvement through work—all the various devices through which an individual can be bound behaviourally, ideationally, and emotionally to a group and a cause—exert their full force on the individual member. The Chinese Communists work on the assumption that if one can force a person to participate in some organised and controlled group, then, whatever the personal inclinations of the individual involved, the proper use of the techniques of "discussion, criticism, and education" will enable one to secure his commitment of one degree and kind or another.

Furthermore, the Chinese Communists never permit participation in group activity to be simply verbal. In most instances "study groups" and "work groups" are one, so that an individual subjected to verbal pressures in one group context will find himself being tested by his concrete work in that same group context. In other words, the party member not only engages verbally with his comrades, but finds himself sent out to do practical party work, like organising, lecturing, interviewing and so on. Both work and talk are forms of participation, and coming together they compound the pressures to involve an individual in the "cause" or organisation in question. It is through the "broadening of democracy" that the party feels it can rely on local party people to make correct decisions, even when an explicit party directive is not forthcoming, or when a party directive is so loosely formulated that the situation explicitly calls for local adaptation. The operation of the latter procedure was seen clearly in the programme of communisation. The decree of August 29, 1958, in no way spelled out in minute detail how communes were to be established. Communes of different types and dimensions arose in various parts of the country. The format of each commune was more often than not the work of the local party cadres. Only in December was there introduced the programme of *Gleichschaltung* which gave the communes a more uniform appearance.

ORIGINS

One might ask what is the historical source of this flexible "dialectical" organisational structure? An organisational history of the Chinese Communists has not yet been written, but there are strong indications that these practices, this mode of thinking, arose in the Yenan period. One has direct indications of this in the writings of Mao Tse-tung on guerrilla warfare. One of the central problems which the Communists faced during that period was the control and manipulation of scattered bands of guerrilla fighters in an overall context of military co-ordination. Actual military conditions did not permit the transformation of these units into regular armies, but on the other hand there always remained the danger of "mountainism," the loosening of central control. Furthermore, both regular and guerrilla warfare had their positive functions. The problem posed itself in terms of "contradictions" and the practices which developed had a "contradictory," "dialectical" character. The intensive use of group pressures—the use of thought control—seems to have developed during the Yenan period. And thought control inculcated the contradictory ideas of centralism and democracy, or, interpreted in military terms, absolute obedience to supreme command coupled with the maximum of independence in guerrilla action.

Contradictions demand resolution, as the ideology of the Chinese Communists teaches. Therefore, one must ask: what are the institutionalised forms of the resolution of contradictions, of the management of intra-organisation tensions? On the everyday level, criticism and self-criticism, and denunciation are mechanisms for resolving intra-organisation tensions. As Mao Tse-tung and Liu Shao-ch'i have repeatedly stated, and as is quite simple to imagine, tensions are generated in the typical organisational setting in which there is a person who leads and people who are led. These tensions have their positive aspects if they induce sufficient anxiety and insecurity in the individual to work out his tensions positively, in work, in study, and in struggle—all sanctioned forms of releasing tension in Communist China. On the other hand, the "contradictions" may begin to impede the orderly functioning of the organisation. Here the mechanisms of denunciation and criticism come in. A cadre is reported to the party through one or another channel. Such reporting is openly encouraged and in many instances denunciation has become a legitimate part of organisational life. Such denunciation will probably be followed by a criticism and self-criticism session in which the denounced becomes the target of criticism.

Aside from the day-to-day programmes of orderly "resolution of contradictions," periodic large-scale movements—"mass movements"—are launched. Mass movements can be launched for many purposes, to implement whatever internal policy the régime wishes carried out. But the "rectification" movements are aimed at solving intra-organisation "contradictions" on a grand scale. Mao's speech of February 1957 ushered in a "rectification" movement. The present, somewhat veiled campaign against rightists in the party seems to be directed against party members who opposed the radicalism of many of the local cadres in the great leap forward and in communisation. Here more is involved than simple elimination of intra-organisation tensions. However, whatever the specific aim of the mass movements, their consequences are usually manifold. In building the party (*chien-tang*), the Communists have always stressed the tremendous importance of participation in mass movements as a training ground for party work. Such participation increases the "democratic aspects" of the party, infuses life and dynamism into its members. In this sense, all mass movements tend to push the pendulum of the dialectic from "centralism" toward "democracy." There is considerable evidence that the present leadership intends to continue to emphasize the importance of "democracy." More than a year ago, voices which suggested the abolition of mass movements in advanced industrial sectors for the sake of rationalised, ordered production were severely attacked by the organs of the Central Committee. The present campaign against the rightists also seems to be directed against those who are calling for moderation or change in organisational methods. However, it seems that Mao Tse-tung and Liu Shao-ch'i are holding fast to those methods and practices of organisation which they helped bring into being during Yenan times and with which they won China and have succeeded in transforming a prostrate, disorganised mass into one of the most powerful, organised, and dynamic countries in the world.

The Chinese Communists grew up on conflict and continue to see conflict as a healthy means of prodding people to change and improve their ways. They have gone further in their recognition of the social utility of conflict than Americans did in their nineteenth century glorification of competitive struggle. Throughout the history of the Movement in China, the overt expression of ideological conflict has actively been nurtured.

There is no question that the present upheaval in China has been officially encouraged. The government went so far as to acknowledge the benefits of "civil war." Red Guard activities and the Maoist "attacks" on anti-Maoists provoked social and political conflict which in some instances has led to violence. If there were any real threat to the stability of a regime, would any government legitimize a disruption of such proportions? From an outsider's point of view it is the courting of disaster if any opposition—even latent—does exist. From a Chinese perspective the situation is quite different. Opposition, if it exists, is more explosive and potentially dangerous to the body politic when left to fester. It must be brought into the open to be overcome.

Theoretically, there are two kinds of opposition: the intransigent and willful opposition of the counter-revolutionary, and the resistance of the ignorant or misled. The former is an enemy of the people and must be handled as such; the latter is capable of change, which is what Mao Tse-tung refers to as a "non-antagonistic contradiction." In the following selection Mao Tse-tung presents a theoretical counterpart to the practical techniques of transforming Chinese society and creating a new Chinese man. The parallel of this amidst the bustle of the cultural revolution is the enjoinder that the aim is to criticize not the person but, specifically, some of his attitudes. People's behaviour and attitudes are amenable to change. The objective of the cultural revolution, therefore, is not to annihilate or crush the human being but to provoke a meta-

morphosis, to change people by eliminating those aspects of their thinking and behavior that inhibit the evolution of the new society. One of the functions of such movements is education on a large scale: to stir the rank and file (who are for the most part, in China, peasants or only one step removed, and therefore not habitually accustomed to change, equalitarianism or the questioning of officialdom) and arouse in them a self-confidence which counteracts their otherwise mute resignation to the status quo.

On the Correct Handling of Contradictions Among the People,* January 1940

OUR GENERAL subject is the correct handling of contradictions among the people. For convenience' sake, let us discuss it under twelve sub-headings. Although reference will be made to contradictions between ourselves and our enemies, this discussion will centre mainly on contradictions among the people.

Never has our country been as united as it is today. The victories of the bourgeois-democratic revolution and the socialist revolution, coupled with our achievements in socialist construction, have rapidly changed the face of old China. Now we see before us an even brighter future. The days of national disunity and turmoil which the people detested have gone for ever. Led by the working class and the Communist Party, and united as one, our six hundred million people are engaged in the great work of building socialism. Unification of the country, unity of the people and unity among our various nationalities—these are the basic guarantees for the sure triumph of our cause. However, this does not mean that there are no longer any contradictions in our society. It would be naive to imagine that there are no more contradictions. To do so would be to fly in the face of objective reality. We are confronted by two types of social contradictions—contradictions between ourselves and the enemy and contradictions among the people. These two types of contradictions are totally different in nature.

If we are to have a correct understanding of these two

* Mao Tse-tung, ON THE CORRECT HANDLING OF CONTRADICTIONS AMONG THE PEOPLE (Peking: Foreign Languages Press, 1964) excerpts.

different types of contradictions, we must, first of all, make clear what is meant by "the people" and what is meant by "the enemy."

The term "the people" has different meanings in different countries, and in different historical periods in each country. Take our country for example. During the War of Resistance to Japanese Aggression, all those classes, strata and social groups which opposed Japanese aggression belonged to the category of the people, while the Japanese imperialists, Chinese traitors and the pro-Japanese elements belonged to the category of enemies of the people. During the War of Liberation, the United States imperialists and their henchmen—the bureaucrat-capitalists and landlord class—and the Kuomintang reactionaries, who represented these two classes, were the enemies of the people, while all other classes, strata and social groups which opposed these enemies, belonged to the category of the people. At this stage of building socialism, all classes, strata and social groups which approve, support and work for the cause of socialist construction belong to the category of the people, while those social forces and groups which resist the socialist revolution, and are hostile to and try to wreck socialist construction, are enemies of the people.

The contradictions between ourselves and our enemies are antagonistic ones. Within the ranks of the people, contradictions among the working people are non-antagonistic, while those between the exploiters and the exploited classes have, apart from their antagonistic aspect, a non-antagonistic aspect. Contradictions among the people have always existed. But their content differs in each period of the revolution and during the building of socialism. In the conditions existing in China today what we call contradictions among the people include the following: contradictions within the working class, contradictions within the peasantry, contradictions within the intelligentsia, contradictions between the working class and the peasantry, contradictions between the working class and peasantry on the one hand and the intelligentsia on the other, contradictions between the working class and other sections of the working people on the one hand and the national bourgeoisie on the other, contradictions within the national bourgeoisie, and so forth. Our people's government is a government that truly represents the interests of the people and serves the people, yet certain contradictions do exist between the government and the masses. These include contradictions between the interests of the state, collective interests and individual interests; between democracy and centralism; between those in positions of leadership and the led, and contradictions arising from the bureaucratic practices of certain state functionaries in their relations with the masses. All these are contradictions among the people. Generally speaking, underlying the contradictions among the people is the basic identity of the interests of the people.

In our country, the contradiction between the working class and the national bourgeoisie is a contradiction among the people. The class struggle waged between the two is, by and large, a class struggle within the ranks of the people. This is because of the dual character of the national bourgeoisie in our country. In the years of the bourgeois-democratic revolution, there was a revolutionary side to their character; there was also a tendency to compromise with the enemy, this was the other side. In the period of the socialist revolution, exploitation of the working class to make profits is one side, while support of the Constitution and willingness to accept socialist transformation is the other. The national bourgeoisie differs from the imperialists, the landlords and the bureaucrat-capitalists. The contradiction between exploiter and exploited, which exists between the national bourgeoisie and the working class, is an antagonistic one. But, in the concrete conditions existing in China, such an antagonistic contradiction, if properly handled, can be transformed into a non-antagonistic one and resolved in a peaceful way. But if it is not properly handled, if, say, we do not follow a policy of uniting, criticizing and educating the national bourgeoisie, or if the national bourgeoisie does not accept this policy, then the contradiction between the working class and the national bourgeoisie can turn into an antagonistic contradiction as between ourselves and the enemy.

Since the contradictions between ourselves and the enemy and those among the people differ in nature, they must be solved in different ways. To put it briefly, the former is a matter of drawing a line between us and our enemies, while the latter is a matter of distinguishing between right and wrong. It is, of course, true that drawing a line between ourselves and our enemies is also a question of distinguishing between right and wrong. For example, the question as to who is right, we or the reactionaries at home and abroad—that is, the imperialists, the feudalists and bureaucrat-capitalists—is also a question of distinguishing between right and wrong, but it is different in nature from questions of right and wrong among the people.

Ours is a people's democratic dictatorship, led by the working class and based on the worker-peasant alliance. What is this dictatorship for? Its first function is to suppress the reactionary classes and elements and those exploiters in the country who range themselves against the socialist revolution, to suppress all those who try to wreck our socialist construction; that is to say, to solve the contradictions between ourselves and the enemy within the country. For instance, to arrest, try and sentence certain counter-revolutionaries, and for a specified period of time to deprive landlords and bureaucrat-capitalists of their right to vote and freedom of speech—all this comes within the scope of our dictatorship. To maintain law and order and safeguard the interests of the people, it is likewise necessary to exercise dictatorship over robbers, swindlers, murderers, arsonists, hooligans and other scoundrels who seriously disrupt social order.

The second function of this dictatorship is to protect our country from subversive activities and possible aggression by the external enemy. Should that happen, it is the task of this dictatorship to solve the external contradiction between ourselves and the enemy. The aim of this dictatorship is to protect all our people so that they can work in peace and build China into a socialist country with a modern industry, agriculture, science and culture. . . .

Our socialist democracy is democracy in the widest sense, such as is not to be found in any capitalist country. Our dictatorship is known as the people's democratic dictatorship, led by the working class and based on the worker-peasant alliance. That is to say, democracy operates within the ranks of the people, while the working class, uniting with all those enjoying civil rights, the peasantry in the first place, enforces dictatorship over the reactionary classes and elements and all those who resist socialist transformation and oppose socialist construction. By civil rights, we mean, politically, freedom and democratic rights.

But this freedom is freedom with leadership and this democracy is democracy under centralized guidance, not anarchy. Anarchy does not conform to the interests or wishes of the people. . . .

As a matter of fact, freedom and democracy cannot exist in the abstract, they only exist in the concrete. In a society where there is class struggle, when the exploiting classes are free to exploit the working people the working people will have no freedom from being exploited; when there is democracy for the bourgeoisie there can be no democracy for the proletariat and other working people. In some capitalist countries the Communist Parties are allowed to exist legally but only to the extent that they do not endanger the fundamental interests of the bourgeoisie; beyond that they are not permitted legal existence. Those who demand freedom and democracy in the abstract regard democracy as an end and not a means. Democracy sometimes seems to be an end, but it is in fact only a means. Marxism teaches us that democracy is part of the superstructure and belongs to the category of politics. That is to say, in the last analysis, it serves the economic base. The same is true of freedom. Both democracy and freedom are relative, not absolute, and they come into being and develop under specific historical circumstances. Within the ranks of our people, democracy stands in relation to centralism, and freedom to discipline. They are two conflicting aspects of a single entity, contradictory as well as united, and we should not one-sidedly emphasize one to the denial of the other. . . .

While we stand for freedom with leadership and democracy under centralized guidance, in no sense do we mean that coercive measures should be taken to settle ideological matters and questions involving the distinction between right and wrong among the people. Any attempt to deal with ideological matters or questions involving right and wrong by administrative orders or coercive measures will not only be ineffective but harmful. We cannot abolish religion by administrative orders; nor can we force people not to believe in it. We cannot compel people to give up idealism, any more than we can force them to believe in Marxism. In settling matters of an ideological nature or controversial issues among the people, we can only use democratic methods, methods of discussion, of criticism, of persuasion and education, not coercive, high-handed methods. In order to carry on their production and studies effectively and to order their lives properly, the people want their government, the leaders of productive work and of educational and cultural bodies to issue suitable orders of an obligatory nature. It is common sense that the maintenance of law and order would be impossible without administrative orders. Administrative orders and the method of persuasion and education complement each other in solving contradictions among the people. Administrative orders issued for the maintenance of social order must be accompanied by persuasion and education, for in many cases administrative orders alone will not work.

In 1942 we worked out the formula "unity—criticism—unity" to describe this democratic method of resolving contradictions among the people. To elaborate, this means to start off with a desire for unity and resolve contradictions through criticism or struggle so as to achieve a new unity on a new basis. Our experience shows that this is a proper method of resolving contradictions among the people. In 1942 we used this method to resolve contradictions inside the Communist Party, namely, contradictions between the doctrinaires and the rank-and-file membership, between doctrinairism and Marxism. . . . The essential thing is to start with a desire for unity. Without this subjective desire for unity, once the struggle starts it is liable to get out of hand. Wouldn't this then be the same as "ruthless struggle and merciless blows"? Would there be any Party unity left to speak of? It was this experience that led us to the formula: "unity—criticism—unity." Or, in other words, "take warning from the past in order to be more careful in the future," and "treat the illness in order to save the patient." We extended this method beyond our Party. During the war it was used very successfully in the anti-Japanese bases to deal with relations between those in position of leadership and the masses, between the army and the civilian population, between officers and men, between different units of the army, and between various groups of cadres. The use of this method can be traced back to still earlier times in the history of our Party. . . . After the liberation of the country, we used this same method—"unity—criticism—unity"—in our relations with other democratic parties and industrial and commercial circles. Now our task is to continue to extend and make still better use of this method throughout the ranks of the people; we want all our factories, co-operatives, business establishments, schools, government offices, public bodies, in a word, all the six hundred million of our people, to use it in resolving contradictions among themselves.

Under ordinary circumstances, contradictions among the people are not antagonistic. But if they are not dealt with properly, or if we relax vigilance and lower our guard, antagonism may arise. . . .

Quite a few people fail to make a clear distinction between these two different types of contradictions—those between ourselves and the enemy and those among the people—and are prone to confuse the two. It must be admitted that it is sometimes easy to confuse them. We had instances of such confusion in our past work. In the suppression of counter-revolution, good people were sometimes mistaken for bad. Such things have happened before, and still happen today. We have been able to keep our mistakes within bounds because it has been our policy to draw a sharp line between our own people and our enemies and where mistakes have been made, to take suitable measures of rehabilitation.

Marxist philosophy holds that the law of the unity of opposites is a fundamental law of the universe. This law operates everywhere, in the natural world, in human society, and in man's thinking. Opposites in contradiction unite as well as struggle with each other, and thus impel all things to move and change. Contradictions exist everywhere, but as things differ in nature, so do contradictions. In any given phenomenon or thing, the unity of opposites is conditional, temporary and transitory, and hence relative; whereas struggle between opposites is absolute. Lenin gave a very clear exposition of this law. In our country, a growing number of people have come to understand it. For many people, however, acceptance of this law is one thing, and its application in examining and dealing with problems is quite another. Many dare not acknowledge openly that there still exist contradictions among the people, which are the very forces that move our society forward. Many people refuse to admit that contradictions still exist in a socialist society, with the result that when confronted with social contradictions they become timid and helpless. They do not understand that socialist society grows more united and consolidated precisely through the ceaseless process of correctly dealing with and resolving contradictions. For this reason, we need to explain things to our people, our cadres in the first place, to help them understand contradictions in a socialist society and learn how to deal with such contradictions in a correct way.

Contradictions in a socialist society are fundamentally different from contradictions in old societies, such as capitalist society. Contradictions in capitalist society find expression in acute antagonisms and conflicts, in sharp class struggle, which cannot be resolved by the capitalist system itself and can only be resolved by socialist revolution. Contradictions in socialist society are, on the contrary, not antagonistic and can be resolved one after the other by the socialist system itself.

The basic contradictions in socialist society are still those between the relations of production and the productive forces, and between the superstructure and the economic base. These contradictions, however, are fundamentally different in character and have different features from contradictions between the relations of production and the productive forces and between the superstructure and the economic base in the old societies. . . .

This is how things stand today: The turbulent class struggles waged by the masses on a large scale characteristic of the revolutionary periods have, in the main, concluded, but class struggle is not entirely over. While the broad masses of the people welcome the new system, they are not yet quite accustomed to it. Government workers are not sufficiently experienced, and should continue to examine and explore ways of dealing with questions relating to specific policies.

In other words, time is needed for our socialist system to grow and consolidate itself, for the masses to get accustomed to the new system, and for government workers to study and acquire experience. It is imperative that at this juncture we raise the question of distinguishing contradictions among the people from contradictions between ourselves and the enemy, as well as the question of the proper handling of contradictions among the people, so as to rally the people of all nationalities in our country to wage a new battle—the battle against nature —to develop our economy and culture, enable all our people to go through this transition period in a fairly smooth way, make our new system secure, and build up our new state.

* * * *

In building a socialist society, all need remoulding, the exploiters as well as the working people. Who says the working class doesn't need it? Of course, remoulding of the exploiters and that of the working people are two different types of remoulding. The two must not be confused. In the class struggle and the struggle against nature, the working class remoulds the whole of society, and at the same time remoulds itself. It must continue to learn in the process of its work and step by step overcome its shortcomings. It must never stop doing so. Take us who are present here for example. Many of us make some progress each year; that is to say, we are being remoulded each year. I myself had all sorts of non-Marxist ideas before. It was only later that I embraced Marxism. I learned a little Marxism from books and so made an initial remoulding of my ideas, but it was mainly through taking part in the class struggle over the years that I came to be remoulded. And I must continue to study if I am to make further progress, otherwise I shall lag behind. Can the capitalists be so clever as to need no more remoulding?

Some contend that the Chinese bourgeoisie no longer has two sides to its character, but only one side. Is this true? No. On the one hand, members of the bourgeoisie have already become managerial personnel in joint state-private enterprises and are being transformed from exploiters into working people living by their own labour. On the other hand, they still receive a fixed rate of interest on their investments in the joint enterprises, that is, they have not yet cut themselves loose from the roots of exploitation. Between them and the working class there is still a considerable gap in ideology, sentiments and habits of life. How can it be said that they no longer have two sides to their character? Even when they stop receiving their fixed interest payments and rid themselves of the label "bourgeoisie," they will still need ideological remoulding for quite some time. . . .

Our industrialists and business men can be thoroughly remoulded only in the course of work; they should work together with the staff and the workers in the enterprises, and make the enterprises the chief centres for remoulding themselves. It is also important for them to change certain of their old views through study. Study for them should be optional. After they have attended study groups for some weeks, many industrialists and business men, on returning to their enterprises, find they speak more of a common language with the workers and the representatives of state shareholdings, and so work better together. They know from personal experience that it is good for them to keep on studying and remoulding themselves. . . .

Contradictions within the ranks of the people in our country also find expression among our intellectuals. Several million intellectuals who worked for the old society have come to serve the new society. The question that now arises is how they can best meet the needs of the new society and how we can help them do so. This is also a contradiction among the people.

China needs as many intellectuals as she can get to carry through the colossal task of socialist construction. We should trust intellectuals who are really willing to serve the cause of socialism, radically improve our relations with them and help them solve whatever problems that have to be solved, so that they can give full play to their talents. Many of our comrades are not good at getting along with intellectuals. They are stiff with them, lack respect for their work, and interfere in scientific and cultural matters in a way that is uncalled for. We must do away with all such shortcomings. . . .

There has been a falling off recently in ideological and political work among students and intellectuals, and some unhealthy tendencies have appeared. Some people apparently think that there is no longer any need to concern themselves about politics, the future of their motherland and the ideals of mankind. It seems as if Marxism that was once all the rage is not so much in fashion now. This being the case, we must improve our ideological and political work. Both students and intellectuals should study hard. In addition to specialized subjects, they should study Marxism-Leninism, current events and political affairs in order to progress both ideologically and politically. Not to have a correct political point of view is like having no soul. . . . Our educational policy must enable everyone who gets an education, to develop morally, intellectually and physically and become a cultured, socialist-minded worker. We must spread the idea of building our country through hard work and thrift. We must see to it that all our young people understand that ours is still a very poor country, that we can't change this situation radically in a short time, and that only through the united efforts of our younger generation and all our people working with their own hands can our country be made strong and prosperous within a period of several decades. It is true that the establishment of our socialist system has opened the road leading to the ideal state of the future, but we must work hard, very hard indeed, if we are to make that ideal a reality. Some of our young people think that everything ought to be perfect once a socialist society is established and that they should be able to enjoy a happy life, ready-made, without working for it. This is unrealistic.

* * * *

"Let a hundred flowers blossom," and "let a hundred schools of thought contend,"* "long-term co-existence and mutual supervision"—how did these slogans come to be put forward?

They were put forward in the light of the specific conditions existing in China, on the basis of the recognition that various kinds of contradictions still exist in a socialist society, and in response to the country's urgent need to speed up its economic and cultural development.

The policy of letting a hundred flowers blossom and a hundred schools of thought contend is designed to promote the flourishing of the arts and the progress of science; it is designed to enable a socialist culture to thrive in our land. Different forms and styles in art can develop freely and different schools in science can contend freely. We think that it is harmful to the growth of art and science if administrative measures are used to impose one particular style of art or school of thought and to ban another. Questions of right and wrong in the arts

* "Let a hundred flowers blossom," and "let a hundred schools of thought contend" are two old Chinese sayings. The word "hundred" does not mean literally the number as such, but simply "numerous."— *Translator*

and sciences should be settled through free discussion in artistic and scientific circles and in the course of practical work in the arts and sciences. They should not be settled in summary fashion. A period of trial is often needed to determine whether something is right or wrong. In the past, new and correct things often failed at the outset to win recognition from the majority of people and had to develop by twists and turns in struggle. Correct and good things have often at first been looked upon not as fragrant flowers but as poisonous weeds. Copernicus' theory of the solar system and Darwin's theory of evolution were once dismissed as erroneous and had to win through over bitter opposition. Chinese history offers many similar examples. In socialist society, conditions for the growth of new things are radically different from and far superior to those in the old society. Nevertheless, it still often happens that new, rising forces are held back and reasonable suggestions smothered. . . .

Marxism can only develop through struggle—this is true not only in the past and present, it is necessarily true in the future also. What is correct always develops in the course of struggle with what is wrong. The true, the good and the beautiful always exist in comparison with the false, the evil and the ugly, and grow in struggle with the latter. As mankind in general rejects an untruth and accepts a truth, a new truth will begin struggling with new erroneous ideas. Such struggles will never end. This is the law of development of truth and it is certainly also the law of development of Marxism. . . .

People may ask: Since Marxism is accepted by the majority of the people in our country as the guiding ideology, can it be criticized? Certainly it can. As a scientific truth, Marxism fears no criticism. . . . Marxists should not be afraid of criticism from any quarter. Quite the contrary, they need to steel and improve themselves and win new positions in the teeth of criticism and the storm and stress of struggle. Fighting against wrong ideas is like being vaccinated—a man develops greater immunity from disease after the vaccine takes effect. Plants raised in hot-houses are not likely to be robust. Carrying out the policy of letting a hundred flowers blossom and a hundred schools of thought contend will not weaken but strengthen the leading position of Marxism in the ideological field. . . .

In 1956, small numbers of workers and students in certain places went on strike. The immediate cause of these disturbances was the failure to satisfy certain of their demands for material benefits, of which some should and could be met, while others were out of place or excessive and therefore could not be met for the time being. But a more important cause was bureaucracy on the part of those in positions of leadership. In some cases, responsibility for such bureaucratic mistakes should be placed on the higher authorities, and those at lower levels should not be made to bear all the blame. Another cause for these disturbances was that the ideological and political educational work done among the workers and students was inadequate. In the same year, members of a small number of agricultural co-operatives also created disturbances, and the main causes were also bureaucracy on the part of the leadership and lack of educational work among the masses.

It should be admitted that all too often some people are prone to concentrate on immediate, partial and personal interests, they do not understand or do not sufficiently understand long-range, nation-wide and collective interests. Because of their lack of experience in political and social life, quite a number of young people can't make a proper comparison between the old and new China; it is not easy for them to thoroughly comprehend what hardships the people of our country went through in the struggle to free themselves from oppression by the imperialists and Kuomintang reactionaries, or what a long period of painstaking work is needed before a happy socialist society can be established. That is why political educational work should be kept going among the masses in an interesting and effective way. We should always tell them the facts about the difficulties that have cropped up and discuss with them how to solve these difficulties. . . .

As I have said, in our society, it is bad when groups of people make disturbances, and we do not approve of it. But when disturbances do occur, they force us to learn lessons from them, to overcome bureaucracy and educate the cadres and the people. In this sense, bad things can be turned into good things. Disturbances thus have a dual character. All kinds of disturbances can be looked at in this way. . . .

Given specific conditions, the two aspects of a contradiction invariably turn into their respective opposites as a result of the struggle between them. Here, the conditions are important. Without specific conditions, neither of the two contradictory aspects can transform itself into its opposite. Of all the classes in the world the proletariat is the most eager to change its position; next comes the semi-proletariat, for the former possesses nothing at all, while the latter is not much better off. The present situation in which the United States controls a majority in the United Nations and dominates many parts of the world is a transient one, which will eventually be changed. China's situation as a poor country denied her rights in international affairs will also be changed—a poor country will be changed into a rich country, a country denied her rights into a country enjoying her rights—a transformation of things into their opposites. Here, the decisive conditions are the socialist system and the concerted efforts of a united people.

* * *

A dangerous tendency has shown itself of late among many of our personnel—an unwillingness to share the joys and hardships of the masses, a concern for personal position and gain. This is very bad. One way of overcoming this dangerous tendency is, in our campaign, to increase production and practise economy, to streamline our organizations and transfer cadres to lower levels so that a considerable number of them will return to productive work. We must see to it that all our cadres and all our people constantly bear in mind that, while ours is a big socialist country, it is an economically backward and poor country, and that this is a very great contradiction. If we want to see China rich and strong, we must be prepared for several decades of intensive effort which will include, among other things, carrying out a policy of building our country through hard work and thrift—of practising strict economy and combating waste. . . .

Long Live the Victory of People's War!*

LIN PIAO

FULL TWENTY YEARS have elapsed since our victory in the great War of Resistance Against Japan. . . .

Of the innumerable anti-imperialist wars waged by the Chinese people in the past hundred years, the War of Resistance Against Japan was the first to end in complete victory. It occupies an extremely important place in the annals of war, in the annals of both the revolutionary wars of the Chinese people and the wars of the oppressed nations of the world against imperialist aggression.

It was a war in which a weak semi-colonial and semi-feudal country triumphed over a strong imperialist country. . . .

* "Long Live the Victory of People's War!" by Lin Piao. Reprinted in *Peking Review*, No. 36, September 3, 1965, pp. 9–30.

How was it possible for a weak country finally to defeat a strong country? How was it possible for a seemingly weak army to become the main force in the war?

The basic reasons were that the War of Resistance Against Japan was a genuine people's war led by the Communist Party of China and Comrade Mao Tse-tung, a war in which the correct Marxist-Leninist political and military lines were put into effect, and that the Eighth Route and New Fourth Armies were genuine people's armies which applied the whole range of strategy and tactics of people's war as formulated by Comrade Mao Tse-tung.

Comrade Mao Tse-tung's theory of and policies for people's war have creatively enriched and developed Marxism-Leninism. The Chinese people's victory in the anti-Japanese war was a victory for people's war, for Marxism-Leninism and the thought of Mao Tse-tung. . . .

Today, the U.S. imperialists are repeating on a world-wide scale the past actions of the Japanese imperialists in China and other parts of Asia. It has become an urgent necessity for the people in many countries to master and use people's war as a weapon against U.S. imperialism and its lackeys. In every conceivable way U.S. imperialism and its lackeys are trying to extinguish the revolutionary flames of people's war. The Khrushchov revisionists, fearing people's war like the plague, are heaping abuse on it. The two are colluding to prevent and sabotage people's war. In these circumstances, it is of vital practical importance to review the historical experience of the great victory of the people's war in China and to recapitulate Comrade Mao Tse-tung's theory of people's war.

* * *

CORRECTLY APPLY THE LINE AND POLICY OF THE UNITED FRONT

In order to win a people's war, it is imperative to build the broadest possible united front and formulate a series of policies which will ensure the fullest mobilization of the basic masses as well as the unity of all the forces that can be united.

History shows that when confronted by ruthless imperialist aggression, a Communist Party must hold aloft the national banner and, using the weapon of the united front, rally around itself the masses and the patriotic and anti-imperialist people who form more than 90 per cent of a country's population, so as to mobilize all positive factors, unite with all the forces that can be united and isolate to the maximum the common enemy of the whole nation. If we abandon the national banner, adopt a line of "closed-doorism" and thus isolate ourselves, it is out of the question to exercise leadership and develop the people's revolutionary cause, and this in reality amounts to helping the enemy and bringing defeat on ourselves.

History shows that within the united front the Communist Party must maintain its ideological, political and organizational independence, adhere to the principle of independence and initiative, and insist on its leading role. Since there are class differences among the various classes in the united front, the Party must have a correct policy in order to develop the progressive forces, win over the middle forces and oppose the die-hard forces. The Party's work must centre on developing the progressive forces and expanding the people's revolutionary forces. This is the only way to maintain and strengthen the united front. "If unity is sought through struggle, it will live; if unity is sought through yielding, it will perish." This is the chief experience gained in our struggle against the die-hard forces. . . .

BUILD A PEOPLE'S ARMY OF A NEW TYPE

"Without a people's army the people have nothing." This is the conclusion drawn by Comrade Mao Tse-tung from the Chinese people's experience in their long years of revolutionary struggle, experience that was bought in blood. This is a universal truth of Marxism-Leninism. . . .

The essence of Comrade Mao Tse-tung's theory of army building is that in building a people's army prominence must be given to politics, *i.e*, the army must first and foremost be built on a political basis. Politics is the commander, politics is the soul of everything. Political work is the lifeline of our army. True, a people's army must pay attention to the constant improvement of its weapons and equipment and its military technique, but in its fighting it does not rely purely on weapons and technique, it relies mainly on politics, on the proletarian revolutionary consciousness and courage of the commanders and fighters, on the support and backing of the masses.

Owing to the application of Comrade Mao Tse-tung's line on army building, there has prevailed in our army at all times a high level of proletarian political consciousness, an atmosphere of keenness to study the thought of Mao Tse-tung, an excellent morale, a solid unity and a deep hatred for the enemy, and thus a gigantic moral force has been brought into being. In battle it has feared neither hardships nor death, it has been able to charge or hold its ground as the conditions require. One man can play the role of several, dozens or even hundreds, and miracles can be performed. . . .

ADHERE TO THE POLICY OF SELF-RELIANCE

The Chinese People's War of Resistance Against Japan was an important part of the Anti-Fascist World War. The victory of the Anti-Fascist War as a whole was the result of the common struggle of the people of the world. By its participation in the war against Japan at the final stage, the Soviet army under the leadership of the Communist Party of the Soviet Union headed by Stalin played a significant part in bringing about the defeat of Japanese imperialism. Great contributions were made by the peoples of Korea, Viet Nam, Mongolia, Laos, Cambodia, Indonesia, Burma, India, Pakistan, Malaya, the Philippines, Thailand and certain other Asian countries. The people of the Americas, Oceania, Europe and Africa also made their contribution. . . .

The common victory was won by all the peoples, who gave one another support and encouragement. Yet each country was, above all, liberated as a result of its own people's efforts. . . .

In order to make a revolution and to fight a people's war and be victorious, it is imperative to adhere to the policy of self-reliance, rely on the strength of the masses in one's own country and prepare to carry on the fight independently even when all material aid from outside is cut off. If one does not operate by one's own efforts, does not independently ponder and solve the problems of the revolution in one's own country and does not rely on the strength of the masses, but leans wholly on foreign aid—even though this be aid from socialist countries which persist in revolution—no victory can be won, or be consolidated even if it is won.

THE INTERNATIONAL SIGNIFICANCE OF COMRADE MAO TSE-TUNG'S THEORY OF PEOPLE'S WAR

The Chinese revolution is a continuation of the Great October Revolution. The road of the October Revolution is the common road for all people's revolutions. The Chinese revolution and the October Revolution have in common the following basic characteristics: (1) Both were led by the working class with a Marxist-Leninist party as its nucleus. (2) Both were based on the worker-peasant alliance. (3) In both cases state power was seized through violent revolution and the dictatorship of the proletariat was established. (4) In both cases the socialist system was built after victory in the revolution. (5) Both were component parts of the proletarian world revolution.

Naturally, the Chinese revolution had its own peculiar

characteristics. The October Revolution took place in imperialist Russia, but the Chinese revolution broke out in a semi-colonial and semi-feudal country. The former was a proletarian socialist revolution, while the latter developed into a socialist revolution after the complete victory of the new-democratic revolution. The October Revolution began with armed uprisings in the cities and then spread to the countryside, while the Chinese revolution won nation-wide victory through the encirclement of the cities from the rural areas and the final capture of the cities.

In the world today, all the imperialists headed by the United States and their lackeys, without exception, are strengthening their state machinery, and especially their armed forces. U.S. imperialism, in particular, is carrying out armed aggression and suppression everywhere.

What should the oppressed nations and the oppressed people do in the face of wars of aggression and armed suppression by the imperialists and their lackeys? Should they submit and remain slaves in perpetuity? Or should they rise in resistance and fight for their liberation?

Comrade Mao Tse-tung answered this question in vivid terms. He said that after long investigation and study the Chinese people discovered that all the imperialists and their lackeys "have swords in their hands and are out to kill. The people have come to understand this and so act after the same fashion." This is called doing unto them what they do unto us.

In the last analysis, whether one dares to wage a tit-for-tat struggle against armed aggression and suppression by the imperialists and their lackeys, whether one dares to fight a people's war against them, is tantamount to whether one dares to embark on revolution. This is the most effective touchstone for distinguishing genuine from fake revolutionaries and Marxist-Leninists.

In view of the fact that some people were afflicted with the fear of the imperialists and reactionaries, Comrade Mao Tse-tung put forward his famous thesis that "the imperialists and all reactionaries are paper tigers." He said,

> All reactionaries are paper tigers. In appearance, the reactionaries are terrifying, but in reality they are not so powerful. From a long-term point of view, it is not the reactionaries but the people who are really powerful.

The history of people's war in China and other countries provides conclusive evidence that the growth of the people's revolutionary forces from weak and small beginnings into strong and large forces is a universal law of development of class struggle, a universal law of development of people's war. A people's war inevitably meets with many difficulties, with ups and downs and setbacks in the course of its development, but no force can alter its general trend towards inevitable triumph.

Comrade Mao Tse-tung points out that we must despise the enemy strategically and take full account of him tactically.

To despise the enemy strategically is an elementary requirement for a revolutionary. Without the courage to despise the enemy and without daring to win, it will be simply impossible to make revolution and wage a people's war, let alone to achieve victory.

It is also very important for revolutionaries to take full account of the enemy tactically. It is likewise impossible to win victory in a people's war without taking full account of the enemy tactically, and without examining the concrete conditions, without being prudent and giving great attention to the study of the art of struggle, and without adopting appropriate forms of struggle in the concrete practice of the revolution in each country and with regard to each concrete problem of struggle.

Dialectical and historical materialism teaches us that what is important primarily is not that which at the given moment seems to be durable and yet is already beginning to die away, but that which is arising and developing, even though at the given moment it may not appear to be durable, for only that which is arising and developing is invincible.

Why can the apparently weak new-born forces always triumph over the decadent forces which appear so powerful? The reason is that truth is on their side and that the masses are on their side, while the reactionary classes are always divorced from the masses and set themselves against the masses.

This has been borne out by the victory of the Chinese revolution, by the history of all revolutions, the whole history of class struggle and the entire history of mankind.

The imperialists are extremely afraid of Comrade Mao Tse-tung's thesis that "imperialism and all reactionaries are paper tigers," and the revisionists are extremely hostile to it. They all oppose and attack this thesis and the philistines follow suit by ridiculing it. But all this cannot in the least diminish its importance. The light of truth cannot be dimmed by anybody.

Comrade Mao Tse-tung's theory of people's war solves not only the problem of daring to fight a people's war, but also that of how to wage it. . . .

It must be emphasized that Comrade Mao Tse-tung's theory of the establishment of rural revolutionary base areas and the encirclement of the cities from the countryside is of outstanding and universal practical importance for the present revolutionary struggles of all the oppressed nations and peoples, and particularly for the revolutionary struggles of the oppressed nations and peoples in Asia, Africa and Latin America against imperialism and its lackeys.

Many countries and peoples in Asia, Africa and Latin America are now being subjected to aggression and enslavement on a serious scale by the imperialists headed by the United States and their lackeys. The basic political and economic conditions in many of these countries have many similarities to those that prevailed in old China. As in China, the peasant question is extremely important in these regions. The peasants constitute the main force of the national-democratic revolution against the imperialists and their lackeys. In committing aggression against these countries, the imperialists usually begin by seizing the big cities and the main lines of communication, but they are unable to bring the vast countryside completely under their control. The countryside, and the countryside alone, can provide the broad areas in which the revolutionaries can manoeuvre freely. The countryside, and the countryside alone, can provide the revolutionary bases from which the revolutionaries can go forward to final victory. Precisely for this reason, Comrade Mao Tse-tung's theory of establishing revolutionary base areas in the rural districts and encircling the cities from the countryside is attracting more and more attention among the people in these regions.

Taking the entire globe, if North America and Western Europe can be called "the cities of the world," then Asia, Africa and Latin America constitute "the rural areas of the world." Since World War II, the proletarian revolutionary movement has for various reasons been temporarily held back in the North American and West European capitalist countries, while the people's revolutionary movement in Asia, Africa and Latin America has been growing vigorously. In a sense, the contemporary world revolution also presents a picture of the encirclement of cities by the rural areas. In the final analysis, the whole cause of world revolution hinges on the revolutionary struggles of the Asian, African and Latin American peoples who make up the overwhelming majority of the world's population. The socialist countries should regard it as their internationalist duty to support the people's revolutionary struggles in Asia, Africa and Latin America. . . .

DEFEAT U.S. IMPERIALISM AND ITS LACKEYS BY PEOPLE'S WAR

Since World War II, U.S. imperialism has stepped into the shoes of German, Japanese and Italian fascism and has been trying to build a great American empire by dominating and enslaving the whole world. It is actively fostering Japanese and West German militarism as its chief accomplices in unleashing a world war. Like a vicious wolf, it is bullying and enslaving various peoples, plundering their wealth, encroaching upon their countries' sovereignty and interfering in their internal affairs. It is the most rabid aggressor in human history and the most ferocious common enemy of the people of the world. Every people or country in the world that wants revolution, independence and peace cannot but direct the spearhead of its struggle against U.S. imperialism.

Just as the Japanese imperialists' policy of subjugating China made it possible for the Chinese people to form the broadest possible united front against them, so the U.S. imperialists' policy of seeking world domination makes it possible for the people throughout the world to unite all the forces that can be united and form the broadest possible united front for a converging attack on U.S. imperialism. . . .

U.S. imperialism is stronger, but also more vulnerable, than any imperialism of the past. It sets itself against the people of the whole world, including the people of the United States. Its human, military, material and financial resources are far from sufficient for the realization of its ambition of dominating the whole world. U.S. imperialism has further weakened itself by occupying so many places in the world, overreaching itself, stretching its fingers out wide and dispersing its strength, with its rear so far away and its supply lines so long. As Comrade Mao Tse-tung has said, "Wherever it commits aggression, it puts a new noose around its neck. It is besieged ring upon ring by the people of the whole world."

When committing aggression in a foreign country, U.S. imperialism can only employ part of its forces, which are sent to fight an unjust war far from their native land and therefore have a low morale, and so U.S. imperialism is beset with great difficulties. The people subjected to its aggression are having a trial of strength with U.S. imperialism neither in Washington nor New York, neither in Honolulu nor Florida, but are fighting for independence and freedom on their own soil. Once they are mobilized on a broad scale, they will have inexhaustible strength. Thus superiority will belong not to the United States but to the people subjected to its aggression. The latter, though apparently weak and small, are really more powerful than U.S. imperialism.

The struggles waged by the different peoples against U.S. imperialism reinforce each other and merge into a torrential world-wide tide of opposition to U.S. imperialism. The more successful the development of people's war in a given region, the larger the number of U.S. imperialist forces that can be pinned down and depleted there. When the U.S. aggressors are hard pressed in one place, they have no alternative but to loosen their grip on others. Therefore, the conditions become more favourable for the people elsewhere to wage struggles against U.S. imperialism and its lackeys.

Everything is divisible. And so is this colossus of U.S. imperialism. It can be split up and defeated. The peoples of Asia, Africa, Latin America and other regions can destroy it piece by piece, some striking at its head and others at its feet. That is why the greatest fear of U.S. imperialism is that people's wars will be launched in different parts of the world, and particularly in Asia, Africa and Latin America, and why it regards people's war as a mortal danger.

U.S. imperialism relies solely on its nuclear weapons to intimidate people. But these weapons cannot save U.S. imperialism from its doom. Nuclear weapons cannot be used lightly. U.S. imperialism has been condemned by the people of the whole world for its towering crime of dropping two atom bombs on Japan. If it uses nuclear weapons again, it will become isolated in the extreme. Moreover, the U.S. monopoly of nuclear weapons has long been broken; U.S. imperialism has these weapons, but others have them too. If it threatens other countries with nuclear weapons, U.S. imperialism will expose its own country to the same threat. For this reason, it will meet with strong opposition not only from the people elsewhere but also inevitably from the people in its own country. Even if U.S. imperialism brazenly uses nuclear weapons, it cannot conquer the people, who are indomitable.

However highly developed modern weapons and technical equipment may be and however complicated the methods of modern warfare, in the final analysis the outcome of a war will be decided by the sustained fighting of the ground forces, by the fighting at close quarters on battlefields, by the political consciousness of the men, by their courage and spirit of sacrifice. Here the weak points of U.S. imperialism will be completely laid bare, while the superiority of the revolutionary people will be brought into full play. The reactionary troops of U.S. imperialism cannot possibly be endowed with the courage and the spirit of sacrifice possessed by the revolutionary people. The spiritual atom bomb which the revolutionary people possess is a far more powerful and useful weapon than the physical atom bomb.

Viet Nam is the most convincing current example of a victim of aggression defeating U.S. imperialism by a people's war. The United States has made south Viet Nam a testing ground for the suppression of people's war. It has carried on this experiment for many years, and everybody can now see that the U.S. aggressors are unable to find a way of coping with people's war. On the other hand, the Vietnamese people have brought the power of people's war into full play in their struggle against the U.S. aggressors. The U.S. aggressors are in danger of being swamped in the people's war in Viet Nam. They are deeply worried that their defeat in Viet Nam will lead to a chain reaction. They are expanding the war in an attempt to save themselves from defeat. But the more they expand the war, the greater will be the chain reaction. The more they escalate the war, the heavier will be their fall and the more disastrous their defeat. The people in other parts of the world will see still more clearly that U.S. imperialism can be defeated, and that what the Vietnamese people can do, they can do too.

History has proved and will go on proving that people's war is the most effective weapon against U.S. imperialism and its lackeys. All revolutionary people will learn to wage people's war against U.S. imperialism and its lackeys. They will take up arms, learn to fight battles and become skilled in waging people's war, though they have not done so before. U.S. imperialism like a mad bull dashing from place to place, will finally be burned to ashes in the blazing fires of the people's wars it has provoked by its own actions. . . .

We are optimistic about the future of the world. We are confident that the people will bring to an end the epoch of wars in human history. Comrade Mao Tse-tung pointed out long ago that war, this monster, "will be finally eliminated by the progress of human society, and in the not too distant future too. But there is only one way to eliminate it and that is to oppose war with war, to oppose counter-revolutionary war with revolutionary war.

All peoples suffering from U.S. imperialist aggression, oppression and plunder, unite! Hold aloft the just banner of people's war and fight for the cause of world peace, national liberation, people's democracy and socialism! Victory will certainly go to the people of the world!

Long live the victory of people's war!

SHORT SELECTIONS FROM MAO TSE-TUNG

The following three short pieces, written by Mao Tse-tung in 1939, 1944 and 1945, are used as basic readings in the cultural revolution. "In Memory of Norman Bethune" and "Serve the People" were testimonials to a Canadian and a Chinese comrade both of whom sacrificed their lives in the Communists' struggle against the Japanese. "The Foolish Old Man Who Removed the Mountains" is an allegorical tale Mao used to emphasize the need for faith and perseverance in the face of all the hardships revolution imposed. By singling out the virtues with which to overcome obstacles, these three pieces contain the central messages of the cultural revolution: (1) the spirit of selflessness in performing one's job with dedication, (2) the spirit of welcoming criticism of one's shortcomings regardless of its source and (3) the conviction that all obstacles no matter how great can be overcome with endurance, hard work and faith in the masses.

In Memory of Norman Bethune*

December 21, 1939

Comrade Norman Bethune, a member of the Communist Party of Canada, was around fifty when he was sent by the Communist Parties of Canada and the United States to China; he made light of traveling thousands of miles to help us in our War of Resistance Against Japan. He arrived in Yenan in the spring of last year, went to work in the Wutai Mountains, and to our great sorrow died a martyr at his post. What kind of spirit is this that makes a foreigner selflessly adopt the cause of the Chinese people's liberation as his own? It is the spirit of internationalism, the spirit of communism, from which every Chinese Communist must learn. . . .

Comrade Bethune's spirit, his utter devotion to others without any thought of self, was shown in his great sense of re-

* Mao Tse-tung, SELECTED WORKS, op. cit., Vol. II, pp. 337-338.

sponsibility in his work and his great warm-heartedness towards all comrades and the people. Every Communist must learn from him. There are not a few people who are irresponsible in their work, preferring the light and shirking the heavy, passing the burdensome tasks on to others and choosing the easy ones for themselves. At every turn they think of themselves before others. When they make some small contribution, they swell with pride and brag about it for fear that others will not know. They feel no warmth towards comrades and the people but are cold, indifferent and apathetic. In truth such people are not Communists, or at least cannot be counted as devoted Communists. No one who returned from the front failed to express admiration for Bethune whenever his name was mentioned, and none remained unmoved by his spirit. In the Shansi-Chahar-Hopei border area, no soldier or civilian was unmoved who had been treated by Dr. Bethune or had seen how he worked. Every Communist must learn this true communist spirit from Comrade Bethune.

Comrade Bethune was a doctor, the art of healing was his profession and he was constantly perfecting his skill, which stood very high in the Eighth Route Army's medical service. His example is an excellent lesson for those people who wish to change their work the moment they see something different and for those who despise technical work as of no consequence or as promising no future.

Comrade Bethune and I met only once. Afterwards he wrote me many letters. But I was busy, and I wrote him only one letter and do not even know if he ever received it. I am deeply grieved over his death. Now we are all commemorating him, which shows how profoundly his spirit inspires everyone. We must all learn the spirit of absolute selflessness from him. With this spirit everyone can be very useful to the people. A man's ability may be great or small, but if he has this spirit, he is already noble-minded and pure, a man of moral integrity and above vulgar interests, a man who is of value to the people.

Serve the People*

September 8, 1944

If we have shortcomings, we are not afraid to have them pointed out and criticized, because we serve the people. Anyone, no matter who, may point out our shortcomings. If he is right, we will correct them. If what he proposes will benefit the people, we will act upon it. The idea of "better troops and simpler administration" was put forward by Mr. Li Ting-ming, who is not a Communist. He made a good suggestion which is of benefit to the people, and we have adopted it. If, in the interests of the people, we persist in doing what is right and correct what is wrong, our ranks will surely thrive.

We hail from all corners of the country and have joined together for a common revolutionary objective. And we need the vast majority of the people with us on the road to this objective. Today, we already lead base areas with a population of 91 million, but this is not enough; to liberate the whole nation more are needed. In times of difficulty we must not lose sight of our achievements, must see the bright future and must pluck up our courage. The Chinese people are suffering; it is our duty to save them and we must exert ourselves in struggle. Wherever there is struggle there is sacrifice, and death is a common occurrence. But we have the interests of the people and the sufferings of the great majority at heart, and when we die for the people it is a worthy death. Nevertheless, we should do our best to avoid unnecessary sacrifices. Our cadres must show concern for every soldier, and all people in the revolutionary ranks must care for each other, must love and help each other.

From now on, when anyone in our ranks who has done some useful work dies, be he soldier or cook, we should have a funeral ceremony and a memorial meeting in his honour. This should become the rule. And it should be introduced among the people as well. When someone dies in a village, let a memorial meeting be held. In this way we express our mourning for the dead and unite all the people.

* Mao Tse-tung, SELECTED WORKS, ibid., Vol. III, pp. 227-228.

The Foolish Old Man
Who Removed the Mountains*

June 11, 1945

We have had a very successful congress. We have done three things. First, we have decided on the line of our Party, which is boldly to mobilize the masses and expand the people's forces so that, under the leadership of our Party, they will defeat the Japanese aggressors, liberate the whole people and build a new-democratic China. Second, we have adopted the new Party Constitution. Third, we have elected the leading body of the Party—the Central Committee. Henceforth our task is to lead the whole membership in carrying out the Party line. Ours has been a congress of victory, a congress of unity. The delegates have made excellent comments on the three reports. Many comrades have undertaken self-criticism and, setting out with unity as the objective, have arrived at unity through self-criticism. This congress is a model of unity, of self-criticism and of inner-Party democracy.

When the congress closes, many comrades will be leaving for their posts and the various war fronts. Comrades, wherever you go, you should propagate the line of the congress and, through the members of the Party, explain it to the broad masses.

Our aim in propagating the line of the congress is to build up the confidence of the whole Party and the entire people in the certain triumph of the revolution. We must first raise the political consciousness of the vanguard so that, resolute and unafraid of sacrifice, they will surmount every difficulty to win victory. But this is not enough; we must also arouse the political consciousness of the entire people so that they may willingly and gladly fight together with us for victory. We should fire the whole people with the conviction that China belongs not to the reactionaries but to the Chinese people. There is an ancient Chinese fable called "The Foolish Old Man Who Removed the Mountains". It tells of an old man who lived in northern China long, long ago and was known as the Foolish Old Man of North Mountain. His house faced

* Mao Tse-tung, SELECTED WORKS, *ibid.*, pp. 321–323.

south and beyond his doorway stood the two great peaks, Taihang and Wanghu, obstructing the way. He called his sons, and hoe in hand they began to dig up these mountains with great determination. Another greybeard, known as the Wise Old Man, saw them and said derisively, "How silly of you to do this! It is quite impossible for you few to dig up these two huge mountains." The Foolish Old Man replied, "When I die, my sons will carry on; when they die, there will be my grandsons, and then their sons and grandsons, and so on to infinity. High as they are, the mountains cannot grow any higher and with every bit we dig, they will be that much lower. Why can't we clear them away?" Having refuted the Wise Old Man's wrong view, he went on digging every day, unshaken in his conviction. God was moved by this, and he sent down two angels, who carried the mountains away on their backs. Today, two big mountains lie like a dead weight on the Chinese people. One is imperialism, the other is feudalism. The Chinese Communist Party has long made up its mind to dig them up. We must persevere and work unceasingly, and we, too, will touch God's heart. Our God is none other than the masses of the Chinese people. If they stand up and dig together with us, why can't these two mountains be cleared away? . . .

> Jean-Louis Vincent, a correspondent for Agence France Presse, returned to Paris after an extended tour of duty in Peking. The following is his collection of observations on the situation in Peking which we can follow only at a great distance through other people's photographic lenses.

Life in Peking: Report from a Long Nose*

JEAN-LOUIS VINCENT

TEN YEARS AGO, in the streets of Peking, European-looking foreigners were greeted with a warm welcome. Chinese children took it for granted that a European in People's China had to be a Soviet expert. Therefore, upon seeing a British diplomat, a West German businessman or a French journalist, some child would cry excitedly: "A Soviet man," and almost immediately hundreds of people would gather, smile, shake hands

* From The New York Times, February 26, 1967. © 1967 by The New York Times Company. Reprinted by permission. Jean Vincent is Correspondent in Peking for Agence France-Presse (AFP).

and say something which sounds like "knee-how" and means "good day." This automatic reaction went on, amazingly, well after the Sino-Soviet quarrel was already in full swing.

Indeed, only last summer, while walking in the heart of Peking on Tien An Men Square among thousands of visiting Red Guards, I had a little chat with two girls from the south and—to tease them and see what their reaction would be—said I was from the Soviet Union. The girls kept smiling and one of them offered some apples she was carrying in a bag. It may well be that they knew nothing about the intricacies of what was still officially an ideological dispute, or simply did not know what the Soviet Union is, or that they thought this particular "Soviet citizen" was one of the happy few who had escaped the "revisionist white terror" and chosen freedom in China.

Whatever the case then, even these two girls probably know by now that when meeting a Soviet citizen smiles and apples are not appropriate. The trouble is, however, that when Chinese children see foreigners they are still convinced that they are looking at Russians, (except, of course, for a small and admirable, but unrecognizable, minority of Albanian comrades). So the children still shout "Soviet man" when a Long Nose appears. And a crowd still gathers. Only now, smiles have been replaced by boos, by angry banging on the foreigner's car and by showers of abuse, which includes heavy spitting.

Until this month, representatives of capitalist countries could stay out of trouble by explaining that they were not from the Soviet Union. For instance, several times, while driving around the Soviet Embassy in what is now called "Antirevisionist Street" (it used to be "The Street of the Growing Prestige"), this correspondent had to proclaim his loyal and faithful attachment to the Western world, especially to France, in order to avoid more spitting, insults and possible violence by Red Guards and other "revolutionary" people.

Now, of course, being French does not help any more. In fact, it became a serious handicap during the first week of February, after two Chinese students had apparently been injured by the Paris police, and after the French Commercial Counselor in Peking and his wife had been detained for seven hours by demonstrators while trying to enter the French Embassy and, in so doing, had "insulted the masses."

A most astonishing point in the Chinese version of this incident is the fact that the counselor, Robert Richard, is supposed to have crushed something like 10 "peaceful demonstrators" with his car. That is an offense that would be serious by anyone's standards, yet all he and his wife would have had to do to be released from the circle of shame in which the crowd kept them prisoner in the darkness and below-freezing cold, under the eyes of unconcerned policemen, was to make a public apology to the masses. It is precisely because they refused to do this that they were kept in the cold, and later spent six hours in a police station.

Other angry explosions have burst out in recent weeks before the Soviet and Yugoslav Embassies also. But to understand properly the extent of the hatred and the meticulous care with which it is implemented, one must go shopping at the diplomats' supermarket at Wai Chiao Ta Lo—the block of apartment buildings reserved for "foreign friends." In this store, where soda, candies, meats, poultry and succulent vegetables are sold—not to speak of caviar packed in cartons labeled "Lily Cup, New York, U.S.A."—a newcomer is struck by what seems to be a festive atmosphere: bunting, signs and multicolored garlands. For those who can read Chinese, or Russian or French, the welcome is less warm. "Down with Franco-Soviet revisionist collusion," proclaims a giant sign set up near the cash desk, while yellow and pink streamers above the counters urge: "Resolutely crush the dog heads Brezhnev, Kosygin and Tito." A refinement: the butcher's counter is decorated with a warning appropriate to his wares —"Slice up Kosygin." Over the fish is a sign in English: "Fry the dog head of Tito." Xenophobia is exercised, though, by another sign that invites the foreigner not to be confused: "Long live the friendship of the Chinese and Soviet peoples."

In truth, whatever their political meaning, the recent anti-Soviet, anti-Yugoslav and anti-French demonstrations in Peking do not seem to reflect any antiforeigner sentiment. The same cooks, chauffeurs, interpreters and other Chinese employes who go on strike to protest the "Facist atrocities" of one government or another and who during these symbolic walkouts demonstrate in front of the offices of their foreign employers, menace them with their fists and occasionally spray them with saliva return to being helpful and irreproachable aides once the strike is over. Demonstrating in Peking is an assignment like any other, just as subject to planning and precise timing.

The Chinese demonstrator knows how to temper fury with discipline. Verbally, he commits the greatest excesses, but, in fact, he keeps his calm. To see him scream, shake fists that come within an inch of the chin of the adversary but never strike—never crossing the invisible limit of his instructions—is to understand that nothing which has not been planned will happen. If the unthinkable should come to pass, it would not be by chance—it would not be by error.

The demonstrators have come in two waves. The first comprised the Red Guards, who flocked to Peking between last August and November. The Red Guard was a youngster. Usually dressed in blue like nearly everyone else, occasionally in khaki, he was 12 to 22 years old. He could be recognized by his red armband on which flashed the three yellow characters *Hung Wei Ping* (Red Guard).

"Revolutionary rebel" workers make up the second group. The revolutionary rebel is generally an adult. He too, can be recognized by his armband. (Practically everyone on the streets of Peking wears an armband of one sort or another.) He is a workman or civil servant; since December, revolutionary rebel groups have been formed in all the Peking factories, in all the Government ministries, at the railway station, airport, hotels, stores and other establishments.

Like the Red Guards, the revolutionary rebels are commanded by group chiefs. These can be readily recognized during the demonstrations because each carries a piece of paper on which are written the slogans that they read out and that everyone repeats.

In addition, the 10 mass demonstrations that took place in Tien An Men Square between Aug. 18 and Nov 26, 1966 (if one counts the Oct. 1 demonstration marking the national holiday) were preceded by rehearsals in all the streets of Peking, where one could see the Red Guards moving about in para-military units, each commanded by a leader, about 40 or 50 youths to a unit.

The precise organization of either the Red Guards or the revolutionary rebels remains something of a mystery. On Aug. 18, foreigners in Peking saw about two million young people leave for Tien An Men Square, without knowing what they were going to see, without being able to go themselves and without the slightest rumor having filtered out on what this first mass meeting of the Cultural Revolution was about. The same was true of the subsequent rallies.

The impression, however, is that in both the revolutionary rebels and the Red Guards, an organic structure parallel to that of the Communist party or the League of Communist Youth is in action. That so secret an organization can function with such precision and efficiency suggests that—in Peking, at least—the Cultural Revolution and its sequels never triggered an opposition dangerous to the regime.

Officially, of course, the purpose of the Cultural Revolution has been to unmask, depose and humiliate a group of leaders of the Communist party who had adopted the "capitalist way," and who thus, in a China that intends to remain pure, risked planting the cursed seeds of "modern revisionism."

The ringleaders of this faction were said to be none other than Peking's Mayor, Peng Chen (then seventh-highest figure in the regime, on the official list); the former Chief of the General Staff, Lo Jui-ching; the former Culture Minister and Chief of the Propaganda Department of the Central Committee, Lu Ting-yi, and Yang Chang-kun—whose position in the Central Committee gave him, if one is to believe the Red Guard press, the opportunity to plant microphones in the private quarters of Chairman Mao Tse-tung and thus communicate savory recordings to the Soviet Ambassador. With them were condemned a group of Peking intellectuals labeled the "black band."

In addition, since the founding of the Red Guard, a second group of villains has been identified. They are labeled the "handful of obstinates applying the bourgeois reactionary line opposed to the proletarian line of Chairman Mao Tse-tung." It is against this handful that the "revolutionary rebels" of industry and the countryside near the large cities are now fighting. According to the hundreds of thousands of posters that garnish the walls of Peking, its principal leaders are the President of the Republic, Liu Shao-chi, and the Secretary General of the Communist party, Teng Hsiao-ping. Hundreds of other responsible officials have been publicly disgraced simply for having carried out the orders of these two. The posters defaming them must lead the Chinese man in the street to distrust everyone—perhaps even himself.

These posters are put up in nearly every district of Peking and its sprawling suburbs—in Tien An Men Square, on the walls enclosing the Forbidden City and the walls near the Gate of Celestial Peace, in Hsi Tan, a shopping street, and Wang Fu Ching Street, which is a sort of Pekingese Fifth Avenue. During the Red Guard phase of the Cultural Revolution, they were put up by youths who could be seen going about the streets at night with cans of paint and large strips of paper. One youth first pasted a strip of paper on the walls, then two others, one with the paint and another with a brush, quickly painted on a text. These posters were called *ta tse bao*, (ta means "big"; *tse*, "character"; *bao*, "journal").

Later, there appeared slogans in giant characters which represented more brutal and brief attacks against the principal leaders. These slogans were also put up by youths, or sometimes painted on the street itself. For example, Tao Chu, who replaced Lu Ting-yi as propaganda chief only to be apparently deposed in turn, was the target of a great campaign which was written mainly in the street—apparently so that passers-by would automatically express their scorn for him by walking on the characters representing his name.

For Mao's purposes, the poster attacks are preferable to the use of the official press and radio because they correspond to the "mass line" of his ideology. Obviously, the movement is highly organized and controlled, but it is also evident that Mao believes the workers and peasants should sometimes be allowed to take some initiatives. Thus, if criticism of Liu, for example, were broadcast by the official radio or published in the newspapers, the whole thing would be over; the workers and peasants would simply say "yes." But because the radio and press say nothing, the masses—workers, peasants, students and every sort of revolutionary rebel and Red Guard—have the appearance of carrying on their own attacks against the leaders of the bourgeois reactionary line. It is a method that serves to demonstrate to the Chinese that the movement stems from the bottom upward.

Each day, several thousand new posters appear in Peking, and almost none have expressed any opposition to the Cultural Revolution. A few slogans did appear criticizing Premier Chou En-lai, and one day in January all the foreign correspondents in Peking roamed the streets trying to find a poster which was said to criticize Chairman Mao's wife, Chiang Ching. If indeed it existed, it had already been covered over when the correspondents arrived on the scene where it had allegedly been spotted by a diplomat. The expatriate American writer Anna Louise Strong reported that a poster criticizing Mao was put up at Tsinghwa University—and that the author of this *ta tse bao* had to be protected from his outraged comrades by the police.

There are some counter-posters. For example, there is a "regiment," or group of revolutionary rebels, of the Peking Aeronautical Institute that calls itself 915, signifying that it was formed on Sept. 15, and another that calls itself 916— that is, that it was formed Sept. 16. These two are rivals in ideological purity, and carry on a poster war, each claiming to be more Maoist than the other. But this war does not seem very serious. Such and such a group may be labeled inferior as not being sufficiently Maoist, but it is never said that Maoism is not good. The word, "Maoism," by the way, has been totally adopted by the Red Guard, although it is never used in the official press.

Not only officials have been victims of the Cultural Revolution. Consider, for example, the strange case of Shih Chuang-hsiang, the élite night-soil collector. His is a trade held in esteem in China because it provides a precious natural fertilizer. In addition, Shih was one of the stars of Chinese propaganda for many years. He represented a Peking district in the National Congress. Even after the disgrace of Mayor Peng, Shih's star continued to shine. The official press continued to carry his bylined articles striking out at "black band" intellectuals. (They had, he complained, opposed the filming of a movie on the life of night-soil collectors for which he had written the scenario.) In September, still in favor with the regime, he undertook to teach Red Guards visiting Peking how to become élite night-soil collectors, and the official news agency Hsinhua published a lyrical dispatch demonstrating that if at least one man could be proud of his good work and excellent ideological orientation, that man was Shih Chuang-hsiang.

Suddenly, on Jan. 15, the élite night-soil collector became an accursed night-soil collector. To the howls of a crowd that saw a prisoner pass every 10 minutes or so, he was driven in a truck through Peking, his head bowed, ridiculously rigged out with a large paper hat and a sign detailing the nature of his revisionist crimes: He had decorated his room with a photograph of himself in the company of Liu Shao-chi instead of with a portrait of Chairman Mao, and, as a parliamentary representative from Peking, he had had culpable dealings with Mayor Peng.

The technique is one that was set out in Mao's 1927 report on the peasant movement in Hunan Province. It is noteworthy that instructions were issued last fall indicating that this report should be studied and its lessons applied. Concerning paper hats and placards of shame, Mao wrote—in reference to the landlords and other defenders of feudalism 30 years ago:

"This sort of thing is very common. A tall paper hat is stuck on the head of one of the local tyrants or evil gentry. . . . He is led by a rope and escorted with big crowds in front and behind. Sometimes brass gongs are beaten and flags waved to attract people's attention. This form of punishment, more than any other, makes the local tyrant and evil gentry tremble.

Anyone who has once been crowned with a tall paper hat loses face altogether and can never again hold up his head."

He goes on: "One ingenious township peasant association arrested an obnoxious member of the gentry and announced that he was to be crowned that very day. The man turned blue with fear. Then the association decided not to crown him that day. They argued that if he were crowned right away he would become case-hardened and no longer afraid, and that it would be better to let him go home and crown him some other day. Not knowing when he would be crowned, the man was in daily suspense—unable to sit down or sleep at ease."

All this suggests that the Cultural Revolution is essentially anti-urban. In recent months, a semiofficial press—speaking in the name of the Red Guards and revolutionary workers—has made its appearance. Its target has been the bourgeois-reactionary "black wind of economism" symbolized by Liu and Teng. Their crime appears to have been to offer industrial workers the carrot of material stimulus: pay increases, yearly bonuses or other benefits. The "black wind" stands for the notion that China's progress should be linked to the progress of industry. It would thus aggravate the contradiction between rural and urban society. In a country whose supreme leaders appear obsessed by such contradictions and by the hope of creating a new man who will be neither worker nor peasant, neither soldier nor intellectual, but all rolled into one, this is a grave sin.

Even before the Cultural Revolution was in full swing, China's cities—not only Peking, but Shanghai and the industrial centers of Manchuria—were suspect and were downgraded in propaganda below the miracle-achievements of the model petroleum field of Taching or the brigade of Tachai. From those two units, born in the desert, where workers became peasants and peasants became workers, where the spirit of the "great leap forward" still lives, the regime has decided that the China of tomorrow must emerge.

Thus, as part of the downgrading of the cities, many posters put up in Peking have underlined the disparity between the incomes of the city workers and those of peasants. According to the revolutionary rebels, this difference can no longer be tolerated; all wages must be leveled to the lowest common denominator. A poster in the Peking station proposed salary reductions of 12 per cent to 60 per cent for railway employes. Similar posters appeared on some factory walls.

The visible effects of the Cultural Revolution on daily life are varied. Certainly, the principal stores are well-supplied with

502   China in the Sixties—Politics as Morality

consumer goods. There are bicycles for $40, radios from $20
to $120, television sets for $200, overcoats and blue cotton
raincoats for $24. But the average wage for an industrial
worker is not more than $32 a month. In the city, incomes run
about $16 a month, and for the peasantry, something like $40
to $80 a year. But food, by Western standards, is incredibly in-
expensive—and so plentiful that ration cards have long been
abandoned.

Entertainment has disappeared. Museums are shut. Parks
and zoos are open only intermittently. The city dweller now
appears to live for nothing but work, food and almost endless
meetings and demonstrations.

After the end of the Peking Opera came the end of the
modern theater, and the abolition of the popular folklore
shows. One wonderful entertainer who disappeared was Ho
Bao-lin, whose specialty had been the subtle mockery of sacred
institutions. Masquerading as a star of the Peking Opera he
would announce to his straight man that he was about to join
the Institute of Irrigation. The straight man would express as-
tonishment. "Why," Ho Bao-lin would say, "don't you know
that to become a great actor or a great orator you must know
how to irrigate your vocal chords with *mao tai?*" *Mao tai*, besides echoing the chairman's name, is a drink as colorless as
gin and much stronger.

Movies have been closed, too, since late last summer, and
even then there were only four being shown in all of China.
Three were documentaries of Mao reviewing the mass demonstrations of Red Guards in Peking. The other was an hour-long
documentary on China's three nuclear explosions. Audiences
read aloud in chorus the quotations from Mao flashed on the
screen, and greeted each mushroom cloud with an incredible
show of gaiety. The sound track of the film explains that atomic
bombs are bombs like any others and that it is easy to escape
them by knowing how to take the proper precautions. As if
to confirm this point of view, the final scene shows a hen, which
had been left in a cage not far from the blast, laying a beautiful egg among the flowers blooming under the immaculate sky
of Sinkiang. Thus ends the first optimistic movie ever made
about the atomic bomb—its message exactly the opposite of
that of Nevil Shute in "On the Beach."

The giants of Western culture—Shakespeare, Beethoven,
Molière—all once adopted by China—have been dismissed as
"revisionist squids." In a speech in November, Mao's wife,
Chiang Ching—speaking in her role as the director of the
cultural department of the Army of Liberation, first assistant

to Chen Po-ta, chief of the Central Committee group in charge of the Cultural Revolution, and first counselor of Marshal Hsui Hsiang-chien, the chief of the group in charge of the Cultural Revolution in the Army of Liberation—roundly condemned cubism, Fauvism, impressionism, jazz and all modern Western art movements. All dissemination, production or presentation of foreign musical, theatrical and literary works has ended. Indeed, all artistic creation seems suspended.

In the major bookstores of Peking there are no Chinese-language works but those of Mao, a few translations of Marx, Engels and Lenin, a few Albanian political studies, and a history of the Indonesian Communist party. The sole foreign-language bookstore offers the same selection, plus the works of Anna Louise Strong and Israel Epstein, another American Marxist-Leninist residing in China.

In effect, nothing is read in China but the works, or excerpts of the works, of Mao. Everywhere, people carry copies of the famous little red book of quotations, "The Thoughts of Mao Tse-tung," that was made up by Lin Piao several years ago for the soldiers of the Liberation Army. They read the book in chorus, in the street, seated on the curbstone, on buses, trains and planes. For foreigners, even veterans of the Cultural Revolution, it remains astonishing to see the chorus of passengers under the leadership of charming, smiling hostesses chant their collective reading and the songs to the glory of Mao to the unexpected rhythm of music from the airplane's loudspeaker system.

It is well to learn quotations of Mao Tse-tung by heart. They are the contemporary version of Chinese universality; they have an answer to everything. Everyone wears one at his buttonhole, inscribed on a small brooch. There is one hung on the handlebars of every bicycle, on cars, and naturally all the walls are loaded with them.

The new China is symbolized by the appearance of a semi-official highly sensational press. It carries such headlines as "The 12 Great Crimes of President Liu Shao-chi," or "The Secretary General of the Party Is a Big Poisonous Plant." It prints such stories as an interview with President Liu's son and daughter accusing their father—China's head of state—of stealing funds from the party to maintain his wife in bourgeois splendor and buy himself such luxuries as a gold shoehorn.

The impact of this sensationalism cannot be grasped by anyone who has not seen Chinese crowds struggling to buy the Red Guard or revolutionary-rebel papers containing such stories. They stand on the curb to read at once the latest scandal, the first since the proclamation of the People's Republic 17 years ago.

Then, as the loudspeakers at every corner roll out the strains of "The Red Orient" or "Navigation on the High Seas Depends on the Pilot," the crowd watches the carts of the condemned roll past or reads the posters relating the misdeeds and the crimes, ever more bloody and unbelievable, of the "black band."

But what is the impact on the masses? Where is China headed? How is the Westerner—diplomat or correspondent—to distinguish the true from the false?

The 11 Japanese correspondents stationed in Peking emerge as the champions of this dead-end quest. They have two trumps: language and gadgets. At night on Hsi Tan, the main commercial artery of Peking, which has become the center of contradictory posters and sensationalist tales, you see them walking—a flashlight in one hand and a bullhorn in the other. A car slowly follows each. They dictate the texts of the posters to their colleagues in the cars, who type them out and announce to the world the latest episodes of a revolution which—as the official writings state every day—is very much "without precedent."

Index